LAND
REGISTRATION
MANUAL

THIRD EDITION

LAND REGISTRATION MANUAL

THIRD EDITION

David W Rees, BSc Econ, LLB, FCIEA

Solicitor
Assistant Land Registrar, HM Land Registry
External Examiner to the Solicitors Regulation Authority and
Bar Standards Board
Chief Examiner to the Chartered Institute of Legal Executives

Wildy, Simmonds & Hill Publishing

© David W Rees, 2018

Contains public sector information licensed under the Open Government Licence v3.0

ISBN: 9780854902491

British Library Cataloguing in Publication Data

A catalogue record for this book is available from the British Library

The right of David W Rees to be identified as the author of this Work has been asserted by him in accordance with sections 77 and 78 of the Copyright, Designs and Patents Act 1988.

Second edition 2014

This edition published in 2018 by

Wildy, Simmonds & Hill Publishing
Wildy & Sons Ltd
Lincoln's Inn Archway
Carey Street
London WC2A 2JD
www.wildy.com

Typeset by Heather Jones, North Petherton, Somerset.
Printed in Great Britain by Ashford Colour Press Ltd.

Preface

The first edition of this book was published in 2003, just as the Land Registration Act 2002 and the Land Registration Rules 2003 were coming into force. Its aim was 'to provide busy conveyancers with the answers to their questions on the law and practice of land registration and dispositions of registered estates, within a logical and straightforward format'. The intervening period has seen not only the settling in of the 2002 Act and 2003 Rules, but also further developments in land registration law and practice in general. In consequence, it was timely to produce a second edition of the *Land Registration Manual* in 2014. Further developments, including amendment of the 2003 Rules in April 2018 so as to further facilitate electronic conveyancing, have meant that a third edition is now appropriate.

This new edition seeks to both update and expand the material in the previous edition, so that not only is the coverage of the legislative framework and of land registration practice and procedures brought up to date, but additional background commentary has also been added.

This edition does, however, retain the features which made the previous edition such a useful book. This includes the alphabetical division of topics and the 'self-contained' approach whereby each topic contains relevant details of which applications are appropriate to that topic and how they may be made.

It is hoped that this book will provide practitioners with a comprehensive and practical source of reference on a wide variety of topics related to land registration.

David Rees
6 April 2018

Contents

Preface   v
Glossary of Terms and Author's Note   xxvii

Access to neighbouring land orders   1
   Notice in respect of a pending land action   2
      Agreed notice   2
      Unilateral notice   2
   Agreed notice in respect of an access order   2
   Agreed notice in respect of an order varying the access order   3
   Restriction in respect of a licence   3
Accretion and diluvion   3
   Registration of agreement   4
Address for service   4
Administrative receivers   5
   Amendment to address for service   6
   Sale or other disposition by an administrative receiver   6
Administrators of a company   8
   Entry of appointment of an administrator in the register   9
   Sale or other disposition by an administrator   9
   Acquisition by company subject to an administration order   11
Adverse possession   11
   Meaning of 'adverse possession'   14
   Registration as a person entitled to be notified of an adverse possession
      application   16
   Application under Land Registration Act 2002, Sch 6, para 1 for
      registration by person in adverse possession of registered land   16
   Notice of an application based on adverse possession under Land
      Registration Act 2002, Sch 6, para 1   19
   Application under Land Registration Act 2002, Sch 6, para 6 for
      registration by person in adverse possession of registered land   21
   Registered charges   22
   Additional defences to actions for possession   23
   Transitional provisions   24
   Application for first registration   25

Adverse possession and leasehold land   27
   Adverse possession of leasehold land   27
   Encroachment from leasehold land onto other land   28
Overriding interests   30
Advowsons   30
Agreement for lease   31
   Agreed notice   32
   Unilateral notice   32
   Restriction   33
Agreement for mortgage   34
   Agreed notice   35
   Unilateral notice   35
   Restriction   36
Agreement to pay further consideration   37
   Restriction   37
Airspace   38
Alteration of the register   39
   Alteration pursuant to a court order   40
   Alteration not pursuant to a court order   40
   Costs and expenses in non-rectification cases   41
Amalgamation of registered titles   42
Annuities   43
   Restriction   44
Applications to HM Land Registry   44
Assents   45
   Unregistered land   45
   Registered land   46
Assets of community value   48

Bankruptcy   49
   Petition in bankruptcy   50
   Bankruptcy order   51
   Bankruptcy entries under the Land Registration Act 1925   52
   Registration of the trustee in bankruptcy   55
   Vacating of office by trustee in bankruptcy   54
   Sale by trustee in bankruptcy   55
   Protection of purchaser from bankrupt   55
   Bankruptcy of a joint proprietor   56
   Administration of an insolvent estate   58
   Cancellation of bankruptcy notice or bankruptcy restriction 59
   Discharge from bankruptcy   60
   Re-vesting of bankrupt's home   61
   Annulment of bankruptcy order   62

After-acquired property   63
Voidable dispositions   64
Bankruptcy and home rights   66
Charging order in favour of trustee in bankruptcy   67
    Agreed notice of the charging order   67
    Unilateral notice of the charging order   68
    Restriction where the charging order is over a beneficial interest   68
Disclaimer by trustee in bankruptcy   69
Insolvency proceedings commenced in another part of the United
    Kingdom   72
Bare trusts   73
Bona vacantia and escheat   74
Boundaries   77
    Determination of the exact line of a boundary   80
    Party Wall etc Act 1996   83
Bulk Applications   83

Cautions against conversion   84
Cautions against dealings   85
    Cautioner showing cause   87
Cautions against first registration   88
    Effect of a caution against first registration   91
    Objection by cautioner   92
    Withdrawal of a caution against first registration 92
    Cancellation of a caution against first registration   92
    Alteration of the cautions register   94
Chancel repair   96
    Caution against first registration   98
    Agreed notice   98
    Unilateral notice   99
Change of gender resulting in a change of name   99
Change of name   99
    Change of name of private individuals   99
    Change of name of corporate bodies   100
Charging orders   100
    Notice in respect of a pending land action   102
        Agreed notice   102
        Unilateral notice   102
    Agreed notice in respect of the charging order   102
    Unilateral notice in respect of the charging order 103
    Restriction where the charging order is over a beneficial interest   103
Charities   104
    Dispositions in favour of charities   106

Dispositions by charities   109
Transfers on sale or leases by non-exempt charities   119
Mortgages by non-exempt charities   113
Dispositions by exempt charities   115
Rentcharge titles   116
Appointment of new trustees   117
Incorporation of trustees of a charity   118
Corporation becoming a non-exempt charity   119
Change of status of charity   119
Change of name of charity   119
Church of England   120
Application of the Charities Act 2011   120
Incumbent of a benefice   122
The Church Commissioners   125
Cathedrals   126
Diocesan boards of finance   128
Diocesan authorities   130
Classes of title   130
Titles to freehold estates   131
Absolute title   131
Qualified title   132
Possessory title   132
Titles to leasehold estates   133
Absolute title   133
Good leasehold title   133
Qualified title   134
Possessory title   134
Coal   135
Collective enfranchisement   136
Notice served under Leasehold Reform, Housing and Urban
    Development Act 1993, s 13   137
Agreed notice   137
Unilateral notice   137
Application for vesting order under Leasehold Reform, Housing
    and Urban Development Act 1993, s 26(1)   138
Agreed notice   138
Unilateral notice   138
Restriction   139
Vesting order under Leasehold Reform, Housing and Urban
    Development Act 1993, s 26(1)   139
Agreed notice   140
Unilateral notice   140
Restriction   140

Vesting order under Leasehold Reform, Housing and Urban
    Development Act 1993, s 24(4) or s 25(6)   141
Transfer or conveyance to nominee or right to enfranchise company   142
Vendor's lien   143
Lease back by nominee or right to enfranchise company   143
Application for acquisition order under Landlord and Tenant Act
    1987, s 28   143
    Agreed notice   144
    Unilateral notice   144
    Restriction   144
Acquisition order under Landlord and Tenant Act 1987, s 28   145
    Agreed notice   145
    Unilateral notice   146
    Restriction   146
Tenants' right of first refusal to purchase the reversion under the
    Landlord and Tenant Act 1987   147
Appointment of manager under the Landlord and Tenant Act 1987   148
Commonhold   148
The commonhold association   149
The commonhold community statement   149
Applying to register a commonhold   150
Winding up or dissolution of a community association   150
Commons   150
First registration of common land   153
Dispositions of registered common land   154
Companies   154
Companies which are a UK company   153
Companies which are not a UK company   154
Dispositions by companies   156
Registration of a charge created by a company   156
Execution of deeds by UK companies   157
    Execution by a company under its common seal   158
    Execution by a company otherwise than under a common seal   158
Execution of deeds by overseas companies   159
    Execution under common seal   159
    Execution in a manner permitted by the local law   159
    Execution by signature of authorised person(s)   160
Related topics   160
Compulsory purchase   160
Deed poll   161
Registered land   161
Unregistered land   162
General vesting declaration   162

Registered land	164
Unregistered land	165
Constructive, resulting and other implied trusts	165
Entry of restrictions	166
Contracts for sale (including sub-sale)	168
Agreed notice	169
Unilateral notice	169
Restriction	170
Conveyancers	171
Copyhold	171
Caution against first registration	173
Agreed notice	173
Unilateral notice	174
Correction of mistakes in an application or accompanying document	174
Costs	175
Costs payable by the Registry	175
Costs payable by a third party	177
Credit unions	178
Day list	179
Delivery and priority of applications	179
Day list information	181
Death of applicant for registration	181
Death of a registered proprietor	182
Death of a sole proprietor	182
Death of a joint proprietor	182
Debentures	183
Deeds amending dispositions of registered titles	185
Amendment before application for registration	185
Amendment after application for registration but before completion of registration	185
Amendment after registration	186
Transfers	186
Leases	186
Charges	187
Related topics	187
Demesne land	187
First registration	189
Cautions against first registration	189
Developing estates	190
Estate boundary approval	190
Estate plan approval	190
Approval of draft transfers and leases	192

Pre- and post-registration services on plot sales | 192
Developing schemes | 193
Disputes | 193
Objections | 194
Referral to the Tribunal | 195
Determination by the Tribunal | 196
Rectification of documents | 199
Division of registered titles | 199

Electronic services | 200
Embankments or sea or river walls | 202
Caution against first registration | 203
Agreed notice | 203
Unilateral notice | 204
Enlargement of long leases | 204
Leasehold title unregistered | 205
Leasehold title registered | 206
Equitable charges | 207
Agreed notice | 208
Unilateral notice | 209
Restriction where the equitable charge is over a beneficial interest | 209
Priority of equitable charges | 210
Orders under Law of Property Act 1925, s 90 | 210
Equitable easements | 212
Agreed notice | 213
Unilateral notice | 213
Equitable interests | 214
Estate, right or interest | 214
European Economic Interest Groupings | 215
European Groupings of Territorial Cooperation | 217
Exclusive use | 219

Fees | 221
First registration | 222
Legal estates capable of first registration | 222
Compulsory first registration | 223
Duty to apply for first registration | 224
Application for first registration | 225
Lodging of title deeds | 227
Appropriate certification | 227
Separate certificate | 228
Original deeds | 228
Examination of title | 229

Floating charges   231
   Agreed notice   232
   Unilateral notice   233
   Crystallisation of floating charge   233
Flying freeholds   234
Foreign law   235
Foreshore   236
Forms   238
Franchises   240
   Caution against first registration   241
   Agreed notice   242
   Unilateral notice   242
   First registration of a franchise   243
   Dispositions of registered franchises   244
Fraud or forgery   245
   Alteration and rectification   245
   Indemnity   246
   Restriction   247
Freezing orders, restraint orders and interim receiving orders   248
   Agreed notice   250
   Unilateral notice   250
   Restriction   251
Friendly societies   251
   Friendly societies registered under the Friendly Societies Act 1974   252
   Friendly societies registered under the Friendly Societies Act 1992   253

Gifts   254
   Unregistered land   254
   Registered land   255

Historical information   256
Home rights   257
   Home rights notice   259
   Renewal of home rights notice   259
   Cancellation of home rights notice   257
   Cancellation of matrimonial home rights caution   260
   Home rights search by a mortgagee   261
Housing action trusts   261
   Restrictions   262
   Disposal of land   262
Housing associations   263
   Registered housing associations   264
   Registration of unregistered housing association as proprietor of land   264

Dispositions by unregistered housing associations 265

Identity evidence 266
Implied covenants 268
    Transfers of pre-1996 leases 270
    Transfer of a registered estate subject to a rentcharge 272
Indemnity 273
    Interest on indemnity 275
Indemnity covenants 276
Individual voluntary arrangements 277
    Agreed notice 278
    Unilateral notice 279
    Restriction 279
Inheritance tax 280
    Liability for death duties 280
    Liability for capital transfer tax/inheritance tax 281
    Nil-rate band discretionary trusts 282
Inhibitions 283
    Effect of an inhibition 284
    Cancellation of an inhibition 284
    Modification or disapplication of an inhibition 285
Internal waters 285

Joint proprietors 286
    Entry of Form A restriction 287
    Death of a joint proprietor 288
    Cancellation of Form A restriction 289
    Related matters 290

Land Registry 290
Land Registry Act 1862 291
Leasehold enfranchisement 291
    Notice under Leasehold Reform Act 1967 292
        Agreed notice 292
        Unilateral notice 293
    Registration of transfer of the freehold 293
    Discharge of registered charges on the freehold title 294
    Rentcharges 294
    Rights and burdens under Leasehold Reform Act 1967, s 10 295
    Estate Management Scheme under the Leasehold Reform Act 1967 295
Leases 296
    Leases granted out of unregistered estates 296
    Leases which are registrable dispositions 297

Leases of land not exceeding 7 years   298
    Agreed notice   299
    Unilateral notice   299
Leases which are incapable of substantive registration   299
Noting of leases   300
Prescribed clauses leases   300
Registration of leases which are registrable dispositions   301
Leases for life or determinable on death, marriage or civil
    partnership   303
Variation of a lease   304
    Deeds of variation varying the term   306
    Deeds of variation varying the extent   306
Acquisition of an extended lease under the Leasehold Reform
    Act 1967   307
    Agreed notice   308
    Unilateral notice   308
    Registration of extended lease   309
Acquisition of a lease under the Leasehold Reform, Housing and
    Urban Development Act 1993   310
    Notice to acquire new lease   311
        Agreed notice   311
        Unilateral notice   311
    Application for vesting order   312
        Agreed notice   312
        Unilateral notice   313
        Restriction   313
    Vesting order   314
        Agreed notice   314
        Unilateral notice   314
        Restriction   315
    Grant of new lease   316
Easements in leases   317
    Easements granted   317
    Easements reserved   318
    Easements in unregistered leases   319
        Easements granted   319
        Easements reserved   319
    Equitable easements in leases   320
Restrictive covenants in leases   320
    Agreed notice   320
    Unilateral notice   321
Apportionment of rent   321

Extensions of leases (other than under the Leasehold Reform Act
    1967 or Leasehold Reform, Housing and Urban Development
    Act 1993)   322
    Where the new lease takes immediate effect   323
    Where the new lease commences on a future date   323
    Determination of registered leases   324
        Form of application   324
        Incumbrances affecting the determined lease   325
        Merger   325
        Surrender by deed   326
        Surrender by operation of law   327
        Disclaimer   328
        Effluxion of time   328
        Forfeiture   328
        Notice   330
        Frustration   331
        Enlargement   331
    Cancellation of a noted lease   331
    Right to determine a registered lease   332
Legal aid   332
Legal charges   333
    Charges of registered land   333
    Charges subsisting at the time of first registration   335
    Approved forms of charge   336
    Further advances   336
    Collateral charges   337
    Priorities   337
    Consolidation   338
    Deeds of variation   338
    Remedies of a registered chargee   339
        Power of sale   339
        Foreclosure   340
    Discharge of registered charge   340
    Sub-charges   342
    Transfer of charge   343
    Related topics   343
Legal easements   343
    Legal easements on first registration   344
        Beneficial easements   344
        Subjective easements   346
    Legal easements arising after first registration   346
    Prescriptive easements   348
    Unregistered legal easements which override registered dispositions   351

Extinguishment of easements   351
Related topics   352
Legal estates   352
Legal interests   352
Licences   353
Limited liability partnerships   354
Registration of a UK limited liability partnership as proprietor   354
Registration of charge created by a UK limited liability partnership 355
Execution of deeds by limited liability partnerships   356
Conversion of a partnership or corporate body to a limited liability
    partnership   356
Dissolution of a limited liability partnership   356
Registration of an overseas limited liability partnership as proprietor   357
Limited owner's charge   357
Limited partnerships   358
Registration and entry of restriction(s)   359
Liquidators   360
Entry of notice of liquidator's appointment   360
Evidence of appointment   361
Creditors' voluntary winding-up   361
Members' voluntary winding-up   361
Winding-up by the court   361
Dispositions by a liquidator   362
Disclaimer by a liquidator   362
Registered disclaimed lease   363
Unregistered disclaimed lease   364
Vesting order relating to registered disclaimed lease   365
Disclaimer of registered freehold estate   365
Dissolution   366
Liquidation of foreign companies   366
Local land charges   367
Lost or destroyed title deeds   369
Application for first registration   369
Circumstances of the loss or destruction   369
Reconstruction of the title   370
Possession of the estate   371
Evidence of identity   371
Class of title   371

Manors   372
Lordship of a manor   372
Transfer of a registered manor   373
Lease of a registered manor   373

Deregistration of a registered lordship of a manor   374
Manorial land   374
Manorial rights   374
Mental incapacity   375
Registered land   376
Registered land held on trust   377
Severance of beneficial joint tenancy of registered land   379
Adverse possession of registered land   379
Mere equities   379
Mines and minerals   380
First registration of mines and minerals   381
Registered surface land   383
Transfer of mines and minerals out of a registered title   383
Lease of mines and minerals out of registered surface land   384
Profits à prendre   384
Overriding interests   384
Indemnity   385
Minors   385
Transfer of land to a minor   385
Transfer of land to a minor jointly with an adult   386
Charge in favour of a minor or to a minor jointly with an adult   387
Mortgage cautions   388

Notices   389
Agreed notice   390
Cancellation of a notice other than a unilateral notice or a home
     rights notice   391
Unilateral notice   392
Registration of new or additional beneficiary of a unilateral notice   393
Removal of a unilateral notice   393
Cancellation of a unilateral notice   393
Notices of deposit   395

Official copies and inspection   396
Personal inspection   398
Official copies   398
Exempt information documents   399
Freedom of Information Act 2000   401
Data Protection Act 1998   403
Official searches   404
Official search with priority   404
Lodging of official search   405
The 'search from' date   405

Official certificate of search   405
Priority period of official search   406
Effect of priority   407
Withdrawal of official search with priority   408
Official search without priority   408
Official search by a mortgagee in Form HR3   408
Outline applications   408
Official searches of the index   409
Search of the index map   409
Search of the index of relating franchises and manors   410
Search of the index of proprietors' names   411
Options   412
Agreed notice   413
Unilateral notice   414
Restriction   414
Options contained in registrable dispositions   415
Overreaching   416
Overriding interests   416
Unregistered interests which override first registration   417
Leasehold estates in land   417
Interests of persons in actual occupation   417
Easements and profits à prendre   418
Customary rights   418
Public rights   418
Local land charges   418
Mines and minerals   418
Franchise   418
Manorial rights   419
Crown rents   419
Non-statutory rights in respect of an embankment or sea or
    river wall   420
Rights to payment in lieu of tithe   420
Rights in respect of the repair of a church chancel   421
Public-private partnership leases relating to transport in London   421
Rights acquired under the Limitation Act 1980   421
Unregistered interests which override registered dispositions   421
Leasehold estates in land   421
Interests of persons in actual occupation   422
Easements and profits à prendre   422
Local land charges   423
Crown rents   423
Rights to payment in lieu of tithe   424
Rights acquired under the Limitation Act 1980   425

Interests which cannot take effect as overriding interests   426
Duty to disclose overriding interests   426
Overseas insolvency proceedings   427
   Insolvency proceedings commenced in another member state of the
     European Union   428
   Cross-Border Insolvency Regulations 2006   429

Partnerships   431
   Registration   431
Party Wall etc Act 1996   432
Pending land actions   433
   Agreed notice   434
   Unilateral notice   434
   Restriction   434
Personal representatives   435
   Registration of personal representative   436
   Entry of restrictions   437
   Dispositions by personal representatives   440
   First registration   441
   Inheritance tax; capital transfer tax; death duties   441
Plans   441
Positive covenants   444
   Restriction   445
   Positive covenants imposed by statute   446
Powers of attorney   446
   General powers under Powers of Attorney Act 1971, s 10   447
   Other general and specific powers   447
   Security powers   447
   Enduring powers of attorney   447
   Lasting powers of attorney   448
   Powers of attorney by joint proprietors and other trustees   449
     Trustee Act 1925, s 25   449
     Trustee Delegation Act 1999, s 1   450
     Trusts of Land and Appointment of Trustees Act 1996, s 9   450
   Gifts and dispositions at undervalue by an attorney   451
   Powers more than 12 months old – evidence of non-revocation   451
   Execution of deeds by an attorney   452
   Powers of attorney given to receivers in debentures   452
Priorities   452
   Basic rule of priority   452
   Special rule of priority   452
     Registrable dispositions of registered estates for valuable
      consideration   453

Registrable dispositions of registered charges for valuable
    consideration   454
Inland Revenue charges   454
Priority of applications   455
Profits à prendre   456
    Legal profits à prendre on first registration   456
        Beneficial profits à prendre   456
        Subjective profits à prendre   458
    Legal profits à prendre arising after first registration   458
    Prescriptive profits à prendre   460
    Unregistered legal profits à prendre which override registered
        dispositions   463
    First registration of profit à prendre in gross   463
    Registration of profit à prendre in gross created over registered land 465
    Dispositions of a registered profit à prendre in gross   466
    Extinguishment of profits à prendre   466
    Related matters   466
Proper office   467
Property adjustment orders   468
    Agreed notice   469
    Unilateral notice   469
    Restriction   470
Proprietary estoppel   471
    Agreed notice   472
    Unilateral notice   472
Public authority certificates of title   472
Public-private partnership leases relating to transport in London   473

Receivers appointed under the Law of Property Act 1925   474
    Address for service   475
    Sale by a receiver   475
Receivers appointed by order of the court   479
    Restriction   479
Rectification   480
    Rectification pursuant to an order of the court   481
    Rectification other than pursuant to an order of the court   482
Registered social landlords and private registered providers   482
    Registration of registered social landlords or private registered
        providers as proprietor   483
    Dispositions by registered social landlords or private registered
        providers   484
Registered societies   485
Rentcharges   486

Rentcharges created out of unregistered land   487
Registration of rentcharge created over registered land   488
Rentcharges granted by a UK company or UK limited liability
    partnership   490
Rentcharges which cannot be registered   491
Entry of notice of rentcharge   491
Dispositions of registered rentcharges   492
Transfer of registered estate subject to a rentcharge   492
Apportionment and redemption of rentcharges   492
Extinguishment of rentcharges   493
Adverse possession of registered rentcharges   494
    Application under Land Registration Act 2002, Sch 6, para 1
      (as modified) for registration by a person in adverse possession
      of registered rentcharge   496
    Application under Land Registration Act 2002, Sch 6, para 6
      (as modified) for registration by person in adverse possession
      of registered rentcharge   497
Transitional provisions   499
Adverse possession of unregistered rentcharges   499
Requisition, rejection and cancellation policy   500
Restrictions   500
Application for entry of restriction   502
Forms of restriction   504
Court order for entry of restriction   505
Obligatory restrictions   505
Compliance with a restriction   506
Application for an order that a restriction be disapplied or
    modified   506
Cancellation of a restriction   506
Withdrawal of a restriction   507
Restrictions entered under the Land Registration Act 1925   508
Inhibitions entered under the Land Registration Act 1925   508
Restrictive covenants   509
Restrictive covenants on first registration   509
Restrictive covenants and registered land   510
    Agreed notice   511
    Unilateral notice   511
Release, waiver or modification of restrictive covenants   511
Positive covenants imposed by statute   512
Retention, destruction and return of documents   513
Right to buy and right to acquire under the Housing Acts   513
Charges on landlord's title   514
Rentcharges   514

Statutory easements   514
Discount charges   514
Right of first refusal   515
Acquisition on rent to mortgage terms   515
Property to which Housing Act 1985, s 37 or s 157 applies   516
Preserved right to buy   516
Right to manage companies   518
Rights of light and air   519
Rights of pre-emption   519
  Agreed notice   521
  Unilateral notice   521
  Restriction   522
  Rights of pre-emption contained in registrable dispositions   523
Rights of reverter   523
  Restriction   525
  Transfer to revertee   526

Sequestrators   526
  Restriction   526
Settlements   527
  Settled land forms of restriction   528
  Transfer of land into settlement   528
  Registered land bought with capital money   529
  Registered land brought into settlement   529
  Proprietor ceasing in his lifetime to be tenant for life   530
  Registration of special personal representatives   530
  Transfer on death of tenant for life   530
  Registration of statutory owner during a minority otherwise than
    on death   531
  Minority where settlement arises under a will or intestacy   531
  Changes to settlement   532
  End of settlement other than on death   532
Severance of a beneficial joint tenancy   533
  Restriction in Form A   533
Shared ownership leases   534
  Registration of the lease   535
  Staircasing   536
Souvenir land   536
  Cancellation of entries relating to souvenir land   538
  Application for registration by a third party   538
Special powers of appointment   538
  Restriction   539
Sporting rights   539

Profits à prendre, franchises and manorial rights   539
Corporeal fisheries   540
Stamp duty land tax   541
Statements of truth   542
Statutory charges   543
    Registration   544
    Restriction   545
Statutory vesting   546
Subrogation   546
    Unilateral notice   547

Time share   547
Title information document   548
Town or village greens   549
    First registration of a town or village green   550
    Dispositions of a registered town or village green   551
Transfers   551
    Registration of transfer   554
    Related topics   554
Tribunal   555
Trusts of land   555
    Registration of trustees   557
    Entry of restrictions   557
    Dispositions by trustees   561
    Powers of attorney granted by trustees   561
    Vesting of registered land in new trustees   562

Unincorporated associations   564
    Registration of trustees   564
    Dispositions by trustees   565
    Change of trustees   565
Upgrade of class of title   565
    Upgrading possessory or qualified freehold to absolute   567
    Upgrading possessory or qualified leasehold to good leasehold   568
    Upgrading good leasehold to absolute   568
    Upgrading possessory or qualified leasehold to absolute   569

Vendor's liens   570
    Agreed notice   571
    Unilateral notice   571

Writs or orders affecting land   571
    Agreed notice   572

Unilateral notice   572
Restriction   573

Appendices
I   HM Land Registry Offices   575
II   List of Forms   577
           Schedule 1 forms   577
           Schedule 3 forms   579
           Commonhold forms   580
           Other forms   580
III   Land Registration Rules 2003, Schedule 1A: Prescribed
       Clauses LR1 to LR14   581
IV   Land Registration Rules 2003, Schedule 4: Standard Forms of
       Restriction   585
V   Land Registration Rules 2003, Schedule 3: Forms Referred to in
       Rule 206   601
VI   Land Registration Rules 2003, Schedule 9: Forms of Execution   613

Index   619

Glossary of Terms and Author's Note

Adjudicator	Adjudicator to HM Land Registry
ANLA 1992	Access to Neighbouring Land Act 1992
BAC	Bulk Application Contact
CAS	Land Registry Commercial Arrangements Section
CCBSA 2014	Co-operative and Community Benefit Societies Act 2014
conveyancer	definition set out in LRR 2003, r 217(A)(1)
CRA 1965	Commons Registration Act 1965
developing estate	registered title consisting of land being developed for residential and/or commercial purposes and disposed of in individual plots or flats
DX	document exchange
ED	electronic discharge
EEIG	European Economic Interest Grouping
EGTC	European Groupings of Territorial Cooperation
European Convention on Human Rights	European Convention for the Protection of Human Rights and Fundamental Freedoms 1950
FCA	Financial Conduct Authority
Fee Order	Land Registration Fee Order 2013 (SI 2013/3174) or (where appropriate) the current Land Registration Fee Order for the time being in force
FLA 1996	Family Law Act 1996
HA 1985	Housing Act 1985
HA 1988	Housing Act 1988
HA 1996	Housing Act 1996
HMRC	HM Revenue and Customs
IA 1986	Insolvency Act 1986
IHT	inheritance tax
IVA	individual voluntary arrangement
Land Registry, the Registry	Her Majesty's Land Registry and (where the context so admits) the Chief Land Registrar of Her Majesty's Land Registry

LBTT	land and buildings transaction tax
LLP	limited liability partnership
LPA receiver	Law of Property Act receiver
LRA 1925	Land Registration Act 1925
LRA 2002	Land Registration Act 2002 (as amended)
LRA (TP) Order 2003	Land Registration Act 2002 (Transitional Provisions) Order 2003 (SI 2003/1953)
LRHUDA 1993	Leasehold Reform, Housing and Urban Development Act 1993
LRR 2003	Land Registration Rules 2003 (SI 2003/1417) (as amended)
LTT	land transaction tax
NLIS	National Land Information Service
PAA 1971	Powers of Attorney Act 1971
PPP	public-private partnership
proper office	office designated under LRA 2002, s 100(3) and the current Land Registration (Proper Office) Order for the receipt of applications or a specified description of application or, if no such order subsists, under the provisions of any relevant direction by the registrar under LRA 2002, s 100(4) as to the address to be used for the delivery of applications
Referral Rules	Land Registration (Referral to the Adjudicator to HM Land Registry) Rules 2003 (SI 2003/2114)
relevant enactments	(in relation to rights of reverter) School Sites Acts of 1841, 1844, 1849, 1851 and 1852; Literary and Scientific Institutions Act 1854; and Places of Worship Sites Act 1873
RTE company	right to enfranchise company, i.e. a private company limited by guarantee, of which all qualifying tenants are entitled to be members, and having as an object the exercise of the right to collective enfranchisement
RTM	right to manage
Sch 1 form	form contained within LRR 2003, Sch 1
Sch 3 form	form contained within LRR 2003, Sch 3
SDLT	stamp duty land tax
SLA 1925	Settled Land Act 1925
standard form restriction	restriction in one of the standard forms set out in LRR 2003, Sch 4; references to a particular form (for example Form A, etc) are to the relevant standard form of restriction set out in Sch 4

statement of truth	statement of truth which complies with the requirements set out in LRR 2003, r 215A
the 1938 Measure	Parsonages Measure 1938
the 1943 Measure	New Parishes Measure 1943
the 1986 Measure	Patronage (Benefices) Measure 1986
the 1999 Measure	Cathedrals Measure 1999
TLATA	Trusts of Land and Appointment of Trustees Act 1996
Tribunal	Land Registration Division of the Property Chamber, First-tier Tribunal
Tribunal Rules	Tribunal Procedure (First-tier Tribunal) (Property Chamber) Rules 2013 (SI 2013/1169)

References to an Act or Statutory Instrument are (if applicable) to that Act or Statutory Instrument as amended.

The commentary in this book is that of the author and not of the Land Registry.

The law is stated as at 6 April 2018, although subsequent changes have been taken into account where possible.

For brevity throughout the book, masculine references are used to represent both masculine and feminine.

ACCESS TO NEIGHBOURING LAND ORDERS

A person who wishes, for the purpose of carrying out works to land, to enter on adjoining or adjacent land and who needs, but does not have, the consent of some other person to that entry, may apply to the court for an access order (Access to Neighbouring Land Act 1992 (ANLA 1992), s 1). 'Land' for this purpose does not include a highway (ANLA 1992, s 8(3)), but does include a party wall (*Dean v Walker* [1996] EWCA Civ 505). The application must be commenced in the county court and constitutes a pending land action (ANLA 1992, s 5(6)). The priority of the pending land action may be protected by entry in the register of an agreed notice or a unilateral notice. In practice, an application for an agreed notice will usually be the appropriate course of action.

Where the result of the application is that the court makes an access order, this should be protected by entry of an agreed notice. It is not possible to protect such an access order by entry of a unilateral notice (Land Registration Rules 2003 (SI 2003/1417) (LRR 2003), r 80).

An access order is (subject, where necessary, to its priority being protected by a notice in the register) binding on the original respondent to the application for the order and his successors in title and all persons who subsequently obtain an estate, right or interest in or over the servient land which is derived under that respondent (ANLA 1992, s 4).

The rights conferred by the access order cannot be an interest belonging to a person in actual occupation falling within Land Registration Act 2002 (LRA 2002), Sch 1, para 2 or Sch 3, para 2 which will override first registration or registered dispositions (ANLA 1992, s 5(5) as substituted by LRA 2002, Sch 11, para 26(4)). A similar exclusion applies to a pending land action (LRA 2002, s 87(3)).

The court may make an order under ANLA 1992, s 6, varying the access order. The variation should also be protected by entry of an agreed notice. The entry made in the register will give details of the variation. It is not possible to protect such a variation by entry of a unilateral notice (LRR 2003, r 80).

Where access to neighbouring land is allowed under a licence from the registered proprietor, it is not possible to protect this by way of a notice in the register. Even a contractual licence does not bind successors in title (*Ashburn Anstalt v W J Arnold and Co* [1988] EWCA Civ 14). If the registered proprietor is prepared to consent, a restriction may be entered in the register of the servient title. A restriction does not confer any priority; it simply prevents an entry being made in the register in respect of any disposition, or a disposition of a specified kind, unless the terms of the restriction have (where applicable) been complied with.

It is also possible to have an easement to enter on another's land for the purpose of carrying out work on a person's own land (see *Equitable easements*, page 212, and *Legal easements*, page 343).

Notice in respect of a pending land action

Agreed notice

In addition to the usual documents required (see *Notices*, page 389), an applicant should deliver to the Registry the claim form sealed by the court and showing the court reference number, or a certified copy of it.

As the consent of the registered proprietor is unlikely to be forthcoming in this situation, this is likely to be sufficient to satisfy the Registry as to the validity of the applicant's claim in accordance with LRA 2002, s 34(3)(c).

The agreed notice in the register will give details of the interest protected.

Unilateral notice

In addition to delivering the usual documents required (see *Notices*, page 389), an applicant should ensure the statement in panel 11 or conveyancer's certificate in panel 12 of Form UN1 is completed on the following lines to show the interest of the applicant:

> applicant in an application under section 1 of the Access to Neighbouring Land Act 1992 in the [*name*] County Court [*set out full court reference and parties*].

The unilateral notice in the register will give brief details of the interest protected and identify the beneficiary of that notice.

Agreed notice in respect of an access order

In addition to the usual documents required (see *Notices*, page 389), an applicant should deliver to the Registry the access order or a certified copy of it.

As the consent of the registered proprietor is unlikely to be forthcoming in this situation, this is likely to be sufficient to satisfy the Registry as to the validity of the applicant's claim in accordance with LRA 2002, s 34(3)(c).

The agreed notice in the register will give details of the interest protected.

Agreed notice in respect of an order varying the access order

In addition to the usual documents required (see *Notices*, page 389), an applicant should deliver to the Registry the order varying the access order or a certified copy of it.

As the consent of the registered proprietor is unlikely to be forthcoming in this situation, this is likely to be sufficient to satisfy the Registry as to the validity of the applicant's claim in accordance with LRA 2002, s 34(3)(c).

The agreed notice in the register will give details of the interest protected.

Restriction in respect of a licence

An applicant should deliver to the Registry the usual documents required (see *Restrictions*, page 500).

Panel 9 of Form RX1 should be completed as to the required restriction(s). A possible form of restriction based on Form N is:

> No disposition of the registered estate (other than a charge) by the proprietor of the registered estate is to be registered without a written consent signed by [*licensee*] of [*address*] or their conveyancer.

A restriction in a standard form contained in LRR 2003, Sch 4 does not require the approval of the Registry to the terms of the restriction under LRA 2002, s 43(3).

ACCRETION AND DILUVION

The doctrine of accretion and diluvion recognises the fact that where land is bounded by water, the forces of nature are likely to cause changes in the boundary between the land and the water. In consequence, where land has a boundary with water, the title of the owner of the land normally extends to any land added by accretion. Equally, where there is erosion, or diluvion, title to the land affected is lost.

This doctrine applies only where the changes are gradual and imperceptible (*Southern Centre of Theosophy Inc v State of South Australia* [1982] AC 706) and where they are natural, not man-made. The doctrine can be excluded if this is the intention of the parties concerned.

If the doctrine applies, the boundary between registered titles abutting a natural non-tidal river or stream will change if the course of the river or stream alters naturally over a period of time. The fact that a registered estate in land is shown in the register as having a particular boundary does not affect the operation of accretion or diluvion (LRA 2002, s 61(1)). This applies whether the registered title has a general boundary or a determined boundary (see *Boundaries*, page 77).

An agreement about the operation of accretion or diluvion in relation to registered land has effect only if it is registered. An application to register such an agreement must be made by, or accompanied by the consent of, the registered proprietor of the land and of any registered charge, but no such consent is required from a person who is party to the agreement (LRR 2003, r 123(1)).

Registration of agreement

An applicant should deliver to the Registry:

(a) an application in Form AP1;
(b) the agreement about the operation of accretion or diluvion or a certified copy of it;
(c) the consent of the registered proprietor of the land and of any registered charge, where such person or persons is/are not party/parties to the agreement; and
(d) the fee payable (see *Fees*, page 221).

On registration of the agreement, a note is made in the property register that the agreement is registered for the purposes of LRA 2002, s 61(2). See also, *Foreshore*, page 236.

ADDRESS FOR SERVICE

The register contains an address for service (including any postcode) of each proprietor of the registered estate and any registered charge. Such an address is also required for certain other persons, including the beneficiary of a unilateral notice; the cautioner under a caution against first registration; the person named in a restriction which requires his consent or certificate or the service of notice upon him; and a person entitled to be notified of an application for adverse possession under LRR 2003, r 194. It is important that a person's address for service is kept up to date, otherwise there is a risk that official notices sent by the Registry might not reach him.

In the case of a proprietor who lives at the registered property, the address to be entered in the register will usually be the full postal address of that property. However, in other cases, such as where the property is acquired for rental purposes, this is not likely to be appropriate and an alternative address should be provided. A person may have up to three addresses, including the address of his conveyancer, entered in the register (LRR 2003, r 198). One address for service must be a postal address but it can be inside or outside the United Kingdom. An address for service will be entered in the register in a format that conforms with official sources such as Royal Mail. Where the Registry sends a notice, the time period for responding to the notice is determined by reference to the date of issue of the notice, not the date it is deemed to have been received. A person providing an overseas address should bear in mind that notice periods are not extended for overseas addresses and there is a risk that he may not receive the notice in time to respond. Up to two additional addresses for service may be provided, which can include a document exchange (DX) box number and/or an electronic address.

An application for a change to an address for service in the register should be made in Form AP1. No fee is currently payable. Unless the application is lodged by a conveyancer, evidence of identity will be required (see *Identity evidence*, page 266). As a security measure, the Registry will enter a note in the register whenever an address for service is changed.

ADMINISTRATIVE RECEIVERS

An administrative receiver is defined as being either: (a) a receiver or manager of the whole (or substantially the whole) of a company's property appointed by or on behalf of the holders of any debentures of the company secured by a charge which, as created, was a floating charge, or by such a charge and one or more other securities; or (b) a person who would be such a receiver or manager but for the appointment of some other person as the receiver of part of the company's property (IA 1986, s 29(2)).

An administrative receiver must be an insolvency practitioner and can be appointed either by the court or under powers contained in a debenture. An important limitation, introduced by the Enterprise Act 2002, is that an administrative receiver cannot (subject to certain limited exceptions) be appointed by the holder of a debenture dated on or after 15 September 2003, notwithstanding any provision contained in the debenture (IA 1986, s 72A). The exceptions are set out in IA 1986, ss 72B to 72GA and include, for example, the circumstances where the company is a registered social landlord or is a project company of a project which is a public-private partnership (PPP).

An entry in respect of the debenture under which the receiver is appointed should already appear in the register of the company's title, as a result of it having been registered as a registered charge or protected by entry of a notice. As the property remains vested in the company, the administrative receiver cannot be registered as proprietor of the title nor is his appointment capable of being noted in the register. The administrative receiver may, however, make an application for any necessary changes to the company's address for service in the register.

Amendment to address for service

The administrative receiver should ensure that the company's address for service shown in the register is such as will allow notices to be received (see *Address for service*, page 4). If an amended address or an additional address for service (up to three are permitted) is required, the administrative receiver should deliver to the Registry:

(a)   an application in Form AP1;
(b)   a certified copy of the appointment of the receiver; and
(c)   a certified copy of the debenture (if not already registered or the subject of a notice in the register with a copy filed in the Registry).

No fee is currently payable.

Sale or other disposition by an administrative receiver

The powers given by the debenture to an administrative receiver are deemed to include the powers specified in IA 1986, Sch 1, except insofar as they are inconsistent with the provisions of the debenture. The powers in Sch 1 include power to sell and to grant, or accept a surrender of, a lease. An administrative receiver has a statutory power to use the company's seal and to execute any deed or other document in the name and on behalf of the company (IA 1986, s 42(1) and Sch 1).

Although it is this statutory power which will normally be used, the debenture will also usually give the administrative receiver the right to sell or otherwise dispose of the company's property. Such a power includes the power to execute in the name and on behalf of the company and will survive liquidation of the company (*Barrows v Chief Land Registrar, The Times*, 20 October 1977).

Alternatively, the debenture may grant a power of attorney in favour of the administrative receiver; such a power is not a security power and will not survive liquidation of the company. If the administrative receiver executes as attorney, even if the power is under 12 months old, the application for registration of the disposition will need to be accompanied by a statutory declaration or statement of truth confirming that the applicant did not, at the time of the completion of the transaction, know of any revocation of the power or know of the occurrence of any event (such as the liquidation of the company) which had the effect of revoking the power. A conveyancer's certificate to the like effect may be provided instead.

An administrative receiver is agent of the company. On liquidation this agency comes to an end but the receiver continues to have power to act for the purposes of holding and disposing of the company's property and may use the company's name for that purpose (*Sowman v David Samuel Trust Ltd* [1978] 1 All ER 616).

Any person dealing with the administrative receiver for value and in good faith does not need to ascertain whether he is acting within his powers (IA 1986, s 42(3)).

An administrative receiver, being the agent of the company not of the debenture holder, has no power to discharge the company's property from any mortgage or charge (including the debenture under which he was appointed), whether or not the mortgage or charge was created after the debenture. Consequently, on a sale of a property by an administrative receiver, the transferee must, where appropriate, ensure that a release is obtained for all mortgages and charges including the debenture itself.

However, an administrative receiver may apply to the court for an order authorising him to dispose of the property free from charges that have priority to the debenture under which he was appointed (IA 1986, s 43). The administrative receiver would need to satisfy the court that the property could be more advantageously disposed of free from the charges.

In the case of a transfer of a registered title by an administrative receiver, the transferee should deliver to the Registry:

(a)   an application in Form AP1;
(b)   the transfer by the company;
(c)   evidence that the power of appointment of an administrative receiver under the debenture has arisen. This may be in the form of a certificate by, or on behalf of, the chargee that the power has arisen. If the debenture is dated on or after 15 September 2003 and the appointment is not made by the court,

evidence that one of the exceptions in IA 1986, ss 72A to 72GA applies will also be required;

(d)   the instrument of appointment of the administrative receiver or a certified copy of it. If joint administrative receivers are appointed, the appointment must state whether they can act jointly and severally;

(e)   the debenture, or a certified copy of it, under which the receiver was appointed (unless already registered or the subject of a notice in the register with a copy filed in the Registry);

(f)   releases or discharges in respect of any charges appearing in the registered title (including the debenture under which the administrative receiver was appointed) and not dealt with under (g) below;

(g)   where the court has made an order allowing the administrative receiver to dispose of the registered title free from charges, an office copy or certified copy of that order;

(h)   evidence of non-revocation, where the administrative receiver executes as attorney of the company;

(i)   details of any challenge to the validity of the debenture by a liquidator of the company, including the name and address of the liquidator;

(j)   any new mortgage or charge entered into by the transferee;

(k)   Form DI, giving the information as to overriding interests required by LRR 2003, r 57, including any documentary evidence of the interests (see 'Duty to disclose overriding interests', page 426);

(l)   the appropriate confirmation or evidence as to identity (see *Identity evidence*, page 266);

(m)   the appropriate SDLT certificate or other evidence (see *Stamp duty land tax*, page 541); and

(n)   the fee payable (see *Fees*, page 221).

ADMINISTRATORS OF A COMPANY

An administrator is a person appointed under Insolvency Act 1986 (IA 1986), s 8 and Sch B1 to manage the affairs, business and property of a company. An administrator must be an insolvency practitioner and can be appointed by either:

(a)   an administration order made by the court;

(b)   the holder of a qualifying floating charge; or

(c)   the company or its directors.

The administrator must perform his functions with the objective of rescuing the company as a going concern or, failing that, achieving a better result for the company's creditors as a whole than would be likely if it were wound up. If neither objective is reasonably practicable, he may realise property in order to make a distribution to one or more secured or preferential creditors (IA 1986, Sch B1, para 3).

The administrator can apply for the administration order and his appointment to be noted in the register (LRR 2003, r 184(2)).

Entry of appointment of an administrator in the register

The administrator should deliver to the Registry:

(a) an application in Form AP1;
(b) an office copy or certified copy of the order of the court appointing the administrator *or* a sealed copy of the prescribed notice of appointment, as the case may be;
(c) the fee payable (see *Fees*, page 221).

Where a new or additional administrator is appointed, a similar application will be required.

The Registry will enter the following note of the appointment in the proprietorship register:

> (*Date*) By [*an order of the court made on*] [*a notice of appointment filed on*] (*date*) [*name of administrator*] of [*administrator's address*] was appointed administrator of [*name of company*].

Although administration normally terminates automatically after one year, this period can be extended. Where the administration has come to an end, an application should be made to cancel the note as to the administrator's appointment. The applicant should deliver to the Registry:

(a) an application in Form AP1;
(b) an office copy or certified copy of a court order; or
(c) a certified copy of the prescribed notice registered with the Companies Registry.

There is currently no fee payable.

Sale or other disposition by an administrator

Whilst a company is in administration its property remains vested in it. The administrator acts as the agent of the company and has powers enabling him to do anything necessary or expedient for the management of the affairs, business and property of the company. This includes the powers specified in IA 1986, Sch 1, which include power to sell and to grant or accept a surrender of a lease. The administrator can use the company seal and execute any deed, receipt or document in the name of and on behalf of the company.

Any person dealing with the administrator for value and in good faith does not need to ascertain whether he is acting within his powers (IA 1986, s 14(6)).

The appointment of an administrator ceases to have effect after one year, unless it has been expressly extended. It can be extended only for a specific time and only by either an order of the court or (once only and for not more than 6 months) the consent of all the secured creditors and a majority of the unsecured creditors of the company. If a disposition is made by an administrator more than one year after the company went into administration, evidence that the administrator's appointment has been extended will therefore be required.

An administrator may dispose of the company's property free from any floating charge to which it is subject (IA 1986, Sch B1, para 70). This extends to any charge which, as created, was a floating charge. It is irrelevant that the charge has, under its terms, crystallised on the service of notice by the administrator (IA 1986, s 251; *Re Brightlife Ltd* [1987] Ch 200).

An administrator may also apply to the court for an order authorising him to dispose of the property free from a charge which, as created, was not a floating charge (IA 1986, Sch B1, para 71).

Where the disposition by an administrator consists of a transfer, the transferee of a registered title from the administrator should deliver to the Registry:

(a)   an application in Form AP1;

(b)   the transfer by the company;

(c)   an office copy or certified copy of the order of the court appointing the administrator *or* a sealed copy of the prescribed notice of appointment, as the case may be (where this has not previously been noted in the register);

(d)   if the transfer is made more than one year after the company went into administration, evidence that the administrator's appointment has been extended, in the form of either (i) an office copy or certified copy of an order of the court; or (ii) a certified copy of a prescribed notice of extension;

(e)   releases or discharges in respect of any charges appearing in the title and not dealt with under (f), (g) or (h) below;

(f)   where a floating charge is noted in the register (other than by way of unilateral notice), Form CN1 signed by the administrator with panel 11 stating that the registered title has been transferred pursuant to the IA 1986, Sch B1, para 70;

(g)   where a floating charge is noted in the register by way of unilateral notice, Form UN2 to remove it or Form UN4 to cancel it;

(h)   where the court has made an order allowing the administrator to dispose of the registered title free from a fixed charge, an office copy or certified copy of that order;

(i)   Form DI giving the information as to overriding interests required by LRR 2003, r 57, including any documentary evidence of the interests (see 'Duty to disclose overriding interests', page 426);

(j)   the appropriate confirmation or evidence as to identity (see *Identity evidence*, page 266);

(k)   the appropriate stamp duty land tax (SDLT) certificate or other evidence (see *Stamp duty land tax*, page 541); and

(l)   the fee payable (see *Fees*, page 221).

Acquisition by company subject to an administration order

Where a company's property has with the authorisation of the court been disposed of free from a charge, the chargee is entitled to his original security in respect of any new property the company acquires with the proceeds (IA 1986, Sch B1, para 70(2)). Accordingly, where a company subject to an administration order is being registered as proprietor of a registered estate, the following entry will be made in the charges register:

> The registered estate is subject to such security or securities as may exist and affect the same by virtue of the provisions of paragraph 70(2) of Schedule B1 to the Insolvency Act 1986.

This entry is not made if the administrator certifies that there are no such securities or that such securities as are affected have been discharged.

ADVERSE POSSESSION

Adverse possession is the mechanism by which a person 'squatting' on land may (in the case of unregistered land) acquire an unregistered legal estate in that land and extinguish that of the documentary title owner or (in the case of registered land) become entitled to be registered as proprietor of the land in place of the existing proprietor.

There are different principles and procedures applicable to an application for registration based upon adverse possession, depending upon whether the application:

(a)   is for first registration; or
(b)   relates to registered land and is made under the transitional provisions of LRA 2002, Sch 12, para 18; or
(c)   relates to registered land and is made under the provisions of LRA 2002, Sch 6.

The different types of application are discussed separately below. However, the underlying principles of adverse possession will be applicable to each of them. Essentially, an application based upon adverse possession must be supported by evidence to satisfy the Registry that:

(a)   the squatter has factual possession of the land;
(b)   the squatter has the necessary intention to possess the land;
(c)   the squatter's possession is without the owner's consent; and
(d)   all of the above have been true of the squatter (and any predecessors through whom he claims) for at least the minimum required period.

For adverse possession in relation to rentcharges, see *Rentcharges*, page 486.

Special considerations apply where the application relates to leasehold land or where the squatter has encroached from their own leasehold land onto other land (see 'Adverse possession and leasehold land', page 27).

Where a person has been in adverse possession of unregistered land for the appropriate period of limitation, the documentary title owner's paper title is extinguished (Limitation Act 1980, s 17). The normal period of limitation for recovery of land is 12 years but this period may be extended in certain circumstances.

The LRA 2002 introduced new provisions for obtaining a title to registered land by virtue of adverse possession, so that the position relating to registered land now differs significantly from that relating to unregistered land. The LRA 2002 provides that no period of limitation under Limitation Act 1980, s 15 (time limits in relation to recovery of land) is to run against any person, other than a chargee, in relation to an estate in land or rentcharge the title to which is registered. No period of limitation under Limitation Act 1980, s 16 (time limits in relation to redemption of land) is to run against any person in relation to such an estate in land or rentcharge. Accordingly, Limitation Act 1980, s 17 (extinction of title on expiry of time limit) does not operate to extinguish the title of any person where, by virtue of this, a period of limitation does not run against him (LRA 2002, s 96).

Instead, under LRA 2002, Sch 6, para 1, a person may apply to be registered as proprietor of a registered estate in land if he has been in adverse possession of the estate for the period of 10 years ending on the date of the application. The estate need not have been registered throughout the period of adverse possession. A person may also apply for registration if he has, in the period of 6 months prior to the application, ceased to be in adverse possession of the estate because of eviction by the registered proprietor or a person claiming under the registered proprietor; and on the day before his eviction he had been in adverse possession for the period of 10 years; and the eviction was not pursuant to a judgment for possession. A person may not make such an application if he is a defendant in proceedings which involve asserting a right to possession of the land, or if judgment for possession of the land has been given against him in the last 2 years.

The Registry must give notice of the application to the proprietor of the registered estate and certain other specified persons. In addition, any person who can satisfy the Registry that he has an interest in a registered estate in land which would be prejudiced by the registration of any other person as proprietor consequent upon an adverse possession application may apply to be registered as a person to be notified of such application (LRR 2003, r 194).

Those persons given notice may then either consent to the application; or give counter-notice to the Registry; or object to the application; or give counter-notice and object. If counter-notice is given, the Registry will reject the application unless the applicant has stated in his application that he intends to rely on one of the three conditions set out in Sch 6, para 5, and the Registry is satisfied that the applicant has shown an arguable case for relying on the specified condition. If the application is rejected, then the registered proprietor is likely either to bring an action to recover the land or to agree with the applicant that he may remain in possession as a tenant or licensee. If, however, the applicant remains in adverse possession for a further 2 years after his first application was rejected, then he may make a further application to the Registry under Sch 6, para 6 and will be entitled to be registered as the new proprietor of the registered estate.

If the applicant is registered as proprietor as a result of a successful application under either para 1 or para 6 of Sch 6, he becomes in effect the successor in title of the former proprietor and therefore takes subject to interests affecting the registered estate, other than (in most cases) registered charges. The unregistered possessory title by virtue of adverse possession which he had at the time of the application is extinguished (LRA 2002, Sch 6, para 9(1)). The registered estate is normally vested in him free of any registered charge affecting the estate immediately before registration, but otherwise his registration does not affect the priority of any interest affecting the registered estate.

Meaning of 'adverse possession'

In the leading case of *J A Pye (Oxford) Ltd v Graham* [2002] UKHL 30, the House of Lords reviewed the law relating to adverse possession and Lord Hope of Craighead said:

> At first sight, it might be thought that the word 'adverse' describes the nature of the possession that the squatter needs to demonstrate. It suggests that an element of aggression, hostility or subterfuge is required. But an examination of the context makes it clear that this is not so. It is used as a convenient label only, in recognition simply of the fact that the possession is adverse to the interests of the paper owner or, in the case of registered land, of the registered proprietor.

As regards the meaning of 'factual possession', in *Powell v McFarlane* (1979) 38 P & CR 452, Slade J said:

> Factual possession signifies an appropriate degree of physical control. It must be a single and [exclusive] possession, though there can be a single possession exercised by or on behalf of several persons jointly. Thus an owner of land and a person intruding on that land without his consent cannot both be in possession of the land at the same time. The question what acts constitute a sufficient degree of exclusive physical control must depend on the circumstances, in particular the nature of the land and the manner in which land of that nature is commonly used or enjoyed. ... Everything must depend on the particular circumstances, but broadly, I think what must be shown as constituting factual possession is that the alleged possessor has been dealing with the land in question as an occupying owner might have been expected to deal with it and that no-one else has done so.

This statement was approved by the House of Lords in *J A Pye (Oxford) Ltd v Graham*.

As regards the meaning of 'intention to possess', in *Buckinghamshire County Council v Moran* [1989] EWCA Civ 11 Hoffmann J stated that what is required is:

> not an intention to own or even an intention to acquire ownership but an intention to possess.

The House of Lords in *Pye* also approved the following statement by Slade J in *Powell v McFarlane* that 'intention to possess' requires an:

intention, in one's own name and on one's own behalf, to exclude the world at large, including the owner with the paper title if he be not himself the possessor, so far as is reasonably practicable and so far as the processes of the law will allow.

As regards the meaning of 'possession without the owner's consent', the squatter must not be in possession of the land with the owner's consent. In *Buckinghamshire County Council v Moran* Slade LJ stated that:

> Possession is never 'adverse' within the meaning of the [Limitation Act] 1980 if it is enjoyed under a lawful title. If, therefore, a person occupies or uses land by licence of the owner with the paper title and his licence has not been duly determined, he cannot be treated as having been in 'adverse possession' as against the owner of the paper title.

The House of Lords' decision in *Pye v Graham* was the subject of an application to the European Court of Human Rights and ultimately the Grand Chamber of that court (*J A Pye (Oxford) Limited v The United Kingdom* (App No 44302/02) [2007] ECHR 700) found that English law on adverse possession is not contrary to the European Convention for the Protection of Human Rights and Fundamental Freedoms 1950 (European Convention on Human Rights). That decision was in relation to the law applicable prior to the coming into force of the LRA 2002; the new regime relating specifically to registered land introduced by Sch 6 to that Act was drafted so as to be compliant with the human rights legislation.

The effect of illegality of the possession by the squatter in relation to adverse possession is not entirely clear. This will be of particular relevance where the land in question comprises a residential building (see Legal Aid, Sentencing and Punishment of Offenders Act 2012, s 144 and Criminal Law Act 1977, s 7) or part of a highway (see Highways Act 1980, s 137 and *R v Smith* [2009] EWHC 328 (Admin)). In *R (Best) v The Secretary of State for Justice* [2015] EWCA Civ 17 the Court of Appeal held that the fact that the 2012 Act made squatting in a residential building a criminal offence would not preclude the right to make an application under LRA 2002, Sch 6 once the squatter had accrued the requisite period of adverse possession.

The fact that the squatter's original entry onto the land constituted a criminal offence would not appear to preclude a relevant period of adverse possession subsequently accruing in favour of the squatter (*Lambeth LBC v Blackburn* [2001] EWCA Civ 912).

Registration as a person entitled to be notified of an adverse possession application

An applicant should deliver to the Registry:

(a)   an application in Form ADV2;
(b)   the fee payable (see *Fees*, page 221).

The interest of the applicant must be set out in the statement of truth in panel 10 of Form ADV2. If the application is in order, the Registry must enter the name of the applicant in the proprietorship register as a person entitled to be notified under LRA 2002, Sch 6, para 2.

Application under Land Registration Act 2002, Sch 6, para 1 for registration by person in adverse possession of registered land

An applicant should deliver to the Registry:

(a)   an application in Form ADV1;
(b)   a statutory declaration or statement of truth made by the applicant not more than one month before the application, together with any necessary supporting statutory declarations, to provide evidence of adverse possession of the land against which the application is made for a period of not less than 10 years ending on the date of application (a statement of truth may be made in Form ST1 in LRR 2003, Sch 1, although its use is not compulsory);
(c)   if the application relates to part only of the land in a registered title, a plan enabling the extent of the land to be fully identified on the Ordnance Survey map, unless that part is referred to in the statutory declaration or statement of truth by reference to the title plan and this enables that part to be so identified; this plan (if required) should be an exhibit to the applicant's statutory declaration or statement of truth;
(d)   any additional evidence which the applicant considers necessary to support the claim;
(e)   a list in duplicate in Form DL of all the documents delivered;
(f)   the appropriate confirmation or evidence as to identity (see *Identity evidence*, page 266); and
(g)   the fee payable (which includes the cost of a survey) (see *Fees*, page 221).

The statutory declaration or statement of truth by the applicant must also contain:

(a)   if reliance is placed on LRA 2002, Sch 6, para 1(2), the facts relied upon with any appropriate exhibits. Paragraph 1(2) allows a person to apply for registration if he has, in the period of 6 months prior to the application, ceased to be in adverse possession of the estate because of eviction by the registered proprietor or a person claiming under the registered proprietor, and on the day before his eviction he had been in adverse possession for the period of 10 years and the eviction was not pursuant to a judgment for possession;

(b) confirmation that LRA 2002, Sch 6, para 1(3) does not apply. Paragraph 1(3) provides that a person may not make an application under Sch 6, para 1 if he is a defendant in proceedings which involve asserting a right to possession of the land, or if judgment for possession of the land has been given against him in the last 2 years;

(c) confirmation that to the best of his knowledge the restriction on applications in LRA 2002, Sch 6, para 8 does not apply. Paragraph 8 provides that no one who has been in adverse possession of a registered estate may apply to be registered as proprietor of that estate during, or before the end of 12 months after the end of, any period in which the existing registered proprietor is for the purposes of the Limitation (Enemies and War Prisoners) Act 1945 an enemy or detained in enemy territory.

Paragraph 8 also provides that no one who has been in adverse possession of a registered estate may apply to be registered as proprietor of that estate during any period in which the existing registered proprietor is unable, because of mental disability, to make decisions about issues of the kind to which such an application would give rise, or unable to communicate such decisions because of mental disability or physical impairment. For these purposes 'mental disability' means a disability or disorder of the mind or brain, whether permanent or temporary, which results in an impairment or disturbance of mental functioning.

Where it appears to the Registry that either of the above restrictions on applications applies to a registered estate in land, it may include a note to that effect in the register;

(d) confirmation that to the best of his knowledge the estate is not, and has not been during any of the period of alleged adverse possession, subject to a trust (other than one where the interest of each of the beneficiaries is an interest in possession); and

(e) if, should a person given notice of the application require that it be dealt with under LRA 2002, Sch 6, para 5, it is intended to rely on one or more of the conditions set out in that paragraph, the facts supporting such reliance. Paragraph 5 and its three conditions are dealt with under 'Notice of an application based on adverse possession under LRA 2002, Sch 6, para 1', below.

The applicant must also supply such additional evidence as the Registry may require after the application has been considered (LRR 2003, r 17). The Registry will normally arrange for an inspection survey of the land to be carried out.

Although LRA 2002, s 96 provides that no period of limitation under Limitation Act 1980, s 15 is to run against any person, other than a chargee, in relation to an estate in registered land, a person is treated as being in adverse possession of an estate in registered land if, but for s 96, a period of limitation under Limitation Act 1980, s 15 would run in his favour in relation to the estate (LRA 2002, Sch 6, para 11). In determining whether for the purposes of para 11 a period of limitation would run under Limitation Act 1980, s 15, the commencement of any legal proceedings is disregarded.

Limitation Act 1980, Sch 1, para 6 provides that where a person is in possession under a lease in writing that reserves a rent of at least £10 and the rent is wrongfully received by some person claiming to be entitled to the immediate reversion, the right of action to recover the land is deemed to have accrued on the date when the rent was first wrongfully received, not on the date of the determination of the lease. In determining whether, for the purposes of LRA 2002, Sch 6, para 11, a period of limitation would run under the Limitation Act 1980, s 15, however, the Limitation Act 1980, Sch 1, para 6 is disregarded.

A person is also to be regarded as having been in adverse possession of an estate in land where he is the successor in title during any period of adverse possession by a predecessor in title to that estate. He is also to be regarded as having been in adverse possession during any period of adverse possession by another person which comes between, and is continuous with, periods of adverse possession of his own.

When an estate in registered land is subject to a trust, a person is not to be regarded as being in adverse possession of that estate unless the interest of each of the beneficiaries is an interest in possession.

Where the registered land consists of foreshore belonging to the Queen in right of the Crown or the Duchy of Lancaster or to the Duchy of Cornwall, the period of adverse possession required before an application may be made is 60 years rather than 10 years.

If the application is in order, the Registry will serve notice of the application upon the registered proprietor and any other relevant persons in accordance with LRA 2002, Sch 6, para 2.

Notice of an application based on adverse possession under Land Registration Act 2002, Sch 6, para 1

The Registry must serve notice of an application under Sch 6, para 1 on:

(a)   the registered proprietor of the land;
(b)   any registered chargee;
(c)   (where the estate is leasehold) the registered proprietor of any superior registered estate;
(d)   any person who is registered as a person to be notified of such an application; and
(e)   (where the registered proprietor is a dissolved company) the Treasury Solicitor (or the Solicitor for the affairs of the Duchy of Lancaster or the Duke of Cornwall, where appropriate).

The notice which is served by the Registry includes notice that, if the application is not required to be dealt with under LRA 2002, Sch 6, para 5, the applicant is entitled to be entered in the register as the new proprietor of the estate. The period allowed for reply is the period ending at 12 noon on the 65th business day after the date of issue of the notice. A business day is a day when the Land Registry is open to the public; that is, every day except Saturdays, Sundays, Christmas Day, Good Friday or any other day either specified or declared by proclamation under Banking and Financial Dealings Act 1971, s 1 or appointed by the Lord Chancellor or certified by the Registry as being an 'interrupted day' due to delay or failure of a communication service or to some other event or circumstance causing substantial interruption in the normal operation of the Registry.

A person given notice of such an application may require that it is dealt with under LRA 2002, Sch 6, para 5. He must do this by giving notice to the Registry in Form NAP, a copy of which will have accompanied the notice of the application. When notice in Form NAP has been given to the Registry requiring that the application be dealt with under para 5, the applicant is entitled to be registered as the new proprietor only if any of the following three conditions is met.

The first condition is that it would be unconscionable, because of an equity by estoppel, for the registered proprietor to seek to dispossess the applicant and the circumstances are such that the applicant ought to be registered as the proprietor. An example might be where a person built on the registered land under the mistaken belief that he was the owner and the registered proprietor acquiesced in that belief, and the person in possession applied for registration after 10 years, having then learnt the true position.

The second condition is that the applicant is for some other reason entitled to be registered as the proprietor of the estate; for example, where a person entered into a valid contract to purchase and paid the purchase money over 10 years before, but the registered title has never been transferred to him.

The third condition (commonly known as the 'mistaken boundary' condition) is the one most likely to be met with in practice. It is that:

(a) the land to which the application relates is adjacent to land belonging to the applicant;

(b) the exact line of the boundary between the two has not been determined under LRR 2003, rr 118 to 122 (see *Boundaries*, page 77);

(c) for at least 10 years of the period of adverse possession ending on the date of the application, the applicant (or any predecessor in title) reasonably believed that the land to which the application relates belonged to him; and

(d) the estate to which the application relates was registered more than one year prior to the date of the application.

Where an application is made after the applicant has been evicted by the registered proprietor or a person claiming under him, the period referred to in (c) of the third condition is to be treated as the period ending on the day before the date of the applicant's eviction.

This third condition under Sch 6, para 5(4) came into force one year after the rest of the LRA 2002. This was so as to allow registered proprietors one year from 13 October 2003 to commence proceedings against any squatter who might come within para 5(4), or regularise the position in some other way so as to end the adverse possession.

If the Registry is required to deal with the matter under Sch 6, para 5 and none of the three conditions is met, then the application will be rejected.

It is also possible for the registered proprietor or other recipient of the notice to use Form NAP to object to the registration on grounds set out in panel 6 of that form; for example that the alleged acts of adverse possession had not happened or that those acts did not constitute adverse possession. Such an objection would be dealt with in accordance with LRA 2002, s 73 (see *Disputes*, page 193). In addition to objecting on Form NAP, the registered proprietor or other recipient of the notice may also require within that form that the application is dealt with under Sch 6, para 5. By doing so, he retains the option of proceeding under para 5 if his objection (which would need to be determined first) is not successful.

Application under Land Registration Act 2002, Sch 6, para 6 for registration by person in adverse possession of registered land

If the application of a person who has been in adverse possession of a registered estate is rejected pursuant to LRA 2002, Sch 6, para 5, he may make a further application to be registered as the proprietor of the estate if he is in adverse possession of the estate from the date of the application until the last day of the period of 2 years beginning with the date of its rejection. A person may not, however, make such an application if:

(a)   he is a defendant in proceedings which involve asserting a right to possession of the land;
(b)   judgment for possession of the land has been given against him in the last 2 years; or
(c)   he has been evicted from the land pursuant to a judgment for possession.

The special form of notice required by Sch 6, para 2 and the right to require the application to be dealt with under Sch 6, para 5 do not apply to such applications. Instead, under LRR 2003, r 17, 15 business days' notice of the application will be served by the Registry on:

(a)   the registered proprietor of the land;
(b)   any registered chargee;
(c)   (where the estate is leasehold) the registered proprietor of any superior registered estate;
(d)   any person who is registered as a person to be notified of such an application; and
(e)   any other person the Registry considers it appropriate to notify.

If a person makes such an application, he is entitled to be entered in the register as the new proprietor of the estate. This is, however, subject to no valid objection being made by the registered proprietor or other person; for example on the grounds that the alleged acts of adverse possession had not happened or that those acts did not constitute adverse possession. Such an objection would be dealt with in accordance with LRA 2002, s 73 (see *Disputes*, page 193).

The applicant should deliver to the Registry:

(a)   an application in Form ADV1;
(b)   a statutory declaration or statement of truth made by the applicant not more than one month before the application (or a certified copy of it), together with any necessary supporting statutory declarations, to provide evidence of adverse possession of the land against which the application is made for a

period of not less than 2 years beginning with the date of rejection of the original application and ending on the date of application (a statement of truth may be made in Form ST1 in LRR 2003, Sch 4, although its use is not compulsory);

(c) if the application relates to part only of the land in a registered title, a plan enabling the extent of the land to be fully identified on the Ordnance Survey map; this plan should be an exhibit to the applicant's statutory declaration or statement of truth. A plan is not needed if the previous rejected application related only to that part, or that part is referred to in the statutory declaration or statement of truth by reference to the title plan and this enables that part to be so identified;

(d) any additional evidence which the applicant considers necessary to support the claim; and

(e) the fee payable (see *Fees*, page 221).

The statutory declaration or statement of truth by the applicant must also contain:

(a) full details of the previous rejected application;

(b) confirmation that to the best of his knowledge the restriction on applications in LRA 2002, Sch 6, para 8 does not apply. The restrictions imposed by para 8 are discussed under 'Application under Land Registration Act 2002, Sch 6, para 1 for registration by person in adverse possession of registered land', page 17;

(c) confirmation that to the best of his knowledge the estate is not, and has not been during any of the period of alleged adverse possession, subject to a trust (other than one where the interest of each of the beneficiaries is an interest in possession); and

(d) confirmation that LRA 2002, Sch 6, para 6(2) does not apply. Paragraph 6(2) provides that a person may not make an application under para 6 if he is a defendant in proceedings which involve asserting a right to possession of the land, or judgment for possession of the land has been given against him in the last 2 years, or he has been evicted from the land pursuant to a judgment for possession.

The applicant must also supply such additional evidence as the Registry may require after the application has been considered (LRR 2003, r 17).

Registered charges

Where a person is registered as proprietor under LRA 2002, Sch 6, para 1 or para 6, the application having been determined other than by reference to whether any of the conditions in Sch 6, para 5 applies, the estate is vested in him free of any registered charge affecting the estate immediately before his registration. If the application proceeded only because one of the three conditions in Sch 6, para 5 was met, the estate remains subject to any registered charges. Where such a charge affects other property as well as the registered estate, the proprietor of the estate may require the chargee to apportion the amount secured by the charge at that time between the estate and the other property on the basis of their respective values. The person requiring the apportionment is entitled to a discharge of his estate from the charge on payment of the amount apportioned to the estate and the costs incurred by the chargee as a result of the apportionment. LRR 2003, rr 194A to 194G contain procedures relating to apportionment.

Where an application is made under LRA 2002, Sch 12, para 18(1), the applicant takes subject to any registered charge in existence when he commenced adverse possession (see 'Transitional provisions', below). The same applies where an application is made for first registration (see 'Application for first registration', below).

Additional defences to actions for possession

LRA 2002, s 98 contains various defences to an action for possession of land. Those defences are additional to any other defences a person may have. That section also sets out when a judgment for possession of land ceases to be enforceable. Where in any proceedings a court determines that a person is entitled to a defence under that section, or that a judgment for possession has ceased to be enforceable against a person by virtue of s 98(4), the court must order the Registry to register that person as the proprietor of the registered estate in respect of which he is entitled to make an application based on adverse possession.

A person has a defence to an action for possession of land if, on the day immediately preceding that on which the action was brought, he was entitled to make an application to be registered as the proprietor of registered land having been in adverse possession for 10 years and, had he made such an application on that day, the third condition in LRA 2002, Sch 6, para 5 would have been satisfied (LRA 2002, s 98(1)).

A judgment for possession of land ceases to be enforceable at the end of the period of 2 years beginning with the date of the judgment if the proceedings in which the judgment is given were commenced against a person who at that time had been in adverse possession for 10 years (LRA 2002, s 98(2)).

A person has a defence to an action for possession of land if, on the day immediately preceding that on which the action was brought, he was entitled to make a further application to be registered as proprietor having been in adverse possession for a period of 2 years from the date of the rejection of his prior application (LRA 2002, s 98(3)).

A judgment for possession of land ceases to be enforceable at the end of the period of 2 years beginning with the date of the judgment if, at the end of that period, the person against whom the judgment was given is entitled to make a further application to be registered as proprietor having been in adverse possession for a period of 2 years from the date of the rejection of his prior application (LRA 2002, s 98(4)).

Transitional provisions

The position under the Land Registration Act 1925 (LRA 1925) was that where a registered proprietor's title had been extinguished by adverse possession, it was open to the squatter to apply for the closure of the registered proprietor's title which was deemed, in the meantime, to be held on trust for the squatter by the registered proprietor (LRA 1925, s 75(1)). The LRA 2002 contains transitional provisions, so that where a registered estate in land was held in trust for a person by virtue of LRA 1925, s 75(1) immediately before the coming into force of the LRA 2002, he is entitled to be registered as the proprietor of the estate (LRA 2002, Sch 12, para 18(1)).

For the period of 3 years beginning with 13 October 2003, the right to be registered under LRA 2002, Sch 12, para 18(1) was an interest which overrode a registered disposition (LRA 2002, Sch 12, para 11).

A person has a defence to any action for the possession of land (in addition to any other defence he may have) if he is entitled to be registered as the proprietor of an estate in the land under LRA 2002, Sch 12, para 18. Where in an action for possession of land a court determines that a person is entitled to such a defence, the court must order the Registry to register him as the proprietor of the estate in question.

An application to be registered as proprietor under these transitional provisions should be made using application Form AP1, not Form ADV1. The applicant should deliver to the Registry:

(a)   an application in Form AP1, specifying that the applicant is applying to be registered as proprietor in accordance with LRA 2002, Sch 12, para 18(1);

(b)   evidence of adverse possession, by way of statutory declaration(s) or statement(s) of truth (a statement of truth may be in Form ST1 in LRR 2003, Sch 4, although its use is not compulsory);

(c) sufficient details, by plan or otherwise, so that the land can be clearly identified on the Ordnance Survey map;

(d) a list in duplicate in Form DL of all the documents delivered; and

(e) the fee payable (which includes the cost of a survey) (see *Fees*, page 221).

Similar limitation periods to those which apply to unregistered land are applicable, but the evidence lodged must *also* demonstrate that the minimum limitation period had expired before 13 October 2003 so that a trust under LRA 1925, s 75 had arisen by that date. In addition, the title to the land must have been registered prior to that date, although not necessarily for the entire period of the adverse possession.

Where the requisite limitation period had expired prior to 13 October 2003 but the land only became registered on or after that date, application cannot be made under the transitional provisions. Instead, application may be made in Form AP1 (accompanied by supporting evidence as above) for alteration of the register to reflect the fact that the documentary owner's title had already been extinguished at the time of first registration of the estate. If the first registered proprietor had notice of the squatter's title or the squatter remained in actual occupation throughout, the registered estate will have vested in that proprietor subject to the squatter's title (LRA 2002, s 11 and Sch 1, para 2).

The Registry will normally arrange for an inspection survey of the land to be carried out. If the application is in order, the Registry will serve notice of it upon the registered proprietor of the land, any registered chargee, and any other person the Registry considers it appropriate to notify. It is open to the registered proprietor or other recipient of the notice to object to the registration; for example, on the grounds that the alleged acts of adverse possession had not happened or that those acts did not constitute adverse possession. Such an objection would be dealt with in accordance with LRA 2002, s 73 (see *Disputes*, page 193).

If the application is successful, the applicant will be registered as proprietor of the land in place of the existing proprietor, with the same class of title.

Application for first registration

Where a person has been in adverse possession of unregistered land for the appropriate limitation period, the documentary title owner's paper title is extinguished (Limitation Act 1980, s 17). The normal period of limitation for recovery of land is 12 years, but this period is extended to 30 years for the Crown and any spiritual or eleemosynary corporation sole. In the case of foreshore owned by the Crown the period is 60 years. The normal period may also be extended where there has been fraud or deliberate concealment of a cause or action, or mistake (Limitation Act 1980, s 32), or where the person entitled to recover the land is under the age of 18 or is of unsound mind (Limitation Act 1980, ss 28 and 38). Where the land is held on trust or is settled land, the legal estate is not extinguished until the rights of action of all the beneficiaries to recover the land have been barred (Limitation Act 1980, s 18).

A squatter cannot, in general, apply for a caution against first registration on the basis of his adverse possession, as he will be a person entitled to an unregistered possessory estate in land which will preclude him from making such an application (LRA 2002, s 15(3) and *Turner v Chief Land Registrar* [2013] EWHC 1382 (Ch)). He may, however, be in a position to apply for such a caution where he is a successor in title to an earlier squatter who transferred the possessory estate to the squatter, and he does not apply for first registration within 2 months of the transfer or does so but the application is cancelled. In that situation, the title to this estate will revert to the transferor, who will then hold it on a bare trust for the squatter. The squatter, having a beneficial interest in this estate and therefore being entitled to an interest affecting a legal freehold estate in land (as opposed to being the owner of such an estate) may therefore be entitled to apply for a caution. This will apply equally whether or not the documentary title has been extinguished by the time of the transfer of the possessory estate (see *Cautions against first registration*, page 88).

An applicant who has been in adverse possession of unregistered land for the appropriate limitation period may apply for first registration of his title. In addition to the usual documents required (see *First registration*, page 222), an applicant should deliver to the Registry evidence as to the adverse possession by way of statutory declaration(s) or statement(s) of truth (a statement of truth may be in Form ST1 in LRR 2003, Sch 4, although its use is not compulsory) and a certified copy of each such declaration or statement, if the applicant wishes for the original to be returned. Also, Land Charges searches against the names of the applicant and any known owners of the paper title (with any entries accounted for and, where applicable, certified by a conveyancer as not affecting the estate), along with any other relevant searches such as a company search or commons registration search where appropriate.

The applicant may be called upon to pay an additional fee to meet the cost of a survey or special enquiries.

The Registry will normally carry out an inspection survey of the land. If the application is in order, the Registry may serve notice of it upon (if known) the owner and any mortgagee of the paper title, and such adjoining owners and others as it considers appropriate. It is open to the recipient of the notice to object to the registration; for example, on the grounds that the alleged acts of adverse possession had not happened or that those acts did not constitute adverse possession. Such an objection would be dealt with in accordance with LRA 2002, s 73 (see *Disputes*, page 193).

If the application is successful, the applicant will be registered as proprietor of the land, but the Registry will normally only grant a possessory title because it will not be in a position to be satisfied with certainty that the adverse possession by the applicant has extinguished the documentary owner's title. A protective entry may be entered in the register if the Registry considers there is a risk that the land may be subject to undisclosed restrictive covenants, easements or rentcharges.

An applicant may be registered with possessory title if the Registry is of the opinion that the applicant is in actual possession of the land, or in receipt of the rents and profits of the land, by virtue of the estate, and that there is no other class of title with which he may be registered (LRA 2002, s 9(5)). The Registry's policy of normally granting a possessory title, rather than an absolute title, on first registration of a title based upon adverse possession has been upheld on judicial review by the High Court as being neither unlawful nor irrational (*R (Diep) v Chief Land Registrar* [2010] EWHC 3315 (Admin)). This was upon the basis that it struck a balance between the economic and social interest in having absolute titles which could be readily marketed on the one hand and the need to protect the public purse against claims for indemnity on the other.

Adverse possession and leasehold land

Adverse possession of leasehold land

If a squatter takes possession of leasehold land, time runs against the tenant, but does not run against the landlord until the lease expires. The exception would be where the adverse possession commenced before the grant of the lease, in which case time will continue to run against the landlord during the term of the lease. Non-payment of rent before the lease expires is of no effect. However, if a third party wrongfully receives the rent from leasehold land for the requisite period, and provided the title to the reversion is unregistered, the lease is in writing and not granted by the Crown and the rent is at least £10 a year, the third party becomes entitled to make an appropriate application to the Registry (Limitation Act 1980, Sch 1, Pt 1, para 6). The position will be similar where the title to the reversion was registered prior to 13 October 2003 and by that date the period of limitation in favour of the third party wrongfully receiving the rent had accrued; in such a case the third party would be entitled to make an application to the registrar for registration as proprietor of the registered reversionary title under the transitional provisions of LRA 2002, Sch 12, para 18(1). However, where the title to the reversion is registered and the third party wrongfully receiving the rent has no entitlement under the transitional provisions, he will not be entitled to apply for registration as proprietor of the registered reversionary title under the Sch 6 procedure. This is because, for the purposes of determining whether a person is in adverse possession of an estate in land for the purposes of the Sch 6 procedure, Limitation Act 1980, Sch 1, para 6 is to be disregarded (LRA 2002, Sch 6, para 11(3)(b)).

In the case of adverse possession of an unregistered leasehold estate the House of Lords, in *Fairweather v St Marylebone Property Co Ltd* [1962] UKHL 1, held that when the tenant has been ousted by a squatter for the full period of limitation, the tenant may still surrender to the landlord who can then take action to recover possession from the squatter. For this reason, the Registry will reject an application for first registration of such an estate on the basis that the tenant – although no longer able to recover possession of the land once the limitation period has expired – may still surrender the lease to the landlord. This is not the case where the lease is registered and the application is made either under LRA 2002, Sch 6 or (where the limitation period expired before 13 October 2003) under the transitional provisions of LRA 2002, Sch 12, para 18(1): *Spectrum Investment Co v Holmes* [1981] 1 All ER 6; *Central London Commercial Estates Ltd v Kato Kagaku Co Ltd* [1998] EWHC Ch 314.

Encroachment from leasehold land onto other land

There is a legal presumption that a tenant who encroaches onto other land does so for the benefit of his landlord (*Smirk v Lyndale Developments Ltd* [1975] Ch 317 and *Tower Hamlets v Barrett* [2005] EWCA Civ 923).

In relation to LRA 2002, Sch 6, one approach to the effect of this presumption is that it means that there can be no adverse possession by the tenant and that any application under Sch 6 should be by the landlord. However, the presumption can be rebutted by evidence that the tenant intended the encroachment to be for his own benefit; in practice, the Registry will treat the fact that the application has been made as sufficient evidence of such an intention. A different approach to the effect of the presumption is that it is only concerned with who might have acquired title at common law to the estate concerned and does not alter the fact that the tenant is in adverse possession, so that it is irrelevant where the application is being made under Sch 6. If an application is made under Sch 6 by a tenant and it is not clear that the applicant is aware of the presumption, the Registry will contact him to explain the position and request confirmation that he wishes to proceed with the application. If he does so, the Registry will in addition to the other relevant notices, also serve notice on the tenant's landlord, referring to the presumption and to the above points.

In relation to encroachment onto unregistered freehold land, where the squatter accepts that the presumption applies, he may make an application for first registration on the basis that the land is to be treated as an accretion to his existing lease, provided there is more than 7 years of the term of the existing lease unexpired (LRA 2002, s 3(3)). Evidence of the squatter's title to that lease, if unregistered, should accompany the application. Any notice served by the Registry will confirm the application is being made on this basis. If the application is completed, the Registry will enter a note in the property register to the effect that, although not originally within the extent demised by the existing lease, the land encroached on is now held for the term of, and as an accretion to, that lease.

Where the squatter does not accept that the presumption applies, he may instead make an application for first registration of a freehold estate, subject to providing evidence of rebuttal of the presumption. In addition to any other notices served, the Registry will serve notice on the landlord of the applicant, confirming that the application is being made on this basis. If the landlord cannot be identified, the Registry will only be able to consider registering with a qualified title. The qualification will be on the lines that the enforcement of any estate, right or interest adverse to, or in derogation of, the proprietor's title subsisting at the time of first registration or then capable of arising is excepted from the effect of registration.

In relation to encroachment by a squatter from leasehold land onto other land which was registered before 13 October 2003 and 12 years' adverse possession had accrued by that date, the tenant squatter cannot be the beneficiary under a trust under LRA 1925, s 75(1) and cannot therefore apply for registration under the transitional provisions of LRA 2002, Sch 12, para 18. However, where the squatter accepts that the presumption applies, he may make an application for first registration on the basis that the land is to be treated as an accretion to his existing lease, provided there are more than 7 years of the term of the existing lease unexpired (LRA 2002, s 3(3)). This is also provided that the title has not been subsequently lost through registration of a registrable disposition of the registered estate for valuable consideration at any time when the leasehold estate was not an overriding interest (LRA 2002, s 29). Evidence of the squatter's title to his existing lease, if unregistered, should accompany the application. Any notice served by the Registry will confirm the application is being made on this basis. If the application is completed, the Registry will enter a note in the property register to the effect that, although not originally within the extent demised by the existing lease, the land encroached on is now held for the term of, and as an accretion to, that lease. Where the encroachment has been onto registered leasehold land and the squatter's existing lease is for a longer term than that of that registered lease, the note will also make it clear that the land is held as an accretion to the squatter's existing lease, but only for the term of years demised by that registered lease.

Where the squatter does not accept that the presumption applies, he may instead make an application under the transitional provisions of LRA 2002, Sch 12, para 18, accompanied by evidence of rebuttal of the presumption. In addition to any other notices served, the Registry will also usually serve notice of the application on the applicant's landlord, confirming that the application is being made on this basis.

Overriding interests

Prior to the coming into force of the LRA 2002, rights acquired, or in the course of being acquired, under the Limitation Acts were overriding interests (LRA 1925, s 70(1)(f)). Although this particular category of overriding interest is not reproduced in the LRA 2002, for the period of 3 years from 13 October 2003 there was included in the list of unregistered interests which override first registration a right acquired under the Limitation Act 1980 before the coming into force of the LRA 2002. For this period therefore, a person who had acquired title by adverse possession continued to have an interest which overrode first registration (LRA 2002, Sch 12, para 7). This would be the case even if he was no longer in actual occupation and gave him a protected period within which he could seek to register his rights. That period of 3 years has now expired, but if such a person *is* in actual occupation of the land then his interest may instead now be an interest which overrides under para 2 of either LRA 2002, Sch 1 or Sch 3.

For the overriding status of the right to be registered as proprietor where a registered estate in land was held in trust for a person by virtue of LRA 1925, s 75(1) immediately before the coming into force of the LRA 2002, see 'Transitional provisions', above.

ADVOWSONS

An advowson is a right to appoint a vicar or rector to a church of the Church of England. It is a property right and was, for the purposes of the LRA 1925, included in the definition of 'land'. As such it was possible to register an advowson. A title number was allocated and a land certificate was issued.

In order to identify existing advowsons and their owners or 'patrons', the General Synod of the Church of England passed the Patronage (Benefices) Measure 1986 (1986/3) (the 1986 Measure). This required the compilation of a new register of rights of advowson to be held by the diocesan registrar in each diocese. Patrons were given a period of 15 months from 1 October 1987 (i.e. until 1 January 1989) to register their advowson with the appropriate diocesan registrar.

The 1986 Measure did not amend the law of real property and in consequence an advowson still remains an interest in land for most purposes. However, the 1986 Measure, s 6(2) amended LRA 1925, s 3 so as to remove the words 'an advowson' from the definition of 'land'. The definition of land in the LRA 2002 does not include an advowson, nor is an advowson a registrable legal estate under that Act.

As a result of the 1986 Measure, after 1 October 1987 no advowson is capable of being registered at the Land Registry; and on 1 January 1989 any existing registered title to an advowson was deemed to have been closed and removed from the register. Any transfer of an advowson for valuable consideration was rendered void.

In Wales and Monmouthshire, advowsons were abolished on 31 March 1920. Any parishes that straddled the boundary between England and Wales could opt to remain under the jurisdiction of the Church of England and if they did so, they subsequently became subject to the 1986 Measure.

AGREEMENT FOR LEASE

An agreement for lease of registered land may be protected by the entry in the register of an agreed notice or a unilateral notice, and possibly also (depending on the terms of the agreement) a restriction. The fact that it is the subject of a notice does not necessarily mean that the agreement for lease is valid, but does mean that the priority of the agreement is protected on any registered disposition for valuable consideration (LRA 2002, ss 29 and 32). A restriction does not confer any priority; it simply prevents an entry being made in the register in respect of any disposition, or a disposition of a specified kind, unless the terms of the restriction have (where applicable) been complied with.

LRA 2002, s 72(6)(a) provides that rules may make provision for priority periods in connection with the noting in the register of a contract for the making of a registrable disposition of a registered estate or charge. No such rules have currently been made.

Although a leasehold estate in land granted for a term not exceeding 7 years from the date of the grant is usually an interest falling within LRA 2002, Sch 3, para 1 and therefore overrides registered dispositions, an agreement to create such a lease is not itself an interest which overrides; its priority therefore needs to be protected by entry of a notice in the register.

However, even where an agreement for lease of registered land is not protected by a notice, it may still override a later registered disposition for valuable consideration if, at the time of that later disposition, the person having the benefit of the agreement for lease is in actual occupation of the land to which the agreement relates. If he is in actual occupation of only part of the land to which the agreement relates, he has an overriding interest only in respect of the part he is occupying (LRA 2002, ss 29 and 30 and Sch 3, para 2).

The interest of the person in actual possession does not override a registered disposition if enquiry was made of him before the disposition and he failed to disclose the agreement for lease when he could reasonably have been expected to do so. Nor does the agreement for lease override a registered disposition if it belongs to a person whose occupation would not have been obvious on a reasonably careful inspection of the land at the time of the disposition, and if the person to whom the disposition is made does not have actual knowledge of the agreement for lease at the time of the disposition (LRA 2002, Sch 3, para 2).

The agreement for lease should be made and signed by the proprietor of the registered estate, or a satisfactory chain of title shown between the person making the agreement and that registered proprietor. For example, if the registered proprietor has contracted to sell a registered freehold title to A, and A then agrees to lease the land in the title to B, B's agreement for lease can be protected by a notice, whether or not A's contract is also protected by a notice.

A mortgage of an agreement for a lease is a general equitable charge and therefore creates a new interest in land which can be protected by a notice independently of the agreement for lease itself, and whether or not the agreement for lease has itself been protected by a notice. The notice can be entered in the prospective landlord's title, providing a satisfactory chain of title is shown (see *Agreement for mortgage*, page 34).

Agreed notice

In addition to the usual documents required (see *Notices*, page 389), an applicant should deliver to the Registry the agreement for lease or a certified copy of it.

Where the consent of the registered proprietor is not available but, for example, the agreement for lease is signed by him, this is likely to be sufficient to satisfy the Registry as to the validity of the applicant's claim in accordance with LRA 2002, s 34(3)(c).

The agreed notice in the register will give details of the interest protected.

An application for entry of a unilateral notice may be preferred, where the applicant does not wish the terms of the agreement for lease to be open to public inspection and copying.

Unilateral notice

In addition to delivering the usual documents required (see *Notices*, page 389), an applicant should ensure that the statement in panel 11 or conveyancer's certificate in panel 12 of Form UN1 is completed on the following lines to show the interest of the applicant:

> intending lessee under an agreement for lease dated [*date*] made between [*registered proprietor*] and [*purchaser/prospective lessee*].

The unilateral notice in the register will give brief details of the interest protected and identify the beneficiary of that notice.

Restriction

As a result of LRA 2002, s 42(2), no restriction may be entered for the purpose of protecting the priority of an interest which is, or could be, the subject of a notice. This does not, however, prevent a restriction being entered in addition to a notice in respect of the agreement for lease. Although the notice protects the priority of the agreement, a restriction may be used to ensure that any conditions in relation to another disposition by the registered proprietor are complied with.

The consent of the registered proprietor to the entry of the restriction is required, unless the agreement for lease contains a provision which limits the registered proprietor's powers to enter into any further disposition.

In addition to delivering the usual documents required (see *Restrictions*, page 500), an applicant should deliver to the Registry (if the application is made by a person who claims that he has a sufficient interest in the making of the entry) a certified copy of the agreement for lease.

The statement in panel 12 of Form RX1 signed by the applicant, or a certificate by his conveyancer in panel 13 of Form RX1, must give details of the nature of the agreement and of the provision in the agreement limiting the registered proprietor's powers to enter into a disposition.

Panel 9 of Form RX1 should be completed as to the required restriction(s). A restriction in a standard form contained in LRR 2003, Sch 4 does not require the approval of the Registry to the terms of the restriction under LRA 2002, s 43(3). A possible form of restriction based on Form L is:

> No disposition of the registered estate by the proprietor of the registered estate is to be registered without a certificate signed by [*intending lessee*] of [*address*] or their conveyancer that the provisions of [*clause, paragraph or other particulars*] of [*details of agreement for lease*] have been complied with or that they do not apply to the disposition.

The Registry must give notice of the application for a restriction to the proprietor of the registered estate or charge concerned, if it has not been made by or with the consent of such proprietor or a person entitled to be registered as such proprietor (LRA 2002, s 45).

AGREEMENT FOR MORTGAGE

An agreement for mortgage of registered land may be protected by the entry in the register of an agreed notice or a unilateral notice, and possibly also (depending on the terms of the agreement) a restriction. The fact that it is the subject of a notice does not necessarily mean that the agreement for mortgage is valid, but does mean that the priority of that agreement is protected on any registered disposition (LRA 2002, ss 29, 30 and 32). A restriction does not confer any priority; it simply prevents an entry being made in the register in respect of any disposition, or a disposition of a specified kind, unless the terms of the restriction have (where applicable) been complied with.

LRA 2002, s 72(6)(a) provides that rules may make provision for priority periods in connection with the noting in the register of a contract for the making of a registrable disposition of a registered estate or charge. No such rules have currently been made.

The agreement for mortgage should be made and signed by the proprietor of the registered estate, or a satisfactory chain of title shown between the person making the agreement and the registered proprietor. For example, if the registered proprietor has contracted to sell a registered freehold title to A, and A then agrees to mortgage the land in the title to B, B's agreement for mortgage can be protected by a notice, whether or not A's contract is also protected by a notice.

Agreed notice

In addition to the usual documents required (see *Notices*, page 389), an applicant should deliver to the Registry the agreement for mortgage or a certified copy of it.

Where the consent of the registered proprietor is not available but, for example, the agreement for mortgage is signed by him, this is likely to be sufficient to satisfy the Registry as to the validity of the applicant's claim in accordance with LRA 2002, s 34(3)(c).

Where the agreement is by an intending purchaser or lessee who has the benefit of a contract for sale or agreement for lease, that contract or agreement, or a certified copy of it, should be lodged with the application. This is not necessary if there is already a notice in the register in respect of that contract or agreement.

The agreed notice in the register will give details of the interest protected.

An application for entry of a unilateral notice may be preferred where the applicant does not wish the terms of the agreement to be open to public inspection and copying.

Unilateral notice

In addition to delivering the usual documents required (see *Notices*, page 389), an applicant should ensure that the statement in panel 11 or conveyancer's certificate in panel 12 of Form UN1 is completed on the following lines to show the interest of the applicant:

intending mortgagee under an agreement for mortgage dated [*date*] made between [*registered proprietor*] and [*prospective mortgagee*].

In the case of an agreement for mortgage given by an intending purchaser who has the benefit of a contract for sale, the statement in panel 11 or conveyancer's certificate in panel 12 of Form UN1 should be completed on the following lines:

intending mortgagee under an agreement for mortgage dated [*date*] made between [*purchaser*] and [*prospective mortgagee*], [*purchaser*] being the purchaser under a contract for sale dated [*date*] made between [*registered proprietor*] and [*purchaser*].

The wording must establish the link between the registered proprietor and the person who is to be shown as the beneficiary of the notice. It must also confirm that an agreement for mortgage exists – a simple statement that monies have been advanced is insufficient, as this does not prove the existence of an interest which affects a registered estate, only the existence of a debt. The position is similar in relation to an agreement for mortgage given by an intending lessee who has the benefit of an agreement for lease.

The unilateral notice in the register will give brief details of the interest protected and identify the beneficiary of that notice.

Restriction

As a result of LRA 2002, s 42(2) no restriction may be entered for the purpose of protecting the priority of an interest which is, or could be, the subject of a notice. This does not, however, prevent a restriction being entered in addition to a notice in respect of the agreement for mortgage. Although the notice protects the priority of the agreement for mortgage, a restriction may be used to ensure that any conditions in relation to another disposition by the registered proprietor are complied with. The consent of the registered proprietor to the entry of the restriction is required, unless the agreement for mortgage contains a provision which limits the registered proprietor's powers to enter into any further disposition.

In addition to delivering the usual documents required (see *Restrictions*, page 500), an applicant should deliver to the Registry (if the application is made by a person who claims that he has a sufficient interest in the making of the entry) a certified copy of the agreement for mortgage.

The statement in panel 12 of Form RX1 signed by the applicant, or a certificate by his conveyancer in panel 13 of Form RX1, must give details of the nature of the agreement and of the provision in the agreement limiting the registered proprietor's powers to enter into a disposition.

Panel 9 of Form RX1 should be completed as to the required restriction(s). A restriction in a standard form contained in LRR 2003, Sch 4 does not require the approval of the Registry to the terms of the restriction under LRA 2002, s 43(3). A possible form of restriction based on Form L is:

> No disposition of the registered estate by the proprietor of the registered estate is to be registered without a certificate signed by [*prospective mortgagee*] of [*address*] or their conveyancer that the provisions of [*clause, paragraph or other particulars*] of [*details of agreement for mortgage*] have been complied with or that they do not apply to the disposition.

The Registry must give notice of the application for a restriction to the proprietor of the registered estate or charge concerned, if it has not been made by or with the consent of such proprietor or a person entitled to be registered as such proprietor (LRA 2002, s 45).

AGREEMENT TO PAY FURTHER CONSIDERATION

A vendor may impose a covenant or provision under which the purchaser is required to pay a further sum or sums. This is sometimes referred to as 'overage'. A common example is where a vendor of undeveloped land is to be paid further sums if planning permission is granted in the future. Another example is where a payment will become due if the use of the land is changed in the future.

Such sums may be secured by a legal charge or an equitable charge (see *Legal charges*, page 333, and *Equitable charges*, page 207). Where the vendor does not take some form of charge to secure payment, the question arises as to whether he can claim that a vendor's lien has arisen. Although this depends on the particular facts, in the main the requirement to pay overage does not give rise to a vendor's lien (*Woolf Project Management v Woodtrek Limited* (1988) 56 P & CR 134). For the situation where a vendor's lien has arisen, see *Vendor's liens*, page 570.

Generally, covenants to pay further sums will be personal covenants because they benefit the vendor personally rather than other neighbouring land owned by the vendor. If the obligation is in the form of a positive covenant, the Registry will make an appropriate entry in the register (see *Positive covenants*, page 444).

If the registered proprietor consents, or if the agreement contains a provision which limits the registered proprietor's powers to enter into any further disposition, application may be made for entry of a restriction in the register. A restriction does not confer any priority; it simply prevents an entry being made in the register in respect of any disposition, or a disposition of a specified kind, unless the terms of the restriction have (where applicable) been complied with.

Restriction

In addition to the usual documents required (see *Restrictions*, page 500), an applicant should deliver to the Registry (if the application is made by a person who claims that he has a sufficient interest in the making of the entry) a certified copy of the agreement to pay further consideration.

The statement in panel 12 of Form RX1 must be signed by the applicant, or a certificate by his conveyancer in panel 13 of Form RX1, giving details of the nature of the agreement and of the provision in the agreement limiting the registered proprietor's powers to enter into a disposition.

Panel 9 of Form RX1 should be completed as to the required restriction(s). A restriction in a standard form contained in LRR 2003, Sch 4 does not require the approval of the Registry to the terms of the restriction under LRA 2002, s 43(3). A possible form of restriction based on Form L is:

> No disposition of the registered estate by the proprietor of the registered estate is to be registered without a certificate signed by [*vendor*] of [*address*] or their conveyancer that the provisions of [*clause, paragraph or other particulars*] of [*details of document containing agreement to pay further consideration*] have been complied with or that they do not apply to the disposition.

Alternatively, where the certificate of the registered proprietor of a specified title number is to be required, a similar restriction based upon Form M may be appropriate.

The Registry must give notice of the application for a restriction to the proprietor of the registered estate or charge concerned, if it has not been made by or with the consent of such proprietor or a person entitled to be registered as such proprietor (LRA 2002, s 45).

AIRSPACE

Unless an entry to the contrary appears in the property register of a registered title, that title includes the airspace above the land identified on the title plan.

In an application for first registration, unless all of the land above the surface is included in that application, the applicant must provide a plan of the surface on, under or over which the land to be registered lies. He must also provide sufficient information to define the vertical and horizontal extents of the land (LRR 2003, r 26). On completion of the registration this information will be reflected by an appropriate entry in the property register. Registrations of airspace, although unusual, are increasing. They can relate to a freehold or leasehold estate, and may be registrations in their own right or form part of the registration of another structure: typically commercial premises such as an office block, an industrial unit or a unit within a shopping complex. Leases of airspace to accommodate solar panels are also becoming increasingly common.

A register of title relating to freehold or leasehold land may describe the land by reference to:

- the Newlyn Datum;
- Ordnance Datum Newlyn; or
- Ordnance Survey Datum.

These are one and the same. Ordnance Survey Datum is mean sea level. The level was based on hourly readings taken by Ordnance Survey on the south pier at Newlyn in Cornwall between 1915 and 1921. Ordnance Survey Datum may also be used in transfers, leases and other deeds as a means of defining the levels or strata within a transfer, demise or grant.

ALTERATION OF THE REGISTER

The LRA 2002 provides for alteration of the register for a number of purposes, either by the Land Registry of its own volition, or in pursuance of an application for alteration, or in pursuance of a court order for alteration (LRA 2002, s 65 and Sch 4).

In considering applications for alteration of the register it is necessary to distinguish between those applications that involve 'rectification' and those that do not. It is also necessary to distinguish alterations made pursuant to a court order for alteration from those which are not made pursuant to such an order.

The LRA 2002 makes a clear distinction between 'alteration' generally and 'rectification' as a specific type of alteration, unlike the LRA 1925 where those two terms were used interchangeably. The distinction between the two is important in relation to both alteration of the register itself (where the power to *rectify* against a 'proprietor in possession' of an estate in land is limited) and entitlement to indemnity (which arises, in relation to alteration for the purposes of correcting a mistake in the register, where the register is rectified or there is a mistake whose correction would involve rectification).

Rectification in this context is an alteration which: (a) involves the correction of a mistake; and (b) prejudicially affects the title of a registered proprietor (LRA 2002, Sch 4 para 1). Rectification is therefore a type of alteration, but not all alterations amount to rectification. For applications involving rectification, see *Rectification*, page 480. For applications relating to payment of indemnity in rectification cases, see *Indemnity*, page 273.

LRA 2002, Sch 4 makes provision for the discretionary payment of costs and expenses in connection with an alteration of the register in non-rectification cases.

Alteration pursuant to a court order

Where in any proceedings the court decides that:

(a)   there is a mistake in the register,
(b)   the register is not up to date, or
(c)   there is an estate, right or interest excepted from the effect of registration that should be given effect to,

it must make an order for alteration of the register (LRA 2002, Sch 4, para 2(1) and LRR 2003, r 126(1)). The court is not, however, obliged to make an order if there are exceptional circumstances that justify not doing so (LRR 2003, r 126(2)). Rule 126 does not apply to an alteration of the register that amounts to rectification.

An estate, right or interest may be excepted from the effect of registration by virtue of the registration of a registered title with qualified, possessory or good leasehold title (LRA 2002, ss 11 and 12) (see *Classes of title*, page 130). Such an estate, right or interest could be the subject of a court order for alteration of the register even though the class of title was not itself changed.

The court order for alteration of the register must state the title number of the title affected and the alteration that is to be made. It must also direct the Registry to make the alteration. If the court makes an order for alteration, the Registry must give effect to the order when it is served on it. Service of the order must be made by making an application to the Registry, accompanied by the order.

An applicant should deliver to the Registry:

(a)   an application in Form AP1;
(b)   the court order for alteration of the register or a sealed copy of the order; and
(c)   the fee (if applicable) (see *Fees*, page 221).

Alteration not pursuant to a court order

The Registry may alter the register for the purpose of:

(a)   correcting a mistake;
(b)   bringing the register up to date;

(c)   giving effect to any estate, right or interest excepted from the effect of registration; or

(d)   removing a superfluous entry.

The alteration may be made as the result of an application or by the Registry of its own volition without an application having been made. The Registry may make such enquiries as it thinks fit and must give notice of the proposed alteration to any person who would be affected by it, unless it is satisfied that such notice is unnecessary (LRR 2003, r 128). Rule 128 does not, however, apply to alteration of the register in the specific circumstances covered by any other rule. An application for alteration by the Registry (otherwise than under a court order) must be supported by evidence to justify the alteration (LRR 2003, r 129).

An applicant for an alteration of the register not pursuant to a court order should deliver to the Registry:

(a)   an application in Form AP1;

(b)   a statement of the alteration being applied for;

(c)   all evidence held by the applicant which is relevant to the application to alter the register; and

(d)   the fee (if applicable) (see *Fees*, page 221).

Costs and expenses in non-rectification cases

If the register is altered under LRA 2002, Sch 4 in a case *not* involving rectification, the Registry may pay such amount as it thinks fit in respect of any costs or expenses reasonably incurred by a person in connection with the alteration which have been incurred with the consent of the Registry (LRA 2002, Sch 4, para 9). Even where the Registry has not consented to the costs or expenses being incurred, it may still make a payment if it appears to the Registry that the costs or expenses had to be incurred urgently and it was not reasonably practicable to apply for its consent. The Registry may also still make a payment if it has subsequently approved the incurring of the costs or expenses.

Costs and expenses are payable under Sch 4, para 9 at the discretion of the Registry and only when the register is actually altered. For costs and expenses in connection with the payment of indemnity in rectification cases, see *Indemnity*, page 273.

AMALGAMATION OF REGISTERED TITLES

An amalgamation is the joining of two or more registered or unregistered estates affecting different extents of land, under a single registered title. The Registry may amalgamate two or more registered titles to form one registered title. It may also add an unregistered estate which is being registered for the first time to an existing registered title. In either case the estates must be of the same kind and vested in the same proprietor (LRR 2003, r 3(4)). The titles must therefore be of the same estate and tenure, and held by the same proprietor in the same capacity. Accordingly, a freehold title cannot be amalgamated with a leasehold title, nor can a possessory title be amalgamated with an absolute title. Nor can amalgamation be effected where the same proprietor holds all the titles, but in a differing capacity; one as beneficial owner and one as trustee, for example.

Amalgamation will most commonly be considered for estates in land. However, it is possible to amalgamate other estates where the estates are of the same kind and are vested in the same proprietor. For example, a proprietor can hold more than one profit à prendre in gross and these can be registered under one title number and set out in a schedule within the property register.

It is possible to amalgamate a title that is subject to a registered charge with one that is not. However, if this is done it will not be possible for the registered chargee to discharge the charge electronically at a later date.

Amalgamation can occur either as the result of an application by the proprietor of the registered estate or of any registered charge over it, or because the Registry considers it desirable for the keeping of the register of title. An application by the proprietor should be made in Form AP1, listing the relevant title numbers in panel 2. For the fee (if any) payable, see *Fees*, page 221.

The Registry has a discretion as to whether or not titles should be amalgamated. It will consider each request on its merits, taking into account the current office work situation; the amount of work and cost involved in amalgamating; and the likely future benefit to the applicant/proprietor and to the Registry in amalgamating.

Where the proprietor has not made an application but amalgamation is effected because the Registry considers it desirable for the keeping of the register of title, it must notify the proprietor of the registered estate and any registered charge, unless they have agreed to the amalgamation. In these circumstances the Registry may make a new edition of any individual register or make entries on any individual register to reflect the amalgamation (LRR 2003, r 3(5)).

LRR 2003, r 70 applies on amalgamation where a registered estate in land includes any mines or minerals but there is no note in the register that they are included, and it is appropriate when describing the amalgamated registered estate to do so by reference to the land where the mines or minerals are or may be situated. In such circumstances the Registry may make an entry in the property register to the effect that such description is an entry made under LRR 2003, r 5(a), and is not a note that the registered estate includes the mines or minerals for the purposes of extending the payment of indemnity to such mines or minerals. LRR 2003, r 5(a) provides that the property register must contain a description of the registered estate (see also *Mines and minerals*, page 380).

ANNUITIES

Strictly, an annuity is not secured on land and so does not require protection at the Land Registry. The term 'annuity' is, however, sometimes used to describe a rentcharge for life, which is an interest under a trust of land or a settlement under the Settled Land Act 1925 (SLA 1925). No notice may be entered in the register in respect of any such interest (LRA 2002, s 33).

In the case of settled land, restrictions are entered in the register for the protection of persons interested in the settled land. The proprietor, or (if there is no proprietor) the personal representatives of a deceased proprietor, must apply for the entry of such restrictions (in addition to a restriction in Forms G, H or I) as may be appropriate. The applicant must state that the restrictions applied for are required for the protection of the beneficial interests and powers under the settlement. The Registry must enter such restrictions without enquiry as to the terms of the settlement (LRR 2003, Sch 7, para 7). Even so, if it does not appear to the Registry that the terms of the proposed restriction are reasonable and that applying the proposed restriction would be straightforward and not place an unreasonable burden on it, it may not approve the application for the restriction (LRA 2002, s 43(3)). For the various restrictions appropriate to settled land, see *Settlements*, page 527.

Where the annuity is an interest under a trust of land, the proprietor of the registered land must apply for entry of a restriction in Form A in LRR 2003, Sch 4, unless one already appears in the register (LRR 2003, r 94). The wording of Form A is set out in Appendix IV, page 585.

Where a restriction in Form A is required but the proprietor of the registered land has not applied for it, any person who has an interest in a registered estate held under a trust of land has a sufficient interest for the purposes of LRA 2002, s 43(1)(c) to apply for that restriction to be entered in the register of that registered estate (LRR 2003, r 93(a)).

An annuity which is a rentcharge for life or lives, or determinable on the dropping of a life, and not arising under a settlement or trust of land, can be overreached by a disposition under SLA 1925, s 72(3) or Law of Property Act 1925, s 2(2) and (3) (as amended by the Law of Property (Amendment) Act 1926). A settled land restriction or Form A restriction would again be appropriate, depending on the circumstances.

Restriction

The applicant should deliver to the Registry the usual documents required (see *Restrictions*, page 500).

Panel 9 of Form RX1 should be completed as to the required restriction(s). A restriction in a standard form contained in LRR 2003, Sch 4 does not require the approval of the Registry to the terms of the restriction under LRA 2002, s 43(3).

The Registry must give notice of the application for a restriction to the proprietor of the registered estate or charge concerned, if it has not been made by or with the consent of such proprietor or a person entitled to be registered as such proprietor (LRA 2002, s 45).

APPLICATIONS TO HM LAND REGISTRY

Applications to the Land Registry must be made in accordance with the provisions of the LRA 2002 and the LRR 2003 and related practice and procedures as laid down by the Registry from time to time.

Many applications are nowadays lodged electronically (see *Electronic services*, page 200). Applicants using e-DRS can only send electronic certified copies of documents.

Under LRR 2003, r 214 (as amended), the originals of scheduled forms and documents which comprise registrable dispositions do not need to be lodged when making an application – instead, only certified copies of deeds or documents need to be provided. This applies not only to electronic applications, but also to postal applications.

Although originals of documents will still be acceptable in the case of postal applications, it is important to bear in mind that, under the revised practice, these will be destroyed once the Registry has made a scanned copy of them for registration purposes. The previous practice, where an original document was lodged, was for the Registry to return the original document if a certified copy of it was provided with the application. The revised practice applies to both originals and certified copies, and to both completed applications and those that are cancelled (see *Retention, destruction and return of documents*, page 513).

For Registry purposes, a 'certified copy' is a copy of a document which has been certified as a true copy of the original document by the applicant, a conveyancer or a person signing on the applicant's behalf. In each case, the person certifying the document should endorse it with his name and address. If it is certified by someone on behalf of the applicant, it should be clear from the certification that that person is signing it on the applicant's behalf.

This practice applies only to postal applications relating to existing registered titles. It does not apply to applications for first registration (see *First registration*, page 222).

ASSENTS

Where a beneficiary is entitled to registered or unregistered land under the will or intestacy of a deceased owner, the personal representative may execute an assent in favour of the beneficiary so as to vest the legal estate in him, whether or not the personal representative has (in the case of registered land) first been registered as proprietor in place of the deceased proprietor. Although the assent must be in writing and signed by all the personal representatives (if more than one), it does not have to be drawn as a deed.

Where an assent relates only to the beneficial share of a deceased proprietor, this does not effect a transfer of the legal estate. Such an assent should not be lodged for registration and, if a transfer of the legal estate is required, this should be effected in the appropriate form and an appropriate application for registration made.

Unregistered land

When the title to land is unregistered, an application for first registration must be made after an assent has transferred a legal freehold estate in the land, or a legal leasehold estate in the land for a term which, at the time of the assent, has more than 7 years to run (LRA 2002, s 4). The requirement to apply for first registration does not apply to mines and minerals held apart from the surface.

The person taking under the assent must apply for first registration within 2 months of the assent. If necessary, he may apply to the Registry for an order that the period for registration ends on a later date, which date will be specified in the order. The Registry will make such an order if it is satisfied that there is good reason for doing so (LRA 2002, s 6(5)).

If the requirement of registration is not complied with following the assent, the legal estate reverts to the personal representative who holds it on a bare trust for the assentee (LRA 2002, s 7). Where an order is made under LRA 2002, s 6(5), this reverter of the legal estate is treated as not having occurred.

If there has to be a further assent because of the failure to apply for first registration following the original assent, the assentee is liable for the proper costs of the personal representative in respect of the new assent (LRA 2002, s 8).

In addition to delivering the usual documents required (see *First registration*, page 222), an applicant for first registration should deliver to the Registry evidence of the appointment of the personal representative, being the original or an office copy or certified copy of the grant of probate, or letters of administration, or order of the court appointing the personal representative.

As to first registration generally, see *First registration*, page 222. The Registry does not have the statutory protection conferred upon a 'purchaser' under Administration of Estates Act 1925, s 36(7) nor does LRR 2003, r 162(2) apply in relation to an application for first registration; the Registry may therefore investigate the will or intestacy if it considers it necessary in order to satisfy itself that the applicant is entitled to apply. In practice, this will not normally be necessary except where a liability for inheritance tax (IHT) may arise (see *Inheritance tax*, page 280).

A restriction in Form A will be entered by the Registry, where necessary, if the assent is in favour of two or more assentees (see *Joint proprietors*, page 286); any other restrictions required should be applied for as appropriate.

Registered land

Where a sole proprietor or the last surviving joint proprietor has died, his personal representative may transfer the deceased's registered estate or registered charge without himself becoming registered as proprietor. LRR 2003, r 162(2) places responsibility on the personal representative in relation to registered land forming part of the deceased's estate, by providing that the Registry is not under a duty to investigate the reasons why any transfer by such a personal representative is made, nor to consider the contents of the will. Provided the terms of any restriction in the register are complied with, the Registry must assume, whether or not it knows the terms of the will, that the personal representative is acting correctly and within his powers.

The assent must be in the appropriate prescribed form, being Form AS1 (assent of whole of land in a registered title), Form AS2 (assent of registered charge), or Form AS3 (assent of part of land in a registered title). Until the assent of the registered estate or registered charge is completed by registration, it does not operate at law (LRA 2002, s 27(1)).

The assentee (not being a 'purchaser') is not able to apply for an official search with priority using Form OS1 or Form OS2, but is able to apply for an official search without priority (see *Official searches*, page 404). In addition, he is able to reserve a period of priority for his substantive application by making an outline application.

A person applying to register an assent of registered land should deliver to the Registry:

(a)   an application in Form AP1;

(b)   Forms AS1, AS2 or AS3 as appropriate;

(c)   evidence of the appointment of the personal representative (unless the personal representative is already registered as proprietor), being the original or an office copy or certified copy of the grant of probate, or letters of administration, or order of the court appointing the personal representative. Alternatively, a certificate from the applicant's conveyancer that he holds the original or an office copy of the grant, letters of administration or court order may be provided (LRR 2003, r 163(2));

(d)   Form DI giving the information as to overriding interests required by LRR 2003, r 57, including any documentary evidence of the interests (see 'Duty to disclose overriding interests', page 426);

(e)   the appropriate confirmation or evidence as to identity (see *Identity evidence*, page 266);

(f)   the appropriate SDLT certificate or other evidence (see *Stamp duty land tax*, page 541); and

(g)   the fee payable (see *Fees*, page 221).

The applicant will be registered subject to any existing entries in the register which are not cancelled or withdrawn, including any existing restrictions. The terms of any such restrictions will, where necessary, need to be complied with before the assent can be completed by registration. Where a restriction in Form C (see *Personal representatives*, page 435) appears in the register, the assent will not be caught by it and it will be automatically cancelled on registration of the assent.

A restriction in Form A in LRR 2003, Sch 4 will be entered by the Registry, where necessary, if the assent is in favour of two or more assentees (see *Joint proprietors*, page 286); any other new restrictions required should be applied for as appropriate.

ASSETS OF COMMUNITY VALUE

Chapter 3 of Localism Act 2011, Pt 5, which deals with 'assets of community value', came into force in England on 21 September 2012, but is not yet in force in Wales. Under s 100 of this Act, local authorities in England must maintain a list of assets of community value, such as a village shop, a pub or a community centre, which further the social well-being or social interests of the local community. The listing of an asset of community value will constitute a local land charge.

Under Localism Act 2011, s 95(1), the owner of listed land is prohibited from entering into a 'relevant disposal' of it unless specified conditions are satisfied. These provide for the owner to give notification to the local authority of his intention to make a relevant disposal, and for a moratorium during which a community interest group may bid for the land, although the owner does not have to accept any such bid.

A 'relevant disposal' is defined as a disposal with vacant possession of a freehold estate or the grant or assignment with vacant possession of a lease granted for a term of at least 25 years. Certain types of relevant disposals are exempted from the right to bid: these include gifts and transfers at nil value; transfers between family members; business-to-business going concern exemptions; and disposals where only part of the land is listed.

LRR 2003, Sch 4 includes a standard form of restriction for use in existing registered titles and on first registration. This is Form QQ, the wording of which is set out in Appendix IV, page 585.

Where the listed land is registered, the relevant local authority is under a duty to apply for the registration of a restriction in Form QQ against the registered estate (LRR 2003, r 94(11)). The local authority must apply as soon as practicable after listing, unless there is an existing Form QQ restriction in respect of the same registered estate.

Where the listed land is currently unregistered, an applicant for first registration of title to the land must at the same time apply for entry of a Form QQ restriction in respect of that land. This includes an applicant who is making the application as mortgagee under a first legal mortgage, the creation of which has triggered compulsory first registration.

Where a person applies for first registration of title to such land and any of the deeds and documents accompanying the application includes a conveyance or lease to the applicant (or to a predecessor in title) made at any time when the land was listed land, the applicant must, in respect of each conveyance or lease, provide a certificate by a conveyancer that the conveyance or lease did not contravene Localism Act 2011, s 95(1).

A transfer or lease in breach of s 95(1) will be ineffective from the outset, unless the owner who made it did not know that the land was listed despite making all reasonable efforts (Assets of Community Value (England) Regulations 2012 (SI 2012/2421), reg 21). A Form QQ restriction only 'catches' transfers and leases, including those taking effect by operation of law. On registration of a transfer or lease, the Registry will not normally cancel the restriction unless a specific application is made in Form RX3 by or with the consent of the relevant local authority.

BANKRUPTCY

The proprietor of a registered estate or charge may become bankrupt and the LRA 2002 contains specific provisions to cover this situation when it occurs. The main statutory provisions relating to insolvency are contained in the IA 1986 and the Insolvency Rules 2016. These are supplemented by specific provisions in the LRA 2002 and the LRR 2003 relating to bankruptcy. The bankruptcy process, where initiated by a creditor, involves two stages: (a) the presentation by a creditor of a bankruptcy petition to the court for a bankruptcy order; and (b) the making of a bankruptcy order by the court. In the alternative, since 1 April 2016 a debtor may make an application for his own bankruptcy to an adjudicator within the Insolvency Service under IA 1986, s 263H. After the bankruptcy order is made, whether by the court or by an adjudicator, a trustee in bankruptcy is appointed who will be either an authorised insolvency practitioner or the Official Receiver.

As an alternative to bankruptcy, a debtor may enter into an individual voluntary arrangement (IVA) with his creditors (see *Individual voluntary arrangements*, page 277).

Petition in bankruptcy

Immediately after the bankruptcy application or petition has been filed, the adjudicator or court must apply to the Land Charges Department for registration of the application or petition in the register of pending actions. As soon as practicable after registration under the Land Charges Act 1972, the Land Registry must enter in the register, in relation to any registered estate or charge which appears to it to be affected, a notice in respect of the pending action (LRA 2002, s 86(2)). This notice is designated a 'bankruptcy notice' (LRR 2003, r 165). No fee is payable.

A bankruptcy notice in relation to a registered estate is entered in the proprietorship register and a bankruptcy notice in relation to a registered charge is entered in the charges register. The notice will be in the following form:

> BANKRUPTCY NOTICE entered under section 86(2) of the Land Registration Act 2002 in respect of a pending action, as the title of the [*proprietor of the registered estate*] *or* [*proprietor of the charge dated ... referred to above*] appears to be affected by a [petition in bankruptcy against [*name of debtor*], presented in the [*name*] Court (Court Reference Number ...)] *or* [bankruptcy application made by [*name of debtor*] (reference ...)] (Land Charges Reference Number PA ...).

The Registry must give notice of the entry of a bankruptcy notice to the proprietor of the registered estate or charge to which it relates.

Unless the bankruptcy notice is cancelled by the Registry, it continues in force until a bankruptcy restriction is entered in the register or the trustee in bankruptcy is entered as proprietor (LRA 2002, s 86(3)). As to cancellation, see 'Cancellation of bankruptcy notice or bankruptcy restriction', below.

Where a bankruptcy notice appears in the register, an application to register a disposition by the registered proprietor after the entry of a bankruptcy notice, such as a transfer, can still be made but, unless it is clear the interest of the disponee has priority over the bankruptcy proceedings, the registration will be made subject to the bankruptcy notice by the entry of a note in the register along the following lines:

> The registration of the proprietor is subject to the rights of all creditors of [*transferor's name*] (a former proprietor) protected by the Bankruptcy Notice(s) referred to above.

This reflects the fact that the priority of the bankruptcy proceedings has been protected by the bankruptcy notice.

Bankruptcy order

Immediately after the adjudicator or court has made a bankruptcy order, at least two sealed copies must be sent to the Official Receiver. On receipt, the Official Receiver must send notice of the making of the order to the Land Charges Department for registration in the register of writs and orders affecting land. As soon as practicable after registration of a bankruptcy order under the Land Charges Act 1972, the Land Registry must enter in the register, in relation to any registered estate or charge which appears to it to be affected, a restriction reflecting the effect of the IA 1986 (LRA 2002, s 86(4)). This restriction is designated a 'bankruptcy restriction' (LRR 2003, r 166). No fee is payable.

A bankruptcy restriction in relation to a registered estate is entered in the proprietorship register and a bankruptcy restriction in relation to a registered charge is entered in the charges register. The restriction will be in the following form:

> BANKRUPTCY RESTRICTION entered under section 86(4) of the Land Registration Act 2002, as the title of [*the proprietor of the registered estate*] *or* [*the proprietor of the charge dated ... referred to above*] appears to be affected by a bankruptcy order made by the [[*name*] Court (Court Reference Number ...)] *or* [adjudicator (reference ...) against [*name of debtor*] (Land Charges Reference Number WO ...).

> No disposition of the registered estate is to be registered until the trustee in bankruptcy of the property of the bankrupt is registered as proprietor of the [*registered estate*] *or* [*charge*].

The Registry must give notice of the entry of a bankruptcy restriction to the proprietor of the registered estate or registered charge to which it relates.

The bankruptcy restriction reflects the position under the IA 1986, s 284 which provides that where a person is adjudged bankrupt, any disposition of property made by him between the making of the bankruptcy application or presentation of the petition and the time at which the property vests in the trustee in bankruptcy is void, except to the extent that it is or was made with the consent of the court, or is or was subsequently ratified by the court.

Where a bankruptcy restriction appears in the register, no disposition (other than the registration of the trustee in bankruptcy) affecting the registered estate or charge can be completed by registration until the restriction is cancelled. The restriction may additionally have the effect of precluding the entry of notices to protect certain third party interests which consist of a disposition by the debtor.

The bankruptcy restriction does not prejudice dealings with, or in right of, interests or charges having priority over the registered estate or registered charge. Thus the proprietor of a registered charge which was registered before a bankruptcy restriction (and any bankruptcy notice) was entered could exercise his power of sale, notwithstanding the entry of the bankruptcy restriction in the proprietorship register. However, the restriction would need to be considered on a disposition by a receiver appointed by the chargee as he would be acting as agent for the debtor/chargor, not the chargee.

Bankruptcy entries under the Land Registration Act 1925

The position prior to the coming into force of the LRA 2002 on 13 October 2003 was that under LRA 1925, s 61, a creditors' notice was entered in the register following the petition in bankruptcy, in a similar way to that in which a bankruptcy notice is now entered. Following the making of the bankruptcy order, a bankruptcy inhibition was entered in the register, in a similar way to that in which a bankruptcy restriction is now entered.

Where a creditors' notice still appears in a registered title, it has the same effect as a bankruptcy notice. A bankruptcy inhibition still appearing in a registered title has the same effect as a bankruptcy restriction (LRA 2002, Sch 12, para 2(1) and (2)).

The form of entry of a creditors' notice in the register in respect of the proprietor of a registered estate was:

> Creditors' Notice entered under section 61(1) of the Land Registration Act 1925 to protect the rights of all creditors, as the title of the proprietor of the land appears to be affected by a petition in bankruptcy against [*name of debtor*], presented in the [*name*] Court (Court Reference Number …) (Land Charges Reference Number PA …).

Where it appeared that the title of the proprietor of a registered charge was affected, the creditors' notice, in a similar form, was entered in the charges register.

The form of entry of a bankruptcy inhibition in the register in respect of the proprietor of a registered estate was:

BANKRUPTCY INHIBITION entered under section 61(3) of the Land Registration Act 1925, as the title of the proprietor of the land appears to be affected by a bankruptcy order made by the [*name*] Court (Court Reference Number …) against [*name of debtor*] (Land Charges Reference Number WO …).

No disposition by the proprietor of the land or transmission is to be registered until the trustee in bankruptcy of the property of the bankrupt is registered.

Where it appeared that the title of the proprietor of a registered charge was affected, the bankruptcy inhibition, in a similar form, was entered in the charges register.

Registration of the trustee in bankruptcy

All the property, including any registered estate or registered charge, owned by the bankrupt for his own benefit at the date of the bankruptcy order automatically vests without any formal transfer in the trustee in bankruptcy when his appointment takes effect (IA 1986, s 306). Property held by the bankrupt on trust for any other person is excluded, whether or not he also holds it on trust for himself (IA 1986, s 283(3)) (see 'Bankruptcy of a joint proprietor', below).

Although the usual rule is that the disposition of a registered estate (even where it occurs by operation of law) does not operate at law until the relevant registration requirements are met, this does not apply to a transfer by operation of law on the bankruptcy of an individual proprietor (LRA 2002, s 27(5)(a)). LRR 2003, r 168 makes provision for registration of the trustee in bankruptcy as proprietor in place of the bankrupt.

A trustee in bankruptcy may apply for the register to be altered by the registration of the trustee in place of the bankrupt proprietor where a sole proprietor has had a bankruptcy order made against him and the bankrupt's registered estate or registered charge has vested in the trustee in bankruptcy.

An applicant should deliver to the Registry:

(a)   an application in Form AP1;
(b)   an office copy of the bankruptcy order relating to the bankrupt;
(c)   a certificate signed by the trustee that the registered estate or registered charge is comprised in the bankrupt's estate;
(d)   (i)   where the Official Receiver is the trustee, a certificate by him to that effect, or (where the trustee is another person)
       (ii)   the trustee's certificate of appointment as trustee by the meeting of the bankrupt's creditors, or

(iii) the trustee's certificate of appointment as trustee by the Secretary of State, or

(iv) an office copy of the order of the court appointing the trustee; and

(e) the fee payable, based upon a certificate as to the value of the registered estate or charge which should accompany the application (see *Fees*, page 221).

Where the Official Receiver is registered as proprietor, the words 'Official Receiver and trustee in bankruptcy of [*name*]' are added to the register. Where another trustee in bankruptcy is registered as proprietor, the words 'Trustee in bankruptcy of [*name*]' are added to the register.

On registration of the trustee in bankruptcy, any bankruptcy notice or bankruptcy restriction appearing in the register will be cancelled.

Vacating of office by trustee in bankruptcy

Where a trustee in bankruptcy, who has been registered as proprietor, vacates his office and the Official Receiver or some other person has been appointed as trustee in bankruptcy, the Official Receiver or that person may apply to be registered as proprietor in place of the former trustee (LRR 2003, r 169).

An applicant should deliver to the Registry:

(a) an application in Form AP1;

(b) (i) where the Official Receiver is the new trustee, a certificate by him to that effect, or (where the trustee is another person)

(ii) the new trustee's certificate of appointment as trustee by the meeting of the bankrupt's creditors, or

(iii) the new trustee's certificate of appointment as trustee by the Secretary of State, or

(iv) an office copy of the order of the court appointing the new trustee;

(c) the fee payable, based upon a certificate as to the value of the registered estate or charge which should accompany the application (see *Fees*, page 221).

Where the Official Receiver is registered as proprietor, the words 'Official Receiver and trustee in bankruptcy of [*name*]' are added to the register. Where another trustee in bankruptcy is registered as proprietor, the words 'Trustee in bankruptcy of [*name*]' are added to the register.

Sale by trustee in bankruptcy

A trustee in bankruptcy may sell the registered estate or charge either as registered proprietor or without having himself been entered in the register as proprietor.

In addition to delivering the usual documents required (see *Transfers*, page 551), the transferee should deliver to the Registry:

(a)   (if appropriate) any new mortgage or charge entered into by the applicant;
(b)   releases or discharges in respect of any charges appearing in the registered title;
(c)   an office copy of the bankruptcy order relating to the bankrupt proprietor;
(d)   a certificate signed by the trustee that the registered estate or registered charge was comprised in the bankrupt's estate;
(e)   (i)   where the Official Receiver is the trustee, a certificate by him to that effect; or (where the trustee is another person)
      (ii)   the trustee's certificate of appointment as trustee by the meeting of the bankrupt's creditors; or
      (iii) the trustee's certificate of appointment as trustee by the Secretary of State; or
      (iv)   an office copy of the order of the court appointing the trustee.

The documentation listed in (c), (d) and (e) can be omitted in a case where the trustee has been registered as proprietor in place of the bankrupt former proprietor.

On registration of the transfer, any bankruptcy notice or bankruptcy restriction will be cancelled.

Protection of purchaser from bankrupt

For the purposes of the LRA 2002, references to an interest affecting an estate or charge do not include a bankruptcy application or petition in bankruptcy or a bankruptcy order (LRA 2002, s 86(1)). Instead, s 86(5) of that Act provides a degree of protection for purchasers in relation to such applications, petitions and orders. This follows the scheme of the IA 1986, even though this brings in the concept of notice in relation to registered land. A person to whom a registrable disposition is made is not required to make any search under the Land Charges Act 1972 (LRA 2002, s 86(7)).

Where the proprietor of a registered estate or charge is adjudged bankrupt, the title of his trustee in bankruptcy is void against a person to whom a registrable disposition of the estate or charge is made if:

(a)   the disposition is made for valuable consideration;
(b)   the person to whom the disposition is made acts in good faith; and
(c)   at the time of the disposition:
    (i)   no bankruptcy notice or bankruptcy restriction is entered in relation to the registered estate or charge; and
    (ii) the person to whom the disposition is made has no notice of the bankruptcy application or petition or the adjudication.

Although this protection applies only if the relevant registration requirements are met in relation to the disposition, as and when they are met it has effect from the date of the disposition.

The fact that a bankruptcy restriction has been entered in the register after the date of the disposition but before application has been made to register it will not prevent the disposition being completed by registration when application has been made, as the provisions of s 86(5)(c) will nevertheless apply in relation to the disposition (*Pick v Chief Land Registrar* [2011] EWHC 206 (Ch)).

Bankruptcy of a joint proprietor

Where one of two or more joint registered proprietors becomes bankrupt neither a bankruptcy notice nor a bankruptcy restriction is entered in the register. This reflects the fact that, as the bankrupt is holding the legal estate as trustee, the legal estate does not automatically vest in the trustee in bankruptcy. Any subsequent transfer of the property will need to be executed by all the joint proprietors in the usual way and not by the trustee on behalf of the bankrupt proprietor. The bankruptcy order does, however, have the effect of severing any beneficial joint tenancy, and the bankrupt's beneficial share vests in the trustee in bankruptcy.

If there is no restriction in Form A already in the register, the trustee in bankruptcy has a sufficient interest for the purposes of LRA 2002, s 43(1)(c) to apply for entry of a restriction in Form A to ensure that a survivor of the joint proprietors (unless a trust corporation) is not able to give a valid receipt for capital money (LRR 2003, 93(a)). The wording of Form A is set out in Appendix IV, page 585.

The trustee in bankruptcy also has a sufficient interest to apply for entry of a restriction in Form J, to ensure that he receives notice of a disposition (LRR 2003, r 93(j)). The wording of Form J is set out in Appendix IV, page 585.

This restriction does not of itself prevent a disposition, provided it is complied with. This is because the interest of the trustee in bankruptcy will be overreached where the requirements of the Form A restriction have been met (Law of Property Act 1925, ss 2 and 27). However, entry of the restriction does help to ensure the trustee is given notice of the disposition so that he can pursue his share of any proceeds of a sale.

The Registry must give notice of an application for entry of a restriction to the proprietor of the registered estate or charge concerned (LRA 2002, s 45).

If applying for entry of a restriction in Form A, the trustee in bankruptcy should deliver to the Registry an application in Form RX1. No fee is currently payable where the application is in respect of a restriction in Form A only.

The statement in panel 12 or the conveyancer's certificate in panel 13 of Form RX1 should be completed on the following lines:

> The interest is that specified in rule 93(a) of the Land Registration Rules 2003, the applicant being the trustee in bankruptcy of [*name of bankrupt joint proprietor*] who is the subject of a bankruptcy order made by the [*name*] Court (Court Reference Number ...) (Land Charges Reference Number WO ...).

Panel 9 of Form RX1 should be completed as to the wording of Form A.

If applying for a restriction in Form J, the trustee in bankruptcy should deliver to the Registry the usual documents required (see *Restrictions*, page 500).

The statement in panel 12 or the conveyancer's certificate in panel 13 of Form RX1 should be completed on the following lines:

> The interest is that specified in rule 93(j) of the Land Registration Rules 2003, the applicant being the trustee in bankruptcy of [*name of bankrupt joint proprietor*] who is the subject of a bankruptcy order made by the [*name*] Court (Court Reference Number ...) (Land Charges Reference Number WO ...).

Panel 9 of Form RX1 should be completed as to the wording of Form J.

A restriction in standard form A or J in LRR 2003, Sch 4 does not require the approval of the Registry to the terms of the restriction under LRA 2002, s 43(3).

Administration of an insolvent estate

If a debtor should die after a bankruptcy application has been made by him or a bankruptcy petition has been presented against him, the proceedings will, unless the court orders otherwise (in the case of a bankruptcy petition), be continued – subject to certain modifications to reflect the death of the debtor – as if he was alive (Administration of Insolvent Estates of Deceased Persons Order 1986 (SI 1986/1999), r 5, Sch 2).

Where a person dies before the making of a bankruptcy application or presentation of a bankruptcy petition, his estate, if insolvent, may be administered in bankruptcy. The relevant provisions of the IA 1986 will (subject to certain modifications to reflect the death of the debtor) apply to the administration of an insolvent estate in bankruptcy (Administration of Insolvent Estates of Deceased Persons Order 1986, r 3, Sch 1).

When an insolvency administration petition is made by creditors or the personal representatives of the deceased debtor, the petition will be registered in the name of the debtor in the Land Charges Department as a pending action under the Land Charges Act 1972, and a bankruptcy notice is then entered in the register of any title where the deceased appears as proprietor of the land or of a registered charge. Following registration of the insolvency administration order in the register of writs and orders under the Land Charges Act 1972, a bankruptcy restriction is entered in the proprietorship register or charges register as appropriate.

Where, as a result of an insolvency administration order, the deceased's registered estate or registered charge has vested in the trustee in bankruptcy, the trustee may apply for the alteration of the register by registering the trustee in place of the deceased proprietor.

An applicant should deliver to the Registry:

(a) an application in Form AP1;
(b) an office copy of the insolvency administration order relating to the deceased debtor's estate;
(c) a certificate signed by the trustee that the registered estate or registered charge is comprised in the deceased debtor's estate;
(d) (i)   where the Official Receiver is the trustee, a certificate by him to that effect; or (where the trustee is another person)
     (ii) the trustee's certificate of appointment as trustee by the meeting of the deceased debtor's creditors; or

(iii) the trustee's certificate of appointment as trustee by the Secretary of State; or

(iv) an office copy of the order of the court appointing the trustee; and

(e) the fee payable, based upon a certificate as to the value of the registered estate or charge which should accompany the application (see *Fees*, page 221).

Where the Official Receiver is registered as proprietor, the words 'Official Receiver and trustee in bankruptcy of [*name*]' are added to the register. Where another trustee in bankruptcy is registered as proprietor, the words 'Trustee in bankruptcy of [*name*]' are added to the register.

On registration of the trustee in bankruptcy, any bankruptcy notice or bankruptcy restriction appearing in the register will be cancelled.

Cancellation of bankruptcy notice or bankruptcy restriction

As mentioned above, a bankruptcy notice (or creditors' notice) and a bankruptcy restriction (or bankruptcy inhibition) will be cancelled on the registration of the trustee in bankruptcy as proprietor or (if he has not become the registered proprietor) on registration of a transfer on sale by him.

A bankruptcy notice (or creditors' notice) will not be cancelled on the production of an order of the court which simply authorises the cancellation of the registration of the bankruptcy application or petition as a pending action in the Land Charges Department. Similarly, a bankruptcy restriction (or bankruptcy inhibition) will not be cancelled on the production of an order of the court which simply authorises the cancellation of the registration of the bankruptcy order at the Land Charges Department. Such an order does not re-vest property in a bankrupt which has automatically vested in his trustee in bankruptcy. Such property will remain vested in the trustee in bankruptcy, subject to the provisions discussed in 'Re-vesting of bankrupt's home', below.

LRR 2003, r 167(1) provides that a bankruptcy notice or bankruptcy restriction will be cancelled if the Registry is satisfied that:

(a) the bankruptcy order has been annulled or rescinded; or

(b) the bankruptcy proceedings have been dismissed or withdrawn with the court's permission; or

(c) the bankruptcy proceedings do not affect or have ceased to affect the registered estate or registered charge in relation to which the bankruptcy notice or restriction has been entered in the register.

Neither an automatic discharge under the provisions of IA 1986, s 279 nor an order for discharge by the court under IA 1986, s 280 operates to re-vest the bankrupt's property. Production of evidence of discharge is not therefore sufficient to enable a bankruptcy notice or bankruptcy restriction to be cancelled, even if accompanied by the consent of the trustee or an order of the court under Land Charges Act 1972, s 1(6) ordering cancellation of Land Charge bankruptcy entries.

The application for cancellation should be made in Form AP1. Where made in the circumstances referred to at (a) and (b) above, it must be accompanied by an office copy of the relevant court order which must expressly authorise the cancellation of the Land Charge bankruptcy entries under the reference number set out in the bankruptcy notice and/or bankruptcy restriction.

Where application for cancellation is made in the circumstances referred to at (c) above, and the proprietor of a registered estate or registered charge is not affected by the bankruptcy proceedings and the entry was made recently, the Registry will normally remove it if the applicant provides a signed disclaimer (as supplied by the Registry) that he was not the subject of the bankruptcy proceedings. In some cases, particularly where the entry was made some years ago, the applicant may be required to supply a statutory declaration or statement of truth to similar effect. Production of a clear Land Charges search showing that the registration of the relevant bankruptcy application or petition and/or bankruptcy order is no longer subsisting is not sufficient without further evidence.

No fee is currently payable for the cancellation of a bankruptcy notice or bankruptcy restriction.

Discharge from bankruptcy

A discharge from bankruptcy releases the bankrupt from his bankruptcy debts, but does not have the effect of re-vesting in him any property which has vested in the trustee in bankruptcy. A certificate of discharge does not allow any bankruptcy notice or bankruptcy restriction to be cancelled.

Special provisions apply in relation to the re-vesting of the bankrupt's home (see 'Re-vesting of bankrupt's home', below), but these do not apply to a registered estate or registered charge in general.

If, unusually, the trustee in bankruptcy is prepared to re-vest registered land in the discharged bankrupt, this should be carried out by means of a formal transfer.

Where the trustee in bankruptcy has not been registered as proprietor, the applicant should, in addition to delivering the usual documents required (see *Transfers*, page 551), deliver to the Registry:

(a) a transfer in Form TR1 or other prescribed form of transfer, as appropriate;
(b) an office copy of the bankruptcy order relating to the discharged bankrupt;
(c) a certificate signed by the trustee that the registered estate or registered charge was comprised in the discharged bankrupt's estate;
(d) (i) where the Official Receiver is the trustee, a certificate by him to that effect; or (where the trustee is another person)
  (ii) the trustee's certificate of appointment as trustee by the meeting of the bankrupt's creditors; or
  (iii) the trustee's certificate of appointment as trustee by the Secretary of State; or
  (iv) an office copy of the order of the court appointing the trustee.

The documentation listed in (b), (c) and (d) can be omitted in a case where the trustee has been registered as proprietor in place of the bankrupt former proprietor.

On registration of the transfer, any bankruptcy notice or bankruptcy restriction in the register relating to the bankruptcy will be cancelled.

Re-vesting of bankrupt's home

Enterprise Act 2002, s 261 introduced a new s 283A into the IA 1986, with effect from 1 April 2004. This applies where the bankrupt's estate includes an interest in a dwelling house which, at the date of the bankruptcy order, was the sole or principal residence of either the bankrupt; the bankrupt's spouse or civil partner; or a former spouse or former civil partner of the bankrupt.

The interest will automatically re-vest in the bankrupt (without any transfer, assignment or conveyance) 3 years after the date of the bankruptcy order, unless the trustee in bankruptcy takes action to deal with the interest in the meantime, for instance by selling it or applying for a possession order. If the bankruptcy order was made before 1 April 2004, the period is 3 years from 1 April 2004.

The 3-year period can be extended by order of the court, or if the debtor fails to inform the trustee in bankruptcy or the Official Receiver of his interest in the property. The 3-year period can also be reduced in certain circumstances. If the trustee in bankruptcy considers that the continuing vesting of the property in the bankrupt's estate is of no benefit to the creditors; or the re-vesting to the bankrupt will facilitate a more efficient administration of the bankrupt's estate, the trustee can send the bankrupt a notice to that effect. The property will then re-vest in the bankrupt one month after the date of the notice.

Where re-vesting occurs where the debtor was a sole proprietor, the trustee in bankruptcy must, within 7 days, make whatever application to the Land Registry is necessary to reflect the re-vesting in the register (Insolvency Rules 1986, r 6237A and B).

In a case where the trustee has not been registered as proprietor in place of the bankrupt, an application should be made in Form RX3 to cancel the bankruptcy restriction (or bankruptcy inhibition), accompanied by:

(a)   a certificate by the trustee stating that the interest has re-vested in the bankrupt under IA 1986, s 283A(2) or s 283A(4) or Enterprise Act 2002, s 261(8); and
(b)   (unless the applicant is the Official Receiver) evidence of the trustee's appointment (see 'Registration of the trustee in bankruptcy', above).

No fee is currently payable.

Any bankruptcy notice (or creditors' notice) which relates to the application or petition under which the bankruptcy order was made will be cancelled, but not any other bankruptcy notice (or creditors' notice) without the evidence specified in 'Cancellation of bankruptcy notice or bankruptcy restriction', above.

In a case where the trustee has been registered as proprietor, an application should be made in Form AP1 for alteration of the register, accompanied by a certificate by the trustee as above. No fee is currently payable.

In a case where the bankrupt is a joint registered proprietor, an application should be made in Form RX4 to withdraw any restriction in Form J, accompanied by a certificate by the trustee as above. No fee is currently payable. The re-vesting will not undo the severance of a beneficial joint tenancy effected by the bankruptcy and therefore any restriction in Form A appearing in the register will not be automatically cancelled.

Annulment of bankruptcy order

A court may annul the bankruptcy order on a number of grounds; for example where the bankruptcy debts and the expenses of the bankruptcy have all been paid or secured (IA 1986, s 282). Where the Registry is satisfied that the bankruptcy order has been annulled, it must as soon as practicable cancel any bankruptcy notice or bankruptcy restriction which relates to that bankruptcy order.

An applicant for cancellation of such entries should deliver to the Registry:

(a) an application in Form AP1; and
(b) an office copy of the court order of annulment, which must expressly authorise the cancellation of the Land Charge bankruptcy entries under the reference number set out in the bankruptcy notice and/or bankruptcy restriction.

No fee is currently payable.

On annulment, any of the bankrupt's estate which is vested in the Official Receiver or trustee in bankruptcy vests in such person as the court appoints. If no other person is appointed, it will vest in the former bankrupt on such terms as the court may direct. Where the Official Receiver or trustee in bankruptcy has been registered as proprietor, an applicant for the former bankrupt to be re-registered should deliver to the Registry:

(a) an application in Form AP1;
(b) an office copy of the court order of annulment, which must expressly authorise the cancellation of the Land Charge bankruptcy entries under the reference number set out in the bankruptcy notice and/or bankruptcy restriction; and
(c) the fee payable, based upon a certificate as to the value of the registered estate or charge which should accompany the application (see *Fees*, page 221).

After-acquired property

A trustee in bankruptcy may claim property which has been acquired by, or devolved on, the bankrupt after the commencement of the bankruptcy and before his discharge. The trustee does this by the service of notice within 42 days beginning on the day when it came to his knowledge that the property had been acquired by, or had devolved on, the bankrupt; this period may be extended by the court (IA 1986, ss 307 and 309).

Where, before or after service of such a notice by the trustee in bankruptcy, a person acquires the property in good faith for value and without notice of the bankruptcy, the trustee has no remedy against the purchaser.

When the trustee has served notice on the bankrupt, he may apply to be registered as proprietor of the after-acquired property in place of the bankrupt. The trustee should deliver to the Registry:

(a)   an application in Form AP1;

(b)   an office copy of the bankruptcy order relating to the bankrupt;

(c)   a certified copy of the notice served by the trustee under the IA 1986, s 307;

(d)   an office copy of any order for extension of time for service of notice made under IA 1986, s 309;

(e)   a certificate signed by the trustee that the registered estate or registered charge is comprised in the bankrupt's estate and that the notice under IA 1986, s 307 was served within the period prescribed by s 309;

(f)   (i)   where the Official Receiver is the trustee, a certificate by him to that effect, or (where the trustee is another person)

      (ii)   the trustee's certificate of appointment as trustee by the meeting of the bankrupt's creditors, or

      (iii) the trustee's certificate of appointment as trustee by the Secretary of State, or

      (iv) an office copy of the order of the court appointing the trustee; and

(g)   the fee payable, based upon a certificate as to the value of the registered estate or charge which should accompany the application (see *Fees*, page 221).

Where the Official Receiver is registered as proprietor, the words 'Official Receiver and trustee in bankruptcy of [*name*]' are added to the register. Where another trustee in bankruptcy is registered as proprietor, the words 'Trustee in bankruptcy of [*name*]' are added to the register.

Where the bankrupt holds the after-acquired property as joint proprietor and the trustee in bankruptcy has served the notice under IA 1986, s 307, the trustee in bankruptcy may apply for a restriction in Form J and, where it does not already appear in the register, in Form A (see 'Bankruptcy of a joint proprietor', above).

Voidable dispositions

The IA 1986 contains provisions to prevent the bankrupt from putting his assets beyond the reach of his creditors after a bankruptcy petition has been presented. It makes certain dispositions of property by the bankrupt void.

The general rule is that when a person has been adjudged bankrupt, any disposition of property made by him between the date of the making of the bankruptcy application or presentation of the bankruptcy petition and the vesting of his estate in the trustee in bankruptcy or in the Official Receiver as trustee is void (IA 1986, s 284(1)). It remains subject to the claim of the trustee in bankruptcy, who may assert his title to it for the benefit of the bankrupt's estate. The rule does not apply, however, where the disposition is made with the consent of, or is subsequently ratified by, the court.

The general rule does not apply to property held on trust (see 'Bankruptcy of a joint proprietor', above). Nor does it apply where a person takes a disposition of property in good faith and without notice that the bankruptcy application has been made or the bankruptcy petition has been presented or the bankruptcy order made (see 'Protection of purchaser from bankrupt', above).

If a void disposition has been completed by registration, the trustee in bankruptcy may apply for alteration of the register so that he is registered as proprietor of the registered estate or charge, as trustee in bankruptcy for the bankrupt former proprietor. The ground of alteration would be to correct the mistaken registration of the void disposition (LRA 2002, Sch 4, paras 2(1)(a) and 5(a)).

The IA 1986 also contains anti-avoidance provisions by which the title of the trustee in bankruptcy can extend to property which was no longer vested in the bankrupt when his bankruptcy commenced, as a result of a voidable disposition by the bankrupt.

Where there has been a transaction at an undervalue for the purposes of IA 1986, s 339, or a preference for the purposes of s 340 of that Act, the trustee in bankruptcy may apply to the court for an order. The court may make such order as it thinks fit for restoring the position to what it would have been had the relevant transaction not taken place. Where the court is satisfied that a transaction at an undervalue constitutes a transaction defrauding creditors for the purposes of IA 1986, s 423, it may make such order as it thinks fit for restoring the position to what it would have been if the transaction had not been entered into and protecting the interests of victims of the transaction.

If the bankrupt has entered into an extortionate credit transaction within the 3 years before the commencement of the bankruptcy, the trustee in bankruptcy may apply to the court for an order (IA 1986, s 343). The court has wide powers to vary or set aside the transaction.

Where an order of the court under ss 339, 340, 343 or 423 requires the register to be altered, the applicant should deliver to the Registry:

(a)   an application in Form AP1;
(b)   the court order or a sealed copy of the court order; and
(c)   the fee payable (see *Fees*, page 221).

It was previously the practice of the Registry, on first registration where the title deduced revealed a possible transaction at undervalue, to make an entry in the register referring to the IA 1986. That practice was discontinued in 2000. When next updating a register, the Registry will cancel automatically any such entries relating to IA 1986, s 339 (or to Bankruptcy Act 1914, s 42).

Bankruptcy and home rights

Nothing occurring in the period between the presentation of the petition for the bankruptcy order and the vesting of the bankrupt's estate in the trustee is to be taken as having given rise to any home rights under the Family Law Act 1996 (FLA 1996) in relation to a dwelling house comprised in the bankrupt's estate (IA 1986, s 336(1)).

Where the home rights of a spouse or civil partner under the FLA 1996 are a charge on the estate or interest of the other spouse or civil partner and the other spouse or civil partner is adjudged bankrupt, the charge continues and binds the trustee in bankruptcy.

The trustee in bankruptcy may apply to the court at any time for an order to restrict or terminate the home rights; any application must be made to the court having jurisdiction in relation to the bankruptcy. On such application the court may make such order as it thinks just and reasonable having regard to the matters set out in IA 1986, s 336(4). However, where such an application is made more than a year after the property vested in the trustee in bankruptcy, the court must assume, unless the circumstances of the case are exceptional, that the interests of the bankrupt's creditors outweigh all other considerations (IA 1986, s 336(5)). Any application for cancellation of a home rights notice (see *Home rights*, page 257) should be accompanied by an office copy of the court order.

Whether or not the bankrupt's spouse or civil partner has any rights of occupation, a bankrupt may himself have rights equivalent to home rights under the FLA 1996 against the trustee in bankruptcy if he was entitled to occupy a dwelling house, and any persons under the age of 18 with whom he occupied the house had their home with him when the bankruptcy application was made or bankruptcy petition was presented and at the commencement of the bankruptcy (IA 1986, s 337). If the bankrupt is in occupation, he has a right not to be evicted or excluded without leave of the bankruptcy court. If he is not in occupation, he has a right, with leave of the bankruptcy court, to enter into occupation.

Such rights are a charge having the same priority as an equitable interest created immediately before the commencement of the bankruptcy, on so much of his estate or interest in the dwelling house as vests in the trustee in bankruptcy. That charge is treated as if it were a charge under the FLA 1996 on the estate or interest of a spouse or civil partner (IA 1986, s 337(3)). To restrict or terminate these rights, the trustee in bankruptcy must apply to the bankruptcy court, which must have regard to the same matters mentioned above.

Where a bankrupt has such rights, these may be protected by entry of an agreed notice notwithstanding the fact that the bankrupt is shown in the register as the registered proprietor.

A bankrupt applying to register an agreed notice should deliver to the Registry an application in Form HR1 (rather than in Form AN1), together with the fee payable (see *Fees*, page 221). In Form HR1 the applicant should state that he is applying pursuant to the provisions of IA 1986, s 337 and that the property is vested in his (named) trustee in bankruptcy.

Charging order in favour of trustee in bankruptcy

Where the trustee in bankruptcy is unable to realise an interest in a dwelling house which forms part of the bankrupt's estate and which is occupied by the bankrupt or his spouse or former spouse, the trustee may apply to the court for a charging order on that dwelling house (IA 1986, s 313). Any such order should also provide for the re-vesting of the interest in the bankrupt, subject to the charging order and any prior charges. Such an order enables any bankruptcy notice or bankruptcy restriction appearing in the register to be cancelled.

Where the bankrupt is the sole proprietor and does not hold as trustee, the trustee in bankruptcy may apply for the entry in the register of an agreed notice or a unilateral notice in respect of the charging order, as it will take effect as a charge on the legal estate. The application should be accompanied by a request for cancellation of any bankruptcy notice and bankruptcy restriction in the register.

Where the debtor's interest was a beneficial interest in a trust of land the charging order will take effect as an equitable charge over the debtor's beneficial interest. In this case, the trustee in bankruptcy may apply for entry of a restriction in Form K restriction.

Agreed notice of the charging order

In addition to the usual documents required (see *Notices*, page 389), an applicant should deliver to the Registry the charging order or a certified copy of it.

As the consent of the registered proprietor is unlikely to be forthcoming in this situation, this is likely to be sufficient to satisfy the Registry as to the validity of the applicant's claim in accordance with LRA 2002, s 34(3)(c).

The agreed notice in the register will give details of the interest protected.

Unilateral notice of the charging order

An applicant should deliver to the Registry the usual documents required (see *Notices*, page 389).

The statement in panel 11 or conveyancer's certificate in panel 12 of Form UN1 should be completed on the following lines to show the interest of the applicant:

> chargee under a charging order of the [name] Court [*set out full court reference and parties*].

The unilateral notice in the register will give brief details of the interest protected and identify the beneficiary of that notice.

Restriction where the charging order is over a beneficial interest

The trustee in bankruptcy will have a sufficient interest for the purposes of LRA 2002, s 43(1)(c) to apply for entry of a restriction in Form K, to ensure that he receives notice of a disposition (LRR 2003, r 93(k)).The wording of Form K is set out in Appendix IV, page 585.

This restriction does not of itself prevent a disposition, provided it is complied with. However, entry of the restriction does help to ensure the trustee is given notice of the disposition so that he can pursue a share of any proceeds of a sale. The restriction will not prevent the interest of the trustee in bankruptcy being overreached where the requirements of Law of Property Act 1925, ss 2 and 27 have been fulfilled.

If applying for a restriction in Form K, the trustee in bankruptcy should deliver to the Registry the usual documents required (see *Restrictions*, page 500).

The statement in panel 12 or the conveyancer's certificate in panel 13 of Form RX1 should be completed on the following lines:

> The interest is that specified in rule 93(k) of the Land Registration Rules 2003, the applicant being the trustee in bankruptcy of [*name of bankrupt joint proprietor*] who

is the subject of a bankruptcy order made by the [*name*] Court (Court Reference Number ...) (Land Charges Reference Number WO ...).

Panel 9 of Form RX1 should be completed as to the wording of Form K.

Disclaimer by trustee in bankruptcy

A trustee in bankruptcy may disclaim any onerous property comprised in the bankrupt's estate. In the case of land it is normally a leasehold estate which is disclaimed, although a trustee may also disclaim a freehold estate, in which case the ownership of the land will revert to the Crown by escheat. The effect of a disclaimer is to determine the rights, interests and liabilities of the bankrupt and his estate in respect of the disclaimed property. It also discharges the trustee from all personal liability for it (IA 1986, s 315(3)).

The trustee disclaims property by authenticating and dating the prescribed form of notice and filing it at the court. In any case where the disclaimer is of registered land, the trustee must send a copy of the notice to the Land Registry. Within 7 days after the date of the notice of disclaimer, the trustee must serve a copy of the notice upon specified categories of person, including those who claim an interest in the disclaimed property or are under any liability in respect of it which will not be discharged by the disclaimer.

Special rules apply to the disclaimer of a leasehold property. The disclaimer is not effective unless a copy of it has been served on any underlessee or mortgagee claiming under the bankrupt. In the case of a dwelling house a copy of the disclaimer must also be served on every person who is in occupation or claims a right to occupy.

Any of the above persons served with notice may apply to the court for a vesting order vesting the property in him or in a trustee on his behalf (IA 1986, s 320). The disclaimer will not take effect unless no person has applied to the court within 14 days of the last notice being served to have the property vested in him, or despite any such application, the court has directed that the disclaimer should take effect.

If no vesting order is made in respect of a leasehold estate, a lease which has been disclaimed vests in the landlord and so will determine. If no vesting order is made in respect of a freehold estate, a freehold which has been disclaimed vests in the Crown by escheat (see *Bona vacantia and escheat*, page 74).

Where the trustee in bankruptcy has disclaimed a registered lease, an applicant should deliver to the Registry:

(a) an application in Form AP1 showing the application as 'Disclaimer of lease'; if the lease is the subject of a notice in a registered superior title the application should also be made in respect of that title so that the notice of the lease may be cancelled at the same time as the disclaimed leasehold title is closed;

(b) the lease;

(c) a certificate signed by the trustee in bankruptcy that he has power to make the disclaimer, that all notices required to be served under the IA 1986 have been served and that he is not aware of any application to the court for a vesting order under IA 1986, s 320;

(d) an office copy of the notice of disclaimer;

(e) (if applicable) a certified copy of any court order directing that the disclaimer should take effect; and

(f) the fee payable (see *Fees*, page 221).

Where the trustee in bankruptcy has not already been registered as proprietor of the leasehold title, the applicant should also deliver to the Registry:

(a) an office copy of the bankruptcy order relating to the bankrupt;

(b) a certificate signed by the trustee that the registered lease is comprised in the bankrupt's estate; and

(c) (i) where the Official Receiver is the trustee, a certificate by him to that effect; or (where the trustee is another person)

(ii) the trustee's certificate of appointment as trustee by the meeting of the bankrupt's creditors; or

(iii) the trustee's certificate of appointment as trustee by the Secretary of State; or

(iv) an office copy of the order of the court appointing the trustee.

As the disclaimer does not affect the rights and liabilities of other persons acquired before the disclaimer, the Registry will not close the disclaimed leasehold title if there is a registered or noted charge in that title, unless the applicant also lodges an application to discharge the registered charge or to cancel the entry of the noted charge; or evidence that the chargee's application for a vesting order has been dismissed; or evidence of forfeiture of the lease.

If the disclaimed leasehold title cannot be closed because there is evidence of a continuing registered or noted charge, the Registry will make appropriate entries in the title for the disclaimed lease and in the landlord's registered title, to refer to the disclaimer. A restriction preventing registration of any disposition of the registered estate will also be entered in the disclaimed leasehold title.

The disclaimed leasehold title may be closed if there is no registered or noted charge, but if there is a registered sub-lease or other third party rights which are the subject of a notice in that title, appropriate entries will be made in the landlord's title and any sub-leasehold title, referring to the disclaimer and to the rights in question.

Where the disclaimed lease has not been registered but is the subject of a notice against a registered superior title, an applicant should deliver to the Registry:

(a) an application in Form CN1, panel 9 being completed by entering details of the lease and placing an 'X' against 'disclaimer';
(b) the lease;
(c) evidence of devolution of title, if the bankrupt is not the original tenant;
(d) a certificate signed by the trustee in bankruptcy that he has power to make the disclaimer, that all notices required to be served under the IA 1986 have been served and that he is not aware of any application to the court for a vesting order under IA 1986, s 320;
(e) an office copy of the notice of disclaimer;
(f) (if applicable) a certified copy of any court order directing that the disclaimer should take effect;
(g) an office copy of the bankruptcy order relating to the bankrupt;
(h) a certificate signed by the trustee that the registered lease is comprised in the bankrupt's estate;
(i) (i) where the Official Receiver is the trustee, a certificate by him to that effect; or (where the trustee is another person)
    (ii) the trustee's certificate of appointment as trustee by the meeting of the bankrupt's creditors; or
    (iii) the trustee's certificate of appointment as trustee by the Secretary of State; or
    (iv) an office copy of the order of the court appointing the trustee;
(j) the fee payable (see *Fees*, page 221).

Where there is no evidence of any charge, sub-lease or other third party rights affecting the disclaimed lease, the notice of the lease in the landlord's title may be cancelled. Otherwise, the notice of the lease cannot be cancelled, but appropriate entries will be made in the landlord's title and any sub-leasehold title, referring to the disclaimer and to the rights in question.

Where the property has been disclaimed and an order has been made by the court vesting the property in some other person, an applicant should deliver to the Registry:

(a) an application in Form AP1;

(b)   an office copy of the court order; and

(c)   the fee payable (see *Fees*, page 221).

Where a property has been disclaimed and the Registry has received notice of the disclaimer but no formal application is made, the Registry may alter the register of its own volition to reflect the disclaimer, for the purposes of bringing the register up to date (LRA 2002, Sch 4, para 5(b)). In the case of a disclaimer of a leasehold estate, the Registry will enter a note of the disclaimer in the register of the disclaimed leasehold title. In the case of a disclaimer of a freehold estate, the Registry will enter a note of the disclaimer in the register to reflect the determination by escheat.

Insolvency proceedings commenced in another part of the United Kingdom

Special provision is made by IA 1986, s 426 whereby an order made by a court in any part of the United Kingdom in the exercise of jurisdiction in relation to insolvency law shall be enforced in any other part of the United Kingdom as if it were made by a court exercising the corresponding jurisdiction in that other part. The courts in England and Wales may not therefore question the jurisdiction of the Scottish or Northern Irish courts to adjudicate a debtor bankrupt. However, nothing in s 426 requires a court in any part of the United Kingdom to enforce, in relation to property situated in that part, any order made by a court in any other part of the United Kingdom. This preserves the principle that the law governing the transfer of land on bankruptcy is the *lex situs*. Thus, for example, registered land in England and Wales owned by a person adjudged bankrupt under the law of Northern Ireland will not vest in the Northern Irish trustee in bankruptcy since the *lex situs* does not have that effect.

Under IA 1986, s 426(4), the courts having jurisdiction in relation to insolvency law in any part of the United Kingdom shall assist the courts having the corresponding jurisdiction in any other part of the United Kingdom. Thus the court in England and Wales may, for example, make an order vesting the bankrupt's legal or equitable estate in land in the trustee in bankruptcy of the other jurisdiction. In practice, the court in England and Wales will generally reseal a bankruptcy order made in Scotland or Northern Ireland. It then becomes an order of the bankruptcy court in England and Wales from the date of the resealing.

For overseas insolvency proceedings, see *Overseas insolvency proceedings*, page 427.

BARE TRUSTS

A bare trust arises where a trustee holds property for a single beneficiary who is of full age and under no legal disability. Where the property consists of or includes land, the trust is a trust of land for the purposes of the Trusts of Land and Appointment of Trustees Act 1996 (TLATA). No notice may be entered in the register in respect of an interest under a trust of land (LRA 2002, s 33(a)).

Where the trustee is, or becomes, the registered proprietor of property held on a bare trust, he must apply for entry of a restriction in Form A (LRR 2003, r 94(1) and (2)). Where the declaration of trust imposes limitations on the powers of the trustee under TLATA, s 8, the trustee must also apply for entry of a restriction in Form B (LRR 2003, r 94(4)). For example, the declaration of trust may require the obtaining of consent to any sale of the property.

If the trustee does not apply for the necessary restriction(s), the beneficiary has a sufficient interest for the purposes of LRA 2002, s 43(1)(c) to do so (LRR 2003, r 93(a) and (c)). The Registry must give notice of the application for a restriction to the proprietor of the registered estate or charge concerned, if it has not been made by or with his consent or a person entitled to be registered as such proprietor (LRA 2002, s 45).

The wording of Forms A, B and II is set out in Appendix IV, page 585.

A restriction in Form B or in Form II does not of itself prevent a disposition, provided it is complied with. This is because the interest of the beneficiary will be overreached where the requirements of the Form A restriction have been met (Law of Property Act 1925, ss 2 and 27).

An applicant for entry of a restriction should deliver to the Registry the usual documents required (see *Restrictions*, page 500).

Panel 9 of Form RX1 should be completed as to the required restriction(s). A restriction in standard forms A, B or II in LRR 2003, Sch 4 does not require the approval of the Registry to the terms of the restriction under LRA 2002, s 43(3).

Form RX1 does not need to be used if the application is for a standard form restriction and is contained in either the 'additional provisions' panel of a prescribed form of transfer or assent, or in clause LR13 of a prescribed clauses lease (or any other lease containing clauses LR1 to LR14 of LRR 2003, Sch 1A) (LRR 2003, r 92(7)).

BONA VACANTIA AND ESCHEAT

Where a company is dissolved, its property (other than that held on trust for another person) vests as bona vacantia in the Crown, under the jurisdiction of the Treasury Solicitor, or in the Duchy of Lancaster or Duchy of Cornwall, under the jurisdiction of the solicitor of the relevant duchy (Companies Act 2006, s 1012; previously Companies Act 1985, s 654). This transfer by operation of law does not constitute a disposition requiring to be completed by registration under LRA 2002, s 27. Pursuant to LRA 2002, s 85, the LRR 2003 contain provisions relating to bona vacantia.

Where a corporation shown as the proprietor of a registered estate or registered charge has been dissolved, the Registry may enter a note of that fact in the proprietorship register or charges register, as appropriate (LRR 2003, r 185). Application may be made by the Crown or the relevant Duchy for registration as proprietor in place of the dissolved company; the Treasury Solicitor or the Solicitor to the Duchy of Lancaster or the Duke of Cornwall will be entered in the register as proprietor, as the case may be. Where an estate that has vested as bona vacantia is subsequently disposed of, a later order reviving the dissolved company will have no effect on the disposition; the revived company may be entitled to compensation.

The Treasury Solicitor and the Solicitors to the Duchies of Lancaster and Cornwall have power to disclaim property that has vested as bona vacantia. The disclaimer is effected by a notice in writing signed by the appropriate solicitor. The effect of the disclaimer is to terminate the rights, interests and liabilities of the company in respect of the disclaimed property. It does not affect the rights and liabilities of other persons acquired before the disclaimer (Companies Act 2006, s 1015).

Although they are not formally required to do so, the Treasury Solicitor or either of the Royal Duchies may send a copy of the notice of disclaimer to the Land Registry, without making a formal application for closure of the relevant title or cancellation of an entry relating to the disclaimed estate or interest. Provided the dissolved company named in the notice is the same as the company registered as proprietor and there is only one proprietor, the Registry will make an entry in the register to reflect the disclaimer. A formal application can, however, be made to close the disclaimed title where appropriate or cancel an entry relating to the disclaimed estate or interest.

As the disclaimer does not affect the rights and liabilities of other persons acquired before the disclaimer, the Registry will not close a disclaimed leasehold title if there is a registered or noted charge in that title, unless the applicant also lodges an application to discharge the registered charge or to cancel the entry of the noted charge; or evidence that the chargee's application for a vesting order has been dismissed; or evidence of forfeiture of the lease. If the disclaimed leasehold title cannot be closed because there is evidence of a continuing registered or noted charge, the Registry will make appropriate entries in the title for the disclaimed lease and in the landlord's registered title, to refer to the disclaimer. A restriction preventing registration of any disposition of the registered estate will also be entered in the disclaimed leasehold title. The leasehold title for a disclaimed lease may be closed if there is no registered or noted charge but there is a registered sub-lease or other third party rights noted in title, in which case appropriate entries referring to the disclaimer will be made in the landlord's title and any registered sub-leasehold title.

Escheat occurs when a freehold estate determines. An escheated estate is usually onerous property of little or no (or even negative) value which is difficult to dispose of because, for example, the land is contaminated. Escheat can arise in different ways, but the most common is where the Treasury Solicitor disclaims a freehold estate passing as bona vacantia, or where the estate is disclaimed by a liquidator or trustee in bankruptcy following insolvency. The freehold estate escheats either to the Crown as demesne land or to one of the Royal Duchies of Cornwall or Lancaster by virtue of their own superior freehold estate. In time, the Crown may re-grant the estate or a Royal Duchy may transfer its freehold estate. The escheat does not constitute a disposition requiring to be completed by registration under LRA 2002, s 27. Pursuant to LRA 2002, s 82, the LRR 2003 contain provisions relating to escheat.

Escheat is based on the feudal principle that land itself is held by the Crown in demesne. Other landowners own a right to possess the land, known as an estate in land. When a leasehold estate determines it merges into the superior estate. When a freehold estate determines, because there is no superior estate, the land reverts to the Crown. For the purposes of the LRA 2002 'demesne land' is defined as land belonging to Her Majesty in right of the Crown which is not held for an estate in fee simple absolute in possession. This does not include land in relation to which a freehold estate in land has determined, but in relation to which there has been no act of entry or management by the Crown (LRA 2002, s 132(1), (2)).

If in the past the Crown has granted a fee simple to one of the Royal Duchies, the determined freehold estate reverts to that Duchy. The Royal Duchies cannot grant a new freehold estate; instead they can transfer their freehold estate in the land to a new owner.

There are various formalities to which the Duchies must adhere when drawing up deeds. For the Duchy of Cornwall, the purchase price or premium needs to be paid into the Bank of England; the Duchy Auditor then endorses a memorandum of the payment on the conveyance or lease. To be effective against the Duke of Cornwall, a conveyance or lease should be enrolled with the Keeper of the Duchy Records who endorses a certificate of enrolment on the deed (Duchy of Cornwall Management Act 1863, s 30). Similar arrangements exist for the Duchy of Lancaster. However, none of the requirements with respect to formalities or enrolment contained in any enactment relating to the Duchy of Lancaster or the Duchy of Cornwall now apply to dispositions by a registered proprietor (LRA 2002, s 84).

The LRA 2002, s 83 makes provision for an 'appropriate authority' to represent, make applications and receive notice on behalf of, Her Majesty and the Duchies of Lancaster and Cornwall. For land vested in Her Majesty in right of the Crown, this may be the Crown Estate Commissioners; or a government department; or such person as Her Majesty may appoint in writing under the Royal Sign Manual. For an interest belonging to Her Majesty in right of the Duchy of Lancaster, the appropriate authority is the Chancellor of the Duchy. For an interest belonging to the Duchy of Cornwall, the appropriate authority is such person as the Duke of Cornwall, or the possessor for the time being of the Duchy of Cornwall, appoints.

On escheat, the Crown and the Royal Duchies take the land subject to all existing incumbrances affecting the determined estate. Where the Crown grants a new estate or a Royal Duchy transfers its estate the new owner is similarly bound by the incumbrances that affected the escheated estate. An application for registration by the new owner would be one for first registration, as opposed to one for registration of a disposition of an existing registered title. Where a registered freehold estate in land has determined on escheat, the Registry may enter a note of that fact in the property register and in the property register of any inferior registered title. If the Registry considers that there is doubt whether a registered freehold estate in land has determined, the entry must be modified by a statement to that effect (LRR 2003, r 173). Where an entry is made under LRR 2003, r 173, the Registry need not close that registered title until a new freehold estate has been registered in respect of the land in which the former estate subsisted.

Under Companies Act 2006, s 1013(2), the Crown or relevant duchy may lose the ability to disclaim bona vacantia by express waiver, taking possession or any act clearly showing the intention to do so. If application was made to register the Treasury Solicitor, the Solicitor to the Duchy of Lancaster or the Duke of Cornwall as proprietor, that could amount to such a waiver. Therefore if the vesting as bona vacantia has already been entered in the register, the escheat entry will be modified to refer to this possibility.

Application may be made in Form AP1 to cancel the escheat entry, if accompanied by either a letter from the Crown Estate Commissioners or the Solicitor for one of the Royal Duchies confirming that escheat has not in fact taken place; or an office copy court order reviving a dissolved company; or an office copy court order reinstating the original freehold estate.

BOUNDARIES

Every property, whether or not it is registered, has exact legal boundaries. That is, lines separating the property owned by one person from that owned by their neighbour. But deeds rarely identify these legal boundaries precisely and often the owners themselves do not know exactly where they are. Trying to fix the boundaries precisely at the time of registration of title would involve a great deal of expense and could cause a dispute that would not otherwise have occurred. For that reason, the boundary of a registered estate as shown for the purposes of the register on the title plan, or otherwise in the register, is a general boundary unless it is shown as determined under LRA 2002, s 60. A general boundary does not determine the exact line of the boundary (LRA 2002, s 60(2)).

There is no definition of a general boundary in the LRA 2002. The Law Commission Report, *Land Registration for the Twenty-First Century: A Conveyancing Revolution* (Law Com No 271) (2001) indicated that it was the intention to retain the so-called 'general boundaries rule', then contained in Land Registration Rules 1925, r 278. Land Transfer Rules 1898, r 213 and Land Transfer Rules 1903, r 274 also provided for general boundaries. Rule 278 of the 1925 Rules stated:

(1) Except in cases in which it is noted in the Property Register that the boundaries have been fixed, the filed plan shall be deemed to indicate the general boundaries only.

(2) In such cases the exact line of the boundary will be left undetermined – as, for instance, whether it includes a hedge or wall and ditch, or runs along the centre of a wall or fence, or its inner or outer face, or how far it runs within or beyond it; or whether or not the land registered includes the whole or any portion of an adjoining road or stream.

(3) When a general boundary only is desired to be entered in the register, notice to the owners of the adjoining lands need not be given.

(4) This rule shall apply notwithstanding that a part or the whole of a ditch, wall, fence, road, stream, or other boundary is expressly included in or excluded from the title or that it forms the whole of the land comprised in the title.

Under the LRR 2003, all registered estates in land, registered rentcharges and registered franchises which are affecting franchises have a title plan. That title plan is based on the Ordnance Survey Map (LRR 2003, r 5). A registered franchise is an affecting franchise if it relates to a defined area of land and is an adverse right affecting, or capable of affecting, the title to an estate or charge (see *Franchises*, page 240).

Prior to the coming into force of the LRA 2002, the title plan was known as the 'filed plan'.

The title plan usually shows the extent of the registered estate by red edging, although other means may be used in particular circumstances. Sometimes the verbal description of the estate in the property register will contain information clarifying the extent. For example, if the title relates to a first floor flat there will be a note in the property register to explain this. Enlargement plans are sometimes provided as part of a title plan, so as to clarify detail beyond the scope of the normal Ordnance Survey scales. For example, to show small juts in boundary walls and different floor levels. Supplementary plans can be annexed to title plans where appropriate; for example to show parts of buildings at different floor levels or to carry complicated reference markings that would cause confusion if shown on the title plan itself.

Where the boundary shown is a general boundary, the legal boundary of the land does not necessarily follow the red edging on the title plan. For example, the so-called 'hedge and ditch rule' may apply. This is a rebuttable presumption that arises when a boundary comprises a hedge and a man-made ditch. It is presumed that the owner of the hedge also owns the ditch beyond it, although this may be rebutted on the facts. The House of Lords applied this presumption in *Alan Wibberley Building Ltd v Insley* [1999] UKHL 15, where Lord Hope of Craighead said:

> Any boundary dispute which leads to litigation as protracted as the dispute has been in this case is regrettable. But no workable system of conveyancing can be expected to eliminate entirely the opportunity for disputes to arise about boundaries. In most cases neighbours are content to accept that absolute precision is unattainable. They recognise that a certain amount of latitude must be given to whatever method has been used to fix the boundaries of their land. That also is the view which has been taken by the legislature. The original system of precise guaranteed boundaries under the Land Registry Act 1862 gave rise to considerable difficulty. It had to be abandoned in view of the expense which was involved in a survey of the precise boundaries and the many disputes which arose between neighbours who had been content until then to accept a certain amount of vagueness as to the precise line of their common boundary. The result was the introduction of the general boundaries rule now contained in rule 278 of the Land Registration Rules 1925.
>
> The use of maps or plans such as those published by the Ordnance Survey is now widespread and has obvious advantages. Ordnance Survey maps are prepared to a

high standard of accuracy and are frequently and appropriately used to fix boundaries by reference, for example, to Ordnance Survey field numbers. But like all maps they are subject to limitations. The most obvious are those imposed by scale. No map can reproduce to anything like the same scale of detail every feature which is found on the ground. Furthermore the Ordnance Survey does not fix private boundaries. The purpose of the survey is topographical, not taxative. Even the most detailed Ordnance Survey map may not show every feature on the ground which can be used to identify the extent of the owner's land. In the present case the Ordnance Survey map shows the hedge, but it does not show the ditch. So there is no reason in principle in this case for preferring the line on the map to other evidence which may be relevant to identify the boundary.

As title plans are based on the Ordnance Survey map, they are limited by the precision with which such maps are prepared. As with any map, Ordnance Survey maps are subject to some limitations which depend upon the scale of the map and the accuracy of the surveying techniques used. These limitations are likely to result in some variation between what is shown on the map and what exists on the ground and as a result, title plans cannot be used to establish the precise position of features on the ground simply by scaling from the title plan. In some cases the nature of particular features on the ground can add to the uncertainty. For example, a mature hedge can be several metres wide, so that it can be difficult to relate it to the single line which represents it on the map.

General boundaries therefore allow flexibility in the relationship between the legal boundaries and any physical features on the Ordnance Survey map that the Land Registry makes reference to when making a reasonable interpretation of the estate comprised within the title deeds.

The nature and effect of registration with general boundaries was considered by the court in *Lee v Barrey* [1957] Ch 251, CA. More recent cases, such as *Derbyshire County Council v Fallon* [2007] EWHC 1326 (Ch), *Strachey v Ramage* [2008] EWCA Civ 384 and *Drake & anor v Fripp* [2011] EWCA Civ 1279, have further emphasised the importance of this point.

Where, on first registration or on the registration of a disposition of a registered estate (such as a transfer of part), an agreement or declaration as to the ownership of boundary structures appears in the relevant deeds, an entry is made in the register reflecting this. Commonly, for example, this may be an agreement that a particular wall is a party wall. Where the entry refers to 'T' marks, these are reproduced on the title plan or otherwise described in the register. But neither a party wall notice, nor a party wall award under the Party Wall etc Act 1996, may be the subject of a notice in the register. Other matters arising under the Party Wall etc Act 1996 may give rise to an entry in the register (see 'Party Wall etc Act 1996', page 83).

LRA 2002, s 61 and LRR 2003, r 123 make provision for accretion or diluvion (see *Accretion and diluvion*, page 3).

Under the LRA 1925, application could be made for a title to be registered with 'fixed boundaries'. The applicant had to bear the cost of this expensive process, and there was no guarantee that it would be possible, as a result of the investigations made, to fix the boundaries. In practice such applications were extremely rare. The LRA 2002 instead contains provision for the exact line of a boundary to be 'determined' instead of it being a general boundary.

Except in those rare cases where the boundary has been fixed or determined, the Land Registry cannot decide or confirm where the exact legal boundary between two properties lies. Therefore, if the exact legal line of the boundary has to be otherwise established, this can only be done either by the adjoining owners reaching an agreement, or by judicial determination.

If the exact line of a boundary is established by agreement and the terms of the agreement are recorded in a formal document, application may be made to the Registry in Form AP1 for such an agreement to be 'noted' in the register of any registered titles affected. However, such an agreement can only *clarify* the position of an existing boundary; it cannot be used to effect a transfer of property and instead a transfer in the prescribed form would be required. Also, such an agreement does not 'determine' a boundary for land registration purposes and it would therefore remain a general boundary in the register. If the exact line of a boundary is established by an order of the court, application may be made to the Registry in Form AP1 for such an order to be 'noted' in the register of any registered titles affected. Such an order does not 'determine' a boundary for land registration purposes and it would therefore remain a general boundary in the register.

Determination of the exact line of a boundary

A proprietor of a registered estate may apply to the Registry for the exact line of the boundary of that registered estate to be determined. The application may be in respect of part only of such a boundary (LRR 2003, rr 117 and 118(1)).

A person applying for the exact line of a boundary to be determined should deliver to the Registry:

(a)   an application in Form DB;
(b)   a plan, or a plan and a verbal description, identifying the exact line of the boundary claimed and showing sufficient surrounding physical features to allow the general position of the boundary to be drawn on the Ordnance Survey map;

(c) the documents and other evidence on which the applicant relies to establish the exact line of the boundary; and

(d) the fee payable (see *Fees*, page 221).

Where the Registry is satisfied that:

(1) the plan, or plan and verbal description, supplied identifies the exact line of the boundary claimed,

(2) the applicant has shown an arguable case that the exact line of the boundary is in the position shown on that plan, or plan and verbal description, and

(3) it can identify all the owners of the land adjoining the boundary to be determined and has an address at which each owner may be given notice,

it must give such adjoining owners notice of the application (LRR 2003, r 119(1)). For these purposes 'owner' means the proprietor of any registered estate or charge affecting land, a person who holds an unregistered legal estate in land which he could apply to register, and, if the land is demesne land, Her Majesty.

Where the evidence supplied in support includes an agreement in writing as to the exact line of the boundary with an owner of the land adjoining the boundary, or a court order determining the line of that boundary, the Registry need not give notice of the application to that owner.

Where the Registry is not satisfied as to (1), (2) and (3) above, it must cancel the application (LRR 2003, r 119(7)).

If no recipient of a notice of the application objects within the relevant period of time, the Registry must complete the application (LRR 2003, r 119(6)). The time for objection fixed by the notice is the period ending at 12 noon on the 20th business day after the date of issue of the notice, or such longer period as the Registry may decide before the issue of the notice. A business day is a day when the Land Registry is open to the public, that is every day except Saturdays, Sundays, Christmas Day, Good Friday or any other day either specified or declared by proclamation under Banking and Financial Dealings Act 1971, s 1, or appointed by the Lord Chancellor, or certified by the Registry as being an 'interrupted day' due to delay or failure of a communication service or to some other event or circumstance causing substantial interruption in the normal operation of the Registry.

Before the period specified in the notice has expired, a recipient of the notice may apply to the Registry for an extension of the period, setting out why an extension should be allowed. On receipt of such a request, the Registry may, if it considers it appropriate, seek the views of the applicant. If, after considering any such views and all other relevant matters, the Registry is satisfied that a longer period should be allowed, it may allow such period as it considers appropriate, whether or not the period is the same as any period requested by the recipient of the notice.

If a valid objection to the application is received which cannot be disposed of by agreement, the matter will have to be dealt with in accordance with LRA 2002, s 73 (see *Disputes*, page 193).

On completion of an application to determine a boundary, there are added to the title plan of the applicant's registered title and, if appropriate, to the title plan of any superior or inferior registered title, and any registered title affecting the other land adjoining the determined boundary, such particulars of the exact line of the boundary as the Registry considers appropriate. Instead of, or as well as, adding such particulars to the title plan(s), the Registry may make an entry in the relevant title(s) referring to any other plan showing the exact line of the boundary.

An entry of the fact of determination of the boundary is also made in the property register of the applicant's registered title. If appropriate, a similar entry is made in the property register of any superior or inferior registered title, and any registered title affecting the other land adjoining the determined boundary.

Where the exact line of only part of the boundary of a registered estate has been determined, the ends of that part of the boundary are not to be treated as determined for the purposes of adjoining parts of the boundary the exact line of which has not been determined (LRR 2003, r 121). By way of example, Figure 1 (below) shows a rectangular piece of land, where A–B is the northern boundary. The part of the boundary between points C and D has been determined but not the rest of the boundary. The determined position for points C and D shown on the title plan determines those points for the boundary C–D but not for the boundaries A–C and B–D. Notice of the application will have been served on the owners of the land adjoining on the south of C–D, but not on the owners of the land adjoining on the east of B–D nor on the owners of the land adjoining on the west of A–C:

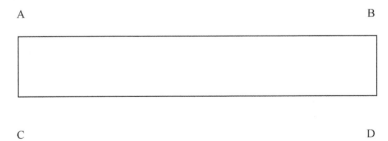

Figure 1

The Registry may determine the exact line of a common boundary without an application being made where there is a transfer of part of a registered estate in land and there is sufficient information in the transfer to enable it to do so. The same applies on a grant of a lease which is a registrable disposition of part of a registered estate in land. A 'common boundary' in this context is any boundary of the land disposed of by the transfer of part or lease of part which adjoins land in which the transferor or landlord, at the date of the transfer or lease, had a registered estate in land or of which such transferor or landlord was entitled to be registered as proprietor (LRR 2003, r 122).

Where the Registry determines the exact line of the common boundary without an application, it must make an entry in the property registers of the affected registered titles stating that the exact line of the common boundary is determined under LRA 2002, s 60. The Registry must also add to the title plan of the transferor's or landlord's affected registered title (whether or not the transferor or landlord is still the proprietor of that title, or still entitled to be registered as proprietor of that title), and to the title plan of the registered title under which the transfer or lease is being registered, such particulars of the exact line of the common boundary as it considers appropriate. Instead of, or as well as, adding such particulars to the title plans, the Registry may make an entry in the property register of the affected registered titles referring to the description of the common boundary in the transfer or lease.

Party Wall etc Act 1996

As to the effect of the Party Wall etc Act 1996, see *Party Wall etc Act 1996*, page 432.

BULK APPLICATIONS

When it is proposed to make a 'large scale application', the applicant should first contact the Bulk Application Contact (BAC) for the relevant Land Registry office, depending on the administrative area in which the applicant is based, to discuss the matter. A large scale application is one comprising a common deed or deeds affecting registered and/or unregistered land in areas covered by one or more Registry office(s) and which either affects more than 200 properties comprising registered titles only or a combination of registered titles and unregistered titles or affects more than 50 unregistered titles. The BAC will provide guidance as to the preparation and lodging of the application and will also arrange for a nominated Registry office to deal with the application or to act as a controller for a group of Land Registry offices nominated to assist with the application. The

BAC will coordinate the processing of the application and provide the applicant with written details of the required steps to take, the timetable of lodgement and the method of calculating the fees. Once the application has been lodged at a Land Registry office, that office will assume the operational responsibility, and the application becomes subject to the normal registration procedures.

When it is proposed to make a 'small scale application', the applicant should first contact the Integrity Manager at the Land Registry office that administers the largest number of affected titles, for further guidance. A small scale application is one comprising a common deed or deeds affecting registered and/or unregistered land in areas covered by more than one Land Registry office, and which affects 200 or fewer registered and/or 50 or fewer unregistered properties. This does not include a follow-up application to an existing large scale application, which must be referred to the BAC as above.

CAUTIONS AGAINST CONVERSION

Where a proprietor was registered with possessory, qualified, or good leasehold title, it was possible under Land Registration Rules 1925, r 215(2) for a caution against conversion to be entered in the register. This had the effect of preventing the title being converted to qualified, good leasehold, or absolute (as appropriate) until notice of the application had been served on the cautioner, allowing him an opportunity to object to the conversion. It is not possible to register a caution against conversion under the LRA 2002, which came into force on 13 October 2003, but there are transitional provisions which apply to pre-existing cautions. Under the LRA 2002 and the LRR 2003, 'conversion' of title is now referred to as 'upgrade' of title (see *Upgrade of class of title*, page 565).

If a caution against conversion has previously been entered in the register and an application is made to upgrade the title, the Registry, before determining the application, must give notice of it to the person named in the caution. Where the cautioner responds to the notice by claiming any estate, right or interest in the land in the title, then, to the extent such estate right or interest subsists and is otherwise enforceable, the claim is treated for the purposes of LRA 2002, s 62(6) as one for an estate, right or interest whose enforceability is preserved by virtue of the existing entry about the class of title (Land Registration Act 2002 (Transitional Provisions) Order 2003 (SI 2003/1953) (LRA (TP) Order 2003), art 15).

LRA 2002, s 62(6) provides that none of the powers to upgrade the title contained in s 62 is exercisable if there is outstanding any claim adverse to the title of the registered proprietor which is made by virtue of an estate, right or interest whose enforceability is preserved by virtue of the existing entry about the class of title.

CAUTIONS AGAINST DEALINGS

LRA 1925, s 54 provided that any person interested in any land or charge registered in the name of any person might lodge a caution to the effect that no dealing with such land or charge is to be registered until notice has been served upon the cautioner.

Although it is not possible to register a caution against dealings under the LRA 2002, which came into force on 13 October 2003, any pre-existing caution against dealings in the register continues to have effect (LRA 2002, Sch 12, para 2(3)).

Notwithstanding their repeal by the LRA 2002, LRA 1925, ss 55 and 56 continue to have effect in respect of existing cautions against dealings, as a result of LRA 2002, Sch 12, para 2(3). Land Registration Rules 1925, rr 215 to 222, which dealt with cautions against dealings, have been replaced by transitional provisions relating to such cautions contained in LRR 2003, rr 218 to 223.

Where a caution has been registered, no registration of any dealing will be completed until notice of it has been served on the cautioner by the Registry (LRA 1925, s 55). The notice may be served by post to the address for service (whether within or outside the United Kingdom), by leaving the notice at the address for service in the United Kingdom, by directing the notice to a DX number entered as the address for service, by electronic transmission to an electronic address for service, or by fax where the cautioner has informed the Registry in writing that he is willing to accept service by fax and of the fax number to which it should be sent. The Registry may also serve the notice by post to an address, other than an address for service, where it believes the addressee is likely to receive it. The same applies to direction by DX to, or leaving the notice at, an address other than an address for service. Whatever method of service is used, the notice period is the period ending at 12 noon on the 15th working day, or ending at 12 noon on such later working day as the Registry may allow, after the date of issue of the notice (LRR 2003, rr 218 and 220(2)). A working day is any day from Monday to Friday (inclusive) which is not Christmas Day, Good Friday or any other day either specified or declared by proclamation under Banking and Financial Dealings Act 1971, s 1 or appointed by the Lord Chancellor, or certified by the Registry as being an 'interrupted day' due to delay or failure of a communication service or to some other event or circumstance causing substantial interruption in the normal operation of the Registry.

The notice warns the cautioner that the caution will cease to have effect at the expiry of the notice period (or such longer period as the Registry may allow), unless an order to the contrary is made by the Registry. That is the only effect of a caution. It does not provide any form of priority or confer validity upon any claim (LRA 1925, s 56(2)). See also *Barclays Bank v Taylor* [1974] Ch 137 and *Clark v Chief Land Registrar* [1994] EWCA Civ 12.

A cautioner may at any time apply for a replacement or additional address, subject to there being, after the application, no more than three addresses, at least one of which is a postal address (LRR 2003, r 198(6)). No fee is currently payable for such an application, which should be made in Form AP1.

Where the caution is registered against the proprietor of the land, this does not allow the cautioner to prevent a registered chargee selling under his power of sale (*Chancery plc v Ketteringham* [1994] EWCA Civ 12). The cautioner will therefore be informed that his caution has been cancelled. This possibility should be borne in mind when a cautioner consents to the registration of a charge.

Although an interest under a trust of land may have been protected by a caution against dealings (*Elias v Mitchell* [1972] Ch 652), a disposition by two or more trustees or a trust corporation which overreaches that interest under Law of Property Act 1925, ss 2 and 27 prevents an objection by a cautioner being sustained, although he will have received notice of the application to register the dealing.

If a caution was lodged without reasonable cause, the cautioner is liable to make, to any person who may have sustained damage by the lodging of the caution, such compensation as may be just. Such compensation is recoverable as a debt by the person who has sustained damage from the person who lodged the caution (LRA 1925, s 56(3)). In practice, the prospects of a successful claim under s 56(3) may be more limited than would appear at first sight. In *Clearbrook Property Holdings v Verrier* [1973] 3 All ER 614, Templeman J said:

> It is at least arguable that a person who genuinely believes he is entitled to specific performance and issues a writ for that purpose under legal advice may say that he lodged his caution with reasonable cause.

Where a cautioner has died, his personal representative may proceed in the same manner as the cautioner (LRA 1925, s 56(4)). The LRR 2003 define 'cautioner' as including his personal representative (LRR 2003, r 218). The personal representative should always consider the need to amend the cautioner's address for service in the register (LRR 2003, r 198(6A)).

The cautioner may apply at any time for the cancellation of the caution (LRR 2003, r 222). The application must be in Form WCT and signed by the cautioner or his conveyancer. If the cautioner has died, the application should be made by his personal representative and a copy of the grant enclosed. Where the cautioner is applying to withdraw the caution as to part only, a plan defining the relevant land should be attached to Form WCT. No fee is currently payable.

A cautioner may make an application for the entry of a notice under LRA 2002, s 34, or for the entry of a restriction under LRA 2002, s 43 in relation to the estate, right, interest or claim in respect of which the caution was lodged only if he also applies for the withdrawal of the caution (LRA 2002, Sch 12, para 17).

The proprietor of the registered estate or charge to which the caution relates may apply for the cancellation of the caution at any time (LRR 2003, r 223). Such an application may also be made by a person who, but for the existence of the caution, would be entitled to be registered as the proprietor of that estate or charge. The application must be in Form CCD. No fee is currently payable. The Registry must give the cautioner notice of the application (LRR 2003, r 223(3)). The notice period is the period ending at 12 noon on the 15th working day, or ending at 12 noon on such later working day as the Registry may allow, after the date of issue of the notice (LRR 2003, rr 218 and 220(2)).

Cautioner showing cause

When the cautioner has received a notice (whether under LRA 1925, s 55 as the result of an application to register a dealing, or under LRR 2003, r 223 as a result of an application to cancel the caution), he may at any time before the expiry of the notice period 'show cause' why the Registry should not give effect to that application. If he does not reply to the notice, or consents unconditionally to the cancellation of the caution, the caution will be cancelled.

To show cause, the cautioner must deliver to the Registry a written statement setting out the grounds relied upon and show that he has a fairly arguable case for the Registry not to give effect to the application in question (LRR 2003, r 221(3)). The written statement must be signed by the cautioner or his conveyancer.

If, after reading the written statement, and making any enquiries it thinks necessary, the Registry is satisfied that cause has been shown, it must order that the caution is to continue until withdrawn or otherwise disposed of under the LRA 2002 or the LRR 2003. The Registry must then give notice to the applicant and the cautioner that it has made the order and that the cautioner is to be treated as having objected under LRA 2002, s 73 to the application that resulted in notice being served (LRR 2003, r 221(5)). The notice given by the Registry under r 221(5) is treated as notice under LRA 2002, s 73(5)(a).

The cautioner and the applicant may still resolve their dispute by agreement. If, however, it is not possible to dispose of the objection by agreement, the matter will have to be dealt with in accordance with LRA 2002, s 73(7) (see *Disputes*, page 193).

Agreement might be reached, for example, that the dealing be registered but with the caution remaining in the register, or that the caution be cancelled and the dealing completed but with the interest to which the caution related being protected by entry of a notice in priority to the dealing. The latter course of action is possible only where the interest is one capable of being protected by a notice and an appropriate application would need to be made.

Where a cautioner is considering agreeing to the registration of a charge on condition that his caution remains in the proprietorship register, he should bear in mind that his caution could be overreached subsequently if the proprietor of the charge sells under his power of sale.

If after service of the notice under LRA 1925, s 55(1) or LRR 2003, r 223(3) the application that resulted in the notice being served is cancelled, withdrawn or otherwise does not proceed, the Registry must make an order that the caution will continue to have effect, unless it has already done so or the caution has been cancelled (LRR 2003, r 221(6)).

Where the notice is served on the cautioner under LRA 1925, s 55 as a result of an application to register a dealing and the cautioner objects but is unable to show cause, or consents to the registration of the dealing but not to cancellation of his caution, the application will be completed but the Registry will normally make an order under s 55 that the caution is to continue until withdrawn or otherwise disposed of under the LRA 2002 or the LRR 2003. No such order will, however, be made where it is clear that the interest protected by the caution has been defeated as a result of the dealing.

CAUTIONS AGAINST FIRST REGISTRATION

A person claiming to be the owner of a qualifying estate or entitled to an interest affecting a qualifying estate may lodge an application for a caution against first registration. For these purposes a 'qualifying estate' is a legal estate which relates to land to which the caution relates and is an estate in land, a rentcharge, a franchise, or a profit à prendre in gross (LRA 2002, s 15). A caution against first registration cannot be entered in the cautions register, however, where the application is by virtue of the applicant's ownership of a freehold estate in land or a leasehold estate in land where more than 7 years of the term are unexpired (LRA 2002, s 15(3)). The limitation on a leaseholder applies equally to a caution in respect of his leasehold estate and a caution in respect of the landlord's estate. The purpose of the limitation is to encourage the owner of a qualifying estate to protect his estate by making an application for substantive registration of his title.

LRA 1925, s 53 contained no limitation equivalent to that in LRA 2002, s 15(3). For the period of 2 years from 13 October 2003 the limitation in s 15(3) did not have effect (LRA 2002, Sch 12, para 14(1)). Any caution lodged under para 14(1), however, ceased to have effect at the end of that period of 2 years, except in relation to applications for first registration made before the end of that period.

Different rules apply to cautions against first registration lodged by the Queen where the land is demesne land (see *Demesne land*, page 187).

A caution against first registration which was lodged under the LRA 1925, s 53 continues to have effect, and the provisions of LRA 2002, other than the limitation in s 15(3) on an owner applying for a caution against first registration, apply to such a caution.

The Registry is obliged to keep a register of cautions against first registration, comprising an individual caution register for each such caution. Each individual caution register has its own caution title number and is divided into two parts; the caution property register and the cautioner's register.

A person applying for a caution against first registration should deliver to the Registry:

(a)   an application in Form CT1;
(b)   a plan allowing the extent of the land to which the caution relates to be identified clearly on the Ordnance Survey map, unless this can be clearly identified from the description in panel 2 on Form CT1;
(c)   (if applicable) any consent in writing of a third party to the lodging of the caution (which may be provided in panel 12 of Form CT1); and
(d)   the fee payable (see *Fees*, page 221).

Either the cautioner (or at least one of them, if there is more than one cautioner), or someone authorised by the cautioner, or the cautioner's conveyancer must make the statement of truth in panel 10 of Form CT1. No documents should be exhibited, as the statement should be self-contained.

The interest stated in the Form CT1 will appear in the caution property register of the individual caution register, together with a description of the legal estate to which the caution relates. The description of the legal estate will refer to a caution plan based on the Ordnance Survey map, unless the legal estate is a relating franchise (see *Franchises*, page 240).

The other part of an individual caution register is the cautioner's register. This contains the name of the cautioner, an address for service and, where appropriate, details of any person consenting to the lodging of the caution. A person consents to the lodging of a caution if, before the caution is entered in the cautions register, he has confirmed in writing that he consents to the lodging of the caution and that consent is produced to the Registry (LRR 2003, r 47).

Where the cautioner is a company registered under the Companies Acts, or a limited liability partnership (LLP) incorporated under the Limited Liability Partnerships Act 2000, its registered number also appears in the cautioner's register.

The cautioner must supply at least one and not more than three addresses for service to which all notices are to be sent. One address must be a postal address, whether or not in the United Kingdom. The other one or two additional addresses may be postal addresses, but may also be a box number at a United Kingdom DX or an email address. The box number referred to must be at a United Kingdom DX to which delivery can be made on behalf of the Registry under arrangements already in existence between the Land Registry and a service provider at the time the box number details are provided to the Registry (LRR 2003, r 198). A cautioner may at any time apply for a replacement or additional address, subject to there being, after the application, no more than three addresses, at least one of which is a postal address. No fee is currently payable for such an application, which should be made in Form AP1.

If a caution against first registration was lodged under the LRA 1925, s 53 without reasonable cause, then the cautioner is liable to make, to any person who may have sustained damage by the lodging of the caution, such compensation as may be just. Such compensation is recoverable as a debt by the person who has sustained damage from the person who lodged the caution (LRA 1925, s 56(3), which continues to have effect in relation to cautions against first registration lodged under that Act as a result of the transitional provisions of LRA 2002, Sch 12, para 4).

A person must not exercise the right to lodge a caution against first registration under LRA 2002, s 15 without reasonable cause (LRA 2002, s 77(1)). This duty to act reasonably is owed to any person who suffers damage in consequence of its breach (LRA 2002, s 77(2)).

For the purposes of the LRA 2002 and the LRR 2003, the 'cautioner' in relation to a caution against first registration means the person who lodged the caution or the person for the time being shown in the cautioner's register, where that person is not the person who lodged the caution (LRA 2002, s 22 and LRR 2003, r 52(1)).

Effect of a caution against first registration

Where an application for first registration relates to a legal estate which is subject to a caution against first registration, the Registry must give the cautioner notice of the application and of his right to object to it. The period in which the cautioner can object is a period ending at 12 noon on the 15th working day after the date of issue of the notice or such longer period as the Registry may allow following a request, provided that the longer period never exceeds a period ending at 12 noon on the 30th working day after the date of issue of the notice (LRR 2003, r 53). The request referred to is one by the cautioner to the Registry setting out why the longer period should be allowed. This request must be made before the period ending at 12 noon on the 15th working day after the date of issue of the notice has expired. After receiving such a request the Registry may, if it considers it appropriate, seek the views of the applicant for first registration; if, after considering any such views and all other relevant matters, the Registry is satisfied that a longer period should be allowed, it may allow such period (not exceeding a period ending at 12 noon on the 30th working day after the date of issue of the notice) as it considers appropriate, whether or not the period is the same as any period requested by the cautioner (LRR 2003, r 53(3)). A working day is any day from Monday to Friday (inclusive) which is not Christmas Day, Good Friday or any other day either specified or declared by proclamation under Banking and Financial Dealings Act 1971, s 1 or appointed by the Lord Chancellor or certified by the Registry as being an 'interrupted day' due to delay or failure of a communication service or to some other event or circumstance causing substantial interruption in the normal operation of the Registry.

The application for first registration cannot be completed within the notice period unless the cautioner has given notice to the Registry that he does not intend to object or unless the cautioner has objected and the objection has been disposed of within the notice period. An example of the latter is where the cautioner objected on the grounds that he had an easement over the land sought to be registered and, still within the notice period, the applicant consented to the making of an entry in the register in respect of the easement.

The above is the only effect of a caution against first registration. In particular, a caution against first registration has no effect on the validity or priority of any interest of the cautioner in the legal estate to which the caution relates (LRA 2002, s 16(3)). The legal estate remains unregistered and registration of a caution against first registration can therefore never supersede the need to register a land charge under the Land Charges Act 1972 in appropriate cases.

Objection by cautioner

Where the cautioner objects to the application for first registration, he must deliver to the Registry at the address indicated in the notice a written statement signed by himself or his conveyancer. That statement must give the full name of the cautioner and state that he objects and set out the grounds for the objection (LRR 2003, r 19). If he wishes communications to be sent to an address other than his address for service, this should be stated.

Unless the Registry is satisfied that the objection is groundless, it must give notice of the objection to the applicant for first registration and may not complete the application for first registration until the objection has been disposed of. The cautioner and the applicant may still resolve their dispute by agreement. If, however, it is not possible to dispose of the objection by agreement, the matter will have to be dealt with in accordance with LRA 2002, s 73 (see *Disputes*, page 193).

Withdrawal of a caution against first registration

The cautioner may withdraw the caution against first registration at any time (LRA 2002, s 17). The cautioner should deliver to the Registry:

(a)   an application in Form WCT; and
(b)   if the withdrawal relates to part only of the land to which the caution relates, a plan or other sufficient details to allow the extent in question to be clearly identified on the Ordnance Survey map.

No fee is currently payable.

Cancellation of a caution against first registration

The owner of the legal estate to which the caution against first registration relates may apply to the Registry for cancellation of the caution (LRA 2002, s 18). In addition the owner of a legal estate which derives out of the legal estate to which the caution against first registration relates may also apply to the Registry for cancellation of the caution (LRR 2003, r 45). If, however, the owner of the legal estate to which the caution against first registration relates consented to the lodging of the caution in accordance with LRR 2003, r 47, he may make an application for cancellation only if the interest claimed by the cautioner has come to an end or if he claims that the consent was induced by fraud, misrepresentation, mistake or undue influence or given under duress. The same limitation on applying for cancellation applies to a person who derives title to the legal estate by operation of law from a person who consented (LRA 2002, s 18(2) and LRR 2003, r 47).

The applicant for cancellation of a caution against first registration should deliver to the Registry:

(a)   an application in Form CCT;
(b)   if the application relates to part only of the land to which the caution relates, a plan or other sufficient details to allow the extent in question to be clearly identified on the Ordnance Survey map;
(c)   evidence that the applicant is the owner of the legal estate to which the caution relates, where he is applying as such owner;
(d)   evidence that the applicant is the owner of a legal estate derived out of the legal estate to which the caution relates, where he is applying as such owner; and
(e)   where the applicant, or a person from whom the applicant derives title to the legal estate by operation of law, has consented to the lodging of the caution, evidence that the interest claimed by the cautioner has come to an end or that the consent was induced by fraud, misrepresentation, mistake or undue influence or given under duress.

No fee is currently payable.

When such an application is received, the Registry must give the cautioner notice of the application and notice that if he does not object to the application within the prescribed period the Registry must cancel the caution. The period within which the cautioner can object is a period ending at 12 noon on the 15th working day after the date of issue of the notice or such longer period as the Registry may allow following a request, provided that the longer period never exceeds a period ending at 12 noon on the 30th working day after the date of issue of the notice (LRR 2003, r 53). The request referred to is one by the cautioner to the Registry setting out why the longer period should be allowed. This request must be made before the period ending at 12 noon on the 15th working day after the date of issue of the notice has expired. After receiving such a request the Registry may, if it considers it appropriate, seek the views of the applicant for cancellation; if, after considering any such views and all other relevant matters, the Registry is satisfied that a longer period should be allowed, it may allow such period (not exceeding a period ending at 12 noon on the 30th working day after the issue of the notice) as it considers appropriate, whether or not the period is the same as any period requested by the cautioner (LRR 2003, r 53(3)). A working day is any day from Monday to Friday (inclusive) which is not Christmas Day, Good Friday or any other day either specified or declared by proclamation under Banking and Financial Dealings Act 1971, s 1 or appointed by the Lord Chancellor or certified by the Registry as being an 'interrupted day' due to delay or failure of a communication service or to some other event or circumstance causing substantial interruption in the normal operation of the Registry.

Only the cautioner, being the person who lodged the caution or the person for the time being shown in the cautioner's register, where that person is not the person who lodged the caution, can object to the cancellation of the caution (LRA 2002, s 73(2)). Where the cautioner shown in the cautioner's register comprises more than one person, each such person has a separate right to object to the cancellation of the caution (LRR 2003, r 52(2)).

Where the cautioner objects to the application for cancellation, he must deliver to the Registry at the address indicated in the notice a written statement signed by himself or his conveyancer. That statement must give the full name of the cautioner and state that he objects and set out the grounds for the objection (LRR 2003, r 19). If he wishes communications to be sent to an address other than his address for service, this should be stated.

Unless the Registry is satisfied that the objection is groundless, it must give notice of the objection to the applicant for cancellation and may not complete the application for cancellation until the objection has been disposed of. The cautioner and the applicant may still resolve their dispute by agreement. If, however, it is not possible to dispose of the objection by agreement, the matter will have to be dealt with in accordance with LRA 2002, s 73 (see *Disputes*, page 193).

Alteration of the cautions register

The LRA 2002 makes provision for alteration of the cautions register. The Registry may alter the cautions register (s 21) or the court may make an order for alteration of the cautions register (s 20). In either case, the alteration must be for the purpose of correcting a mistake or bringing the register up to date.

There was no machinery under the LRA 1925 allowing a successor by operation of law to the cautioner to be shown in the register in place of the cautioner. In such circumstances a new application for a caution against first registration was required. The LRR 2003, however, makes specific provision for this and r 51(1) provides that a person who claims that the whole of the relevant interest recorded in an individual cautions register is vested in him by operation of law as successor to the cautioner may apply for the register to be altered to substitute him as cautioner in the cautioner's register, in place of the cautioner. In addition to delivering the usual documents required (see *Alteration of the register*, page 39), the applicant should deliver to the Registry written details of the grounds on which he claims that the whole of the relevant interest recorded in the cautions register is vested in him by operation of law as successor to the cautioner.

Before the Registry alters the cautioner's register to show the new cautioner it must serve a notice on the existing cautioner giving details of the application, unless it is satisfied that service of the notice is unnecessary (LRR 2003, r 50(2)). If the Registry is so satisfied and does not serve notice or if the existing cautioner does not object within the time specified in any notice if served, the Registry must alter the cautioner's register to show the new cautioner in place of the existing cautioner. The new cautioner is then treated as 'the cautioner' for the purposes of the LRA 2002.

The Registry may also alter the cautions register for the purpose of bringing it up to date in some other manner, or for the purpose of correcting a mistake (LRA 2002, s 21). For example, to alter the cautioner's register in circumstances where the whole of the relevant interest has vested in another person other than by operation of law. The Registry is not, however, under an obligation to alter the cautions register in such circumstances (LRR 2003, r 49(2)).

A person who wishes to apply for an alteration under LRA 2002, s 21 should deliver to the Registry the usual documents required (see *Alteration of the register*, page 39) along with any supporting documents.

Before the Registry alters the cautions register it must serve a notice on the cautioner giving details of the application, unless it is satisfied that service of the notice is unnecessary (LRR 2003, r 50(2)). If the Registry is satisfied that the cautioner does not own the relevant interest, or owns only part, or that such interest did not exist or has come to an end wholly or in part, it must on application alter the cautions register under LRA 2002, s 21(1) (LRR 2003, r 49(1)). Where an alteration is made under LRA 2002, s 21, the Registry may pay such amount as it thinks fit in respect of any costs reasonably incurred by a person in connection with the alteration (LRA 2002, s 21(3)). This is most likely to arise where there has been a mistake in the cautions register.

The court may make an order for alteration of the cautions register for the purpose of bringing it up to date in some other manner, or for the purpose of correcting a mistake (LRA 2002, s 21). If, in any proceedings, the High Court or a county court decides that a cautioner does not own the interest claimed by the cautioner, or owns only part, or that such interest either wholly or in part did not exist or has come to an end, the court must make an order for the alteration of the cautions register (LRR 2003, r 48(1)). If the court makes an order for alteration of the cautions register, the order must state the caution title number of the individual cautions register affected, describe the alteration that is to be made, and direct the Registry to make the alteration. The order must be served on the Registry by making an application for it to give effect to the order.

In addition to delivering the usual documents required (see *Alteration of the register*, page 39), the applicant should deliver to the Registry the order of the court or a certified copy of it

CHANCEL REPAIR

Chancel repair liability is a liability of the owner of land to pay for the repair of the chancel of a parish church. The liability is mediaeval in origin and arises in relation to certain churches of the Church of England and the Church in Wales, so that there may be a liability where land was formerly attached to a rectory. Such former rectorial land is not necessarily close to a church building or situated within a rural area. In England, the parochial church council and, in Wales, the Representative Body of the Church in Wales, have the right to enforce the liability.

In the majority of cases the liability is joint and several as between the respective owners of the parts of the land burdened by the right, so that each owner is potentially liable for the whole of the cost of repairs to the chancel, subject to a right of contribution from others similarly liable. In a minority of cases the liability may be limited to only a proportion of the cost of repair of the chancel; this would be the case where, in particular, the title to a parcel of land is one in which a tithe rentcharge has previously merged pursuant to the Tithe Act 1936. Further details as to the background to chancel repair liability are contained in a report by the Law Commission, *Property Law – Liability for Chancel Repairs* (Law Com No 152) (1985).

In certain cases, it may be possible to obtain a release from any further liability for chancel repair; for example, by means of a 'composition' under the Diocesan Dilapidations Measure 1923 (1923/3). Also, if a parish church of the Church of England is declared redundant, any liability of a parochial church council or rector (including a lay rector) ceases upon a declaration of redundancy taking effect (Mission and Pastoral Measure 2011 (2011/3), s 61(3), which re-enacted the Pastoral Measure 1983, s 49(3)).

The benefit of a right in respect of the repair of a church chancel is not capable of being registered, as it is not a legal estate which can be registered as appurtenant to a registered estate. Until 12 October 2013, the burden of such a right was an unregistered interest which overrode first registration and registered dispositions (LRA 2002, Sch 1, para 13 and Sch 3, para 13). Such a right was therefore protected notwithstanding that there was no entry in the register in respect of it (LRA 2002, ss 11, 12, 29 and 30). After the period of 10 years beginning on 13 October 2003, the protection of the burden of the right as an overriding interest ceased.

On first registration of title, the Registry will enter a notice in the register as to the burden of such a liability, if it appears from its examination of the title to affect the land.

The liability for chancel repair was an overriding interest under LRA 1925, s 70(1)(c). In *Aston Cantlow and Wilmcote with Billesley Parochial Church Council v Wallbank* [2001] EWCA Civ 713, the Court of Appeal held that the modern liability of lay owners of what was once the glebe lands of a rectory to defray the unmet cost of repairs to the chancel of the parish church was a form of taxation which operated arbitrarily. This was held to have breached the defendants' right to peaceful enjoyment of their possessions under Article 1 of the First Protocol to the European Convention on Human Rights (as set out in Human Rights Act 1998, Sch 1), and so was unenforceable.

As a result of this decision, the liability for chancel repair was not originally included in the list of unregistered interests which override set out in LRA 2002, Schs 1 and 3. However, the decision of the Court of Appeal was reversed by the House of Lords in *Aston Cantlow and Wilmcote with Billesley Parochial Church Council v Wallbank* [2003] UKHL 37, and in consequence the liability for chancel repair was added to the list of unregistered interests which overrode first registration and registered dispositions set out in LRA 2002, Schs 1 and 3 (Land Registration Act 2002 (Transitional Provisions) (No 2) Order 2003 (SI 2003/2431), art 2(1) and (2)).

There was therefore a duty to disclose a liability for chancel repair under LRR 2003, r 28 or r 57 (see 'Duty to disclose overriding interests', page 426). The 10-year period referred to above having now expired, such liability no longer takes effect as an interest which overrides.

The person having the benefit of the right (if its priority has not already been previously defeated and it continues to subsist) should where necessary protect it. If he does not do so, the priority of the right is liable to be defeated on a subsequent first registration of unregistered burdened land or on a subsequent registration of a registrable disposition of registered burdened land for valuable consideration (LRA 2002, ss 11, 12, 29 and 30), as the case may be. If the burdened land is unregistered he should apply for a caution against first registration. If the burdened land is registered he should apply for the entry of a notice if one does not already appear in the register. Until 12 October 2013, no fee was payable for such an application, but the normal fee will now apply.

Caution against first registration

An applicant should deliver to the Registry the usual documents required (see *Cautions against first registration*, page 88).

The statement of truth in panel 10 of Form CT1 should be completed on the following lines to show the interest of the applicant:

> the person entitled to enforce a liability [*to repair*] [*to contribute towards the cost of repair*] of the chancel of [*specify the church in question*] *arising by reason of* [*summarise the basis on which the interest arises*] and payable by [*name of registered proprietor*].

The interest stated in the Form CT1 will appear in the caution register, together with a description of the legal estate to which the caution relates. For the effect of a caution against first registration, see *Cautions against first registration*, page 88.

Agreed notice

An applicant should deliver to the Registry the usual documents required (see *Notices*, page 389).

Documentary evidence of the creation or existence of the right in respect of the repair of a church chancel will normally be in the form of a statutory declaration or statement of truth containing details of how the right arose and how it has devolved to the applicant.

The agreed notice in the register will give details of the interest protected.

Where the registered proprietor does not consent to the entry in the register of an agreed notice and evidence to satisfy the Registry as to the validity of the applicant's claim cannot be lodged, an application for entry of a unilateral notice may still be made.

Unilateral notice

An applicant should deliver to the Registry the usual documents required (see *Notices*, page 389).

The statement in panel 11 or conveyancer's certificate in panel 12 of Form UN1 should be completed on the following lines to show the interest of the applicant:

> the person entitled to enforce a liability [*to repair*] [*to contribute towards the cost of repair*] of the chancel of [*specify the church in question*] arising by reason of [*summarise the basis on which the interest arises*] and payable by [*name of registered proprietor*].

The unilateral notice in the register will give brief details of the interest protected and identify the beneficiary of that notice.

CHANGE OF GENDER RESULTING IN A CHANGE OF NAME

An applicant should deliver to the Registry:

(a) an application in Form CNG;
(b) evidence of change of gender, in the form of a Gender Recognition Certificate, a New Birth Certificate or a UK Medical Practitioner's letter.

No fee is currently payable.

CHANGE OF NAME

It is important that the registered proprietor of a registered estate or charge ensures that his name, as well as his address for service, is kept up to date and that, where necessary, an application is made for alteration of the register to reflect any change in name. Such a change may be effected by a private individual or by a corporate body.

Change of name of private individuals

An applicant should deliver to the Registry:

(a) an application in Form AP1;
(b) evidence of change of name, which may be in the form of:
   (i) an original or official copy of a marriage certificate or civil partnership certificate or (unless the certificate was from outside the United Kingdom, in which case a certified copy is required) a conveyancer's certificate confirming the names of the couple (including the wife's or civil partner's former name) and the date and place of the marriage or civil partnership,
   (ii) a deed poll or a certified copy of it, or
   (iii) a statutory declaration or statement of truth (and a certified copy, if the applicant wishes the original to be returned);
(c) the appropriate confirmation or evidence as to identity (see *Identity evidence*, page 266).

No fee is currently payable.

Change of name of corporate bodies

An applicant should deliver to the Registry:

(a) an application in Form AP1;
(b) evidence of change of name, in the form of the original or a certified copy of the certificate of incorporation of change of name.

No fee is currently payable. Satisfactory alternative evidence may be required where the proprietor is an overseas company or LLP.

CHARGING ORDERS

A charging order is an order, usually of the court, imposing a charge upon a person's property to secure the payment of money that is due. Most charging orders are made under the Charging Orders Act 1979, but such orders can also arise under other statutes. For example, the court can make a charging order on a bankrupt's home in favour of a trustee in bankruptcy under the provisions of the IA 1986 in certain circumstances (see *Bankruptcy*, page 49). A charging order takes effect as an equitable charge.

Although the process under the Charging Orders Act 1979 involves two separate orders, it appears that there is only one equitable charge. At the interim charging order stage, the charge is conditional and if the charging order is made absolute then the charge becomes unconditional.

A person who has obtained a charging order against the legal estate in registered land may apply for the entry in the register of a notice in respect of the charging order. This is so whether it is an interim charging order or a final charging order. Such a charging order will arise where it is one made against a sole proprietor who is the sole legal and beneficial owner, or against joint proprietors expressly as 'trustees'. The applicant cannot apply for an official search with priority using Form OS1 or Form OS2, as the making of the charging order is not a protectable disposition, but is able to reserve a period of priority for his application by making an outline application.

Where the charging order is over a beneficial interest in registered land held under a trust of land, a notice cannot be entered in the register (LRA 2002, s 33(a)). Such a charging order will arise, for example, where it is made against the beneficial interest of one of two or more registered proprietors. In this situation, it is instead possible to apply for the entry of a restriction in Form K (LRA 2002, s 42(4) and LRR 2003, r 93(k)). This is an exception to the general principle that a person with the benefit of an equitable charge upon such a beneficial interest does not have a right or claim which would give him a sufficient interest to apply for entry of any restriction, other than one in Form A (if one does not already appear in the register) to reflect the severance of any beneficial joint tenancy which such a charge will normally effect.

Separate charging orders made against joint proprietors in the same court proceedings will not be treated as charging the legal estate and separate applications for a restriction in Form K would therefore need to be made instead. The applications may be made within a single Form RX1.

An application for entry of a notice may be for an agreed notice or a unilateral notice. In the case of an agreed notice, the Registry may approve the application without the consent of the proprietor where it is satisfied of the validity of the applicant's claim (LRA 2002, s 34(3)). Normally the production of the charging order enables the Registry to be so satisfied.

Where an application for a charging order against the legal estate is pending before the court, this will represent a 'pending land action' within the meaning of Land Charges Act 1972, s 17(1). A pending land action is treated as an interest affecting an estate or charge for the purposes of the LRA 2002 (LRA 2002, s 87(1)). It cannot, however, be an interest belonging to a person in actual occupation falling within LRA 2002, Sch 1, para 2 or Sch 3, para 2 which will override first registration or registered dispositions (LRA 2002, s 87(3)). The priority of the pending land action may be protected by application for entry of an agreed notice or a unilateral notice (LRA 2002, s 87(1) and LRR 2003, r 172). However, an application for a charging order over a beneficial interest in land held under a trust of land would not appear to be a pending land action for this purpose and is not therefore protectable by entry of a notice. Nor is it protectable by entry of a restriction, as at this stage the applicant for the charging order has no interest in the beneficial interest in question.

Notice in respect of a pending land action

Agreed notice

In addition to the usual documents required (see *Notices*, page 389), an applicant should deliver to the Registry the sealed claim form and notice of issue or a certified copy of it.

As the consent of the registered proprietor is unlikely to be forthcoming in this situation, this is likely to be sufficient to satisfy the Registry as to the validity of the applicant's claim in accordance with LRA 2002, s 34(3)(c).

The agreed notice in the register will give details of the interest protected.

Unilateral notice

An applicant should deliver to the Registry the usual documents required (see *Notices*, page 389).

The statement in panel 11 or conveyancer's certificate in panel 12 of Form UN1 should be completed on the following lines to show the interest of the applicant:

> applicant in an application for a charging order in the [*name of court*] Court [*set out full court reference and parties*].

The unilateral notice in the register will give brief details of the interest protected and identify the beneficiary of that notice.

Agreed notice in respect of the charging order

In addition to the usual documents required (see *Notices*, page 389), an applicant should deliver to the Registry the charging order or a certified copy of it.

As the consent of the registered proprietor is unlikely to be forthcoming in this situation, this is likely to be sufficient to satisfy the Registry as to the validity of the applicant's claim in accordance with LRA 2002, s 34(3)(c).

The agreed notice in the register will give details of the interest protected.

Unilateral notice in respect of the charging order

An applicant should deliver to the Registry the usual documents required (see *Notices*, page 389).

The statement in panel 11 or conveyancer's certificate in panel 12 of Form UN1 should be completed on the following lines to show the interest of the applicant:

> chargee under a charging order of the [*name of court*] Court dated [*date*] [*set out full court reference and parties*].

The unilateral notice in the register will give brief details of the interest protected and identify the beneficiary of that notice.

Restriction where the charging order is over a beneficial interest

If there is no restriction in Form A already in the register, a person having the benefit of a charging order over a beneficial interest under a trust of land has a sufficient interest for the purposes of LRA 2002, s 43(1)(c) to apply for entry of a restriction in Form A, to ensure that a survivor of the joint proprietors (unless a trust corporation) will not be able to give a valid receipt for capital money (LRR 2003, r 93(a)). The wording of Form A is set out in Appendix IV, page 585.

The person having the benefit of a charging order over a beneficial interest under a trust of land also has a sufficient interest to apply for entry of a restriction in Form K to ensure that he receives notice of a disposition (LRR 2003, rule 93(k)). The wording of Form K is set out in Appendix IV, page 585.

This restriction does not of itself prevent a disposition, provided its terms are complied with. This is because the interest of the person having the benefit of a charging order will be overreached where the requirements of Form A have been met (Law of Property Act 1925, ss 2 and 27).

The Registry must give notice of an application for a restriction to the proprietor of the registered estate or charge concerned, if it has not been made by or with the consent of such proprietor or a person entitled to be registered as such proprietor (LRA 2002, s 45).

A restriction does not confer any priority; it simply prevents an entry being made in the register in respect of any disposition, or a disposition of a specified kind, unless the terms of the restriction have (where applicable) been complied with.

If applying for entry of a restriction in Form A, an applicant should deliver to the Registry an application in Form RX1, accompanied by the charging order or a certified copy of it. No fee is currently payable where the application is in respect of a restriction in Form A only.

As the application is unlikely to be made by or with the consent of the registered proprietor in this situation, the statement in panel 12 or conveyancer's certificate in panel 13 of Form RX1 should be completed on the following lines:

> The interest is that specified in rule 93(a) of the Land Registration Rules 2003, the applicant being the person with the benefit of [an interim *or* a final] charging order on the beneficial interest of [*name of judgment debtor*] made by the [*name of court*] on [*date*] (Court reference [*insert reference*]).

Panel 9 of Form RX1 should be completed as to the wording of Form A.

If applying for a restriction in Form K, an applicant should deliver to the Registry the usual documents required (see *Restrictions*, page 500).

As the application is unlikely to be made by or with the consent of the registered proprietor in this situation, the statement in panel 12 or conveyancer's certificate in panel 13 of Form RX1 should be completed on the following lines:

> The interest is that specified in rule 93(k) of the Land Registration Rules 2003, the applicant being the person with the benefit of [an interim *or* a final] charging order on the beneficial interest of [*name of judgment debtor*] made by the [*name of court*] on [*date*] (Court reference [*insert reference*]).

Panel 9 of Form RX1 should be completed as to the wording of Form K.

A restriction in standard Form A or K in LRR 2003, Sch 4 does not require the approval of the Registry to the wording of the restriction under LRA 2002, s 43(3).

CHARITIES

In addition to the requirements of the LRA 2002 and the LRR 2003, the requirements of the Charities Act 2011 need to be borne in mind when making applications to register dispositions by or in favour of charities. The Charities Act 1960 was repealed by the Charities Act 1993, which was subsequently amended by the Charities Act 2006 which effected numerous changes in relation to the law relating to charities generally. The Charities Act 1993 was repealed by the Charities Act 2011, which came into force on 14 March 2012.

For the purposes of the Charities Act 2011, a 'charity' is defined as any institution, corporate or not, which is established for charitable purposes only and is subject to the control of the High Court in the exercise of the court's jurisdiction with respect to charities (Charities Act 2011, s 1). 'Charitable purposes' is defined as a purpose which falls within s 3(1) of that Act (which lists 13 descriptions of purposes) and is for the public benefit. 'Charity trustees' is defined as being the persons having the general control and management of the administration of a charity. 'Charity' and 'charity trustees' have the same meaning in the LRR 2003 (LRR 2003, r 217). Although LRR 2003, rr 176 to 180 were not amended by the Charities Act 2011, by virtue of Sch 8 to that Act the prescribed statements and certificates set out in those rules should be interpreted as referring to the corresponding relevant provisions of the Charities Act 2011 rather than to the relevant provisions of the Charities Act 1993.

Most charities are subject to the jurisdiction of the Charity Commission (previously 'the Charity Commissioners') and are referred to as 'non-exempt' charities, as opposed to the minority of charities, referred to as 'exempt charities', which are covered by the Charities Act 2011 for some purposes, but are largely exempted from the jurisdiction of the Charity Commission. Exempt charities are those which are listed in Charities Act 2011, Sch 3 (or which are an exempt charity by virtue of any other enactment) and include certain universities and colleges and the board of trustees of certain museums, for example.

The trustees of non-exempt charities are generally allowed to sell, mortgage or otherwise dispose of the charity's land without an order of the court or of the Charity Commission, if they follow the correct procedures. These procedures are not binding on exempt charities, nor do they apply to certain specific transactions.

All dispositions of an estate *in favour of a charity* must contain an appropriate statement as to whether the charity is exempt or non-exempt and, if the latter, as to the restrictions on dispositions imposed by the Charities Act 2011.

All dispositions of a registered estate *by a charity* must contain an appropriate statement. In the case of a non-exempt charity the disposition may also need to contain a certificate by the charity trustees.

The statements enable the Land Registry, when registering a non-exempt charity or its trustees as proprietors of land, to enter an appropriate restriction; and when registering a disposition by a non-exempt charity, to be satisfied that the restriction has been complied with.

A transfer of a registered or unregistered estate on or in consequence of the appointment of a new charity trustee is not a 'disposition' for the purposes of the Charities Act 2011. Therefore, none of the statements or the certificate are required to be included in a deed that appoints a new trustee or is made in consequence of the appointment of a new charity trustee. In the case of an unregistered estate, the appointment of a new charity trustee may 'trigger' compulsory first registration.

The Charities Act 2011 does not apply to land held by corporations in the Church of England in cases where they hold the land as part of their corporate property for ecclesiastical purposes, or where a diocesan board of finance is holding glebe land of the diocese (see *Church of England*, page 120).

The Charity Commission is regarded as having a sufficient interest to apply for a restriction in relation to registered land held on charitable trusts (LRA 2002, s 43(1)(c) and LRR 2003, r 93(f)).

Dispositions in favour of charities

Any disposition of registered land in favour of a charity which requires to be registered, and any disposition in favour of a charity which 'triggers' first registration, must contain a statement in one of the following forms (Charities Act 2011, s 122(8) and LRR 2003, r 179), depending upon whether it is an exempt or a non-exempt charity:

(a)   The land transferred (*or as the case may be*) will, as a result of this transfer (*or as the case may be*) be held by [*or in trust for*] (*name of charity*), an exempt charity.

(b)   The land transferred (*or as the case may be*) will, as a result of this transfer (*or as the case may be*) be held by [*or in trust for*] (*name of charity*), a non-exempt charity, and the restrictions on disposition imposed by sections 117 to 121 of the Charities Act 2011 will apply to the land (subject to section 117(3) of that Act).

The appropriate statement should be made in the contract as well as in the document effecting the disposition.

None of the above applies to a mortgage in favour of a charity, nor do any of the restrictions discussed below need to be entered where a charity is registered as proprietor of a charge.

The application to register the disposition is not required to be in any special form merely because the applicants are charity trustees. In the case of an exempt charity the Registry is not under an obligation to enter a restriction. An application for an appropriate restriction must therefore be made, if such a restriction is required because of limitations on the powers of the charity.

In the case of a non-exempt charity, the Registry is under an obligation to enter a restriction that reflects the powers of the charity as registered proprietor (Charities Act 2011, s 123 and LRR 2003, r 176).

In the event of a voluntary application for first registration by a non-exempt charity, the conveyance or other instrument will not contain one of the above statements and therefore LRR 2003, r 176 provides that the application must be accompanied by an application for entry of the appropriate restriction in Form E.

Application for the appropriate restriction must also be made where application is made to register a transfer which does not contain the necessary statement set out above or application is made under LRR 2003, r 161 to register the vesting of a registered estate in a person by operation of law.

Where the disposition is in favour of an exempt charity, the application must be accompanied by the document creating the trust or a certified copy of it (LRR 2003, r 182(1)). This requirement does not apply in the case of a disposition to a non-exempt charity (LRR 2003, r 182(2)). However, where the charity is incorporated otherwise than under the Charities Acts 2011 or 1993 or under the Companies Acts, evidence of the charity's constitution or trusts (or a conveyancer's certificate in the appropriate form specified in LRR 2003, r 183, being Form 7 or Form 8 in Sch 3 as the case may be, see Appendix V, page 593) should be lodged.

If the disposition is in favour of charity trustees incorporated under Charities Act 2011, Pt 12 or Charities Act 1993, Pt VII, they must be described as 'a body corporate under Part 12 of the Charities Act 2011 (*or* Part VII of the Charities Act 1993)' and the application to register the disposition must be accompanied by the certificate granted by the Charity Commission under Charities Act 2011, s 251 or Charities Act 1993, s 50 (LRR 2003, r 177). These requirements apply equally to a disposition of a registered charge in favour of charity trustees.

Where the application is to register the Official Custodian for Charities as proprietor of a registered estate or registered charge, the application must be accompanied by:

(a) an order of the court made under Charities Act 2011, s 90(1) or Charities Act 1993, s 21(1); or

(b) an order of the Charity Commission made under Charities Act 2011, s 9(1)(c) or s 76(3) or Charities Act 1993, ss 16 or 18; and

(c) (in cases where the land is vested in the Official Custodian by virtue of a vesting order under Charities Act 2011, s 76 or Charities Act 1993, s 18) an application in Form RX1 for entry of a restriction in Form F. This situation may arise where, for example, the Charity Commission has intervened as a result of misconduct or mismanagement in the administration of the charity.

The wording of Form F is set out in Appendix IV, page 585.

Where the Official Custodian for Charities is registered as proprietor of a registered estate or a registered charge, the address of the charity trustees or, where the registered estate or charge is held on behalf of a charity which is a corporation, the address of the charity, must be entered in the register as his address for service (LRR 2003, r 178(3)). However, this does not apply where the estate or charge is vested in him by virtue of an order under Charities Act 2011, s 76 or Charities Act 1993, s 18, in which case the address of the Official Custodian will be entered as the address for service.

Where the Official Custodian is not being registered as proprietor, there is no limit to the number of trustees of a charity who can be registered as proprietors (Trustee Act 1925, s 34(3)). Where charity trustees are individuals the Registry will, if requested, enter the names of the trustees in the proprietorship register followed by an appropriate description such as:

> the trustees of the charity known as [*name of charity*].

If the charity trustees have been incorporated under Charities Act 2011, Pt 12 or Charities Act 1993, Pt VII, this fact will be stated in the proprietorship entry.

Where the charity is a corporation, the Registry will enter its name and address in the register, together with the company registration number if applicable.

Where the charity being registered as proprietor is an exempt charity, it is not compulsory for any restriction to be entered in the register. In the case of an application to register a non-exempt charity, or trustees of a non-exempt charity, as proprietor(s), it must be accompanied by an application for the appropriate restriction (LRR 2003, r 176). The application may be made in Form RX1 or set out in the additional provisions panel of Forms TP1, TP2, TR1, TR2, TR4, TR5, AS1, AS2 or AS3 or in clause LR13 of a prescribed clauses lease (or any other lease containing clauses LR1 to LR14 of LRR 2003, Sch 1A). No additional fee is currently payable for the application for the restriction.

The appropriate restriction is Form E, the wording of which is set out in Appendix IV, page 585.

Where the estate is vested in the Official Custodian for Charities under Charities Act 2011, s 76 or Charities Act 1993, s 18, in addition to a restriction in Form E, a restriction in Form F is required for the reasons explained above.

In all cases where two or more trustees of the charity are registered as proprietors the Registry will enter a restriction in Form A in the register (LRA 2002, s 44(1)). Where a sole or last surviving trustee or custodian trustee of the charity applies to be registered as proprietor of the land held on a trust of land, he must apply for entry of a restriction in Form A in addition to any charity restriction (LRR 2003, r 94).

The wording of Form A is set out in Appendix IV, page 585.

Dispositions by charities

A disposition by a charity of registered land, or of unregistered land which 'triggers' first registration, is required to contain a statement about the land and the charity (Charities Act 2011, ss 122 and 125). The type of statement to be included depends upon whether the charity is exempt or non-exempt and whether or not the disposition is a mortgage. The deed effecting the disposition and the contract for such disposition must contain any appropriate statement. Any disposition of registered land by a charity which is required to be registered must also comply with any restrictions which appear in the register, including any restriction in Form E. In the case of a disposition by a non-exempt charity, this may require the disposition to also contain an appropriate certificate.

The disposition will need to be executed by the charity. Where the charity is a body corporate incorporated under the Companies Acts, it should execute a disposition in the form appropriate for a company. Where the charity consists of individual trustees, a disposition must normally be executed by them all. However, subject to the trusts of the charity, charity trustees may confer on two or more of their number authority to execute deeds and instruments in the names and on behalf of the trustees (Charities Act 2011, s 333). This also allows execution on behalf of the Official Custodian for Charities, unless a contrary intention appears. Where a deed is expressed to be executed under Charities Act

2011, s 333 and the disposition is in favour of a person acquiring in good faith for money or money's worth an interest in or charge on land, it is not necessary to deliver to the Registry evidence of the authority to execute under that section.

Where the registered proprietor is a charitable company and its name does not include the words 'charity' or 'charitable', the deed effecting the disposition must contain a statement that the company is a charity (Charities Act 2011, s 194).

Where the charity is an incorporated body under Charities Act 2011, Pt 12 or Charities Act 1993, Pt VII, it can execute deeds using its common seal, if it has one, in the presence of appropriate officers of the charity. If the charity chooses not to use or does not have a common seal, two other methods of execution are provided by Charities Act 2011, s 260:

(a) by being signed by a majority of the trustees of the charity and expressed to be executed by the incorporated body; or

(b) by being executed by two or more of the trustees authorised (under Charities Act 2011, s 261) to execute in the name and on behalf of the incorporated body.

This also allows execution on behalf of the Official Custodian for Charities, unless a contrary intention appears. In favour of a purchaser (including a lessee or mortgagee) in good faith and for valuable consideration, a document is deemed to be duly executed by an incorporated body which is a charity if it purports to be executed by either of the two methods mentioned above (Charities Act 2011, s 260(5)). Where this applies, no evidence that the trustees are a majority, or of their authority, needs be delivered to the Registry.

Where the Official Custodian for Charities is the registered proprietor, he will no longer execute deeds in person. Instead, the charity trustees have full power to execute the disposition, except where the estate has been vested in the Official Custodian under Charities Act 2011, s 76 or Charities Act 1993, s 18 and a restriction in Form F appears in the register. A deed may be executed by the charity trustees, either by all of them, or under the provisions of Charities Act 2011, s 260 or s 333 referred to above.

If the Charity Commissioners have appointed a receiver and manager under Charities Act 2011, s 76, a certified copy of the order must accompany any application in respect of a deed executed by him.

The charity trustees must in any event execute the disposition, for the purposes of giving any required certificate (as discussed below), using one of the methods of execution outlined above.

Transfers on sale or leases by non-exempt charities

Under Charities Act 2011, ss 117 to 121, a non-exempt charity is required to go through certain procedural steps before disposing of land, such as taking advice from a qualified surveyor. Once these steps have been taken then, provided that it has power under the trusts of the charity to make the disposal and the transaction is not in favour of a connected person (as defined in the Charities Act 2011), the charity can dispose of the land without an order of the Charity Commission or the court. In all other cases such an order is required.

However, dispositions falling within Charities Act 2011, s 117(3) are not subject to those restrictions and so these will not need to be complied with nor will the consent of the Charity Commission or the court be required. The categories of disposition covered by s 117(3)(a) to (d) are:

(a) any disposition for which general or special authority is expressly given by a statutory provision or a legally established scheme;
(b) any disposition for which the authorisation or consent of the Secretary of State is required under the Universities and Colleges Estates Act 1925;
(c) any disposition of an estate in land which:
    (i)   is made to another charity otherwise than for the best price; and
    (ii) is authorised to be made by the trusts of the disposing charity;
(d) any disposition by way of lease to a beneficiary under the trusts of the charity which:
    (i)   is granted for less than the best rent that can be obtained; and
    (ii) is intended to enable the demised premises to be occupied for the purposes of the charity.

Where the charity's land is registered, the requirements of the Charities Act 2011, which apply notwithstanding anything in the trusts of the charity, are reflected in the register by the restriction in Form E. Providing any disposition by a non-exempt charity contains the relevant statement confirming whether or not the restrictions imposed by the Charities Act 2011 apply and, if they do apply, also contains a certificate by the charity trustees confirming that those restrictions have been complied with, the requirements of the restriction in Form E will be met and the disposition can be registered.

LRR 2003, r 180 specifies the alternative forms of statement to be included. The statements for dispositions other than mortgages are either:

(1) The land transferred (*or as the case may be*) is held by [(*proprietors*) *in trust for*] (*charity*), a non-exempt charity, and this transfer (*or as the case may be*) is not one falling within paragraph (a), (b), (c) or (d) of section 117(3) of the

Charities Act 2011, so that the restrictions on disposition imposed by sections 117–121 of that Act apply to the land; or

(2)   The land transferred (*or as the case may be*) is held by [(*proprietors*) *in trust for*] (*charity*), a non-exempt charity, but this transfer (*or as the case may be*) is one falling within paragraph (a), (b), (c) or (d) (*as the case may be*) of section 117(3) of the Charities Act 2011.

Where a restriction in Form E appears in the register, in addition to the appropriate statement the disposition must also contain a certificate where it is a disposition to which Charities Act 2011, ss 117 to 121 apply. There is no prescribed form of certificate, but it should normally reflect the appropriate statement in the deed effecting the disposition, depending upon whether the charity trustees have complied with the relevant provisions of the Charities Act 2011 (so far as applicable to the disposition). The alternative to complying with the provisions of the Charities Act 2011 is to obtain an order of the Charity Commission or the court authorising the disposition.

Where the charity trustees have complied with Charities Act 2011, ss 117 to 121, a suitable form of certificate would be:

[*Description of charity trustees and capacity in which they certify*] certify that they have power under its trusts to effect this disposition and that they have complied with the provisions of the said sections 117–121 so far as applicable to this disposition.

Where the disposition has been sanctioned by an order of the Charity Commission or the court, a suitable form of certificate would be:

[*Description of charity trustees and capacity in which they certify*] certify that this disposition has been sanctioned by an order of the Charity Commission (*or* the court).

Where a disposition contains any such certificate, when a person acquires an interest in land for money or money's worth it shall be conclusively presumed that the facts are as stated in the certificate (Charities Act 2011, s 122(4)). The certificate must be given by the charity trustees; if they are not also the registered proprietors, they will therefore need to join in and execute the disposition in order to give the certificate.

A certificate will not be required where the disposition is one falling within Charities Act 2011, s 117(3), as will be confirmed by the appropriate statement in the disposition. Also, a certificate should not be included in a deed that is not a 'disposition' for the purposes of the Charities Act 2011, such as a deed that appoints a new trustee.

Where charity land is unregistered, the restrictions on dispositions apply in much the same way as they would do if the title were registered. Therefore, when examining a title on first registration, the Registry will apply the principles outlined above as if the appropriate restriction in Form E had applied. The requirement that the disposition contains statements about the land, the charity and the nature of the disposition also applies to dispositions of unregistered land. A disposition of unregistered land by a non-exempt charity, to which Charities Act 2011, ss 117 to 121 apply, should therefore contain an appropriate certificate as described above.

Any other restrictions appearing in the register, including a restriction in Form A, will need to be complied with as necessary. If a restriction in Form F appears in the register and the disposition has been executed in the name of and on behalf of the Official Custodian by the charity trustees, an order of the Charity Commission will be required to authorise the disposition (Charities Act 2011, s 91(4)). If this is the case, the disposition should include a certificate stating that it has been sanctioned by an order of the Charity Commission or of the court, as appropriate (and the certificate should accompany any application for registration). The restriction does not apply to dispositions executed by the Official Custodian.

A restriction in the register in Form A, Form E or Form F will be cancelled automatically where an application is made to register a transfer of the title by the charity provided that the restriction has been complied with and the application is otherwise in order. If the charity will remain as proprietor following registration of a disposition, such as a lease or a charge, the restrictions will remain in the register.

Mortgages by non-exempt charities

Generally, non-exempt charities are subject to the restrictions on mortgaging under Charities Act 2011, s 124, which requires the charity to go through certain procedural steps before mortgaging its land, such as taking advice on whether the loan is necessary and its terms are reasonable. However, mortgages falling within Charities Act 2011, s 124(9) are not subject to those restrictions and so these will not need to be complied with. The categories of mortgage covered by s 124(9)(a) and (b) are:

(a)   any disposition for which general or special authority is expressly given by a statutory provision or a legally established scheme;
(b)   any disposition for which the authorisation or consent of the Secretary of State is required under the Universities and Colleges Estates Act 1925.

Where the charity's land is registered, the requirements of the Charities Act 2011, which apply notwithstanding anything in the trusts of the charity, are reflected in the register by the restriction in Form E. Providing any mortgage by a non-exempt charity contains the relevant statement confirming whether or not the restrictions imposed by the Charities Act 2011 apply and, if they do apply, also contains a certificate by the charity trustees confirming that those restrictions have been complied with, the requirements of the restriction in Form E will be met and the mortgage can be registered.

LRR 2003, r 180 specifies the alternative forms of statement to be included. The statements for mortgages are either:

(1)   The land charged is held by (*or* in trust for) (*charity*), a non-exempt charity, and this charge (*or* mortgage) is not one falling within section 124(9) of the Charities Act 2011, so that the restrictions imposed by section 124 of that Act apply; or

(2)   The land charged is held by (*or* in trust for) (*charity*), a non-exempt charity, but this charge (*or* mortgage) is one falling within section 124(9) of the Charities Act 2011.

In addition, a mortgage by a non-exempt charity that 'triggers' compulsory first registration should also contain the following statement:

The restrictions on disposition imposed by sections 117–121 of the Charities Act 2011 also apply to the land (subject to section 117(3) of that Act).

Where a restriction in Form E appears in the register, in addition to the appropriate statement the mortgage must also contain a certificate where it is a disposition to which Charities Act 2011, s 124 applies. There is no prescribed form of certificate, but it should normally reflect the appropriate statement in the deed effecting the disposition, depending upon whether the charity trustees have complied with the relevant provisions of the Charities Act 2011 (so far as applicable to the mortgage). The alternative to complying with the provisions of the Charities Act 2011 is to obtain an order of the Charity Commission or the court authorising the mortgage.

Where the charity trustees have complied with Charities Act 2011, s 124, a suitable form of certificate would be:

[*Description of charity trustees and capacity in which they certify*] certify that they have power under its trusts to effect this charge and that they have obtained and considered such advice as is mentioned in section 124(2) of the said Act.

Where the mortgage has been sanctioned by an order of the Charity Commission or the court, a suitable form of certificate would be:

> [*Description of charity trustees and capacity in which they certify*] certify that this charge has been sanctioned by an order of the Charity Commission (*or* the court).

Where a mortgage contains any such certificate, when a person acquires an interest in land for money or money's worth (whether under the mortgage or afterwards) it shall be conclusively presumed that the facts are as stated in the certificate (Charities Act 2011, s 125(3)). The certificate must be given by the charity trustees; if they are not also the registered proprietors, they will therefore need to join in and execute the mortgage in order to give the certificate.

A certificate will not be required where the disposition is one falling within Charities Act 2011, s 124(9), as will be confirmed by the appropriate statement in the disposition.

Where charity land is unregistered, the restrictions on mortgages apply in much the same way as they would be if the title were registered. Therefore, when examining a title on first registration, the Registry will apply the principles outlined above as if the appropriate restriction in Form E had applied. The requirement that the mortgage contains statements about the land, the charity and the nature of the mortgage also applies to mortgages of unregistered land. A mortgage of unregistered land by a non-exempt charity, to which Charities Act 2011, s 124 applies, should therefore contain an appropriate certificate as described above when it is appropriate to the circumstances – in particular, when the mortgage 'triggers' first registration.

Any other restrictions appearing in the register, including a restriction in Form A, will need to be complied with as necessary. If a restriction in Form F appears in the register and the mortgage has been executed in the name of and on behalf of the Official Custodian by the charity trustees, an order of the Charity Commission will be required to authorise the mortgage (Charities Act 2011, s 91(4)). If this is the case, the mortgage should include a certificate stating that it has been sanctioned by an order of the Charity Commission or of the court, as appropriate (and the certificate should accompany any application for registration). The restriction does not apply to mortgages executed by the Official Custodian.

Dispositions by exempt charities

The Registry will not have been obliged to enter a charity restriction on the registration of a disposition to an exempt charity. However, an application may have been made to enter an appropriate restriction to reflect any limitation on the powers of disposition of the charity. Any restriction which does appear in the proprietorship register must be complied with.

Even where there is no restriction in the register, an appropriate statement must be included in any disposition of registered land, or of unregistered land which 'triggers' compulsory first registration, by the exempt charity.

The statement required in the case of a disposition which is not a charge is (LRR 2003, r 180(1)):

> The land transferred (*or as the case may be*) is held by [(*proprietors*) *in trust for*] (*charity*), an exempt charity.

The statement required in the case of a charge is (LRR 2003, r 180(2)):

> The land charged is held by [*or in trust for*] (*charity*), an exempt charity.

Rentcharge titles

Where there is a release of a registered rentcharge falling within the Charities Act 2011, s 127, which provides that the restrictions on dispositions do not apply to the release of a rentcharge given in consideration of a sum which is not less than ten times the annual amount of the rentcharge or to a redemption of a registered rentcharge under Rentcharges Act 1977, ss 8 to 10, no certificate as to compliance with the Charities Act 2011 is required. In either of these situations the statement required in the instrument effecting the release of the registered rentcharge is (LRR 2003, r 180(1)):

(a)   in the case of an exempt charity:

> The rentcharge released is held by [(*proprietors*) *in trust for*] (*charity*), an exempt charity.

(b)   in the case of a non-exempt charity:

> The rentcharge released is held by [(*proprietors*) *in trust for*] (*charity*), a non-exempt charity, but this release is one falling within paragraph (a) of section 117(3) of the Charities Act 2011.

Any other disposition of a rentcharge title should be dealt with in the same way as a disposition of registered land, as set out above.

Appointment of new trustees

Where a charity is registered as proprietor, application should be made to reflect any relevant changes to the charity in the register, as appropriate. For example, if there is a change in the individual charity trustees following an appointment and/or discharge, or a change in the name of the charity. The general law relating to the appointment and discharge of trustees also applies to charities. In addition, Charities Act 2011, s 334 provides that where under the trusts of a charity its trustees may be appointed or discharged by resolution of a meeting of the charity trustees, members or other persons, a memorandum declaring a trustee to have been so appointed or discharged operates as a vesting declaration under Trustee Act 1925, s 40, provided:

(a) the memorandum is executed as a deed;
(b) the execution is effected either at the meeting by the person presiding or in some other manner directed by the meeting;
(c) the memorandum is attested by two persons present at the meeting; and
(d) the memorandum relates to land to which Trustee Act 1925, s 40 applies.

The exclusions relating to charges and leases referred to in Trustee Act 1925, s 40 also apply to this procedure under Charities Act 2011, s 334.

Where an application is made to register the new trustees as proprietors and this procedure has been used, the applicant should deliver to the Registry:

(a) an application in Form AP1;
(b) the memorandum;
(c) a certificate from the charity's conveyancer that it has power to use the procedure set out in Charities Act 2011, s 334;
(d) evidence of the death of any deceased trustee; and
(e) the fee payable (see *Fees*, page 221).

Where the appropriate restriction does not appear in the register, this should be applied for using Form RX1 (see *Restrictions*, page 500).

A transfer merely vesting the estate in new trustees does not need to contain a statement or certificate under the Charities Act 2011 as it is not a 'disposition' for the purposes of that Act.

The Charity Commission has the same powers as the High Court of appointing, discharging or removing a trustee of a charity. Where such powers are exercised and affect the registered proprietors, the applicant should deliver to the Registry:

(a)   an application in Form AP1;
(b)   a certified copy of the order of the Charity Commission; and
(c)   the fee payable (see *Fees*, page 221).

Where the appropriate restriction does not appear in the register, this should be applied for using Form RX1 (see *Restrictions*, page 500).

Incorporation of trustees of a charity

Where the Charity Commissioners grant a certificate of incorporation to the trustees of a charity under Charities Act 2011, s 251, the property of the charity, other than any vested in the Official Custodian for Charities, vests in the new body corporate (Charities Act 2011, s 252). An application should be made to amend the register of all affected titles. The applicant should deliver to the Registry:

(a)   an application in Form AP1;
(b)   a certified copy of the certificate of incorporation; and
(c)   the fee payable (if applicable) (see *Fees*, page 221).

Where the appropriate restriction does not appear in the register, this should be applied for using Form RX1 (see *Restrictions*, page 500).

Where an incorporated body is dissolved under Charities Act 2011, s 263, the order has the effect of vesting the land in the trustees of the charity where it has up to then been held by the body corporate or by any other person (apart from the Official Custodian) on trust for the charity. The order may also direct that particular land be vested in a specified person as trustee for, or nominee of, the charity or in such persons other than the charity trustees as the Charity Commission may specify.

An application should be made to amend the register of all affected titles. The applicant should deliver to the Registry:

(a)   an application in Form AP1;
(b)   a certified copy of the order of the Charity Commission;
(c)   where the order does not state in whom the land is vested, a certificate by the charity's conveyancer as to who are the trustees of the charity; and
(d)   the fee payable (if applicable) (see *Fees*, page 221).

Where the appropriate restriction does not appear in the register, this should be applied for using Form RX1 (see *Restrictions*, page 500).

Corporation becoming a non-exempt charity

Where a registered estate is held by or in trust for a corporation and the corporation becomes a non-exempt charity, the charity trustees must apply for a restriction in Form E (LRR 2003, r 176(3)).

The charity trustees should deliver to the Registry:

(a)   an application in Form RX1; and
(b)   the fee payable (see *Fees*, page 221).

Panel 9 of Form RX1 should be completed as to the required restriction. A restriction in standard Form E in LRR 2003, Sch 4 does not require the approval of the Registry to the terms of the restriction under LRA 2002, s 43(3).

Change of status of charity

Where an exempt charity ceases to be exempt, or registered land not previously so held becomes held in trust for a non-exempt charity as a result of a declaration of trust by the proprietor, an application must be made using Form RX1 (as above) to ensure the appropriate restriction is entered in the register (Charities Act 2011, s 123(5)). Where a non-exempt charity becomes exempt, an application to cancel any Form E restriction should be made in Form RX3 accompanied by evidence of the change of status (see further *Restrictions*, page 500).

Change of name of charity

Where a charity changes its name, whether of its own volition or at the direction of the Charity Commission, an application to change the name of the charity or its description in the register should be made. The applicant should deliver to the Registry:

(a)   an application in Form AP1; and
(b)   a new certificate of incorporation (where the charity is incorporated), or (if not incorporated) a certificate by the charity or its conveyancer as to its new name.

No fee is currently payable for reflecting a change in the name, address or description of a registered proprietor.

CHURCH OF ENGLAND

The Church of England owns a significant of amount of land, which may be vested in one of several ecclesiastical bodies and is subject to various ecclesiastical statutes and measures governing its acquisition and disposal. In addition, the restrictions upon disposition contained in the Charities Act 2011 apply to some, but not all, of such land.

Certain of the statutes relating to the acquisition of church land contain rights of reverter; for example, the Consecration of Churchyards Act 1867. A right of reverter allowed individuals to donate land for certain purposes on the basis that, if the land ever ceased to be used for the stated purpose, it would revert to the donor or his successor (see *Rights of reverter*, page 523).

Application of the Charities Act 2011

Charities Act 2011, ss 117 to 121 and s 124 contain restrictions upon mortgages and other dispositions of charity land (see *Charities*, page 104). The Charities Act 2011 does not in general apply to:

(a)   any ecclesiastical corporation sole or corporation aggregate in the Church of England which is established for spiritual purposes in respect of its corporate property, except a corporation aggregate having some purposes which are not ecclesiastical in respect of its corporate property held for those purposes. This does not therefore include a diocesan board of finance, nor does it include a parochial church council, as these are not established for spiritual purposes;

(b)   a diocesan board of finance (or any subsidiary thereof) in respect of the diocesan glebe land of the diocese; or

(c)   any trust of property for purposes for which the property has been consecrated (Charities Act 2011, s 10(2)).

Land in this category includes land held by:

(a)   the body corporate of a cathedral (formerly the dean and chapter of a cathedral or the cathedral chapter of a parish church cathedral) in respect of the corporate property of the cathedral, other than any property held for purposes which are not ecclesiastical;

(b)   the incumbent of a benefice in respect of the parsonage house and grounds and the church and churchyard vested in him;

(c)   the bishop of a diocese in respect of parsonage land vested in him during a vacancy in the benefice;

(d) the diocesan board of finance of a diocese in respect of diocesan glebe land vested in it.

Therefore, when registering one of the above bodies as proprietor of a registered estate in such land, a restriction in Form E will not be entered in the register. However, dispositions by the above corporations are subject to the requirements of ecclesiastical law as discussed below.

Where a corporation aggregate in the Church of England has some purposes which are ecclesiastical and some which are not, the Charities Act 2011 applies in respect of its corporate property held for non-ecclesiastical purposes. For example, where land is vested in the incumbent and churchwardens of a parish for the purposes of an educational trust, the Charities Act 2011 applies. Equally, where an ecclesiastical corporation such as a bishop is an *ex officio* trustee of a charity, the trust property is not corporate property of the ecclesiastical corporation and the Charities Act 2011 applies. The Church of England Pensions Board is a charity to which the Charities Act 2011 applies, as was the Central Board of Finance of the Church of England until it was dissolved in 2008. That Act also applies where land which is not glebe land is vested in a diocesan board of finance and where a diocesan authority (which may be the diocesan board of finance or, in some dioceses, a separate diocesan trust) is holding land on behalf of the parochial church council or the incumbent and churchwardens of a parish. The appropriate statement and certificate should therefore be included in any disposition, whether in favour of or by the ecclesiastical corporation. A restriction in Form E will be entered upon registration of such a corporation as proprietor of a registered estate or charge in these circumstances.

The Church Commissioners was formerly an exempt charity but the Church Commissioners and any institution that is administered by it became non-exempt on 1 June 2010 when the Charities Act 2006, s 11(7) came into force. Consequently, the restrictions on dispositions and on mortgaging contained in the Charities Act 2011 apply to dispositions on or after 1 June 2010. The appropriate statement and certificate should therefore be included in any disposition, whether in favour of or by the Church Commissioners or any institution administered by it. A restriction in Form E will be entered upon registration of the Church Commissioners or such an institution as proprietor of a registered estate or charge.

Where a corporation or body of trustees holding on charitable, ecclesiastical or public trusts applies to be registered as proprietor of a registered estate or registered charge, the application must be accompanied by the document creating the trust or a certified copy of it (LRR 2003, r 182(1)). It may be necessary to make an application to enter an appropriate restriction to reflect any limitations on the power of disposition contained in that trust document. The requirement in

LRR 2003, r 182(1) does not apply in the case of an estate or a charge held by or in trust for a non-exempt charity (LRR 2003, r 182(2)).

For details of the relevant statements and certificates required under the Charities Act 2011 and the LRR 2003, and of the relevant forms of restriction, see *Charities*, page 104.

Incumbent of a benefice

The incumbent of a benefice (who may be a vicar or a rector, depending upon whether the benefice is a vicarage or a rectory) is an ecclesiastical corporation sole and usually has the parsonage house and grounds, and the church and churchyard, vested in him. Land may be transferred directly to an incumbent or it may become vested in him in his corporate capacity by virtue of the operation of a particular statute or measure.

As regards the acquisition of land in connection with churches and churchyards, the New Parishes Measure 1943 (1943/1) (the 1943 Measure), s 13 enables land to be acquired for (inter alia) use as a church or as a site for a new church or as a new churchyard or extension to an existing churchyard, or as land for providing access to or improving the amenities of any church or churchyard. Previously, such land would initially be transferred to the Church Commissioners, but the Church of England (Miscellaneous Provisions) Measure 2010 (2010/1) amended the 1943 Measure so that, with effect from 1 September 2010, a diocesan board of finance, not the Church Commissioners, will be the acquiring body under the 1943 Measure. From 1 September 2010, the consent of the Church Commissioners will not be required for acquisitions and disposals under the 1943 Measure, unless the transaction is with a 'connected person' (defined in the 1943 Measure, s 17) or where the person or body purchasing the subject property has not obtained or considered a written report from a qualified surveyor to say that the proposed terms of the sale are the best that can reasonably be obtained.

Under the 1943 Measure, s 16, church property acquired by a diocesan board of finance (formerly by the Church Commissioners) under the 1943 Measure automatically vests in the incumbent of the benefice on a transfer to the diocesan board of finance (formerly to the Church Commissioners).

In the transfer of the land the diocesan board of finance will be shown as transferee, but the 'additional provisions' panel of the transfer (for example panel 11 of Form TR1) should include an appropriate statement to explain the statutory authority for the transfer and a request that the land be registered in the name of the incumbent. Under LRR 2003, r 174 a certificate in Form 4 in LRR 2003,

Sch 3 should either accompany, or be included in, the transfer (see Appendix V, page 593).

As regards the acquisition of land in connection with parsonage houses (which will be a rectory or a vicarage, as the case may be), the 1943 Measure, s 13 enables land to be acquired for (*inter alia*) use as a parsonage house, or as an extension to a parsonage house, or as land for providing access to or improving the amenities of a parsonage house.

Previously, such land would initially be transferred to the Church Commissioners, but the Church of England (Miscellaneous Provisions) Measure 2010 amended the 1943 Measure so that, with effect from 1 September 2010, a diocesan board of finance, not the Church Commissioners, will be the acquiring body under the 1943 Measure.

Under the 1943 Measure, s 16, parsonage land acquired by a diocesan board of finance (formerly by the Church Commissioners) under the 1943 Measure automatically vests in the incumbent of the benefice on a transfer to the diocesan board of finance (formerly to the Church Commissioners).

The diocesan board of finance will be shown as transferee, but the 'additional provisions' panel of the transfer (for example panel 11 of Form TR1) should include an appropriate statement to explain the statutory authority for the transfer and a request that the land be registered in the name of the incumbent. Under LRR 2003, r 174 a certificate in Form 4 in LRR 2003, Sch 3 should either accompany, or be included in, the transfer (see Appendix V, page 593).

A parsonage house may also be acquired by an incumbent (or a bishop during a vacancy in the benefice) under the Parsonages Measure 1938 (1938/3) (the 1938 Measure), s 2, in which case the transfer will be to the incumbent (or bishop) direct.

In each of the above cases, the incumbent will be registered as proprietor in the following form:

> The incumbent of the benefice of (*name of benefice*) in the county of (*county*) in the diocese of (*name of diocese*) and the incumbent's successors of (*address for service*).

When making an application to register the incumbent of a benefice as proprietor, the applicant should also make an application to enter a restriction in Form D. LRR 2003, r 93(g) provides that the Church Commissioners, the parsonages board and the diocesan board of finance are to be regarded as having a sufficient interest under LRA 2002, s 43(1)(c) to apply for such a restriction. The wording of Form D in this case will be:

No disposition of the registered estate is to be registered unless made in accordance with [*in the case of parsonage land* the Parsonages Measure 1938] [*in the case of church or churchyard land* the New Parishes Measure 1943] or some other Measure or authority.

If the area within which the land is situated is subsequently constituted a new parish, the land automatically vests in the incumbent of the new parish and application should be made to bring the register up to date to reflect this by registering the new incumbent in place of the existing incumbent. The diocesan board of finance or diocesan registrar should certify the facts, and confirm that the land is vested in the incumbent of the new parish.

As regards a disposition of registered land by an incumbent, his authority to make such a disposition will arise under certain statutory provisions. Under the 1938 Measure the incumbent (or the bishop during a vacancy), may sell or exchange parsonage land, subject to the consent of the diocesan parsonages board (or where designated as such, the diocesan board of finance) and the bishop. From 1 September 2010 the consent of the Church Commissioners is no longer required unless the sale is to a 'connected person' (as defined in the 1943 Measure, s 17) or where the transferor has not obtained or considered a written report from a qualified surveyor to say that the proposed terms of the sale are the best that can reasonably be obtained. These restrictions on the incumbent's power to deal with the property under the 1938 Measure will be satisfied by one of the following:

(a) The document giving effect to the disposition being sealed by the relevant board; or

(b) A statement in a document made pursuant to the 1938 Measure, s 9(2A) that the Church Commissioners have consented to the terms of the transaction under the Measure, signed by the secretary or other duly authorised officer of the Church Commissioners; and (where the disposition is by the incumbent), the written consent of the bishop; and either the written consent of the relevant board, signed by its secretary, or a statement in the document giving effect to the disposition made pursuant to the 1938 Measure, s 9(2B) that the consent of the board to the terms of the transaction is not required under the 1938 Measure, s 1(3)(ii), sealed or signed on behalf of the board by a duly authorised person; or

(c) A statement in the document giving effect to the disposition made pursuant to the 1938 Measure, s 9(2B) that the consent of the Church Commissioners to the terms of the transaction is not required under the 1938 Measure, s 1(3)(ii), sealed or signed on behalf of the relevant board, by a duly authorised person; and (where the disposition is by the incumbent), the written consent of the bishop; and either the written consent of the relevant board, signed by its secretary, or a statement in the document giving effect to the disposition made pursuant to the 1938 Measure, s 9(2B) that the consent of the board to the terms of the transaction is not required under the 1938 Measure, s 1(3)(ii), sealed or signed on behalf of the board by a duly authorised person.

Sometimes a disposal of church land may be made under another provision, for example, under the 1943 Measure, s 17, which relates to land acquired for use as a church or burial ground but which is no longer required for that purpose. The disposal may require the consent of: (a) the incumbent (if any) and the bishop (in respect of any land vested in the Church Commissioners); or (b) the bishop (in respect of any land vested in the incumbent). The consent of the Church Commissioners is not required for transactions dated on or after 1 September 2010, unless the disposal is in favour of a 'connected person' or where a surveyor's report has not been obtained.

The terms of any Form D restriction appearing in the register will need to be complied with before any disposition can be registered. The restriction will be cancelled by the Registry if the appropriate evidence has been lodged to comply with the restriction and registration of the disposition will mean that the incumbent will no longer be the registered proprietor. If, however, the incumbent is to remain in the register after completion of the application (for example, following registration of a transfer of part of the land in the title), the restriction will not be cancelled.

Prior to 13 October 2003 an inhibition was entered in the proprietorship register when an incumbent was registered (Land Registration Rules 1925, r 232). The wording of the inhibition was:

> No disposition of the land shall be registered except on production of a certificate from the Church Commissioners in accordance with section 99 of the Land Registration Act 1925.

Where this appears, the Registry will accept evidence of compliance with the relevant Measure or other authority referred to above as sufficient to meet the requirements of such an inhibition. Such an inhibition will be cancelled by the Registry if registration of the disposition will mean that the incumbent will no longer be the registered proprietor. If, however, the incumbent is to remain in the register after completion of the application the inhibition will not be cancelled.

The Church Commissioners

By the Church Commissioners Measure 1947 (1947/2), the Ecclesiastical Commissioners and Queen Anne's Bounty were dissolved on 1 April 1948 and all property vested in either of them was transferred to and vested in the Church

Commissioners for England without the need for any deed. The Church Commissioners and any institution which is administered by them are now non-exempt charities as a result of Charities Act 2006, s 11(7) which came into force on 1 June 2010 (see 'Application of the Charities Act 2011', above).

An application to register the Church Commissioners as proprietors by virtue of:

(a)   a scheme of the Church Commissioners, or
(b)   an instrument taking effect on publication in the London Gazette made pursuant to any Act or Measure relating to or administered by the Church Commissioners, or
(c)   any transfer authorised by any such Act or Measure,

should include a certificate in Form 5 in LRR 2003, Sch 3 (LRR 2003, r 175) (see Appendix V, page 593). The certificate may be given either in a transfer or in a separate document.

In addition one of the following, as appropriate, should be lodged:

(a)   a sealed copy of the scheme of the Church Commissioners;
(b)   a copy of the London Gazette publishing the instrument; or
(c)   the transfer.

An example of where this might apply is a scheme made under the Mission and Pastoral Measure 2011 (2011/3). No application for entry of a restriction is normally necessary. In other respects the application should be dealt with as in *Charities*, page 104. Similarly, in respect of an application to register a disposition by the Church Commissioners.

Cathedrals

The Cathedrals Measure 1999 (1999/1) (the 1999 Measure) brought about a single form of governance to the cathedrals in England (other than Oxford, which is part of Christ Church). The effect of the 1999 Measure, s 9(1)(a) is that each cathedral will have a body corporate consisting of the members for the time being of the council, chapter and college of canons. The body corporate will hold property for the cathedral and the cathedral chapter has power to sell, lease, exchange or acquire such property on behalf of the body corporate under the 1999 Measure, s 4(9). The body corporate of a cathedral established under the 1999 Measure is an ecclesiastical corporation for the purpose of Charities Act 2011, s 10(2) (see 'Application of the Charities Act 2011', page 120).

By virtue of the 1999 Measure, s 13, any property that was vested in the dean and chapter of a cathedral (or the cathedral chapter of a parish church with cathedral status) immediately before the relevant date automatically vests in the body corporate of the cathedral. The relevant date is that upon which the relevant provisions of the 1999 Measure took effect in relation to the individual cathedral concerned. In addition, the 1999 Measure, s 14 permits the Church Commissioners to set up a scheme providing for the transfer of property by the Church Commissioners to a cathedral. Any such scheme requires the consent of the cathedral chapter.

When making an application to register the body corporate of a cathedral, the applicant may also apply for entry of a suitable restriction. A possible form of restriction based on Form L in LRR 2003, Sch 4 is:

> No disposition by the proprietor of the registered estate is to be registered without a certificate signed on behalf of the [*name of body corporate of cathedral*] by its administrator or conveyancer that the provisions of the Cathedrals Measure 1999 have been complied with or that they do not apply to the disposition.

Prior to the coming into force of the LRA 2002 on 13 October 2003, the appropriate form of restriction would have been:

> No disposition by the proprietor of the registered estate is to be registered unless made in accordance with the Cathedrals Measure 1999 or some other Measure or authority.

This form of restriction may therefore appear in a registered title where cathedral property was registered prior to that date.

Subject to certain exceptions, the 1999 Measure, s 15 provides that any acquisition or disposal requires the consent of the Church Commissioners for England. Acceptable evidence of consent will depend on the nature of the restriction in the register.

Where a restriction in Form L appears in the register, the certificate referred to in the restriction is the acceptable evidence.

Where the earlier form of restriction referred to above appears in the register, the sealing of the document by the Church Commissioners is conclusive evidence that the Commissioners have given their consent to the disposition as required by the 1999 Measure, s 15 and that the requirements of the restriction have been complied with.

The 1999 Measure, s 15(1) contains a number of exceptions where the consent of the Church Commissioners is not required. These exceptions include a gift *inter vivos* or by will to the cathedral, or a grant of a lease to a clerk in Holy Orders holding office in the cathedral or to any person employed in connection with the cathedral. In addition, the Church Commissioners may by order exempt disposals of certain classes of property from the requirement to obtain their consent. Where the Church Commissioners consent is not required and a restriction in Form L appears in the register, the certificate referred to in the restriction will be required. Where the earlier form of restriction referred to above appears in the register, a statement in a document sealed by the cathedral chapter that the Commissioners' consent is not required is sufficient evidence of that fact.

Special considerations apply if the disposal is of a house of residence, where additional consents may be required under the 1999 Measure, s 15(1)(a) or (b) (for example, those of the dean or residentiary canon who usually occupies the house).

Diocesan boards of finance

A diocesan board of finance is a limited company empowered to hold real and personal property for purposes connected to the Church of England. It is a non-exempt charity and therefore, apart from glebe land, the restrictions on dispositions contained in the Charities Act 2011 normally apply to all land vested in such a board (see 'Application of the Charities Act 2011', above). Such land may, for example, consist of its own corporate property held in accordance with its memorandum and articles of association; property held as trustee for all purposes on specific charitable trusts; and property vested for disposal under schemes made under the Mission and Pastoral Measure 2011. For property held as custodian trustee under the Parochial Church Councils (Powers) Measure 1956 (1956/3), s 6 and property held under the Incumbents and Churchwardens (Trusts) Measure 1964 (1964/2), see 'Diocesan authorities', below.

Glebe land is land owned by the diocesan board of finance as an investment. Historically, its function was to provide an income for the benefice to which it was attached and its incumbent. Much of such glebe land consisted of small parcels of agricultural land and was vested in the incumbent. Since 1 April 1978, glebe land has been vested in the diocesan board of finance of the relevant diocese (Endowments and Glebe Measure 1976 (1976/4), s 15). The board has power to acquire land as glebe land; typically this may consist of a house of residence for a curate, for example.

A diocesan board of finance may sell, exchange, lease, mortgage or otherwise deal with the diocesan glebe land of the diocese. It must serve notice of any proposed disposition upon the incumbent of the benefice in which the glebe land in question is situated. The consent of the Church Commissioners is not required provided no objection has been made by the incumbent, the disposition is not to a connected person (or a trustee for or nominee of a connected person), and various requirements (including as to the obtaining and considering of advice) are complied with. Evidence of this compliance or consent will consist of either:

(a)   a statement in a document signed by the secretary or other duly authorised officer of the Church Commissioners that the Commissioners have consented to the transaction; or

(b)   a statement in the document giving effect to the disposition, sealed by the diocesan board of finance or signed on its behalf by a duly authorised person, that all the requirements of the Endowments and Glebe Measure 1976 with respect to the transaction have been complied with.

Where a diocesan board of finance is to be registered as proprietor of land, application may be made for entry of an appropriate form of restriction. Where the land consists of glebe land the appropriate form of restriction is in Form D, the wording of which in this case will be:

> No disposition by the proprietor of the registered estate is to be registered unless made in accordance with the Endowments and Glebe Measure 1976 or some other Measure or authority.

When glebe land previously vested in an incumbent became vested in a diocesan board of finance under the Endowments and Glebe Measure 1976, s 15, it was vested subject to all such rights in the nature of easements as were necessary for the reasonable enjoyment of any parsonage land belonging to the benefice or any church land which had been previously exercisable by the incumbent in right of his benefice (s 15(1)(b)). Such rights became legal easements appurtenant to the parsonage or church land (s 15(2)). In consequence, where title devolved to the diocesan board of finance under s 15, the Registry will on first registration of title to the land make the following entry in the charges register:

> The land is subject to such easements as affect the same by virtue of section 15(1)(b) of the Endowments and Glebe Measure 1976.

The Mission and Pastoral Measure 2011, s 75 confers power, when selling a redundant church or the site of a redundant church, to impose such covenants as to the use of the building or land as it thinks necessary. Covenants imposed under this section (which re-enacts the Pastoral Measure 1983, s 62) are enforceable as if the vendors were the owners of adjacent land and, in the case of covenants of a positive character, as if they were negative and will therefore bind future owners. The Mission and Pastoral Measure 2011 expressly provides that, unlike other restrictive covenants relating to land, such covenants cannot be varied or released on application to the Upper Tribunal (Lands Chamber).

Diocesan authorities

A diocesan authority may be the diocesan board of finance of the diocese, although in some dioceses, it will be a separate body. A diocesan authority may, as custodian trustee under the Parochial Church Councils (Powers) Measure 1956, s 6, hold land on behalf of a parochial church council of a parish. It may also hold land as custodian trustee under the Incumbents and Churchwardens (Trusts) Measure 1964, on behalf of the incumbent and churchwardens of a parish. In either case such land may consist, for example, of a church hall or a house of residence for a curate. Under the provisions of each of those Measures, any such land (other than a lease of less than one year or from year to year) must be vested in the diocesan authority, with the parochial church council or the incumbent and churchwardens (as the case may be) acting as the managing trustees. Neither the parochial church council or the incumbent and churchwardens may acquire or dispose of any property held or to be held on permanent trusts without the consent of the diocesan authority.

The restrictions on dispositions contained in the Charities Act 2011 would appear to apply to all land vested in a diocesan authority (see 'Application of the Charities Act 2011', above).

Where a diocesan authority is to be registered as proprietor of land, application may be made for entry of an appropriate form of restriction. For example, a restriction in Form A would appear to be appropriate given that the diocesan authority will be holding the land as custodian trustee.

CLASSES OF TITLE

The LRA 2002 provides that, on first registration, the Registry may grant one of a number of different classes of title. The best class of title is absolute title, but the Registry has a discretion to grant a lesser class of title if it thinks appropriate. Under the LRA 1925 the court had no jurisdiction to overrule the Registry if it was not prepared to register a title as absolute, or indeed to register it with any class of title (*Dennis v Malcolm* [1934] Ch 244). Similarly there is no provision under the LRA 2002 for an appeal to either a court or the Land Registration Division of the Property Chamber, First-tier Tribunal (the Tribunal) in respect of such a decision of the Registry. The Registry's policy of normally granting a possessory title, rather than an absolute title, on first registration of a title based upon adverse possession was upheld on judicial review by the High Court as being neither unlawful nor irrational (*R (Diep) v Chief Land Registrar* [2010] EWHC 3315 (Admin)). This was upon the basis that it struck a balance between the economic and social interest in having absolute titles which could be readily marketed on the one hand and the need to protect the public purse against claims for indemnity on the other.

Titles to freehold estates

There are three classes of title with which a proprietor of a freehold estate may be registered: absolute title, qualified title and possessory title.

Absolute title

A person may be registered with absolute title if the Registry is of the opinion that the person's title to the freehold estate is such as a willing buyer could properly be advised by a competent professional adviser to accept (LRA 2002, s 9(2)). In applying s 9(2), the Registry may disregard the fact that a person's title appears to it to be open to objection if it is of the opinion that the defect will not cause the holding under the title to be disturbed (s 9(3)).

First registration of a proprietor with absolute title has the following effects:

(a) the estate is vested in the proprietor together with all interests subsisting for the benefit of the estate (LRA 2002, s 11(3)); and
(b) the estate is vested in the proprietor subject to the following interests affecting the estate at the time of registration:
  (i) interests which are the subject of an entry in the register in relation to the estate,
  (ii) unregistered interests falling within LRA 2002, Sch 1, and
  (iii) interests acquired under the Limitation Act 1980 of which the proprietor has notice (LRA 2002, s 11(4)).

For details of the types of unregistered interest which fall within LRA 2002, Sch 1 (see *Overriding interests*, page 416).

If, on first registration, the proprietor is not entitled to the estate for his own benefit, or not entitled solely for his own benefit, then, as between himself and the persons beneficially entitled to the estate, the estate is vested in him subject to such of their interests as he has notice of (LRA 2002, s 11(5)).

Qualified title

A person may be registered with qualified title if the Registry is of the opinion that the person's title to the estate has been established for a limited period only, or is subject to certain reservations which cannot be disregarded as defects which will not cause the holding under the title to be disturbed (LRA 2002, s 9(4)). Qualified titles are rarely met with in practice. A qualified title might be given, for example, where the conveyance to the applicant for first registration constituted a breach of trust.

Registration with qualified title has the same effect as registration with absolute title, except that it does not affect the enforcement of any estate, right or interest which appears from the register to be excepted from the effect of registration (LRA 2002, s 11(6)).

It is possible for a qualified title to be upgraded to absolute under LRA 2002, s 62(1), if the Registry is satisfied as to the title to the estate (see *Upgrade of class of title*, page 565).

Possessory title

A person may be registered with possessory title if the Registry is of the opinion:

(a) that the person is in actual possession of the land, or in receipt of the rents and profits of the land, by virtue of the estate; and

(b) that there is no other class of title with which he may be registered (LRA 2002, s 9(5)).

The most common examples of situations where the Registry may grant a possessory title on first registration are where the applicant has been in adverse possession for 12 years or more; and where the applicant has lost the deeds and documents to prove his title. For further details as to such applications, see *Adverse possession*, page 11, and *Lost or destroyed title deeds*, page 369.

Registration with possessory title has the same effect as registration with absolute title, except that it does not affect the enforcement of any estate, right or interest adverse to, or in derogation of, the proprietor's title subsisting at the time of registration or then capable of arising (LRA 2002, s 11(7)).

It is possible for a possessory title to be upgraded to absolute under LRA 2002, s 62(1), if the Registry is satisfied as to the title to the estate (see *Upgrade of class of title*, page 565).

Titles to leasehold estates

There are four classes of title with which a proprietor of a leasehold estate may be registered: absolute title, good leasehold title, qualified title and possessory title.

Absolute title

A person may be registered with absolute title if the Registry is of the opinion that the person's title to the leasehold estate is such as a willing buyer could properly be advised by a competent professional adviser to accept and the Registry approves the landlord's title to grant the lease (LRA 2002, s 10(2)). In applying s 10(2), the Registry may disregard the fact that a person's title appears to it to be open to objection if it is of the opinion that the defect will not cause the holding under the title to be disturbed (LRA 2002, s 10(4)).

First registration of a proprietor with absolute title has the following effects:

(a)   the estate is vested in the proprietor together with all interests subsisting for the benefit of the estate (LRA 2002, s 12(3)); and
(b)   the estate is vested subject only to the following interests affecting the estate at the time of registration:
  (i)   implied and express covenants, obligations and liabilities incident to the estate,
  (ii) interests which are the subject of an entry in the register in relation to the estate,
  (iii) unregistered interests falling within LRA 2002, Sch 1, and
  (iv) interests acquired under the Limitation Act 1980 of which the proprietor has notice (LRA 2002, s 12(4)).

For details of the types of unregistered interest which fall within LRA 2002, Sch 1, see *Overriding interests*, page 416.

If, on first registration, the proprietor is not entitled to the estate for his own benefit, or not entitled solely for his own benefit, then, as between himself and the persons beneficially entitled to the estate, the estate is vested in him subject to such of their interests as he has notice of (LRA 2002, s 12(5)).

Good leasehold title

A person may be registered with good leasehold title if the Registry is of the opinion that the person's title to the leasehold estate is such as a willing buyer could properly be advised by a competent professional adviser to accept (LRA 2002, s 10(3)). In applying s 10(3), the Registry may disregard the fact that a person's title appears to it to be open to objection if it is of the opinion that the defect will not cause the holding under the title to be disturbed (LRA 2002, s 10(4)).

Registration with good leasehold title has the same effect as registration with absolute title, except that it does not affect the enforcement of any estate, right or interest affecting, or in derogation of, the title of the landlord to grant the lease (LRA 2002, s 12(6)).

It is possible for a good leasehold title to be upgraded to absolute under LRA 2002, s 62(2), if the Registry is satisfied as to the superior title (see *Upgrade of class of title*, page 565).

Qualified title

A person may be registered with qualified title if the Registry is of the opinion that the person's title to the estate, or the landlord's title to the reversion, has been established only for a limited period or subject to certain reservations which cannot be disregarded as defects which will not cause the holding under the title to be disturbed (LRA 2002, s 10(5)). Qualified titles are rarely met with in practice. A qualified title might be given, for example, where the assignment to the applicant for first registration constituted a breach of trust.

Registration with qualified title has the same effect as registration with absolute title, except that it does not affect the enforcement of any estate, right or interest which appears from the register to be excepted from the effect of registration (LRA 2002, s 12(7)).

It is possible for a qualified title to be upgraded to good leasehold under LRA 2002, s 62(3), if the Registry is satisfied as to the title to the estate; and to absolute if it is satisfied both as to the title to the estate and as to the superior title (see *Upgrade of class of title*, page 565).

Possessory title

A person may be registered with possessory title if the Registry is of the opinion:

(a)   that the person is in actual possession of the land, or in receipt of the rents and profits of the land, by virtue of the estate; and

(b) that there is no other class of title with which he may be registered (LRA 2002, s 10(6)).

The most common example of a situation where the Registry may grant a possessory title is where the applicant has lost the deeds and documents to prove his title. For further details as to such an application, see *Lost or destroyed title deeds*, page 369.

Registration with possessory title has the same effect as registration with absolute title, except that it does not affect the enforcement of any estate, right or interest adverse to, or in derogation of, the proprietor's title subsisting at the time of registration or then capable of arising (LRA 2002, s 12(8)).

It is possible for a possessory title to be upgraded to good leasehold under LRA 2002, s 62(3), if the Registry is satisfied as to the title to the estate; and to absolute if it is satisfied both as to the title to the estate and as to the superior title (see *Upgrade of class of title*, page 565).

COAL

Following the privatisation of the coal industry in 1994, the ownership of almost all coal is now vested in the Coal Authority, which is a non-departmental public body. The main functions of the Coal Authority are to manage the coal resources under its control and grant licences for coal exploration and extraction; to provide effective management of subsidence damage claims; and to provide information on past, present and proposed future coal mining activities.

An interest in any coal or coal mine, the rights attached to any such interest and the rights of any person under Coal Industry Act 1994, ss 38, 49 or 51 are unregistered interests which override both first registration and registered dispositions (LRA 2002, Sch 1, para 7 and Sch 3, para 7). Such interests are therefore protected notwithstanding that there is no entry in the register in respect of them (LRA 2002, ss 11, 12, 29 and 30). Coal Industry Act 1994, s 38 deals with rights to withdraw support after the service of notices, s 49 with rights to work coal in land that was formerly copyhold land after the service of notices, and s 51 with rights attaching to underground land. These interests were similarly overriding interests under LRA 1925, s 70(1) (as amended by Coal Industry Act 1994, Sch 9).

It is not possible to enter a notice in the register in respect of an interest in any coal or coal mine, the rights attached to any such interest and the rights of any person under Coal Industry Act 1994, ss 38, 49 or 51 (LRA 2002, s 33(e)). It was similarly not possible to register or lodge any notice or caution relating to such interests under the LRA 1925. In consequence, such interests are not subject to the duty to disclose overriding interests under LRR 2003, rr 28 and 57 (see 'Duty to disclose overriding interests', page 426).

See also *Mines and minerals*, page 380.

COLLECTIVE ENFRANCHISEMENT

The Leasehold Reform, Housing and Urban Development Act 1993 (LRHUDA 1993), as amended by the Commonhold and Leasehold Reform Act 2002, confers on qualifying tenants of flats the right to have the freehold of the building containing the flats acquired on their behalf by their nominee. This right applies whether or not the landlord wishes to sell. The nominee may be a right to enfranchise (RTE) company (i.e. a private company limited by guarantee, of which all qualifying tenants are entitled to be members, and having as an object the exercise of the right to collective enfranchisement) for the purposes of that Act, of which the tenants are the members. When Commonhold and Leasehold Reform Act 2002, s 121 comes into force, the nominee will have to be an RTE company. A person is a 'qualifying tenant' if he is a tenant under a long lease for a term exceeding 21 years whether or not it is determinable by notice or re-entry. The LRHUDA1993 also lays down a framework within which negotiations take place with the aim of entering into a contract for sale in the normal way. Where tenants acquire the premises outside the legislation, by independent negotiation, the provisions of LRHUDA 1993 do not apply.

The Landlord and Tenant Act 1987 confers certain rights on tenants of flats as against their landlord that continue to exist in addition to the provisions of LRHUDA 1993. These include provision for compulsory acquisition by tenants of their landlord's interest in certain circumstances. Where a landlord of a building containing flats is in breach of his obligations to his tenants with regard to the maintenance or management of the premises, the court may, on the application of the tenants, make an acquisition order (Landlord and Tenant Act 1987, ss 25, 28 and 29). If granted, the order will provide for the tenant's nominee to be entitled to acquire the landlord's interest in the premises on such terms as may be agreed, or, failing agreement, on such terms as a leasehold valuation tribunal may determine (Landlord and Tenant Act 1987, ss 30 and 31).

Notice served under Leasehold Reform, Housing and Urban Development Act 1993, s 13

Any right of a tenant arising from a notice served under LRHUDA 1993, s 13 claiming to exercise the right of collective enfranchisement is not capable of being an interest within the LRA 2002, Sch 1, para 2 or Sch 3, para 2, which overrides first registration or registered dispositions (LRHUDA 1993, s 97(1)). However, it may be protected by the entry of a notice as if it were an estate contract. Where the freehold is registered, application may be made for the entry of an agreed notice or a unilateral notice.

Agreed notice

In addition to the usual documents required (see *Notices*, page 389), an applicant should deliver to the Registry a certified copy of the notice under LRHUDA 1993, s 13.

As the consent of the registered proprietor is unlikely to be forthcoming in this situation, this is likely to be sufficient to satisfy the Registry as to the validity of the applicant's claim in accordance with LRA 2002, s 34(3)(c).

The agreed notice in the register will give details of the interest protected.

Unilateral notice

An applicant should deliver to the Registry the usual documents required (see *Notices*, page 389).

The statement in panel 11 or conveyancer's certificate in panel 12 of Form UN1 should be completed on the following lines to show the interest of the applicant:

> [*nominee*] *or* [*RTE company*], notice of collective enfranchisement under section 13 of the Leasehold Reform, Housing and Urban Development Act 1993 having been served by [*tenants*] on [*date*] to [*name and address of landlord*].

The unilateral notice in the register will give brief details of the interest protected and identify the beneficiary of that notice.

Application for vesting order under Leasehold Reform, Housing and Urban Development Act 1993, s 26(1)

If the qualifying tenants wish to exercise their right to collective enfranchisement but the landlord cannot be found or his identity cannot be ascertained, the court may make a vesting order (LRHUDA 1993, s 26(1)). An application for such a vesting order is treated as a pending land action (LRHUDA 1993, s 97(2)(b)) and cannot therefore be an interest within LRA 2002, Sch 1, para 2 or Sch 3, para 2, which overrides first registration or registered dispositions (LRA 2002, s 87(1) and(3)). Such an application may, however, be protected by entry of an agreed notice or a unilateral notice, and a restriction.

Agreed notice

In addition to the usual documents required (see *Notices*, page 389), the applicants should deliver to the Registry the application to the court for the vesting order or a certified copy of it.

As the consent of the registered proprietor is unlikely to be forthcoming in this situation, this is likely to be sufficient to satisfy the Registry as to the validity of the applicants' claim in accordance with LRA 2002, s 34(3)(c).

The agreed notice in the register will give details of the interest protected.

Unilateral notice

The applicants should deliver to the Registry the usual documents required (see *Notices*, page 389).

The statement in panel 11 or conveyancer's certificate in panel 12 of Form UN1 should be completed on the following lines to show the interest of the applicants:

> qualifying tenants in an application under section 26(1) of the Leasehold Reform, Housing and Urban Development Act 1993 in the [*name* County Court] *or* [*name* Division of the High Court of Justice] [*state full court reference and parties*].

The unilateral notice in the register will give brief details of the interest protected and identify the beneficiaries of that notice.

Restriction

The applicants for a vesting order under LRHUDA 1993, s 26(1) are to be regarded as having a sufficient interest in relation to a registered estate or charge for the purposes of LRA 2002, s 43(1)(c) if they are applying for a restriction in Form N (LRR 2003, r 93(q)). The Registry must give notice of the application for a restriction to the proprietor of the registered estate concerned, if it has not been made by or with his consent or a person entitled to be registered as such proprietor (LRA 2002, s 45). A restriction does not confer any priority; it simply prevents an entry being made in the register in respect of any disposition, or a disposition of a specified kind, unless the terms of the restriction have (where applicable) been complied with.

In addition to delivering the usual documents required (see *Restrictions*, page 500), the applicants should deliver to the Registry the application to the court for the vesting order or a certified copy of it.

As the application is unlikely to be made by or with the consent of the registered proprietor in this situation, the statement in panel 12 or conveyancer's certificate in panel 13 of Form RX1 must be completed, confirming that the applicants' interest is that specified in LRR 2003, r 93(q) and setting out details of the application to the court. Any supporting documents should be listed in panel 5 of Form RX1 or in a separate Form DL.

Panel 9 of Form RX1 should be completed as to the appropriate restriction. A possible form of restriction based on the wording of Form N is:

> No [disposition or specify type of disposition] of the registered estate by the proprietor of the registered estate [or by the proprietor of any registered charge, not being a charge registered before the entry of this restriction] is to be registered without a written consent signed by [name] of [address] [or [their conveyancer or specify appropriate details]].

A restriction in standard Form N in LRR 2003, Sch 4 does not require the approval of the Registry to the wording of the restriction under LRA 2002, s 43(3).

Vesting order under Leasehold Reform, Housing and Urban Development Act 1993, s 26(1)

Where the court makes a vesting order under LRHUDA 1993, s 26(1), the LRA 2002 applies in relation to that order as it applies in relation to an order affecting land which is made by the court for the purpose of enforcing a judgment or recognisance (LRHUDA 1993, s 97(2)(a)). Such a vesting order cannot be an interest within LRA 2002, Sch 1, para 2 or Sch 3, para 2, which overrides first registration or registered dispositions (LRA 2002, s 87(1) and (3)), but it may be protected by an entry of an agreed notice or a unilateral notice, and a restriction.

Agreed notice

In addition to the usual documents required (see *Notices*, page 389), an applicant should deliver to the Registry the vesting order or a certified copy of it.

As the consent of the registered proprietor is unlikely to be forthcoming in this situation, this is likely to be sufficient to satisfy the Registry as to the validity of the applicants' claim in accordance with LRA 2002, s 34(3)(c).

The agreed notice in the register will give details of the interest protected.

Unilateral notice

An applicant should deliver to the Registry the usual documents required (see *Notices*, page 389).

The statement in panel 11 or conveyancer's certificate in panel 12 of Form UN1 should be completed on the following lines to show the interest of the applicants:

> [*qualifying tenants*] *or* [*nominee*] *or* [*RTE company*] having the benefit of an order under section 26(1) of the Leasehold Reform, Housing and Urban Development Act 1993 made by the [*name* County Court] *or* [*name* Division of the High Court of Justice] [*state full court reference and parties*].

The unilateral notice in the register will give brief details of the interest protected and identify the beneficiaries of that notice.

Restriction

A person who has obtained a vesting order under LRHUDA 1993, s 26(1) is to be regarded as having a sufficient interest in relation to a registered estate or charge for the purposes of LRA 2002, s 43(1)(c) if he is applying for a restriction in Form L or Form N (LRR 2003, r 93(p)). The Registry must give notice of the application for a restriction to the proprietor of the registered estate concerned if it has not been made by or with his consent or a person entitled to be registered as such proprietor (LRA 2002, s 45). A restriction does not confer any priority; it simply prevents an entry being made in the register in respect of any disposition, or a disposition of a specified kind, unless the terms of the restriction have (where applicable) been complied with.

In addition to delivering the usual documents required (see *Restrictions*, page 500), an applicant should deliver to the Registry the vesting order or a certified copy of it.

As the application is unlikely to be made by or with the consent of the registered proprietor in this situation, the statement in panel 12 or conveyancer's certificate in panel 13 of Form RX1 must be completed, confirming that the applicants' interest is that specified in LRR 2003, r 93(p) and setting out details of the vesting order made by the court. Any supporting documents should be listed in panel 5 of Form RX1 or in a separate Form DL.

Panel 9 of Form RX1 should be completed as to the appropriate restriction(s). A possible form of restriction based on the wording of Form L is:

> No [*disposition or specify type of disposition*] of the registered estate by the proprietor of the registered estate [*or by the proprietor of any registered charge not being a charge registered before the entry of this restriction*] is to be registered without a certificate signed by [*name*] of [*address*] [or [*their conveyancer or specify appropriate details*]] that the provisions of [*specify clause, paragraph or other particulars*] of [*specify details*] have been complied with [*or that they do not apply to the disposition*].

A possible form of restriction based on the wording of Form N is:

> No [*disposition or specify type of disposition*] of the registered estate by the proprietor of the registered estate [*or by the proprietor of any registered charge not being a charge registered before the entry of this restriction*] is to be registered without a written consent signed by [*name*] of [*address*] [or [*their conveyancer or specify appropriate details*]].

A restriction in standard Form L or N in LRR 2003, Sch 4 does not require the approval of the Registry to the wording of the restriction under LRA 2002, s 43(3).

Vesting order under Leasehold Reform, Housing and Urban Development Act 1993, s 24(4) or s 25(6)

Although there is no provision in the LRHUDA 1993 relating to the protection of vesting orders made under s 24(4) or s 25(6) in circumstances where there is a dispute between the parties, such orders may be capable of being protected in a manner similar to that relating to vesting orders under s 26(1) as described above.

Transfer or conveyance to nominee or right to enfranchise company

Once the nominee or RTE company has taken a transfer or conveyance of the freehold estate, an application for registration should be made in the normal way (see *Transfers*, page 551, or *First registration*, page 222, as appropriate). Where the acquisition is made under the provisions of the LRHUDA 1993, the transfer or conveyance must contain a statement in the following terms (LRHUDA 1993, s 34(10) and LRR 2003, r 196(1)):

> This conveyance (or transfer) is executed for the purposes of Chapter 1 of Part 1 of the Leasehold Reform, Housing and Urban Development Act 1993.

The LRHUDA 1993 does not contain any provision for the grant or reservation of statutory easements (unlike the Leasehold Reform Act 1967), and so the parties must include any necessary easements in the conveyance or transfer.

Where the court has made a vesting order under LRHUDA 1993, ss 24(4), 25(6) or 26(1), a certified copy of the order should accompany the application for registration.

Unless there is a contrary agreement, the transfer or conveyance is effective to discharge the property from any mortgage and from the operation of any order made by a court for the enforcement of the mortgage, and to extinguish any term of years created for the purpose of the mortgage (LRHUDA 1993, s 35). It is the duty of the nominee or RTE company to apply the consideration payable, in the first instance, in or towards the redemption of any such mortgage or charge and, if there are more than one, then according to their priorities (LRHUDA 1993, s 35 and Sch 8, para 2). The application for registration must be accompanied by the normal evidence of discharge (for example, in Form DS1) or by a statutory declaration or statement of truth establishing that the nominee or RTE company has applied a sufficient part of the purchase money in discharge of the mortgage or charge direct to the chargee or into court. The Registry may serve notice of the application upon the chargee, if it considers it necessary. If such evidence is not lodged the Registry will assume that the mortgage or charge is subsisting.

The transfer or conveyance will normally take effect subject to any existing rentcharge affecting the freehold estate. The landlord may either procure a release of the rentcharge from the rentcharge owner, or require, subject to the reasonable consent of the tenant, that the land be exonerated or the rentcharge apportioned.

The Registry will not automatically cancel notices where an application is received to register a transfer of the freehold and so the applicant for registration should at the same time apply for cancellation or removal of notices previously entered to protect the interest under the LRHUDA 1993, using either Form CN1 or UN2 as appropriate (see *Notices*, page 389).

Vendor's lien

A vendor's lien is capable of arising on the transfer to the nominee or RTE company, where an amount remains outstanding. The vendor's lien for the price payable extends to amounts which, at the time of the transfer or conveyance, are due to him from his tenants in respect of their leases or any collateral agreements. The lien also extends to sums payable to the vendor under LRHUDA 1993, s 18(2) (relating to increases in the price where the RTE company has not disclosed the existence of agreements in accordance with s 18(1)) and to any costs of the enfranchisement payable to him under LRHUDA 1993, s 33 (LRHUDA 1993, s 32(2)).

For the protection of a vendor's lien by entry of an agreed notice, see *Vendor's liens*, page 570. Since the items referred to in the last paragraph (other than the price payable) do not arise under the contract as such, it would appear that the vendor could apply for a notice in respect of the lien in respect of those items after the transfer had been completed.

Lease back by nominee or right to enfranchise company

Under certain circumstances as set out in LRHUDA 1993, Sch 9, the nominee or RTE company is required to grant a lease back to the person from whom the freehold has been acquired (LRHUDA 1993, s 36). For example, a lease back is required where the former freeholder was the immediate landlord of a tenant of a flat let under a secure tenancy. The lease back will be for 999 years at a peppercorn rent (LRHUDA 1993, Sch 9, para 8), unless the nominee or RTE company and the freeholder have agreed otherwise with the approval of a leasehold valuation tribunal (LRHUDA 1993, Sch 9, para 4(1)). Such a lease itself requires registration (see *Leases*, page 296).

Application for acquisition order under Landlord and Tenant Act 1987, s 28

An application for an acquisition order under Landlord and Tenant Act 1987, s 28 is treated as a pending land action (Landlord and Tenant Act 1987, s 28(5)) and cannot therefore be an interest within LRA 2002, Sch 1, para 2 or Sch 3, para 2, which overrides first registration or registered dispositions (LRA 2002, s 87(1) and (3)). Such an application may be protected by entry of an agreed notice or a unilateral notice, and a restriction.

Agreed notice

In addition to the usual documents required (see *Notices*, page 389), the applicants should deliver to the Registry the application to the court for the acquisition order or a certified copy of it.

As the consent of the registered proprietor is unlikely to be forthcoming in this situation, this is likely to be sufficient to satisfy the Registry as to the validity of the applicants' claim in accordance with LRA 2002, s 34(3)(c).

The agreed notice in the register will give details of the interest protected.

Unilateral notice

The applicants should deliver to the Registry the usual documents required (see *Notices*, page 389).

The statement in panel 11 or conveyancer's certificate in panel 12 of Form UN1 should be completed on the following lines to show the interest of the applicant:

> qualifying tenants in an application under section 28 of the Landlord and Tenant Act 1987 in the [*name*] Court [*state full court reference and parties*].

The unilateral notice in the register will give brief details of the interest protected and identify the beneficiaries of that notice.

Restriction

The applicants for an acquisition order under Landlord and Tenant Act 1987, s 28 are to be regarded as having a sufficient interest in relation to a registered estate or charge for the purposes of LRA 2002, s 43(1)(c) if they are applying for a restriction in Form N (LRR 2003, r 93(o)). The Registry must give notice of the application for a restriction to the proprietor of the registered estate concerned if it has not been made by or with his consent or a person entitled to be registered as such proprietor (LRA 2002, s 45). A restriction does not confer any priority; it simply prevents an entry being made in the register in respect of any disposition, or a disposition of a specified kind, unless the terms of the restriction have (where applicable) been complied with.

In addition to delivering the usual documents required (see *Restrictions*, page 500), the applicants should deliver to the Registry the application to the court for the acquisition order or a certified copy of it.

As the application for a restriction is unlikely to be made by or with the consent of the registered proprietor in this situation, the statement in panel 12 or conveyancer's certificate in panel 13 of Form RX1 must be completed, confirming that the applicants' interest is that specified in LRR 2003, r 93(o) and setting out details of the application to the court. Any supporting documents should be listed in panel 5 of Form RX1 or in a separate Form DL.

Panel 9 of Form RX1 should be completed as to the appropriate restriction. A possible form of restriction based on the wording of Form N is:

> No [disposition or specify type of disposition] of the registered estate by the proprietor of the registered estate [or by the proprietor of any registered charge, not being a charge registered before the entry of this restriction] is to be registered without a written consent signed by [name] of [address] [or [their conveyancer or specify appropriate details]].

A restriction in standard Form N in LRR 2003, Sch 4 does not require the approval of the Registry to the wording of the restriction under LRA 2002, s 43(3).

Acquisition order under Landlord and Tenant Act 1987, s 28

Where the court makes an acquisition order under Landlord and Tenant Act 1987, s 28, the LRA 2002 applies in relation to that order as it applies in relation to an order affecting land which is made by the court for the purpose of enforcing a judgment or recognisance (Landlord and Tenant Act 1987, s 30(6)). Such an order cannot be an interest within LRA 2002, Sch 1, para 2 or Sch 3, para 2 which overrides first registration or registered dispositions (LRA 2002, s 87(1) and (3)), but it may be protected by entry of an agreed notice or a unilateral notice, and a restriction.

Agreed notice

In addition to the usual documents required (see *Notices*, page 389), the applicants should deliver to the Registry the acquisition order or a certified copy of it.

As the consent of the registered proprietor is unlikely to be forthcoming in this situation, this is likely to be sufficient to satisfy the Registry as to the validity of the applicants' claim in accordance with LRA 2002, s 34(3)(c).

The agreed notice in the register will give details of the interest protected.

Unilateral notice

The applicants should deliver to the Registry the usual documents required (see *Notices*, page 389).

The statement in panel 11 or conveyancer's certificate in panel 12 of Form UN1 should be completed on the following lines to show the interest of the applicant:

> qualifying tenants having the benefit of an acquisition order under section 28 of the Landlord and Tenant Act 1987 made by the [*name*] Court [*state full court reference and parties*].

The unilateral notice in the register will give brief details of the interest protected and identify the beneficiaries of that notice.

Restriction

A person who has obtained an acquisition order under Landlord and Tenant Act 1987, s 28 is to be regarded as having a sufficient interest in relation to a registered estate or charge for the purposes of LRA 2002, s 43(1)(c) if he is applying for entry of a restriction in Form L or Form N (LRR 2003, r 93(n)). The Registry must give notice of the application for a restriction to the proprietor of the registered estate concerned if it has not been made by or with his consent or a person entitled to be registered as such proprietor (LRA 2002, s 45). A restriction does not confer any priority; it simply prevents an entry being made in the register in respect of any disposition, or a disposition of a specified kind, unless the terms of the restriction have (where applicable) been complied with.

In addition to delivering the usual documents required (see *Restrictions*, page 500), an applicant should deliver to the Registry the acquisition order or a certified copy of it.

As the application is unlikely to be made by or with the consent of the registered proprietor in this situation, the statement in panel 12 or conveyancer's certificate in panel 13 of Form RX1 must be completed, confirming that the applicants' interest is that specified in LRR 2003, r 93(n) and setting out details of the acquisition order made by the court. Any supporting documents should be listed in panel 5 of Form RX1 or in a separate Form DL.

Panel 9 of Form RX1 should be completed as to the appropriate restriction(s). A possible form of restriction based on the wording of Form L is:

No [*disposition or specify type of disposition*] of the registered estate by the proprietor of the registered estate [*or by the proprietor of any registered charge not being a charge registered before the entry of this restriction*] is to be registered without a certificate signed by [*name*] of [*address*] [*or [their conveyancer or specify appropriate details]*] that the provisions of [*specify clause, paragraph or other particulars*] of [*specify details*] have been complied with [*or that they do not apply to the disposition*].

A possible form of restriction based on the wording of Form N is:

No [*disposition or specify type of disposition*] of the registered estate by the proprietor of the registered estate [*or by the proprietor of any registered charge not being a charge registered before the entry of this restriction*] is to be registered without a written consent signed by [*name*] of [*address*] [*or [their conveyancer or specify appropriate details]*].

A restriction in standard Form L or N in LRR 2003, Sch 4 does not require the approval of the Registry to the wording of the restriction under LRA 2002, s 43(3).

Following a transfer or conveyance of the freehold estate pursuant to the acquisition order, an application for registration should be made in the normal way (see *Transfers*, page 551, or *First registration*, page 222, as appropriate).

Where the landlord cannot be found, Landlord and Tenant Act 1987, s 33 enables the court to order the vesting of the landlord's interest in a nominated person and for the payment of the purchase money into court. Following the vesting, the appropriate application to register the vesting may be made as above, accompanied by the court order and court receipt for the purchase money.

Tenants' right of first refusal to purchase the reversion under the Landlord and Tenant Act 1987

A landlord of a building containing flats must not dispose or contract to dispose of an interest in those premises unless he has served a notice of his intention on the tenants giving them collectively a right of first refusal (Landlord and Tenant Act 1987, ss 1(1), 4A and 5(1)). The 1987 Act contains detailed definitions and prescribed procedures in this regard.

As any offer and any acceptance are deemed to be 'subject to contract', there is at that stage no interest capable of being protected in the register. However, once a contract has been entered into, the tenants can protect their interest by applying for entry in the landlord's title of an agreed notice, using Form AN1 or a unilateral notice, using Form UN1 (see *Notices*, page 389).

Where a landlord has disposed of an interest in the premises in contravention of the tenants' right of first refusal, the tenants have additional rights such as, where applicable, the right to take the benefit of the contract or to compel the purchaser to sell to them. The notice by which the right is exercised does not itself give an interest that can be protected in the register, but when a binding contract has been entered into in pursuance of the tenants' rights, their interest may, in the case of registered land, be protected by application for entry in the landlord's title of an agreed notice, using Form AN1 or a unilateral notice, using Form UN1 (see *Notices*, page 389).

Appointment of manager under the Landlord and Tenant Act 1987

A tenant of a building containing flats may apply to a leasehold valuation tribunal for the appointment of a manager if the landlord has failed to manage the premises in accordance with his obligations or the service charges are unreasonable (Landlord and Tenant Act 1987, s 21). It may, in the case of registered land, be possible to protect such an application as a pending land action by application for entry in the landlord's title of an agreed notice, using Form AN1 or a unilateral notice, using Form UN1 (see *Notices*, page 389).

The leasehold valuation tribunal may then, if it thinks fit, make an order appointing a manager to carry out functions in connection with management or functions of a receiver. Any such order may, in the case of registered land, be protected by entry of a suitable non-standard restriction in the register of the landlord's title (see *Restrictions*, page 500).

COMMONHOLD

Commonhold is a form of freehold ownership of properties which share common parts. It was introduced by Commonhold and Leasehold Reform Act 2002, Pt 1, which came into force on 27 September 2004. Until it was introduced such properties were normally held as leasehold because positive covenants to maintain common parts were enforceable under a lease, but not where the land was owned freehold.

Commonhold must be registered at the Land Registry in accordance with the Commonhold (Land Registration) Rules 2004 (SI 2004/1830) and can only be created out of a freehold estate in land registered with absolute title. It must consist of a minimum of two residential, commercial or industrial units which share common parts. It cannot be a flying freehold; agricultural land; or a title which could in certain circumstances revert to someone other than the registered proprietor.

Unit-holders in a commonhold development own the freehold of their own unit and are members of a commonhold association, which owns and manages the common parts. A commonhold unit is each property in the commonhold, as defined in the commonhold community statement. Common parts are all parts of the commonhold which are not a unit.

A commonhold can be created either where there are no unit-holders and a new development is planned or where freeholders or leaseholders agree to convert an existing development into a commonhold. If the title is not yet registered, an application for first registration can be accompanied by an application to register the commonhold.

The commonhold association

A commonhold association is a private company limited by guarantee incorporated under the Companies Act 1985 or the Companies Act 2006. The members of the company are the unit-holders with each unit being represented by one member.

The two documents which govern a commonhold are the memorandum and articles of association (or, as from 1 October 2009, the articles of association) of the commonhold association and the commonhold community statement. The form and contents of those two documents are prescribed by the Commonhold Regulations 2004 (SI 2004/1829). The memorandum and articles (or articles) define the powers of the association and contain the rules, for example as to voting rights and meetings, under which it operates. Neither document can be designated as an exempt information document (Commonhold (Land Registration) Rules 2004, r 3(3)(c)).

The commonhold community statement

The commonhold community statement defines the extent of the commonhold and the extent of the units by reference to a plan; sets out the framework for the commonhold including the regulations for the use and maintenance of the units and the rights and duties of the association and the unit-holders; and describes how management decisions will be taken.

Applying to register a commonhold

An application to register a freehold estate in commonhold land must be made in Form CM1. Application can be for registration either without unit-holders, when it is a new development, or with unit-holders when an existing leasehold or freehold development is being converted to commonhold. The application must be accompanied by the relevant documentation, including consent to registration in Form CON1 from relevant interest holders (including the registered proprietor of the freehold estate in the land) or, in appropriate circumstances, a court order dispensing with consent.

Winding up or dissolution of a community association

If a community association is the subject of a voluntary winding up, or a winding up order by the court and no successor community association has been appointed, application may be made to the Registry to remove the commonhold entries from the common parts and all the unit titles. The titles will then be ordinary freehold titles and unit-holders will not be able to rely on the rights contained in the commonhold community statement and will need to make arrangements with the liquidator, or whoever the common parts are transferred to, to ensure that new deeds are completed granting them any necessary rights, etc.

COMMONS

Common land is defined in the Commons Registration Act 1965 (CRA 1965) as land subject to rights of common and waste land of a manor not subject to rights of common. There are more than 500,000 hectares of common land in England and Wales.

The purpose of the CRA 1965 was to establish a record of land in England and Wales which was either common land, a town green or a village green; the rights of common existing over such land; and the ownership of the land. The Commons Act 2006 is not fully in force yet, but when it is, it will repeal the CRA 1965 and the regulations passed under its authority. When s 6 of that Act comes into force, a right of common will not be capable of creation by prescription, and will be capable of creation by express grant only if the benefit is attached to identifiable land, so that it will not be a profit à prendre in gross. As to town and village greens, see *Town or village greens*, page 549.

As a result of the CRA 1965, all common land in England and Wales was required to be registered with the appropriate council specified in that Act during a period expiring on 31 July 1970. After that date no land capable of being registered under the CRA 1965 is deemed to be common land unless so registered.

Registration under the CRA 1965 was of land which is common land, the rights of common over that land, and of the persons claiming to be or found to be owners of that land. No person was to be registered as owner of any land the freehold estate to which was already registered at the Land Registry. Once the ownership had been registered under the CRA 1965 (unless provisionally only), the land was subject to compulsory registration at the Land Registry on sale, even in areas which at that time were not compulsory areas. The application had to be made within 2 months of the sale. Where this requirement has been overlooked, an application may be made to the Registry for an order under LRA 2002, s 6(5) extending the period for registration. The application may be made by letter and should explain the reasons why the period for registration should be extended.

Where a town or village green was registered under the CRA 1965 and the Commons Commissioner, following enquiry, was not satisfied that any person was the owner of the land, he could direct the registration authority to register as owner the parish council or other appropriate local authority as set out in CRA 1965, s 8. On registration under that section, the land vested in that local authority. Any such direction should be revealed on a subsequent application for first registration of the land.

Once common land is registered at the Land Registry, the Registry notifies the appropriate council accordingly. The council then deletes the registration of ownership and indicates that the land is registered at the Land Registry.

Rights of common, subject to the exceptions stated below, ceased to exist if they were not registered under the CRA 1965. CRA 1965, s 1 provides that no rights of common over land which is capable of being registered under that Act may be registered in the register of title at the Land Registry. The express grant or reservation of a right which is capable of being registered under the CRA 1965 is not required to be completed by registration at the Land Registry (LRA 2002, s 27(2)(d)). No notice may be entered in the register at the Land Registry in respect of any interest which is capable of being registered under the CRA 1965 (LRA 2002, s 33(d)). Accordingly it is not possible to register or enter a notice in respect of any right of common at the Land Registry. This applies whether the right is in gross or appurtenant to land (including where an appurtenant right of pasture is severable, as in *Bettison v Langton* [2001] UKHL 24) and whether the right was registered under the CRA 1965 or the Commons Registration (New Land) Regulations 1969 (SI 1969/1843). However, as rights held for a term of years or from year to year are not registrable under the CRA 1965, it follows that leasehold profits à prendre can be registered under the LRA 2002, even if they are of a kind that could otherwise be registered under the CRA 1965. The limitation under the LRA 2002 does not prejudice the effect of registration of any rights of common under the LRA 1925.

Common rights can broadly be described as rights that a person has to take part of the natural produce of another person's land and are in general a kind of profit à prendre which may exist in gross or as appurtenant for the benefit of another parcel of land (see *Profits à prendre*, page 456). However, land affected by cattlegates is sometimes vested in the cattlegate owners as tenants in common (*R v Whixley Inhabitants* (1786) 1 Term Rep 137).

There are six principal categories of common rights which may be encountered:

(a)   rights of common of pasture (rights to turn out sheep or other animals to graze);
(b)   rights of pannage (rights to turn out pigs to eat acorns and beechmast);
(c)   rights of turbary (rights to dig turf or peat for fuel);
(d)   rights of estovers (rights to take underwood for fuel or bedding);
(e)   rights of piscary (rights to fish); and
(f)   rights of common in the soil (rights to dig for sand, stone, coals and minerals).

CRA 1965, s 11 exempts from the effect of that Act the New Forest, Epping Forest and the Forest of Dean and any land exempted by an order of the Minister. Such orders were made in respect of the following areas:

> Austenwood Common (Amersham), Brooks Hill Common (Esher), Cassiobury Common (Watford), Cippenham Village Green Common (Slough), Coleshill Common (Amersham), Coulsdon Common (Croydon), Downside Common (Esher), Farthing Down Common (Croydon), Gold Hill Common (Amersham), Gosford Green (Coventry), Greyfriars Green (Coventry), Hearsall Common (Coventry), Hyde Heath (Amersham), Kenley Common (Croydon), Keresley Common (Coventry), Leigh Hill Common (Esher), Ley Hill Common (Amersham), Little Heath Common (Esher), Lower Tilt Common (Esher), Micklegate Stray (York), Mitcham Common (Merton), Old Common (Esher), Otterbourne Hill Common (Hampshire), Oxshott Heath (Esher), Radford Common (Coventry), Riddlesdown Common (Croydon), Shenfield Common (Brentwood), Sowe Common (Coventry), Spring Park (Bromley), Stivichall Common (Coventry), Stoke Commons (Coventry), The Links Common (Whitley Bay), The Stray (Harrogate), Thorpe Green (Egham), Top Green

(Coventry), Upper Tilt Common (Esher), Victoria Gardens (Portland), West End Road Recreation Ground (Southampton), West Wickham Common (Bromley), and Whitley Common (Coventry).

Where a profit affects land exempted from the CRA 1965, it should be dealt with in the usual way (see *Profits à prendre*, page 456).

The Common Land (Rectification of Registers) Act 1989 made provision for removal from the register of common land, on application by the owner, of dwelling houses and land ancillary to dwelling houses. Any such application had to be made by 22 July 1992. A copy of any order made under that Act should be lodged with any application for first registration of the land in question.

First registration of common land

In addition to the usual documents required (see *First registration*, page 222), an applicant should deliver to the Registry a copy of the entries in the commons register.

If there are any rights, interests or claims affecting the estate which are known to the applicant, other than those disclosed in the title deeds or Form DI, these should be disclosed in Form FR1. This would include, for example, any rights in the course of being acquired over the estate by adverse possession, or a disputed third party claim relating to the estate.

In examining the title, the Registry may have regard to any examination by a conveyancer prior to the application and to the nature of the property. It may make searches and enquiries and give notice to other persons, direct that searches and enquiries be made by the applicant, and advertise the application (LRR 2003, r 30).

Any discrepancy between the commons registration ownership register and the deeds must be accounted for. Registration as owner under the CRA 1965 is not conclusive proof of ownership; evidence of the applicant's title must be produced to the Land Registry in the normal way. The applicant may be registered with absolute title if the Registry is of the opinion that the applicant's title is such as a willing buyer could properly be advised by a competent professional adviser to accept. In considering the applicant's title, the Registry may disregard the fact that the title appears to it to be open to objection if it is of the opinion that the defect will not cause the holding under the title to be disturbed.

Dispositions of registered common land

Once the title to common land has been the subject of first registration, any subsequent registrable disposition of the land should be completed by registration in the normal way (see generally *Transfers*, page 551, *Leases*, page 296, and *Legal charges*, page 333).

COMPANIES

A company may be registered as proprietor of a registered estate or registered charge, and may make a disposition of that registered estate or charge, as is the case with an individual. However, certain special provisions apply in the case of a company. The effect of those provisions in relation to a particular company depends upon the type of company concerned and whether or not it is a UK company.

Companies which are a UK company

Where a UK company (i.e. one registered in England, Wales, Scotland or Northern Ireland under the Companies Acts or in Northern Ireland under the Companies (Northern Ireland) Order 1986 (SI 1986/1032)), applies to be registered as proprietor of a registered estate or registered charge, the application must state its registered number including any prefix. This number will appear in the entry of the company as proprietor in the register. No evidence of the company's powers to hold, sell or otherwise deal with land will normally be required. The same applies to a UK LLP (i.e. one incorporated in the United Kingdom under the Limited Liability Partnerships Act 2000 or the Limited Liability Partnerships Act (Northern Ireland) 2002) (see *Limited liability partnerships*, page 354).

Where a corporation or body of trustees holding on charitable, ecclesiastical or public trusts (other than a non-exempt charity) applies to be registered as proprietor of a registered estate or charge, the application must be accompanied by the document creating the trust (LRR 2003, r 182) (see *Charities*, page 104, as to charities generally).

If the company is, or holds on trust for, a registered social landlord within the meaning of the Housing Act 1996 (HA 1996), the application must include a certificate to that effect (LRR 2003, r 183A(1)). Similarly, if the company is, or holds on trust for, a private registered provider of social housing, the application must include a certificate to that effect (LRR 2003, r 183A(1A)).

If the company is, or holds on trust for, an unregistered housing association within the meaning of the Housing Associations Act 1985 and the application relates to grant-aided land as defined in Sch 1 to that Act, the application must include a certificate to that effect (LRR 2003, r 183A(2)).

Companies which are not a UK company

Where a corporate body, which is not either:

(a)   a UK company; or
(b)   a UK LLP; or
(c)   the trustee of a public, ecclesiastical or charitable trust (other than a non-exempt charity),

applies to be registered as proprietor of a registered estate or registered charge, evidence of the extent of its powers to hold and sell, mortgage, lease, and otherwise deal with land, and, in the case of a charge, to lend money on mortgage must be lodged (LRR 2003, r 183(1)). The evidence must include the document(s) constituting the corporation, or a certified copy, and any further evidence the Registry may require (r 183(2)). If the evidence is in a language other than English or Welsh, a certified translation must be provided.

Alternatively, a certificate in Form 7 (for a corporation incorporated outside the United Kingdom) may be given by a qualified lawyer practising in the territory of incorporation or in Form 8 (for a corporation incorporated within the United Kingdom) may be given by the applicant's conveyancer. Forms 7 and 8 are contained in LRR 2003, Sch 3 (see Appendix V, page 593).

These provisions enable the Registry to be satisfied that the applicant has the necessary power to hold, sell and otherwise deal with the registered estate (or to lend money on mortgage, in the case of a registered charge) and to enter any appropriate restrictions in the register.

An application for registration of an overseas company (i.e. one incorporated outside the United Kingdom) must be accompanied by details of its territory of incorporation and its registered number in the United Kingdom.

If the corporation is, or holds on trust for, a registered social landlord within the meaning of the HA 1996, the application must include a certificate to that effect (LRR 2003, r 183A(1)). Similarly, if the corporation is, or holds on trust for, a private registered provider of social housing, the application must include a certificate to that effect (LRR 2003, r 183A(1A)).

If the corporation is, or holds on trust for, an unregistered housing association within the meaning of the Housing Associations Act 1985 and the application relates to grant-aided land as defined in Sch 1 to that Act, the application must include a certificate to that effect (LRR 2003, r 183A(2)).

Dispositions by companies

In the absence of any restriction in the register, no evidence of a company's power to transfer land or otherwise deal with land of which it is the registered proprietor is required. Although a search in the Companies Registry is not normally necessary in relation to a registered estate, a purchaser of registered land from a UK company may wish to consider making such a search for the purposes of checking that the company which is shown as the registered proprietor has not been dissolved, or that the company purporting to sell the property is that shown in the register (i.e. that the company registration number and/or other details correspond).

Registration of a charge created by a company

In the case of a UK company, registration of the charge at the Companies Registry should precede an application for registration to the Land Registry. Registration of a charge of registered land at the Companies Registry alone is not sufficient – it should also be completed by registration in accordance with LRA 2002, s 27, if it is to take effect at law and be protected in the register. Conversely, registration of a charge in a debenture at the Land Registry does not remove the need for it to be registered under the Companies Act 2006.

Although LRA 2002, s 121 allows the Lord Chancellor to make rules about the transmission, by the Land Registry to the Registrar of Companies, of applications for registration of charges under the Companies Act 2006, no such rules have yet been made. The application to the Companies Registry must therefore be made separately. Since 6 April 2013, such application may be made electronically, in which case the certificate of registration will be issued electronically. It is still possible to apply in paper form and the certificate of registration will be issued in paper form; the charge itself will no longer be stamped with the Companies Registry stamp.

When making an application for registration of a charge created by a UK company, the applicant must produce to the Registry the certificate issued under Companies Act 2006, s 859I that the charge has been registered at the Companies Registry under s 859A of that Act (LRR 2003, r 111), together with a Companies Registry official copy of the charge or a certificate or confirmation in writing by the lender or a conveyancer that the charge lodged for registration is identical to the copy charge filed at the Companies Registry and is the charge to which the certificate of registration relates.

If the certificate is not produced, the Registry must enter a note in the register stating that no evidence of registration of the charge in accordance with Companies Act 2006, s 859A has been lodged. Similar provisions applied prior to 6 April 2013 in relation to Companies Act 2006, s 860 or s 878 and, prior to 1 October 2009, in relation to Companies Act 1985, s 395 or s 410 or the Companies (Northern Ireland) Order 1986 as the case may be, with any necessary note in the register referring to the relevant provision. The note reflects the fact that where the charge is not registered with the Companies Registry within the prescribed period, the charge is void against the liquidator or administrator of the company and any creditor of the company.

An application for registration of a charge created by an overseas company (i.e. one incorporated outside the United Kingdom), which is dated on or after 1 October 2009 and before 1 October 2011, must be accompanied by evidence to satisfy the Registry that the charge has been registered in the Companies Registry under Overseas Companies (Execution of Documents and Registration of Charges) Regulations 2009 (SI 2009/1917), Pt 3, or the charge must include a statement that the charge, when created, did not require to be so registered (LRR 2003, r 111A). In default of this, the Registry must enter a note in the register to the effect that no evidence has been lodged either that the charge has been so registered or that such registration was not required.

A fixed legal charge or mortgage of registered land in a debenture can be registered as a registered charge (see *Legal charges*, page 333). A fixed equitable charge or floating charge in a debenture may be capable of protection by entry of a notice in the register (see *Debentures*, page 183).

Execution of deeds by UK companies

On 6 April 2008, Companies Act 2006, s 44 came into force and applies to deeds executed on or after that date by a UK company. The formalities for execution depend upon whether or not a company executes a deed using a company seal. A deed which has been executed by a company must also be delivered in order to be effective. In practice, the Land Registry will assume that a document has been delivered as a deed unless there is some indication to the contrary.

Execution by a company under its common seal

Where this form of execution is adopted, the common seal will normally be affixed to the deed in the presence of the company secretary and one director, or two directors, who attest the sealing by countersigning the deed and describing themselves by their respective offices. If this is done, a purchaser is (from 15 September 2005) protected by Law of Property Act 1925, s 74(1) which provides that, in favour of a 'purchaser' (as defined in s 205(1)(xxi) of that Act), an instrument executed in this manner shall be deemed to have been duly executed.

In transfers of registered land and other deeds whose form is prescribed, the attestation clause in Form C in LRR 2003, Sch 9 must be used when a company executes a deed under its common seal.

Most companies have articles of association that authorise the affixing of the company seal to a deed in the presence of people other than a director and the secretary. The protection provided by Law of Property Act 1925, s 74(1) is limited to cases where the seal is affixed in the presence of a director and the secretary or two directors. Where a deed is executed by a company affixing its seal in the presence of persons other than a director and the secretary or two directors, the Land Registry may therefore call for evidence that the persons attesting the affixing of the seal are duly authorised by the company's articles to do so. Where their authority also depends upon a decision by the directors of the company, a certified copy of the board resolution may also be required. Prior to 1 October 2009 similar provisions were contained in Companies Act 1985, s 36(A)(2).

Execution by a company otherwise than under a common seal

A different method of execution can be used by a company which either has no seal or chooses not to use it. Companies Act 2006, s 44(2)(a) and (3) provides that a document is validly executed by a company if it is signed on its behalf by two 'authorised signatories', being every director of the company and (in the case of a private company with a secretary or a public company) the secretary, or any joint secretary, of the company.

In transfers of registered land and other deeds whose form is prescribed, the attestation clause in Form D(i) in LRR 2003, Sch 9 must be used when a company executes a deed in this way (see Appendix VI, page 605).

In addition, for deeds executed on or after 6 April 2008, Companies Act 2006, s 44(2)(b) provides that a company may execute a document by a single director, if that signature is witnessed and attested. In transfers of registered land and other deeds whose form is prescribed, the attestation clause in Form D(ii) in LRR 2003, Sch 9 must be used when a company executes the deed in this way (see Appendix VI, page 605).

Companies Act 2006, s 44(4) and (5) provides that a document signed in accordance with s 44(2) of that Act and expressed, in whatever words, to be executed by the company has the same effect as if executed under the common seal of the company and that in favour of a 'purchaser' (as defined in s 44(5) of that Act), a document is deemed to have been duly executed by a company if it purports to be signed in accordance with s 44(2) of that Act.

For deeds executed before 6 April 2008, Companies Act 1985, s 36(A)(4) provided that a document signed by a director and secretary of a company, or by two directors of a company and expressed (in whatever form of words) to be executed by the company had the same effect as if executed under the common seal of the company. Also, Companies Act 1985, s 36(A)(6) provided that, in favour of a 'purchaser' (as defined in that sub-section), a document should be deemed to have been duly executed by a company if it purported to be signed by a director and the secretary of the company, or by two directors of the company.

Execution of deeds by overseas companies

For deeds executed on or after 6 April 2008, 'overseas companies' are those incorporated outside the United Kingdom. For deeds executed on or after 1 October 2009 the Overseas Companies (Execution of Documents and Registration of Charges) Regulations 2009 (SI 2009/1917) provide that a foreign corporation can execute a deed using one of the following three methods.

Execution under common seal

An overseas company possessing a common seal may execute a deed using that seal. The points made above in relation to a UK company apply if a deed is executed in this way.

Execution in a manner permitted by the local law

A deed can be executed in any manner permitted by the laws of the territory in which the company is incorporated for the execution of documents by such a company. If this method is used, the Land Registry will require evidence (for example, a letter from a qualified lawyer practising in or familiar with the laws of the territory of incorporation) to establish that the manner of execution used is effective according to the laws of the territory of incorporation. Any documentation in a language other than English or Welsh will need to be accompanied by a certified translation.

Execution by signature of authorised person(s)

A deed may be signed by a person who, in accordance with laws of the territory in which the company is incorporated, is acting under the express or implied authority of the company and expressed (in whatever form of words) to be executed by the company. A deed executed in this way has the same effect as it would have in relation to a company incorporated in England and Wales or Northern Ireland if executed under the common seal of a company so incorporated (see above). In transfers of registered land and other deeds whose form is prescribed, the attestation clause in Form E in LRR 2003, Sch 9 must be used when a foreign corporation executes a deed in this way (see Appendix VI, page 605).

Prior to 1 October 2009 similar provisions were contained in the Foreign Companies (Execution of Documents) Regulations 1994 (SI 1994/950).

Related topics

In addition to the matters discussed above in respect of companies, reference should be made, as appropriate, to *Administrators of a company*, page 8; *Administrative receivers*, page 5; *Bona vacantia and escheat*, page 74; *Debentures*, page 183; *Floating charges*, page 231; *Liquidators*, page 360; and *Receivers appointed under the Law of Property Act 1925*, page 474.

COMPULSORY PURCHASE

The Crown, government ministers, local and other authorities require the power to acquire land for the public benefit (for example the building of new roads, schools and hospitals) and to be able to do so, where necessary, without the agreement of the owner. Initially, the acquiring authority will seek the agreement of the owner to the purchase in return for a payment. If the parties agree on the sale and the amount of the purchase money, there is then a conveyance or transfer in the usual way. However, where the authority cannot reach an agreement, it is instead able to acquire the land compulsorily. The Acquisition of Land Act 1981 deals with the making and confirmation of compulsory purchase orders. The

Compulsory Purchase Act 1965 deals with the process following the confirmation; in particular, the service of notice to treat (i.e. negotiate) and the payment of compensation. Under the Compulsory Purchase Act 1965 there is provision for the vesting of title by deed poll in the event of the owner failing to convey the land. Alternatively, an acquiring authority can rely on the Compulsory Purchase (Vesting Declarations) Act 1981 and make a general vesting declaration. The Housing and Planning Act 2016 made wide-ranging changes to the compulsory purchase regime, including to compensation provisions and access arrangements for acquiring authorities.

Deed poll

Where an owner refuses to accept the compensation, or does not show a good title, or refuses to convey or release the land, or is absent from the United Kingdom, or cannot be found after diligent enquiry, the acquiring authority may execute a deed poll to vest the land in itself (Compulsory Purchase Act 1965, s 9). The acquiring authority pays the compensation into court for the benefit of the owners.

The deed poll must contain a description of the land in respect of which the payment into court was made, and declare the circumstances under which, and the names of the parties to whose credit, the payment into court was made (Compulsory Purchase Act 1965, s 9(3)).

The effect of the deed poll is to vest absolutely in the acquiring authority all the estate and interest in the land of the parties for whose use the compensation was paid into court (Compulsory Purchase Act 1965, s 9(4)). The acquiring authority does not, however, acquire the interests of others and so any existing easements and restrictive covenants will not be extinguished by virtue of the deed poll itself.

Registered land

Where, in the case of a registered title, the recitals in the deed poll show that the statutory procedures have been followed correctly, this will be sufficient evidence of the disposition for the purpose of LRR 2003, r 161. The deed poll is a registrable disposition under the LRA 2002, s 27. In addition to the usual documents required in the case of a transfer (see *Transfers*, page 551), the acquiring authority should deliver to the Registry the deed poll or a certified copy of it.

Unregistered land

In the case of unregistered land, the execution of a deed poll does not trigger compulsory first registration, as the vesting of the land takes effect by operation of law. A voluntary application for first registration may nevertheless be made. In addition to the usual documents required (see *First registration*, page 222), the acquiring authority should deliver to the Registry the deed poll and all other deeds and documents relating to the title that are in the control of the applicant, including relevant Land Charges searches (with any entries accounted for and, where applicable, certified by a conveyancer as not affecting the estate).

If there are any rights, interests or claims affecting the estate which are known to the applicant, other than those disclosed in the title deeds or Form DI, these should be disclosed in Form FR1. If the title deeds are not produced by the applicant, although this may not preclude the grant of an absolute title, the Registry will normally make a 'protective' entry in the register in respect of the possible existence of undisclosed incumbrances; the entry will state that the land is subject to such easements and restrictive covenants as may have been created or imposed prior to the date of the deed poll and are still subsisting and enforceable. A 'certificate of title' under an arrangement with a local authority will not normally be appropriate in relation to a vesting by deed poll, because of the absence of a full investigation of title.

General vesting declaration

When authorised to acquire land under a compulsory purchase order, an acquiring authority can vest the land in itself by way of a general vesting declaration (Compulsory Purchase (Vesting Declarations) Act 1981, s 1). The acquiring authority must follow the relevant provisions laid down in that Act and in the relevant Regulations. This enables the authority to obtain title to the land more quickly, as vesting is not dependent on the payment or deposit of the compensation money. The effect of the declaration is that the land vests in the acquiring authority at the end of the period specified in the declaration, as if the authority had on that date executed a deed poll. The acquiring authority does not, however, acquire the interests of others and so any existing easements and restrictive covenants will not be extinguished by virtue of the declaration itself.

Prior to 3 February 2017 (in the case of land that is situated in England) and 6 April 2017 (in the case of land that is situated in Wales), the form of declaration was as set out in the Schedule to the Compulsory Purchase of Land (Vesting Declarations) Regulations 1990 (SI 1990/497). That form may still be relevant where a compulsory purchase order was 'authorised' prior to certain dates.

On 3 February 2017 (in the case of land that is situated in England) the Compulsory Purchase of Land (Vesting Declarations) (England) Regulations 2017 (SI 2017/3) came into force. The form of declaration in respect of such land, for compulsory purchase orders which are 'authorised' on or after 3 February 2017, is prescribed within those regulations. The question of whether a compulsory purchase order was 'authorised' on or after that date is set out in those regulations.

On 6 April 2017 (in the case of land that is situated in Wales) the Compulsory Purchase of Land (Vesting Declarations) (Wales) Regulations 2017 (SI 2017/362) came into force. The form of declaration in respect of such land, for compulsory purchase orders which are 'authorised' on or after 6 April 2017, is prescribed within those regulations. The question of whether a compulsory purchase order was 'authorised' on or after that date is set out in those regulations.

No declaration can be executed, however, until at least 2 months after a notice of intention to make a declaration (a 'preliminary notice') has been served on any owner, lessee or occupier. Also, where an acquiring authority has served a notice to treat in respect of a property it cannot execute a declaration in respect of that land without having first withdrawn it (Housing and Planning Act 2016, s 185).

As soon after the execution of the declaration as is possible the acquiring body must serve notices in the prescribed form on every occupier of the land and anyone else who has given information to the acquiring body of any entitlement to compensation.

The period stated in the declaration after which the land will vest in the acquiring body must be at least 28 days from the service of such notices. The notices must specify the effect of the declaration. Unlike a notice to treat, a declaration cannot be withdrawn and once made the acquiring authority is obliged to proceed with the purchase of the land. A declaration must be made within 3 years of the service of the preliminary notice. It is possible to challenge the making of a declaration and serving statutory notice of it by way of judicial review.

Housing and Planning Act 2016, s 184 and Sch 15 simplify the requirements regarding the steps to be taken prior to a declaration taking effect. Of particular note, a declaration must specify the date on which the land comprised in it will vest in the acquiring authority and that date must not be less than 3 months from the date on which notices that must be served by the acquiring authority under Compulsory Purchase (Vesting Declarations) Act 1981, s 6 have been served.

If the declaration comprises part only of a house, building or factory, or of a park or garden belonging to a house, any person who is able to sell the whole of the property in question may serve a 'counter-notice' upon the acquiring authority (prior to the 2016 Act coming into force this was called a notice of objection to severance and it may still be relevant while transitional provisions associated with the changes made in the 2016 Act take effect) requiring the authority to purchase the whole. If this notice is served, the part concerned will not vest until the notice has been disposed of. This means, in effect, that the acquiring authority must decide whether to give up its acquisition of the part, acquire the whole, or refer the matter to the Upper Tribunal (Lands Chamber). A 'counter-notice' requiring the acquiring authority to purchase an owner's interest in the whole of his land (formerly a 'notice of objection to severance') must normally be served within 28 days of the date on which the acquiring authority serves notice of the execution of the declaration on him.

Registered land

Where the title to the land is registered, the acquiring authority is not able to apply for an official search with priority using Form OS1 or Form OS2 as it is not a 'purchaser' for that purpose, but it may reserve a period of priority by making an outline application.

In the case of a registered title, the declaration will be sufficient evidence of the disposition for the purpose of LRR 2003, r 161. The declaration is a registrable disposition under the LRA 2002, s 27. In making its application for registration the acquiring authority should, in addition to the usual documents required in the case of a transfer (see *Transfers*, page 551), deliver to the Registry:

(a) the general vesting declaration or a certified copy of it (showing the stamp duty impressed on the original, if made on or before 30 November 2003) in the form prescribed in Form 1 in the Schedule to the Compulsory Purchase of Land (Vesting Declarations) Regulations 1990, and including a plan if only part of the land in the title is affected;

(b) a certificate by the authority's chief executive officer or conveyancer that the service of notice required by Compulsory Purchase (Vesting Declarations) Act 1981, s 6 was completed on a specified date; and

(c) (where appropriate) confirmation by the chief executive officer that no notice of objection to severance has been served.

If compensation has been fixed or the value of the land agreed so that the Land Registry fee can be assessed, it must be paid on delivery of the application. If compensation has not been fixed so that the Land Registry fee cannot be assessed, a minimum sum towards the fee must be paid on delivery of the application and an undertaking lodged at the same time to pay the balance, if any, on demand.

Unregistered land

In the case of unregistered land, the execution of a general vesting declaration does not 'trigger' compulsory first registration, as the vesting of the land takes effect by operation of law. A voluntary application for first registration may nevertheless be made. In addition to the usual documents required (see *First registration*, page 222), the acquiring authority should deliver to the Registry:

(a) the general vesting declaration (showing the stamp duty impressed on the original, if made on or before 30 November 2003) in the form prescribed in Form 1 in the Schedule to the Compulsory Purchase of Land (Vesting Declarations) Regulations 1990;

(b) a certificate by the authority's chief executive officer or conveyancer that the service of notice required by Compulsory Purchase (Vesting Declarations) Act 1981, s 6 was completed on a specified date; and

(c) (where appropriate) confirmation by the chief executive officer that no notice of objection to severance or counter-notice has been served.

If compensation has been fixed or the value of the land agreed so that the Land Registry fee can be assessed, it must be paid on delivery of the application. If compensation has not been fixed so that the Land Registry fee cannot be assessed, a minimum sum towards the fee must be paid on delivery of the application and an undertaking lodged at the same time to pay the balance, if any, on demand.

If there are any rights, interests or claims affecting the estate which are known to the applicant, other than those disclosed in the title deeds or Form DI, these should be disclosed in Form FR1. If the title deeds are not produced by the applicant, although this may not preclude the grant of an absolute title, the Registry will normally make a 'protective' entry in the register in respect of the possible existence of undisclosed incumbrances; the entry will state that the land is subject to such easements and restrictive covenants as may have been created or imposed prior to the date of the general vesting declaration and are still subsisting and enforceable. A 'certificate of title' under an arrangement with a local authority will not normally be appropriate in relation to a vesting under a general vesting declaration, because of the absence of a full investigation of title.

CONSTRUCTIVE, RESULTING AND OTHER IMPLIED TRUSTS

An implied trust in relation to land arises where, in relation to a conveyance of land, a trust arises by operation of equity. The equitable interest of a beneficiary is recognised in equity in circumstances where it would be unfair not to do so. A resulting trust is a form of implied trust and can arise where a payment was made in or towards the purchase price at the time of acquisition of the land; in equity it will then be presumed that the legal estate will be held on a trust of land, with the contributing person or persons having a beneficial interest proportionate to their contribution to the purchase price. This presumption is rebuttable on evidence to the contrary; for example, where it is shown that the contribution was made by way of gift. A constructive trust is another form of implied trust and can arise where, for example, a person has acted to his detriment in reliance upon a common intention that he will acquire an interest in the land. The case law in this area continues to develop and in recent years has been the subject of leading decisions by senior courts; in particular the decision of the House of Lords in *Stack v Dowden* [2007] UKHL 17 and of the Supreme Court in *Jones v Kernott* [2011] UKSC 53.

Any constructive, resulting or other implied trust which consists of or includes land is a trust of land (TLATA, s 1). The creation of constructive, resulting, or other implied trusts is not required to be in writing (Law of Property Act 1925, s 53(2) and Law of Property (Miscellaneous Provisions) Act 1989, s 2(5)). The Land Registry is not, however, affected with notice of a trust (LRA 2002, s 78).

No notice may be entered in the register in respect of any interest under a trust of land (LRA 2002, s 33(a)). Where a constructive, resulting or other implied trust has arisen, it may be protected by entry of a restriction. A restriction does not confer any priority; it simply prevents an entry being made in the register in respect of any disposition, or a disposition of a specified kind, unless the terms of the restriction have (where applicable) been complied with.

Entry of restrictions

Where a registered estate becomes subject to a trust of land, other than on a registrable disposition, or where the estate is held on a trust of land and there is a change in the trusts, and a sole or last surviving trustee will not be able to give a valid receipt for capital money, the registered proprietor must apply for entry of a restriction in Form A (LRR 2003, r 94(1) and (2)). Where there are two or more persons registered as proprietor of the estate, an application by one or more of them satisfies the obligation to apply for entry of the restriction. If such an application is not made, a person having a beneficial interest under a trust of land has a sufficient interest for the purposes of LRA 2002, s 43(1)(c) to apply for entry of a restriction in Form A, to ensure that a survivor of the joint proprietors (unless a trust corporation) will not be able to give a valid receipt for capital money (LRR 2003, r 93(a)). The wording of Form A is set out in Appendix IV, page 585.

The person having a beneficial interest under a trust of land also has a sufficient interest for the purposes of LRA 2002, s 43(1)(c) to apply for entry of a restriction in Form II to ensure that he receives notice of a disposition. The wording of Form II is set out in Appendix IV, page 585.

This restriction does not of itself prevent a disposition, provided its terms are complied with. This is because the interest of the beneficiary will be overreached where the requirements of Form A have been met (Law of Property Act 1925, ss 2 and 27).

The Registry must give notice of an application for a restriction to the proprietor of the registered estate or charge concerned if it has not been made by or with his consent or a person entitled to be registered as such proprietor (LRA 2002, s 45).

An application for a restriction in Form N, requiring the consent of the beneficiary, will not normally be appropriate as it would effectively confer upon the beneficiary a right to which he was not entitled and could undermine the principle of overreaching pursuant to the LRA 2002, ss 42(1)(b) and 44(1) and the Law of Property Act 1925, ss 2 and 27.

An applicant for a restriction should deliver to the Registry the usual documents required (see *Restrictions*, page 500).

If the application is made by a person who claims that he has a sufficient interest in the making of the entry, Form RX1 should include a statement in panel 12 of Form RX1 signed by the applicant or a certificate by his conveyancer in panel 13, giving details of the nature of the applicant's interest in the entry of the required restriction(s) (or, if the interest is one of those specified in LRR 2003, r 93, stating which of them) and details of how the applicant's interest arose, including details of how the beneficiary's interest under the constructive, resulting or other implied trust of land arose. Any supporting documents should be listed in panel 5 of Form RX1 or in a separate Form D.

No fee is currently payable where the application is in respect of a restriction in Form A only.

Panel 9 of Form RX1 should be completed as to the required restriction(s). A restriction in standard Form A or II in LRR 2003, Sch 4 does not require the approval of the Registry to the terms of the restriction under LRA 2002, s 43(3).

Form RX1 does not need to be used if the application is for a standard form restriction and is contained in either the 'additional provisions' panel of a prescribed form of transfer or assent, or in clause LR13 of a prescribed clauses lease (or any other lease containing clauses LR1 to LR14 of LRR 2003, Sch 1A) (LRR 2003, r 92(7)).

CONTRACTS FOR SALE
(INCLUDING SUB-SALE)

A contract for sale of registered land may be protected by the entry in the register of an agreed notice or a unilateral notice and possibly also (depending on the terms of the contract) a restriction. A notice does not necessarily mean that the contract is valid but does mean that the priority of the contract will be protected on any registered disposition (LRA 2002 ss 29, 30 and 32). A restriction does not confer any priority; it simply prevents an entry being made in the register in respect of any disposition, or a disposition of a specified kind, unless the terms of the restriction have (where applicable) been complied with.

LRA 2002, s 72(6)(a) provides that rules may make provision for priority periods in connection with the noting in the register of a contract for the making of a registrable disposition of a registered estate or charge. No such rules have currently been made.

A contract for sale is not itself an interest within LRA 2002, Sch 1 or Sch 3 which overrides either first registration or a registered disposition. Its priority therefore needs to be protected by entry of a notice in the register. However, even where a contract for sale of registered land is not protected by a notice, it may still override a later registered disposition for valuable consideration if, at the time of that later disposition, the person having the benefit of the contract is in actual occupation of the land to which the contract relates. If he is in actual occupation of only part of the land to which the contract relates, he has an overriding interest only in respect of the part he is occupying (LRA 2002, ss 29 and 30 and Sch 3, para 2).

The interest of the person in actual possession does not override a registered disposition if enquiry was made of him before the disposition and he failed to disclose the contract for sale when he could reasonably have been expected to do so. Nor does the contract for sale override a registered disposition if it belongs to a person whose occupation would not have been obvious on a reasonably careful inspection of the land at the time of the disposition, and if the person to whom the disposition is made does not have actual knowledge of the contract for sale at the time of the disposition (LRA 2002, Sch 3, para 2).

The contract for sale should be made and signed by the proprietor of the registered estate, or a satisfactory chain of title between the person making the contract and the registered proprietor shown. For example, if the registered proprietor has contracted to sell a registered title to A, and A then agrees to sell the land in the title to B by way of sub-sale, B's contract for sub-sale can be protected by a notice, whether or not A's contract is also protected by a notice.

A mortgage of a contract for sale is a general equitable charge and therefore creates a new interest in land which can be protected by a notice independently of the contract for sale itself, and whether or not the contract for sale has itself been protected by a notice. The notice can be entered in the current proprietor's title, providing a satisfactory chain of title is shown (see *Agreement for mortgage*, page 34).

Agreed notice

In addition to the usual documents required (see *Notices*, page 389), an applicant should deliver to the Registry the contract or a certified copy of it.

Where the consent of the registered proprietor is not available but, for example, the original agreement is signed by him, this is likely to be sufficient to satisfy the Registry as to the validity of the applicant's claim for the purposes of LRA 2002, s 34(3)(c).

Where the contract is in respect of a sub-sale, the earlier contract or a certified copy of it should be included with the application. This is not necessary if there is already a notice of the earlier contract in the register.

The agreed notice in the register will give details of the interest protected.

An application for entry of a unilateral notice may be preferred, where the applicant does not wish the terms of the contract to be open to public inspection and copying.

Unilateral notice

An applicant should deliver to the Registry the usual documents required (see *Notices*, page 389).

The statement in panel 11 or conveyancer's certificate in panel 12 of Form UN1 should be completed on the following lines to show the interest of the applicant:

> purchaser under a contract for sale dated [*date*] made between [*registered proprietor*] and [*purchaser*].

In the case of a sub-sale both contracts should be referred to:

> purchaser under a contract for sale dated [*date*] made between [*purchaser*] and [*sub-purchaser*], [*purchaser*] being the purchaser under a contract for sale dated [*date*] made between [*registered proprietor*] and [*purchaser*].

The wording must establish the link between the registered proprietor and the person who is to be shown as the beneficiary of the notice.

The unilateral notice will give brief details of the interest protected and identify the beneficiary of that notice.

Restriction

As a result of LRA 2002, s 42(2) no restriction may be entered for the purpose of protecting the priority of an interest which is, or could be, the subject of a notice. This does not, however, prevent a restriction being entered in addition to a notice of the contract. Although the notice protects the priority of the contract, a restriction may be used to ensure that any conditions in relation to another disposition by the registered proprietor are complied with.

The consent of the registered proprietor to the entry of the restriction is required, unless the contract for sale contains a provision which limits the registered proprietor's powers to enter into any further disposition. The Registry must give notice of the application for a restriction to the proprietor of the registered estate or charge concerned, if it has not been made by or with the consent of such proprietor or a person entitled to be registered as such proprietor (LRA 2002, s 45).

In addition to the usual documents required (see *Restrictions*, page 500), an applicant should deliver to the Registry (if the application is made by a person who claims that he has a sufficient interest in the making of the entry) a certified copy of the contract for sale.

The statement in panel 12 or conveyancer's certificate in panel 13 of Form RX1 must be completed, setting out details of the contract and of the provision in the contract limiting the registered proprietor's powers to enter into a disposition.

Panel 9 of Form RX1 should be completed as to the required restriction(s). A restriction in a standard form contained in LRR 2003, Sch 4 does not require the approval of the Registry to the terms of the restriction under LRA 2002, s 43(3). A possible form of restriction based on Form L in LRR 2003, Sch 4 is:

No disposition of the registered estate by the proprietor of the registered estate is to be registered without a written certificate signed by [*purchaser*] of [*address*] or their conveyancer that the provisions of [*clause, paragraph or other particulars*] of [*details of contract for sale*] have been complied with or that they do not apply to the disposition.

CONVEYANCERS

The LRR 2003 refer in various contexts to 'conveyancer', including provision for a conveyancer's certificate to be given in relation to certain matters. The definition of 'conveyancer' in LRR 2003, r 217A(1) effectively includes:

(a)   solicitors and firms of solicitors;
(b)   licensed conveyancers;
(c)   barristers;
(d)   duly certificated notaries public;
(e)   alternative business structures (licensed bodies);
(f)   organisations which employ a person who is a conveyancer and will undertake or direct or supervise conveyancing activities;
(g)   a person carrying out conveyancing activities in the course of his duties as a public officer.

This list does not currently include legal executives, because their regulating authority (the Chartered Institute of Legal Executives) is not currently permitted to authorise legal executives to carry out conveyancing activities. Where legal executives do prepare and submit applications to the Registry, this would therefore need to be in their capacity as employees of a conveyancer (such as a firm of solicitors).

Where a rule, form or restriction does not specify that a form or a certificate has to be signed by an individual conveyancer, it can be signed in the name of the conveyancer by an employee. However, r 217(A)(2) limits the definition of 'conveyancer' in certain contexts.

COPYHOLD

Copyhold was an ancient form of tenure, where the owner was the tenant of the lord of the manor. A copyholder would take his grant of land at the manor court of the lord of the manor and the steward would record the admittance on the court roll and give the tenant a copy of the entry – hence the name 'copyhold'. A copyholder was not allowed to transfer his land by conveyance. Instead, if he wanted to sell the land he had to return to the manor court and surrender the land back into the hands of the lord of the manor on condition that he grant it to the purchaser.

Copyholds could always be enfranchised (i.e. turned into a freehold) by a conveyance of the freehold from the lord of the manor to the copyholder. Various 19th-century statutes allowed for compulsory enfranchisement and the Law of Property Act 1922 abolished copyhold and converted all existing copyholds into freehold land. Any copyhold land then remaining in existence was enfranchised on 1 January 1926 (Law of Property Act 1922, s 128). Such enfranchisement did not affect any rights of the lord or tenant in any mines and minerals or ancillary rights, or any rights of the lord in respect of fairs, markets or sporting rights (Law of Property Act 1922, Sch 12). Copyhold Act 1852, s 48 and Copyhold Act 1894, s 23 excepted similar rights in respect of enfranchisements made under those Acts.

Where on first registration the title deduced reveals that the rights of the lord have been preserved under the Law of Property Act 1922 or the earlier Copyhold Acts, the Registry will enter a notice to that effect in the property register. The absence of such a notice is not, however, conclusive that the land was not formerly copyhold. Applications are sometimes made to the Registry to have such a notice cancelled on the grounds that Law of Property Act 1922, s 128 and Sch 12 have been repealed by the Statute Law (Repeals) Act 1969. Such applications are misconceived because the repeal of an enactment does not, unless the contrary intention appears, affect any right, privilege, obligation or liability acquired, accrued or incurred under that enactment (Interpretation Act 1978, s 16). No contrary intention appears in the Statute Law (Repeals) Act 1969.

Any unregistered manorial rights were interests which overrode both first registration or a registered disposition (LRA 2002, Sch 1, para 11 and Sch 3, para 11). Such interests were therefore protected notwithstanding that there was no entry in the register in respect of them (LRA 2002, ss 11, 12, 29 and 30). There was therefore a duty to disclose the burden of such rights under LRR 2003, r 28 or r 57 (see 'Duty to disclose overriding interests', page 426).

However, such rights ceased to have overriding status at the end of 10 years from 13 October 2003 (LRA 2002, s 117). The person having the benefit of a manorial right (if its priority has not already been previously defeated and it continues to subsist) should therefore protect it in the register. If he does not do so, the priority of the right is liable to be defeated in favour of a subsequent registrable disposition for valuable consideration which is completed by registration (LRA 2002, s 29). If the burdened land is unregistered he should apply for a caution against first registration. If the burdened land is registered he should apply for the entry of a notice if one does not already appear in the register. Until 12 October 2013, no fee was payable for such an application, but the normal fee will now apply.

Caution against first registration

A person applying for a caution against first registration should deliver to the Registry the usual documents required (see *Cautions against first registration*, page 88).

No documents should be exhibited, as the statement should be self-contained. The statement of truth in panel 10 of Form CT1 should be completed on the following lines to show the interest of the applicant:

> the person entitled to a manorial right affecting that estate being [*set out nature of the manorial right*].

The interest stated in the Form CT1 will appear in the caution register, together with a description of the legal estate to which the caution relates. For the effect of a caution against first registration, see *Cautions against first registration*, page 88.

Agreed notice

An applicant should deliver to the Registry the usual documents required (see *Notices*, page 389).

To establish the validity of his claim for the purposes of entry of an agreed notice, the applicant will normally need to produce evidence:

(a)   that the land in question was previously copyhold of the manor in question (usually in the form of a copy of the deed of enfranchisement or compensation agreement);

(b)   that it was the custom of the manor in question that the lord had the rights claimed (for example by evidence from the court rolls);

(c)   that the rights in question survived enfranchisement (usually in the form of a copy of the deed of enfranchisement or compensation agreement); and

(d)   of the applicant's title to the particular manorial rights claimed (usually in the form of an abstract or epitome of title showing the applicant's title to the lordship of the manor and that the rights have not been severed from the lordship).

The agreed notice in the register will give details of the interest protected.

Where the registered proprietor does not consent to the entry in the register of an agreed notice and evidence to satisfy the Registry as to the validity of the applicant's claim cannot be lodged, an application for entry of a unilateral notice may still be made.

Unilateral notice

An applicant should deliver to the Registry the usual documents required (see *Notices*, page 389).

The statement in panel 11 or conveyancer's certificate in panel 12 of Form UN1 should be completed on the following lines to show the interest of the applicant:

> the person having the benefit of a manorial right being [*set out nature of the manorial right*].

The unilateral notice will give brief details of the manorial right protected and identify the beneficiary of that notice.

CORRECTION OF MISTAKES IN AN APPLICATION OR ACCOMPANYING DOCUMENT

Where an application or an accompanying document contains a mistake, the Registry may, if it thinks fit, make an alteration to correct the mistake (LRR 2003, r 130). In the case of a mistake of a clerical or like nature, the alteration has effect in all circumstances as if made by the applicant or other interested party or parties. In the case of any other mistake, the alteration has effect as if made by the applicant or other interested party or parties only if the applicant and any other interested party has requested, or consented to, the alteration (LRR 2003, r 130(2)).

If an applicant discovers such a mistake either during the course of an application or after it has been completed, he should draw it to the attention of the Registry and, if appropriate, request the Registry to correct the mistake. An applicant cannot insist that an alteration is made pursuant to r 130 – it is entirely at the discretion of the Registry as to whether it will make the alteration. The effect of the alteration must not prejudice any other person and must normally be requested within one year of the date of completion of an application. Any alteration should reflect the original agreement between the parties and must not constitute an attempt to redraft a document after completion (for example when matters have been overlooked or when a change of circumstances makes alterations desirable) by means of an application under r 130.

Alterations to documents under r 130 can only be made if the original deed is lodged at the Registry or if the Registry holds the original of the deed in its file or as a scanned image.

LRR 2003, r 130(2)(a) relates to the alteration in the case of a mistake of a clerical or like nature. For example, where a name has been misspelt in a document lodged for registration and the correct name can be clearly shown.

Where an alteration does not comprise a mistake of a clerical or like nature the alteration cannot be made under r 130(2)(a). However, in some circumstances it may be possible to make an alteration under r 130(2)(b) provided the applicant and any other interested party has requested or consented to the alteration.

Where an alteration is made under r 130, it may be necessary to consider whether consequential amendments to the register are required. In straightforward cases, such as where a transfer has been altered due to a misspelt name, the register should reflect what is in the transfer and may be altered by the Registry under LRA 2002, Sch 4, para 5(b) for the purposes of 'bringing the register up to date'. In other circumstances, an application in Form AP1 may be required.

If a proposed alteration does not fall within the scope of LRR 2003, r 130, a deed of rectification or corrective disposition may be necessary (see *Deeds amending dispositions of registered titles*, page 185).

COSTS

The LRA 2002 makes provision for the payment of costs, both by the Land Registry and by a third party. In the case of costs payable by the Registry, these may involve costs arising in connection with indemnity, or alternatively the payment of 'non-rectification' costs which do not involve indemnity.

Costs payable by the Registry

If the register is altered under LRA 2002, Sch 4 in a case *not* involving rectification, the Registry may pay such amount as it thinks fit in respect of any costs or expenses reasonably incurred by a person in connection with the alteration which have been incurred with the consent of the Registry. Even where the Registry has not consented to the incurring of costs or expenses, it may still make a payment if it appears to it that the costs or expenses had to be incurred urgently and it was not reasonably practicable to apply for the Registry's consent. The Registry may also still make a payment if it has subsequently approved the incurring of the costs or expenses (see *Alteration of the register*, page 39).

Where a person is entitled to be indemnified by the Registry under LRA 2002, Sch 8 (including cases involving rectification), an indemnity under that schedule is payable in respect of loss consisting of costs or expenses incurred by the claimant in relation to the matter only if such costs or expenses were reasonably incurred by the claimant with the consent of the Registry. The requirement for consent does not, however, apply where the costs or expenses must be incurred by the claimant urgently and it is not reasonably practicable to apply for the Registry's consent. If the Registry approves the incurring of costs or expenses after they have been incurred, they are treated as having been incurred with its consent. The consent of the Registry to the incurring of costs or expenses does not mean that it will necessarily pay all, or indeed any, of those costs or expenses. See *Indemnity*, page 273, as to when a person is entitled to be indemnified by the Registry.

Interest is payable on indemnity for costs or expenses at the applicable rate for the period from the date when the claimant pays them to the date of payment (LRR 2003, r 195). In calculating the exact period in respect of which interest is payable, the date when the claimant pays the costs or expenses is excluded, but the date of payment by the Registry is included.

If no indemnity is payable to a claimant under LRA 2002, Sch 8, the Registry may pay such amount as it thinks fit in respect of any costs or expenses reasonably incurred by the claimant in connection with the claim which have been incurred with the consent of the Registry. Even where the Registry has not consented to the incurring of costs or expenses, it may still make such a payment if it appears to it that the costs or expenses had to be incurred urgently and it was not reasonably practicable to apply for the Registry's consent. It may also still make a payment if it has subsequently approved the incurring of the costs or expenses.

The consent of the Registry to the incurring of costs or expenses does not mean that it will necessarily pay all, or indeed any, of those costs or expenses.

Where a claim to indemnity for costs or expenses under LRA 2002, Sch 8 cannot be resolved by agreement with the Registry, a person may apply to the High Court or a county court for the determination of any question as to whether he is entitled to such indemnity or as to the amount of the indemnity. The requirement that the

Registry consents to the incurring of costs or expenses does not apply to the costs of such an application to the court or of any legal proceedings arising out of such an application.

Costs payable by a third party

Any person who has incurred costs in relation to proceedings before the Registry may request the Registry to make an order requiring a party to those proceedings to pay the whole or part of those costs (LRA 2002, s 76 and LRR 2003, r 202). The Registry may make such an order only where those costs were occasioned by the unreasonable conduct of the party in question in relation to the proceedings.

This power relates only to proceedings before the Registry, not to proceedings before the Tribunal, as to which the Tribunal has power to make an order as to costs (see *Disputes*, page 193).

The request for the payment of costs must be made by delivering to the Registry a written statement by 12 noon on the 20th business day after the completion of the proceedings to which the request relates. A business day is a day when the Land Registry is open to the public, that is every day except Saturdays, Sundays, Christmas Day, Good Friday or any other day either specified or declared by proclamation under Banking and Financial Dealings Act 1971, s 1 or appointed by the Lord Chancellor, or certified by the Registry as being an 'interrupted day' due to delay or failure of a communication service or to some other event or circumstance causing substantial interruption in the normal operation of the Registry.

The statement must identify the party against whom the order is sought and include an address where notice may be served on that party; state in full the grounds for the request; give an address to which communications may be sent; and be signed by the person making the request or his conveyancer.

The Registry must give notice of the request to the party against whom the order is sought at the address stated and also at any address for service for him stated in a registered title that relates to the proceedings. The notice gives the recipient a period ending at 12 noon on the 20th business day after the issue of the notice, or such other period as the Registry thinks appropriate, to deliver a written response to the Registry by the method and to the address stated in the notice.

The response must state whether or not the recipient opposes the request; if he does, he must state in full the grounds for that opposition and give an address to which communications may be sent. The response must be signed by the recipient or his conveyancer.

The Registry must determine the matter on the basis of the written request and any response submitted to it; all the circumstances including the conduct of the parties; and the result of any enquiries the Registry considers it necessary to make. The Registry may make an order requiring the party against whom it is made to pay to the requesting party the whole, or such part as the Registry thinks fit, of the costs incurred in the proceedings by the person who made the request. The order may specify the sum to be paid or require the costs to be assessed by the court (if not otherwise agreed), and specify the basis of the assessment to be used by the court.

The Registry must send all parties its written reasons for any such order it makes. Such an order is enforceable as an order of the court (LRA 2002, s 76(4)). A person aggrieved by the order may appeal to a county court, which may make any order which appears appropriate (LRA 2002, s 76(5)).

CREDIT UNIONS

The main provisions of the Credit Unions Act 1979 came into operation on 20 August 1979 and enabled certain savings and loan societies to be registered under the Industrial and Provident Societies Act 1965 as 'credit unions'. A society registered under the Industrial and Provident Societies Act 1965 as a credit union in accordance with the Credit Unions Act 1979 is a body corporate with perpetual succession and a common seal (Industrial and Provident Societies Act 1965, s 3). The name of a credit union must include the words 'credit union' or, provided its registered office is in Wales, 'undeb credyd'.

A credit union may hold, purchase or take on lease in its own name any land for the purpose of conducting its business thereon but for no other purpose; it may sell, exchange, mortgage or lease any such land, and erect, alter or pull down buildings on it (Credit Unions Act 1979, s 12). It can also hold an interest in land as a mortgagee.

As credit unions have statutory powers to deal with and hold land that does not depend upon their rules, it will not normally be necessary to lodge a copy of the rules when application is made to register such a body as proprietor of registered land.

By virtue of Credit Unions Act 1979, s 11, a credit union has the power, under its rules, to make a loan to a member for a provident or productive purpose with or without security. Section 11 imposes limits as to the amount that may be lent, the repayment period and the chargeable rate of interest. If an application is made to register a charge in favour of a credit union, it must therefore be supported by a certificate by its secretary or conveyancer, confirming that the charge is in accordance with the provisions of the Credit Unions Act 1979. The Registry will accept this certificate as evidence of compliance not only with the Act but also with the rules of the credit union.

By virtue of Credit Unions Act 1979, s 21, a credit union may by special resolution amalgamate with, transfer its engagements to, or accept a transfer of engagements from, another credit union. When application is made to register such a disposition, evidence of such amalgamation or transfer should take the form of a certified copy of Form CU24 (Acknowledgement of Registration of Copy of Special Resolution) issued pursuant to the Industrial and Provident Societies (Credit Unions) Regulations 1979 (SI 1979/937) (see *Registered societies*, page 485).

DAY LIST

The day list is a record of the date and time at which every pending application is made and of every application for an official search with priority (LRR 2003, r 12). For this purpose 'pending application' does not include an application under LRR 2003, Pt 13 (which covers 'Information etc' such as applications for official copies), except an application to designate a document an exempt information document under LRR 2003, r 136. Notice of an application for an official search with priority remains on the day list until the priority period allowed by the search comes to an end. If the Registry proposes to alter the register without having received an application, it must enter its proposal on the day list and, when so entered, it will have the same effect as if it were an application made at the date and time of its entry.

Delivery and priority of applications

Unless lodged electronically or in accordance with a written arrangement as to delivery made between the Registry and the applicant or his conveyancer, all applications and correspondence should be delivered to the 'proper office', as designated by an order of the Lord Chancellor as the proper office for the receipt of applications (LRA 2002, s 100(3)) or if no such order subsists, to the Registry under the provisions of any relevant direction by the registrar under LRA 2002, s 100(4) as to the address to be used for the delivery of applications (LRR 2003, r 15(3)(a)) (see *Proper office*, page 467). An application is 'received' by the Registry when it is delivered:

(a)   to the proper office; or

(b)   in accordance with a written arrangement as to delivery made between the Registry and the applicant or his conveyancer; or

(c)   electronically where that is authorised (LRR 2003, r 15(3)).

This does not apply to an application under LRR 2003, Pt 13 other than an application to designate a document an exempt information document under LRR 2003, r 136.

An application received *on* a business day is taken as made at the earlier of:

(a)   the time of the day that notice of it is entered in the day list; or

(b)   midnight marking the end of:
   (i)   the day it was received if the application was received before 12 noon; or
   (ii)   the next business day after the day it was received if the application was received at or after 12 noon (LRR 2003, r 15(1)).

An application received on a day which is *not* a business day is taken as made at the earlier of:

(a)   the time of the day that notice of it is entered in the day list; or

(b)   midnight marking the end of the next business day after the day it was received (LRR 2003, r 15(2)).

A business day is a day when the Registry is open to the public, that is every day except Saturdays, Sundays, Christmas Day, Good Friday or any other day either specified or declared by proclamation under Banking and Financial Dealings Act 1971, s 1 or appointed by the Lord Chancellor or certified by the Registry as being an 'interrupted day' due to delay or failure of a communication service or to some other event or circumstance causing substantial interruption in the normal operation of the Registry.

Entries made in the register on first registration, or on the registration of a disposition required to be completed by registration or entries made, removed or altered as a result of any other application have effect from the time the application is made (LRA 2002, s 74 and LRR 2003, r 20).

Where two or more applications relating to the same registered title are taken as having been made at the same time the order in which they should rank in priority as between each other is determined in accordance with the provisions of LRR 2003, r 55.

Day list information

LRR 2003, r 141 provides for applications for day list information. This includes historic day list information to be provided as well as current day list information. Historic day list information is information that was, but is no longer, kept on the day list. Such applications may be made only during the currency of a relevant notice given under LRR 2003, Sch 2, and subject to and in accordance with the limitations contained in the notice. The Registry must provide the historic day list information in the manner specified in the relevant notice.

DEATH OF APPLICANT FOR REGISTRATION

If an applicant dies before an application to the Registry has been completed, the application may be continued by his personal representative (LRR 2003, r 18). The personal representative should lodge a copy of the probate or letters of administration to show that he is the person to whom the applicant's interest has devolved by operation of law and thus entitled to continue the application.

In relation to registered land, where the deceased applicant was applying to be registered as proprietor, the personal representative should consider whether to be registered as proprietor himself or whether to deal with the registered estate or registered charge without being registered as proprietor (see *Personal representatives*, page 435).

In relation to unregistered land, it is not possible to make an application for first registration in the name of a deceased estate owner (including a deceased mortgagor), as the deceased is not a 'person' for the purpose of LRA 2002, s 9(2), (4) or (5) or s 10(2), (3) or (5); a deceased owner cannot therefore be entered in the register as proprietor. The vesting of the legal estate in a deceased owner's personal representative by operation of law does not trigger compulsory first registration. The personal representative should consider whether to apply for voluntary first registration of title and be registered as proprietor himself or whether to deal with the unregistered estate or charge without making such an application (see *Personal representatives*, page 435).

Where unregistered land is subject to a mortgage, LRR 2003, r 21 allows a mortgagee under any protected first legal mortgage of a qualifying estate (as defined in LRA 2002, s 4) to apply for registration of the estate charged, whether or not the estate owner consents. This applies only where the mortgage itself is the trigger for compulsory first registration. The mortgagee must apply to register either the executors as proprietor (if the deceased left a will, whether or not a grant has been issued) or the Public Trustee (where the deceased died intestate but no grant of letters of representation has been issued) or the administrators (where the deceased died intestate and a grant has been issued). In the case of any other charge, the mortgagee cannot apply for registration without an estate owner's consent, unless authorised to apply under the mortgage terms or conditions.

DEATH OF A REGISTERED PROPRIETOR

The effect of the death of a registered proprietor of a registered estate, and the steps which may be taken to reflect the death, will depend upon whether the deceased was a sole proprietor or one of two or more joint registered proprietors.

Death of a sole proprietor

On the death of the proprietor, the legal estate will have vested in his personal representative by operation of law. As an interim measure, before any further action is taken in relation to the title, application may be made to note the death in the proprietorship register. This is not obligatory, but it helps to keep the register up to date and reduce the possibility of fraud, particularly if there is likely to be some delay in obtaining a grant of representation.

The application should be made in Form AP1, citing 'death of sole proprietor'. There is currently no fee payable, but the application must be accompanied by evidence of the death in the form of the original or an office copy of the death certificate or grant of representation (if any). Alternatively, written confirmation of the fact of death in a certificate from a conveyancer may (except where the deceased died abroad) be provided.

On completion of the application, the Registry will enter a simple note of the death in the register. No change will be made to the address for service, even if requested, unless the personal representative applies to be registered as proprietor at the same time.

Once a grant of representation has been obtained, the personal representative may either apply to register himself as proprietor, execute an assent of the registered estate in favour of the beneficiaries or transfer the property to a third party (see *Personal representatives*, page 435).

Death of a joint proprietor

See *Joint proprietors*, page 286.

DEBENTURES

A debenture is used by companies and usually contains one or more charges by way of security by the company to secure money raised by way of loan. If the debenture does not in fact charge land it cannot be protected at the Land Registry. If a debenture does contain a charge, this may comprise a legal charge, a fixed equitable charge and/or a floating charge. A legal charge of registered land created by a debenture can be registered as a registered charge (see *Legal charges*, page 333). A fixed equitable charge or a floating charge cannot be substantively registered, but may be capable of protection by an entry in the register (see *Equitable charges*, page 207, and *Floating charges*, page 231). If a company has created a debenture containing a fixed equitable or a floating charge on its assets, the existence of the charge must be disclosed when the company makes an application for the first registration of its title to an estate affected by the debenture. A notice of the charge will be entered in the register, and the copy of the debenture will be filed (LRR 2003, r 35).

Where a company that has created a debenture acquires a registered estate or a registered charge, or where a company that is already the proprietor of a registered estate or a registered charge creates a debenture, no entry will be made in the register to protect any charge created by the debenture (whether registered in the Companies Registry or not) in the absence of a specific application.

In the case of a UK company (i.e. one registered in England, Wales, Scotland or Northern Ireland under the Companies Acts or in Northern Ireland under the Companies (Northern Ireland) Order 1986), registration of the charge at the Companies Registry should precede an application for registration to the Land Registry. Registration of a charge of registered land at the Companies Registry alone is not sufficient – it should also be completed by registration in accordance with LRA 2002, s 27, if it is to take effect at law and be protected in the register. Conversely, registration of a charge in a debenture at the Land Registry does not remove the need for it to be registered under the Companies Act 2006.

Although LRA 2002, s 121 allows the Lord Chancellor to make rules about the transmission, by the Land Registry to the Registrar of Companies, of applications for registration of charges under the Companies Act 2006, no such rules have yet been made. The application to the Companies Registry must therefore be made separately. Since 6 April 2013, such application may be made electronically, in which case the certificate of registration will be issued electronically. It is still possible to apply in paper form and the certificate of registration will be issued in paper form; the charge itself will no longer be stamped with the Companies Registry stamp.

When making an application for registration of a charge created by a UK company, the applicant must produce to the Registry the certificate issued under Companies Act 2006, s 859I that the charge has been registered at the Companies Registry under s 859A of that Act (LRR 2003, r 111), together with a Companies Registry official copy of the charge or a certificate or confirmation in writing by the lender or a conveyancer that the charge lodged for registration is identical to the copy charge filed at the Companies Registry and is the charge to which the certificate of registration relates.

If the certificate is not produced, the Registry must enter a note in the register stating that no evidence of registration of the charge in accordance with Companies Act 2006, s 859A has been lodged. Similar provisions applied prior to 6 April 2013 in relation to Companies Act 2006, s 860 or s 878 and, prior to 1 October 2009, in relation to Companies Act 1985, s 395 or s 410, with any necessary note in the register referring to the relevant section. The note reflects the fact that where the charge is not registered with the Companies Registry within the prescribed period, the charge is void against the liquidator or administrator of the company and any creditor of the company.

An application for registration of a charge created by an overseas company (i.e. one incorporated outside the United Kingdom), which is dated on or after 1 October 2009 and before 1 October 2011, must be accompanied by evidence to satisfy the Registry that the charge has been registered in the Companies Registry under Overseas Companies (Execution of Documents and Registration of Charges) Regulations 2009, Pt 3, or the charge must include a statement that the charge, when created, did not require to be so registered (LRR 2003, r 111A). In default of this, the Registry must enter a note in the register to the effect that no evidence has been lodged either that the charge has been so registered or that such registration was not required.

The Registry is required to enter one of the above notes only where a legal charge is being registered, not when notice of a charge is being entered in the register.

A purchaser taking a transfer of registered land from a company registered with absolute title or good leasehold title is not concerned to search that company's file at the Companies Registry in respect of debentures. If any had been created before the company became registered proprietor of the estate, a notice should appear in the register and if the company had created a debenture and then acquired a registered estate, or had become proprietor of a registered estate and then created a debenture, a purchaser of the registered land would not be concerned with any charge created by the debenture unless it was registered or protected in the register (LRA 2002, s 29).

Where a company is the proprietor of a registered estate and a notice of a fixed equitable charge under a debenture by the company appears in the register, any application to register a lease by the company with absolute leasehold title must be accompanied by the consent of the chargee, otherwise a protective entry may be made in the register (see *Classes of title*, page 130).

Where a notice of a floating charge under a debenture by a company appears in the register and a transfer on sale of the estate by the chargor company is being registered, a certificate of non-crystallisation will normally be required (see *Floating charges*, page 231). Where a lease by the chargor company is being registered with absolute leasehold title, the consent of the chargee under the floating charge will be required, otherwise a protective entry may be made in the register (see *Classes of title*, page 130).

DEEDS AMENDING DISPOSITIONS OF REGISTERED TITLES

It may sometimes be necessary, due to a clerical error or change of circumstances for example, to correct or otherwise amend a deed which has effected a disposition of a registered estate or charge. The need for correction or amendment may arise before the deed has been completed by registration, or subsequent to such registration.

Amendment before application for registration

If the need to amend an original deed is discovered after it has been executed but before any application to register it has been made, the original deed should be altered so as to give effect to the parties' true intentions before it is lodged for registration. All alterations to the deed must be authenticated by the signatures of all the parties against each amendment made. If a plan to the original deed is amended or substituted, all the parties should sign the plan. Priority for any additional land added to a disposition effected by the deed should, where necessary, be protected by an official search.

Amendment after application for registration but before completion of registration

It may be that the need for the amendment of an original deed is not discovered until after the application to register it has been lodged at the Registry. This may result in the application being rejected, or the subject of a requisition, by the

Registry and an amendment to the deed is made (as above) in consequence. In other cases, the applicant may request the temporary return of the original deed for amendment, provided the request is made before completion of the application and the intended variation is compatible with keeping the application on the day list.

Amendment after registration

Where the original deed has been registered, different considerations apply. This is because once the register has been changed to give legal effect to a registrable disposition and reflect the information contained in the deed, it records the existence of the relevant registered estates, charges and legal interests that subsist and the identity of the persons in whom, as registered proprietors, the estates and charges are vested. In consequence, if a further disposition of a registered title is needed, this must be effected by means of a further registrable deed. This must where necessary be in the appropriate prescribed form (LRA 2002, s 25 and LRR 2003, r 206(1)) and be completed by registration in order to take effect at law (LRA 2002, s 27).

Transfers

If an original transfer transferred the incorrect extent of a registered estate, the correction must be effected by one or more transfers in the prescribed form. Appropriate adjusting provisions may, where necessary, be included in those transfer(s) in relation to easements or covenants, etc contained in the original transfer. If the extent transferred by the original transfer was correct so that no adjusting transfer is required, but other provisions within it require amendment, this may be effected by a deed of variation. There is no prescribed form for such a deed. It must, however, be completed by registration where necessary – for example, if it grants or reserves an easement. In other cases, the appropriate form of application to reflect the deed in the register should be made. Appropriate steps should be taken in relation to any existing registered charges and other existing register entries, including compliance with any restriction(s) where necessary.

Leases

If a registered lease has demised the incorrect extent or term, see 'Variation of a lease', page 304. In other cases, where certain terms in a registered lease require amendment, this may be effected by a deed of variation. There is no prescribed form for such a deed. It must, however, be completed by registration. Appropriate steps should be taken in relation to any existing registered charges and other existing register entries, including compliance with any restriction(s) where necessary.

Charges

Where a registered charge should have included additional registered land that was not referred to in the original charge, the parties may either execute a further deed creating a legal charge over the additional land as additional security for the borrowing secured by the original charge; or replace the existing registered charge with a fresh legal charge that charges both the land charged by the original deed and the additional land as security. In either case, the charge would need to be completed by registration and in the latter case the existing charge would need to be discharged.

Where a registered charge includes registered land that should not have been included, the parties should apply to cancel the registration of the charge against the land in question. This should be a discharge of the whole, or the relevant part of the registered charge, as appropriate.

Where the extent charged by a registered charge is correct but certain terms within it require amendment, the parties may either replace the existing registered charge with a fresh legal charge that incorporates the revised terms; or execute a deed of variation by which they agree to amend the original charge. There is no prescribed form for a deed of variation. The fresh charge or deed of variation would need to be completed by registration and in the former case the existing charge would need to be discharged.

Related topics

For the correction of mistakes in applications, see *Correction of mistakes in an application or accompanying document*, page 174. For leases, see *Leases*, page 296. For transfers, see *Transfers*, page 551. For registered charges, see *Legal charges*, page 333. For the rectification or setting aside of a document by an order of the Tribunal, see *Tribunal*, page 555.

DEMESNE LAND

For the purposes of the LRA 2002 'demesne land' is defined as land belonging to Her Majesty in right of the Crown which is not held for an estate in fee simple absolute in possession. This does not include land in relation to which a freehold estate in land has determined, but in relation to which there has been no act of entry or management by the Crown (LRA 2002, s 132(1), (2)). The demesne land of the Crown includes:

(a)   the foreshore around England and Wales, except where it has been granted away or it has vested in a private owner;
(b)   land which has escheated to the Crown (see *Bona vacantia and escheat*, page 74); and
(c)   the ancient lands of the Crown which it has never granted away.

Demesne land held by the Crown is not land held for an estate in fee simple and therefore was not capable of registration under the LRA 1925. LRA 2002, s 79 provides that Her Majesty may grant an estate in fee simple out of demesne land to Herself. Such a grant must be followed by an application for first registration or the grant is to be regarded as not having been made (LRA 2002, s 79(2)), in which case the land will continue to be held as demesne land.

The period in which the application for first registration must be made is 2 months beginning with the date of the grant. If, on the application of Her Majesty, the Registry is satisfied that there is a good reason for doing so, it may by order extend the period for registration. If the Registry makes an order extending the period for registration where LRA 2002, s 79(2) has already applied, that application of s 79(2) is treated as not having occurred (LRA 2002, s 79(5)). Grants of legal estates in land by the Queen out of demesne land to other parties are normally subject to compulsory registration (LRA 2002, s 80). Compulsory registration applies to:

(a)   a grant by Her Majesty out of demesne land of a freehold estate (otherwise than to Herself under s 79); and
(b)   leases out of demesne land for more than 7 years from the date of the grant which are for valuable or other consideration; by way of gift (including a grant for the purpose of constituting a trust under which Her Majesty does not retain the whole of the beneficial interest); or in pursuance of an order of the court. Compulsory registration does not apply to a grant of an estate in mines and minerals held apart from the surface.

See further *First registration*, page 222.

LRA 2002, s 83 makes provision for an 'appropriate authority' to represent, make applications and receive notice on behalf of, Her Majesty and the Duchies of Lancaster and Cornwall. For land vested in Her Majesty in right of the Crown, this may be the Crown Estate Commissioners; or a government department; or such person as Her Majesty may appoint in writing under the Royal Sign Manual.

The LRA 2002 also includes provision for registration of cautions against first registration in respect of demesne land, so that LRA 2002, s 15 (which confers a right to lodge a caution) shall apply as if demesne land were held by Her Majesty for an unregistered estate in fee simple absolute in possession (LRA 2002, s 81).

The LRA 2002 binds the Crown (LRA 2002, s 129). On any application relating to a registered estate the Crown must therefore comply with its provisions.

First registration

Applications for first registration should be made using Form FR1 with such modifications as are appropriate and have been approved by the Registry (LRR 2003, r 23(2)). The Queen will be entered as the registered proprietor in the following form:

> THE QUEEN'S MOST EXCELLENT MAJESTY IN RIGHT OF HER CROWN of the Crown Estate Commissioners, Crown Estate Office, Whitehall, London SW1.

Cautions against first registration

For the period of 10 years from 13 October 2003, the Queen could lodge a caution against first registration of demesne land as if she held the demesne land for an unregistered estate in fee simple absolute in possession (LRA 2002, s 81 and Sch 12, para 15(1)). The application had to be made in Form CT1 and contain sufficient details, by plan or otherwise, so that the extent of the demesne land to which the caution relates could be identified clearly on the Ordnance Survey map.

Any such caution lodged under LRA 2002, s 15 (as applied by s 81 of that Act), ceased to have effect at the end of the period of 10 years from 13 October 2003, except in relation to applications for first registration made before the end of that period (LRA 2002, Sch 12, para 15(2)).

Where the land to which a caution against first registration related was demesne land, either the Queen or the owner of a legal estate affecting the demesne land could apply for the cancellation of the caution. Where the Queen was applying for cancellation, the application had to be made in Form CCT with such modifications as were appropriate and had been approved by the Registry.

In other respects cautions against first registration of demesne land operated in the same way as other cautions against first registrations (see *Cautions against first registration*, page 88).

DEVELOPING ESTATES

A registered title may sometimes consist of land which is intended to be developed for residential or commercial purposes and divided into plots or units which will be individually transferred or leased. The Registry provides a number of services relating to such 'developing estate' titles and developers are encouraged to utilise these, both to minimise the scope for problems as the estate is being developed and to facilitate registration of subsequent transfers and leases. Those services are:

(a)   estate boundary approval;
(b)   estate plan approval;
(c)   approval of draft transfers and leases;
(d)   pre- and post-registration services on plot sales.

These services are designed to complement each other, but may be used independently if preferred. There are currently no fees for any of these services.

Estate boundary approval

This service is for use *before* design of the estate layout. It ensures that the developer's initial site survey plan corresponds with the extent of his registered title. Any discrepancies can then be identified and resolved. Advice can also be given on easements intended to be granted. The initial site survey plan showing the extent of the land included in the development should be sent in duplicate to the appropriate Registry office. If it is satisfied that the external boundaries shown on the site survey plan agree with those shown on the title plan and the latest Ordnance Survey map, the Registry will give estate boundary approval. Such approval cannot be given until the developer's title has been registered.

Estate plan approval

As early as possible before the first transfer or lease of part is likely to be lodged for registration, the developer or his conveyancer should send the estate plan in duplicate to the appropriate Registry office, for approval of its use in connection with official searches of the register and official certificates of inspection of the title plan. Where the estate boundary approval service has been used, the estate plan should be based upon the same plan.

The estate plan should show the final layout of the proposed development and must show sufficient detail to enable it to be accurately related to the title plan of the developer's title and the surrounding boundary features. It must be drawn to a suitable scale, usually 1:500; its true scale and orientation must be shown and it must clearly and precisely define each plot or property and identify it by a plot number or other reference. Plans marked '*For identification only*' or with some similar phrase are not acceptable, nor are those bearing a statement of disclaimer intended to comply with the Property Misdescriptions Act 1991.

Where a property comprises more than one parcel (for example a house and separate garage) each parcel must be distinguished on the estate plan by a separate number. If two or more floors of a purpose-built block of flats are co-extensive and the layout of the flats on each floor is identical, it is usually sufficient to lodge the plan of a single floor, but this plan must show the reference numbers distinguishing each flat on each floor. Common areas should be identified. All buildings, drives and pathways should be shown in their correct positions. If approved, one copy of the plan will be retained by the Registry. The other, marked as officially approved, will be returned to the developer or his conveyancer. The advantages of obtaining estate plan approval are that:

(a) negotiations for the sale of individual plots can proceed without an official copy of the title plan;

(b) applications for official searches of the register and for official certificates of inspection of the title plan may describe the land being purchased by reference to the plot number(s) on the approved plan, so avoiding the need to provide separate plans; and

(c) the approved plan, or extracts from it, can form the basis of transfer or lease plans, ensuring consistency throughout the transaction.

Problems can be avoided if, before contract, the developer checks the position of plot fences on the ground against the approved estate plan. The developer should notify the Registry immediately of any change in the layout of the estate and should return the duplicate approved estate plan to the Registry with a new estate plan for approval (in duplicate) showing the changes. Failure to do this may lead to the withdrawal of approval of the obsolete part of the plan and in turn to the cancellation of applications for official searches against individual plots. It may also lead to difficulties in the registration of transfers or leases based on the obsolete part of the estate plan.

The Registry should be kept informed of the progress of the development periodically so that new surveys can be made as necessary.

Approval of draft transfers and leases

The appropriate form of transfer in LRR 2003, Sch 1, such as Form TP1 or TP2, should be used for transfers of individual plots. In the case of leases of individual plots, the lease will normally need to be in the form of a prescribed clauses lease and contain the prescribed clauses set out in LRR 2003, Sch 1A. A draft of the proposed form of transfer or lease (with plan) for general use may be sent, in duplicate, to the appropriate Registry office for approval. This will ensure consistency and help avoid difficulties in connection with easements and the development generally. If the draft is approved, it should be used as the basis for all plot transfers or leases on the development.

Pre- and post-registration services on plot sales

Land Registry plans are based on the Ordnance Survey map and surveys of developing estates are made at frequent intervals so that the Registry's plans can be revised to show all new buildings, fences, roads and other physical features.

If a draft transfer or lease for the estate has been approved, the Registry will, where appropriate, supply a letter to the developer, which may be passed to purchasers, confirming that if easements are granted in the approved form they will be registered as appurtenant to the purchaser's title. This avoids the need for each purchaser to inspect the title plan to ensure that the developer has power to grant the easements.

Although a developer may have been under a duty to disclose any existing overriding interests when he was registered as proprietor of the land, it may be that further overriding interests may subsequently arise or come to light. If these affect more than one plot, they will have to be disclosed with each application to register a transfer or lease of an individual plot. There may therefore be an advantage in a developer applying voluntarily to enter a notice of the burden of any such overriding interests in the register where appropriate, before the development of the estate and sales of individual plots or flats commences (see *Overriding interests*, page 416).

For details of official copies and certificate of official inspection of the title plan, see *Official copies and inspection*, page 396.

DEVELOPING SCHEMES

Where a local authority or company or similar purchaser acquires a large extent of land in a piecemeal manner over a period of time, a request may be made to the Registry for each parcel of land to be incorporated into a single registered title, known as a 'developing scheme title', as and when it is acquired. This avoids the applicant becoming the proprietor of a large number of individual registered titles and subsequently having to request amalgamation of those titles. A developing scheme title may be appropriate where, for example, a local authority is in the process of acquiring a large number of individual properties by compulsory purchase, as part of a redevelopment scheme.

Development schemes have taken the place of 'scheme titles', and are based on revised registration processes. Existing scheme titles that are in progress and remain active will continue to be processed as agreed with the applicant.

The applicant will need to contact the Registry with all the relevant facts before a decision can be made as to whether a development scheme will be appropriate and what extent it will cover. The title to the land to be acquired may be wholly registered, wholly unregistered or a mixture of both.

On receipt of the first application to register a parcel of land within the proposed development, the Registry will allocate a title number. Subsequent additions will be made by amalgamation with this title. The Registry will register leasehold interests and rentcharges within the development scheme separately. When all the land has been acquired and added to the scheme, the applicant should inform the Registry that the scheme is complete, and as to whether or not the land within the scheme has been redeveloped, so that the Registry has the opportunity (if necessary) to complete a survey.

If the development scheme will constitute a large scale application, the applicant should initially contact a bulk application contact (see *Bulk applications*, page 83).

DISPUTES

Although the vast majority of applications to the Land Registry are completed without becoming contentious, provision is needed to enable the minority of cases, where an objection to an application is received from a third party, to be determined.

The Registry's internal dispute procedures may assist in resolving disputed applications, but ultimately it may be necessary for the matter to be determined judicially. This judicial determination may be carried out by the court or, on reference from the Registry, by the Tribunal (see *Tribunal*, page 555). Before 13 October 2003, objections and disputes were referred to the Solicitor to HM Land Registry, who was a senior lawyer within the Registry. The LRA 2002 instead created a new independent post of Adjudicator to Her Majesty's Land Registry (LRA 2002, s 107). On 1 July 2013 the functions of the Adjudicator were transferred to the Tribunal, the office of the Adjudicator was abolished and consequential amendments were made to the LRA 2002 (Transfer of Tribunal Functions Order 2013 (SI 2013/1036)).

Objections

In general anyone may object to an application to the Registry (LRA 2002, s 73(1)). This is, however, subject to the exceptions specified in s 73.

In the case of an application for the cancellation of a caution against first registration under LRA 2002, s 18, only the person who lodged the caution in question, or (where that person is not the person who lodged the caution) the person for the time being shown as cautioner in the cautioner's register, may object (LRA 2002, s 73(2) and LRR 2003, r 52). Where the cautioner shown in the cautioner's register comprises more than one person, each such person has a separate right to object to the cancellation of the caution (LRR 2003, r 52(2)).

In the case of an application for the cancellation of a unilateral notice under LRA 2002, s 36, only the person shown in the register as the beneficiary of the notice in question, or a person entitled to be registered as the beneficiary of that notice, may object (LRA 2002, s 73(3) and LRR 2003, r 86(7)). Where there are two or more persons shown in the register as the beneficiary of the unilateral notice, or two or more persons entitled to be registered as beneficiary, each such person has a right to object to the cancellation of the unilateral notice (LRR 2003, r 86(8)).

An objection to an application must be made by delivering to the Registry (at the appropriate local office) a written statement signed by the objector or his conveyancer (LRR 2003, r 19). The statement must state that the objector objects to the application, state the grounds for the objection and give the full name of the objector. If he wishes communications to be sent to an address other than his address for service, this should be stated. The objection may be delivered in paper form, or by email or by fax.

Where an objection is made the Registry must give notice of it to the applicant and may not determine the application until the objection has been disposed of.

An objection may be disposed of if it is withdrawn, or settled by agreement, or determined by a decision of the Tribunal or of the court. If, however, the Registry is satisfied that the objection is groundless, it need not give notice of it to the applicant and may determine the application (LRA 2002, s 73(5) and (6)).

A notice of objection served upon the applicant by the Registry will invite him to either withdraw his application or indicate that he wishes to proceed. If the applicant does not respond to the notice it will be assumed that he does not wish to proceed and the application will be cancelled. If the applicant indicates that he does wish to proceed, the parties will be allowed time to negotiate. In order to avoid long running, unresolved disputes the Registry allows 6 months for a disputed application to be resolved before it refers the matter to the Tribunal. Land Registry lawyers will be able to exercise a discretion to extend this period in exceptional, unavoidable circumstances when cogent reasons have been given for the need for additional time.

During the 6-month period the Registry will only contact the parties twice: once after 3 months of the 6-month period have elapsed, and again after 5 months have elapsed. On each occasion, it will ask if negotiations are continuing. If one or all of the parties say they are not, or do not reply, the Registry must refer the matter to the Tribunal (LRA 2002, s 73(7)).

Additionally, at the 5-month stage a draft case summary will be sent to the parties for comment in advance of the referral to the Tribunal being made at the end of the 6-month period. This provides brief details of the disputed application, which will be sent to the Tribunal as part of the referral process.

Referral to the Tribunal

Referral to the Tribunal is made under the provisions of the Land Registration (Referral to the Adjudicator to HM Land Registry) Rules 2003 (SI 2003/2114) (the Referral Rules). These rules were amended by the Transfer of Tribunal Functions Order 2013, to reflect the transfer of the functions of the Adjudicator to the Tribunal. The referral is effected by means of a written notice to the Tribunal informing it that the matter is being referred under LRA 2002, s 73(7), accompanied by a case summary and copies of the documents listed in that case summary (the Referral Rules, r 5(2) and (3)).

The Registry prepares the case summary which is sent to the Tribunal. This must contain the names and addresses of the parties, details of their legal or other representatives, a summary of the core facts, details of the disputed application, details of the objection, a list of any documents that will be copied to the Tribunal, and any other information the Registry considers appropriate (the Referral Rules, r 3(2)). Before sending the case summary to the Tribunal, the Registry must send a copy of it and a list of the accompanying documents to the parties, who may comment on anything in it. The Registry may amend the summary in the light of any comments, but is not required to do so. The case summary does not form part of the pleadings in the proceedings before the Tribunal and does not set out the parties' detailed arguments or deal with their evidence. However, it may be used by the Tribunal to assist in the identification of the matter referred to it for determination.

When the case summary has been finalised the Registry will send it, with copies of the documents listed in it, to the Tribunal under cover of the written notice informing it that the matter is being referred to the Tribunal under s 73(7). The provisions relating to withdrawal of a case which has been referred to the Tribunal are considered in the next paragraph.

Once a matter has been referred to the Tribunal, an objector cannot bring the proceedings to an end by simply withdrawing his objection, as the matter is thenceforth within the jurisdiction of the Tribunal, not the Registry (*Chief Land Registrar and Silkstone v Tatnall* [2011] EWCA Civ 801). It would appear that a similar principle would apply in relation to a withdrawal of the application itself.

Determination by the Tribunal

The Tribunal will deal with the matter in accordance with the Tribunal Procedure (First-tier Tribunal) (Property Chamber) Rules 2013 (SI 2013/1169) (the Tribunal Rules), the overriding objective of which is to enable the Tribunal to deal with matters fairly and justly.

The case summary gives the Tribunal sufficient information to allow it to make an initial decision as to whether it will hear the case. The Tribunal may, instead of deciding a matter itself, direct a party to the dispute to commence proceedings in court, within a specified period, for the purpose of obtaining the court's decision on the matter (LRA 2002, s 110(1)). In that case, the proceedings before the Tribunal are automatically stayed pending the outcome of the court proceedings. Following a final decision by the court, the Tribunal proceedings are to be regarded as stayed (except in relation to any question of costs), although the Tribunal may make a decision, including as to the lifting of such a stay, if such a decision is necessary to implement the final court order (the Tribunal Rules, r 39).

The Tribunal Rules make provision for either of the parties to give notice of withdrawal of his case or any part of it, either orally at a hearing or by lodging with the Tribunal a written notice of withdrawal (the Tribunal Rules, r 22). The notice of withdrawal will not take effect unless the Tribunal consents to the withdrawal. The Tribunal may make such directions or impose such conditions on withdrawal as it considers appropriate. Application may be made for re-instatement of a case, or part of it, subject to certain time limits as set out in r 22.

The Tribunal has broad case management powers and may give directions to enable the parties to prepare for a hearing or to assist the Tribunal to conduct the proceedings or determine any question in the proceedings with or without a hearing (the Tribunal Rules, r 6). The Tribunal may impose a sanction upon a party who fails to comply with a direction, including a sanction that the application be cancelled in whole or part or that the Registry should give effect to the application as if the objection had not been made, as the case may be (the Tribunal Rules, r 8). Also, the Tribunal has power to stay proceedings.

The parties will each be required to provide to the Tribunal and each other party a statement of case and copies of the documents referred to in it (the Tribunal Rules, rr 28 and 30). The Tribunal has power to strike out a party's case in certain circumstances, including where the Tribunal considers that the applicant or respondent has no reasonable prospect of succeeding in the proceedings (the Tribunal Rules, r 9).

The Tribunal will normally hold a hearing, although in some circumstances it can also determine a dispute without holding a hearing. Hearings before the Tribunal must be held in public, except where the Tribunal gives a direction that a hearing (or part of it) is to be held in private (the Tribunal Rules, r 33).

The Tribunal may make an order for costs in proceedings before it (the Tribunal Rules, r 13).

The Tribunal may, at the request of the parties but only if it considers it appropriate, make a consent order disposing of the proceedings and making such other appropriate provision as the parties have agreed (the Tribunal Rules, r 35).

The Tribunal must provide to each party as soon as reasonably practicable after making a decision which finally disposes of all issues in the proceedings (or of a preliminary issue):

(a) a decision notice stating the Tribunal's decision;
(b) written reasons for the decision; and
(c) notification of any right of appeal against the decision and the time within which, and the manner in which, such right of appeal may be exercised (the Tribunal Rules, r 36).

The Tribunal must send written notice to the Registry of any direction which requires the Registry to take action (the Tribunal Rules, r 40). Where the Tribunal has made a decision, that decision may include a direction to the Registry to:

(a)   give effect to the original application in whole or in part as if the objection to that original application had not been made; or
(b)   cancel the original application in whole or in part.

Such a direction must be in writing, must be sent or delivered to the Registry and may include:

(a)   a condition that a specified entry be made on the register of any title affected; or
(b)   a direction to reject any future application of a specified kind by a named party to the proceedings either unconditionally or unless that party satisfies specified conditions.

If a decision does not need to be served by the Tribunal upon the Registry then the parties should send a copy of the decision to the Registry so that it can take any appropriate action in the light of it.

A requirement of the Tribunal is enforceable as an order of the court (LRA 2002, s 112).

The Tribunal Rules, r 50 provides a conventional 'slip rule'. Rule 51 allows the Tribunal to set aside a decision (or part of a decision) which disposes of proceedings if it is in the interests of justice to do so and one of a number of conditions is fulfilled, such as a document not being received by the Tribunal at the appropriate time or other procedural irregularity.

A person aggrieved by a decision of the Tribunal may appeal to the Upper Tribunal, subject to permission to appeal being granted by the Tribunal. When applying for permission to appeal, a party may at the same time apply for a stay of the implementation of the decision. An appeal (other than on a point of law) arises under LRA 2002, s 111; an appeal on a point of law arises under Tribunals, Courts and Enforcement Act 2007, s 11.

Where, in determining a dispute relating to an application under LRA 2002, Sch 6, para 1 for the registration of a person who has been in adverse possession of registered land, the Tribunal determines that it would be unconscionable because of an equity by estoppel for the registered proprietor to seek to dispossess the applicant, but that the circumstances are not such that the applicant ought to be registered as proprietor, the Tribunal must determine how the equity due to the applicant is to be satisfied. It may for that purpose make any order that the High Court could make in the exercise of its equitable jurisdiction (LRA 2002, s 110(4)).

If, on an appeal to the High Court relating to an application under LRA 2002, Sch 6, para 1 for the registration of a person who has been in adverse possession of registered land, the court determines that it would be unconscionable because of an equity by estoppel for the registered proprietor to seek to dispossess the applicant, but that the circumstances are not such that the applicant ought to be registered as proprietor, the court must determine how the equity due to the applicant is to be satisfied (LRA 2002, s 111(3)).

Rectification of documents

The Tribunal may also, on application, make any order which the High Court could make for the rectification or setting aside of a document which:

(a) effects a registrable disposition of a registered estate or registered charge;
(b) effects a disposition in respect of a registered estate or registered charge which creates an interest which may be the subject of a notice in the register;
(c) is a contract to make a disposition falling within (a) or (b) above; or
(d) effects a transfer of an interest which is the subject of a notice in the register (LRA 2002, s 108(2) and (3)).

Any such application must be made direct to the Tribunal and not to the Registry. The general law about the effect of an order of the High Court for the rectification or setting aside of a document applies to any such order of the Tribunal (LRA 2002, s 108(4)).

DIVISION OF REGISTERED TITLES

It may sometimes be necessary or desirable for a registered title to be divided. LRR 2003, r 3 provides that on first registration, the Registry may open an individual register for each separate area of land affected by the proprietor's registered estate as it designates. Subsequently, the Registry may open an individual register for part of the registered estate in a registered title and retain the existing register for the remainder. Such a subsequent division of a registered title may be as the result of an application by the proprietor of the registered estate and of any registered charge over it; or because the Registry considers it desirable for the keeping of the register of title; or on the registration of a charge of part of the registered title (LRR 2003, r 3(3)). The Registry's power to divide a title is always discretionary, even in relation to charges of part. Thus an application for division may be refused where it relates to land which is being developed as a residential estate and the division would result in a 'fractured' title making official searches and registrations in respect of transfers of individual plots more difficult.

An application by the proprietor which does not relate to a charge of part should be made in Form AP1. It should be accompanied by a plan identifying the division sought. For the position where the application is for a charge of part, see *Legal charges*, page 333.

Where the proprietor has not made an application but division is effected because the Registry considers it desirable for the keeping of the register of title, the Registry must notify the proprietor of the registered estate and of any registered charge, unless they have agreed to the division. In these circumstances the Registry may make a new edition of any individual register or make entries on any individual register to reflect the division (LRR 2003, r 3(5)).

LRR 2003, r 70 will apply on division where a registered estate in land includes any mines or minerals but there is no note in the register that they are included, and it is appropriate, when describing any of the registered estates created on division, to do so by reference to the land where the mines or minerals are or may be situated. In such circumstances the Registry may make an entry in the property register to the effect that such description is an entry made under LRR 2003, r 5(a) and is not a note that the registered estate includes the mines or minerals for the purposes of extending the provision for payment of indemnity under the LRA 2002, Sch 8, para 2 to such mines or minerals. LRR, rule 5(a) provides that the property register must contain a description of the registered estate (see *Mines and minerals*, page 380).

ELECTRONIC SERVICES

The LRA 2002 contains provisions which authorise the establishment of a Land Registry network to facilitate a system of e-conveyancing (LRA 2002, ss 91 to 95 and Sch 5). Various consultation exercises on such a system have been carried out by the Registry in recent years, as a result of which it has been concluded that the system should be introduced in stages over a period of time rather than in one major change.

The Registry's 'Business e-services' are accessed through the Land Registry portal, which is the Registry's web-based electronic channel, and are divided into three service groups each governed by an agreement between the Registry and the user:

(a) 'Information Services' provide online access to information about the register, title plan and day list. These can be used to lodge searches of the index map with supporting plans, official searches of whole or part and outline applications, and to conduct land charges and bankruptcy searches in the Land Charges Department. There is no interaction with the register.

(b) 'Network Services' are available to users who have applied for and been granted a network access agreement. These permit the creation and lodgment of e-documents and electronic substantive applications directly with the Registry. This includes the facility to use e-signatures, where appropriate and for the electronic attachment of supporting documents and certificates of compliance, if necessary. A subscriber to Network Services also has access to Information Services. Network access agreements are dealt with in LRA 2002, s 92 and Sch 5 and the Land Registration (Network Access) Rules 2008 (SI 2008/1748).

(c) 'Lender Services' provides an automated discharge service that allows mortgage lenders, or their appointed agents, to lodge electronic applications to discharge registered charges (see 'Discharge of registered charge', page 340).

The Registry's electronic Document Registration Service (known as e-DRS) is available through its portal and also through its 'business to business' channel called 'Business Gateway'. By using the e-DRS, applicants who would otherwise submit postal applications are able to submit the majority of them electronically through the portal. The system is intended to provide a number of benefits, such as increased speed, reduced costs and environmental impact and also an electronic audit trail which can provide a useful tool in the prevention of fraud.

Business e-services have been developed for business users and are not available to individual members of the public. Instead, the Registry provides a range of services for use by the general public collectively known as *'Find a property'*. Copies of title registers, title plans and Flood Risk Indicator results for more than 22 million registered properties in England and Wales can be purchased and downloaded as part of these services.

Due to the increasing demand for electronic services, to enable conveyancing and registration to be carried out entirely online, the LRR 2003 were amended with effect from 6 April 2018 to provide more flexibility for the introduction of new electronic conveyancing and registration services. LRR 2003, rr 54A to 54D specify that all transactions of registered land that have to be registered can be carried out using electronic documents with electronic signatures, once the registrar is satisfied that adequate arrangements are in place, and publishes a notice to that effect. This allows for the incremental introduction of new digital conveyancing and registration services (such as a new digital mortgage service), without rule changes for each new service.

Up-to-date information is available on the Land Registry's website at www.gov.uk/government/publications.

EMBANKMENTS OR SEA OR RIVER WALLS

Liabilities in respect of embankments or sea or river walls include, but are not limited to, the liabilities of owners whose properties front the sea or a river to repair and maintain sea walls and river banks. Until 12 October 2013, the benefit of a non-statutory right in respect of an embankment or sea or river wall was an unregistered interest which overrode first registration and registered dispositions (LRA 2002, ss 11, 12, 29 and 30, Sch 1, para 13 and Sch 3, para 13). In order to take effect as interests which overrode, liabilities in respect of embankments and sea and river walls must have arisen by proprietary means; that is, by virtue of custom, prescription, grant, a covenant supported by a rentcharge, or tenure (see *London & North-Western Railway Co v Fobbing Sewers Commissioners* [1896] 75 LT 629).

A contractual obligation, not being proprietary (see *Eton Rural District Council v Thames Conservators* [1950] Ch 540), was not an interest which overrode. Nor was a liability imposed by statute; for example one arising under the Coast Protection Act 1949, the Land Drainage Act 1991 or Water Resources Act 1991, Pt VI.

On first registration of title, the Registry will enter a notice in the register as to the burden of such a right, if it appears from its examination of the title to affect the land. Until 12 October 2013 there was a duty to disclose a non-statutory right in respect of an embankment or sea or river wall under LRR 2003, r 28 or s 57 (see 'Duty to disclose overriding interests', page 426).

After the period of 10 years beginning on 13 October 2003, the automatic protection as an overriding interest ceased (LRA 2002, s 117(1)).The person having the benefit of the right (if its priority has not already been previously defeated and it continues to subsist) should therefore protect it in the register. If he does not do so, the priority of the right is liable to be defeated on a subsequent first registration of unregistered burdened land or on a subsequent registration of a registrable disposition of registered burdened land for valuable consideration (LRA 2002, ss 11, 12, 29 and 30), as the case may be. If the burdened land is unregistered he should apply for a caution against first registration. If the burdened land is registered he should apply for the entry in the register of a notice.

Until 12 October 2013, no fee was payable for such an application, but the normal fee will now apply.

Caution against first registration

A person applying for a caution against first registration should deliver to the Registry the usual documents required (see *Cautions against first registration*, page 88).

The statement of truth in panel 10 of Form CT1 should be completed on the following lines to show the interest of the applicant:

> the person entitled to enforce a liability [*to repair*] or [*to contribute towards the cost of repair*] of [*specify the embankment or wall in question*] arising by reason of [*summarise the basis on which the interest arises*] and payable by [*specify relevant details*].

The interest stated in the Form CT1 will appear in the caution register, together with a description of the legal estate to which the caution relates. For the effect of the caution against first registration, see *Cautions against first registration*, page 88.

Agreed notice

An applicant should deliver to the Registry the usual documents required (see *Notices*, page 389).

Documentary evidence of the creation or existence of the non-statutory right in respect of an embankment or sea or river wall will normally be in the form of a statutory declaration or statement of truth containing details of how the right arose and how it has devolved to the applicant.

The agreed notice in the register will give details of the interest protected.

Where the registered proprietor does not consent to the entry in the register of an agreed notice and evidence to satisfy the Registry as to the validity of the applicant's claim cannot be lodged, an application for entry of a unilateral notice may still be made.

Unilateral notice

An applicant should deliver to the Registry the usual documents required (see *Notices*, page 389).

The statement in panel 11 or conveyancer's certificate in panel 12 of Form UN1 should be completed on the following lines to show the interest of the applicant:

> the person entitled to enforce a liability [*to repair*] or [*to contribute towards the cost of repair*] of [*specify the embankment or wall in question*] arising by reason of [*summarise the basis on which the interest arises*] and payable by [*specify relevant details*].

The unilateral notice in the register will give brief details of the interest protected and identify the beneficiary of that notice.

ENLARGEMENT OF LONG LEASES

A lease originally created for a term of not less than 300 years of which at least 200 years remain unexpired may, if it meets the other requirements in Law of Property Act 1925, s 153, be enlarged into a fee simple. The other requirements in s 153 are:

(a)   there must not be any trust or right of redemption affecting the term in favour of the owner of the reversionary estate;

(b)   there must not be any rent payable other than a peppercorn or other rent having no monetary value; or, a rent having been payable (not being a peppercorn rent or other rent having no monetary value), the rent has been released or become barred by lapse of time, or has in any other way ceased to be payable; and

(c)   there must not be any right of re-entry affecting the leasehold estate or any superior leasehold estate out of which it was created.

Enlargement cannot be effected where the lease sought to be enlarged is an underlease and the headlease is itself incapable of enlargement. A yearly rent not exceeding £1 that has not been collected or paid for 20 years or more is deemed to have ceased to be payable (Law of Property Act 1925, s 153(4)).

In a majority of cases, leases which are capable of enlargement tend to be of relatively ancient origin. This reflects the fact that many such leases were deliberately granted in certain areas in order to avoid extending the voting franchise, as formerly only freeholders were entitled to vote. However, some modern leases may also be capable of enlargement; in these cases, the landlord may have granted a long lease instead of conveying the freehold, in an attempt to ensure that positive covenants, which do not normally bind successors in title of a freehold estate, continue to run with the land.

The enlargement is usually effected by either the execution of a deed poll or endorsement on one of the unregistered title deeds. On enlargement, the land remains subject to the same trusts and covenants that affected the original lease.

Where the conditions for enlargement are not met, it may still be possible to acquire the freehold under the Leasehold Reform Act 1967 (see *Leasehold enfranchisement*, page 291).

Leasehold title unregistered

Where the existing leasehold title is unregistered (regardless of whether or not the freehold estate is registered), in addition to the usual documents required (see *First registration*, page 222), an applicant should deliver to the Registry:

(a) the lease or a certified copy or examined abstract of it; and
(b) (where applicable) a statutory declaration or statement of truth as to non-payment of the rent over a period of 20 years, where it is necessary to show that a rent not exceeding £1 is deemed to have ceased to be payable.

Where the freehold title is registered, whether or not the lease is the subject of a notice in the register, that freehold title will not be closed. Instead, the Registry will leave the existing freehold title open and enter a note in the property register confirming that if the effect of the enlargement is to determine the former landlord's estate, then the estate has determined. This practice reflects the fact that the effect of enlargement under s 153 upon the landlord's legal estate is uncertain and in particular as to whether it extinguishes the landlord's estate or whether the landlord's estate continues alongside the tenant's new freehold estate. Previously, the practice of the Registry was to close the former landlord's title.

On completion of the application for registration, an entry is made in the property register of the new freehold title to show that the fee simple has been acquired by enlargement and is therefore subject to the matters set out in Law of Property Act 1925, s 153(8). The entry will instead refer to Conveyancing and Law of Property Act 1881, s 65(4), if the date of the deed of enlargement is prior to 1 January 1926. Any charges or other relevant entries affecting the leasehold title will be reflected in the charges register of the new freehold title.

Where the applicant is unable to produce full details of the lease so that it is not certain that the conditions for enlargement have been met, the Registry may refuse an application for enlargement; for example where it is not clear whether the lease was originally created for a term of not less than 300 years of which at least 200 years remain unexpired. In some cases, the Registry will accept the application for enlargement, but will only grant a qualified class of title (see *Classes of title*, page 130). In such a case, the qualification shown in the proprietorship register will be on the following lines:

> As neither the Lease dated *[date]* referred to in the Property Register nor full evidence of its contents was produced on first registration it is possible that the term was not capable of being enlarged. There are excepted from the effect of registration all estates rights and interests vested in any other person or persons if and so far as the enlargement was ineffective.

This entry (which will be in addition to that referring to the matters set out in Law of Property Act 1925, s 153(8) specified above) makes clear that the registered title is subject to all estates rights and interests vested in any other person or persons if and so far as the enlargement was ineffective. The previous practice of the Registry under the LRA 1925, of granting an absolute title but subject to a qualification in the above form, no longer applies under the LRA 2002.

Leasehold title registered

Where the existing leasehold title is registered (regardless of whether or not the freehold estate is registered), an applicant should deliver to the Registry:

(a)   an application in Form AP1;
(b)   the deed of enlargement or a certified copy of it;
(c)   the lease or a certified copy or examined abstract of it;
(d)   (if applicable) a statutory declaration or statement of truth as to non-payment of the rent over a period of 20 years, where it is necessary to show that a rent not exceeding £1 is deemed to have ceased to be payable; and
(e)   the fee payable (see *Fees*, page 221).

Where the freehold title is registered, whether or not the lease is the subject of a notice in the register, that freehold title will not be closed. Instead, the Registry will leave the existing freehold title open and enter a note in the property register confirming that if the effect of the enlargement is to determine the former landlord's estate, then the estate has determined. This practice reflects the fact that the effect of enlargement under s 153 upon the landlord's legal estate is uncertain as to whether it extinguishes the landlord's estate or whether the landlord's estate continues alongside the tenant's new freehold estate. Previously, the practice of the Registry was to close the former landlord's title.

On completion of the application for registration, if the leasehold title is already registered, it will be closed. An entry is made in the property register of the new freehold title to show that the fee simple has been acquired by enlargement and is therefore subject to the matters set out in Law of Property Act 1925, s 153(8). The entry will instead refer to Conveyancing and Law of Property Act 1881, s 65(4), if (unusually) the date of the deed of enlargement is prior to 1 January 1926. Any charges or other relevant incumbrances affecting the leasehold title will be reflected in the charges register of the new freehold title.

EQUITABLE CHARGES

An equitable charge (or mortgage) may arise where, for example, the charge is created in writing other than by deed; or if it charges only an equitable interest; or if it takes effect as a contract to create a legal mortgage. Where the land is registered, the creation of such a charge on the land is not a registrable disposition which is required to be completed by registration. Where an equitable charge on land is created and the charged land is unregistered, that charge will need to be protected by way of a Land Charge (normally Class C(iii)). An equitable charge can also arise in relation to registered land where, although it is created by deed and is capable of registration as a legal charge, it cannot be completed by registration. This could occur where, for example, there is a restriction in the register requiring the consent of a prior chargee to the registration and that consent is not forthcoming. The grant of a legal charge of registered land must be completed by registration (LRA 2002, s 27(2)(f)) and until then it takes effect as an equitable charge of the legal estate. On registration it becomes a legal charge and the chargee is entered in the register as proprietor of the registered charge (LRA 2002, Sch 2, para 8).

A charge which takes effect in equity only cannot be substantively registered as a registered charge. A person who has obtained an equitable charge against the legal estate in registered land may apply for the entry in the register of a notice in respect of the equitable charge. The equitable chargee is not able to apply for an official search with priority using Form OS1 or Form OS2, but may reserve a period of priority by making an outline application.

Where an equitable charge is in respect only of a beneficial interest in registered land held under a trust of land, a notice cannot be entered in the register (LRA 2002, s 33(a)). In that case it is possible to apply for the entry of a restriction. A restriction does not confer any priority; it simply prevents an entry being made in the register in respect of any disposition, or a disposition of a specified kind, unless the terms of the restriction have (where applicable) been complied with.

An application for a notice may be for an agreed notice or a unilateral notice. In the case of an application for an agreed notice, the Registry may approve the application without the consent of the proprietor where it is satisfied of the validity of the applicant's claim. A unilateral notice may be preferred where the applicant does not wish the terms of the charge to be open to public inspection and copying.

Agreed notice

In addition to the usual documents required (see *Notices*, page 389), an applicant should deliver to the Registry the equitable charge or a certified copy of it.

Where the consent of the registered proprietor is not available but, for example, the equitable charge is signed by him, this is likely to be sufficient to satisfy the Registry as to the validity of the applicant's claim in accordance with LRA 2002, s 34(3)(c).

The agreed notice in the register will give details of the interest protected.

If the equitable charge is subsequently discharged, an application in Form CN1 to cancel the agreed notice should be made, accompanied by an appropriate form of receipt or other evidence of the discharge. This may consist of either a Form DS1 or Form DS3; or an endorsed receipt on the instrument of charge; or a letter from the chargee addressed to the Registry, confirming that the charge has been satisfied and including where appropriate confirmation that there has been no assignment of the benefit of the charge. If an assignment has been made, the normal conveyancing evidence of devolution of title should be lodged.

Unilateral notice

An applicant should deliver to the Registry the usual documents required (see *Notices*, page 389).

The statement in panel 11 or conveyancer's certificate in panel 12 of Form UN1 should be completed on the following lines to show the interest of the applicant:

equitable chargee under [*specify the document creating the equitable charge*] dated [*date*] and made between [*registered proprietor*] and [*beneficiary of the unilateral notice*].

The unilateral notice in the register will give brief details of the interest protected and identify the beneficiary of that notice.

If the equitable charge is subsequently discharged, an application to cancel the unilateral notice in Form UN2 should be made by the beneficiary of the notice. If the beneficiary fails to do so, the registered proprietor of the land may apply in Form UN4 for the cancellation of the unilateral notice (see *Notices*, page 389).

Restriction where the equitable charge is over a beneficial interest

If there is no restriction in Form A in the register, a person having the benefit of an equitable charge over a beneficial interest under a trust of land has a sufficient interest for the purposes of LRA 2002, s 43(1)(c) to apply for entry of a restriction in Form A to ensure that a survivor of the joint proprietors (unless a trust corporation) will not be able to give a valid receipt for capital money (LRR 2003, r 93(a)). The wording of Form A is set out in Appendix IV, page 585.

This restriction does not of itself prevent a disposition, provided it is complied with. This is because the interest of the person having the benefit of the equitable charge will be overreached where the requirements of Form A have been met (Law of Property Act 1925, ss 2 and 27).

The Registry must give notice of an application for a restriction to the proprietor of the registered estate concerned, if it has not been made by or with his consent or a person entitled to be registered as such proprietor (LRA 2002, s 45).

No other form of restriction may be applied for, because such a charge is not a right or claim in relation to a registered estate within LRA 2002, s 42(1)(c) – it is a right or claim in relation to the beneficial interest under a trust of land and not in relation to the registered estate. Such a charge does not fall within the exception applicable to charging orders, which may be protected by entry of a restriction in Form K (see *Charging orders*, page 100).

In addition to the usual documents required (see *Restrictions*, page 500), if applying for a restriction in Form A, the person having the benefit of an equitable charge over a beneficial interest under a trust of land should deliver to the Registry the equitable charge or a certified copy of it.

No fee is payable where the application is in respect of a restriction in Form A only.

The statement in panel 12 or conveyancer's certificate in panel 13 of Form RX1 should be completed on the following lines:

> The interest is that specified in rule 93(a) of the Land Registration Rules 2003, the applicant having the benefit of a charge over a beneficial interest in the registered estate.

Panel 9 of Form RX1 should be completed as to the wording of Form A, as set out above. A restriction in a standard Form A in LRR 2003, Sch 4 does not require the approval of the Registry to the terms of the restriction under LRA 2002, s 43(3).

Priority of equitable charges

There are no specific provisions in the LRA 2002 dealing with the priority of competing equitable charges. In the light of the basic rule as to priorities set out in LRA 2002, s 28, the priority of such charges accords with the dates when they were created, the first in time having priority. The priority of such charges in relation to registered dispositions (including the grant of a legal charge) for valuable consideration will be governed by the special rule of priority set out in LRA 2002, s 29 (see *Priorities*, page 452).

Orders under Law of Property Act 1925, s 90

Where an order for sale is made by the court in reference to an equitable mortgage on land, the court may, in favour of a purchaser, make a vesting order conveying the land; or appoint a person to convey the land; or create and vest in the mortgagee a legal term of years absolute to enable him to carry out the sale (Law of Property Act 1925, s 90).

If the court has made a vesting order transferring registered land, this must be completed by registration (LRA 2002, s 27). The applicant should, in addition to the usual documents required in the case of a transfer (see *Transfers*, page 551), deliver to the Registry the court order or a sealed copy of that order or a certified copy of it.

If the court has made an order appointing a person to convey the land, that order, or a sealed copy of it, should be lodged in support of the application to register a transfer executed by that person.

Where the court has made an order vesting in the equitable mortgagee a legal term of years absolute to enable him to carry out a sale, the charge takes the form of a demise. The demise is usually for 3,000 years if a freehold estate has been charged or, if a leasehold estate has been charged, for one day less than the original term granted by the lease. If a leasehold estate is being charged, care should therefore be taken that the term of the demise does not extend beyond the term granted in the lease.

Although LRA 2002, s 23(1)(a) removed the power of the owner of a registered estate to create a mortgage by demise or sub-demise, this does not affect the ability of the courts to do so. Such a charge created by the court order would appear to be a registrable disposition which is required to be completed by registration (LRA 2002, s 27(2)(f) and(5)); it must therefore be substantively registered if it is to take effect at law.

The mortgagee should deliver to the Registry:

(a)   an application in Form AP1;
(b)   the court order or a sealed copy of that order or a certified copy of it; and
(c)   the fee payable (see *Fees*, page 221).

However, as s 90 provides that the mortgage will take effect 'as if the mortgage had been created by deed by way of legal mortgage', the registered estate can effectively be transferred under the power of sale without the mortgage created under s 90 being registered. This reflects the decision in *Swift 1st Limited v Colin* [2011] EWHC 2410 (Ch), which provides that if a charge of the registered estate is by deed expressed to be by way of legal mortgage but is not completed by registration, the chargee still has a statutory power of sale. The sale will override all rights over which the charge has priority and the transfer will be of the registered estate. A copy of the order of the court under Law of Property Act 1925, s 90 must accompany an application to register a transfer made under the chargee's power of sale in such circumstances. As to the exercise of a power of sale, see *Legal charges*, page 333.

In determining the priority of a mortgage created under Law of Property Act 1925, s 90, account would need to be taken of the wording in s 90(1) which states that the creation of the mortgage is 'without prejudice to any encumbrance having priority to the equitable mortgage' and also the effect of LRA 2002, ss 28 and 29. In some circumstances, the mortgage may have priority over an existing registered charge shown in the register. For example, if the mortgage under s 90 was created in respect of a charging order which pre-dated the registered charge and its priority had been protected by a notice in the register for the purposes of LRA 2002, s 29 when the registered charge was registered, the mortgage under s

90 would appear to have priority over the existing registered charge. That priority would need to be reflected by an entry in the register pursuant to LRA 2002, s 48 and LRR 2003, r 101. The Registry would, before making such an entry, serve notice on the registered proprietor of the existing registered charge unless he had consented to the making of the entry (LRR 2003, r 128).

EQUITABLE EASEMENTS

If an easement is granted or reserved in writing other than by deed, or other than for a period equivalent to a fee simple absolute in possession or a term of years absolute, it will be equitable. Where the burdened land is registered, the grant or reservation of such an easement is not a registrable disposition which is required to be completed by registration. Where an easement is granted or reserved and the burdened land is unregistered, that easement will need to be protected by way of a Class D(iii) Land Charge. Equitable easements can arise in relation to leases as well as freehold land; if the lease is merely in writing but not by deed, any easement granted or reserved within it can only be equitable. The express grant or reservation of a legal easement out of registered land must be completed by registration (LRA 2002, s 27(2)(d)) and until then it takes effect as an equitable easement. On registration it becomes a legal easement and a notice of it is entered in the register of the servient land (LRA 2002, Sch 2, para 7).

As to the benefit of equitable easements, the LRA 2002 makes provision only for the registration of legal interests (LRA 2002, s 2) and therefore the Registry will not enter the benefit of an equitable interest in the register of the benefiting estate, either on first registration or subsequently.

As to the burden of equitable easements, this will, if it is disclosed within the application, be the subject of a notice in the register on first registration of the burdened estate (LRR 2003, r 35). If the burdened estate is already registered, an application may be made to enter an agreed notice or a unilateral notice in respect of the burden of the equitable easement.

Where an equitable easement is granted in a transfer, lease or other disposition of registered land, the Registry will enter a notice of the burden of the easement in the register of a registered burdened estate, providing the title number is entered in panel 2 of the Form AP1, or clause LR2.2 in the case of a prescribed clauses lease; otherwise, a separate application must be made (LRR 2003, rr 72(4) and (5), 72A(4) and 72C(2) and (3)).

Before the coming into force of the LRA 2002 on 13 October 2003, equitable easements that were openly exercised and enjoyed as appurtenant to the dominant tenement could take effect as overriding interests on the registered servient title under Land Registration Rules 1925, r 258 (*Celsteel Ltd v Alton House Holdings Ltd* [1985] 2 All ER 562). By virtue of transitional provisions, any such equitable easement which was an overriding interest in relation to a registered estate immediately before 13 October 2003 is treated as an unregistered interest which overrides registered dispositions within LRA 2002, Sch 3, para 3 (LRA 2002, Sch 12 para 9).

All other equitable easements are not interests which override either first registration under Sch 1 or registered dispositions under LRA 2002, Sch 3 and must therefore be protected by way of notice in the register. The overriding status conferred by LRA 2002, Sch 1, para 3 and Sch 3, para 3 relates only to legal easements.

Agreed notice

In addition to the usual documents required (see *Notices*, page 389), an applicant should deliver to the Registry the document creating the equitable easement or a certified copy of it.

Where the consent of the registered proprietor is not available but, for example, the document creating the easement is signed by him, this is likely to be sufficient to satisfy the Registry as to the validity of the applicant's claim in accordance with LRA 2002, s 34(3)(c).

The agreed notice in the register will give details of the interest protected.

Unilateral notice

An applicant should deliver to the Registry the usual documents required (see *Notices*, page 389).

The statement in panel 11 or conveyancer's certificate in panel 12 of Form UN1 should be completed on the following lines to show the interest of the applicant:

> the person having the benefit of an equitable right of [*specify the easement*] created by a [*description of document*] dated [*date*] and made between [*parties*].

The unilateral notice in the register will give brief details of the interest protected and identify the beneficiary of that notice.

EQUITABLE INTERESTS

Any interest in land that does not qualify as a legal estate or interest is an equitable interest (Law of Property Act 1925, s 1(3)). Equitable interests include, for example:

(a)   the interest of a beneficiary under a trust;
(b)   interests arising under a contract for sale;
(c)   interests that do not meet the formal requirements for the creation of a legal interest (for example an easement not created by deed); and
(d)   restrictive covenants.

The benefit of equitable interests cannot be registered. However, the burden of the interest can be protected by the entry of a notice and/or restriction (as appropriate) in the register of an affected registered title (see *Notices*, page 389, and *Restrictions*, page 500).

ESTATE, RIGHT OR INTEREST

When a vendor has doubts as to his title to a piece of land, he may convey or transfer it for such 'estate, right or interest (if any)' as he may have in it. For example, he may believe either that he has lost, or is losing, his title to the land by adverse possession; or conversely that he has recently acquired, or is in the process of acquiring, title to the land by adverse possession. A conveyance containing such wording would not be a good root of title to such land, since a good root must show nothing to cast doubt on the title of the disposing party.

Where the land conveyed or transferred for 'estate right or interest' is unregistered, any application for first registration of title to it should be supported by sufficient evidence to show title to that land. This is normally by way of statutory declaration or statement of truth; for example a statement of truth in Form ST1 in LRR 2003, Sch 4. Even though the title is open to objection, it may still be registered with absolute freehold, absolute leasehold, or good leasehold title (as the case may be) if the Registry is of the opinion that the defect will not cause the holding under the title to be disturbed (LRA 2002, ss 9(3) and 10(4)) (see *Classes of title*, page 130).

However, if a third party is in possession of the land and the applicant for first registration cannot account for that possession (for example, by providing details of a subsisting lease or licence granted by the applicant or his predecessor in title), the Registry may not be prepared to grant any class of title in respect of that land and will exclude it from the registered title.

A vendor may convey or transfer his 'estate right or interest' in land where he is in adverse possession of the land but has been so for less than the requisite period. Where an applicant for first registration has not been in adverse possession for the requisite period under the Limitation Act 1980, no class of title can be granted. Similarly, where a person has not been in adverse possession for the requisite period specified in LRA 2002, Sch 6, no application to be registered as proprietor of a registered estate in land can be made under that Schedule (see *Adverse possession*, page 11).

EUROPEAN ECONOMIC INTEREST GROUPINGS

A European Economic Interest Grouping (EEIG) is formed of two or more legal bodies or natural persons, which have their central administrations or carry on their principal activities in different member states of the European Union. They are intended to be an alternative way to establish links in other EU countries without losing the individual identity of the members. Advantages of EEIGs include the greater flexibility of financing, which makes it easier for non-profit-making organisations to join; the main disadvantage is the unlimited joint and several liability of its members. An EEIG must have at least two members from different EU states and can be formed by companies, firms or other legal entities and, in certain circumstances, individuals. It must have a registered office within the EU. UK-registered EEIGs may not use the words 'Limited', 'Unlimited' or 'Public Limited Company' (or their Welsh equivalents) in their name.

The contract of formation of an EEIG must include the name of the grouping followed by an EEIG identifier; the official address; the objects of the grouping; the name, business name, permanent address or registered office and number and place of registration of any member of the grouping; and its duration, unless it is indefinite. The contract must be filed at the companies registry of the member state in which the 'official address' is situated; for official addresses in England and Wales, the registration authority is the Companies Registry in Cardiff, and for official addresses in Scotland it is the Companies Registry in Edinburgh.

An EEIG registered in the United Kingdom is a body corporate, whether or not it is treated so in the country of registration (European Economic Interest Grouping Regulations 1989 (SI 1989/638), reg 3). Only the manager (or, where there are two or more, each of the managers) may represent the EEIG in respect of dealings with third parties (Council Regulation (EEC) No 2137/85, art 20). Where the manager is not a natural person it must designate one or more natural persons to represent it (European Economic Interest Grouping Regulations 1989, reg 5). Accordingly execution of a deed by an EEIG should be on the following lines:

> Signed as a deed by [*name of natural person*] the [sole] *or* [*joint*] [*representative of the*] manager(s) of [*name of EEIG*] in the presence of ...

An application to register an EEIG as the proprietor of a registered estate or of a registered charge should be supported by the usual documentation, accompanied by the result of a recent search in the Companies Registry against the EEIG and evidence of appointment of the manager or the natural person designated as representative.

In view of the nature of an EEIG and the restrictions on its powers contained in Council Regulation (EEC) No 2137/85 and the European Economic Interest Grouping Regulations 1989, a restriction on the following lines may be applied for, if required, using Form RX1:

> No disposition of the [*registered estate*] *or* [*registered charge dated date*] by the proprietor of [*the registered estate*] *or* [*that registered charge*] is to be registered without a certificate signed by the conveyancer to [*name of EEIG*] that the manager or managers or its representative who has or have executed the deed, has or have been duly appointed and has or have the power to bind the proprietor; that the proprietor is not in receivership or administrative receivership and has not been wound up or dissolved and generally that the provisions of Council Regulation (EEC) No 2137/85 and the European Economic Interest Grouping Regulations 1989 (SI 1989/ 638) have been complied with.

Where the EEIG does not have an indefinite duration, a restriction on the following lines may also be applied for if required, using Form RX1 (see *Restrictions*, page 500):

> No disposition by the proprietor of the [*registered estate*] *or* [*registered charge dated date*] completed on or after [*date when duration of EEIG ceases*] is to be registered unless its conveyancer has certified that the duration of the proprietor has been extended and that it remained a body corporate on the date of such disposition.

In the light of Council Regulation (EEC) No 2137/85, art 25, all deeds entered into by an EEIG must indicate legibly:

(a) the name of the grouping preceded or followed either by the words 'European Economic Interest Grouping' or by the initials 'EEIG', unless those words or initials already occur in the name;

(b)   the location of the registry in which the grouping is registered, together with the grouping's entry at that registry; and

(c)   the grouping's official address.

European Economic Interest Grouping Regulations 1989, reg 19(1) provides that IA 1986, Pt III applies to EEIGs, and their establishments, registered under those Regulations, as if they were companies registered under the Companies Act 2006. A receiver or manager or administrative receiver may be appointed, but not an administrator. The matters set out under *Administrative receivers*, page 5, *Liquidators*, page 360, and *Receivers appointed under the Law of Property Act 1925*, page 474, therefore apply. At the end of 3 months from the date of receipt by the companies registry of a notice of the conclusion of the liquidation of an EEIG, the EEIG is dissolved (European Economic Interest Grouping Regulations 1989, reg 8(2)). There is no automatic dissolution if the number of members falls below two – the EEIG must be formally wound up.

EUROPEAN GROUPINGS OF TERRITORIAL COOPERATION

European Groupings of Territorial Cooperation (EGTCs) are cross-border associations of EU member states or of public authorities of EU member states, which may be created for various reasons, including the administration of EU grants. They must have participants from at least two member states. An EGTC has legal personality and can own land in its own name. Its registered office must be in the member state of one of the participants. There is no requirement for the letters EGTC to be included in the name. In English law EGTCs are similar to unregistered companies, so that the same restrictions on UK public authorities participating in companies will apply to EGTCs.

There are two sources of legislation governing an EGTC and its participants. The primary source is Regulation (EC) No 1082/2006 of the European Parliament and of the Council of 5 July 2006 on a European Grouping of Territorial Cooperation. Regulations have also been made in the United Kingdom to ensure the effective application of the EC Regulation; these are the European Grouping of Territorial Cooperation Regulations 2015 (SI 2015/1493). The UK Regulations apply to prospective members of an EGTC who are formed under UK laws, and to EGTCs whose registered office is located in the United Kingdom.

A UK public authority must seek approval of its proposed membership of an EGTC from the Secretary of State for Business, Energy & Industrial Strategy.

An EGTC can decide which member state its registered office will be in, but it must be the member state of one of the participants. For example, an EGTC made up of British and Dutch authorities can only be registered in the United Kingdom or the Netherlands.

The governing documents of an EGTC are the convention and the statutes. The convention includes details of the EGTC's registered office, the extent of the territory in which the EGTC may execute its tasks, the specific objectives and tasks of the EGTC, its duration and the conditions governing its dissolution and the list of the EGTC members. The statutes include further details about the decision-making procedures, and the operating provisions of the 'organs' that comprise the EGTC. An EGTC must have at least the following organs:

(a)   an assembly of representatives of its members; and
(b)   a director who represents the EGTC and acts on its behalf.

The statutes may provide for additional organs with clearly defined powers.

An EGTC can choose to register its statutes, or publicise them. A UK-domiciled EGTC will not be registered at the Companies Registry. Instead, EGTCs with a registered office in England and Wales must publish the statutes in the London Gazette. The EGTC acquires legal personality from the date of publication in the Gazette.

An EGTC has the power to buy and sell land, and to lend and borrow money, but this may be limited by its convention. An application to register an EGTC as the proprietor of a registered estate or of a registered charge should therefore be supported by:

(a)   a copy of the convention and statutes and evidence of registration or publication of statutes; or
(b)   a certificate in Form 7 given by a qualified lawyer practising in the territory of incorporation of the EGTC if it is incorporated outside the United Kingdom; or
(c)   a certificate in Form 8 given by the applicant's conveyancer if the EGTC is incorporated within the United Kingdom.

Form 7 and Form 8 are contained in LRR 2003, Sch 3 (see Appendix V, page 593).

A restriction on the following lines may be applied for, if required, using Form RX1 (see *Restrictions*, page 500):

> No disposition of the [*registered estate*] *or* [*registered charge dated date*] by the proprietor of [*the registered estate*] *or* [*that registered charge*] is to be registered without a certificate signed by the conveyancer to [*name of EGTC*] that the provisions of Council Regulation (EC) No 1082/2006 and the European Grouping of Territorial Cooperation Regulations 2015 (SI 2015/1493) have been complied with.

Where the EGTC does not have an indefinite duration, a restriction on the following lines may also be applied for if required, using Form RX1:

> No disposition by the proprietor of the [*registered estate*] *or* [*registered charge dated date*] completed on or after [*date when duration of EGTC ceases*] is to be registered unless its conveyancer has certified that the duration of the proprietor has been extended and that it remained a body corporate on the date of such disposition.

In principle a UK EGTC has unlimited powers of borrowing, subject to any limits within its statutes. However, the position with regard to non-UK domiciled EGTCs will depend upon the individual territory of the member state.

Deeds may be executed by an EGTC in a similar way to an unregistered company, or in some other way in accordance with the convention and statutes. In this context a 'director' may be the director of either the EGTC or any of its assembly members. Evidence of appointment of director or assembly member executing a deed on behalf of an EGTC should be lodged with any application for registration.

An EGTC may be wound up in the same manner as an unregistered company. An unregistered company may not voluntarily wind itself up. For EGTCs domiciled in England and Wales, the High Court is the designated court to make such an order (European Grouping of Territorial Cooperation Regulations 2015, art 6).

EXCLUSIVE USE

Historically, particularly in the Midlands and the North of England, it has sometimes been the practice to include in a conveyance or lease of a dwelling house the exclusive use of or exclusive right to use other adjacent premises such as a lavatory or coal shed. Modern conveyances or leases also occasionally include reference to exclusive use, particularly in relation to the use of certain parts of a purpose-built development such as a bin store or car parking space. The legal nature and effect of a grant of 'exclusive use' remains largely undefined by either statute or case law. It follows that it can be difficult, when considering how to treat such a grant for land registration purposes, to determine whether the grant takes effect as a transfer or demise, or merely as an easement.

In *Reilly v Booth* (1890) 44 Ch D 12 (CA), exclusive use of a gateway was granted, and Lopes LJ said, in a passage later cited with approval by the House of Lords in *Metropolitan Railway Company v Fowler* [1893] AC 416 (HL):

> The exclusive or unrestricted use of a piece of land, I take it, beyond all question passes the property or ownership in that land, and there is no easement known to law which gives exclusive and unrestricted use of a piece of land. It is not an easement in such a case, it is property that passes.

If, when applying for registration, the applicant specifically applies for the grant of the exclusive use to be registered as an estate in land, the Registry will consider it on that basis. However, for the grant to be treated as a transfer or demise of the land in question, the following conditions will need to be satisfied:

(a)   the grantor must intend the grantee to have exclusive use of the land. If the grantor retains the ability to exercise a degree of control, so that the grantee cannot exclude all others from the land, the grant cannot operate as a transfer of the land. However, the grant may still operate as a transfer or demise if the grantor retains an interest in the boundaries or structures only that delimit the area (such as the ceilings, walls and floors), or the grantor's retained property has a right of support, or the grant imposes covenants to protect the grantor's retained property; and

(b)   the area the subject of the grant must be well-defined. This will clearly be the case where the description includes details of the area's length, width and height or where the purpose of the grant (for example exclusive use of a storage room) in itself defines the area.

If the exclusive use *is* treated as a transfer or demise of the legal estate, it will be included within the property description in the property register of the grantee's registered title having the benefit of the exclusive use. Where necessary a reference to it will be made on the title plan, to supplement this. In the grantor's registered title, the land will be either excluded from the registered title (in the case of a transfer) or included in the notice of the burden of the lease (in the case of a demise).

The land will be limited to the area over which exclusive use has been granted; it will not therefore include the airspace over it or the soil beneath it, as the purpose of such a grant (rather than the transfer or demise of the entirety of the land outright) is presumably to except everything lying above or below it.

In other cases, the Registry will treat the grant of exclusive use as an easement but, because of its exclusive nature, it will make specific entries on both the grantee's and grantor's titles in relation to it. The land over which it is granted will not be included within the red edging on the title plan of the grantee's registered title (other than where the land overlaps with the footprint of the red edging). Nor will it be included within the property description in the property register. Instead a separate entry will be made in the grantee's registered title in respect of the benefit of the grant of exclusive use. The entry will be along the lines of:

> A [*details of deed containing the grant of exclusive use*] dated [*date*] made between [*parties*] grants the exclusive use of the [*describe land, for example basement store room*] shown [*plans reference*] on the title plan.

Reference will be made on the title plan to the land subject to the grant, if it is necessary to supplement the description of that land within the register entry. A separate entry will be made even if the deed containing the grant also grants other easements.

The land subject to the grant of exclusive use will be included within the grantor's registered title and a specific notice as to the burden of the grant will be made in the grantor's title, even if the deed containing the grant also grants other easements.

FEES

Fees are prescribed by the Land Registration Fee Order, currently the Land Registration Fee Order 2013 (SI 2013/3174) (the Fee Order).

A fee calculator for all types of application is on the Land Registry's website at www.gov.uk/guidance/hm-land-registry-registration-services-fees.

Fees are normally required to be paid on delivery of the application to which they relate by means of a cheque or postal order crossed and made payable to the Land Registry (the Fee Order, art 13). Where a fee is paid by a cheque which is not honoured the application may be cancelled (LRR 2003, r 16(4)).

Applicants who have made prior arrangements may pay fees for substantive applications by direct debit.

When two or more instruments relating to the same land are delivered for registration as part of the same application, a separate fee is payable in respect of each; but when a sale and a sub-sale are effected by one instrument of transfer only one fee, assessed on the price paid by the purchaser or the sub-purchaser, whichever is the greater, is payable (the Fee Order, art 3(4)). There are special provisions for 'large scale' applications involving large numbers of 'land units', as defined in the Fee Order.

FIRST REGISTRATION

The LRA 2002 makes provision for first registration of title to certain unregistered legal estates. Title to an estate in land may be capable of either voluntary or compulsory first registration. Title to a rentcharge, a franchise or a profit à prendre in gross may be capable of voluntary first registration, but is not currently subject to compulsory first registration; nor is land consisting of mines and minerals held apart from the surface.

Legal estates capable of first registration

An application for first registration of title may be made in respect of an unregistered legal estate which is either an estate in land, a rentcharge, a franchise, or a profit à prendre in gross (LRA 2002, s 3(1)). It is no longer possible to apply for first registration of title to an unregistered manor. If the application is in respect of a leasehold estate in land, the lease must be either for a discontinuous period or for a term of which more than 7 years are unexpired. In calculating the duration of the lease for this purpose, a person holding in the same right both a lease in possession and a lease to take effect in possession on, or within a month of, the end of the lease in possession, may, to the extent they relate to the same land, treat them as one continuous term.

The applicant may apply to be registered as proprietor of the legal estate on first registration if the estate is vested in him or he is entitled to require the estate to be vested in him. For example, a person entitled solely and absolutely under a trust of land may apply. A person who has contracted to buy an unregistered legal estate, however, cannot apply to be registered as proprietor before completion of the contract (LRA 2002, s 3(6)). A person with a leasehold estate vested in him as mortgagee may not apply in respect of that leasehold estate while there is a subsisting right of redemption (LRA 2002, s 3(5)).

No application for first registration of a leasehold estate under a PPP lease can be made (LRA 2002, s 90(1)). A PPP lease is one within the meaning given by Greater London Authority Act 1999, s 218, which makes provision about leases created for PPPs relating to transport in London.

Compulsory first registration

It is compulsory to apply for first registration of any freehold estate in land, or leasehold estate in land with more than 7 years left to run, on the occurrence of any of the following:

(a) a transfer, conveyance or assignment for valuable or other consideration (if the estate transferred has a negative value, it is regarded as transferred for valuable or other consideration (LRA 2002, s 4(6));

(b) a transfer, conveyance or assignment by way of gift (including for the purposes of constituting a trust under which the settlor does not retain the whole of the beneficial interest, or uniting the bare legal title and the beneficial interest in property held under a trust under which the settlor did not, on constitution, retain the whole beneficial interest);

(c) a transfer, conveyance or assignment in pursuance of an order of any court;

(d) an assent (including a vesting assent);

(e) a transfer, conveyance or assignment giving effect to a partition of land subject to a trust of land;

(f) a deed that appoints (or by virtue of Charities Act 2011, s 334 has effect as if it appointed) a new trustee;

(g) a vesting order under Trustee Act 1925, s 44 that is consequential on the appointment of a new trustee;

(h) a transfer, conveyance or assignment where Housing Act 1985 (HA 1985), s 171A applies (disposal by a landlord leading to a person's ceasing to be a secure tenant; the preserved right to buy applies);

(i) a first legal mortgage protected by the deposit of the title deeds (other than a mortgage of a lease with no more than 7 years to run at the date of the mortgage); and

(j) a grant by Her Majesty out of demesne land of an estate in fee simple absolute in possession, other than a grant to Herself.

It is compulsory to apply for first registration on the grant of any of the following leases out of an unregistered freehold estate in land or out of an unregistered leasehold estate in land where the lease has more than 7 years left to run at the date of the grant:

(a) a lease for more than 7 years from the date of the grant for valuable or other consideration (if the estate granted has a negative value, it is regarded as granted for valuable or other consideration (LRA 2002, s 4(6));

(b) a lease for more than 7 years from the date of the grant by way of gift;

(c) a lease for more than 7 years from the date of the grant in pursuance of an order of any court;

(d)   a lease for any length of term, which takes effect in possession more than 3 months from the date of the grant (in the case of a sub-lease it is compulsory to register only if the lease out of which it is granted has, at the date of that grant, more than 7 years to run);

(e)   a lease for any length of term in pursuance of HA 1985, Pt 5 (the right to buy);

(f)   a lease where the HA 1985, s 171A applies (disposal by a landlord leading to a person's ceasing to be a secure tenant; the preserved right to buy applies); and

(g)   a lease by Her Majesty out of demesne land for more than 7 years.

It is *not* compulsory to apply for first registration in respect of any of the following:

(a)   an assignment of a mortgage term;

(b)   an assignment or surrender of a lease to the owner of the immediate reversion where the term is to merge in that reversion;

(c)   a mortgage by demise which is not a first legal mortgage protected by the deposit of the title deeds;

(d)   any transaction relating to a rentcharge;

(e)   any transaction relating to a franchise;

(f)   any transaction relating to a profit à prendre in gross;

(g)   a transfer or grant creating a trust where the settlor retains the whole of the beneficial interest;

(h)   a transfer or grant uniting the bare legal title and the beneficial interest in property held under a trust under which the settlor retained the whole of the beneficial interest;

(i)   any transaction relating solely to mines and minerals held apart from the surface;

(j)   a transfer or grant of a lease that is a relevant social housing tenancy (as defined by LRA 2002, s 132(1));

(k)   a transfer by operation of law (for example, the vesting of a deceased's estate in his personal representatives); and

(l)   a general vesting declaration under the Compulsory Purchase (Vesting Declarations) Act 1981.

Duty to apply for first registration

Where compulsory first registration applies, the estate owner, or his successor in title, must apply for first registration within 2 months of the event triggering the duty to apply. Where the event triggering compulsory first registration is a mortgage, it is the mortgagor, not the mortgagee, who is required to apply. In such circumstances, however, the mortgagee may make an application for first registration in the name of the mortgagor, whether or not the mortgagor consents (LRR 2003, r 21). Where the mortgage is not a first legal mortgage protected by the deposit of the title deeds, the mortgagee may not apply for first registration without the consent of the mortgagor.

Any interested party may apply to the Registry for an order extending the period of 2 months in which the application for first registration must be made. Such application may be made by way of letter setting out the reasons why the order should be made. No fee is payable. If the Registry is satisfied there is good reason for doing so, it may by order provide that the period for registration ends on such later date as it may specify in the order (LRA 2002, s 6(5)).

Where it is compulsory to apply for first registration but an application has not been made within 2 months, or by any later date stated in an order of the Registry, the transfer, grant or creation of a legal estate becomes void as regards the transfer, grant or creation of that legal estate (LRA 2002, s 7(1)). In the case of a transfer, the title to the legal estate reverts to the transferor who holds it on a bare trust for the transferee. In the case of a lease or first mortgage, the grant or creation has effect as a contract made for valuable consideration to grant or create the legal estate concerned.

If the Registry makes an order extending the period for registration where LRA 2002, s 7(1) has already applied, that application of s 7(1) is treated as not having occurred (LRA 2002, s 7(3)). The possibility of reverter arising under s 7(1) is disregarded for the purposes of determining whether a fee simple is a fee simple absolute.

If the legal estate is retransferred, re-granted or recreated because of a failure to comply with the requirement for first registration, the transferee, grantee or mortgagor is liable to the other party for all the proper costs of and incidental to the retransfer, re-grant or recreation of the legal estate. That person is also liable to indemnify the other party in respect of any other liability reasonably incurred by him because of the failure to comply with the requirement of registration (LRA 2002, s 8).

Application for first registration

An applicant should deliver to the Registry:

(a) an application in Form FR1;
(b) sufficient details, by plan or otherwise, so that the land can be clearly identified on the Ordnance Survey map;

(c)   in the case of a leasehold estate, the lease, if in the control of the applicant (and a certified copy, if the applicant wishes for the original to be returned);

(d)   all deeds and documents relating to the title that are in the control of the applicant, including relevant Land Charges searches (with any entries accounted for and, where applicable, certified by a conveyancer as not affecting the estate);

(e)   a list in duplicate in Form DL of all the documents delivered;

(f)   Form DI giving the information as to overriding interests required by LRR 2003, r 28 including any documentary evidence of the interests (see 'Duty to disclose overriding interests', page 426);

(g)   the appropriate confirmation or evidence as to identity (see *Identity evidence*, page 266);

(h)   the appropriate SDLT certificate or other evidence (see *Stamp duty land tax*, page 541); and

(i)   the fee payable (see *Fees*, page 221).

If there are any rights, interests or claims affecting the estate which are known to the applicant, other than those disclosed in the title deeds or Form DI, these should be disclosed in the Form FR1. This would include, for example, any rights in the course of being acquired over the estate by adverse possession, or a disputed third party claim relating to the estate.

On an application to register a rentcharge, franchise or profit à prendre in gross, the land to be identified under (b) above is the land affected by that estate.

For the position where the application is for first registration of an estate in mines and minerals held apart from the surface, see *Mines and minerals*, page 380.

Unless all the land above and below the surface is included in the application for first registration, the applicant must supply a plan of the surface on, under or over which the land to be registered lies, and sufficient information to define the vertical and horizontal extents of the land (LRR 2003, r 26). This requirement does not apply where only mines and minerals are excluded from the application.

Where the applicant for first registration is unable to produce a full documentary title, the application must be supported by evidence to satisfy the Registry that the applicant is entitled, or required, to apply for first registration and, where appropriate, to account for the absence of documentary evidence of title (LRR 2003, r 27). This means that the evidence must show that the applicant has the legal estate vested in him or that he is entitled to require the legal estate to be vested in him. In practice the evidence is usually in the form of a statutory declaration or statement of truth, exhibiting any appropriate supporting documents. A statement of truth may be in Form ST3 in LRR 2003, Sch 1 (see *Lost or destroyed title deeds*, page 369).

Where the applicant for first registration comprises more than one person, panel 9 of Form FR1 should be completed to confirm the basis of the trusts upon which the property will be held. This enables the Registry to decide whether the entry of a restriction in Form A will be necessary (see *Joint proprietors*, page 286).

The Registry will assume that the applicant requests the return of all documents relating to the title except any statutory declaration, statement of truth, subsisting lease, subsisting charge, SDLT certificate, or the latest document of title (for example the conveyance to the applicant). Those documents will be returned if the applicant lodges a certified copy with the application for first registration; he does not need to lodge certified copies of the other documents accompanying the application.

Lodging of title deeds

Since 2016 conveyancers have been able to lodge first registration applications without lodging original deeds and documents. The Chief Land Registrar made a Direction under LRR 2003, r 24 that, providing certain conditions are met, only certified copy deeds and documents need to be lodged. This option is voluntary, so that conveyancers who choose to do so can still lodge original deeds and documents with applications if they prefer. The required conditions are as follows.

Appropriate certification

Each copy of any deed or document must bear the appropriate certification from the three listed below, signed by a conveyancer and dated no more than 3 months before the application is made for the purposes of LRR 2003, r 15:

I/We certify this is a true copy of the original document.

I/We certify this is a true copy of a document which is certified by a conveyancer to be a true copy of the original.

This is a true copy of an uncertified copy deed or document that is in the control of the applicant.

The conveyancer who signs the certificate must add his name and address. All copy deeds and documents must be as clear and legible as the originals. They must also be complete copies, including any memoranda. Any plans accompanying the application, including plans contained within deeds or documents, must be full sized colour copies and must not be reduced in scale or size from the original.

Separate certificate

In addition, a separate certificate in the form below, signed and dated by an individual conveyancer and including his roll, licence, authorisation or membership number as allocated by his approved regulator or licensing authority, must accompany the application:

> I certify on behalf of my organisation that this application is accompanied by certified copies of all deeds and documents relating to the title that are in the control of the applicant (as listed in the Form DL). My organisation will comply with any Land Registry request to lodge the originals of such deeds and documents until such time as Land Registry notifies us that the application is completed.

If this certificate does not accompany the application, the application will be considered to be substantially defective, and may be rejected or cancelled pursuant to LRR 2003, r 16(3).

Original deeds

The Land Registry may request that original deeds are lodged for quality assurance purposes. If they are not provided then the application may be cancelled. Any renewed application must then be lodged with the original deeds requested.

Notwithstanding this change, it should be borne in mind that:

- it is still only possible to lodge first registrations by way of post, DX and personal delivery, not electronically;
- the change of policy only relates to applications lodged by conveyancers, not other customers; and
- the Land Registry policy relating to first registrations where deeds and documents have been lost or destroyed, or where title is based upon adverse possession of unregistered land, has not changed. These types of applications will still need to be lodged in line with *Lost or destroyed title deeds*, page 369 or *Adverse possession*, page 11. However, where such applications consist only of Form FR1 and the statutory declaration or statement of truth and any exhibits, the applicant may lodge certified copies of these instead of the originals.

Examination of title

In examining the title shown by the documents accompanying an application for first registration, the Registry may have regard to any examination by a conveyancer prior to the application and to the nature of the property (LRR 2003, r 29). The Registry may make searches and enquiries and give notices to other persons, direct that searches and enquiries be made by the applicant and advertise the application (LRR 2003, r 30).

The applicant may be registered with absolute title if the Registry is of the opinion that the applicant's title to the estate is such as a willing buyer could properly be advised by a competent professional adviser to accept and (in the case of a leasehold estate) if the Registry approves the landlord's title to grant the lease. The Registry may disregard the fact that the title appears to it to be open to objection if it is of the opinion that the defect will not cause the holding under the title to be disturbed (LRA 2002, ss 9(2) and (3), 10(2) and (4)).

For the classes of title which may be granted as a result of the examination of title and the effect of first registration with a particular class of title, see *Classes of title*, page 130.

The benefit of an appurtenant right may be entered in the register on first registration if, on examining the title, the Registry is satisfied that the right subsists as a legal estate and benefits the registered estate (LRR 2003, r 33). Where the existence of the appurtenant right is not apparent on the face of the title deeds, a written application may accompany Form FR1 providing details of the right and evidence of its existence; this evidence may be in the form of a statement of truth in Form ST4 in LRR 2003, Sch 1. This application should be listed in panel 5 of Form FR1. If the Registry is satisfied that the right subsists as a legal estate and benefits the registered estate, it may enter it in the register. If the Registry is not so satisfied, it may enter details of the right claimed in the property register with such qualification as it considers appropriate; such an entry does not guarantee the validity of the claimed right.

On first registration the Registry, whenever practicable, enters in the proprietorship register the price paid or value declared. That entry will remain until there is a change of proprietor or some other change in the register of title which the Registry considers would render the entry misleading (LRR 2003, r 8(2) and (3)).

The Registry must enter a notice in the register of the burden of any interest which appears from its examination of title to affect the registered title (LRR 2003, r 35). This does not apply to interests that, under LRA 2002, s 33 or s 90(4), cannot be protected by notice. Such interests are:

(a)   interests under a trust of land or under an SLA 1925 settlement;
(b)   a leasehold estate in land granted for 3 years or less from the date of the grant and which is not required to be registered;
(c)   a restrictive covenant between lessor and lessee, so far as relating to the demised premises;
(d)   an interest which is capable of being registered under the CRA 1965;
(e)   an interest in any coal or coal mine, or the rights attached to any such interest, or the rights of any person under Coal Industry Act 1994, ss 38, 49 or 51; and
(f)   leases created for PPPs relating to transport in London, within the meaning given by Greater London Authority Act 1999, s 218.

Rule 35 also does not apply to public rights and local land charges. Nor does it apply to an interest which appears to the Registry to be of a trivial or obvious character, or the entry of a notice which would be likely to cause confusion or inconvenience.

Where the applicant has provided information to the Registry in Form DI about a disclosable overriding interest that affects the estate to which the application relates, the Registry may enter a notice in the register in respect of that interest (LRR 2003, r 28(4)).

If it appears to the Registry on first registration that an agreement prevents the acquisition of rights of light or air for the benefit of the registered estate, it may make an entry in the property register of that estate (LRR 2003, r 36).

In defined circumstances, before completing an application for first registration with absolute title of a leasehold title, the Registry must serve notice of the application on the proprietor of the registered reversionary estate. Those circumstances are where:

(a)   the lease was granted out of an unregistered legal estate, or the reversion was registered but the grant of the lease was not required to be completed by registration;
(b)   at the time of the application the immediate reversion to the lease is registered;
(c)   the lease is not noted in the register of that reversionary title; and
(d)   it is not apparent from the application that the proprietor of that reversionary title consents to the registration.

On completing registration of the leasehold estate the Registry must enter notice of the lease in the register of that reversionary title (LRR 2003, r 37).

Where a first legal mortgage is the event that triggers compulsory first registration, the Registry must enter the mortgagee as the proprietor of that charge if it is satisfied of that person's entitlement (LRR 2003, r 22). As regards any other legal mortgage which is either a charge on the legal estate that is being registered or a charge on such a charge, the Registry must enter the mortgagee as the proprietor of that charge if it is satisfied of that person's entitlement (LRR 2003, r 34).

If, while a person is required to apply for first registration of a legal estate, there is a dealing with that estate, LRA 2002 applies to that dealing as if the dealing had taken place after the date of first registration. Where the dealing is delivered for registration with the application for first registration, it has effect from the time of making that application (LRR 2003, r 38).

FLOATING CHARGES

Debentures are used by companies to secure money raised by way of loan. A debenture may create a legal charge or an equitable charge; if equitable, it may be in the form of a fixed equitable charge or a floating charge (see *Companies*, page 154, and *Debentures*, page 183). A floating charge cannot be substantively registered, but may be capable of protection by an entry in the register.

If a company has created a debenture containing a floating charge on its assets, the existence of the charge must be disclosed when the company makes an application for the first registration of its title to an estate affected by the debenture. A certified copy of the debenture must be lodged with the application if the applicant wishes the original to be returned (LRR 2003, r 203). Where, on first registration of land held by a company, it appears to the Registry from its examination of the title that it is subject to a floating charge, it will enter a notice of it in the charges register (LRR 2003, r 35). If the debenture creating the floating charge contains a proviso which prohibits the creation of any other charges ranking in priority to or *pari passu* with the floating charge, a note of that proviso is included in the notice of the floating charge. The entry of a notice in respect of a floating charge in the charges register does not remove the need for it to be registered under the Companies Act 2011.

Where a company that has created a debenture acquires a registered estate or a registered charge, or where a company that is already the proprietor of a registered estate or a registered charge creates a debenture, no entry will be made in the register to protect any floating charge created by the debenture (whether registered in the Companies Registry or not) in the absence of a specific application.

When a floating charge relating to registered land is created, the chargee is not able to apply for an official search with priority using Form OS1 or Form OS2, but may reserve a period of priority by making an outline application.

A floating charge relating to registered land may be protected by an application for entry of an agreed notice or a unilateral notice.

Agreed notice

In addition to the usual documents required (see *Notices*, page 389), an applicant for entry of an agreed notice should deliver to the Registry the debenture creating the floating charge or a certified copy of it.

Where the consent of the registered proprietor is not available but, for example, the original debenture has been executed by it, this is likely to be sufficient to satisfy the Registry as to the validity of the applicant's claim for the purposes of LRA 2002, s 34(3)(c).

The agreed notice in the register will give details of the interest protected.

If the floating charge is subsequently discharged, an application in Form CN1 to cancel the agreed notice (see *Notices*, page 389) should be made accompanied by an appropriate evidence of the discharge. This may consist of either:

(a) a copy of a declaration of satisfaction in Companies Registry Form 403A stamped as 'registered'; or
(b) a letter from the Companies Registry confirming that the charge has been satisfied; or
(c) a letter from the chargee addressed to the Land Registry confirming that the charge has been satisfied and including (where appropriate) confirmation that there has been no assignment of the benefit of the charge. If an assignment has been made, the normal conveyancing evidence of devolution of title must be lodged.

Where a purchaser from the chargor company is seeking to have the notice of the floating charge cancelled, he should deliver application Form CN1 to the Registry at the same time as his application to register the transfer. The application for cancellation should be supported by a letter signed by the company's secretary or conveyancer to the effect that no event has occurred which would crystallise the charge. This will normally be accepted by the Registry as sufficient evidence for the cancellation of the notice. A certificate to like effect from the chargee or his conveyancer would also usually be accepted. Where a lease by the chargor company is being registered with absolute leasehold title, the consent of the chargee under the floating charge will be required, otherwise a protective entry may be made in the register (see *Classes of title*, page 130). This applies whether the floating charge is protected by an agreed notice or a unilateral notice.

Unilateral notice

Application for entry of unilateral notice may be preferred where the applicant does not wish the terms of the charge to be open to public inspection and copying. The applicant should deliver to the Registry the usual documents required (see *Notices*, page 389).

The statement in panel 11 or conveyancer's certificate in panel 12 of Form UN1 should be completed on the following lines to show the interest of the applicant:

> chargee having the benefit of a floating charge created by a [*specify the document creating the floating charge*] dated [*date*] made between [*registered proprietor*] and [*beneficiary of the unilateral notice*].

The unilateral notice in the register will give brief details of the interest protected and identify the beneficiary of that notice.

If the floating charge is subsequently discharged, an application to cancel the unilateral notice in Form UN2 should be made by the beneficiary of the notice. If the beneficiary fails to do so, the registered proprietor of the land may apply in Form UN4 for the cancellation of the unilateral notice (see *Notices*, page 389). Evidence of discharge would not need to accompany either of these applications.

Crystallisation of floating charge

If a floating charge crystallises, an application should be made for an additional notice in respect of the variation of the existing interest. This will show that the charge has become a fixed charge (LRR 2003, r 84(4)). An applicant may apply for entry of an agreed notice or a unilateral notice, as above. Where the application is for entry of an agreed notice, evidence of the crystallisation should accompany the application. It will not normally be appropriate to apply to cancel or remove any existing notice, as the date of entry of that notice will be relevant for priority purposes (see *Priorities*, page 452).

FLYING FREEHOLDS

It sometimes happens that the owner of a freehold property may own some or all of his property at one level or stratum, but not at all levels or strata. This can give rise to a so-called 'flying freehold'. A common example occurs where a room above a passageway is owned as part of a property, but the passageway itself is owned by the adjoining property.

When an application for first registration is made, unless all the land above and below the surface is included in the application for first registration, the applicant must provide a plan of the surface on, under or over which the land to be registered lies, and sufficient information to define the vertical or horizontal extents of the land (LRR 2003, r 26(1)). This does not apply where it is only mines and minerals that are excluded from the application.

Where the application for first registration shows that the land being registered is affected by a flying freehold, an appropriate entry is made in the property register. An example of such an entry is:

> NOTE: As to the part tinted blue on the title plan only the rooms over the passageway which form part of 15 Friar Street are included in the title.

Where a title was registered under LRA 1925, r 251 of the Land Registration Rules 1925 provided that the registration of a person as proprietor of land vested in him all appurtenances appertaining or reputed to appertain to the land or any part of it, or, at the time of registration, demised, occupied, or enjoyed with the land, or reputed or known as part or parcel of or appurtenant to the land or any part of it. The 1925 Rules, r 251 also provided that this included the appropriate rights and interests which, had there been a conveyance of the land, would have passed under Law of Property Act 1925, s 62.

LRA 2002, ss 11(3) and 12(3) now provide that the registered freehold or leasehold estate is vested in the proprietor together with all interests subsisting for the benefit of the estate. In addition, LRA 2002, s 60 provides that where the boundary of a registered estate is a general boundary, that general boundary does not determine the exact line of the boundary. The result of these provisions is that if, for example, there is a room projecting over an adjoining owner's land or a cellar projecting under that land, this is usually included in the occupying owner's registered title even though it falls outside the red edging on the title plan, no details of the flying freehold having been supplied to the Registry at the time of registration.

Where a flying freehold has not been reflected by an entry in the property register, an application may be made for an alteration to the register by the making of such an entry on the title or titles affected. The applicant should deliver to the Registry:

(a)   an application in Form AP1;
(b)   a statement of the alteration being applied for;
(c)   all relevant evidence held by the applicant which is relevant to the application to alter the register; and
(d)   the fee payable (if applicable) (see *Fees*, page 221).

The Registry may make such enquiries as it thinks fit, which may include a survey where necessary, and must give notice of the proposed alteration to any person who would be affected by it, unless it is satisfied that such notice is unnecessary (LRR 2003, r 128). Rule 128 does not, however, apply to alteration of the register in the specific circumstances covered by any other rule. An application for alteration by the Registry (otherwise than under a court order) must be supported by evidence to justify the alteration (LRR 2003, r 129) (see *Alteration of the register*, page 39).

FOREIGN LAW

In general, the law relating to land is the law of the state in which the land is situated, i.e. the *lex situs*. In relation to registered estates under the LRA 2002, 'foreign law' is that of any country outside England and Wales; this therefore includes the law of Scotland, Northern Ireland, the Channel Islands and the Isle of Man. Issues of foreign law may, for example, sometimes arise in relation to a foreign power of attorney, divorce or bankruptcy. Any such issue will be considered by the Registry on an individual basis. For example, in the case of a foreign power of attorney, the Registry will consider whether the power is valid for land registration purposes and authorises the execution of the disposition in question.

A signature in foreign characters still constitutes a signature complying with the requirements for a valid deed. However, where any instrument is executed in foreign (i.e. non-Roman) characters, such as Arabic or Chinese characters, the Registry will require either:

(a)   the words of execution to be expanded to confirm that the signatory understands English or has familiarised himself with its contents (for example by having had it read out to him in his native language); or

(b)   a separate certificate to that effect given by a conveyancer acting for the signatory.

FORESHORE

The foreshore is the shore and bed of the sea and of any tidal water, below the line of the medium high tide between the spring and neap tides (LRA 2002, Sch 6, para 13(3)). In addition to the sea, tidal waters occur in river estuaries, harbours and any other water feature that adjoins the sea. There is a presumption that the Crown owns the foreshore in demesne, although in practice extensive tracts of the foreshore are in fact owned by other parties such as port authorities, local authorities or even private individuals.

In the light of this presumption, where it appears to the Registry that any of the land in an application for first registration comprises foreshore, it must serve notice of the application on the Crown Estate Commissioners (LRR 2003, r 31). It must also serve notice on the Chancellor of the Duchy of Lancaster in the case of land in the county palatine of Lancaster and on the Port of London Authority in the case of land within its jurisdiction. In the case of land in the counties of Devon and Cornwall and the Isles of Scilly, the Registry must also serve notice on such person as the Duke of Cornwall, or the possessor for the time being of the Duchy of Cornwall, appoints. Where the land is within the jurisdiction of the Port of London Authority, the Registry must also serve notice of the application on such person as the Duke of Cornwall, or the possessor for the time being of the Duchy of Cornwall, appoints.

The notice must allow a period ending at 12 noon on the 20th business day after the date of issue of the notice in which to object to the application. A business day is a day when the Land Registry is open to the public, that is every day except Saturdays, Sundays, Christmas Day, Good Friday or any other day either specified or declared by proclamation under Banking and Financial Dealings Act 1971, s 1 or appointed by the Lord Chancellor or certified by the Registry as being an 'interrupted day' due to delay or failure of a communication service or to some other event or circumstance causing substantial interruption in the normal operation of the Registry.

Such a notice need not be served where, if it was served, it would be served on the applicant for first registration (LRR 2003, r 31(3)).

Where the registered title comprises only foreshore, or comprises land and a separate parcel of foreshore, the description of the registered estate in the property register will describe the foreshore as such. It will not, however, be separately referred to where the registered estate comprises a single parcel of land which includes foreshore.

The effect of accretion and diluvion also applies to foreshore, so that the position of foreshore is moveable due to deposition and erosion. Sudden or violent changes, for example through the effects of a storm or the building of sea walls, do not affect the owner's rights. The Registry will therefore make an entry in the property register to reflect the effect of accretion and diluvion. Where the application for first registration includes an agreement as to the effect of accretion and diluvion, this will only have effect if registered (LRA 2002, s 61(2)). The Registry will make an entry in respect of it in the register and add a note to confirm that it is registered for the purposes of s 61(2). If there is no such agreement, the Registry will enter a note to confirm that the boundary of the registered estate is subject to the effect of accretion and diluvion (LRR 2003, r 123).

In relation to registered land which comprises or includes foreshore, LRR 2003, r 123 requires that an application to register an agreement about the operation of accretion and diluvion in relation to a registered estate in land must be made by, or be accompanied by the consent of, the proprietor of the registered estate and of any registered charge, unless they are party to the agreement.

Where registered land consists of foreshore belonging to the Queen in right of the Crown or the Duchy of Lancaster or to the Duchy of Cornwall, the period of adverse possession required before an application may be made under LRA 2002, Sch 6, para 1(1) is 60 years rather than 10 years (LRA 2002, Sch 6, para 13). For these purposes land is treated as foreshore if it has been foreshore at any time in the 10 years before the application by the squatter for registration. A similar period applies in respect of Crown foreshore which is unregistered (Limitation Act 1980, s 15 and Sch 1, para 11(1)). The normal limitation periods apply to foreshore which is not Crown land. For foreshore which is Crown land, see also *Demesne land*, page 187.

Registration of title to foreshore does not affect existing public rights over foreshore. Such public rights are typically fishing and navigation (*Blundell v Catterall* [1821] 5 B & Ald 268), although there may be other rights in a particular locality. Public rights are interests which override both first registration and registered dispositions (LRA 2002, Sch 1, para 5 and Sch 3, para 5). Such interests are therefore protected notwithstanding that there is no entry in the register in respect of them (LRA 2002, ss 11, 12, 29 and 30).

Public rights are not disclosable overriding interests under LRR 2003, r 28 or r 57. See also *Accretion and Diluvion*, page 3.

FORMS

LRA 2002, s 25(1) provides that a registrable disposition of a registered estate or registered charge only has effect if it complies with the requirements in the LRR 2003 as to form and content. LRR 2003, Sch 1 contains numerous prescribed forms of application and disposition (Sch 1 forms) and Sch 3 contains a small number of miscellaneous forms which must be used in all matters to which they refer (Sch 3 forms), but which can be adapted with the Registry's consent. LRR 2003, Sch 9 contains approved forms of execution of Sch 1 and Sch 3 forms, which can be adapted with the Registry's consent. The Registry also publishes Welsh language versions of these scheduled forms. Specific forms are referred to under the relevant headings elsewhere in this book. See Appendix II, page 577 for a list of forms. See Appendix V, page 593 for the Sch 3 forms. See Appendix VI, page 605 for the Sch 9 forms.

Most types of application and disposition have a prescribed form and LRR 2003, r 206(1) requires that the prescribed form must be used. Thus LRR 2003, r 58 states that a transfer must be in Form TP1, TP2, TR1, TR2, TR5, AS1 or AS3, as appropriate. Also, r 59 prescribes the forms of transfer which must be used to effect a transfer by way of exchange and deals with the need for a receipt for equality money and suitable additional wording in the transfer. LRR 2003, r 60 covers transfers of leasehold land where the rent is being apportioned or the land is being exonerated.

A document affecting a registered title must refer to the title number (LRR 2003, r 212(3)). The Registry may permit a person to make an application relying on a document that is not in the relevant Sch 1 or Sch 3 form if that person cannot obtain and lodge the relevant scheduled form or it is only possible to do so at unreasonable expense, if the Registry is satisfied that neither the rights of any person nor the keeping of the register are likely to be materially prejudiced by allowing the alternative document to be relied upon.

Any application or document in one of the Sch 1 forms must:

(a) be printed on durable A4 size paper;
(b) be reproduced as set out in Sch 1 as to its wording, layout, ruling, font and point size (except for Forms ST1, ST2, ST3 and ST4 where the special forms of execution provided in r 215A(4) and (5) may be used instead);
(c) contain all the information required in an easily legible form; and

(d)   if it consists of more than one sheet of paper, or refers to an attached plan or a continuation sheet, be securely fastened together.

An 'additional provisions' panel may be used, where provided within a Sch 1 form. If (other than in Form DL) the necessary information will not fit in the panel provided, the panel must be continued on a continuation sheet in Form CS.

Where a form is produced electronically:

(a)   the depth of a panel may be increased or reduced to fit the material to be comprised in it, and a panel may be divided at a page break;
(b)   the text outside of the panels (other than the name and description of the form at the top of the page, and any text after the final panel) may be omitted;
(c)   inapplicable certificates and statements may be omitted;
(d)   the plural may be used instead of the singular and the singular instead of the plural;
(e)   panels which would contain only the panel number and the panel heading may be omitted, but such omission must not affect the numbering of subsequent panels;
(f)   'X' boxes may be omitted where all inapplicable statements and certificates have been omitted;
(g)   the sub-headings in an additional provisions panel may be added to, amended, repositioned or omitted;
(h)   'Seller' may be substituted for 'Transferor' and 'Buyer' for 'Transferee' in a transfer on sale;
(i)   the vertical lines which define the left and right boundaries of the panel may be omitted.

If no form is prescribed, the document must be in such form as the Registry may direct or allow.

The Registry's approval of a draft document may be sought:

(a)   when it is desired to adapt a Sch 3 form for a particular matter (LRR 2003, r 206(2)); or
(b)   when it is a document for which no form is prescribed (LRR 2003, r 212); or
(c)   when it is desired to make an application for which there is a prescribed Sch 1 or Sch 3 form, but the applicant wishes to rely on an alternative document instead (LRR 2003, r 209).

The draft (with plan if any) and a copy should be sent to the appropriate Registry office. No fee is currently payable. Approval will be limited to matters of form;

the person lodging the document for registration will be responsible for ensuring that it carries out the intention of the parties and for all other matters of substance, due execution, etc.

Where several associated dispositions relating to a particular registered title are delivered for registration together, the application forms may be numbered consecutively (for example when there are five applications: 1/5, 2/5, 3/5, 4/5 and 5/5), so that Registry staff will readily identify that they should be dealt with together and in the order indicated. The appropriate number should be endorsed prominently at the top of the first page of each form.

FRANCHISES

A franchise is 'an incorporeal hereditament which has been authoritatively defined as a royal privilege or branch of the royal prerogative subsisting in the hands of a subject, by grant from the King' (*Spook Erection Ltd v Secretary of State for the Environment* [1988] 2 All ER 667 (CA)). A franchise is normally created by a grant from the Crown in the form of a charter or letters patent, although it may also be claimed by prescription. A franchise does not carry with it ownership of the physical land to which it relates and is distinct from the freehold or leasehold estates in that land. The most common franchise is the right to hold a market or fair. A right of market confers on the owner a monopoly right, in the form of the exclusive right to hold markets within a certain radius. A fair is a market held at rarer intervals. A franchise can be confiscated by the Crown or abolished by Act of Parliament; for example, franchises of forest, free chase, park or free warren were abolished by Wild Creatures and Forest Laws Act 1971, s 1(1). Franchises were not capable of registration under the LRA 1925, but may now be the subject of voluntary registration (LRA 2002, s 3). It is not, however, compulsory to apply for first registration of the title to a franchise.

The LRR 2003 differentiate between an 'affecting franchise' and a 'relating franchise' (LRR 2003, r 217). An affecting franchise is one which relates to a defined area of land and is an adverse right affecting, or capable of affecting, the title to an estate or charge. A relating franchise is defined as one which is not an affecting franchise.

The view of the Registry is that most franchises are considered to be relating franchises and as such will not constitute interests which override, because they do not affect an estate or charge. Thus in the case of a market franchise, it is considered that this will be a relating franchise because even if it relates to a definable area, it does not appear to give the franchisee the right to enter the land without the landowner's consent and so does not confer property rights adversely affecting the title to any estate or charge. Relating franchises cannot, therefore, be the subject of an application for entry of a notice in the register.

In the case of an affecting franchise, it is possible to register a caution against first registration both of that franchise and of any estate in land that it affects. Although it is possible to register a caution against first registration of a relating franchise (rather than against the land to which it relates), such a caution will not provide protection in relation to an application for first registration of the land to which it relates, as it does not 'affect' that land for the purposes of LRA 2002, s 15(1)(b).

Until 12 October 2013, the benefit of an affecting franchise was an unregistered interest which overrode first registration and registered dispositions (LRA 2002, ss 11, 12, 29 and 30, Sch 1, para 13 and Sch 3, para 13). There was a duty to disclose the burden of an affecting franchise under LRR 2003, r 28 or r 57. On first registration of title, the Registry will enter a notice in the register as to the burden of an affecting franchise, if it appears from its examination of the title to affect the land.

After the period of 10 years beginning on 13 October 2003, the automatic protection of an affecting franchise as an overriding interest ceased (LRA 2002, s 117(1)).The person having the benefit of the affecting franchise (if its priority has not already been previously defeated and it continues to subsist) should therefore protect it in the register. If he does not do so, the priority of the affecting franchise is liable to be defeated on a subsequent first registration of unregistered burdened land or on a subsequent registration of a registrable disposition of registered burdened land for valuable consideration (LRA 2002, ss 11, 12, 29 and 30), as the case may be. If the burdened land is unregistered he should apply for a caution against first registration. If the burdened land is registered he should apply for the entry of a notice in the register. Until 12 October 2013, no fee was payable for such an application, but the normal fee will now apply.

Caution against first registration

An applicant should deliver to the Registry the usual documents required (see *Cautions against first registration*, page 88).

No documents should be exhibited, as the statement should be self-contained. The statement of truth in panel 10 of Form CT1 should be completed on the following lines to show the interest of the applicant:

> owner of the following franchise affecting the land: [*set out details of the franchise, including details of the grant under which it arose*].

The interest stated in the Form CT1 will appear in the caution register, together with a description of the legal estate to which the caution relates. For the effect of a caution against first registration, see *Cautions against first registration*, page 88.

Agreed notice

An affecting (but not a relating) franchise may be protected by entry of an agreed notice. In addition to the usual documents required (see *Notices*, page 389), an applicant should deliver to the Registry the deed, order or instrument giving rise to the interest claimed or a certified copy of it, or (if there is no such deed, order or instrument) other details of the interest claimed so as to satisfy the Registry as to the nature of the applicant's claim.

Documentary evidence of the creation or existence of the franchise will normally be in the form of a certified copy (together with a certified translation if the copy document is in Latin) of the Charter or Letters Patent, together with evidence to demonstrate that the franchise is now vested in the applicant and remains actively exercised. Where the franchise is claimed by prescription, evidence by way of statutory declaration or statement of truth of at least 20 years' prescriptive use will be required.

The agreed notice in the register will give details of the interest protected.

Where the registered proprietor does not consent to the entry in the register of an agreed notice and evidence to satisfy the Registry as to the validity of the applicant's claim cannot be lodged, an application for entry of a unilateral notice may still be made.

Unilateral notice

An affecting (but not a relating) franchise may be protected by entry of a unilateral notice. An applicant should deliver to the Registry the usual documents required (see *Notices*, page 389).

The statement in panel 11 or conveyancer's certificate in panel 12 of Form UN1 should be completed on the following lines to show the interest of the applicant:

> owner of the following franchise affecting the land: [*set out details of the franchise, including details of the grant under which it arose*].

The unilateral notice in the register will give brief details of the interest protected and identify the beneficiary of that notice.

First registration of a franchise

Both a relating franchise and an affecting franchise may be the subject of an application for first registration of title. However, to be capable of registration, a franchise must constitute a legal estate and be either perpetual or for a term of years absolute with more than 7 years unexpired. The applicant should make clear whether he is applying for registration of a relating franchise or an affecting franchise.

In addition to the usual documents required (see *First registration*, page 222), an applicant should deliver to the Registry:

(a) (in the case of an affecting franchise) sufficient details, by plan or otherwise, so that the area of land to which the franchise relates can be clearly identified on the Ordnance Survey map;

(b) (in the case of a relating franchise) details of the current administrative area (i.e. the county or unitary authority) in which the franchise operates;

(c) the original (together with a certified translation if the document is in Latin) of the Charter or Letters Patent, or a certified copy; and

(d) (in the case of a franchise claimed by prescription) evidence by way of statutory declaration or statement of truth (which may be in Form ST4 in LRR 2003, Sch 1) of at least 20 years' prescriptive use.

Where the applicant for first registration is unable to produce a full documentary title, the application must be supported by evidence to account for this, usually in the form of a statutory declaration or statement of truth, exhibiting any appropriate supporting documents. A statement of truth may be in Form ST3 in LRR 2003, Sch 1 (see *Lost or destroyed title deeds*, page 369).

Where two or more persons apply to be registered as proprietors of a franchise and a sole proprietor or the survivor of joint proprietors will not be able to give a valid receipt for capital money, application must be made for entry of a restriction in Form A (LRR 2003, r 94(2A)) (see *Joint proprietors*, page 286).

The Registry will normally serve notice of an application for registration of a franchise upon the Crown. The applicant should lodge any relevant correspondence with the Crown as part of the application. In the case of an affecting franchise, the Registry will also serve notice on all the registered proprietors of estates in land, charges and relevant franchises within the defined area of the franchise and (where appropriate) on any known unregistered owners, chargees and relevant franchise-holders.

On first registration of an affecting franchise, a title plan based on the Ordnance Survey map is created and referred to in the description of the registered estate in the property register. The area identified on the title plan is indexed on the index map and will then be revealed on the result of an official search of the index map in respect of the land affected, made under LRR 2003, r 145. An application for an official search of the index map is made in Form SIM (see *Official searches of the index*, page 409).

On first registration of a relating franchise, no title plan is created. The franchise is indexed in the index of relating franchises and manors. This is an index of verbal descriptions of registered franchises which are relating franchises, pending applications for first registration of such franchises, and registered manors. It also includes cautions against first registration where the subject of the caution is a relating franchise, and pending applications for such cautions. The index contains the relevant title numbers, arranged by administrative area. Registered relating franchises are not revealed on an official search of the index map, but are revealed on the result of an official search of the index of relating franchises and manors made under LRR 2003, r 146. An application for an official search of the index of relating franchises and manors is made in form SIF (see *Official searches of the index*, page 409).

For first registrations generally, see *First registration*, page 222. For the classes of title which may be granted as a result of the examination of title and the effect of first registration with a particular class of title, see *Classes of title*, page 130.

Registration of a franchise does not prejudice a right of the Crown to forfeit the franchise, and the priority of that right is automatically protected for the purposes of LRA 2002, s 29 (LRR 2003, r 196B).

Dispositions of registered franchises

The transfer or grant of a lease of a registered franchise is a registrable disposition which must be completed by registration and will not operate at law until the registration requirements have been met (LRA 2002, s 27(1) and (2)(c)). This applies regardless of the length of the term of any such lease.

In the case of a transfer, the appropriate application for registration should be made in the normal way (see *Transfers*, page 551).

Where there is a grant out of a lease of a registered franchise, the form of application depends upon the length of the term of the lease. If the lease is for a term of more than 7 years from the date of the grant, the application is completed by the entry in the register of:

(a)   the grantee (or his successor in title) as proprietor of the lease; and
(b)   a notice in respect of the lease.

If the lease is for a term not exceeding 7 years from the date of the grant, the application is completed only by the entry of a notice in respect of the lease (LRA 2002, Sch 2, paras 4 and 5). An application for entry of a notice of a lease which is for a term not exceeding 7 years from the date of the grant may be made in Form AP1 or AN1 (LRR 2003, r 90).

A lease of a franchise is not required to be in the form of a prescribed clauses lease. An applicant should deliver to the Registry the usual documents required (see *Leases*, page 296).

FRAUD OR FORGERY

Property fraud can potentially occur in relation to registered land as well as unregistered land. However, separate principles apply in relation to registered estates. In particular, in contrast to the position in unregistered land, the entry of a person in the register as the proprietor of a registered legal estate vests the legal estate in him even where it would not otherwise have vested in him (LRA 2002, s 58). Accordingly if, for example, a person is registered as proprietor as the result of a forged or fraudulent transfer, the legal estate is still vested in him. This is the case whether the transfer is void or merely voidable. This principle reflects the importance of the fact of registration, but this does not mean that a person who has been the victim of fraud or forgery has no recourse.

Alteration and rectification

Although the legal estate has so vested, this does not prevent an application being made for alteration of the register under LRA 2002, Sch 4 (see *Alteration of the register*, page 39, and *Rectification*, page 480). An alteration of the register will constitute 'rectification' if it involves the correction of a mistake and prejudicially affects the title of a registered proprietor. Rectification is therefore a specific form of alteration, upon which the LRA 2002 imposes certain limitations in relation to rectification of a registered estate in land against a 'proprietor in possession'. Under LRA 2002, s 131, land is in the possession of a proprietor if it is physically in his possession, or in that of a person who is entitled (other than as an adverse possessor under Sch 6 to that Act) to be registered as the proprietor of the registered estate. In the following cases land which is (or is treated as being) in the possession of the second-mentioned person is to be treated for these purposes as in the possession of the first-mentioned person: landlord and tenant; mortgagor and mortgagee; licensor and licensee; trustee and beneficiary.

Where an alteration which would constitute rectification affects the title of the proprietor of a registered estate in land, no order may be made by the court or the Registry without that proprietor's consent in relation to land in his possession, unless he has by fraud or lack of proper care caused or substantially contributed to the mistake, or it would be unjust for any other reason for the alteration not to be made. For example, if a husband and wife were the registered proprietors of land and the husband forged the wife's signature on a transfer into his sole name, on registration of the transfer the legal estate would vest in him alone. Because of his fraud, an order for alteration to the register to show the husband and wife as registered proprietors would normally be made, even though the husband had remained in possession. However, if an innocent purchaser from the husband was registered as proprietor before the forgery came to light, an order for rectification would not usually be made so as to affect that proprietor if he was in possession of the land. In that situation, the husband may be entitled to indemnity from the Registry for the loss he has suffered.

Indemnity

The distinction between rectification and alteration in general is also important in relation to entitlement to indemnity under LRA 2002, Sch 8. Where the register is rectified as a result of fraud or forgery, the question arises whether a person who has suffered loss by reason of the rectification is entitled to be indemnified by the Registry. For these purposes, LRA 2002, Sch 8, para 1(2)(b) provides that the proprietor of a registered estate or charge claiming in good faith under a forged disposition is, where the register is rectified, to be regarded as having suffered loss by reason of such rectification as if the disposition had not been forged.

Conversely, where the register is not rectified notwithstanding fraud or forgery, for example because of the protection conferred upon a proprietor in possession of land referred to above, a person who has suffered loss by reason of the fraud or forgery may be entitled to be indemnified by the Registry.

No indemnity is payable by the Registry, however, for any loss suffered wholly or partly as a result of the claimant's own fraud, or wholly as a result of his own lack of proper care. Where any loss is suffered by a claimant partly as a result of his own lack of proper care, any indemnity payable to him is to be reduced to such extent as is fair having regard to his share in the responsibility for the loss. For these purposes, any fraud or lack of proper care on the part of a person from whom the claimant derives title (otherwise than under a disposition for valuable consideration which is registered or protected by an entry in the register) is to be treated as if it were fraud or lack of care on the part of the claimant (LRA 2002, Sch 8, para 5) (see *Indemnity*, page 273).

Restriction

Where it is believed that there is the possibility of an attempt to register a forged or fraudulent disposition, application may be made for entry of a restriction in Form LL. This provides an element of protection against forgery or fraud by requiring a conveyancer's certificate to be lodged with an application, certifying that he is satisfied that the person who executed the document submitted for registration as disponor is the same person as the proprietor. The wording of Form LL is set out in Appendix IV, page 585.

Where it is considered that there is a higher risk of forgery or fraud, application may be made under LRA 2002, s 42(1)(a) for entry of a non-standard restriction in the following form:

> No disposition of the registered estate by the registered proprietor is to be registered.

This form of restriction is intended to effectively 'freeze' the register, so that no disposition by the proprietor can be registered until the restriction is cancelled under LRR 2003, r 97 or disapplied by the Registry under LRA 2002, s 41(2). Such a restriction would not, however, prevent a disposition by a registered chargee in exercise of its power of sale.

The registered proprietor should deliver to the Registry the usual documents required (see *Restrictions*, page 500).

Panel 9 of Form RX1 should be completed as to the required restriction(s). A restriction in a standard form LL in LRR 2003, Sch 4 does not require the approval of the Registry to the terms of the restriction under LRA 2002, s 43(3).

The statement in panel 12 or conveyancer's certificate in panel 13 of Form RX1 should be completed as to the reasons for the application.

If the applicant is a private individual and does not live at the property, he may apply for entry of a restriction in Form LL using Form RQ. No fee is currently payable if this form is used.

Instead of applying for a non-standard restriction in Form RX1, a company may apply in Form RQ(Co) for entry of a specific non-standard counter-fraud restriction in titles of which it is the registered proprietor. The Registry will currently enter the restriction in up to three titles without a fee. The wording of the restriction requires a conveyancer to certify that he is satisfied the company transferring or mortgaging the property is the same company as the owner. The conveyancer must also certify that he has taken reasonable steps to establish that anyone who executed the deed on behalf of the company held the stated office at the time of execution.

It is also important that a registered proprietor ensures that their address for service in the register is kept up to date, so as to ensure that notices and other correspondence from the Registry are delivered to them.

FREEZING ORDERS, RESTRAINT ORDERS AND INTERIM RECEIVING ORDERS

Where a person has the benefit of a freezing order or an undertaking given in place of a freezing order affecting a registered estate or charge, he has a sufficient interest to apply for entry of a restriction in Form AA or Form BB, as appropriate (LRR 2003, r 93(h)).Where a person has applied to the court for a freezing order affecting a registered estate or charge, he has a sufficient interest to apply for entry of a restriction in Form CC or Form DD, as appropriate (LRR 2003, r 93(i)).

This applies equally where the International Criminal Court applies for entry of a restriction in Forms AA, BB, CC or DD in respect of a freezing order, or an application for a freezing order, under International Criminal Court Act 2001, Sch 6 (LRR 2003, r 93(r)). The LRA 2002 applies in relation to freezing orders under the International Criminal Court Act 2001, as it applies in relation to orders affecting land made by the court for the purpose of enforcing judgments or recognisances, except that no notice may be entered in the register of title in respect of such orders (LRA 2002, Sch 11, para 40).

An application for a freezing order does not, in general, constitute a pending land action. This is because it relates to an application to restrain the registered proprietor from exercising his powers of disposition, rather than to a proprietory claim (see *Pending land actions*, page 433). However, certain statutes expressly provide that certain actions are to be treated, for the purposes of the LRA 2002, as pending land actions. These include an application for a restraint order under Proceeds of Crime Act 2002, s 41 or Terrorism Act 2000, Sch 4, para 5(1) or (2); an application for a freezing order under the International Criminal Court Act 2001; and an application for an interim receiving order under Proceeds of Crime Act 2002, s 246. In these cases, the application to the court may be protected as a pending land action, by application for entry of an agreed notice or a unilateral notice; this may be in addition to protection by the entry of an appropriate restriction. These statutory exceptions only relate to the application to the court; any order made by the court will not usually constitute a pending land action capable of protection by entry of a notice, but it may be capable of being protected by entry of a restriction.

A person who has obtained a restraint order under Terrorism Act 2000, Sch 4, para 5(1) or (2) or Proceeds of Crime Act 2002, s 41 affecting a registered estate or charge may apply for entry of a restriction in Form EE or Form FF, as appropriate (LRR 2003, r 93(l)). A person who has applied for such a restraint order may apply for entry of a restriction in Form GG or Form HH, as appropriate (LRR 2003, r 93(m)).

A person who has obtained an interim receiving order under Proceeds of Crime Act 2002, s 246 affecting a registered estate or charge may apply for entry of a restriction in Form EE or Form FF, as appropriate (LRR 2003, r 93(u)). A person who has applied for such an interim receiving order may apply for entry of a restriction in Form GG or Form HH, as appropriate (LRR 2003, r 93(v)).

Under LRA 2002, s 46 if the court considers it necessary or desirable to do so for the purposes of protecting a right or claim in relation to a registered estate or charge, it may make an order requiring the Registry to enter a restriction in the register. The court may include in such an order a direction that an entry made in pursuance of the order is to have overriding priority; and may make the exercise of its power to make such a direction subject to such terms and conditions as it thinks fit. A restriction having overriding priority shall be in such form as the Registry determines so as to ensure the priority of the restriction ordered by the court is apparent from the register, and if entered during the priority period of a prior official search, the Registry must give notice of the entry to the person who applied for the search unless satisfied such notice is unnecessary (LRA 2002, s 46(4) and LRR 2003, r 100).

The applicant for entry of a restriction is not able to apply for an official search with priority using Form OS1 or Form OS2, but may reserve a period of priority by making an outline application.

The Registry must give notice of an application for a restriction to the proprietor of the registered estate or charge concerned, if it has not been made by or with his consent or a person entitled to be registered as such proprietor (LRA 2002, s 45). However, the Registry is not obliged to give notice where the application reflects a limitation under an order of the court, or an undertaking given in place of such an order (LRA 2002, s 45(3)(c)).

Under the LRA 1925, freezing orders were usually protected by inhibitions. The LRA 2002 applies to any inhibitions entered under the 1925 Act as it applies to restrictions under the 2002 Act (LRA 2002, Sch 12, para 2(2)).

Agreed notice

Where the applicant wishes to apply for an agreed notice to protect a pending land action he should, in addition to the usual documents required (see *Notices*, page 389), deliver to the Registry a certified copy of the application to the court.

As the consent of the registered proprietor is unlikely to be forthcoming in this situation, this is likely to be sufficient to satisfy the Registry of the validity of the applicant's claim in accordance with LRA 2002, s 34(3)(c).

The agreed notice in the register will give details of the interest protected.

Unilateral notice

Where the applicant wishes to apply for a unilateral notice to protect a pending land action he should deliver to the Registry the usual documents required (see *Notices*, page 389).

The statement in panel 11 or conveyancer's certificate in panel 12 of Form UN1 should be completed on the following lines to show the interest of the applicant:

> applicant in an application for a [*restraint*] or [*freezing*] or [*interim receiving*] order in the [*name of court*] [*set out full court reference and parties*] to be made under [*state statutory provision*].

The unilateral notice in the register will give brief details of the interest protected and identify the beneficiary of that notice.

Restriction

In addition to the usual documents required (see *Restrictions*, page 500), the applicant for entry of a restriction should deliver to the Registry a certified copy of the court order, or of the application to the court, as the case may be.

As the consent of the registered proprietor is unlikely to be forthcoming in this situation, the statement in panel 12 or the conveyancer's certificate in panel 13 of Form RX1 as to the nature of the applicant's interest should be completed on the following lines:

> The interest is that specified in rule 93 [*(h) of the Land Registration Rules 2003, the applicant being a person with the benefit of a freezing order or an undertaking given in place of a freezing order (as appropriate)*] or [*(i) of the Land Registration Rules 2003, the applicant being a person who has applied for a freezing order*] or [*(r) of the Land Registration Rules 2003, the application being in respect of a freezing order or application for a freezing order (as appropriate) under Schedule 6 to the International Criminal Court Act 2001*].

Panel 9 of Form RX1 should be completed as to the wording of the appropriate restriction.

The wording of Forms AA, BB, CC, DD, EE, FF, GG and HH is set out in Appendix IV, page 585.

A restriction in standard Forms AA, BB, CC, DD, EE, FF, GG or HH in LRR 2003, Sch 4 does not require the approval of the Registry to the wording of the restriction under LRA 2002, s 43(3).

FRIENDLY SOCIETIES

Friendly societies were originally started by groups of individuals who joined together to make mutual provision for welfare issues that could affect individual members, such as sickness, disability or retirement, at a time when there were no general welfare provisions provided by the state. Although state welfare benefits and private insurance schemes are now available, friendly societies often offer other discretionary benefits to members in financial or other difficulties, in addition to providing tax-free savings policies, and therefore still exist and attract members. Various legislation was introduced to control and regulate the activities of friendly societies, culminating in the Friendly Societies Act 1974 and the Friendly Societies Act 1992.

The Friendly Societies Act 1992 provided a new framework for friendly societies, by allowing them to incorporate, conferring a wider range of powers on incorporated societies, and providing for more supervision to protect members. The 1992 Act came into force on 1 February 1993 and since that date no new friendly societies may be registered under the Friendly Societies Act 1974.

Friendly societies which are registered under the Friendly Societies Act 1992 are incorporated, while those still registered under the Friendly Societies Act 1974 are unincorporated. A friendly society which is not registered under either of those Acts will be an unincorporated association. If a friendly society was in existence on 1 February 1993, it can choose to become incorporated under the Friendly Societies Act 1992. If a friendly society is a charity, it is an exempt charity, see *Charities*, page 104.

Friendly societies registered under the Friendly Societies Act 1974

A friendly society registered under the 1974 Act may acquire land if this is permitted by its rules. The transfer should be to all the trustees. There is no limit to the number of trustees of a friendly society who can be registered as proprietors. The names of the trustees in the proprietorship register may be followed by an appropriate description such as: 'the trustees of the [*name*] Friendly Society'. If a trustee company has been appointed as trustee of a friendly society, the trustee company will be registered as proprietor.

The business address of the society should be given as an address for service.

If the survivor of the trustees will not be able to give a valid receipt for capital money, a restriction in Form A is required in the register. The wording of Form A is set out in Appendix IV, page 585.

A disposition by a friendly society should be executed by the current trustees of the society. If these are not also the existing registered proprietors, and the signatures have not been witnessed by the society's secretary, the society's solicitor or secretary should certify that they are the present trustees. A person dealing with the trustees is not required to enquire as to their authority to dispose of or deal with land (Friendly Societies Act 1974, s 53(1) as substituted by the Friendly Societies Act 1992).

Where an unincorporated friendly society which is a registered proprietor has become incorporated under the Friendly Societies Act 1992, the trustees cease to hold office and the property formerly held by them on trust for the society automatically vests in the incorporated society (Friendly Societies Act 1992, s 6(2)). An application should therefore be made for an alteration to bring the register up to date. The friendly society should deliver to the Registry:

(a)   an application in Form AP1;
(b)   the original or a certified copy of the certificate of incorporation; and
(c)   the fee payable (see *Fees*, page 221).

A branch of a friendly society registered under the Friendly Societies 1974 can acquire land only if its rules permit it to do so. Land, or a charge, acquired by a branch of a friendly society registered under the 1974 Act (whether or not the branch itself is so registered) vests in the trustees of the branch. Where a friendly society registered under the 1974 Act incorporates under the Friendly Societies Act 1992, the property of its branches vests in the incorporated society unless a scheme to the contrary is made under s 6(5) of the 1992 Act.

Friendly societies registered under the Friendly Societies Act 1992

All friendly societies registered under the Friendly Societies Act 1992 are incorporated societies and have power to acquire, hold, charge and dispose of land. The last word of the name of an incorporated friendly society is 'Limited' or 'Cyfyngedig'. In the case of an incorporated friendly society which is a collecting society the last three words of the name are 'Collecting Society Limited' or 'Cymdeithas Casglu Cyfyngedig'.

Where a friendly society registered under the Friendly Societies Act 1992 is registered as proprietor of registered land or of a registered charge, no restriction is usually required to be entered in the register because of the protection afforded to a purchaser in good faith of property from a friendly society (Friendly Societies Act 1992, s 9(4) and (5)).

An incorporated friendly society may execute a deed by either:

(a)   its common seal being affixed to a document that is expressed to be a deed in the presence of, and attested by, two persons who are stated to be either two members of the committee of management of the society or one such member and the secretary; or
(b)   the document being signed by two persons who are stated to be either two members of the committee of management of the society or one such member and the secretary, and expressed (in whatever form of words) to be executed by the society as a deed.

In favour of a purchaser in good faith for valuable consideration, a document executed in accordance with (b) above is deemed to have been duly executed by the society (Friendly Societies Act 1992, Sch 6, para 2).

If the society executes a deed using a different method, a certificate by either a conveyancer, or the secretary or a member of the committee of management of the society, will need to be lodged with any application for registration. The certificate must confirm that the deed has been duly executed in the manner authorised by the instrument constituting the society or regulating its affairs.

GIFTS

To pass a legal estate, a gift of land must be made by a deed. When the title to the land is unregistered, the gift may trigger compulsory first registration of title if it constitutes the transfer of a qualifying estate for the purposes of LRA 2002, s 4. When the title to the land is registered, a transfer by way of gift must be in the appropriate prescribed form (LRR 2003, r 58) and will constitute a registrable disposition which is required to be completed by registration under LRA 2002, s 27.

Unregistered land

When the title to land is unregistered, an application for first registration must be made if the gift 'triggers' compulsory first registration. The events triggering compulsory first registration under LRA 2002, s 4 include the transfer by way of gift (whether by conveyance, assignment, transfer or otherwise) of a freehold estate in land, or of an existing leasehold estate in land with more than 7 years to run at the time of the transfer. Also, the grant of a new leasehold estate in land out of a qualifying estate for a term of years absolute which is for a term of more than 7 years from the date of the grant, and which is by way of gift. For the purposes of s 4, a 'gift' includes a transfer or grant for the purposes of constituting a trust under which the settlor does not retain the whole of the beneficial interest, or uniting the bare legal title and the beneficial interest in property held under a trust under which the settlor did not, on constitution, retain the whole beneficial interest. 'Land' for the purposes of s 4 does not include mines and minerals held apart from the surface (s 4(9)), so the requirement to apply for first registration does not apply to a gift in respect of such mines and minerals.

The donee, as the person taking under the gift, must apply for first registration within 2 months of the gift. Where necessary, he may apply to the Registry for an order that the period for registration ends on a later date, which date will be specified in the order, if made. The Registry will make such an order if it is satisfied that there is good reason for doing so (LRA 2002, s 6(5)).

If the requirement of registration is not complied with, the transfer or lease becomes void as regards the transfer or grant of a legal estate (LRA 2002, s 7(1)). In consequence, in the case of a transfer by way of gift, the legal estate reverts to the donor who holds it on a bare trust for the donee; in the case of the grant of a lease, the grant takes effect as a contract for valuable consideration to grant the lease (s 7(2)). Where an order is made under LRA 2002, s 6(5), the application of s 7(1) is treated as not having occurred.

If there has to be a further deed because of the failure to apply for first registration following the original deed of gift, the donee will be liable for the proper costs of the donor in respect of the new deed (LRA 2002, s 8).

A donee applying for first registration should deliver to the Registry the usual documents required (see *First registration*, page 222).

For first registration generally, see *First registration*, page 222.

It was previously the practice of the Land Registry to make an entry in the register referring to the IA 1986 when first registration was 'triggered' by a gift. That practice was discontinued as from 15 November 1999, when a gift of land became a 'trigger' for compulsory first registration under the LRA 1925, s 123 (as amended).

Registered land

A transfer by way of gift of registered land must be made in the appropriate prescribed form. This will be either Form TR1 (for the whole of the land in a registered title); Form TR4 (for a registered charge or a portfolio of charges); Form TR5 (for a portfolio of titles as to whole or part); or Form TP1 (for part of the land in a registered title). Until the transfer of the registered estate or registered charge is completed by registration, it does not operate at law (LRA 2002, s 27(1)).

The donee (not being a 'purchaser) is not able to apply for an official search with priority using Form OS1 or Form OS2, but may reserve a period of priority by an outline application.

A donee applying to register a transfer of registered land should deliver to the Registry the usual documents required (see *Transfers*, page 551).

The priority of any interest affecting the registered estate is not affected by a gift of registered land (not being a disposition for valuable consideration), whether or not the interest or the gift is registered (LRA 2002, s 28).

Where a donee is seeking indemnity from the Registry under LRA 2002, Sch 8 (following rectification of the register, for example), any fraud or lack of proper care by the donor is treated as fraud or lack of proper care by the donee for the purposes of Sch 8, para 5 and may therefore preclude or reduce the payment of indemnity (see *Indemnity*, page 273).

For the position where an order of the court under IA 1986, ss 339, 340, 343 or 423 requires the register to be altered following the bankruptcy of the donor, see *Bankruptcy*, page 49.

HISTORICAL INFORMATION

The register of title only provides current details of the title at a particular point in time – it does not show how the title has changed historically. In most conveyancing transactions it is not necessary to consider historical editions of the registered title, but these may be relevant where, for example, consideration is being given to whether certain registered titles were at some point in common ownership, so as to extinguish easements or restrictive covenants by unity of seisin. Another example is where consideration is being given to whether a former owner is liable on implied covenants for title, the benefit of which runs with the registered estate under Law of Property (Miscellaneous Provisions) Act 1994, s 7.

It is possible to apply for historical information about a registered title (including the title plan) where this is held by the Registry in electronic form (LRA 2002, s 69 and LRR 2003, r 144). This includes information that was but is no longer in the register. The Registry is not under an obligation to hold previous editions of a registered title in electronic form and register history information *may* be available for dates after 4 May 1993 and title plan information *may* be available for dates after 13 October 2003. Limited information is held about title plans before this date. The application should be made in Form HC1 and should specify the date of the edition in question and indicate whether it is the last edition on that date, or all editions on that date, which are required. An application which does not specify such a date may be rejected. A fee is payable (see *Fees*, page 221).

Where the Registry is keeping in electronic form an edition of the registered title as it existed at the date specified in the application, it must issue a copy of it. If only part of the edition requested is kept by the Registry in electronic form, it must issue a copy of that part.

If the required information is not held in electronic form, the Registry may hold paper copies of earlier editions of the register or title plan and may be able to provide copies of these in response to an application under the Freedom of Information Act 2000 (see 'Freedom of Information Act 2000', page 401). Such an application should provide as much information as possible about the enquiry and the reason why the information is required. This will enable the Registry to determine if it is able to provide the information required.

HOME RIGHTS

'Home rights' means the rights of occupation of the home conferred upon a spouse or civil partner by FLA 1996, s 30. 'Home' means the dwelling house constituting the matrimonial or civil partnership home to which the home rights attach.

The Civil Partnership Act 2004 created a new legal relationship of civil partnership, which two people of the same sex can form by signing a registration document. It also amended the FLA 1996 to extend to civil partners the same rights of occupation of their home as apply to a matrimonial home.

The Marriage (Same Sex Couples) Act 2013 came into force on 29 March 2014. As well as enabling same sex couples to marry, it also contained provision for existing civil partners to convert their partnership to a marriage.

Home rights under the FLA 1996 constitute a charge on the home (FLA 1996, s 31) which, if the title to the home is registered, should be protected by the entry of a notice, which must be in the form of an agreed notice (LRR 2003, r 80(a)). Such a notice is referred to in the LRR 2003 as a 'home rights notice' (LRR 2003, r 217). Prior to the Civil Partnership Act 2004, a right of occupation was conferred only upon a spouse, and a notice in respect of such a right was referred to as a 'matrimonial home rights notice'. In the context of this topic, 'the spouse or civil partner' means the person whose home rights are protected or in need of protection; and 'the owning spouse or civil partner' means the other spouse or civil partner, who is the owner of the home.

A home rights charge arises on whichever is the latest of:

(a) the date when the owning spouse or civil partner acquires the home;
(b) the date of the marriage or civil partnership; and
(c) 1 January 1968 (being the date of commencement of the Matrimonial Homes Act 1967).

Where the owning spouse or civil partner is not the registered proprietor (or sole registered proprietor) of the home, but is entitled to occupy the home by virtue of a beneficial interest under a trust, the spouse or civil partner may still be entitled to home rights which are capable of protection against the trustees' registered title. However, this will only be the case where the property is held on trust for:

(a)   the owning spouse or civil partner only; or
(b)   the owning spouse or civil partner and the spouse or civil partner only (FLA 1996, s 31(4) and (5)).

Home rights will only continue so long as the marriage or civil partnership subsists, unless the court directs otherwise during the subsistence of the marriage or civil partnership by means of an order under FLA 1996, s 33(5). If the court makes such an order and those home rights have not already been protected in the register, an application for a home rights notice should be made. If the court makes such an order, and the home rights have already been protected in the register, an application for renewal of the registration in respect of home rights should be made.

A spouse's or civil partner's home rights may be brought to an end in the following ways:

(a)   by the death of either spouse or civil partner (FLA 1996, s 31(8)(a)), but subject to the power of the court to make an order under FLA 1996, s 33(5);
(b)   by the ending of the marriage or civil partnership otherwise than by death (FLA 1996, s 31(8)(b)), but subject to the power of the court to make an order under FLA 1996, s 33(5);
(c)   by an order of the court (FLA 1996, Sch 4, para 4(1)(c)); or
(d)   by the spouse or civil partner voluntarily releasing the home rights in writing (FLA 1996, Sch 4, para 5(1)).

As to bankruptcy and home rights, see *Bankruptcy*, page 49.

No protection under the FLA 1996 is necessary when the home is held jointly, both legally and beneficially, by both the spouses or civil partners. The protection of a home rights notice is only available in respect of one home at any one time. Prior to 14 February 1983, matrimonial home rights could also be protected by the entry of a caution against dealings (see *Cautions against dealings*, page 85). The registration of a Class F Land Charge is relevant only to unregistered land and will confer no protection in relation to registered land.

The right of a spouse or civil partner to occupy the home conferred by the FLA 1996 is not capable of falling within LRA 2002, Sch 1, para 2 or Sch 3, para 2, which deal with the overriding status of interests of persons in actual occupation (FLA 1996, s 31(10) as substituted by LRA 2002, Sch 11, para 34(2)). Even if the spouse or civil partner is occupying the home, such a right will not therefore constitute an interest which overrides first registration or registered dispositions and will need to be protected by entry of a home rights notice.

Home rights notice

A person applying to enter a home rights notice should deliver to the Registry an application in Form HR1. No fee is currently payable. As home rights may subsist in respect only of one property at a time, any previous registration must be revealed in Form HR1 and will be cancelled (FLA 1996, Sch 4, para 2). Where the application is made after the court has made an order under FLA 1996, s 33(5), an office copy of that order must be lodged with Form HR1. Alternatively a conveyancer may certify in panel 10 of Form HR1 that he holds such an office copy. The Registry will serve notice of the application to the registered proprietor.

Renewal of home rights notice

Where the court has made an order under FLA 1996, s 33(5), directing that the home rights shall not be brought to an end by the termination of the marriage or civil partnership, whether by death or otherwise, and those rights have already been protected in the register by means of a home rights notice or (prior to 14 February 1983) by a caution against dealings, an application should be made for the renewal, by way of entry of a home rights notice, of the registration of the existing notice or caution so that the making of the order can be protected in the register.   .

A person applying to renew the registration of a home rights notice should deliver to the Registry:

(a)   an application in Form HR2;
(b)   an office copy of the court order made under FLA 1996, s 33(5). Alternatively, a conveyancer may certify in panel 8 of Form HR2 that he holds such an office copy.

No fee is currently payable. The priority of the application may be reserved by lodging an outline application.

The renewal will be effected by the entry of a home rights notice referring to the order. It will not affect the priority of the original home rights charge (FLA 1996,

Sch 4, para 4(5)). The Registry will serve notice of the application for renewal upon the registered proprietor.

Cancellation of home rights notice

An application to cancel a home rights notice must be made in Form HR4, accompanied by the evidence required by FLA 1996, Sch 4, para 4. That evidence will normally consist of:

(a)   the death certificate or other sufficient evidence of death of either spouse or civil partner (but see also (e) below); or

(b)   an office copy of a decree absolute of divorce, dissolution or nullity (but see also (e) below). If a decree of divorce by an overseas court is lodged, additional evidence as to residence, domicile or nationality, may be required and, if the decree is not in English, a notarially certified translation should be provided; or

(c)   an office copy of an order of the court terminating the home rights; or

(d)   a written release of the home rights by the spouse or civil partner; and

(e)   where the supporting evidence is evidence of the spouse's or civil partner's death or a copy of a decree absolute produced in accordance with (a) or (b) above and the court has made an order under FLA 1996, s 33(5) and that order is referred to on the register, satisfactory evidence that the order has ceased to have effect.

No fee is currently payable.

Cancellation of matrimonial home rights caution

Where matrimonial home rights have been protected by a caution against dealings, application for removal of the caution may be made in one of the following ways:

(a)   by application for cancellation in Form CCD by the registered proprietor or a person who, but for the caution, would be entitled to be registered as proprietor; or

(b)   by withdrawal of the caution in Form WCT signed by the spouse or civil partner (or by their personal representative where appropriate) or by their conveyancer; or

(c)   by letter, accompanied by the appropriate evidence confirming one of the events described in (a), (b) or (c) in 'Cancellation of home rights notice', above. If the court has made an order under FLA 1996, s 33(5) which is referred to in the register, the applicant must also supply satisfactory evidence that this order has ceased to have effect.

No fee is currently payable. As to cautions against dealings generally, see *Cautions against dealings*, page 85.

Home rights search by a mortgagee

A mortgagee of a dwelling house who brings an action to enforce his security is obliged, under FLA 1996, s 56, to serve notice of the action on a spouse or civil partner whose rights of occupation are protected at the relevant time by a notice or caution in the register. A mortgagee of registered land that consists of or includes all or part of a dwelling house may apply in Form HR3 or by telephone or electronically for an official certificate of the result of a search (LRR 2003, r 158). This will reveal if there is a home rights notice or a matrimonial home rights caution registered, or a pending application for entry of a home rights notice on the day list. The search will confer priority for a period of 15 days (FLA 1996, s 56(5)). A fee is payable (see *Fees*, page 221).

HOUSING ACTION TRUSTS

Housing action trusts are established by the Secretary of State or, in Wales, the Welsh Ministers in relation to a designated area which may be added to and which does not need to be contiguous (Housing Act 1988 (HA 1988), Pt III, ss 60 to 92 and Sch 11). Broadly, the aims of a housing action trust are to renovate an area of run down housing and its general environment. In pursuance of this objective, the trust, which is a body corporate, has power to acquire, hold, manage, reclaim and dispose of land and other property and to carry on any business or undertaking and generally do anything necessary or expedient for the purposes of that objective. A housing action trust may acquire land in the following ways:

(a) by order of the Secretary of State or the Welsh Ministers ordering a transfer of housing accommodation from a local housing authority, a county council, a waste disposal authority, a joint body established under Local Government Act 1985, Pt IV or a residuary body established under Pt VII of that Act;

(b) by statutory vesting by an order of the Secretary of State or Welsh Ministers and, where appropriate, a minister of land which is owned by a public body or a statutory undertaker; or

(c) by agreement, or, provided the Secretary of State or Welsh Ministers consent, compulsorily.

While a housing action trust can dispose of land with the consent of the Secretary of State or Welsh Ministers, it may not dispose of a house which is for the time being subject to a secure tenancy, except to a registered social landlord or to a local housing authority or other local authority (HA 1988, s 79(2)). This does not, however, prevent a disposal of a house under the right to buy provisions in HA 1985, Pt 5.

Restrictions

In the light of the limitations on disposals by housing action trusts, when registering such a trust as the proprietor of a registered estate, application should be made for entry of a restriction on the following lines:

> No disposition by the proprietor of the registered estate (other than a charge) is to be completed by registration without the consent of the [*Secretary of State*] or [*Welsh Ministers*] unless either:
>
> (a)   it is a disposition of a house or flat under Part 5 of the Housing Act 1985 (Right to Buy); or
> (b)   it is a disposition to one or more individuals and contains a certificate that it consists of a single house or flat; or
> (c)   it contains a certificate that no part of the land consists of a house or a flat.

An application to register a disposition by a housing action trust should include the necessary evidence to meet the requirements of this restriction.

Disposal of land

A housing action trust has power, subject to any directions by, and with the consent of, the Secretary of State or Welsh Ministers, to dispose of any land that it owns. However, this is subject to limitation in relation to a house or flat which is the subject of a secure tenancy unless it is sold under the right to buy (HA 1988, s 79). All disposals of land require the consent of the Secretary of State or Welsh Ministers which may be given generally or specifically. A disposal of land which includes a house or flat made without such consent is void unless the disposal is to an individual or to two or more individuals, and the disposal does not extend to any other house. Where the land does not consist of a house or flat, then a purchaser is not concerned to enquire whether or not consent has been given and the disposal is not invalid.

In the case of a disposal of a house subject to a secure tenancy, the sale must be either to an 'approved person' or to a housing authority or other local authority. If the sale is to an approved person, the requirement in the HA 1988, s 81 that the consent of the Secretary of State or Welsh Ministers be obtained to any subsequent disposal of the house by the approved person applies. The transfer effecting the disposal must state that the requirement applies to any such disposal. Where the land has been mortgaged, this requirement for consent also applies to a disposal in exercise of the power of sale.

Where a transfer contains the statement required by HA 1988, s 81, the Registry is obliged to enter a restriction in Form X (HA 1988, s 81(10) and LRR 2003, r 95(2)(d)). The wording of Form X is set out in Appendix IV, page 585.

Exempt disposals as defined by HA 1988, s 81(8) are:

(a)   the disposal of a dwelling house to a person having the right to buy it under HA 1988, Pt 5 (whether the disposal is in fact made under that Part or otherwise);

(b)   the disposal of a dwelling house to a person having the right to buy it under HA 1996, Pt I (whether or not the disposal is in fact made under provisions having effect by virtue of s 17 of that Act);

(c)   a compulsory disposal within the meaning of HA 1985, Pt 5;

(d)   the disposal of an easement or rentcharge;

(e)   the disposal of an interest by way of security for a loan;

(f)   the grant of a secure tenancy or what would be a secure tenancy but for any of HA 1985, Sch 1, paras 2 to 12;

(g)   the grant of an assured tenancy or an assured agricultural occupancy, within the meaning of HA 1988, Pt I, or what would be such a tenancy or occupancy but for any of Sch 1, paras 4 to 8 to that Act; and

(h)   the transfer of an interest held on trust for any person where the disposal is made in connection with the appointment of a new trustee or in connection with the discharge of any trustee.

HOUSING ASSOCIATIONS

The law relating to housing associations is largely contained in the Housing Associations Act 1985 in respect of unregistered housing associations and in the HA 1996 in respect of registered housing associations. In England, but not in Wales, the regulation of social housing was further amended by the Housing and Regeneration Act 2008, and again by the Localism Act 2011. Housing associations are therefore affected by different regulatory regimes depending upon whether they are English or Welsh.

Housing Associations Act 1985, s 1 defines a housing association as a society, body of trustees or company:

(a)   which is established for the purpose of, or amongst whose objects or powers are included those of, providing, constructing, improving or managing, or facilitating or encouraging the construction or improvement of, housing accommodation, and

(b)   which does not trade for profit or whose constitution or rules prohibit the issue of capital with interest or dividend exceeding such rate as may be prescribed by the Treasury, whether with or without differentiation as between share and loan capital.

Most housing associations are charities and some of them are registered societies (see *Charities*, page 104, and *Registered societies*, page 485). Registered housing associations will be private registered providers (in England) and registered social landlords (in Wales). Some housing associations were either never registered, or were registered but subsequently became deregistered. Different regulatory regimes will apply to a housing association, depending upon whether or not it is registered.

Registered housing associations

For housing associations which are private registered providers or registered social landlords, see *Registered social landlords and private registered providers*, page 482.

Registration of unregistered housing association as proprietor of land

Where an unregistered housing association acquires land, it may be grant-aided land. Grant-aided land is defined in Housing Associations Act 1985, Sch 1 as land:

(a)   in respect of which a payment by way of annual grant or subsidy under the statutory provisions referred to in Sch 1, para 2 falls or fell to be made in respect of a period ending after 24 January 1974; or

(b)   on which is, or has been, secured a loan made under the statutory provisions referred to in Sch 1, para 3, in respect of which a repayment (by way of principal or interest or both) falls or fell to be made after 24 January 1974.

A disposition of grant-aided land by an unregistered housing association requires the consent of the Homes and Communities Agency, if the land is in England, or of the Welsh Ministers, if the land is in Wales. Previously, the required consent was that of the Housing Corporation or (in England only) the Office for Tenants and Social Landlords (Tenant Services Authority) depending upon the date of the disposition.

If an applicant for registration as proprietor of a registered estate or registered charge is, or holds on trust for, an unregistered social landlord within the meaning of the Housing Associations Act 1985 and the application relates to grant-aided land as defined in Sch 1 to that Act, the application must include a certificate to that effect (LRR 2003, r 183A(2)). This is in addition to any requirements arising from the fact that the applicant is a charity, a registered society or a company, for which see *Charities*, page 104; *Registered societies*, page 485; or *Companies*, page 154, respectively. Where such a certificate is given, application should be made for entry of a restriction to the following effect in the proprietorship register in the case of land in England:

> No disposition of the registered estate by the proprietor of the registered estate is to be completed by registration without a certificate by the registered proprietor signed by their secretary or by two trustees if a charitable trust or by their conveyancer that the provisions of section 172 of the Housing and Regeneration Act 2008 have been complied with or that they do not apply to the disposition.

In the case of grant-aided land in Wales the restriction is to the following effect:

> No disposition by the proprietor of the registered estate is to be registered without the consent of the Welsh Ministers when such consent is required under the provisions of section 9 of the Housing Associations Act 1985.

If a registered estate in land is held on trust for an unregistered housing association and two or more trustees are being entered as proprietors, a restriction in Form A will be entered in the register. If an unregistered housing association is a charity, a charity restriction will be entered where appropriate.

Dispositions by unregistered housing associations

Applications to register dispositions by unregistered housing associations should meet the requirements of any restriction in the register. Where a restriction refers to the consent of Homes England (previously the Homes and Communities Agency), or the Welsh Ministers, under Housing Associations Act 1985, s 9, evidence of that consent need not be lodged where the disposal is an exempt disposal or other form disposal where such consent is not required.

If an unregistered housing association is a charity, the appropriate charity statement should be included within the disposition where necessary (see *Charities*, page 104).

IDENTITY EVIDENCE

To reduce the risk of registration fraud, the Registry requires confirmation or evidence of identity to be provided in respect of parties to certain dispositions and transactions which are the subject of an application for registration. The Registry's requirements will depend upon whether an application is lodged by a conveyancer or by a lay-person. For the definition of 'conveyancer', see *Conveyancers*, page 171.

Evidence of identity will be required in relation to the following types of application:

(a) registration of a transfer of a registered estate or registered charge (whether or not for valuable consideration and including transfers to appoint or remove a trustee and assents by personal representatives);

(b) registration of a lease (whether or not for valuable consideration) of a registered estate;

(c) closure of a registered leasehold title on surrender of the registered lease;

(d) first registration of freehold or leasehold land (including a voluntary application where the title documents have been lost or destroyed);

(e) registration of a legal charge of a registered estate or sub-charge of a registered charge or registration of such on first registration of the land;

(f) discharge or release of a registered charge in paper form (Form DS1 or Form DS3); and

(g) alteration of the register following an individual's change of name by deed poll, statutory declaration or statement of truth.

Although the Registry will not routinely require confirmation of identity in other situations, it may request this if it considers it necessary or desirable (LRR 2003, r 17). The evidence will be required in respect of the transferor and transferee, landlord and tenant, or mortgage lender, as the case may be. Evidence will also be required for an attorney of any of those parties.

Certain exceptions may apply:

(a) *The 'low-value' exception*, which applies where the true value of the land which is the subject of the disposal, discharge or release is £6,000 or less. In these cases, the conveyancer may instead lodge a certificate confirming the value of the land.

(b) *The 'insolvency official, etc' exception*, which applies in respect of a person acting in the capacity of a trustee in bankruptcy, liquidator, supervisor, administrator or administrative receiver appointed under the IA 1986; or as a receiver under the Law of Property Act 1925; or as a deputy appointed under the Mental Health Act 2005; or as a personal representative who assents or transfers the land.

(c)   *The 'not practicable' exception*, which applies where it is not practicable to provide evidence of identity. For example, where a tenant has 'disappeared' and application is made to close the leasehold title following its surrender by operation of law. The conveyancer should enclose a covering letter with the application explaining why it is not practicable to provide evidence of identity. Mere 'inconvenience' is not sufficient.

(d)   *The 'Land Registry facility letter' exception*, which applies where the Registry has issued a facility letter in respect of the identity of a private individual or corporate body dealing regularly with the Registry. A copy of the facility letter may be enclosed with any application in place of evidence of identity.

(e)   *The 'retained evidence of identity' exception*, which applies where the Land Registry has approved draft forms of transfers and leases of part for specific developments (see *Developing estates*, page 190). Evidence of identity for any attorney acting for the transferor or landlord does not have to be lodged with each individual transfer or lease for registration where that evidence has been lodged with the draft for approval and has been retained by the Registry.

(6)   *The 'Legal charge up to £10,000 to a local authority in respect of a service charge loan' exception*, which applies where an application is made to register a legal charge to a local authority, the value of the charge as stated on the charge deed or application form is up to £10,000, and the charge is in respect of a service charge loan and this is clearly stated in the charge deed or on the application form.

Confirmation of identity by a conveyancer should, in relation to most applications, be provided by completing the relevant panel(s) in Forms AP1, FR1 or DS2 as the case may be. This will be in relation to the conveyancer's own client (the applicant) and the other party or parties involved. For any unrepresented party, the conveyancer must either confirm that sufficient steps have been taken to verify that party's identity or provide evidence of identity for that party using Form ID1 (for a private individual) or Form ID2 (for a corporate body). Completed Forms ID1 and ID2 are not open to public inspection or copying and normally a person may not apply for an official copy of them (LRR 2003, rr 133 and 135 (see *Official copies and inspection*, page 396). In the case of an application for change of name by an individual which is not combined with any other application, a conveyancer may either confirm that sufficient steps have been taken to verify that party's identity or provide evidence of identity for that party using Form ID1 (see *Change of name*, page 99).

Where an application has been lodged by a lay-person, confirmation of identity cannot be provided by that person (as he is not a conveyancer) and instead evidence of identity of that applicant and of any other unrepresented party will need to be provided using Form ID1 or Form ID2 as appropriate.

Further guidance as to the Registry's requirements is contained in its Practice Guide 67 – *Evidence of identity – conveyancers*. This is available to view and download at www.gov.uk/government/publications.

IMPLIED COVENANTS

A registrable disposition may be expressed to be made either with full title guarantee or with limited title guarantee or, in the case of an instrument in the Welsh language, *gyda gwarant teitl llawn* or *gyda gwarant teitl cyfyngedig* (LRR 2003, r 67(1)). The effect of using these expressions is to imply covenants by the person making the disposition, as set out in Law of Property (Miscellaneous Provisions) Act 1994, Pt I.

A disposition '*with full title guarantee*' or '*gyda gwarant teitl llawn*' implies the following covenants:

(a)   that the person making the disposition has the right (with the concurrence of any other person conveying the property) to dispose of the property as he purports to;

(b)   that the person making the disposition will at his own cost do all that he reasonably can to give the person to whom he disposes of the property the title he purports to give;

(c)   that the person making the disposition is disposing of the property free from all charges and incumbrances (whether monetary or not) and all other rights exercisable by third parties, other than any charges, incumbrances or rights which that person does not and could not reasonably be expected to know about;

(d)   (where the disposition is of leasehold land) that the lease is subsisting at the time of the disposition and there is no subsisting breach of a condition or tenant's obligation, and nothing which at that time would render the lease liable to forfeiture;

(e)   (where the disposition is a mortgage of property subject to a rentcharge) that the mortgagor will fully and promptly observe and perform all the obligations under the instrument creating the rentcharge that are for the time being enforceable with respect to the property by the owner of the rentcharge in his capacity as such; and

(f) (where the disposition is a mortgage of leasehold land) that the mortgagor will fully and promptly observe and perform all the obligations under the lease subject to the mortgage that are for the time being imposed on him in his capacity as tenant under the lease.

A disposition '*with limited title guarantee*' or '*gyda gwarant teitl cyfyngedig*' implies the covenants set out at (a), (b), (d), (e) and (f) above, and the following covenant:

(g) that the person making the disposition has not since the last disposition for value:

(i) charged or incumbered the property by means of any charge or incumbrance which subsists at the time when the disposition is made, or granted third party rights in relation to the property which so subsist, or

(ii) suffered the property to be so charged or incumbered or subjected to any such rights,

and that he is not aware that anyone else has done so since the last disposition for value.

Law of Property (Miscellaneous Provisions) Act 1994, s 6 provides that the implied covenantor in a registrable disposition made with either full or limited title guarantee is not liable under the implied covenants referred to in (a), (c) (d) or (g) above in respect of any particular matter to which the disposition is expressly made subject or which, at the time of the disposition, was entered in the register in relation to the interest in question. Nor for anything that at the time of the disposition is within the actual knowledge, or which is a necessary consequence of facts that are within the actual knowledge, of the purchaser (for which purpose Law of Property Act 1925, s 198 is to be disregarded, so that registration in the Land Charges Department will not be deemed to constitute actual notice of an interest).

The operation of any covenant implied in an instrument by virtue of Law of Property (Miscellaneous Provisions) Act 1994, Pt I may be limited or extended by a provision of that instrument (Law of Property (Miscellaneous Provisions) Act 1994, s 8(1)). One of the covenants referred to above is that contained in s 4(1)(b) of that Act which implies, in a disposition of leasehold land made with full title guarantee or limited title guarantee, a covenant that there is no subsisting breach of a condition or tenant's obligation, and nothing which at that time would render the lease liable to forfeiture. If the disposition is the grant of an underlease, the reference in the implied covenant to 'lease' is to the lease out of which the underlease is granted. Where a document effecting a registrable disposition contains a provision which limits or extends a covenant implied under Law of Property (Miscellaneous Provisions) Act 1994, s 4(1)(b), that document must do so by express reference to that section of that Act (LRR 2003, r 68). The form of statement is not prescribed, but may for example be in one of the following forms:

> The covenant set out in section 4(1)(b) of the Law of Property (Miscellaneous Provisions) Act 1994 shall [*not*] extend to [*insert relevant details*].

> The [*transferor*] or [*lessor*] shall not be liable under any of the covenants set out in section 4(1)(b) of the Law of Property (Miscellaneous Provisions) Act 1994.

Where a registrable disposition of leasehold land limits or extends the implied covenant under Law of Property (Miscellaneous Provisions) Act 1994, s 4(1)(b), a reference to this may be made in the register (LRR 2003, r 67(6)). The form of entry will be along the following lines:

> The covenant implied under s 4(1)(b) of the Law of Property (Miscellaneous Provisions) Act 1994 in the disposition to the proprietor is modified.

No other reference to any covenant implied by Law of Property (Miscellaneous Provisions) Act 1994, Pt I will be made in the register in any other circumstances. No reference will be made to any covenant implied by Law of Property Act 1925, s 76 as applied by Law of Property (Miscellaneous Provisions) Act 1994, s 11(1)) (LRR 2003, r 67(5)).

Right to buy transfers and leases must be made with full title guarantee, which should not be modified (HA 1985, Pt I, Sch 6, para 4A).

The benefit of the implied covenants runs with the purchaser's estate or interest, so that a successor in title is able to enforce them (Law of Property (Miscellaneous Provisions) Act 1994, s 7). However, the liability under the implied covenants does not attach to land retained by the vendor and so does not pass to his successors in title.

Transfers of pre-1996 leases

Landlord and Tenant (Covenants) Act 1995, s 1(3) defines a 'new tenancy' as a lease granted on or after 1 January 1996 otherwise than in pursuance of an agreement entered into, an option granted or a court order made before that date. An 'old tenancy' will therefore be a tenancy granted before 1 January 1996 or in pursuance of an agreement entered into, an option granted or a court order made before that date. Unless the contrary intention is expressed, the following covenants are implied in a transfer of a registered leasehold estate which is an 'old tenancy' rather than a 'new tenancy' for the purposes of Landlord and Tenant (Covenants) Act 1995, s 1 (LRA 2002, Sch 12, para 20):

(a) (in the case of a transfer of the whole of the land comprised in the registered lease) the transferee covenants with the transferor that during the residue of the term granted by the registered lease the transferee and the persons deriving title under him will:

   (i)   pay the rent reserved by the lease,
   (ii) comply with the covenants and conditions contained in the lease, and
   (iii) keep the transferor and the persons deriving title under him indemnified against all actions, expenses and claims on account of any failure to comply with clauses (i) and (ii);

(b) (in the case of a transfer of part of the land comprised in the registered lease) the transferee covenants with the transferor that during the residue of the term granted by the registered lease the transferee and the persons deriving title under him will:

   (i)   where the rent reserved by the lease is apportioned, pay the rent apportioned to the part transferred,
   (ii) comply with the covenants and conditions contained in the lease so far as affecting the part transferred, and
   (iii) keep the transferor and the persons deriving title under him indemnified against all actions, expenses and claims on account of any failure to comply with clauses (i) and (ii);

(c) (in the case of a transfer of part of the land comprised in the registered lease where the transferor continues to hold land under that lease) the transferor covenants with the transferee that during the residue of the term granted by the registered lease the transferor and the persons deriving title under him will:

   (i)   where the rent reserved by the lease is apportioned, pay the rent apportioned to the part retained,
   (ii) comply with the covenants and conditions contained in the lease so far as affecting the part retained, and
   (iii) keep the transferee and the persons deriving title under him indemnified against all actions, expenses and claims on account of any failure to comply with clauses (i) and (ii).

Where a transfer of such a registered leasehold estate modifies or negatives any of the covenants implied under paragraphs (a) and (b) above, an entry must be made in the register that the covenants have been so modified or negatived (LRR 2003, r 66).

As original tenant liability was abolished for new tenancies, the covenants implied into a transfer of an old tenancy will not, therefore, be implied into the transfer of a new tenancy. However, transfers of new tenancies will be subject to the implied covenants for title set out in the Law of Property (Miscellaneous Provisions) Act 1994 referred to above.

Transfer of a registered estate subject to a rentcharge

In addition to the covenants implied under Law of Property (Miscellaneous Provisions) Act 1994, Pt I, where a registered estate is transferred subject to a rentcharge, the covenants referred to in Law of Property Act 1925, s 77 and Sch 2 (as modified by LRR 2003, r 69) are also implied.

In a transfer for valuable consideration of the whole of the land affected by a rentcharge, there is implied a covenant by the transferee with the transferor that the transferee or the persons deriving title under him will at all times, from the date of the transfer or other date therein stated:

(a) duly pay the rentcharge and observe and perform all the covenants, agreements and conditions contained in the deed or other document creating the rentcharge, and thenceforth on the part of the owner of the land to be observed and performed; and

(b) save harmless and keep indemnified the transferor and his estate and effects from and against all proceedings, costs, claims and expenses on account of any omission to pay the rentcharge or any part thereof, or any breach of the said covenants, agreements and conditions.

Where a rentcharge has been apportioned in respect of any land, with the consent of the owner of the rentcharge, these covenants are implied in the transfer in the like manner as if the apportioned rentcharge were the rentcharge referred to and the document creating the rentcharge related solely to that land.

In a transfer for valuable consideration of part of the land affected by a rentcharge, subject to a part of that rentcharge which has been or is by that transfer apportioned (but in either case without the consent of the owner of the rentcharge) in respect of the land transferred, there is implied a covenant by the transferee with the transferor that the transferee or the persons deriving title under him will at all times, from the date of the transfer or other date therein stated:

(a) pay the apportioned rent and observe and perform all the covenants (other than the covenant to pay the entire rent) and conditions contained in the deed or other document creating the rentcharge, so far as the same relate to the land conveyed; and

(b) save harmless and keep indemnified the transferor and his respective estate and effects from and against all proceedings, costs, claims and expenses on account of any omission to pay the said apportioned rent, or any breach of any of the said covenants and conditions, so far as the same relate as aforesaid.

On a transfer of a registered estate subject to a rentcharge, any covenant implied by Law of Property Act 1925, s 77(1)(A) or (B) may be modified or negatived by adding suitable words to the transfer (LRR 2003, r 69(4)).

The implied covenants referred to above do not apply to a rentcharge falling within Rentcharges Act 1977, s 2(3)(a) (i.e. family charges), in relation to which different covenants are implied (Rentcharges Act 1977, s 11).

INDEMNITY

The LRA 2002 contains provisions relating to the payment of indemnity (i.e. statutory compensation) by the Registry under the 'state guarantee of title' in appropriate cases (LRA 2002, s 103 and Sch 8). A person is entitled to be indemnified by the Registry if he suffers loss by reason of:

(a) rectification of the register;

(b) a mistake the correction of which would involve rectification of the register;

(c) a mistake in an official search;

(d) a mistake in an official copy;

(e) a mistake in a document kept by the Registry which is not an original and is referred to in the register;

(f) the loss or destruction of a document lodged at the Registry for inspection or safe custody;

(g) a mistake in the cautions register; or

(h) failure by the Registry to perform its duty under LRA 2002, s 50 to give notice of the creation of a statutory charge.

'Rectification' for these purposes means an alteration of the register which involves the correction of a mistake and prejudicially affects the title of a registered proprietor. References to a mistake in something include anything mistakenly omitted from it as well as anything mistakenly included in it (LRA 2002, Sch 8, para 11(1)).

A person who suffers loss by reason of the upgrade of a title under LRA 2002, s 62 is treated for the purposes of an indemnity claim as having suffered loss by reason of rectification of the register (see *Upgrade of class of title*, page 565).

Where the register is rectified following a forgery, the proprietor of a registered estate or charge claiming in good faith under the forged disposition is treated for the purposes of an indemnity claim as having suffered loss by reason of such rectification as if the disposition had not been forged (LRA 2002, Sch 8, para 1(2)(b)).

No indemnity, however, is paid in the following cases:

(a) on account of any mines or minerals or the existence of any right to work or get mines or minerals, unless it is noted in the register that the registered title includes the mines and minerals;
(b) on account of any loss suffered by a claimant wholly or partly as a result of his own fraud; or
(c) on account of any loss suffered by the claimant wholly as a result of his own lack of proper care.

Where any loss is suffered by a claimant partly as a result of his own lack of proper care, any indemnity payable to him is reduced to such extent as is fair having regard to his share in the responsibility for the loss (LRA 2002, Sch 8, para 5(2)).

When deciding whether there has been any fraud or lack of care on the part of the claimant, any fraud or lack of care on the part of a person from whom he derives title is treated as if it were the claimant's fraud or lack of care. This does not apply, however, where the claimant derives title from such a person under a disposition for valuable consideration which is registered or protected by an entry in the register.

Where the indemnity is payable in respect of an estate, interest or charge, the value of such estate, interest or charge is regarded, in a case where there is rectification, as not exceeding its value immediately before the rectification (but as if there were to be no rectification). Where correcting a mistake would involve rectification of the register but there is to be no rectification, the value of such estate, interest or charge is regarded as its value at the time when the mistake which caused the loss was made (LRA 2002, Sch 8, para 6).

For the position where indemnity is being sought in respect of costs, see *Costs*, page 175.

Where a claim to indemnity under LRA 2002, Sch 8 cannot be resolved by agreement with the Registry, a person may apply to the High Court or a county court for the determination of any question as to whether he is entitled to such indemnity or as to the amount of the indemnity. The requirement that the registrar consents to the incurring of costs or expenses does not apply to the costs of such an application to the court or of any legal proceedings arising out of such an application (LRA 2002, Sch 8, para 7).

Interest on indemnity

Interest is payable on the amount of any indemnity paid at the applicable rate (LRR 2003, r 195). Where there has been rectification, interest is payable for the period from the date of rectification to the date of payment. Where there has not been rectification, interest is payable for the period from the date the loss is suffered by reason of the relevant mistake, loss, destruction or failure to the date of payment. No interest is payable for any period or periods where the Registry or the court is satisfied that the claimant has not taken reasonable steps to pursue with due diligence the claim for indemnity or, where relevant, the application for rectification.

In calculating the exact period in respect of which interest is payable, the date of payment is included but the date of the rectification, or the date the loss is suffered, is excluded.

The applicable rate of interest will be calculated as follows:

(a)   Where the relevant period starts on or after 10 November 2008, at 1 per cent above the applicable Bank of England base rate or rates.
(b)   Where the relevant period starts before that date:

   (i)   for the part of the period before 10 November 2008, at the applicable rate or rates set for court judgment debts, and
   (ii) for the part of the period on or after 10 November 2008, at 1 per cent above the applicable Bank of England base rate or rates.

For the purposes of r 195, 'Bank of England base rate' means: (a) the rate announced from time to time by the Monetary Policy Committee of the Bank of England as the official dealing rate, being the rate at which the Bank is willing to enter into transactions for providing short-term liquidity in the money markets; or (b) where an order under Bank of England Act 1998, s 19 is in force, any equivalent rate determined by the Treasury under that section.

For the purposes of the Limitation Act 1980, a liability to pay an indemnity under LRA 2002, Sch 8 is a simple contract debt and the cause of action arises at the time when the claimant knows, or but for his own default might have known, of the existence of his claim (LRA 2002, Sch 8, para 8).

When an indemnity is paid, including interest on an indemnity, the Registry is entitled to recover the amount paid from any person who caused or substantially contributed to the loss by his fraud. The Registry is also, for the purpose of recovering that amount, entitled to enforce the following rights of action:

(a) any right of action (of whatever nature and however arising) which the claimant would have been entitled to enforce had the indemnity not been paid; and

(b) where the register has been rectified, any right of action (of whatever nature and however arising) which the person in whose favour the register has been rectified would have been entitled to enforce had it not been rectified.

This is without prejudice to any other rights the Registry may have (LRA 2002, Sch 8, para 10). For example, the Registry may be able to recover indemnity by enforcing an implied covenant for title given by the person who purported to transfer the estate to the claimant. There are also specific provisions under the Housing Acts that provide for a right of recourse against a local authority, if indemnity is paid where land has been registered in reliance on the accuracy of a certificate of title and there was an error in that certificate. Similar rights arise in cases where reliance has been placed on a certificate given by a housing action trust.

INDEMNITY COVENANTS

Where the proprietor of a registered estate has given an indemnity covenant, the Registry may make an entry in respect of it in the proprietorship register (LRR 2003, r 65). This applies whether the indemnity covenant is given in respect of a restrictive covenant or other matter that affects the registered estate or in respect of a positive covenant that relates to that estate.

If the existence of the indemnity covenant is apparent from the register in some other way, the Registry need not make an entry. This might arise where the indemnity covenant is included amongst restrictive covenants and is set out with them in the charges register. Where the Registry does make an entry, it must, where practicable, refer to the deed or document that contains the indemnity covenant.

There is no need to make a specific application for an entry in respect of an indemnity covenant when this is included in a deed or document lodged as part of an application in respect of a registrable disposition. The entry will be made by the Registry if it considers it appropriate.

Where an entry has been made in respect of an indemnity covenant, the Registry must remove it from the register if it appears to the Registry that the covenant does not bind the current proprietor of the registered estate (LRR 2003, r 65(3)).

INDIVIDUAL VOLUNTARY ARRANGEMENTS

An IVA with creditors (as an alternative to bankruptcy) consists of either a composition in satisfaction of debts or a scheme of arrangement of affairs. In either case it must be approved by a meeting of creditors and is implemented by a licensed insolvency practitioner as the 'supervisor' of the IVA (IA 1986, Pt VIII). The effect of an IVA, if any, on the debtor's property depends on its terms. All of the debtor's property will be included in the arrangement, unless specifically excluded (Insolvency (England and Wales) Rules 2016, r 8.2 or r 8.3).

An IVA is different to a deed of arrangement (now abolished). The effect of an IVA, if any, on the debtor's property depends upon its terms. If the IVA is simply an agreement to pay regular sums to the supervisor, then any registered estate or registered charge of the debtor will be unaffected and neither a notice nor a restriction can be applied for.

If the debtor is the sole proprietor of a registered estate or registered charge which he holds for his own benefit and the IVA creates an equitable charge, a contract for sale, option, or right of pre-emption in favour of the supervisor affecting that registered estate or registered charge, an application may be made for entry of an agreed notice or unilateral notice, in respect of the interest created.

If the debtor has a beneficial interest under a trust of land of a registered estate and the IVA creates an equitable charge, a contract for sale, option, or right of pre-emption in favour of the supervisor affecting that interest, or if the effect of the IVA is to create a trust and it affects a registered estate, the interest created cannot be protected by an agreed notice or unilateral notice (LRA 2002, s 33(a)). However, it may be possible to protect this by an application for entry of a restriction. The appropriate form of restriction which can be applied for will depend upon the circumstances.

If the debtor is a sole registered proprietor who was holding the registered estate on trust for his own benefit before the IVA and is holding the property on trust for the creditors under the voluntary arrangement, an application may be made for entry of a restriction in Form A or Form II.

If the IVA contains a provision that the debtor will not transfer, charge or otherwise deal with the property without the consent of the supervisor then, in addition to a restriction in Form A, application may also be made for a restriction in Forms L, N, or NN. In the case of a registered charge, application may be made for a restriction in Forms S, T or OO.

Where the registered estate is held by joint registered proprietors (one of whom may be the debtor) on trust for the debtor and others before the IVA, and the IVA contains a charge or assignment of the debtor's beneficial interest, or creates a trust in favour of the supervisor, an application may be made for the entry of a restriction in Form A, if such a restriction has not already been entered in the register. The supervisor may also apply for a restriction in Form II if the IVA contains an assignment of a debtor's beneficial interest, or if the debtor holds his beneficial share on a bare trust for the supervisor.

If the interest is held on trust by the debtor for the creditors or charged to the supervisor, no form of restriction other than a restriction in Form A (in relation to a registered estate, if not already entered in the register) can be applied for, as the interest of the supervisor or creditors will be derivative and will not therefore constitute a right or claim in relation to a registered estate or charge for the purposes of LRA 2002, s 42(1)(c).

No other form of restriction may be applied for without the consent of the registered proprietor(s).

A restriction does not confer any priority; it simply prevents an entry being made in the register in respect of any disposition, or a disposition of a specified kind, unless the terms of the restriction have (where applicable) been complied with.

Agreed notice

In addition to the usual documents required (see *Notices*, page 389), an applicant should deliver to the Registry a certified copy of the IVA.

Where the consent of the registered proprietor is not available, the certified copy of the IVA is likely to be sufficient to satisfy the Registry as to the validity of the applicant's claim for the purposes of LRA 2002, s 34(3)(c).

The agreed notice in the register will give details of the interest protected.

Unilateral notice

An applicant should deliver to the Registry the usual documents required (see *Notices*, page 389).

The statement in panel 12 or conveyancer's certificate in panel 13 of Form UN1 should be completed to show details of the IVA, including the date of the agreement, the debtor's name and details of the provisions in the IVA claimed to give the supervisor an interest in the registered estate or charge.

The unilateral notice in the register will give brief details of the interest protected and identify the beneficiary of that notice.

Restriction

Where the supervisor is applying for a restriction he should, in addition to the usual documents required (see *Restrictions*, page 500), deliver to the Registry (if the application is made by a person who claims that he has a sufficient interest in the making of the entry) a certified copy of the IVA.

The statement in panel 12 or conveyancer's certificate in panel 13 of Form RX1 must be completed, setting out details of the IVA, including the provisions in the IVA claimed to give the supervisor an interest in the registered estate or charge.

Panel 9 of Form RX1 should be completed to show the wording of the appropriate restriction(s). A restriction in a standard form contained in LRR 2003, Sch 4 does not require the approval of the Registry to the terms of the restriction under LRA 2002, s 43(3).

The wording of Forms A and II is set out in Appendix IV, page 585.

A restriction in Form II does not of itself prevent a disposition, provided its terms are complied with. This is because the interest of the beneficiary will be overreached where the requirements of Form A have been met (Law of Property Act 1925, ss 2 and 27).

A possible form of restriction based on the wording of Form L is:

> No [disposition or specify type of disposition] of the registered estate by the proprietor of the registered estate [or by the proprietor of any registered charge not being a charge registered before the entry of this restriction] is to be registered without a certificate signed by [name] of [address] [or [their conveyancer or specify appropriate details]] that the provisions of [specify clause, paragraph or other

particulars] of [specify details] have been complied with [or that they do not apply to the disposition].

A possible form of restriction based on the wording of Form N is:

> No [disposition or specify type of disposition] of the registered estate by the proprietor of the registered estate [or by the proprietor of any registered charge not being a charge registered before the entry of this restriction] is to be registered without a written consent signed by [name] of [address] [or [their conveyancer or specify appropriate details]].

A possible form of restriction based on the wording of Form NN is:

> No [disposition *or specify type of disposition*] of the registered estate [(other than a charge)] by the proprietor of the registered estate [, or by the proprietor of any registered charge, not being a charge registered before the entry of this restriction,] is to be registered without a written consent signed by [*name*] of [*address*] [or [*their conveyancer or specify appropriate details*]], or a certificate signed by [*name*] of [*address*] [or [*their conveyancer or specify appropriate details*]] that the provisions of [*specify clause, paragraph or other particulars*] of [*specify details*] have been complied with [or that they do not apply to the disposition].

The equivalent restrictions to those in Forms L, N and NN relating to a registered estate will, in the case of a registered charge, be Forms S, T and OO, respectively.

The Registry must give notice of such an application to the proprietor of the registered estate or charge concerned if it has not been made by or with his consent or a person entitled to be registered as such proprietor (LRA 2002, s 45).

INHERITANCE TAX

In some circumstances a registered estate may be subject to a liability for IHT (formerly known as capital transfer tax) in respect of deaths occurring after 12 March 1975. This tax replaced death duties (in practice only estate duty) which applied in respect of deaths occurring on or before that date. The entry and/or removal of entries relating to IHT or death duties may therefore be relevant (see also *Personal representatives*, page 435).

Liability for death duties

Where the proprietor of a registered estate died before 13 March 1975 and it appeared that the registered estate was subject to a charge for death duties, the

Registry would make the following entry (known as a notice in Form 60) in the register:

> Until the registration of a disposition in favour of a purchaser for money or money's worth, the land is liable to such death duties as may be payable or arise by reason of the death of [*name*] of [*address*] who died on [*date*].

The Registry will automatically cancel this entry upon the registration of a transfer of the registered estate on sale or other disposition for value. However, application to cancel this entry may be made at any time by lodging Form CN1 completed by the Commissioners of HM Revenue and Customs (HMRC) (the Commissioners). No fee is currently payable.

Liability for capital transfer tax/inheritance tax

When IHT is due to the Commissioners, a statutory charge in their favour is imposed on the registered estate that is the subject of the gift. The Registry will not automatically make any entry in respect of this, but the Commissioners can, if they so wish, apply in Form AN1 to protect this charge by entering in the register an agreed notice (LRR 2003, rr 80 and 81) in the following form:

> Notice of an Inland Revenue charge (Reference number –) in respect of such tax as may arise.

LRA 2002, s 31 provides that the effect of a disposition of a registered estate or charge on a charge under Inheritance Tax Act 1984, s 237 is to be determined not in accordance with LRA 2002, ss 28 to 30, but in accordance with Inheritance Tax Act 1984, ss 237(6) and 238 (under which a purchaser in good faith for money or money's worth takes free from the charge in the absence of registration). A disposition of the registered estate therefore takes subject to a subsisting Inland Revenue charge unless:

(a) the disposition is in favour of a purchaser within the meaning of the Inheritance Tax Act 1984; and
(b) the charge is not, at the time of registration of the disposition, protected by a notice in the register.

Such a notice will not be cancelled by the Registry, even when registering a transfer on sale, without receipt of Form CN1 completed by the Commissioners. If the Commissioners have certified in the Form CN1 that the application for cancellation is only to take effect upon the registration of a disposition to a purchaser, then the Registry will cancel the entry only when the Form CN1 is accompanied by a proper application to register the transfer, or other specified disposition, in favour of the purchaser.

On an application for first registration not based on a disposition for value and where a gift has been made within 8 years of the date of the application, where no charge is disclosed and no Class D(i) Land Charge is registered, consideration will be given by the Registry as to whether any liability to capital transfer tax or IHT has arisen.

Where the value of the estate is above the IHT threshold, a certified copy (or probate copy) of the will or a statutory declaration or statement of truth as to entitlement under an intestacy, together with any relevant deed of family arrangement or variation must be lodged in order to satisfy the Registry as to the applicant's entitlement to apply.

If it appears from the application that the property being registered may be subject to a charge for IHT, the Registry will inform the applicant that it intends to make the following entry in the register:

> Notice of the possibility of an Inland Revenue charge in respect of such inheritance tax as may arise as a result of the death of [*name*] who died on [*date*].

However, if the applicant confirms in writing details of the surrounding circumstances of the case and that either no IHT was ever payable, or that it has been paid in full, the entry will not be made. Alternatively, the applicant may supply a certificate of discharge from the Commissioners, or a letter from the Commissioners addressed to the Registry confirming the same.

Nil-rate band discretionary trusts

A nil-rate band discretionary trust is sometimes used in estate planning to reduce liability to IHT on the death of a surviving joint proprietor. The trustees have discretion as to the application of the trust income and how the trust assets will ultimately be distributed among a class of beneficiaries. Commonly, a property comprising the family home is an asset used in relation to such a trust. If the trust is created before the first death of a joint proprietor and the property is not already held under a tenancy in common, the proprietors sever their joint tenancy (see *Severance of a beneficial joint tenancy*, page 533).

If the trust is created after the first death, the surviving proprietor and his family may enter into a deed of family arrangement to vary the disposition of the property comprised in the deceased's estate (for example under a right of survivorship) by effecting a post-death 'severance'. Provided this is done within 2 years after the first death, it has effect for tax purposes as though it had been made by the deceased proprietor (Inheritance Tax Act 1984, s 142). However, such a 'severance' has no effect in general property law, so that the surviving beneficial joint tenant acquires the deceased's equitable share by survivorship in the normal way. An application to enter a Form A restriction on the basis of such a 'severance' will not therefore be appropriate. The property may, however, become the subject of a trust as a result of other steps taken.

Typically, the value of the deceased proprietor's equitable share in the property will form part of the assets to be put into the nil-rate band discretionary trust. The value of this share cannot be realised without selling the property, and if the surviving proprietor wishes to carry on residing there, the deceased's personal representatives may instead charge the share to the trustees of the trust to satisfy the bequest. The personal representatives may then make an assent of the share, subject to the charge, to the beneficiary. Such an assent cannot be registered as it does not relate to the legal estate. The equitable charge of the equitable share cannot be registered or protected by notice (LRA 2002, s 33). Following such a charge and an assent, an application to cancel any existing Form A restriction would not be appropriate, given the charge created on the equitable share.

On the death of the deceased joint proprietor, an application should be made to remove his name from the register (see *Joint proprietors*, page 286). In most cases, the relevant form of application to reflect the existence of the nil-rate band discretionary trust will be for entry of any appropriate restriction(s). For example, a restriction in Form A (if one does not already appear in the register) and in Form B, if the trust contains limitations on the trustees' powers (see *Trusts of land*, page 555).

INHIBITIONS

An inhibition is an entry which was made in the register under LRA 1925, s 57 preventing the registration or entry of any dealing with registered land or with a registered charge. Inhibitions were usually entered to reflect an obligation not to deal with a registered estate or charge arising out of court proceedings, most often pursuant to a freezing injunction, or an undertaking given in lieu of such an injunction, or a restraint order (see *Freezing orders, restraint orders and interim receiving orders*, page 248). In rare cases, inhibitions were also entered by the Registry for other reasons – for example, where a land certificate had been stolen or where there was other reason to believe that there was a risk of an application being made following an incident of fraud or forgery.

No new inhibitions can be entered in the register since the coming into force of the LRA 2002 on 13 October 2003. By virtue of transitional provisions, any pre-existing inhibitions remain in the register, but the LRA 2002 applies to any such inhibitions as it applies to restrictions entered under that Act (LRA 2002, Sch 12, para 2(2)). Special rules apply to bankruptcy inhibitions (see *Bankruptcy*, page 49). As to an inhibition entered in the register under LRA 1925, s 99 where the incumbent of a benefice was the registered proprietor, see *Church of England*, page 120.

Effect of an inhibition

An inhibition will normally prevent the registration of a disposition. However, it cannot prevent the entry of a unilateral notice. Whether it prevents the entry of an agreed notice will depend upon the wording of the individual inhibition in the register. Thus an inhibition that no disposition is to be 'registered' (without further wording) will not prevent the entry of an agreed notice. However, an inhibition that no disposition is to be 'registered or noted' will prevent the entry of an agreed notice in respect of a disposition, although it will not, for example, prevent the entry of such a notice in respect of a charging order as it is not a 'disposition'. An inhibition entered against a registered estate will not prevent the registration of a disposition by the proprietor of a registered charge in exercise of its power of sale, where the charge was registered prior to the entry of the inhibition.

Cancellation of an inhibition

An application to cancel an inhibition must be made in Form RX3 and be accompanied by evidence to satisfy the Registry that the inhibition is no longer required (see *Restrictions*, page 500). Where the inhibition was entered pursuant to an order of the court, normally it will be cancelled only pursuant to an order for its cancellation obtained from the court. If the inhibition was entered in pursuance of an order of the court under the Criminal Justice Act 1988, the Drug Trafficking Act 1994 or the Terrorism Act 2000, the written release by any prosecutor (as defined in those Acts) suffices in place of a court order.

An application in Form RX4 to withdraw an inhibition will not normally be appropriate, given the circumstances in which inhibitions were usually entered in the register.

Modification or disapplication of an inhibition

The Registry may make an order modifying or disapplying an inhibition in relation to a specified disposition or class of dispositions (LRA 2002, s 41(2)). An application for such an order must be made in Form RX2 (see *Restrictions*, page 500). The application must state whether it is to modify or disapply the inhibition, give details of the order sought (including details of the disposition or the kind of dispositions in question), explain why the applicant has a sufficient interest in the inhibition, and state why the applicant considers that the Registry should make the order.

A note of the terms of any order made by the Registry under LRA 2002, s 41(2) must (if appropriate) be entered in the register.

INTERNAL WATERS

The LRA 2002 extends to England and Wales only (LRA 2002, s 136(3)). It applies to land covered by internal waters of the United Kingdom which are within England and Wales (LRA 2002, s 130(a)). 'England' means, subject to any alteration of the boundaries under Local Government Act 1972, Pt IV, the area consisting of the counties established by s 1 of that Act, Greater London and the Isles of Scilly, while 'Wales' means the combined area of the counties which were created by Local Government Act 1972, s 20 as originally enacted, but subject to any alteration made under s 73 of that Act (consequential alteration of boundary following alteration of watercourse) (Interpretation Act 1978, s 5 and Sch 1). 'Internal waters' means waters to the landward side of the baseline used for defining the territorial limits of the United Kingdom and fixed in accordance with the Convention on the Territorial Sea of 1958. This baseline is normally, but not always, the low-water mark.

A coastal county or other administrative area normally extends up to the low-water mark on its seaward side (*R v Keyn* (1876) 2 Ex D 63). In the case of estuaries, the county boundary is at the seaward limit of the estuary shown by the Ordnance Survey. The Channel Tunnel (as far as the frontier) is incorporated into England by Channel Tunnel Act 1987, s 10(1).

It is possible for the Lord Chancellor to extend by order the application of the LRA 2002 to other land covered by internal waters of the United Kingdom which is adjacent to England and Wales (LRA 2002, s 130(b)). No such order has currently been made. Until such an order is made, land which falls within internal waters but outside the county boundaries of England and Wales is not registrable.

JOINT PROPRIETORS

Where joint proprietors are registered as proprietors of registered land, they hold the legal estate as joint tenants on a trust of land, whether or not they also hold the equitable interest as joint tenants (Law of Property Act 1925, ss 34 and 36). In relation to registered land, the register records the ownership of the legal estate not the beneficial interests, and the Registry is not affected by notice of such a trust (LRA 2002, s 78). No more than four joint proprietors can be entered in the proprietorship register at any one time, unless the land is vested in trustees for charitable, ecclesiastical, or public purposes (Trustee Act 1925, s 34).

The legal estate can never be severed and can only be held by two or more persons as beneficial joint tenants (Law of Property Act 1925, ss 1(6) and 34). If one joint owner dies, the legal estate will pass by 'survivorship' and vest automatically in the surviving joint owner(s), regardless of the devolution of the equitable interest.

However, the equitable interest may, where there are two or more beneficiaries, be held as between themselves as beneficial joint tenants or tenants in common. In the case of a beneficial joint tenancy, the whole equitable interest is held equally and the right of 'survivorship' applies so that, if one joint tenant dies, his interest passes automatically to the survivor(s). In the case of a beneficial tenancy in common, the equitable interest may be held in either equal or unequal undivided shares and the right of 'survivorship' does not apply, so that, if one tenant in common dies, his share passes under the terms of his will or intestacy. A tenant in common may also assign or dispose of his share during his lifetime.

Since 1926, a purchaser of land (as defined in Law of Property Act 1925, s 205(1)(xxi), which for this purpose includes a mortgagee) need only be concerned with the legal estate, the devolution of which on death is clear, and does not need to investigate or be concerned with the equitable interest provided that, where necessary, 'overreaching' is effected.

Overreaching occurs where there is a disposition of land, which is subject to a trust of land, and capital money arises; for example on a sale of the property. It is the mechanism under which the capital money is paid to not less than two trustees (or to a sole personal representative acting as such) or to a trust corporation, so that the equitable interests of the beneficiaries under the trust are transferred to the capital monies (such as the proceeds of sale), leaving the purchaser to take free of those interests (Law of Property Act 1925, ss 2 and 27).

If there is only a sole trustee of land held on a trust of land, that trustee (unless a trust corporation or a sole personal representative acting as such) will therefore need to appoint a co-trustee to act jointly with him in respect of a sale of the land, so that there is a valid receipt for the capital money by not less than two trustees and overreaching is effected.

Only certain equitable interests can be overreached, being those which relate to an equitable interest under a trust of land rather than to the legal estate. For example, an equitable share in land, or an equitable charge on an equitable share in land, such as a charging order on the beneficial share of one of joint owners of land. Other equitable interests which relate to the legal estate cannot be overreached; for example a restrictive covenant, equitable easement or equitable charge affecting the legal estate. Legal estates and interests, such as a leasehold estate in land or a legal easement, cannot be overreached.

A person dealing with a registered proprietor can assume that he has unlimited power to dispose of the registered estate or registered charge concerned, free from any limitation affecting the validity of the disposition, unless there is a restriction or other entry in the register limiting his powers, or a limitation imposed by or under the LRA 2002 (LRA 2002, s 26). In the context of a trust of land, this means that, if two or more persons are registered as joint proprietors, a purchaser can safely acquire the legal estate from them, or from the survivor of them, unless there is a restriction or other entry to the contrary in the register.

Entry of Form A restriction

If the Registry enters two or more registered proprietors of a registered estate in land, it must enter a Form A restriction in the register where the survivor of them will not be able to give a valid receipt for capital money. The prescribed forms of transfer or assent of registered land (Forms AS1, AS3, TR1, TR2, TR5, TP1 and TP2) and clause LR14 of a prescribed clauses lease all contain a panel headed 'Declaration of trust' containing the following alternative declarations where the transferee is more than one person:

(a) The transferees are to hold the property on trust for themselves as joint tenants.
(b) The transferees are to hold the property on trust for themselves as tenants in common in equal shares.
(c) The transferees are to hold the property on trust [*to be completed as necessary*].

The appropriate option should be selected, depending upon whether the transferees are to hold the registered estate on trust for themselves as joint tenants beneficially, or as tenants in common in equal shares, or upon some other trust. Completion of the declaration in the transfer and execution of the transfer by the transferees is important, so that the transferees make an appropriate declaration as to the trusts upon which the registered estate will be held by them. This was emphasized by the House of Lords in *Stack v Dowden* [2007] UKHL 17 and by the Supreme Court in *Jones v Kernott* [2011] UKSC 53. A declaration of trust in a separate document may be executed if desired. The 'trust information' panel in application Forms FR1 and ADV1 also include provision for similar confirmation to be given as to the trusts upon which the property is to be held. As an alternative to completing the relevant panel in a prescribed form, a declaration in Form JO may be lodged instead. The completed and signed Form JO must be lodged with the relevant application for registration to which it relates.

Unless the transferees declare (or it is otherwise apparent from the application) that they are holding the property on trust for themselves as beneficial joint tenants, the Registry will enter a restriction in Form A, the wording of which is set out in Appendix IV, page 585.

The purpose of the Form A restriction is to reflect the existence of a trust of land and ensure that overreaching is effected on a disposition for value of the land (LRA 2002, s 42(1)(b)). The restriction will not 'catch' a disposition where no capital money arises, for example on the appointment of a new trustee.

In the case of other types of registered estate, as opposed to an estate in land, LRR 2003, r 94(2A) provides that where two or more persons apply to be registered as proprietors of an estate which is a rentcharge, profit à prendre in gross, franchise or manor, they must also apply for entry of a restriction in Form A if a sole (surviving) proprietor will not be able to give a valid receipt for capital money.

The Registry will not enter a restriction in Form A in respect of a registered charge, because although a charge can be held on trust, the survivor of the registered chargees is always able to give a valid receipt for the money secured by it. This reflects LRA 2002, s 56 which provides that where a registered charge has two or more proprietors, a valid receipt for the money secured by it may be given by:

(a)   the registered proprietors;
(b)   the survivors or survivor of the registered proprietors; or
(c)   the personal representative of the last survivor of the registered proprietors.

Death of a joint proprietor

Where a joint proprietor of a registered estate or a registered charge dies, an application may be made for alteration of the register by the removal of the deceased joint proprietor. The application may conveniently be made in application Form AP1 or Form DJP, although this is not essential. The application must be accompanied by evidence of the death (LRR 2003, r 164). Such an application can also be lodged electronically by a conveyancer, who must certify that he has seen the appropriate evidence of the death.

The Registry will delete the name of the deceased joint proprietor, leaving the names of the survivor(s) in the register. The only exception is where there is a 'partnership' restriction in Form Q (or similar) requiring the consent of the deceased proprietor's personal representative to any disposition. Where such a restriction appears, the Registry will leave the name of the deceased in the register, but enter a note of his death.

Cancellation of Form A restriction

Where a restriction in Form A appears in the register, this will not be automatically cancelled on the death of a joint proprietor. If the trust of land continues to subsist and a sole survivor of joint proprietors remains as proprietor of land with a restriction in Form A in the register, a new trustee can be appointed and registered as proprietor jointly with him. This appointment will not be 'caught' by the restriction, which will remain in the register to reflect the fact the registered estate is still subject to a trust of land.

If, however, the sole surviving joint proprietor has become legally and beneficially entitled to the whole of the estate, he may apply for the cancellation of the restriction. The application should be made in Form RX3 (see *Restrictions*, page 500) and supported by evidence of the equitable title showing that the surviving proprietor can give a valid receipt for capital money arising on a disposition of the estate. Usually, the Registry will accept a statutory declaration or statement of truth by the survivor (which may be in Form ST5 in LRR 2003, Sch 1), or a certificate by a conveyancer with personal knowledge of the facts, which shows how he has become the sole beneficial owner by:

(a) explaining what has happened to the beneficial interest protected by the restriction;
(b) if it has devolved to the surviving proprietor, explaining how it has so devolved;
(c) confirming, if such be the case, that no one other than the surviving proprietor now has a beneficial interest in the property; and
(d) confirming, if such be the case, that no beneficial interest in the property has been encumbered (other than by a charge that is also of the legal estate).

can be used as evidence to show how the beneficial interest protected by the restriction has devolved and how the trust of land has come to an end, so that the restriction is no longer needed. The declaration, statement or certificate should be accompanied by any available documentary evidence, such as an assent relating to an undivided share. No fee is currently payable for the cancellation of the restriction.

If all the registered proprietors have died, the personal representatives of the last surviving proprietor can make a similar application adjusting the terms of the statutory declaration, statement of truth or certificate according to the individual circumstances.

An application for cancellation of the restriction may also be made, where appropriate, in other circumstances. For example, where a registered estate has been transferred into the sole name of one of the former joint proprietors and he has become legally and beneficially entitled to the whole of the estate. Or where the trusts upon which the joint proprietors hold the property have been replaced or amended, so that they now hold the registered estate upon trust for themselves as beneficial joint tenants rather than as tenants in common. Alternatively a court order requiring the registrar to cancel the restriction may be lodged.

In certain circumstances, a restriction in Form A may be cancelled automatically following completion of a disposition by registration. Thus a restriction in Form A will be cancelled on registration of a transfer on sale by two or more trustees or a trust corporation (except where the transfer is to one or more of the existing proprietors) under LRR 2003, r 99. A restriction in Form A cannot normally be withdrawn (LRR 2003, r 98(3)).

Related matters

In addition to the matters discussed above in respect of joint proprietors, reference should be made, as appropriate, to *Constructive, resulting and other implied trusts*, page 165; *Restrictions*, page 500; *Severance of a beneficial joint tenancy*, page 533; and *Trusts of land*, page 555.

LAND REGISTRY

Land registration is administered by Her Majesty's Land Registry and is carried out principally under the authority of the LRA 2002 and the LRR 2003, and in accordance with the Registry's own practice and procedures.

The Registry, which was established in 1862, is a government agency whose main purpose is to register title to land and other registrable estates in England and Wales and to record dispositions, such as sales and mortgages, with registered titles. It also provides information in relation to registered titles and related data. It has a head office and a number of local offices, details of which are set out in Appendix I, page 575.

LAND REGISTRY ACT 1862

The Land Registry Act 1862 was the first statute under which the title to land could be registered. Application for registration was voluntary and the requirements for registration of title were stringent. The 1862 Act did not require subsequent dispositions of registered land to be registered and it was not essential for a land certificate to be issued. The Land Registry Act 1862 is now repealed (LRA 2002, s 122). Even before that repeal, Land Transfer Act 1875, s 125 and subsequently LRA 1925, s 137(1) provided that no application for the registration of an estate under the 1862 Act was to be entertained.

The Land Registry Act 1862 was largely replaced by the Land Transfer Act 1875 which (as subsequently amended by the Land Transfer Act 1897 to make provision for compulsory registration of title) introduced the land registration system which largely operated until 2003. The LRA 1925 was an important part of the great property reform legislation of 1925 which also included the Law of Property Act 1925. The LRA 2002 replaced the earlier legislation and came into force on 13 October 2003.

Any land which is registered under the Land Registry Act 1862 is now treated as being unregistered land and may be registered under the LRA 2002 by an application for first registration in the usual way (see *First registration*, page 222). If a land certificate issued under the 1862 Act is available, it should be lodged with the application for first registration.

If a person requires a copy of any information included in a record of title made under the Land Registry Act 1862, he should apply to the Registry by way of a letter setting out what is required. Although the Registry may supply a copy of a register and title plan relating to such a title, these will not be official copies for the purposes of LRA 2002, s 67. An official search may not be made in respect of such a title.

LEASEHOLD ENFRANCHISEMENT

The Leasehold Reform Act 1967 confers upon qualifying tenants of a house held for the last 2 years under a long tenancy at a low rent the right to acquire the freehold or an extended lease. 'House' does not include flats in a horizontally divided building and 'premises' includes any garage, outhouse, garden, yard and appurtenances let with the house (Leasehold Reform Act 1967, s 2(1) to (3)). 'Long tenancy' means any tenancy originally granted for a term exceeding 21 years whether or not it is determinable by notice or re-entry (s 3 of the 1967 Act). There are further conditions and exceptions that apply in particular circumstances.

Such a right may also be exercised by the personal representatives of a tenant who held the right at his death, so long as the tenancy is vested in them (Commonhold and Leasehold Reform Act 2002, s 142). The personal representatives may not give notice of their desire to have the freehold or an extended lease later than 2 years after the grant of probate or letters of administration. For extended leases under the Leasehold Reform Act 1967 or under the LRHUDA 1993, see *Leases*, page 296. For collective enfranchisement under the LRHUDA 1993, see *Collective enfranchisement*, page 136.

Enfranchisement under the Leasehold Reform Act 1967 may be possible in circumstances where the details of the lease and of the landlord are not fully known and enlargement of the lease under Law of Property Act 1925, s 153 is precluded (see *Enlargement of long Leases*, page 296).

Notice under Leasehold Reform Act 1967

Any right of a tenant or his personal representatives arising from a notice served on the landlord under the Leasehold Reform Act 1967 is not capable of being an interest within LRA 2002, Sch 1 or Sch 3 which overrides first registration and registered dispositions (Leasehold Reform Act 1967, s 5(5)). However, it may be the subject of a notice as if it were an estate contract and, where the landlord's reversionary title is registered, application may be made for the entry of an agreed notice or a unilateral notice.

Agreed notice

In addition to the usual documents required (see *Notices*, page 389), an applicant should deliver to the Registry a certified copy of the notice under the Leasehold Reform Act 1967.

Where the consent of the registered proprietor is not available, the notice under the 1967 Act is likely to be sufficient to satisfy the Registry as to the validity of the applicant's claim in accordance with LRA 2002, s 34(3)(c).

The agreed notice in the register will give details of the interest protected.

Unilateral notice

An applicant should deliver to the Registry the usual documents required (see *Notices*, page 389).

The statement in panel 11 or conveyancer's certificate in panel 12 of Form UN1 should be completed on the following lines to show the interest of the applicant:

> intending purchaser, notice of enfranchisement under the Leasehold Reform Act 1967 having been given on [*date*] to [*name and address of landlord*].

Where the applicant has taken an assignment from the tenant of the benefit of the rights under notice in accordance with Leasehold Reform Act 1967, s 5(2), Form UN1 should be completed on the following lines to show the interest of the applicant:

> assignee of rights under the Leasehold Reform Act 1967 by virtue of an assignment dated [*date*] made between [*former tenant*] and [*applicant*], the rights having arisen on [*date*] by the service of notice of enfranchisement on [*name and address of landlord*].

The unilateral notice in the register will give brief details of the interest protected and identify the beneficiary of that notice.

Any subsequent assignment of rights under the Leasehold Reform Act 1967 should not be included in a transfer of a registered leasehold estate but should instead be effected by a separate instrument 'off the register'. No entry of such an assignment will be made in the register, but if the rights are already protected in the register by a unilateral notice, the assignee should apply in Form UN3 to be registered as the new beneficiary of the notice (see *Notices*, page 389).

Registration of transfer of the freehold

The application for the registration of the transfer of the freehold reversion should be made in the usual way (see *First registration*, page 222 or *Transfers*, page 551, as appropriate). The application should show, either by a statement in the transfer or on the application form, that the transfer is made under the Leasehold Reform Act 1967.

Any necessary request for merger should be included in the application. Where a deed of substituted security transferring a legal charge on a merged lease to the freehold estate is lodged, the charge will normally be registered against the tenant's freehold title. If the charge is only to be noted, Form AN1 (for entry of an agreed notice) or Form UN1 (for entry of a unilateral notice) should be lodged (see *Notices*, page 389).

Certain special considerations also apply, as discussed below.

Discharge of registered charges on the freehold title

The landlord's chargee may have expressly discharged the charge or released the land from it in the usual way. If not, and the tenant claims that he has paid to the chargee enough money to discharge the house from the charge, a verified copy of the chargee's (appropriately worded) receipt must be lodged. Alternatively, if sufficient money to discharge or release the house from the charge has been paid into court by the tenant under Leasehold Reform Act 1967, s 13, there must be lodged a verified copy of the affidavit the tenant will have made for that purpose, and a verified copy of the court's official receipt.

If there has been an express discharge or release, or if, on the receipt of the appropriate evidence of payment to the chargee or into court the Registry is satisfied that the tenant may be registered as the freehold proprietor free from the charge, no entry of it will appear in the register of the tenant's freehold title. In appropriate cases, the Registry may serve notice upon the chargee explaining the nature of the transaction and inviting him to consent. If in response to the notice the chargee provides arguable grounds for objection, the application cannot proceed until the objection is disposed of either by agreement or in accordance with LRA 2002, s 73 (see *Disputes*, page 193).

In the case of a floating charge created by a landlord, a certificate by the solicitor, secretary or other responsible officer of the landlord company or of the debenture holder that the charge had not crystallised at the date of the conveyance or transfer on enfranchisement will be accepted as sufficient evidence for the registration of the tenant's freehold title free from the charge.

Rentcharges

The transfer or conveyance will normally take effect subject to any pre-existing rentcharges affecting the title. However, where the rentcharge is more than the amount payable as rent under the lease, the tenant can require the landlord to discharge the house and premises from the rentcharge to the extent of the excess. The appropriate evidence of discharge should be lodged. Where difficulties arise in paying the redemption price, provision is made for payment into court under Leasehold Reform Act 1967, s 11(4), in which case evidence of such payment should be lodged in the form of a verified copy of the tenant's or landlord's affidavit and a verified copy of the court's receipt.

Rights and burdens under Leasehold Reform Act 1967, s 10

Leasehold Reform Act 1967, s 10(2) provides that the benefit and burden of certain rights that affect the leasehold interest shall automatically continue on enfranchisement, but without prejudice to any rights that may be expressly granted or reserved. The rights passing under s 10(2) take effect so far as the landlord is capable of granting them and consist of rights of support, rights of access of light and air and rights to the passage, use or maintenance of the usual common services, such as water, drainage, electricity, etc.

If the Registry is aware that a conveyance or transfer has been made under the Leasehold Reform Act 1967, appropriate entries will be made in the register as to the benefit and burden of rights passing under s 10(2) of that Act. If the conveyance or transfer expressly excludes or restricts any of the benefiting rights, this will be reflected in the entry. If the conveyance or transfer includes new easements or restrictive covenants under s 10(3) or (4) of the 1967 Act, entries will be made in the register in respect of these.

The applicant should ensure that where the reversionary title over which the easement is granted is registered in the name of the landlord but under a different title number to that of the house, application is also made against the burdened title, or that where the title is unregistered, satisfactory evidence of title is lodged.

In some instances rights originally granted or reserved affecting the leasehold interest will, by virtue of s 10 of the 1967 Act, now affect the freehold estate. If reference to the deed which granted or reserved those rights is required to be made in the register, this should be expressly requested and the original deed, or a certified copy or examined abstract of it, should be lodged.

Estate Management Scheme under the Leasehold Reform Act 1967

In certain circumstances on enfranchisement, Leasehold Reform Act 1967, s 19 provides for the retention of management powers by the landlord for the general benefit of the neighbourhood, exercised by means of a scheme authorised by the Secretary of State and approved by the High Court. To be effective, such a scheme must be registered as a local land charge. Given the nature of the scheme, entry of a notice would not normally be appropriate. An exception to this would be where a scheme imposes a statutory charge, in which case this may be the subject of a notice in the register, although such a charge would have to be registered before it could be realised (LRA 2002, s 55). Rights under local land charges, unless and until registered or protected in the register of title, take effect as overriding interests under LRA 2002, Schs 1 and 3 (see *Local land charges*, page 367).

LEASES

Certain leases of unregistered estates are capable of being the subject of an application for first registration, which may be either a voluntary application or a compulsory application as a result of a 'trigger' for first registration having occurred. In the case of registered estates, certain leases are registrable dispositions which are required to be completed by registration if they are to take effect at law. Some leases may not be capable of substantive registration, but may be the subject of a notice in the register. Other leases may not be capable of either substantive registration or protection by the entry of a notice in the register.

Leases granted out of unregistered estates

A lease granted out of unregistered land is not required to contain the prescribed clauses which are required wording for a prescribed clauses lease (see 'Prescribed clauses leases', page 300), but these clauses can be used voluntarily if desired. If the prescribed clauses are used, application for entry of a standard restriction may be made in clause LR13 rather than by using Form RX1 (LRR 2003, r 92). The provisions as to entries made in respect of registrable leases of registered land, contained in LRR 2003, r 72A, do not apply to such leases. Such a lease may be subject to compulsory first registration upon its grant or assignment or may be the subject of a voluntary application for first registration (see *First registration*, page 222, for leases granted out of unregistered estates, and *Classes of title*, page 130 for details of the various classes of leasehold title).

The Registry will enter a notice of the burden of an unregistered lease if it is disclosed on an application for first registration of the landlord's reversionary title, provided it is capable of being noted (LRR 2003, r 35).

If the landlord's title is registered and no notice of the lease appears in the register, the Registry must, when completing an application for first registration of the lease, enter a notice of the lease in the landlord's title (LRR 2003, r 37).

Where a lease granted out of unregistered land is not subject to compulsory first registration, the burden of it will be an interest which overrides first registration and registered dispositions (LRA 2002, Sch 1, para 1 and Sch 3, para 1). An application may nevertheless be made for entry of a notice in the landlord's title, if registered, provided the lease is granted for a term of more than 3 years (LRA 2002, ss 33(b) and 34). A PPP lease cannot be noted (LRA 2002, s 90).

Leases which are registrable dispositions

By virtue of the owner's powers conferred by LRA 2002, s 23(1) a proprietor of a registered estate has full power to grant a lease (or, if it is a leasehold estate, an underlease for any term of years absolute of less duration than his own registered estate), subject to any entry in the register to the contrary. Under LRA 2002, s 26, a person's right to exercise owner's powers are, in favour of a tenant, taken to be free from any limitation affecting the validity of the lease, subject to any entry to the contrary in the register or any limitation imposed by or under that Act. For example, a restriction in the landlord's title may have to be complied with, or a registered chargee's consent obtained. Where an existing lease is registered with less than absolute class of leasehold title, see *Classes of title*, page 130.

Where the registered estate is an estate in land, the following grants of terms of years absolute are required to be completed by registration (LRA 2002, s 27(2)):

(a)   for a term of more than 7 years from the date of the grant;
(b)   to take effect in possession after the end of the period of 3 months beginning with the date of the grant;
(c)   under which the right to possession is discontinuous;
(d)   in pursuance of the right to buy under HA 1985, Pt V; or
(e)   in circumstances where the HA 1985, s 171A applies (disposal by a landlord which leads to a person's no longer being a secure tenant; preserved right to buy).

Where the registered estate is a franchise or manor, the grant of any lease must be completed by registration (see *Franchises*, page 240, and *Manors*, page 372).

LRA 2002, Sch 2 sets out the registration requirements. Where there is a grant out of an estate in land of a term of years absolute which is required to be completed by registration, the grantee, or his successor in title, must be entered in the register as the proprietor of the lease and a notice in respect of the lease must be entered in the register of the reversionary title. In the case of a grant out of a registered franchise or manor of a lease for a term of more than 7 years from the date of the grant, the grantee, or his successor in title, must be entered in the register as the proprietor of the lease and a notice in respect of the lease must be entered in the register of the reversionary title. In the case of a grant out of a registered franchise or manor of a lease for a term not exceeding 7 years from the date of the grant, a notice in respect of the lease must be entered in the register of the reversionary title.

No form of lease was prescribed by the LRR 2003 as originally made. However, in 2006 the LRR 2003 were amended by the introduction of provisions relating to 'prescribed clauses leases'. Most registrable dispositions consisting of a lease of a registered estate in land must be now be in the form of a prescribed clauses lease (see 'Prescribed clauses leases', below). Where a lease of a registered estate is not required to be in the form of a prescribed clauses lease, it may be in any form provided that it refers to the landlord's title number (LRR 2003, r 212) and, if it is a lease of part of the registered estate, it must normally have attached to it a plan enabling the demised premises to be identified on the title plan of the landlord's title, unless it is already identified on that title plan (LRR 2003, r 13). The route of any easements and other rights must similarly be clearly identified.

Leases of land not exceeding 7 years

A leasehold estate in land granted for a term not exceeding 7 years from the date of the grant cannot usually be registered or, if for 3 years or less, noted in the register. It is an interest which overrides first registration and registered dispositions (LRA 2002, Sch 1, para 1 and Sch 3, para 1). However, the following leases not exceeding 7 years are registrable dispositions and do not take effect as overriding interests:

(a) a grant of a term of years absolute to take effect in possession after the end of the period of 3 months beginning with the date of the grant;
(b) a grant of a term of years absolute under which the right to possession is discontinuous;
(c) a grant of a term of years absolute in pursuance of the right to buy under HA 1985, Pt V; or
(d) a grant of a term of years absolute in circumstances where the HA 1985, s 171A applies (disposal by a landlord which leads to a person no longer being a secure tenant; preserved right to buy).

Prior to the coming into force of the LRA 2002, leases granted for a term not exceeding 21 years were overriding interests under the LRA 1925. A lease which was an overriding interest under the LRA 1925 immediately before 13 October 2003 continues to be an unregistered interest overriding both first registration and registered dispositions (LRA 2002, Sch 12, para 12).

For the position where a lease not exceeding 7 years is an overriding interest and the lease contains an option to renew or to purchase the reversion, or a right of pre-emption, see *Options*, page 412, and *Rights of pre-emption*, page 519.

A notice may be entered in respect of a lease exceeding 3 years even when that lease is not required to be registered.

Agreed notice

In addition to the usual documents required (see *Notices*, page 389), an applicant for an agreed notice should deliver to the Registry the lease or a certified copy of it.

Where the consent of the registered proprietor is not available but the lease is signed by him, this is likely to be sufficient to satisfy the Registry as to the validity of the applicant's claim for the purposes of LRA 2002, s 34(3)(c).

The agreed notice in the register will give details of the interest protected.

Unilateral notice

An applicant for a unilateral notice should deliver to the Registry the usual documents required (see *Notices*, page 389).

The statement in panel 11 or conveyancer's certificate in panel 12 of Form UN1 should be completed on the following lines to show the interest of the applicant:

> person having the benefit of a lease dated [*date*] made between [*names*].

Where the lease was granted by a person who is not the current proprietror, the wording must establish the link between the current registered proprietor and the person who is to be shown as the beneficiary of the notice.

The unilateral notice in the register will give brief details of the interest protected and identify the beneficiary of that notice.

Leases which are incapable of substantive registration

There are certain leasehold interests created out of registered land which are incapable of substantive registration. These are:

(a)　a lease granted for a term of 7 years or less, except for those mentioned in 'Leases of land not exceeding 7 years', above;

(b)　a lease for which a rent or premium is payable where the term commences more than 21 years from the date of the lease and the lease is void by virtue of Law of Property Act 1925, s 149(3);

(c)　leases with no certain start date, so that the lease is not for a term of years certain;

(d)　leases where the landlord and tenant are the same person and therefore of no effect (see *Rye v Rye* [1962] AC 496); and

(e)　PPP leases (LRA 2002, s 90).

Noting of leases

On substantive registration of a lease, the Registry will enter a notice of the lease in the landlord's registered title. Where a lease granted out of a registered estate in land is not capable of substantive registration, the burden of it will be an interest which overrides registered dispositions, under LRA 2002, Sch 3, para 1. An application may nevertheless be made for entry of a notice in the landlord's registered title provided the lease is granted for a term of more than 3 years (LRA 2002, ss 33(b) and 34) (see *Notices*, page 389). A PPP lease cannot be noted (LRA 2002, s 90).

Prescribed clauses leases

As from 19 June 2006 use of a prescribed clauses lease has (with certain limited exceptions) been compulsory for any lease granted out of a registered estate in land which is a registrable disposition under LRA 2002, s 27(2)(b) and therefore required to be completed by registration (LRR 2003, r 58A(1)).

A prescribed clauses lease is defined by LRR 2003, r 58A(4) as a lease granted out of a registered estate in land on or after 19 June 2006 which is a registrable disposition required to be completed by registration under LRA 2002, s 27(2)(b) and which is not granted in a form *expressly* required:

(a)　by an agreement entered into before 19 June 2006;

(b)　by an order of the court;

(c)　by or under an enactment;

(d)　by a necessary consent or licence for the grant of a lease given before 19 June 2006.

A lease by virtue of a variation of a lease which is a deemed surrender and re-grant is not a prescribed clauses lease; this exemption does not apply where a deed *expressly* provides for the surrender of an existing lease and the grant of a new lease in substitution.

A prescribed clauses lease must begin with the required wording (referred to below) or that wording must appear immediately after any front sheet. 'Front sheet' means a front cover sheet, or a contents or index sheet at the beginning of the lease, or a front cover sheet and contents or index sheet where the contents or index sheet is immediately after the front cover sheet.

'Required wording' means the wording in clauses LR1 to LR14 of LRR 2003, Sch 1A completed in accordance with the instructions in that schedule as appropriate for the particular lease. These clauses are set out in Appendix III, page 581. If a prescribed clauses lease is an electronic document to which LRA 2002, s 91 applies, the required wording will be such as is required by the relevant notice given under LRR 2003, r 54C; that wording must be to like effect to that given in paper form.

The prescribed clauses are therefore a standard set of clauses that must appear at the beginning of all such leases, containing relevant details which will assist in the registration of the lease. It is important that these clauses are correctly completed, as the Registry will prepare the register entries to complete registration of the lease from the information provided in the clauses. Also, if a clause is not completed this may result in any entry not being made (see 'Registration of leases which are registrable dispositions', below). The remainder of the lease can be in whatever form the parties require.

Registration of leases which are registrable dispositions

A person applying to register a lease granted out of a registered estate should deliver to the Registry:

(a) an application in Form AP1;

(b) the lease or a certified copy of it;

(c) any consents or certificates required in respect of mortgages, charges or restrictions in the landlord's title;

(d) Form DI giving the information as to overriding interests required by LRR 2003, r 57, including any documentary evidence of the interests (see 'Duty to disclose overriding interests', page 426);

(e) the appropriate confirmation or evidence as to identity (see *Identity evidence*, page 266);

(f) the appropriate SDLT certificate or other evidence (see *Stamp duty land tax*, page 541); and

(g) the fee payable (see *Fees*, page 221).

On registration of the lease, it is allotted its own title number. Notice of the registered lease is entered in the landlord's registered title without any need for a separate application or further fee.

LRR 2003, r 72A specifies certain entries which the Registry is obliged to make on registration of a lease granted out of a registered estate in land on or after 19 June 2006 which is required to be registered under LRA 2002, s 27(2)(b). Rule 72A also specifies situations where the Registry is required to make no entry. This applies to both prescribed clauses leases and other registrable leases.

Under r 72A(2), on completion of such a lease by registration the Registry must (where appropriate) make entries in the relevant individual register in respect of interests contained in the lease which are of the nature referred to in clauses LR9 (rights of acquisition, etc), LR10 (restrictive covenants by the landlord in respect of other land), LR11 (easements granted or reserved) and LR12 (estate rentcharge). The requirement to make an entry in respect of an interest referred to in clause LR12 is satisfied by entry, where appropriate, of notice of the interest created.

Under r 72A(3), where the lease is a prescribed clauses lease and contains a prohibition or restriction on disposing of the lease of the nature referred to in clause LR8 or it contains interests of the nature referred to in clauses LR9, LR10, LR11 and LR12, but the prohibition or restriction or the interests are not specified or referred to in those clauses, or the lease does not contain the required wording in respect of them, then the Registry need take no action in respect of them unless a separate application is made. LRR 2003, r 6(2), which requires the Registry to make an entry on registration in respect of a prohibition or restriction on disposing of a lease, is amended accordingly.

Under r 72A(4), the Registry need not make entries in respect of interests of the nature referred to in clauses LR9, LR10 or LR11 or a standard form of restriction set out in clause LR13 where:

(a) in the case of a prescribed clauses lease, the title numbers of the individual registers have not been given in clause LR2.2; or

(b) in any other case, the title numbers of the individual registers required by clause LR2.2 have not been given in panel 2 of the Form AP1 lodged for the purpose of completing the lease by registration,

unless a separate application is made in respect of the interests or restriction.

Under r 72A(5), where a separate application is made in Form AP1 in respect of either a prohibition or restriction on disposal of the lease or the grant or reservation of an easement, the Form AP1 must specify the particular clause, schedule or paragraph of a schedule, where the prohibition or restriction or easement is contained in the lease.

Under LRR 2003, r 58A(3), if it appears to the Registry that a lease is not a prescribed clauses lease, then the required wording is not necessary and r 72A(3) shall not apply to that lease, even though the lease would otherwise be a prescribed clauses lease.

An application for entry of a restriction may be made, where appropriate, contemporaneously with the application for registration of the lease. For example, a restriction in Form PP where a certificate signed by the landlord will be required before any disposition may be registered (see Appendix IV, page 585). LRR 2003, r 92 relaxes the requirement for a Form RX1 to be lodged, where application for the entry of a standard restriction is made in clause LR13 of a 'relevant lease' which is defined as:

(a) a prescribed clauses lease; or
(b) any other lease which complies with the requirements as to form and content of a prescribed clauses lease and which either is required to be completed by registration under LRA 2002, s 27(2)(b) or is the subject of an application for first registration of the title to it.

Under LRR 2003, r 72B, on completion of the lease by registration, the Registry must enter a notice or other appropriate entry in respect of any interest which, at the time of registration, is the subject of a notice in the landlord's registered title and which the Registry considers may affect the registered lease.

Under LRR 2003, r 77, where a right of re-entry is derived in a grant of a lease and the lease is a registrable disposition which is completed by registration, that is also sufficient to complete the grant of the right of re-entry (being itself a registrable disposition under LRA 2002, s 27(2)(e)) by registration, without any specific entry being made in relation to it in the register.

Leases for life or determinable on death, marriage or civil partnership

A lease may be expressed to:

(a) be for a life or lives;
(b) come to an end on the death of any person; or

(c)   come to an end on the marriage or formation of civil partnership of the tenant.

Such a lease may fall within Law of Property Act 1925, s 149(6) if it terminates *automatically* on the specified event (i.e. on death, marriage or civil partnership) and is granted at a rent or in consideration of a premium. A lease falling within s 149(6) takes effect as a lease for 90 years determinable after the death, marriage or civil partnership, as the case may be, by giving at least one month's notice. Such a lease should be in the form of a prescribed clauses lease, where necessary (see above).

A lease which terminates *automatically* on the specified event but does not fall within s 149(6) generally constitutes only an equitable interest, which is incapable of substantive registration, although it may be the subject of a notice in the landlord's title (if registered). However, it is possible that a lease by way of a gift of a term of years subject to automatic determination on the marriage or civil partnership of the tenant may take effect at law (see Law of Property Act 1925, s 205(1)(xxvii)), in which case the lease should be in the form of a prescribed clauses lease, where necessary (see above).

A lease for a specified term determinable by the *service of notice* following death or marriage or civil partnership will not fall within s 149(6) (see *Bass Holdings v Lewis* [1986] EWCA Civ 2). Accordingly, it does not take effect as a lease for 90 years and instead takes effect for the term referred to in the lease, subject to the provision for determination. Such a lease should be in the form of a prescribed clauses lease, where necessary (see above).

Variation of a lease

An application to register the variation of a registered lease must be accompanied by the instrument effecting the variation and evidence to satisfy the Registry that the variation has effect at law (LRR 2003, r 78). In construing a deed of variation of a lease, a court gives effect to the intention of the parties, unless it is compelled, by the nature of the changes made, to hold that the effect of the deed is to bring about a surrender and re-grant by operation of law. This occurs only where the variation affects the legal estate and either increases the extent of the premises demised or the term for which they are held (*Friends' Provident Life Office v British Railways Board* [1996] 1 All ER 336 (CA)).

An applicant for registration of a deed of variation of a registered lease (other than one which takes effect as a surrender and re-grant) should deliver to the Registry:

(a)   an application in Form AP1;

(b)   the deed of variation or a certified copy of it;

(c)   any consents or certificates required in respect of mortgages, charges or restrictions in the lessor's title;

(d)   where the landlord's title is unregistered, evidence of that title;

(e)   any other necessary evidence to show that the variation takes effect at law and;

(f)   the fee payable (see *Fees*, page 221).

Where the variation has been made by an order pursuant to Landlord and Tenant Act 1987, s 35, that order should be lodged in place of the deed of variation.

If satisfied that the variation has effect at law, the Registry will make an entry relating to the deed in the property register of the tenant's title, together with a notice in the landlord's title (if registered).

If a chargee's consent is not lodged when required, the following note will be added to the register entry of the relevant title(s):

> NOTE: The proprietor of the registered charge dated [*date*] [*of the landlord's/tenant's title number* ...] was not a party to the deed nor was evidence of its consent to the deed produced to the registrar.

An application may be made for entry of either an agreed notice using Form AN1 or a unilateral notice using Form UN1 in respect of a deed of variation, even when the lease is substantively registered, if sufficient evidence cannot be provided to satisfy the Registry that the variation takes effect at law under LRR 2003, r 129 (see *Notices*, page 389).

If notice of an unregistered lease is entered in a landlord's title, an application may be made to enter a notice in respect of a variation of the lease. Such an application can be for entry of an agreed notice using Form AN1, if the deed of variation can be provided and the lease is already protected by an agreed notice. Alternatively, application may be made in Form UN1 for entry of a unilateral notice; for example, if the lease is already protected by way of unilateral notice or if the lease or/and the deed of variation cannot be provided (see *Notices*, page 389).

If the deed of variation contains easements which constitute a registrable disposition under LRA 2002, s 27, these will not operate at law until completed by registration.

The position regarding deeds of variation is similar in relation to a deed of rectification, where a lease is rectified so as to give effect to the original intention of the parties. For example, by the addition of covenants which were omitted from the lease by mistake.

Any party to a long lease of a flat may apply to a leasehold valuation tribunal for an order varying the lease on the grounds that the lease fails to make satisfactory provision with respect to repair, maintenance, the provision of services, insurance, the recovery of expenses or the computation of service charges (Landlord and Tenant Act 1987, s 35). The leasehold valuation tribunal may then make an appropriate order that will be binding on the parties to the lease and any other persons concerned (Landlord and Tenant Act 1987, ss 38 and 39). Where an application is to be made for entry of a notice in respect of any variation of a lease effected by or under Landlord and Tenant Act 1987, s 38 (including any variation as modified by an order under s 39(4) of that Act), it must be for an agreed notice using application Form AN1 (LRR 2003, r 80(d)).

Deeds of variation varying the term

If a tenant takes a new lease of the same property before the existing lease has expired then the original lease is treated as surrendered immediately before the new lease. As the term of a lease cannot be altered by means of a deed of variation, the Registry will treat any deed purporting to vary the term of a registered lease as being a new lease which will, therefore, have the effect of surrendering the original lease. The proper application in such a case will be for closure of the title to the original lease and registration of the new lease (if as varied, it is a registrable disposition). The deed of variation, in such a case, does not have to be in the form of a prescribed clauses lease. For surrenders of leases, see 'Determination of registered leases', below. For the position where the existing lease is not registered but is noted on the landlord's registered title, see 'Cancellation of a noted lease', below. For details of applications to register a new lease where it is granted out of unregistered land, see *First registration*, page 222. For details of applications to register a new lease where it is out of registered land, see 'Registration of leases which are registrable dispositions', above. As an alternative to use of a deed of variation, an extension of a lease may be granted (see 'Extensions of leases (other than under the Leasehold Reform Act 1967 or Leasehold Reform, Housing and Urban Development Act 1993)', below).

Deeds of variation varying the extent

A deed of variation which *reduces* the extent of the premises demised by a lease will be treated as a surrender of the part in question.

As the extent of the premises demised by a lease cannot be *extended* by means of a deed of variation, the Registry will treat any deed purporting to increase the extent of the demised premises in a registered lease as being a new lease which will, therefore, have the effect of surrendering the original lease. The proper application in such a case will be for closure of the title to the original lease and registration of the new lease (if as varied, it is a registrable disposition). The deed of variation, in such a case, does not have to be in the form of a prescribed clauses lease. As an alternative to use of a deed of variation, a supplemental lease may be granted or the existing lease surrendered and replaced with a new lease of the combined extent. A prescribed clauses lease should be used where necessary and application made to register the lease and any surrender.

For surrenders of leases, see 'Determination of registered leases', below. For the position where the existing lease is not registered but is noted on the landlord's registered title, see 'Cancellation of a noted lease', below. For details of applications to register a new lease where it is granted out of unregistered land, see *First registration*, page 222. For details of applications to register a new lease where it is out of registered land, see 'Registration of leases which are registrable dispositions', above.

Acquisition of an extended lease under the Leasehold Reform Act 1967

The Leasehold Reform Act 1967 confers on a tenant of a house held for the last 2 years under a long tenancy at a low rent the right to acquire either the freehold on enfranchisement (see *Collective enfranchisement*, page 136); or an extended lease of the house and premises expiring 50 years after the date on which the existing term is due to expire (Leasehold Reform Act 1967, s 1). 'House' does not include flats in a horizontally divided building and 'premises' includes any garage, outhouse, garden, yard and appurtenances let with the house (Leasehold Reform Act 1967, s 2(1) to (3)). 'Long tenancy' means any tenancy originally granted for a term exceeding 21 years whether or not it is determinable by notice or re-entry (Leasehold Reform Act 1967, s 3). There are further conditions and exceptions that apply in particular circumstances. Where the tenant holds under a sub-lease, there are complicated provisions in Sch 1 to the 1967 Act to determine which landlord is to act as reversioner on behalf of all the landlords where there are sub-leases.

Any right of a tenant or his personal representatives arising from a notice served on the landlord under the Leasehold Reform Act 1967 is not capable of being an interest within LRA 2002, Sch 1 or Sch 3 which overrides first registration or registered dispositions (Leasehold Reform Act 1967, s 5(5)). It may, however, be the subject of a notice as if it were an estate contract and where the landlord's reversionary title is registered, application may be made for the entry of an agreed notice or a unilateral notice.

Agreed notice

In addition to the usual documents required (see *Notices*, page 389), an applicant should deliver to the Registry a certified copy of the notice under the Leasehold Reform Act 1967.

Where the consent of the registered proprietor is not available, this is likely to be sufficient to satisfy the Registry as to the validity of the applicant's claim for the purposes of LRA 2002, s 34(3)(c).

The agreed notice in the register will give details of the interest protected.

Unilateral notice

An applicant should deliver to the Registry the usual documents required (see *Notices*, page 389).

The statement in panel 11 or conveyancer's certificate in panel 12 of Form UN1 should be completed on the following lines to show the interest of the applicant:

> tenant having on [*date*] given notice under the Leasehold Reform Act 1967 to [*name and address of the landlord*] in respect of the grant of an extended lease.

The unilateral notice in the register will give brief details of the interest protected and identify the beneficiary of that notice.

Where the applicant has taken an assignment from the tenant of the benefit of the rights under notice in accordance with Leasehold Reform Act 1967, s 5(2), no entry of such an assignment will be made in the register. However, if the rights are already protected in the register by a unilateral notice, the assignee should apply in Form UN3 to be registered as the new beneficiary of the notice. Panel 11 of Form UN3 should be completed on the following lines to show the entitlement of the applicant:

> assignee of rights under the Leasehold Reform Act 1967 by virtue of an assignment dated [*date*] made between [*name of former tenant*] and the applicant, the rights having arisen on [*date*] by the service of notice on [*name and address of the landlord*] in respect of the grant of an extended lease.

Registration of extended lease

The application for registration of the extended lease should be made in the usual way (see *First registration*, page 222 or 'Leases which are registrable dispositions', above, as the case may be). The application should show, either by a statement in the lease or on the application form, that the lease is made under the Leasehold Reform Act 1967.

In general, any prior mortgagee's consent to the extended lease is implied. A mortgagee's consent to the extended lease does not therefore normally need to be lodged with the application. However, the consent of the landlord's mortgagee (and any other person interested in the mortgage) should be lodged where the existing lease:

(a)   was granted on or after 1 January 1968;
(b)   was made subsequent to the date of the landlord's mortgage; and
(c)   would not have been binding on the persons interested in the mortgage (i.e. it was outside the mortgagor's leasing powers and the mortgagee did not concur in it).

Where any necessary consent is not lodged, a protective entry will be made in the property register of the new title (see *Classes of title*, page 130).

When the applicant's title to his existing lease is unregistered, satisfactory evidence of this should accompany an application for first registration of the extended lease, so that appropriate entries can be made in the register of title to the extended lease as to any rights of a mortgagee of the existing lease.

If the extended lease incorporates the terms of an unregistered existing lease, a certified copy or examined abstract of the existing lease should be lodged for filing in the Registry.

If an interest is protected in the register of a registered existing lease but does not affect the new extended lease, application should be lodged as appropriate for the withdrawal or cancellation of the existing entry in respect of it. If the interest affects the extended lease, an application to protect it by means of a suitable entry in the register of the new title should accompany the application to register the extended lease.

Where the extended lease is being granted under the Leasehold Reform Act 1967, a mortgage secured on the existing lease does not transfer automatically to the extended lease and should, therefore, be either discharged and replaced, or transferred to the extended lease by using a deed of substituted security.

Where the existing lease is registered, any chargees of the applicant's existing lease should be contacted prior to completion of the extended lease and the necessary arrangements made. If the mortgage is discharged then the appropriate form of discharge should be lodged with the application for registration. If a deed of substituted security is used, the deed should be lodged. Any new mortgage (with a certified copy, if the applicant wishes the original to be returned) should be lodged with the application for registration.

Where the existing lease is unregistered, if the mortgage is discharged then the discharged mortgage or other evidence of discharge should be lodged with the application for registration. If a deed of substituted security is used, the mortgage and the deed should be lodged. Any new mortgage (with a certified copy, if the applicant wishes the original to be returned) should be lodged with the application for registration.

If the mortgagee's co-operation cannot be secured, the Registry will endeavour to serve notice on him, and any other person appearing to be interested in the mortgage, giving relevant details of the applicant and the nature of the application. If there is no response to the notice, the application will be completed and a protective entry will be made to the effect that the extended lease is subject to such rights as may be subsisting in favour of the persons interested in a charge of the existing lease. The entry will not be a registration of the charge, but will take effect as a notice which will protect the priority of the charge in the register.

If, in response to the notice, the mortgagee lodges the original mortgage, either it will be registered or a notice will be entered in respect of it, as appropriate.

Where the existing lease is registered, an application should also be made to close that registered title and cancel the notice in respect of that lease in the landlord's registered title (see 'Determination of registered leases', below).

For the position where the existing lease is not registered but is noted in the landlord's registered title (see 'Cancellation of a noted lease', below).

Acquisition of a lease under the Leasehold Reform, Housing and Urban Development Act 1993

The LRHUDA 1993 confers upon a qualifying tenant of a flat an individual right to acquire from the landlord a new lease in substitution for an existing lease. Such right may also be exercised by the personal representatives of a tenant who held the right at his death, so long as the tenancy is vested in them (Commonhold and Leasehold Reform Act 2002, s 132). The personal representatives may not give notice of their desire to acquire the new lease later than 2 years after the grant of probate or letters of administration. If the immediate landlord does not have sufficient interest to grant such a lease, the new lease must be granted by the nearest landlord whose lease is sufficient. For the right to collective enfranchisement conferred upon qualifying tenants by the LRHUDA 1993, see *Collective enfranchisement*, page 136.

The new lease is at a peppercorn rent for a term expiring 90 years after the term date of the existing lease (LRHUDA 1993, s 56). A premium, calculated under LRHUDA 1993, Sch 13, is payable.

Notice to acquire new lease

The notice served by a qualifying tenant under LRHUDA 1993, s 42 claiming to exercise the right to acquire a new lease of the flat is not capable of being an interest within LRA 2002, Sch 1, para 2 or Sch 3, para 2 which overrides first registration or registered dispositions (LRHUDA 1993, s 97(1)). However, it may be the subject of a notice as if it were an estate contract and where the landlord's reversionary title is registered, application may be made for the entry of an agreed notice or a unilateral notice.

AGREED NOTICE

In addition to the usual documents required (see *Notices*, page 389), an applicant should deliver to the Registry a certified copy of the notice under LRHUDA 1993, s 42.

Where the consent of the registered proprietor is not available, this is likely to be sufficient to satisfy the Registry as to the validity of the applicant's claim for the purposes of LRA 2002, s 34(3)(c).

The agreed notice in the register will give details of the interest protected.

UNILATERAL NOTICE

An applicant should deliver to the Registry the usual documents required (see *Notices*, page 389).

The statement in panel 11 or conveyancer's certificate in panel 12 of Form UN1 should be completed on the following lines to show the interest of the applicant:

> qualifying tenant having given notice under section 42 of the Leasehold Reform, Housing and Urban Development Act 1993 on [*date*] to [*name and address of the landlord*] [and to [*name and address of any third party in the tenant's existing lease*]].

The unilateral notice in the register will give brief details of the interest protected and identify the beneficiary of that notice.

Where the applicant has taken an assignment from the tenant of the benefit of the rights under notice in accordance with LRHUDA 1993, s 42, no entry of such an assignment will be made in the register. However, if the rights are already protected in the register by a unilateral notice, the assignee should apply in Form UN3 to be registered as the new beneficiary of the notice. Panel 11 of Form UN3 should be completed on the following lines to show the entitlement of the applicant:

> assignee of rights under the Leasehold Reform, Housing and Urban Development Act 1993 by virtue of an assignment dated [*date*] made between [*name of former tenant*] and the applicant, the rights having arisen on [*date*] by the service of notice on [*name and address of the landlord*] in respect of the grant of a new lease.

Application for vesting order

If the qualifying tenant wishes to make a claim to exercise the right to acquire a new lease of his flat but the landlord cannot be found or his identity cannot be ascertained, the court may make a vesting order (LRHUDA 1993, s 50(1)). Such an order provides for the surrender of the tenant's lease of his flat and for the granting to him of a new lease of it on such terms as may be determined by a leasehold valuation tribunal to be appropriate, with a view to the lease being granted to him as if he had given notice under LRHUDA 1993, s 42. An application for such a vesting order is treated as a pending land action (LRHUDA 1993, s 97(2)(b)) and cannot therefore be an interest within LRA 2002, Sch 1, para 2 or Sch 3, para 2 which overrides first registration or registered dispositions (LRA 2002, s 87(1) and (3)). Such an application may, however, be protected by entry of an agreed notice or a unilateral notice, and a restriction.

AGREED NOTICE

In addition to the usual documents required (see *Notices*, page 389), an applicant should deliver to the Registry the application to the court for the vesting order or a certified copy of it.

As the consent of the registered proprietor is unlikely to be forthcoming in this situation, this is likely to be sufficient to satisfy the Registry as to the validity of the applicants' claim in accordance with LRA 2002, s 34(3)(c).

The agreed notice in the register will give details of the interest protected.

UNILATERAL NOTICE

An applicant should for a unilateral notice deliver to the Registry the usual documents required (see *Notices*, page 389).

The statement in panel 11 or conveyancer's certificate in panel 12 of Form UN1 should be completed on the following lines to show the interest of the applicant:

> qualifying tenants in an application under section 50(1) of the Leasehold Reform, Housing and Urban Development Act 1993 in the [*name* County Court] *or* [*name* Division of the High Court of Justice] [*state full court reference and parties*].

The unilateral notice in the register will give brief details of the interest protected and identify the beneficiaries of that notice.

RESTRICTION

The applicant for a vesting order under LRHUDA 1993, s 50(1) is to be regarded as having a sufficient interest in relation to a registered estate or charge for the purposes of LRA 2002, s 43(1)(c) if he is applying for a restriction in Form N (LRR 2003, r 93(q)). The Registry must give notice of the application for a restriction to the proprietor of the registered estate or charge concerned, if it has not been made by or with the consent of such proprietor or a person entitled to be registered as such proprietor (LRA 2002 s 45).

A restriction does not confer any priority; it simply prevents an entry being made in the register in respect of any disposition, or a disposition of a specified kind, unless the terms of the restriction have (where applicable) been complied with.

In addition to the usual documents required (see *Restrictions*, page 500), the applicant should deliver to the Registry the application to the court for the vesting order or a certified copy of it.

As the application for a restriction is unlikely to be made by or with the consent of the registered proprietor in this situation, the statement in panel 12 or conveyancer's certificate in panel 13 of Form RX1 must be completed, confirming that the applicants' interest is that specified in LRR 2003, r 93(q) and setting out details of the application to the court.

Panel 9 of Form RX1 should be completed as to the appropriate restriction. A possible form of restriction based on the wording of Form N is:

> No [disposition *or specify type of disposition*] of the registered estate by the proprietor of the registered estate [*or by the proprietor of any registered charge, not being a charge registered before the entry of this restriction*] is to be registered

without a written consent signed by [*name*] of [*address*] [or [*their conveyancer or specify appropriate details*]].

A restriction in standard Form N in LRR 2003, Sch 4 does not require the approval of the Registry to the wording of the restriction under LRA 2002, s 43(3).

Vesting order

Where the court makes a vesting order under LRHUDA 1993, s 50(1), the LRA 2002 applies in relation to that order as it applies in relation to an order affecting land which is made by the court for the purpose of enforcing a judgment or recognisance (LRHUDA 1993, s 97(2)(a)). Such a vesting order cannot be an interest within LRA 2002, Sch 1, para 2 or Sch 3, para 2 which overrides first registration or registered dispositions (LRA 2002, s 87(1) and (3)), but it may be protected by entry of an agreed notice or a unilateral notice, and a restriction.

AGREED NOTICE

In addition to the usual documents required (see *Notices*, page 389), an applicant should deliver to the Registry the vesting order or a certified copy of it.

As the consent of the registered proprietor is unlikely to be forthcoming in this situation, this is likely to be sufficient to satisfy the Registry as to the validity of the applicants' claim in accordance with LRA 2002, s 34(3)(c).

The agreed notice in the register will give details of the interest protected.

UNILATERAL NOTICE

An applicant should deliver to the Registry the usual documents required (see *Notices*, page 389).

The statement in panel 11 or conveyancer's certificate in panel 12 of Form UN1 should be completed on the following lines to show the interest of the applicant:

> qualifying tenant having the benefit of an order under section 50(1) of the Leasehold Reform, Housing and Urban Development Act 1993 made by the [*name* County Court] *or* [*name* Division of the High Court of Justice] [*state full court reference and parties*].

The unilateral notice in the register will give brief details of the interest protected and identify the beneficiaries of that notice.

RESTRICTION

A person who has obtained a vesting order under the LRHUDA 1993, s 50(1) is to be regarded as having a sufficient interest in relation to a registered estate or charge for the purposes of LRA 2002, s 42(1)(c) if he is applying for a restriction in Form L or Form N (LRR 2003, r 93(p)). The Registry must give notice of the application for a restriction to the proprietor of the registered estate or charge concerned, if it has not been made by or with the consent of such proprietor or a person entitled to be registered as such proprietor (LRA 2002, s 45).

A restriction does not confer any priority; it simply prevents an entry being made in the register in respect of any disposition, or a disposition of a specified kind, unless the terms of the restriction have (where applicable) been complied with.

In addition to the usual documents required (see *Restrictions*, page 500), the applicant should deliver to the Registry the vesting order or a certified copy of it.

As the application for a restriction is unlikely to be made by or with the consent of the registered proprietor in this situation, the statement in panel 12 or conveyancer's certificate in panel 13 of Form RX1 must be completed, confirming that the applicant's interest is that specified in LRR 2003, r 93(p) and setting out details of the vesting order made by the court.

Panel 9 of Form RX1 should be completed as to the appropriate restriction. A possible form of restriction based on the wording of Form L is:

> No [disposition *or specify type of disposition*] of the registered estate by the proprietor of the registered estate [*or by the proprietor of any registered charge not being a charge registered before the entry of this restriction*] is to be registered without a certificate signed by [*name*] of [*address*] [or [*their conveyancer or specify appropriate details*]] that the provisions of [*specify clause, paragraph or other particulars*] of [*specify details*] have been complied with [or that they do not apply to the disposition].

A possible form of restriction based on the wording of Form N is:

> No [disposition *or specify type of disposition*] of the registered estate by the proprietor of the registered estate [*or by the proprietor of any registered charge not being a charge registered before the entry of this restriction*] is to be registered without a written consent signed by [*name*] of [*address*] [or [*their conveyancer or specify appropriate details*]].

A restriction in standard Form L or Form N in LRR 2003, Sch 4 does not require the approval of the Registry to the wording of the restriction under LRA 2002, s 43(3).

Grant of new lease

The new lease, which takes effect in substitution for the existing lease, is to be on the same terms as the existing lease but with such modifications as may be required or appropriate. A lease granted under the LRHUDA 1993 must contain a statement in the following form (LRR 2003, r 196(2)):

> This lease is granted under section 56 of the Leasehold Reform, Housing and Urban Development Act 1993.

Where the lease is a prescribed clauses lease, this statement must be referred to in prescribed clause LR5.1.

Once the new lease has been granted to the tenant it must be registered. The application for registration should be made in the usual way (see *First registration*, page 222 or 'Leases which are registrable dispositions', above, as the case may be).

Unless the existing lease falls within the limited exception in LHRUDA 1993, s 58(2), the new lease is binding on the persons interested in any mortgage on the landlord's title, even where the grant of such a lease is otherwise unauthorised (LRHUDA 1993, s 58(1)). It is therefore usually unnecessary to include consents of mortgagees with the application to register the new lease. However, the consent of the landlord's mortgagee (and any other person interested in the mortgage) should be lodged where the existing lease:

(a)   was granted on or after 1 November 1993;
(b)   was made subsequent to the date of the landlord's mortgage; and
(c)   would not have been binding on the persons interested in the mortgage (i.e. it was outside the mortgagor's leasing powers and the mortgagee did not concur in it).

Where any necessary consent is not lodged, a protective entry will be made in the property register of the new title (see *Classes of title*, page 130).

If the existing lease is subject to a mortgage or charge immediately before surrender, on the grant of a new lease the mortgage or charge will attach to the new lease (LRHUDA 1993, s 58(4)). The application for registration should therefore include an application in respect of the registration of an existing mortgage or charge against the title of the new lease.

If the charge is to be protected by entry of a notice only, application should be made either for entry of an agreed notice, using Form AN1 or for entry of a unilateral notice, using Form UN1 as appropriate (see *Notices*, page 389). The

Registry will serve notice on a chargee before closing the existing leasehold title, if registered. Any other entries in the register of the existing leasehold title, if registered, must be considered and the appropriate steps taken.

If the tenant's existing lease is unregistered and is subject to a mortgage entitling the mortgagee to possession of the documents of title relating to the existing lease, then, within one month of the registration of the new lease, it must be delivered to that mortgagee by the tenant (LRHUDA 1993, s 58(5)). Failure to do this has the same effect as the breach of an obligation under the existing mortgage (LRHUDA 1993, s 58(6)).

Easements in leases

From 19 June 2006, the register heading of a registered leasehold estate states that:

> This register describes the land and estate comprised in the title.

This is supplemented by the following entry in the property register:

> Unless otherwise mentioned the title includes any legal easements granted by the registered lease(s) but is subject to any rights that it reserves, so far as those easements and rights exist and benefit or affect the registered land.

Where a lease is lodged for registration, the Registry will where appropriate make an entry in the register in respect of easements granted and/or reserved by the lease. Where necessary, the entry will include any note qualifying or excluding an easement. The benefit of an equitable easement cannot be registered in the registered leasehold title, but the burden of it can be the subject of a notice in any registered burdened title.

Easements granted

In the case of a prescribed clauses lease, LRR 2003, r 72A(3) applies and the Registry need only consider any easements granted that are referred to in clause LR11.1. If the lease is not a prescribed clauses lease, the Registry will consider any easements granted in the lease and make the appropriate entry in the register.

Where the easement is granted over other land within the landlord's registered title out of which the lease is granted, a notice of the easements will appear in the register by virtue of the standard entry made in the landlord's title on registration of the lease:

The parts of the land affected thereby are subject to the leases set out in the schedule of leases hereto. The leases grant and reserve easements as therein mentioned.

If the easement is granted over land within other registered titles, the title numbers must be stated in clause LR2.2 (in the case of a prescribed clauses lease) or panel 2 of form AP1 (in the case of other leases), otherwise LRR 2003, r 72A(4) applies and the Registry need make no entry in those other titles. In that event, unless a separate application is made against each registered title comprising the burdened land, the easements will not have been completed by registration for the purposes of LRA 2002, s 27 and the Registry will not be able to register the benefit of the easement in the registered leasehold title as it will not have taken effect at law.

If the easement is granted over unregistered burdened land, any legal easement will bind any subsequent purchaser and the burden of it will take effect as an interest which overrides on first registration (LRA 2002, Sch 1, para 3). Satisfactory evidence of the grantor's unregistered title will need to be lodged before the benefit of the easement can be registered in the registered leasehold title.

Easements reserved

The entry in the property register of a registered leasehold title, referred to above, also refers to easements reserved. Thus there is a notice entered in the register of the leasehold title in respect of any easements reserved in the registered lease. If the lease contains no beneficial easements (or these are not being registered because clause LR11.1 of a prescribed clauses lease has not been completed correctly) an entry will be made in the charges register of the leasehold title in respect of the easements reserved by the lease.

In the case of a prescribed clauses lease, LRR 2003, r 72A(3) applies and the Registry need only consider any easements reserved (or granted for the benefit of land owned by a third party) in the lease which are referred to in clause LR11.2, unless separate application is made. If the lease is not a prescribed clauses lease, the Registry will consider any easements reserved (or granted for the benefit of land owned by a third party) in the lease and make the appropriate entries in the register.

If the easements are reserved for the benefit of other land within the landlord's registered reversionary title, the easement is included in that title by virtue of the standard entry in the register of that registered title referred to above.

If the easement is reserved for the benefit of land in other registered titles, the title numbers must be stated in clause LR2.2 (in the case of a prescribed clauses lease) or panel 2 of Form AP1 (in the case of other leases), otherwise LRR 2003, r 72A(4) applies and the Registry need make no entry in those other titles unless separate application is made.

Where the benefiting land is unregistered, the benefit of the easement will subsist for the benefit of that land. On first registration of the benefiting estate, the estate will vest in the proprietor together with the benefit of the easement (LRA 2002, ss 11(3) and 12(3)).

Easements in unregistered leases

Easements may be granted or reserved in 'unregistered leases', being leases:

(a) the grant of which is not a registrable disposition;
(b) the grant or assignment of which does not trigger compulsory first registration; and
(c) that are not the subject of voluntary first registration.

EASEMENTS GRANTED

Where the burdened land is registered, the grant of such easements is a registrable disposition which must be completed by registration, even if the lease itself will not be substantively registered or the subject of a notice in the register of the landlord's title. An application should therefore be made in Form AP1 to complete the grant of the easement by registration.

Where the lease itself *is* capable of being noted, details of it may be provided in a Form DI accompanying the application, and the Registry will normally then enter a notice in the register in respect of the lease at the same time.

If the easement is granted over unregistered burdened land, there is no register entry to be made; any legal easement will bind any subsequent purchaser and the burden of it will take effect as an overriding interest on first registration of the burdened estate (LRA 2002, Sch 1, para 3).

EASEMENTS RESERVED

As the burdened leasehold land is unregistered, the reservation is not a registrable disposition. Any legal easement will bind any subsequent purchaser and the burden of it will take effect as an overriding interest on first registration of the burdened estate (LRA 2002, Sch 1, para 3).

Application can, however, be made in Form AP1 for the benefit of a legal easement to be registered in the register of any registered benefiting title (LRR 2003, r 73A(1)(a)).

Equitable easements in leases

An easement may be equitable rather than legal. For example, if the lease is merely in writing but not by deed, any easement granted or reserved within it can only be equitable. The effect of this is that:

(a)   Where the burdened land is registered, the grant or reservation of such an easement is not a registrable disposition which is required to be completed by registration, although it is capable of being noted.
(b)   The benefit of such an easement cannot be registered in the register of any registered benefiting title.
(c)   Where an easement is granted or reserved and the burdened land is unregistered, that easement will need to be protected by way of a Class D(iii) Land Charge.

Restrictive covenants in leases

On registration of a person as proprietor of a leasehold estate, that estate is vested in him together with all interests subsisting for the benefit of the estate, but subject to implied and express covenants, obligations and liabilities incident to that estate (LRA 2002, s 12(4)(a)). It is not possible to enter a notice in the register in respect of the burden of restrictive covenants made between a landlord and tenant, so far as relating to the demised premises (LRA 2002, s 33(c)). However, where a restrictive covenant between a landlord and tenant does not relate to the demised premises, an application should be made for a notice to be entered in the affected title. This might arise where the landlord is covenanting in respect of a neighbouring property which he owns, as in *Oceanic Village Ltd v United Attractions Ltd* [2000] Ch 234, or where a tenant covenants not to open a competing business within a certain radius of the demised premises. The application may be for an agreed notice or a unilateral notice.

Agreed notice

In addition to the usual documents required (see *Notices*, page 389), an applicant should deliver to the Registry the document containing the restrictive covenant or a certified copy of it.

Where the consent of the registered proprietor is not available but, for example, the original document is signed by him, this is likely to be sufficient to satisfy the Registry as to the validity of the applicant's claim for the purposes of LRA 2002, s 34(3)(c).

The agreed notice in the register will give details of the interest protected.

Unilateral notice

An applicant should deliver to the Registry the usual documents required (see *Notices*, page 389).

The statement in panel 11 or conveyancer's certificate in panel 12 of Form UN1 should be completed on the following lines to show the interest of the applicant:

> person having the benefit of a restrictive covenant contained in a [*Lease*] *or* [*Deed*] dated [*date*] and made between [*parties*] which, although made between a landlord and tenant, does not relate to the demised premises.

The unilateral notice in the register will give brief details of the interest protected and identify the beneficiaries of that notice.

Apportionment of rent

A transfer of a registered leasehold estate in land containing a legal apportionment of, or exoneration from, the rent reserved by the lease must include the statement prescribed by LRR 2003, r 60(1). Where the landlord does not consent to the apportionment, it will take effect in equity only. The statement must be in the additional provisions panel of the transfer and may contain any necessary alterations and additions. The statement is:

> Liability for the payment of [*if applicable the previously apportioned rent of (amount) being part of*] the rent reserved by the registered lease is apportioned between the Transferor and the Transferee as follows:
>
> — (*amount*) shall be payable out of the Property and the balance shall be payable out of the land remaining in title number (*title number of retained land*) or
> — the whole of that rent shall be payable out of the Property and none of it shall be payable out of the land remaining in title number (*title number of retained land*) or
> — the whole of that rent shall be payable out of the land remaining in title number (*title number of retained land*) and none of it shall be payable out of the Property.

Where in a transfer of part of a registered leasehold estate which is held under an old tenancy, that part is, without the consent of the landlord, expressed to be exonerated from, or charged with, the entire rent, the covenants in LRA 2002, Sch 12, para 20(3) or (4), if implied, are modified (LRR 2003, r 60(2) and (3)).

An 'old tenancy' is a tenancy which is not a new tenancy for the purposes of Landlord and Tenant (Covenants) Act 1995, s 1 (see also *Implied covenants*, page 268, as to when such covenants are implied).

The covenants in para 20(3) as modified are:

> The transferee covenants with the transferor that during the residue of the term granted by the registered lease the transferee and the persons deriving title under him will:
>
> (a)   pay the entire rent,
> (b)   comply with the covenants and conditions contained in the lease so far as affecting the part transferred but extended to a covenant to pay the entire rent, and
> (c)   keep the transferor and the person deriving title under him indemnified against all actions, expenses and claims on account of any failure to comply with paragraphs (a) and (b).

The covenants in para 20(4) as modified are:

> The transferor covenants with the transferee that during the residue of the term granted by the registered lease the transferor and the persons deriving title under him will:
>
> (a)   pay the entire rent,
> (b)   comply with the covenants and conditions contained in the lease so far as affecting the part retained but extended to a covenant to pay the entire rent, and
> (c)   keep the transferee and the persons deriving title under him indemnified against all actions, expenses and claims on account of any failure to comply with paragraphs (a) and (b).

Where a transfer of such a registered leasehold estate modifies or negatives any of the covenants implied under LRA 2002, Sch 12, para 20(3), an entry must be made in the register that the covenants have been so modified or negatived (LRR 2003, r 66).

Extensions of leases (other than under the Leasehold Reform Act 1967 or Leasehold Reform, Housing and Urban Development Act 1993)

Aside from the grant of an extended lease under the provisions of the Leasehold Reform Act 1967 or the LRHUDA 1993 discussed above, or the variation of an existing lease which takes effect as a deemed surrender and re-grant (see

'Variation of a lease', above), an existing lease may be extended by the grant of a new lease, either to take immediate effect or to commence on a future date.

Where the new lease takes immediate effect

In this case, the tenant is deemed to have surrendered his existing lease immediately before the new lease commences. This applies irrespective of the intention of the parties, because the new lease is inconsistent with the existing lease and therefore the tenant is estopped from denying that the existing lease has come to an end.

The surrender of the existing lease must be effected in the register and the new lease registered in its place.

Before completing the new lease, the tenant should contact any chargee of the existing lease to ascertain his requirements. The chargee may prefer either to release his existing charge and take a fresh charge over the new leasehold estate, or to use a deed of substituted security.

However, if the new lease is made *expressly subject* to the existing lease, the Registry will accept that surrender of the existing lease does not occur, as the new lease (as a lease of the landlord's reversionary interest) is not inconsistent with the existing lease. In this event, the existing leasehold title, if registered, will not be closed. When registering such a new lease, the Registry will have regard to the possibility that any chargee of the existing lease has an interest in the new lease. Accordingly, when making an application to register such a new lease, it is also necessary to lodge any charges affecting the old lease or list them in panel 10 of Form FR1 or panel 10 of Form AP1. Where appropriate, an entry on the following lines will be made in the charges register of the registered title of the new lease:

> The land is subject to such rights as may be subsisting in favour of the persons interested in a charge dated (*date*) made between (*parties*) of the lease dated (*date*) referred to in the Schedule of leases hereto.

Where the new lease commences on a future date

The new lease may, when granted at a rent or for a premium, commence at any time up to 21 years from the date of the grant (Law of Property Act 1925, s 149(3)). Therefore, if the existing lease has less than 21 years to run, the new lease may be granted to commence on its expiry. However, if the existing lease has more than 21 years to run, it will have to be shortened, either by a separate deed of variation, or by suitable wording in the new lease, so that the existing lease determines just before the commencement of the new lease.

For surrenders of leases, see 'Determination of registered leases', below. For the position where the existing lease is not registered but is noted on the landlord's registered title, see 'Cancellation of a noted lease', below. For details of applications to register a new lease where it is granted out of unregistered land, see *First registration*, page 222. For details of applications to register a new lease where it is out of registered land, see 'Registration of leases which are registrable dispositions', above.

Determination of registered leases

There are various ways in which a leasehold estate in land may come to an end. The evidence required in support of an application following the determination of a lease depends on the manner in which the leasehold estate has determined and upon whether the leasehold estate and/or the landlord's reversionary estate are registered.

Form of application

In addition to any documents that may be specified in the individual paragraphs set out below relating to the particular method by which the lease has been determined, an applicant for closure of a registered leasehold title should deliver to the Registry:

(a)   an application in Form AP1 to close the registered leasehold title on determination and (where applicable) to cancel the notice of that lease on the registered reversionary title;

(b)   the original lease and/or counterpart lease, if in the applicant's possession;

(c)   (if the reversionary estate is unregistered) an examined abstract or epitome of the landlord's unregistered title;

(d)   (in the case of an application to close a registered leasehold title on surrender) the appropriate confirmation or evidence as to identity (see *Identity evidence*, page 266); and

(e)   the fee payable (see *Fees*, page 221).

The Registry will, where appropriate, serve notice of the application on any person appearing to be affected by it.

If the determined lease is unregistered but is the subject of a notice in a registered reversionary title, application may be made for cancellation or removal of that notice (see 'Cancellation of a noted lease', below).

Incumbrances affecting the determined lease

Any incumbrances affecting the leasehold estate being determined will need to be considered and any necessary action taken in respect of them, as follows:

(a)   If a lease is determined by notice, effluxion of time, forfeiture or frustration, all incumbrances will normally end automatically with the determination of the lease. This is subject to the exception, in the case of determination by effluxion of time, to inferior leases which have been extended by either the Landlord and Tenant Act 1954 or the Local Government and Housing Act 1989 and which may therefore affect the reversionary estate (see (c) below).

(b)   If a lease is being determined by merger, surrender or disclaimer, all incumbrances affecting the leasehold estate which is being determined must be dealt with as appropriate. Thus registered or noted charges, restrictions and cautions should be either discharged, withdrawn or cancelled, and the appropriate documentation lodged to effect this. Where an incumbrance consists of a registered charge, it may be possible to deal with the matter by way of a deed of substituted security, and an application made to register it against a registered reversionary title, where appropriate. Other incumbrances such as subjective easements and restrictive covenants will normally be carried forward to any registered reversionary title, unless they are already substantially repeated on that title.

(c)   Where a lease has been determined by notice, forfeiture or frustration, any inferior leases (such as any underleases derived from that lease) will also determine. Where a lease has been determined by disclaimer, see *Bankruptcy*, page 49 or *Liquidators*, page 360. In other cases, any inferior leases will continue to subsist and may affect the reversionary estate, in which case they will be noted against any registered reversionary title unless evidence is produced that the inferior lease has also determined and, if the inferior lease is registered, an application is made to close that registered title.

(d)   Where a leasehold estate is registered with a possessory leasehold class of title, it will not be possible to determine that registered leasehold title unless the applicant also lodges Form UT1, or the title is otherwise capable of being upgraded to absolute leasehold title, see *Upgrade of class of title*, page 565. This reflects the fact that such a lease may be subject to other unregistered interests which might prevent determination.

Merger

Merger occurs where a leasehold estate and the reversionary estate come into the same ownership and are held in the same capacity, so that the lease is absorbed by the reversionary estate and thus determined. There must be an intention to merge the estates, so that even where a leasehold estate and its immediate reversionary title have become vested in the same person in the same capacity, it is a matter of intention as to whether or not the leasehold estate is to be determined on merger. The applicant should therefore always make it clear within the application that merger is intended.

Where a restriction in Form A appears in a registered leasehold title and/or in a registered reversionary title, it will not be possible to determine the registered leasehold title by merger unless the applicant is able to lodge satisfactory evidence that he holds both estates upon the same trusts. Similarly, if the leasehold estate or the reversionary estate is unregistered and there is an indication of a trust, the applicant must lodge satisfactory evidence that he holds both estates upon the same trusts.

As regards any benefiting easements affecting the leasehold estate, it needs to be considered whether the reversionary estate has the benefit of an equivalent easement where necessary and if not, whether the two estates should continue to be held separately and the lease not determined. In *Wall v Collins* [2007] EWCA Civ 444, the Court of Appeal held that an easement must be appurtenant to a dominant tenement, but not necessarily to a particular interest in that dominant tenement. In consequence, when a lease is extinguished on merger, the tenant may not automatically lose any benefiting easements granted for the benefit of the leasehold estate and those easements may continue to exist and to be exercisable by the occupier of the dominant tenement for the period for which they were granted. The Registry will not automatically enter the benefit of such easements in the registered title to the reversionary estate (if registered). However, an application may be made to register the benefit of such easements in the registered title to the reversionary estate, either at the time of merger or subsequently (see *Legal easements*, page 343).

Surrender by deed

When a tenant surrenders his lease to his immediate landlord, who accepts the surrender, the lease is absorbed by the reversionary estate and thus determined. A deed effecting a surrender of a leasehold estate must contain wording which clearly shows that the tenant is surrendering the lease. The application must be accompanied by the original deed of surrender and, as it will normally be a land transaction, the appropriate SDLT evidence (see *Stamp duty land tax*, page 541). Evidence of the landlord's consent to the surrender (if he has not executed the deed and is not the applicant) must also be lodged. Where a restriction in Form A appears in the registered leasehold title, the surrender is a 'disposition' for the purposes of that restriction. If capital money arises and the surrender is by a sole registered proprietor, the disposition will be caught by the terms of the restriction and the registered leasehold title cannot be closed.

Surrender by operation of law

Instead of surrender by deed, a surrender of a lease may be effected by operation of law, that is, as a result of the actions of both of the parties. For example, where the tenant gives up possession of the premises to the landlord, who then grants a new lease of the premises to a third party with the tenant's consent. It can also occur where the landlord grants a new lease of the same premises to the existing tenant. The application must be accompanied by satisfactory evidence of the acts which imply surrender (LRR 2003, r 161(1)). This will normally consist of a statutory declaration or statement of truth made by a suitable person with full knowledge of the facts, together with any other available evidence relating to the surrender, such as a receipt for money paid for the surrender. If the tenant was occupying the property and has given vacant possession to the landlord, the statutory declaration or statement of truth must describe when and how the premises were vacated and the keys returned to the landlord. If a sub-tenant was occupying the property, the statutory declaration or statement of truth must contain evidence that the landlord is receiving the rent directly from that sub-tenant.

A statutory declaration or statement of truth will not be required where either the landlord grants a new lease of the same premises to the existing tenant; or the leasehold estate and the reversionary estate are both registered and the application is made by or with the consent of the registered proprietors of both titles, provided the determined leasehold estate is registered with an absolute leasehold or a good leasehold class of title.

Confirmation must be given that no deed of surrender was entered into.

A surrender by operation of law is a land transaction for SDLT purposes and by virtue of Finance Act 2000, s 128 any document evidencing the surrender, including consents, statutory declarations, statements of truth or Land Registry application forms, will represent an instrument of surrender. The appropriate SDLT evidence should therefore be lodged (see *Stamp duty land tax*, page 541).

Where a restriction in Form A appears in the registered leasehold title, the surrender is a 'disposition' for the purposes of that restriction. If capital money arises and the surrender is by a sole registered proprietor, the disposition will be caught by the terms of the restriction and the registered leasehold title cannot be closed.

Disclaimer

When a person becomes bankrupt or a company becomes insolvent, either a trustee in bankruptcy or a liquidator respectively may, by giving the prescribed notice, disclaim certain onerous property, including leases. This has the effect of determining the lease. For disclaimer by a trustee in bankruptcy, see *Bankruptcy*, page 49. For disclaimer by a liquidator, see *Liquidators*, page 360.

Effluxion of time

A lease for a fixed term will automatically determine when the fixed term expires, unless it is prolonged by virtue of the provisions of either the Landlord and Tenant Act 1954 or the Local Government and Housing Act 1989. The application must therefore be accompanied by confirmation that neither of those Acts affect the lease or that it has determined in accordance with their provisions. If the tenant has an option to renew the lease, satisfactory evidence that the option has not been, and cannot now be, exercised must also be lodged.

Forfeiture

A lease containing a proviso for re-entry or 'forfeiture clause' may enable a landlord to forfeit the lease by taking court proceedings or by peaceable re-entry, because the tenant either has not paid the rent or has breached some other covenant(s) in the lease. An interested person may apply to the court for relief from forfeiture. However, this is not in itself a valid ground for objection to an application based upon determination on forfeiture.

If the forfeiture is based on a *court order*, the application must be accompanied by:

(a)   the claim form, indicating the reason for the forfeiture;
(b)   a certified copy of the court order directing the forfeiture of the lease; and
(c)   the sheriff's return, or a statutory declaration or statement of truth, proving the facts which are stated to amount to re-entry on a stated date.

If the forfeiture is based on *peaceable re-entry*, the application must be accompanied by evidence in the form of a statutory declaration or statement of truth by a suitable person with full knowledge of the facts, proving the facts which, it is claimed, amount to a lawful re-entry on a specified date.

If the forfeiture is for *non-payment of rent*, the statutory declaration or statement of truth must establish whether a formal demand was required and, if so, whether it was made. Confirmation of the amount of rent arrears and that this was sufficient to trigger the proviso for re-entry must also be provided.

If the forfeiture is for *breach of covenant other than non-payment of rent*, the statutory declaration or statement of truth must establish:

(a) That the landlord served the requisite notice under Law of Property Act 1925, s 146(1) upon the tenant on a stated date. If the leasehold estate is not registered, satisfactory evidence that the person served was the tenant must be lodged.

(b) In the case of a breach of a repairing covenant, that the service of the notice was known to the tenant, or to a sub-tenant where the tenant has only a nominal reversion, or to the person who last paid the rent due under the lease, either on his own behalf or as agent for the tenant or sub-tenant, and that a time reasonably sufficient to enable the repairs to be executed had subsequently elapsed (see Landlord and Tenant Act 1927, s 18(2)).

(c) In the case of a breach of a repairing covenant contained in a lease of which 3 years or more remained unexpired at the date of the notice served under Law of Property Act 1925, s 146, that the notice contained the required statement that the tenant was entitled to serve a counter-notice claiming the benefit of the Leasehold Property (Repairs) Act 1938 and did not do so.

(d) That the tenant failed to comply with the notice served under Law of Property Act 1925, s 146.

If the demised premises are let as a dwelling, the only lawful method of enforcing a right of re-entry while anyone is lawfully residing there is by obtaining a court order (Protection from Eviction Act 1977, s 2). Therefore, if the demised premises comprise a dwelling, the statutory declaration or statement of truth must establish either that no one was residing in the premises or any part of them, or if someone was, that he was not lawfully residing there.

If the lease is a residential lease, the statutory declaration or statement of truth must establish that the following provisions either do not apply or have been complied with:

(a) HA 1996, s 81 which limits the landlord's right to forfeit a residential lease where there are arrears of service charges which are disputed by the tenant.

(b) Commonhold and Leasehold Reform Act 2002, s 166 which provides that a tenant under a long lease of a dwelling is not liable to make a payment of rent under the lease unless the landlord has given the tenant a notice relating to the payment and the date on which he is liable to make the payment is specified in the notice.

(c)   Commonhold and Leasehold Reform Act 2002, s 167 which provides that a landlord under a long lease of a dwelling may not forfeit the lease for failure by the tenant to pay rent, service charge or administration charges unless the amount exceeds a prescribed sum (currently £350), or has been unpaid for a period in excess of a prescribed period (currently 3 years).

(d)   Commonhold and Leasehold Reform Act 2002, s 168 which provides that a landlord under a long lease of a dwelling may not serve a notice under Law of Property Act 1925, s 146 for breach of covenant by the tenant unless the tenant has admitted the breach, or a period of 14 days has elapsed after a leasehold valuation tribunal or court has determined that the breach has occurred.

An assured tenancy (including an assured shorthold tenancy) is a tenancy of a home created after 15 January 1989 which meets the conditions of HA 1988, s 1. HA 1988, Sch 1 contains a number of exceptions which prevent a tenancy becoming an assured tenancy. A landlord can determine an assured tenancy only by obtaining a court order for possession under HA 1988, s 7 or, in the case of a fixed-term tenancy, by notice under a 'break clause'; it cannot be determined by forfeiture. Because the tenancy is not determined by forfeiture it is not possible to claim relief against forfeiture. An assured tenancy will determine when the court order is executed (HA 1988, s 5(1A)). Any incumbrances against the leasehold interest will determine when the lease itself determines. An application to determine a lease on the basis of an order for possession made under HA 1988, s 7 should be accompanied by:

(a)   a certified copy of the court order, and
(b)   the sheriff's return, or a statutory declaration or statement of truth confirming that the order has been executed.

Notice

A lease for a fixed term may contain an option, usually called a 'break clause', allowing either one or both parties to the lease to determine the lease before the expiry of the fixed term. The option is usually only exercisable by written notice. The application must be accompanied by evidence of the determination of the lease by notice in accordance with the terms of the lease, such as a copy of the receipted notice, or a statutory declaration or statement of truth by the applicant, or a certificate by the applicant's conveyancer confirming the relevant facts.

Frustration

A lease may be determined under the doctrine of frustration, i.e. the occurrence of an unforeseen event that makes performance of the lease impracticable. Such cases will be rare and any application will be considered on its individual facts. This situation should be distinguished from the determination of a lease by notice on the occurrence of an event (such as the damage of the premises by fire so as to be beyond repair) referred to in a 'frustration clause' in the lease.

Enlargement

A tenant who holds the residue of a long lease of land may, under certain conditions, 'enlarge' it into a freehold. This is usually achieved by either the execution of a deed poll, or endorsement on one of the unregistered title deeds relating to an unregistered lease. On enlargement, the land remains subject to the same trusts and covenants that affected the original lease (see *Enlargement of long leases*, page 204).

Cancellation of a noted lease

Where a registered lease is determined, the notice of that lease in the landlord's registered title is cancelled at the same time as the closure of the leasehold title. Where an unregistered lease is determined and a notice of the lease appears in the landlord's registered title, an application should be made for that notice to be cancelled. An applicant should deliver to the Registry:

(a) an application in Form CN1 (completing panels 9 and 10 as appropriate);
(b) documentary evidence to prove that the unregistered leasehold estate has determined;
(c) the original lease and/or counterpart lease, or an account for its absence;
(d) satisfactory evidence of title to the determining leasehold estate, consisting of either documents similar to those required on first registration or (where the applicant is the landlord) the counterpart lease and copies of any assignments;
(e) a Land Charges search against the name of the tenant (with any entries accounted for and, where applicable, certified by a conveyancer as not affecting the estate);
(f) a list in duplicate in Form DL of all the documents delivered; and
(g) the fee payable (see *Fees*, page 221).

If the lease is noted by way of a unilateral notice, an application must be made either to remove the unilateral notice using Form UN2 or to cancel it using Form UN4 (see *Notices*, page 389).

Right to determine a registered lease

Where it appears to the Registry that a right to determine a registered estate is exercisable, it may enter the fact in the property register of the affected title (LRA 2002, s 64 and LRR 2003, r 125(1)). Where a right to determine a registered leasehold estate has arisen, an applicant may apply for such an entry to be made by delivering to the Registry:

(a) an application in Form AP1;
(b) evidence to satisfy the Registry that the applicant has the right to determine the registered leasehold estate and that the right is exercisable; and
(c) the fee payable (see *Fees*, page 221).

Before making an entry, the Registry must give notice of the application to the proprietor of the registered estate to which the application relates and the proprietor of any registered charge on that estate.

When such an entry has been made, an application to cancel it must be supported by evidence to satisfy the Registry that the right to determine the leasehold estate is not exercisable. The application for cancellation may be made by:

(a) the person entitled to determine the registered estate;
(b) the proprietor of the registered estate to which the entry relates;
(c) a person entitled to be registered as proprietor of that estate; or
(d) any other person whom the Registry is satisfied has an interest in the removal of the entry.

LEGAL AID

The Legal Aid, Sentencing and Punishment of Offenders Act 2012 came into force on 1 April 2013 and made significant changes in relation to legal aid, although it preserved the principle that where legal aid services are made available to an individual, the aid provided constitutes a first charge on any property recovered or preserved by the individual in proceedings, or in any compromise, settlement or dispute in connection with which the services were provided, whether the property is recovered or preserved for the individual or another person. The system for legal aid is administered by the Legal Aid Agency on behalf of the Lord Chancellor. Previously, it was administered by the Legal Services Commission under the Access to Justice Act 1999 and, prior to that, by the Legal Aid Board under the Legal Aid Act 1988. Originally, it was administered by The Law Society. A charge in favour of the Lord Chancellor may be:

(a)   a statutory charge arising under Legal Aid, Sentencing and Punishment of Offenders Act 2012, s 25(1) (previously, Legal Aid Act 1988, s 16(6) or Access to Justice Act 1999, s 10(7)) (see *Statutory charges*, page 543);

(b)   a contractual charge, which normally arises when the individual moves to a new property (see *Legal charges*, page 333);

(c)   a voluntary charge, entered into voluntarily by the individual as security for monies owed (see *Legal charges*, page 333); or

(d)   a sub-charge of an existing charge in favour of the individual (see *Legal charges*, page 333).

LEGAL CHARGES

A registered proprietor of a registered estate has power to create a charge expressed to be by way of legal mortgage and to charge the estate at law with the payment of money. It is no longer possible to charge a registered estate by a mortgage by demise or sub-demise (LRA 2002, s 23). A legal charge of a registered estate may be made in Form CH1 (LRR 2003, r 103), although its use is not compulsory. The grant of a legal charge must be completed by registration if it is to operate at law; until then it takes effect in equity only (LRA 2002, s 27). Registration of a charge is effected when the chargee or his successor in title is entered in the register as the proprietor of the charge (LRA 2002, Sch 2, para 8). On completion of registration, the charge has effect, if it would not otherwise do so, as a charge by deed by way of legal mortgage (LRA 2002, s 51).

For the position where a charge drawn as a legal charge cannot be registered, see *Equitable charges*, page 207. An example of when this might occur is where a consent is required under a restriction but that consent is not forthcoming.

Charges of registered land

An applicant to register a legal charge should deliver to the Registry:

(a)   an application in Form AP1;

(b)   the charge (and a certified copy, if the applicant wishes for the original to be returned);

(c)   where applicable, application for entry of a restriction (see below);

(d)   Form DI giving the information as to overriding interests required by LRR 2003, r 57, including any documentary evidence of the interests (see 'Duty to disclose overriding interests', page 426);

(e)   the appropriate confirmation or evidence as to identity (see *Identity evidence*, page 266); and

(f)   the fee payable (see *Fees*, page 221).

Where an application is made to register a charge created by a company or an LLP, the applicant must produce to the Registry a certificate that the charge has been registered under Companies Act 2006 LRR 2003, r 111(1)) (see *Companies*, page 154, and *Limited liability partnerships*, page 354). In addition, special evidence may be required in relation to particular kinds of chargors and chargees, such as charities (see *Charities*, page 104). If the Registry needs to see an incorporated document in order to complete the registration, a copy will be requested.

On a charge of part of a registered estate, under LRR 2003, r 72 the Registry must:

(a)   make an entry in the chargor's title as to the removal of the estate comprised in that charge (where the charged part is registered under a separate title from the uncharged part), or make a new edition of that title; and

(b)   where appropriate, make entries in the relevant individual registers in respect of any rights, restrictive covenants, provisions or other matters created by the charge which are capable of being so entered. However, the Registry need make no such entries where the relevant title numbers have not been given in panel 2 of the Form AP1, unless separate application is made in respect of them.

Charges of part of a registered estate sometimes contain the grant and/or reservation of rights in the nature of easements over the part of the land that has not been charged. Such rights are not easements as they do not have all the necessary characteristics of easements; in particular the benefiting land and burdened land remain in the same ownership. In consequence, they do not constitute registrable dispositions under LRA 2002, s 27 and cannot be registered as appurtenant to a registered title. They may take effect as quasi-easements and as such, if the chargee were to subsequently exercise his power of sale, they could become easements either under the rule in *Wheeldon v Burrows* (1879) LR 12 Ch D 31 or by virtue of Law of Property Act 1925, s 62. When registering such a charge of part, the Registry will not therefore make any entry as to the benefit of such rights. It will, however, make an entry in the title affected by the charge, referring to the fact that the charge contains provisions relating to the rights in question. In the alternative, specific application may be made using Form UN1 for entry of a notice in the affected title as to the burden of such rights (see *Notices*, page 389).

If the chargee requires the entry of a restriction preventing registration of a disposition by the registered proprietor of the registered estate without the consent of the chargee, the application must be made in Form RX1 (see *Restrictions*, page 500). Alternatively, if a standard form of restriction is sought, the application may be contained in panel 8 of Form CH1 or in an electronic document to which LRA 2002, s 91 applies where the form of the document (including the application for the restriction) has first been approved by the Registry, or in an approved charge. An 'approved charge' for these purposes is one the form of which (including the application for the restriction) has first been approved by the Registry (LRR 2003, r 92). A possible form of restriction based on Form P is:

> No [disposition *or specify type of disposition*] of the registered estate [(other than a charge)] by the proprietor of the registered estate [, or by the proprietor of any registered charge, not being a charge registered before the entry of this restriction,] is to be registered without a written consent signed by the proprietor for the time being of the charge dated [*date*] in favour of [*chargee*] referred to in the charges register [or [*their conveyancer or specify appropriate details*]].

A restriction in a standard form contained in LRR 2003, Sch 4 does not require the approval of the Registry to the terms of the restriction under LRA 2002, s 43(3).

Charges subsisting at the time of first registration

In the case of an unregistered estate in land, the creation of a protected first legal mortgage may be a 'trigger' for first registration (see *First registration*, page 222). Where a charge or mortgage subsists at the time of first registration, it must be disclosed in the application for first registration. The charge will be registered under LRR 2003, r 22 (in the case of a protected first legal mortgage) or r 34 (in the case of a subsequent legal charge).

Where a charge or mortgage has been created contemporaneously with the purchase of land which has triggered compulsory first registration, under LRR 2003, r 38 this will need to be completed by registration as a 'dealing' taking place prior to completion of the first registration. In such a case, the charge should be lodged for registration with the application for first registration of the estate and it will be registered on completion of the first registration; under r 38(2) the registration of the charge has effect from the time of the making of the application for first registration.

If a charge accompanies an application for first registration in Form FR1, no separate application or fee for its registration will be necessary.

Approved forms of charge

The Registry has a facility to approve standard forms of charge (not being in Form CH1) and major lenders are encouraged to apply for such approval. An approved form of charge is given a unique 'MD reference', which assists in the processing of an application to register the charge. Re-approval is necessary if changes are made to the approved form. Application is made in Form ACD and no fee is currently payable.

Further advances

The proprietor of a registered charge may make further advances on the security of the charge ranking in priority to a subsequent charge if he has not received from the subsequent chargee notice of the creation of the subsequent charge (LRA 2002, s 49(1)). Such notice is treated as having been received at the time when, in accordance with LRR 2003, r 107, it ought to have been received. Rule 107 sets out details of various methods of the giving of the notice and of the time when the notice ought to have been received when given by one of those methods.

The proprietor of a registered charge may also make further advances on the security of the charge ranking in priority to a subsequent charge if the advance is made pursuant to an obligation and, at the time of the creation of the subsequent charge, the obligation was entered in the register (LRA 2002, s 49(3)). Where the proprietor of a registered charge, or a person applying to be so registered, is under an obligation to make further advances on the security of that charge, he may apply for the obligation to be entered in the register. The application must be in Form CH2 unless it is contained in panel 8 of Form CH1, or in an electronic legal charge, or in a charge the form of which has been approved by the Registry (LRR 2003, r 108).

The proprietor of a registered charge may also make further advances on the security of the charge ranking in priority to a subsequent charge if the parties to the prior charge have agreed a maximum amount for which the charge is security and, at the time of the creation of the subsequent charge, the agreement was entered in the register (LRA 2002, s 49(4)). Where the parties have agreed such a maximum amount, the proprietor of a registered charge, or a person applying to be registered as proprietor, may apply for such agreement to be entered in the register. The application must be made in Form CH3.

Other than as set out above, tacking in relation to a charge over registered land is possible only with the agreement of the subsequent chargee (LRA 2002, s 49(6)).

Collateral charges

A collateral charge is one that runs parallel to another charge (i.e. the primary security) secured on other property. It usually arises where a lender is only prepared to advance additional money to the borrower if additional security is provided. It does not in itself secure any new money but merely extends the lender's security to include the property subject to the collateral charge. The lender will protect his interest in the additional security by registering a collateral charge on it (see 'Charges of registered land', above).

Priorities

Subject to any entry in the register to the contrary, registered charges on the same registered estate, or on the same registered charge, are taken to rank as between themselves in the order shown in the register (LRA 2002, s 48(1) and LRR 2003, r 101).

Where a deed or other document alters the priority between registered charges, an application should be made for an entry in the register to reflect that altered priority. Such a deed is often referred to as a 'deed of postponement'. The application must be made by or with the consent of the proprietor, or a person entitled to be registered as the proprietor, of any registered charge whose priority is adversely affected by the alteration (LRR 2003, r 102). However, such consent is not required from a person who has executed the deed or document which alters the priority.

The applicant should deliver to the Registry:

(a) an application in Form AP1;
(b) the deed or document altering the priority of the registered charges or a certified copy of it;
(c) any consent required (or a conveyancer's certificate confirming that he holds any necessary consents); and
(d) the fee payable (see *Fees*, page 221).

In relation to deeds of postponement in respect of a registered charge and a noted charge, the Registry may, on application, make an entry in the register referring to an agreement which it is claimed relates to priorities between a registered charge and a charge which is the subject of a notice in the register (LRR 2003, r 116).

Consolidation

A chargee who has a right of consolidation in relation to a registered charge may apply for an entry in respect of that right to be made in the register in which the charge is registered (LRR 2003, r 110). The chargee should deliver to the Registry:

(a)   an application in Form AP1 (or Form FR1, if part of an application for first registration);
(b)   Form CC;
(c)   certified copies of any unregistered charges that are consolidated; and
(d)   the fee payable (see *Fees*, page 221).

Deeds of variation

An application to register a deed or other document varying the terms of a registered charge must be made by, or with the consent of, the proprietor of the registered charge and the proprietor of the estate charged. It must be accompanied by the consent of the proprietor, or a person entitled to be registered as proprietor, of any registered charge of equal or inferior priority (and the proprietor of any sub-charge derived directly or indirectly from such a charge) that is prejudicially affected by the variation (LRR 2003, r 113). However, such consent is not required from any person who has executed the deed of variation or whose consent is not required under the terms of his charge (or sub-charge).

The applicant should deliver to the Registry:

(a)   an application in Form AP1;
(b)   the deed of variation of the registered charge or a certified copy of it;
(c)   any consent required (or a conveyancer's certificate confirming that he holds any necessary consents); and
(d)   the fee payable (see *Fees*, page 221).

A note of the variation is made in the register if the Registry is satisfied that the proprietor of any other registered charge of equal or inferior priority to that of the varied charge who is prejudicially affected by the variation is bound by it. If the Registry is not so satisfied, it may make an entry to the effect that a deed which is expressed to vary the terms of the registered charge has been entered into.

Remedies of a registered chargee

A registered chargee will have a number of methods of enforcing his security. Unless there are entries in the register to the contrary, the proprietor of a registered charge is taken to have the powers of disposition conferred by law on the owner of a legal mortgage (LRA 2002, s 52(1)). This has effect only for the purpose of preventing the title of a disponee being questioned and does not affect the lawfulness of a disposition (s 52(2)).

No period of limitation under Limitation Act 1980, s 16 shall run against any person in relation to a registered estate in land or rentcharge (LRA 2002, s 96(2)). Accordingly, even where a mortgagee is in possession, the mortgagor does not lose his right to redeem.

A mortgagee is required by FLA 1996, s 56 to serve notice on a spouse or civil partner, who is not a party to the action and who has the benefit of a homes right notice or a matrimonial homes right caution, of an action for enforcement of the mortgagee's security. The mortgagee may apply in Form MH3 for an official search certificate of the result of search for this purpose, which will reveal whether a home rights notice or matrimonial home rights caution is entered in the register, and whether there is a pending application for the entry of a home rights notice (see *Home rights*, page 257).

The most common method of enforcing the security of a registered chargee is the exercise of the chargee's power of sale. An order for foreclosure may also be applied for. A legal mortgagee also has a statutory power to appoint a receiver under Law of Property Act 1925, s 101 (see *Receivers appointed under the Law of Property Act 1925*, page 474).

Power of sale

A transfer of a registered estate by the proprietor of a registered charge under the power of sale must be in Form TR2 (for a transfer of whole) or TP2 (for a transfer of part). The transfer must be completed by registration if it is to operate at law (see *Transfers*, page 551).

A sale by the chargee is subject to any matters which appear in the register and have priority over the charge under which the power of sale is being exercised. It overreaches any caution registered in the proprietorship register, other than a matrimonial home rights caution registered prior to the charge and not subsequently postponed to the charge. Interests in existence at the time of registration of the charge which took effect as interests which override first registration or registered dispositions under LRA 2002, Sch 1 or Sch 3 are not overreached by a transfer under the power of sale.

A transfer by a chargee in exercise of his power of sale is subject to any charges which have priority over the chargee's charge (for which a discharge will therefore be required if it is to be removed from the register), but otherwise the purchaser will take free of any other legal or equitable charges, which will be cancelled automatically upon registration of the transfer.

Where the chargee has a surplus arising from the sale after discharging prior charges, the expenses of the sale and his own charge, he holds it on trust to pay it to the person entitled to the mortgaged property (Law of Property Act 1925, s 105). LRA 2002, s 54 provides that for the purposes of Law of Property Act 1925, s 105, a person is taken to have notice of anything in the register immediately before the disposition on sale. As a result, the chargee should inspect the register to ascertain whether there is any subsequent chargee to whom he should pay the balance of the proceeds of sale.

Foreclosure

Foreclosure is a judicial procedure by which a chargee acquires the land freed from the chargor's interest in it. Where a person has obtained an order for foreclosure absolute, he should deliver to the Registry:

(a)   an application in Form AP1;
(b)   the foreclosure order absolute or an office copy of it or a certified copy of it (or a conveyancer's certificate confirming that he holds such order or office copy); and
(c)   the fee payable (see *Fees*, page 221).

On completion of the application, the registration of the charge in respect of which the order was made, and any entry in respect of an interest over which that charge has priority, will be cancelled. The applicant is entered as proprietor of the registered estate (LRR 2003, r 112).

Discharge of registered charge

A discharge of a registered charge, in documentary form, should be in Form DS1 and a release of part of the registered estate from a registered charge should be in Form DS3. Forms DS1 and DS3 must be executed as deeds or authenticated in such other manner as the Registry may approve. The Registry is also entitled to accept and act upon any other proof of satisfaction of a charge that it may regard as sufficient (LRR 2003, r 114).

Where a charge is registered in the name of two or more proprietors, a valid receipt for the money secured by it may be given by:

(a)   the registered proprietors;
(b)   the survivors or survivor of the registered proprietors; or
(c)   the personal representative of the last survivor of the registered proprietors.

A person applying to register the discharge or release of a registered charge should deliver to the Registry:

(a)   an application in Form AP1 or Form DS2 (for use with Form DS1 only);
(b)   a discharge in Form DS1 or DS3;
(c)   where necessary, the appropriate confirmation or evidence as to identity (see *Identity evidence*, page 266); and
(d)   any evidence necessary to show that the correct person has executed Form DS1 or Form DS3.

No fee is currently payable.

Discharges of part of a registered charge sometimes contain the grant and/or reservation of rights in the nature of easements over the part of the land that has not been charged. Such rights are not easements. Similar comments apply to those in relation to such rights contained in charges of part of a registered estate (see 'Charges of registered land', above).

LRR 2003, r 115 provides for discharges and releases of registered charges in electronic form. The release of part of a registered charge in electronic form is not currently permitted. The electronic discharge (ED) method is used by a number of major lending institutions. An ED cancels the charge entries automatically and, in most cases, immediately. No DS1 and no formal paper application to discharge the charge is therefore required and the process is completely automated. The ED method has been supplemented by the introduction of the e-DS1, which is an electronic form of discharge submitted through the Land Registry portal. The e-DS1 acts as both the evidence of discharge and the application to cancel the charge from the register. Currently, the e-DS1 service is designed for corporate chargees and their agents only.

Generally, any restriction that specifically relates to the charge being discharged will be cancelled automatically when the charge is discharged. However, if a restriction in favour of the chargee does not specifically refer to the charge being discharged, a separate withdrawal of that restriction in Form RX4 must be lodged, otherwise the restriction will remain in the register.

In relation to the discharge of registered charges, a policy of 'early completion' was introduced by the Registry on 3 August 2009 with the purpose of ensuring that individual applications for registration are, where possible, completed rather than being delayed as a result of failure to provide evidence of satisfaction of an existing registered charge. The policy applies to all situations where an application for a discharge of the whole has been made with another application, but evidence of satisfaction of the charge has not been provided. For example, it applies in the common scenario where an application is made in Form AP1 for the registration of a discharge of an existing charge, a transfer and a new charge. Three distinct applications are being made. Without evidence of satisfaction of the existing charge, the Registry will reject the application for discharge but complete the other applications where possible. The entries relating to the existing charge will be left in the register until evidence of satisfaction is provided.

If there is a restriction registered in favour of the existing chargee which provides that no disposition and/or that no charge of the registered estate shall be registered without the consent of that chargee, the Registry will requisition for evidence of discharge or evidence that the terms of the restriction have been met. If the requisition is not dealt with the Registry will, in the case of a restriction against the registration of any disposition, cancel not only the application for discharge but also the application to register the transfer and charge. In the case of a restriction against the registration of a charge only, the Registry will complete the registration of the transfer, cancelling the other applications and leaving the entries relating to the existing charge in the register. A 'stand alone' application made only for discharge of a registered charge is substantially defective if evidence of satisfaction is not lodged with the application and will therefore be rejected.

Sub-charges

A proprietor of a registered charge has power to charge at law with the payment of money indebtedness secured by the registered charge. A sub-charge of a registered charge may not be created in any other way (LRA 2002, s 23(2)(b) and (3)). The grant of a sub-charge of a registered charge must be completed by registration, with the sub-chargee or his successor in title being entered in the register as proprietor of the sub-charge (LRA 2002, s 27(3)(b) and Sch 2, para 11).

The registered proprietor of a sub-charge has the same powers as the sub-chargor in relation to the property subject to the principal charge or any intermediate charge (LRA 2002, s 53).

An applicant to register a sub-charge should deliver to the Registry:

(a)   an application in Form AP1;
(b)   the sub-charge or a certified copy of it; and
(c)   the fee payable (see *Fees*, page 221).

Transfer of charge

The transfer of a registered charge must be in Form TR4 or Form AS2, as appropriate (LRR 2003, r 116). The transfer must be completed by registration with the transferee, or his successor in title, being entered in the register as proprietor of the charge (LRA 2002, s 27(3)(a) and Sch 2, para 10).

An applicant to register a transfer of a registered charge should deliver to the Registry the usual documents required (see *Transfers*, page 551).

Related topics

As to equitable charges, see *Equitable charges*, page 207. As to charges created by debenture, see *Debentures*, page 183. As to statutory charges, see *Statutory charges*, page 543.

LEGAL EASEMENTS

An easement is a right which one piece of land has over another piece of land. For an easement to subsist at law, there are four essential characteristics which must be present:

(a)   there must be a benefiting tenement and a burdened tenement, as an easement cannot exist in gross;
(b)   the easement must benefit the benefiting land by making it a better and more convenient property, rather than it being a purely personal right;
(c)   the benefiting land and burdened land must not be both owned *and* occupied by the same person. A landowner cannot have an easement over his own land – rights exercised by him over part of his land will take effect only as quasi-easements. This does not, however, prevent an easement arising in

favour of a tenant over other land of his landlord, as the landlord does not own *and* occupy both tenements; and

(d)   the easement must be capable of forming the subject matter of a grant. No right can exist as an easement unless it could have been validly granted by deed. This principle in turn has four elements:

   (i)   the right must be within the general nature of rights capable of being granted as easements;
   (ii)   the right must be sufficiently definite;
   (iii) there must be a capable grantor; and
   (iv)   there must be a capable grantee.

Most easements are expressly granted or reserved, in either a deed of grant, a transfer or a lease, but they can also arise through implication or through long use. Implied easements are easements arising by implication:

(a)   under the Law of Property Act 1925, s 62; or
(b)   under the rule in *Wheeldon v Burrows* (1879) LR 12 Ch D 31; or
(c)   by virtue of necessity; or
(d)   by virtue of being 'intended easements', i.e. easements which were intended to be granted or reserved, but which for some reason were not expressly set out in the conveyance or other deed.

Prescriptive easements are legal easements which arise by virtue of user as of right (i.e. without permission, force, or secrecy) over a long period of time, as opposed to having arisen by way of a formal grant or by implication.

A legal easement must subsist for an interest equivalent to an estate in fee simple absolute in possession or a term of years absolute (Law of Property Act 1925, s 1(2)(a)).

Legal easements on first registration

Beneficial easements

On first registration of title, the estate is vested in the registered proprietor together with all interests subsisting for the benefit of the estate (LRA 2002, ss 11(3) and 12(3)). This includes the benefit of any subsisting legal easements, whether or not these are the subject of an entry in the register. If, at the time of first registration, the Registry is satisfied that a right subsists as a legal estate and benefits the registered estate, it may enter the benefit of that appurtenant right in the register (LRR 2003, r 33(1)). This will be as the result of the Registry's examination of the title or its consideration of a written application providing details of the right and evidence of its existence. Where the easement arose by prescription or is an implied easement, the evidence will usually be in the form of a statutory declaration or statement of truth (see 'Prescriptive easements', below). If the Registry is not satisfied that the right subsists as a legal interest benefiting the registered estate, it may enter details of the right claimed in the property register with such qualification as it considers appropriate (LRR 2003, r 33(2)). The applicant must therefore lodge evidence that the grantor had power to grant the right, otherwise the Registry may either omit the right or enter a qualification note to an entry in the register relating to the right.

Where the burdened estate is registered, the consent of any chargee of the burdened estate whose charge has priority over the grant of the easement and who has not joined in the grant, should be lodged. If the chargee has not consented to the grant, the easement is liable to be overridden if the chargee exercises his power of sale. If the consent cannot be lodged, the application may be completed but with a note along the following lines being added to the register entry for the benefiting title:

> NOTE: The consent of the proprietor of the charge dated [*date*] in favour of [*name*] affecting title(s) [*title number(s)*] was not produced on registration and the rights [*referred to above or as the case may be*] may be overridden in the event of the exercise of the power of sale.

The note can be cancelled without fee if an application is subsequently made in Form AP1 enclosing the consent. Any restriction (including a restriction in favour of a chargee) in the register of the burdened title must be complied with as necessary. If there is a caution against dealings or a notice of (intended) deposit in the register of the burdened title and the consent to the registration of the easement does not accompany the application, the Registry may serve notice upon the cautioner or depositee.

Where the burdened estate is unregistered, evidence of the grantor's title to it, commencing with a good root more than 15 years old at the date of the application, must accompany the application. The consent of any legal mortgagee of the burdened estate to the grant of the easement should also be lodged, unless he has joined in the grant. If this consent is not lodged, the application may be completed but with a note being added to the register entry for the benefiting title in the form referred to above.

If the easement was granted over an unregistered estate that has since been registered, it may be necessary for a notice as to the burden of the easement to be entered in the register of the burdened title at the same time as the benefit is entered in the register of the benefiting title. This will be done by the Registry as part of the first registration, normally after service of notice on the proprietor of the burdened title.

Subjective easements

On first registration, the estate is vested in the registered proprietor subject to any easements which are an interest which overrides first registration under LRA 2002, Sch 1, or are the subject of an entry in the register in relation to the estate, and/or, in the case of a leasehold title, which are incident to the leasehold estate (LRA 2002, ss 11(4)(a) and 12(4)(a) and (b)). The Registry must enter a notice in the register of the burden of any easement which appears from its examination of the title to affect the registered estate, except any which appear to it to be of a trivial or obvious character, or the entry of a notice in respect of which would be likely to cause confusion or inconvenience (LRR 2003, r 35). Even where no entry is made as to a subjective legal easement on first registration, it is an interest falling within LRA 2002, Sch 1, para 3, which therefore overrides first registration.

A person applying for first registration must provide information to the Registry in Form DI about any legal easements which are within his actual knowledge and affect the estate to which the application relates, including any documentary evidence of the interests (see 'Duty to disclose overriding interests', page 426). The Registry may enter a notice in the register in respect of any such legal easement (LRR 2003, r 28).

Legal easements arising after first registration

The express grant or reservation of a legal easement over registered land (other than a grant as a result of the operation of Law of Property Act 1925, s 62) must be completed by registration if it is to operate at law. Registration is completed by the entry of a notice of the easement in the register of the burdened title and, if the title to the benefiting estate is registered, by an entry in the property register of that title (LRA 2002, s 27(2)(d) and (7) and Sch 2, para 7). Until completed by registration, such an easement is only equitable.

The benefit of a legal easement can be entered in the register only as appurtenant to a registered estate; it cannot be registered independently (LRA 2002, s 59(1)).

If the grant of an easement over a registered burdened estate is a registrable disposition, an application to complete the grant by registration *must* be made in Form AP1 or AN1 in order to meet the registration requirements. This is the case even if only the burdened estate is registered (LRR 2003, rr 13 and 90). Therefore an application for entry of an agreed notice or unilateral notice in Form UN1 will *not* meet the registration requirements. In that event, a subsequent application may be made in Form AP1 to complete the easement by registration so that it does take effect at law. Until then, it takes effect in equity only and the benefit cannot be registered in the property register of the benefiting estate (if registered).

Where the easement is contained in a transfer or charge of part of a registered title, only an application to register the transfer or charge is necessary; no separate application in respect of the easements is required. The Registry will make the necessary entries as a matter of course when registering the transfer, provided the relevant title numbers are provided in panel 2 of the Form AP1 or separate application is made (LRR 2003, r 72(4) and (5)). In the case of a charge of part, such entries are made only if the Registry decides that the charged part is to be comprised in a registered title separate from the uncharged part.

An applicant for registration of an easement contained in a deed of grant should deliver to the Registry:

(a)   an application in Form AP1;
(b)   the deed of grant or a certified copy of it;
(c)   any consents or certificates required in respect of mortgages, charges or restrictions relating to the burdened title;
(d)   (if the right is granted over an unregistered estate) an abstract or epitome showing the grantor's title to the burdened estate;
(e)   the appropriate confirmation or evidence as to identity (see *Identity evidence*, page 266);
(f)   the appropriate SDLT certificate or other evidence (see *Stamp duty land tax*. page 541); and
(g)   the fee payable (see *Fees*, page 221).

The title numbers of all the registered titles involved must be specified in panel 2 of Form AP1, otherwise the Registry is not obliged to make any entry unless separate application is made (LRR 2003, r 72C(3)). The easement will be completed by registration, with entries being made in the register of the burdened estate and (if registered) the benefiting estate (r 72C(2)).

Where the grant or reservation of an easement is not a registrable disposition, it will be effective at law when made. However, an application may be made for the benefit of the easement to be registered as appurtenant to the benefiting estate, if registered (LRR 2003, r 73A(1)(a)). The application must be made in Form AP1, accompanied by an abstract or epitome showing the grantor's title to the unregistered burdened estate and any consents or certificates required in respect of mortgages, charges or restrictions relating to the burdened estate. Where the Registry is not satisfied that the right claimed subsists as a legal estate appurtenant to the applicant's registered estate, it may enter details of the right claimed in the property register with such qualification as it considers appropriate.

Where the benefiting estate is unregistered, application may be made for the entry of a notice in respect of an easement affecting a registered title. Where it appears to the Registry that a registered estate is subject to a legal easement, it may enter a notice in the register in respect of that easement (LRA 2002, s 37). In that case the Registry must give notice to the registered proprietor and to any person who appears to it to be entitled to the interest protected by the notice or whom the Registry otherwise considers appropriate (LRR 2003, r 89). However, if the registered proprietor applies for the entry of the notice, or consents to an application for such an entry, the Registry is not obliged to give notice to him. The Registry is also not obliged to give notice under r 89 to any person who has applied for, or consented to, the entry of the notice, nor is it so obliged if that person's name and address for service are not set out in the registered title in question.

Prescriptive easements

Prescription is the acquisition of a right through long use or enjoyment (user) so that the law presumes that the right was lawfully granted. There are three methods of acquiring an easement by prescription: at common law; by lost modern grant; and under the Prescription Act 1832. Whichever method is relied on, the user must have been exercised:

(a)   for at least 20 years;
(b)   as of right, i.e. without force, without secrecy and without permission;
(c)   by or on behalf of a freehold owner against another freehold owner, so that where the burdened land is occupied by a tenant, the user must normally have started before the tenancy began; and
(d)   continuously, with no long, unexplained periods of non-user. Where the claim is made under the Prescription Act 1832, a break is not treated as an 'interruption' in user for the purposes of that Act until acquiesced in for one year.

In addition, the right claimed must be one that could have been lawfully granted. This point was considered by the House of Lords in *Bakewell Management Ltd v Brandwood* [2004] UKHL 14. In consequence, if the right could not have been lawfully granted by deed (for example, a right to pollute a river contrary to a statutory prohibition), then it cannot be acquired by prescription.

Law of Property Act 1925, s 193(4) makes it a criminal offence to drive a vehicle over a common. Road Traffic Act 1988, s 34 makes it a criminal offence to drive a motor vehicle over land that is not a road and that is a restricted byway or over which a public footpath or bridleway runs. However, both offences are only committed if driving over the land is 'without lawful authority'. Since a right to drive over the land concerned *could* in most cases have been lawfully granted, it can in those cases be acquired by prescription.

Previously, the Vehicular Access Across Common and Other Land (England) Regulations 2002 (SI 2002/1711) and the Vehicular Access Across Common and Other Land (Wales) Regulations 2004 (SI 2004/248) (made under the Countryside and Rights of Way Act 2000, s 68), provided for the creation of a legal easement, giving a right of way for vehicles, in cases where the user would have given rise to a prescriptive easement had it not constituted an offence. Those regulations lapsed when Commons Act 2006, s 51 came into force on 1 October 2006.

A prescriptive easement over a registered estate that has arisen by prescription does not have to be completed by registration to take effect at law and it will subsist for the benefit of any registered or unregistered estate to which it is appurtenant, notwithstanding that it is not the subject of an entry in the register. However, its validity will only be guaranteed for registration purposes if it is registered as appurtenant to a registered estate.

An application for registration of the benefit of a prescriptive easement may be made in either Form FR1 at the time of an application for first registration of the benefiting estate (LRR 2003, r 33); or Form AP1 at any time subsequently (LRR 2003, r 73A). If the burdened land is registered, the title number must be given in the application form. Where the application is only to note the burden of an easement in the register of a registered burdened estate (for example where the benefiting estate is unregistered), the application should be made in Form AN1 for entry of an agreed notice or Form UN1 for entry of a unilateral notice, as appropriate (see *Notices*, page 389).

The application must be accompanied by satisfactory supporting evidence, normally in the form of a statement of truth (which may be in Form ST4 in LRR 2003, Sch 1) or statutory declaration by the applicant and any predecessors in title setting out the relevant details of the user of the easement claimed, for the requisite period of 20 years or more (and a certified copy of each, if the applicant wishes for the original to be returned). If the title to the applicant's estate is unregistered, he should lodge evidence of his title. Similarly, the applicant should lodge evidence of title in respect of the burdened estate if that is unregistered. If an inspection of the land is necessary, an additional fee to cover the cost of this will also be payable.

If the application is completed, the register entries made by the Registry will depend upon whether both the benefiting estate and burdened estate are registered or only one of them is registered. Also, where the burdened estate is unregistered, whether satisfactory evidence of title to it has been lodged.

Where both the benefiting estate and the burdened estate are registered, the Registry will give notice of the application to the registered proprietor and any registered chargee of the burdened title. If no objection is received, the benefit of the easement will be registered as appurtenant to the benefiting title and a notice as to the burden will be entered in the burdened title.

Where the benefiting estate is registered but the burdened estate is unregistered, if the applicant lodges evidence of title to the burdened estate and the address of the freehold owner, the Registry will give notice of the application to the freehold owner and any other person who may have an interest in the burdened estate. If no objection is received, the benefit of the easement will be registered as appurtenant to the benefiting estate. However, if (as may often be the case) the applicant is not able to lodge evidence of title to the burdened estate and the address of the freehold owner, the Registry is likely to make only a note in the register to the effect that the applicant claims the benefit of the easement (LRR 2003, r 73A(5)). This entry will be in the following form:

> The registered proprietor claims that the land has the benefit of a right [*terms of right as claimed by claimant*]. The right claimed is not included in this registration. The claim is supported by [*dates and details of statement(s) of truth or statutory declaration(s) and who has made them*].

Where the burdened estate is registered but the benefiting estate is unregistered, the Registry will give notice of the application to the registered proprietor and any registered chargee of the burdened estate. If no objection is received, a notice as to the burden will be entered in the burdened estate in the appropriate form, depending upon whether the application is for an agreed notice or a unilateral notice.

Where the benefit of a prescriptive easement is entered in the register of a registered benefiting estate, the entry will indicate that the right was acquired through long user and will refer to the statement(s) of truth or statutory declaration(s) lodged in support of the application, which will be open to inspection and copying.

If a valid objection is received in response to a notice of an application which cannot be disposed of by agreement, the matter will have to be dealt with in accordance with LRA 2002, s 73 (see *Disputes*, page 193).

Unregistered legal easements which override registered dispositions

Although all legal easements override first registration, the position is not the same for registered dispositions. In the light of LRA 2002, Sch 3, para 3, a legal easement (not being one registered under the CRA 1965) overrides a registered disposition only if:

(a) at the time of the disposition it is within the actual knowledge of the person to whom the disposition is made; or
(b) at the time of the disposition it would have been obvious on a reasonably careful inspection of the land over which the easement is exercisable; or
(c) the person entitled to the easement proves that it has been exercised in the period of one year ending with the day of the disposition.

However, any easement which was an overriding interest immediately before 13 October 2003, but which would not fall within LRA 2002, Sch 3 para 3 if created on or after 13 October 2003, continues to be an overriding interest (LRA 2002, Sch 12, para 9). For a period of 3 years beginning on 13 October 2003, any unregistered legal easement overrode a registered disposition (LRA 2002, Sch 12, para 10). An unregistered easement over registered land arising on or after 13 October 2003 is a legal easement only if it is an implied or prescriptive easement; the grant of an easement which constitutes a registrable disposition will be equitable unless completed by registration.

A person applying to register a registrable disposition of a registered estate must provide information to the Registry in Form DI about any legal easements falling within LRA 2002, Sch 3, para 3 which are within his actual knowledge and affect the estate to which the application relates (see 'Duty to disclose overriding interests', page 426). The applicant must produce to the Registry any documentary evidence of the existence of any such legal easements as is under his control. The Registry may enter a notice in the register in respect of any such legal easements (LRR 2003, r 57).

Extinguishment of easements

When an easement is referred to in the register of title and has been extinguished, an appropriate application may be made for the relevant entry or entries to be removed. Extinguishment may arise where, for example, there has been a deed of release, or through unity of ownership of both the benefiting and burdened estates, or through abandonment. The application should be accompanied by evidence to satisfy the Registry that the easement has been extinguished.

Where the benefit of the easement has been registered in a registered benefiting title, the application should be made in Form AP1; otherwise (where only the burden has been noted in the register of a registered burdened title) the application should be in Form CN1 (for cancellation of an agreed notice) or Form UN2 (for removal of a unilateral notice) or Form UN4 (for cancellation of a unilateral notice) as appropriate (see *Notices*, page 389).

Related topics

As to equitable easements, see *Equitable easements*, page 212. As to profits à prendre, see *Profits à prendre*, page 456. As to easements in leases, see 'Easements in leases', page 317.

LEGAL ESTATES

There can only be two legal estates in land (Law of Property Act 1925, s 1(1)):

(a)   an estate in fee simple absolute in possession (the freehold estate); and
(b)   a term of years absolute (the leasehold estate).

These two legal estates may be registered with their own individual title if they fall within the categories of registrable estates prescribed by the LRA 2002 (see *First registration*, page 222).

LEGAL INTERESTS

There are five types of legal interest in land (Law of Property Act 1925, s 1(2)):

(a)   easements, rights or privileges;
(b)   rentcharges;
(c)   charges by way of legal mortgage;
(d)   certain charges not created by an instrument (for example a statutory charge);
(e)   rights of entry (for example under the terms of a lease or rentcharge).

These interests are only legal interests if they take effect at law. So, for example, an easement granted by deed may take effect at law and be a legal interest, but if granted in writing (but not by deed) it will take effect only in equity and be an equitable interest. Where it is a registrable disposition, the grant of the easement would need to be completed by registration in order to take effect at law; until then, it operates in equity only (LRA 2002, s 27).

Of these legal interests, only rentcharges, profits in gross and franchises can be registered with their own individual title (see *First registration*, page 222).

The remaining interests, being easements, profits appurtenant (i.e. a profit that exists for the benefit of a piece of land) and charges by way of legal mortgage, can be registered by way of entry in an existing registered title (see *Legal easements*, page 343; *Legal charges*, page 333, and *Profits à prendre*, page 456).

LICENCES

Bare licences and contractual licences are not, without more, interests in land binding on a purchaser, even if he has notice (*Ashburn Anstalt v W J Arnold and Co* [1988] EWCA Civ 14). For the position where, on the facts of a particular case, a constructive trust or an equity by estoppel has arisen, see *Constructive, resulting and other implied trusts*, page 165, and *Proprietary estoppel*, page 471.

Whether a licence coupled with an interest (that is, a licence collateral to a proprietary interest) is an interest which overrides first registration and also overrides registered dispositions depends on the status of that interest. For example, where a person has a licence to enter on land in the exercise of a legal profit à prendre, the legal profit is capable of being an interest which overrides under LRA 2002, Sch 1, para 3 or Sch 3, para 3 and the licence has the same status. If the profit is only equitable, then neither it nor the licence has overriding status and should be protected by entry of a notice, where the burdened estate is registered. The entry of a notice in respect of the profit in practice protects the licence as well, since this is irrevocable while the interest subsists. If the burdened estate is unregistered, application for registration of a caution against first registration should be made. For the protection of a profit à prendre generally, see *Profits à prendre*, page 456.

The benefit of a licence is not in itself capable of being registered, as it is not a legal estate which can be registered as appurtenant to a registered estate.

For the purposes of the LRA 2002, land in the possession of a licensee is treated as being in the possession of the licensor (LRA 2002, s 131). This applies, for example, when establishing that the proprietor is in possession for the purposes of upgrading a possessory title under LRA 2002, s 62(5), or when establishing whether the proprietor is in possession for the purposes of LRA 2002, Sch 4, paras 3(2) or 6(2) where rectification of the register is sought.

LIMITED LIABILITY PARTNERSHIPS

An LLP incorporated in England and Wales or in Scotland under the Limited Liability Partnerships Act 2000 has full powers to deal with land. It is a body corporate with a legal personality separate from that of its members and is registered at the Companies Registry. The name of an LLP must end with one of the following expressions or abbreviations: limited liability partnership, llp or LLP or (being the Welsh equivalents) partneriaeth atebolrwydd cyfyngedig, pac, or PAC. The Limited Liability Partnerships Act (Northern Ireland) 2002 applied to LLPs incorporated in Northern Ireland, which are registered at the Companies Registry in Belfast. However, as a result of the Companies Act 2006, the Limited Liability Partnerships Act 2000 now also applies to LLPs incorporated in Northern Ireland. A UK LLP is one incorporated in the United Kingdom under the Limited Liability Partnerships Act 2000 or the Limited Liability Partnerships Act (Northern Ireland) 2002.

The Limited Liability Partnerships (Application of Companies Act 2006) Regulations 2009 (SI 2009/1804) came into force on 1 October 2009 and apply provisions of the Companies Act 2006 to UK LLPs. Those Regulations replaced the Limited Liability Partnerships Regulations 2001 (SI 2001/1090) and the Limited Liability Partnerships Regulations (Northern Ireland) 2004 (SI 2001/307) which applied to LLPs' provisions of the Companies Act 1985 and the Companies (Northern Ireland) Order 1986.

An LLP should not be confused with a partnership or a limited partnership (see *Partnerships*, page 431, and *Limited partnerships*, page 358).

Registration of a UK limited liability partnership as proprietor

Where a UK LLP applies to be registered as proprietor of a registered estate or a registered charge, the application must state the LLP's registered number. In practice the registered number is usually stated in a prescribed form of disposition or application, such as panel 5 of a transfer in Form TR1 or in panel 6 of application Form FR1. The registered number commences 'OC' for LLPs registered in England and Wales, 'SO' for LLPs registered in Scotland, or 'NILLP' for LLPs registered in Northern Ireland. The LLP itself, not its individual members, will be registered as proprietor. The registered number is included in the entry of the LLP as proprietor in the proprietorship register or charges register (LRR 2003, r 8(1)(b)).

Registration of charge created by a UK limited liability partnership

In the case of a UK LLP, registration of the charge at the Companies Registry within 21 days of its creation should precede an application for registration to the Land Registry. Registration of a charge of registered land at the Companies Registry alone is not sufficient – it should also be completed by registration in accordance with LRA 2002, s 27, if it is to take effect at law and be protected in the register. Conversely, registration of a charge in a debenture at the Land Registry does not remove the need for it to be registered under the Companies Act 2006.

Although LRA 2002, s 121 allows the Lord Chancellor to make rules about the transmission, by the Land Registry to the Registrar of Companies, of applications for registration of charges under the Companies Act 2006, no such rules have yet been made. The application to the Companies Registry must therefore be made separately. Since 6 April 2013, such application may be made electronically, in which case the certificate of registration will be issued electronically. It is still possible to apply in paper form and the certificate of registration will be issued in paper form; the charge itself will no longer be stamped with the Companies Registry stamp.

When making an application for registration of a charge created by a UK LLP, the applicant must produce to the Registry the certificate issued under Companies Act 2006, s 859I that the charge has been registered at the Companies Registry under s 859A of that Act (LRR 2003, r 111), together with a Companies Registry official copy of the charge or a certificate or confirmation in writing by the lender or a conveyancer that the charge lodged for registration is identical to the copy charge filed at the Companies Registry and is the charge to which the certificate of registration relates.

If the certificate is not produced, the Registry must enter a note in the register stating that no evidence of registration of the charge in accordance with Companies Act 2006, s 859A has been lodged. Similar provisions applied prior to 6 April 2013 in relation to Companies Act 2006, s 860 or s 878 and, prior to 1 October 2009, in relation to Companies Act 1985, s 395 or s 410, with any necessary note in the register referring to the relevant section. The note reflects the fact that where the charge is not registered with the Companies Registry within the prescribed period, the charge is void against the liquidator or administrator of the LLP and any creditor of the LLP.

An LLP, like a limited company, may create a debenture (see *Debentures*, page 183).

Execution of deeds by limited liability partnerships

Like a limited company, an LLP can execute a deed under seal or under the provisions of Companies Act 1985, s 36A for deeds executed before 6 April 2008 and under Companies Act 2006, s 44 for deeds executed on and after 6 April 2008. In transfers of registered land and other deeds whose form is prescribed, the attestation clause in Form F(i) or F(ii) of LRR 2003, Sch 9 must be used when an LLP executes a deed. If instead an LLP uses a seal, the Registry can accept this provided the attestation clause is in similar form to Form C in LRR 2003, Sch 9, but with two members witnessing the affixing of the seal.

Conversion of a partnership or corporate body to a limited liability partnership

Under the Limited Liability Partnerships Act 2000, existing partnerships and companies may choose to convert to LLP status. Any two or more persons associated for carrying on business can become an LLP. An LLP is formed when those persons incorporate as an LLP by registration at the Companies Registry. This is a similar process to company incorporation.

When an existing corporate body or partnership becomes an LLP, property of the former corporate body or partnership which is to be held by the LLP will need to be transferred to the newly formed LLP. If the property comprises a registered estate or charge, it should be transferred in the normal way to the LLP. If the estate is unregistered and the transfer triggers compulsory first registration, the appropriate application should be made. If the transfer does not trigger compulsory first registration, a voluntary application may still be made (see *First registration*, page 222).

Dissolution of a limited liability partnership

Under the Limited Liability Partnerships (Application of Companies Act 2006) Regulations 2009, Companies Act 2006, s 1012 is modified to apply to a UK LLP. On dissolution, therefore, all the property and rights of a UK LLP (other than property held on trust for another) are deemed to be bona vacantia and will belong to the Crown or to the Duchy of Lancaster or the Duke of Cornwall, as the case may be (Companies Act 2006, s 1012 as from 1 October 2006; previously Companies Act 1985, s 654). Where a corporation which is the proprietor of a registered estate or registered charge has been dissolved, the Registry may enter a note of that fact in the proprietorship register or charges register, as appropriate (LRR 2003, r 185).

Registration of an overseas limited liability partnership as proprietor

Where an LLP, which is not a UK LLP, applies to be registered as proprietor of a registered estate or registered charge, evidence of the extent of its powers to hold and sell, mortgage, lease, and otherwise deal with land, and, in the case of a charge, to lend money on mortgage, must be lodged (LRR 2003, r 183(1)). The evidence must include the document(s) constituting the corporation, or a certified copy, and any further evidence the Registry may require (r 183(2)). If the evidence is in a language other than English or Welsh, a certified translation must be provided. Alternatively, a certificate in Form 7 in LRR 2003, Sch 3 may be given by a qualified lawyer practising in the territory of incorporation of the LLP. These provisions enable the Registry to be satisfied that the applicant has the necessary power to hold, sell and otherwise deal with the registered estate (or to lend money on mortgage, in the case of a registered charge) and to enter any appropriate restriction(s) in the register.

LIMITED OWNER'S CHARGE

A limited owner's charge arises where a tenant for life or statutory owner of settled land discharges IHT or any other liabilities to which special priority is given by statute. The charge may be overreached by a disposition under SLA 1925, s 72(3) or Law of Property Act 1925, s 2(2) and (3). As to settled land generally, see *Settlements*, page 527.

No notice may be entered in the register in respect of a limited owner's charge (LRA 2002, s 33(a)). The relevant form of protection for a limited owner's charge is the entry of a restriction in Forms G, H or I, as appropriate, to ensure capital money arising under the settlement is paid to at least two trustees or a trust corporation. If there is no such restriction entered in the proprietorship register, the person having the benefit of the limited owner's charge is entitled to apply for entry of the appropriate restriction (LRR 2003, Sch 7, para 3(2)).

The Registry must give notice of an application for a restriction to the proprietor of the registered estate or charge concerned if it has not been made by or with his consent or a person entitled to be registered as such proprietor (LRA 2002, s 45).

A restriction does not confer any priority; it simply prevents an entry being made in the register in respect of any disposition, or a disposition of a specified kind, unless the terms of the restriction have (where applicable) been complied with.

If applying for entry of a restriction in Forms G, H or I, the person having the benefit of a limited owner's charge should deliver to the Registry the usual documents required (see *Restrictions*, page 500).

If the application is made by a person who claims that he has a sufficient interest in the making of the entry, the statement in panel 12 or a conveyancer's certificate in panel 13 of Form RX1 must be completed, setting out details of the limited owner's charge and confirming that 'the applicant's interest is an interest in settled land as specified in Schedule 7 paragraph 3(2) of the Land Registration Rules 2003'. Any supporting documents should be listed in panel 5 of Form RX1 or in a separate Form DL.

Panel 9 of Form RX1 should be completed as to the wording of the restriction in Forms G, H or I, as appropriate. The wording of Forms G, H and I is set out in Appendix IV, page 585.

Form G is applicable where the tenant for life is the registered proprietor of the settled land and there are trustees of the settlement.

Form H is applicable where the statutory owners are the trustees of the settlement and registered proprietors of the settled land.

Form I is applicable where the tenant for life is the registered proprietor of the settled land and there are no trustees of the settlement.

A restriction in Forms G, H or I in LRR 2003, Sch 4 does not require the approval of the Registry under LRA 2002, s 43(3).

LIMITED PARTNERSHIPS

A partnership is the relationship which subsists between persons carrying on a business in common with a view to profit (Partnership Act 1890, s 1). A limited partnership is a special type of partnership set up under the Limited Partnership Act 1907. It enables a person, who has contributed financially to the partnership but is not involved with the management of it, to become a 'sleeping' partner with only a limited liability to creditors of the partnership. In a limited partnership, there must be at least one partner whose liability is not limited in this way. A limited partnership therefore consists of one or more 'general' partners, who are liable for all debts and obligations of the firm, and one or more 'limited' partners, who contribute a sum or sums of money as capital, or property valued at a stated amount. Limited partners are not liable for the debts and obligations of the partnership beyond the amount contributed (Limited Partnership Act 1907, s 4(2)). The Companies Registry maintains an index and a register of limited partnerships. When a limited partnership is formed, it must be registered with the Companies Registry, otherwise it will be regarded as a general partnership and both the general and the limited partners will be equally responsible for any debts and obligations of the partnership. A limited partnership registered at the Companies Registry has a registration number with the prefix 'LP'.

A limited partnership created under the Limited Partnership Act 1907 is not a separate legal entity. It does not have the corporate status of an LLP incorporated under the Limited Liability Partnerships Act 2000 (see *Limited liability partnerships*, page 354). Different principles apply to a limited partnership in Scotland, and to overseas limited partnerships.

The Limited Partnership Act 1907 was amended by the Legislative Reform (Private Fund Limited Partnerships) Order 2017 (SI 2017/514) so as to introduce a new form of limited partnership: the private fund limited partnership. This is for use by private investment funds (i.e. funds that may not be promoted to retail consumers, for example private equity and venture capital funds) that are structured as a limited partnership, and is intended to reduce the administrative and financial burdens previously affecting private funds that use a limited partnership structure. The designation as a private fund limited partnership on original registration of the limited partnership, or the change from an existing limited partnership to a private fund limited partnership, has effect from the date shown in the certificate of registration (or designation) issued by the Companies Registry (Limited Partnership Act 1907, s 8C).

Registration and entry of restriction(s)

A transfer or charge to a limited partnership must be to the individual partners, not to the partnership name. If there are more than four partners the transfer should be to four of them to hold the legal estate on trust for the partnership. No reference to the partnership is made in the register, nor is its registration number as a limited partnership set out in the register. However, the proprietors may specifically apply to have any trading name entered in the proprietorship register. This will appear after the last address for service in the entry of the proprietors, in the form 'trading as [*trading name*]'.

In the case of a registered estate in land, as the beneficial interests are held under a tenancy in common, the Registry will enter a restriction in Form A in the proprietorship register in accordance with its obligation under LRA 2002, s 44(1). In the case of other registered estates, the proprietors should make an application for entry of such a restriction (LRR 2003, r 94(2A)).

The partners may also, if they wish, apply for entry of a restriction in Form Q.

If the partnership deed contains specific provisions requiring any consent to be obtained to a disposition, application should be made for entry of a restriction in Form B (TLATA, s 8(2) and LRR 2003, r 94(4)).

The wording of Forms A, B and Q is set out in Appendix IV, page 585.

An application for entry of a restriction should normally be made in Form RX1. However, Form RX1 does not need to be used if the application is for a standard form restriction and is contained in either the 'additional provisions' panel of a prescribed form of transfer or assent, or in clause LR13 of a prescribed clauses lease (or any other lease containing clauses LR1 to LR14 of LRR 2003, Sch 1A) (LRR 2003, r 92(7)). A restriction in a standard form contained in LRR 2003, Sch 4 does not require the approval of the Registry to the terms of the restriction under LRA 2002, s 43(3).

LIQUIDATORS

Where a company which is the registered proprietor of a registered estate or registered charge is in liquidation, its liquidator may apply for an entry to be made in the register as to his appointment. Such an entry will not be made automatically by the Registry and a specific application is therefore required. The application must be supported by evidence of the liquidator's appointment (LRR 2003, r 184). In the alternative, a liquidator may instead provide evidence of his appointment to a purchaser or other disponee, which should be lodged with the application for registration of the transfer or other disposition.

Entry of notice of liquidator's appointment

The liquidator should deliver to the Registry:

(a) an application in Form AP1;

(b) evidence of appointment (see 'Evidence of appointment', below); and

(c) the fee payable (see *Fees*, page 221).

When notice of the appointment is entered in the register, the liquidator may also make an application for entry of any appropriate restriction(s) required.

Evidence of appointment

The evidence required varies depending on the type of liquidation. The same evidence is required whether for entry of a notice of the liquidator's appointment or for the registration of a transfer or other disposition by him.

Creditors' voluntary winding-up

The following documents are required:

(a) a certified copy of the resolution passed at the company's meeting that the company be wound up and appointing a liquidator; and

(b) either a certified copy of a resolution passed at the creditor's meeting appointing the liquidator, or a certificate by the liquidator appointed at the company's meeting (or his conveyancer) that the meeting of the creditors was duly held in accordance with IA 1986, s 98(1) at which either the appointment of the liquidator by the company's meeting was confirmed or no resolution nominating a liquidator was passed.

Members' voluntary winding-up

The following documents are required:

(a) a certified copy of the resolution passed by the general meeting of the company appointing the liquidator; and

(b) a certificate by the secretary of the company (or his conveyancer) or by the liquidator (or his conveyancer) that a statutory declaration of solvency complying with the requirements of IA 1986, s 89 has been filed with the Companies Registry.

Winding-up by the court

The following documents are required:

(a)   a certified copy of the winding up order and either;
(b)   a certified copy of the order of the court appointing the liquidator; or
(c)   a certified copy of the appointment of the liquidator by the Secretary of State; or
(d)   a certified copy of the order of the court appointing the liquidator; or
(e)   a certified copy of the resolution passed at the contributories' meeting appointing the liquidator, and a certificate by the liquidator appointed at the contributories' meeting (or his conveyancer) that the meeting of the creditors was duly held at which either the appointment of the liquidator by the contributories' meeting was confirmed or no resolution nominating a liquidator was passed.

Dispositions by a liquidator

If a transfer or other disposition of a registered estate or registered charge by or in favour of a company in liquidation is lodged for registration (and notice of the appointment has not previously been entered, in the case of a disposition by the company), evidence of the liquidator's appointment as set out above will be required. This will also apply in relation to an application for first registration. A disposition by a company in liquidation should be executed by the liquidator either by affixing the company seal and signing the document to attest that the seal has been affixed in his presence or by signing the document as a deed in the name and on behalf of the company.

Disclaimer by a liquidator

A liquidator may disclaim any onerous property comprised in the insolvent estate and is entitled to do so even if he has taken possession of the property or attempted to sell it (IA 1986, s 178). In the case of land, it is normally a leasehold estate which is disclaimed, although disclaimer of a registered freehold estate is also possible. The notice operates to determine the rights, interests and liabilities of the company in respect of the property. It does not, however, otherwise affect the rights or liabilities of any other person. The disclaimer of a lease is not effective unless a copy of it has been served on any sub-tenant or mortgagee claiming under the company and either no application for a vesting order is made to the court within a period of 14 days from the day on which the last copy notice was served, or the court has directed that the disclaimer is to take effect (IA 1986, s 179).

Any person claiming an interest in the disclaimed property may apply to the court for a vesting order vesting the property in him or in a trustee on his behalf (IA 1986, s 181). A person who is under a liability in respect of a disclaimed property, which liability will not be discharged by the disclaimer, may also apply for a vesting order.

If no vesting order is made, a lease which has been disclaimed vests in the landlord and so will determine. If no vesting order is made, a freehold which has been disclaimed vests in the Crown or the relevant Royal Duchy by escheat.

Under the Insolvency Rules 1986 (SI 1986/1925), r 4.187(3A), the liquidator must send to the Land Registry a copy of the notice of disclaimer of a registered estate or of a registered charge as soon as reasonably practicable after it has been authenticated (i.e. signed) and dated by the liquidator. No formal application in Form AP1 is necessary at this stage and no fee is payable. The Registry will make the following note in the register:

> A notice dated [*date*] by the liquidator of [*name of company*] stated that the [*registered estate in this title*] or [*registered charge dated [date] referred to above*] was being disclaimed under section 178 of the Insolvency Act 1986.

A liquidator who has disclaimed a registered lease may apply for formal notice of the disclaimer to be entered in the register with or without an application to close the title under LRR 2003, r 79. Where the disclaimed lease is unregistered but has been noted against a registered title, application may be made to cancel notice of the unregistered lease in the landlord's title.

Registered disclaimed lease

Where a liquidator has disclaimed a registered lease, an applicant should deliver to the Registry:

(a) an application in Form AP1;
(b) a copy of the notice of disclaimer, unless the note referred to above already appears in the register;
(c) evidence of the appointment of the liquidator (see 'Evidence of appointment', above);
(d) the original lease, or a satisfactory explanation of why it cannot be lodged; and
(e) the fee payable (see *Fees*, page 221).

The Registry will serve notice of the application on the registered proprietor of the freehold or other superior leasehold title in which the disclaimed lease is noted, on any chargee or sub-tenant and on any other party whose interest would be affected by closure of the title.

If there is no evidence of any registered or noted charge, sub-lease or other third party rights affecting the disclaimed leasehold title, or satisfactory evidence is supplied that every such interest has also come to an end, the Registry will close the leasehold title and cancel any notice of the lease in the landlord's registered title.

However, as determination of a lease by disclaimer does not affect the rights and liabilities acquired before the disclaimer by persons other than the tenant, the Registry will not close the registered leasehold title if there is a registered or noted charge in the disclaimed leasehold title, unless the application includes an application either to discharge the registered charge or to cancel the entry of the noted charge; or evidence that the chargee's application for a vesting order has been dismissed (so that the chargee is excluded from all interest in the property); or evidence of forfeiture of the lease.

If the registered leasehold title cannot be closed (or the application is only for a formal notice of the disclaimer to be entered in the register), the Registry will make the following entries in the property register of the disclaimed leasehold title:

> This lease was disclaimed by the liquidator of the registered proprietor on [*date*] pursuant to section 178 of the Insolvency Act 1986.

A restriction will at the same time be entered in the proprietorship register, to the effect that no disposition of the registered estate is to be completed by registration.

The Registry will also add the following note to the notice of the disclaimed lease in the landlord's title:

> This lease was disclaimed by the liquidator of the registered proprietor on [*date*]. The registered leasehold title has not been closed because there is a subsisting [*registered*] or [*noted*] charge in favour of [*name*] dated [*date*].

The leasehold title for a disclaimed lease may be closed if there is no registered or noted charge but there is a registered sub-lease or other third party rights noted in title, in which case appropriate entries referring to the disclaimer will be made in the landlord's title and any registered sub-leasehold title.

Unregistered disclaimed lease

Where the disclaimed lease has not been registered but has been noted against a registered title, an applicant should deliver to the Registry:

(a)   an application in Form CN1, panel 9 being completed by entering details of the lease and placing an 'X' against 'disclaimer';

(b)   the original lease or a satisfactory explanation of why it cannot be lodged;

(c)   the deeds and documents relating to the leasehold title;

(d)   a copy of the notice of disclaimer, unless the note referred to above already appears in the register;

(e)   evidence of the appointment of the liquidator (see 'Evidence of Appointment', above); and

(f)   the fee payable (see *Fees*, page 221).

Where there is no evidence of any charge, sub-lease or of other third party rights affecting the disclaimed noted lease, then the notice of the lease in the landlord's title may be cancelled.

Where there is evidence of a continuing charge, sub-lease or other third party rights affecting the disclaimed noted lease, the notice of the lease cannot be cancelled, but appropriate entries referring to the disclaimer will be made in the landlord's title and any registered sub-leasehold title.

Vesting order relating to registered disclaimed lease

Where the property has been disclaimed and an order has been made by the court vesting the property in some other person, an applicant should deliver to the Registry:

(a)   an application in Form AP1;

(b)   an office copy of the court order; and

(c)   the fee payable (see *Fees*, page 221).

Disclaimer of registered freehold estate

In the unusual situation where a registered freehold estate has been disclaimed, application may be made for formal notice of the disclaimer to be entered in the register of the freehold title under LRR 2003, rr 79 and 173. The requirements are similar to those where application is made to close a registered leasehold title following disclaimer (see above). The Registry will not close the registered title unless and until it registers either a grant from the Crown of a new freehold estate or a transfer from one of the Royal Duchies (see *Bona vacantia and escheat*, page 74). In the interim, it will make the following entry in the property register:

The registered estate in this title has determined on disclaimer by the liquidator of the registered proprietor on [*date*] pursuant to section 178 of the Insolvency Act 1985.

If the escheated freehold title is subject to a registered lease or other inferior interest, the following entry will be made in the property register for that title:

The [*landlord's (or as the case may be)*] registered estate has determined on disclaimer by the liquidator on [*date*] pursuant to section 178 of the Insolvency Act 1986 but the entries relating to the estate continue in the register.

The Registry may qualify the above entries where there is some doubt as to whether escheat has in fact taken place.

Dissolution

On dissolution, all the property and rights of a company (other than property held on trust for another) are deemed to be bona vacantia and will belong to the Crown or to the Duchy of Lancaster or the Duke of Cornwall, as the case may be (Companies Act 2006, s 1012 as from 1 October 2006; previously Companies Act 1985, s 654). Where a company which is the proprietor of a registered estate or registered charge has been dissolved, the Registry may enter a note of that fact in the proprietorship register or charges register, as appropriate (LRR 2003, r 185) (see *Bona vacantia and escheat*, page 74).

Liquidation of foreign companies

In the case of an overseas liquidation, the liquidation of a foreign company in its country of incorporation is recognised by English law. An application to register a disposition made by or on behalf of such a company must be made in Form AP1, accompanied by appropriate evidence of the liquidation and of its effect. Certified translations should be supplied of any documents not in English or Welsh.

In the case of a liquidation in the United Kingdom, a foreign company that has been carrying on business in the United Kingdom may be wound up as an unregistered company under the IA 1986 even though it may already have been dissolved or otherwise ceased to exist under the law of its country of incorporation. The winding up will be by order of the court and the relevant evidence specified in 'Evidence of liquidation', above would need to be lodged.

LOCAL LAND CHARGES

The Local Land Charges Act 1975 and the Local Land Charges Rules 1977 govern the operation of local land charges. A local land charge is an unregistered interest which overrides both first registration and registered dispositions (LRA 2002, Sch 1, para 6 and Sch 3, para 6). This includes a local land charge the status of which as an overriding interest under the LRA 1925 was preserved by Local Land Charges Act 1975, s 19(3) (LRA 2002, Sch 12, para 13). The duty to disclose information about interests which override on an application for first registration or on an application to register a registrable disposition does not apply to information about local land charges (LRR 2003, rr 28(2)(d) and 57(2)(c)) (see 'Duty to disclose overriding interests', page 426).

Although a local land charge is an interest which overrides, it may be protected by entry of a notice or restriction. If it is protected by a notice, it ceases to be an interest which overrides, and does not revert to being an overriding interest if the notice is subsequently cancelled (LRA 2002, ss 29(3) and 30(3)). In practice, a local land charge is usually registered in the local land charges registers but is not entered in the register at the Land Registry.

Some local land charges create monetary charges. These are charges on a property imposed under various statutes, such as Public Health Act 1936, s 291, to recover costs incurred by a local authority. For example, the costs of cleansing and clearing land, or repairing or demolishing buildings, structures and services, which are a hazard to health or safety. Such a charge is a statutory charge and, although not created by a deed executed by the owner, takes effect as a charge by way of legal mortgage when registered as a local land charge, but without prejudice to its priority (Local Land Charges Act 1975, s 7).

A charge over registered land which is a local land charge may be protected by entry of a notice, but may be realised only if the charge is registered (LRA 2002, s 55). An application to register the title to such a charge must be supported by evidence of the charge (LRR 2003, r 104). As there will be no formal deed of charge, such evidence may be the declaration in writing creating the charge, where that is required by legislation, or a sealed resolution of the local authority which recites the facts giving rise to the charge and resolves that application is made for its registration.

When applying for substantive registration of a monetary local land charge, the applicant authority should deliver to the Registry:

(a)   an application in Form AP1;
(b)   documentary evidence of the charge or a certified copy of it; and

(c)   the fee payable (see *Fees*, page 221).

If the statutory charge has effect to postpone a charge which is already entered in the register or is the basis for an entry in the register, the applicant authority must also deliver Form SC with the application (LRA 2002, s 50 and LRR 2003, r 105(1)). The usual basis for claiming priority over an existing charge is that a statutory provision expressly provides that the charge is a charge on the premises and on all estates and interests in it (and is thus a charge on a prior registered charge); or that the charge secures the cost of works which have resulted in an improvement to the property, which has benefited not only the proprietor of the registered estate but also others who have an interest in it.

Where the applicant satisfies the Registry that the statutory charge has the priority specified in Form SC, an entry must be made in the charges register showing that priority. If the applicant does not satisfy the Registry that the statutory charge has that priority, but the Registry considers that the applicant has an arguable case, an entry may be made in the charges register that the applicant claims that priority. In either case the Registry must give notice to the registered proprietor of any existing registered charge and any person who appears to the Registry to be entitled to a charge protected by a notice. In the case of a charge protected by a notice, the Registry is obliged to serve notice only if the chargee's name and address for service appear in the register of the title in question. A person who suffers loss by reason of a failure by the Registry to give such notice may be entitled to indemnity (see *Indemnity*, page 273).

Where an entry as to claimed priority has been made, LRR 2003, r 105(5) to (8) makes provision for an application to be made for the entry to be removed, or to be replaced with an entry that the statutory charge in question does have the priority specified in the Form SC. The applicant must provide evidence to satisfy the Registry that it should take the action sought by the applicant. The Registry must serve notice of the application upon the proprietors of registered charges affected by the application.

Infrastructure Act 2015, s 34 and Sch 5 make provision for the Chief Land registrar to become the sole registering authority and holder of a local land charges register and index, which may be kept in electronic form. The intention is that, ultimately, there will be a single local land charges register and index for the whole of England and Wales, and that it will be held in electronic form. However, the Infrastructure Act 2015 provides that the registrar may take over responsibility for the individual registers, currently held by each local authority, on a 'staged' basis, by means of the service of a notice by the registrar upon a local authority under Infrastructure Act 2015, Sch 5, para 40. The notice will specify the date upon which the registrar is to assume responsibility. Currently, no such notices have been served.

LOST OR DESTROYED TITLE DEEDS

Where the unregistered title deeds have been lost or destroyed, an application for first registration must be supported by evidence to satisfy the Registry that the applicant is entitled to apply voluntarily for first registration under LRA 2002, s 3(2) because the unregistered legal estate sought to be registered is vested in him or he is entitled to require the estate to be vested in him; or (as the case may be) that he is required to apply for compulsory first registration under LRA 2002, s 6(1) on the occurrence of a 'trigger' for compulsory registration listed in s 4 of that Act. The supporting evidence must also account for the absence of the deeds (LRR 2003, r 27). The evidence may consist of, or include, a statutory declaration or statement of truth (which may be in Form ST3 in LRR 2003, Sch 1), setting out the facts and exhibiting any appropriate supporting documents. The evidence required in each individual case will depend on the particular facts, but it will need to cover the following:

(a) the circumstances of the loss or destruction;
(b) the reconstruction of the title;
(c) possession of the estate; and
(d) evidence of identity of the applicant, where necessary.

Application for first registration

In addition to the usual documents required (see *First registration*, page 222), an applicant should deliver to the Registry evidence as to the applicant's title by way of statutory declaration(s) or statement(s) of truth (which may be in Form ST3) and a certified copy of each, if the applicant wishes for the original to be returned.

The applicant may be called upon to pay an additional fee to meet the cost of a survey or special enquiries.

Circumstances of the loss or destruction

The evidence lodged must cover:

(a) where and by whom the deeds were held immediately before their loss or destruction;

(b) why the person in possession had custody of the deeds; for example, whether they were held for safekeeping or as security for a loan;

(c) the full circumstances of their loss or destruction;

(d) the efforts made to recover the deeds;

(e) whether or not at the time of the loss or destruction the applicant had created any mortgage, charge or lien on the property or deposited the deeds with any person, firm or body as security for money;

(f) whether the applicant is in occupation of the estate or in receipt of the rents and profits from it; and

(g) that the applicant is entitled to apply for first registration as the legal estate is vested in him or he is entitled to require it to be vested in him.

If the deeds were lost or destroyed whilst in the custody of (or being sent in the post from) a conveyancer, building society, bank or other well-known institution, the above information should normally be supplied by a member of that firm or organisation.

Reconstruction of the title

The best available secondary evidence of how title has devolved to the applicant must be produced. The nature and quality of this will vary depending on the circumstances of the individual case. Copies or drafts of lost deeds may often be obtained from solicitors or other conveyancers who acted at the time of a previous sale or purchase of the property. If the property is mortgaged, evidence of the mortgage should be included. If there is no mortgage on the property, the declaration should specifically confirm that at the time of the loss or destruction the owner had not created any mortgage, charge or lien on the land and had not deposited the deeds by way of security for money.

Where the property is leasehold, copies of the deeds may be available from the landlord, who should also be able to confirm who has paid the rent. The landlord may also have details as to licences to assign, where this is a requirement of the lease.

Where the land falls within the areas covered by any of the former deeds registries for Middlesex or Yorkshire, copies of deeds or of memorials of deeds may be available from the appropriate archive service. Memorials did not, though, normally show whether the land was subject to restrictive covenants.

Possession of the estate

The applicant should also provide satisfactory evidence that since the date of acquisition he has been in actual occupation of the whole of the estate or in receipt of its rents and profits (particulars of which, supported by copies of leases, rent books or receipts, should be given) without any adverse claim. Any other relevant facts should be provided. The registrar may, if it considers it necessary, arrange for an inspection survey of the land.

Evidence of possession is relevant not only in helping to satisfy the Registry that the applicant is entitled to apply for registration, but because a possessory title (which is the most commonly granted class of title in these circumstances) can only be granted where the Registry is satisfied that the applicant is in actual possession of the land or in receipt of the rents and profits from it (LRA 2002, ss 9(5) and 10(6)).

Evidence of identity

In some cases, the Registry may require evidence of identity. This can assist in demonstrating that the applicant does hold the legal estate and in combating property fraud. Such evidence is not required when the application is lodged by:

(a) a conveyancer who is applying for registration because the title deeds were lost or destroyed whilst in his custody; or
(b) a major mortgage lender, where the deeds were being held as security for the lender's mortgage and were lost whilst in its custody; or
(c) a duly authorised official of a local authority, government department or nationally well-known body, where the deeds relating to its land, or land on which it holds a mortgage, were lost whilst in its custody; or
(d) a receiver or liquidator of a company, where evidence of the appointment is supplied, together with a certified copy of the mortgage or charge where the applicant is a receiver appointed under such a deed.

Where the applicant is required to provide evidence of identity, see *Identity evidence*, page 266.

Class of title

Where the Registry is satisfied as to the applicant's title and the circumstances of the loss or destruction, a registered title may be granted. Although each application is considered on its merits, normally absolute title will not be granted (nor good leasehold title, in the case of a leasehold estate) where the loss or destruction of the deeds cannot be adequately explained. Instead a possessory title will usually be granted. An applicant may be registered with possessory title if the Registry is of the opinion that the applicant is in actual possession of the land, or in receipt of the rents and profits of the land, by virtue of the estate, and that there is no other class of title with which he may be registered (LRA 2002, ss 9(5) and 10(6)). If the applicant remains in possession of the registered estate for the requisite period, or if the title deeds are subsequently found, application may be made to upgrade the class of title (see *Upgrade of class of title*, page 565).

A protective entry may be entered in the register if the Registry considers there is a risk that the land may be subject to undisclosed restrictive covenants, easements or rentcharges. An entry in respect of the benefit of legal easements will only be made in the register if the applicant has shown satisfactory evidence of title to them (LRR 2003, r 33).

MANORS

Manors are of ancient origin dating from pre-Norman times, with the extent of each manor normally being determined by the original grant from the Crown or superior lord. A manor was self-contained with its own customs and rights within its defined area. A manor can comprise three separate elements which may affect registered land:

(a)   The title of lord of the manor, which confers the right upon the person holding the title to refer to himself as lord of that manor; for example, 'Lord of the manor of [*name of manor*]'.

(b)   Manorial land, comprising the freehold or leasehold land within the defined area of the manor.

(c)   Manorial rights, comprising rights which were part of the manorial title and which were usually retained by the lord on any disposal of part of the manorial land; for example, the right to hunt, shoot or fish.

The lordship title cannot be sub-divided, but the manorial land and the manorial rights can be, so that these three elements may remain combined or they may have become separated. When dealing with a manor, it is therefore important to consider, and where necessary distinguish between, each of these elements.

Lordship of a manor

The lordship of a manor is an incorporeal hereditament. It is no longer possible to register the title to a lordship of a manor (LRA 2002, s 3). Manors which were registered under the LRA 1925 remain in the register, but the proprietor of a registered manor may apply for the title to the manor to be removed from the register (LRA 2002, s 119).

The registered title to a manor has no title plan and the Registry does not hold any definitive record of the extent of the original manor. Registrations of manors are listed in the index of franchises and manors, which can be searched in respect of any particular administrative area using Form SIF (LRR 2003, r 146). The result of such a search does not, however, reveal any caution against first registration of a manor which may have been in existence on 13 October 2003. To ascertain whether there is such a caution, a search of the index map using Form SIM is required (see *Official searches of the index*, page 409). No caution against first registration in respect of a manor may be lodged under the LRA 2002.

Transfer of a registered manor

A transfer of a registered manor is a registrable disposition which must be completed by registration if it is to operate at law (LRA 2002, s 27) (see *Transfers*, page 551).

Lease of a registered manor

Where there is a grant of a lease out of a registered manor, an application must be made to register the lease (LRA 2002, s 27(2)(c)). Any lease, however short, out of a registered manor is required to be registered. If this is not desired, consideration should be given to deregistering the manor (see below).

If the lease is for a term of more than 7 years from the date of the grant, the application is completed by the entry in the register of the grantee (or his successor in title) as proprietor of the lease; and a notice in respect of the lease.

If the lease is for a term not exceeding 7 years from the date of the grant, the application is completed only by the entry of a notice in respect of the lease (LRA 2002, Sch 2, paras 4 and 5). An application for entry of a notice of a lease which is for a term not exceeding 7 years from the date of the grant may be made in Form AP1 or Form AN1 (LRR 2003, r 90).

An applicant should deliver to the Registry the usual documents required (see *Leases*, page 296).

For registration of leases generally, see *Leases*, page 296.

Deregistration of a registered lordship of a manor

An applicant for the title to a lordship of a manor to be removed from the register should deliver to the Registry:

(a)   an application in Form AP1, showing the nature of application as 'deregistration of manor'; and

(b)   the land certificate.

No fee is currently payable for the removal of a registered lordship of a manor from the register. Upon deregistration the lordship continues to subsist, but not as a registered estate.

Manorial land

Manorial land is the land that was originally part of the landholdings of the lordship of the manor and which has not been separated from the lordship title. Manorial land can be extensive if the manor remains largely intact, or if the manor has been broken up it can consist of a collection of small pieces of land remaining in the manor and scattered across a large area, including manorial waste, such as some highway verges. Manorial land is subject to the same requirements as to compulsory first registration, and the completion of registrable dispositions by registration, as any other corporeal land (see *First registration*, page 222, and *Transfers*, page 551).

Registrations of manorial land are recorded in the index map, which can be searched in respect of any particular administrative area using Form SIM (LRR 2003, r 145) (see *Official searches of the index*, page 409).

Manorial rights

A lord of the manor may exercise certain rights usually known as 'manorial rights' or 'manorial incidents'. Such rights could no longer be created after 1925. Manorial rights are not defined in the LRA 2002, but were defined in the LRA 1925 as having the same meaning as in Law of Property Act 1922, Pt V. They include:

(a)   any right of the lord or tenant in or to any mines, minerals, limestone, lime, clay, stone, gravel, pits, or quarries, and any associated rights of search, winning, working and carrying away;

(b)   the rights, franchises, royalties, or privileges of the lord in respect of any fairs, markets, rights of chase or warren, piscaries, or other rights of hunting, shooting, fishing, fowling, or otherwise taking game, fish or fowl; and

(c)   any liability subsisting on 1 January 1926 for the construction, maintenance, cleansing, or repair of any dykes, ditches, canals, sea or river walls, piles, bridges, levels, ways and other works required for the protection or general benefit of any land within a manor or for abating nuisances therein.

Manorial rights arise in relation to land which was formerly copyhold, being rights which were reserved to the lord of the manor on enfranchisement (see *Copyhold*, page 171).

Where on first registration the title deduced reveals that the land is subject to manorial rights, the Registry will enter a notice to that effect in the property register.

Any unregistered manorial rights were interests which overrode both first registration or a registered disposition (LRA 2002, Sch 1, para 11 and Sch 3, para 11). Such interests were therefore protected notwithstanding that there was no entry in the register in respect of them (LRA 2002, ss 11, 12, 29 and 30). There was therefore a duty to disclose the burden of such rights under LRR 2003, r 28 or r 57 (see 'Duty to disclose overriding interests', page 426).

However, such rights ceased to have overriding status at the end of 10 years from 13 October 2003 (LRA 2002, s 117). The person having the benefit of a manorial right (if its priority has not already been previously defeated and it continues to subsist) should therefore protect it in the register. If he does not do so, the priority of the right is liable to be defeated in favour of a subsequent registrable disposition for valuable consideration which is completed by registration (LRA 2002, s 29). If the burdened land is unregistered, he should apply for a caution against first registration. If the burdened land is registered, he should apply for the entry of a notice if one does not already appear in the register. Until 12 October 2013, no fee was payable for such an application, but the normal fee will now apply.

As to an application for a caution against first registration, or an application for entry of a notice in the register, to protect manorial rights, see *Copyhold*, page 171.

MENTAL INCAPACITY

Where a person is suffering from a lack of mental capacity, either permanently or temporarily, it is necessary for someone to be appointed to manage his property on his behalf. A mentally incapacitated person is not barred from holding registered land and any registered land held by him when he became incapacitated remains vested in him. However, he will lack capacity to effect a valid disposition of that registered land. Any valid enduring power or lasting power of attorney given by a person is not revoked by his subsequent mental incapacity and the attorney can therefore act on his behalf (see *Powers of attorney*, page 446). However, in the absence of such a power of attorney, special provision may need to be made by the court in relation to the management of the incapacitated person's property and affairs.

Prior to 1 October 2007, mental incapacity in relation to property was dealt with under Mental Health Act 1983, Pt VII, under which the Court of Protection could, by order, appoint a 'receiver' or other authorised person to deal with the incapacitated person's property. Since 1 October 2007, mental incapacity in relation to property has been dealt with under the Mental Capacity Act 2005, which repealed Mental Health Act 1983, Pt VII and established a new Court of Protection together with a new statutory office of Public Guardian. Where a person is suffering from mental incapacity, the court may by order make decisions on behalf of that person or may appoint a 'deputy' to make decisions on his behalf. A deputy will have such powers as the court confers upon him in relation to the personal welfare and the property and affairs of the incapacitated person, including powers in relation to real property (Mental Capacity Act 2005, ss 16 and 18). A deputy will therefore normally have power to buy and sell property on behalf of the incapacitated person.

The appointment of a receiver under the Mental Health Act 1983 remains effective notwithstanding the repeal of that Act by the Mental Capacity Act 2005. However, the 2005 Act applies as if the receiver were a deputy appointed by the court for the incapacitated person, but with the functions that he had as a receiver. Orders made under the 1983 Act did not always empower the receiver to buy or sell property on behalf of the incapacitated person; where this is the case, a further order of the court authorising the disposition will be required.

Registered land

Where the incapacitated person is the sole proprietor of registered land, any transfer or other registrable disposition by him should be signed by the deputy in the name of the incapacitated individual and their own name and duly witnessed. An application to register such a disposition must be accompanied by the order appointing the deputy or a certified copy of it. Where a deputy is a receiver appointed under the Mental Health Act 1983, a certified copy of the order appointing him must be provided, together with (where necessary) a certified copy of the order authorising the sale or other disposition.

Notwithstanding his mental incapacity, property may be acquired on behalf of an incapacitated person. Where unregistered land is acquired for an incapacitated person and this triggers compulsory first registration of title, the deputy should apply for first registration in the name of the incapacitated person. Similarly, where registered land is acquired for an incapacitated person, the deputy should apply for registration in the name of the incapacitated person. He must lodge with the application a certified copy of the order appointing him to act as deputy and also a certified copy of the order authorising the acquisition, which may be a separate order or form part of the powers conferred within the order appointing the deputy. Where a deputy is a receiver appointed under the Mental Health Act 1983, a certified copy of the order appointing him must be provided, together with (where necessary) a copy of the order authorising the acquisition.

Prior to 1 October 2007, the receiver of an incapacitated person could apply to be registered as proprietor of that person's property. A restriction was normally entered against the title of the receiver, preventing the registration of any disposition unless the disposition was made pursuant to an order of the Court under the Mental Health Act 1983. Since 1 October 2007, the deputy of an incapacitated person may not apply to be registered as proprietor, unless specifically authorised by the Court of Protection. The Registry will not enter a restriction reflecting a proprietor's mental incapacity unless the deputy expressly applies for this. A deputy is entitled to apply for entry of a restriction in Form RR (LRR 2003, r 93(aa)). The wording of Form RR is set out in Appendix IV, page 585.

Any application for cancellation of such a restriction should be made using Form RX3, accompanied by an appropriate order or direction of the Court of Protection. An application to withdraw such a restriction may be made by the deputy using Form RX4. No fee is currently payable for the cancellation or withdrawal of a restriction (see *Restrictions*, page 500).

Registered land held on trust

It may be that a mentally incapacitated person holds registered land on trust. A deputy cannot be given power to act on behalf of a patient in respect of trust property (Mental Capacity Act 2005, s 20(3)). Where a patient is a trustee, a deputy should not therefore make the disposition on behalf of the patient in conjunction with the other trustee(s). Instead, when a trustee is unfit to act, or incapable of acting, in respect of the trusts conferred upon him, a new trustee should be appointed in his place. This power would lie first with any person whom the trust instrument nominated to do so. If there is no one to make the appointment, or no one who is willing and able to do so, then the continuing trustees may appoint a new trustee in his place (Trustee Act 1925, s 36(1)). If a trustee who is incapable is also entitled to some beneficial interest in the trust property, only the person nominated by the trust instrument may appoint a new trustee in his place, unless the Court of Protection has given leave to the continuing trustees to make the appointment (Trustee Act 1925, s 36(9)). If both or all the trustees are mentally incapacitated, an order of the court under the Trustee Act 1925, s 41 will be required.

If a trustee who is incapable does not have an entitlement to some beneficial interest in the trust property and there is no one who is entitled or willing to appoint a trustee in his place, the beneficiaries may give a deputy of the incapacitated trustee a written direction to appoint the person named in the direction to be the trustee in place of the incapable person (TLATA, s 20(2)). The beneficiaries may only give this direction if they are of full age and capacity, and are together absolutely entitled to the trust property. They may also give a similar direction to a person authorised for this purpose by the Court of Protection, or to the donee of an enduring power or lasting power of attorney with authority to act on behalf of the incapacitated trustee where the power has been registered under the Mental Capacity Act 2005.

An incapable trustee should generally be removed and a new one appointed before the trustees deal with the legal estate. However, even without taking those steps, the trustees may deal with the legal estate if the donee of an enduring power or lasting power of attorney is entitled to act in the dealing on the incapable trustee's behalf (Law of Property Act 1925, s 22(3)). While this power subsists, it would not be necessary to discharge the incapable trustee or appoint a new trustee.

An attorney for an incapacitated trustee or incapacitated trustees under an enduring power or lasting power of attorney which has been registered under the Mental Capacity Act 2005 may have power to make an appointment of an additional trustee on behalf of the trustee or trustees (Trustee Act 1925, s 36(6)(b), (6A), (6B), (6C), (6D)). This power would not appear to enable such an attorney to appoint himself as such a trustee.

An appointment of a new trustee is a disposition required to be completed by registration (LRA 2002, s 27).

A trustee of a registered estate or registered charge that requires the consent of the Court of Protection to any disposition, is entitled to apply for entry of a restriction in Form SS (LRR 2003, r 93(bb)). The wording of Form SS is set out in Appendix IV, page 585.

Severance of beneficial joint tenancy of registered land

An application may be made by a deputy for the entry of a restriction in Form A following the severance of a beneficial joint tenancy where the incapacitated person is one of the beneficial owners. The application must be supported, where necessary, by evidence to satisfy the Registry that the deputy has power to make the application. An order made under the Mental Capacity Act 2005 giving the deputy general authority includes (unless otherwise qualified in the order) the power to sever the joint tenancy of a patient. If the deputy is a receiver appointed under the Mental Health Act 1983, his power to sever the joint tenancy will depend on the terms of the order. If the order does not specifically authorise the receiver to sever the joint tenancy, the written authority of the court to do this will be required. If the deputy has the power to sever the joint tenancy, any application should be made in the patient's name and the usual evidence of severance will be required (see *Severance of a beneficial joint tenancy*, page 533).

Adverse possession of registered land

No one who has been in adverse possession of a registered estate may apply to be registered as proprietor of that estate during any period in which the existing registered proprietor is unable because of mental disability to make decisions about issues of the kind to which such an application would give rise, or unable to communicate such decisions because of mental disability or physical impairment. Where it appears to the Registry that this applies, it may include a note to that effect in the register. For these purposes 'mental disability' means a disability or disorder of the mind or brain, whether permanent or temporary, which results in an impairment or disturbance of mental functioning (LRA 2002, Sch 6, para 8(2), (3) and (4)). Where it is desired that the Registry should make such a note in the register, application should be made using application Form AP1, supported by appropriate evidence of the mental disability or physical impairment. As to adverse possession of registered land generally, see *Adverse possession*, page 11.

MERE EQUITIES

A mere equity is an equitable right which falls short of being an equitable interest. The courts have not laid down what distinguishes an equitable interest from a mere equity but the latter appears usually to involve a claim to discretionary relief in equity which relates to property. Examples are the right to rectify a deed for mutual mistake, a right to set aside a transfer for fraud or undue influence, and a right to seek relief from forfeiture of a lease after peaceable re-entry.

LRA 2002, s 116 declares, for the avoidance of doubt, that in relation to registered land, a mere equity has effect from the time the equity arises as an interest capable of binding successors in title, subject to the rules about the effect of dispositions on priority. For the rules about the effect of dispositions on priority, see *Priorities*, page 452.

The purchaser of a later equitable interest in the registered title does not therefore take free from the mere equity, even though he has no notice of it. This is different from the position with unregistered land, where the purchaser would take free in this case (*Phillips v Phillips* (1861) 4 De GF & J 208).

LRA 2002, s 116 applies to mere equities which arose both before and after the section came into force on 13 October 2003.

To protect the priority of a mere equity affecting registered land against a registrable disposition made for valuable consideration, application may be made for entry of a notice in the register. Given the inchoate nature of a mere equity, in the absence of the consent of the registered proprietor it will normally be appropriate to make an application for entry of a unilateral notice rather than an agreed notice, due to the difficulty of being able to satisfy the Registry of the validity of the applicant's claim under LRA 2002, s 34(3)(c). For example, in the case of a claimed right to have a deed rectified for mutual mistake.

An applicant for entry of a unilateral notice should deliver to the Registry the usual documents required (see *Notices*, page 389).

The statement in panel 11 or conveyancer's certificate in panel 12 of Form UN1 should be completed on the following lines to show the interest of the applicant:

> person having the right [*insert details of the mere equity, for example to have a Transfer dated (date) made between (parties) rectified for mutual mistake*].

The unilateral notice in the register will give brief details of the interest protected and identify the beneficiary of that notice.

MINES AND MINERALS

Mines and minerals are 'land' for the purposes of the LRA 2002 (LRA 2002, s 132(1)) and are rebuttably presumed to be included in the registered title of a registered estate in the surface land. This is in accordance with the common law position regarding mines and minerals where the surface land is unregistered. However, no indemnity is payable in respect of mines and minerals unless there is a specific note in the register that title to them is included (LRA 2002, Sch 8, para 2). Such a note can be entered as a result of a specific application either on first registration or subsequently and will only be made where evidence of title to the mines and minerals sufficient to satisfy the Registry that those mines and minerals are included in the registered estate is lodged (LRR 2003, r 71).

Where a note cannot be made in the register that the title to the registered estate includes mines and minerals, but the description of the registered estate makes reference to mines and minerals, the Registry may make the following entry (LRR 2003, r 70):

> NOTE: The description of the registered estate is an entry made under rule 5(a) of the Land Registration Rules 2003 and is not a note to which paragraph 2 of Schedule 8 to the Land Registration Act 2002 refers that the registered estate includes the mines or minerals. The mines and minerals under the land are only included in the registration to the extent that they were included in [*title number*].

LRR 2003, r 5(a) provides that the property register must contain a description of the registered estate. Such an entry may be used, for example, where a transfer of part of a registered estate is expressed to include the mines and minerals, but the register of the transferor's title does not include a note for the purposes of LRA 2002, Sch 8, para 2. The Registry will therefore wish to ensure that any reference to mines and minerals in the description in the transferee's property register is not a note for the purposes of Sch 8, para 2.

Under the general law, as part of the Crown's prerogative, all mines of gold and silver belong to the Crown other than, exceptionally, where they have been granted to a subject. Petroleum in its natural state is also vested in the Crown. Most interests in coal are vested in the Coal Authority (see *Coal*, page 135). The Coal Authority may also have title to other mines and minerals in coal mining areas. A registered estate will not therefore include any of these interests.

First registration of mines and minerals

Although a voluntary application may be made, it is never compulsory to apply for first registration of mines and minerals held apart from the surface (LRA 2002, ss 3 and 4(9)). Where the mines and minerals constitute the surface of land, the normal rules regarding compulsory first registration apply.

Where an application for first registration of mines and minerals is made, investigation of title often needs to go beyond the normal 15-year root. Evidence, typically by way of statutory declaration(s) or statement(s) of truth, as to the working of the mines and minerals will assist in showing a good title. If the land was formerly copyhold, evidence to show the effect of enfranchisement on the mines and minerals should be lodged. Mines and minerals were often retained by the lord on enfranchisement. In many areas, mines and minerals were reserved to the Crown on the original grant of the land; where appropriate, a disclaimer of ownership by the Crown might be lodged. If the land was subject to inclosure, the Inclosure Act and Award should be considered, since these often deal with the ownership of mines and minerals.

In addition to the usual documents required (see *First registration*, page 222), an applicant for first registration of mines and minerals should deliver to the Registry:

(a)   a plan of the surface under which the mines and minerals lie;
(b)   any other sufficient details, by plan or otherwise, so that the mines and minerals can be clearly identified; and
(c)   full details of rights incidental to the working of the mines and minerals.

Items (a), (b) and (c) are requirements imposed by LRR 2003, r 25. As to first registration generally, see *First registration*, page 222.

Due to the difficulties in establishing a good title to mines and minerals, the Registry will in many cases only be in a position to grant a qualified, rather than an absolute, class of title. The qualification will be on the following lines:

> The inclusion of all or any of the mines and minerals and powers of working and getting them in this title does not affect or prejudice the enforcement of any estate right or interest therein existing before [*date of first registration*].

In the case of an application for first registration of a lease of mines and minerals, where the landlord's title to the mines and minerals cannot be satisfactorily established, a good leasehold class of title will be granted, rather than title absolute (see *Classes of title*, page 130).

Where the Registry is satisfied, on first registration of an estate comprising or including the land beneath the surface, that the mines and minerals are included in or excluded from the applicant's title, it must make an appropriate note in the register (LRR 2003, r 32).

Registered surface land

If a registered estate includes mines or minerals but there is no note in the register to that effect, the registered proprietor of that estate may apply for a note to be entered that the registered estate includes the mines or minerals or specified mines or minerals (LRR 2003, r 71). The applicant should deliver to the Registry:

(a) an application in Form AP1;
(b) evidence (in similar form to that outlined above in respect of first registration) to satisfy the Registry that the mines or minerals were vested in the applicant for first registration of the registered estate at the time of first registration and were so vested in the same capacity as the remainder of the estate in land then sought to be vested; and
(c) the fee payable (see *Fees*, page 221).

Where the Registry is satisfied that those mines and minerals are included in the registered estate, it must enter the appropriate note in the register. The form of the note will be:

> NOTE: For the purposes of paragraph 2 of Schedule 8 to the Land Registration Act 2002 [*details of mines and minerals*] are included in this title.

Transfer of mines and minerals out of a registered title

Where a transfer of mines and minerals is granted out of a registered title to mines and minerals, or to surface land, which contains a note regarding the inclusion of those mines and minerals, the new title will be registered with the same class of title as the existing class of title. Where there is no such note, the new title will be registered with the same class of title as the existing class of title but with the entry referred to above being made in the register under LRR 2003, r 70. Such a transfer will be a registrable disposition which must be completed by registration if it is to operate at law (LRA 2002, s 27).

Where a registered title contains a note that expressly includes mines and minerals or is silent as to the inclusion or exclusion of mines and minerals, any transfer of or out of that title that excepts the mines and minerals will have the effect of severing the mines and minerals from the surface land. In such circumstances, if the transfer is of the whole of the registered title, a new title will be created for the mines and minerals retained by the transferor. If the transfer is of part of the registered title, the mines and minerals will be retained by the transferor in the existing registered title.

Lease of mines and minerals out of registered surface land

Where a lease of mines and minerals is a registrable disposition and is granted out of an absolute registered title where there is a note in the title regarding the inclusion of those mines and minerals within the landlord's registered title, an absolute leasehold title can be granted. Where there is no such note and the landlord is registered with an absolute title, then an absolute leasehold title can still be granted but with the following entry being made after the description of the registered estate (LRR 2003, r 70):

> NOTE: The description of the registered estate is an entry made under rule 5(a) of the Land Registration Rules 2003 and is not a note to which paragraph 2 of Schedule 8 to the Land Registration Act 2002 refers that the registered estate includes the mines or minerals under the land. The mines and minerals under the land are only included in the registration to the extent that they were included in [*title number of the landlord's title*].

The purpose of this note is discussed above. In those cases where the landlord is registered with a qualified or possessory title, a good leasehold title will be registered. As to leases generally, see *Leases*, page 296.

Profits à prendre

A right to enter on to land and extract minerals may in some instances constitute a profit à prendre, rather than a freehold or leasehold estate in land, depending upon the nature and terms of the grant or reservation. Thus rights in respect of mines and minerals reserved to the lord of the manor on enfranchisement under Copyhold Act 1852, s 48, Copyhold Act 1894, s 23, or Law of Property Act 1922, Sch 12, para 5 do not constitute a freehold estate in land, but may constitute a profit in gross (see *Copyhold*, page 171, and *Profits à prendre*, page 456).

Overriding interests

The burden of certain rights and interests relating to mines and minerals may take effect as an interest which overrides both first registration and registered dispositions notwithstanding that there is no entry in the register in respect of them. LRA 2002, Schs 1 and 3 specify such rights and interests which have overriding status. These are:

(a)   Interests in any coal or coal mine, the rights attached to any such interest and the rights of any person under Coal Industry Act 1994, ss 38, 49 or 51

(LRA 2002, Sch 1, para 7 and Sch 3, para 7). No notice may be entered in the register in respect of any such rights (LRA 2002, s 33(e)) (see *Coal*, page 135).

(b)   In the case of land which was registered before 1898, unregistered rights to mines and minerals and incidental rights created before 1898 override both first registration and registered dispositions (LRA 2002, Sch 1, para 8 and Sch 3, para 8).

(c)   In the case of land which was registered between 1898 and 1925 inclusive, unregistered rights to mines and minerals and incidental rights created before the date of registration of the title override both first registration and registered dispositions (LRA 2002, Sch 1, para 9 and Sch 3, para 9).

As to manorial rights relating to mines and minerals, see *Copyhold*, page 171, and *Manors*, page 372.

Indemnity

No indemnity under LRA 2002, Sch 8 is payable on account of any mines or minerals or the existence of any right to work or get mines or minerals, unless it is noted in the register that the title of the registered estate concerned includes the mines and minerals (LRA 2002, Sch 8, para 2). Although mines and minerals are rebuttably presumed to be included in a registered title if there is no entry excluding them in the register, this does not of itself give any entitlement to indemnity if, for example, it subsequently transpires that the title does not in fact include them. There must be a specific note in the register that they are included in the title. As to indemnity generally, see *Indemnity*, page 273.

MINORS

A minor is a person who has not attained the age of majority. A person attains the age of majority at the first moment of the 18th anniversary of his birth (Family Law Reform Act 1969, s 9). A minor cannot hold a legal estate in land (Law of Property Act 1925, s 1(6)). He may hold an equitable interest only. Nevertheless situations do arise where, through inadvertence, a legal estate or legal charge is purported to be vested in a minor.

Transfer of land to a minor

After 1996 a purported transfer to one or more minors is not effective to pass the legal estate but operates as a declaration that the land is held in trust for the minor or minors (or if it purports to transfer it to the minors in trust for any persons, for those persons) (TLATA, s 2(6) and Sch 1, para 1(1)). Such a transfer is not, therefore, capable of registration, but an application should be made in Form RX1 for entry of a restriction in Form A, if this does not already appear in the register. The wording of Form A is set out in Appendix IV, page 585.

Application may also be made in Form RX1 for entry of a restriction in Form B (LRR 2003, r 93(c). The wording of Form B is set out in Appendix IV, page 585.

Since no evidence of the age of an applicant is required to be produced to the Registry, a conveyancer may discover that a person is under the age of 18 only after he has been registered as proprietor. This will represent a mistake in the register and an application for alteration of the register should be made to reinstate the previous proprietor and enter a Form A restriction if this does not already appear in the register. Application may also be made in Form RX1 for entry of a restriction in Form B.

An applicant for alteration of the register should deliver to the Registry:

(a) an application in Form AP1;
(b) a statement by the conveyancer briefly summarising the facts and stating the alteration sought;
(c) evidence of minority (for example a birth certificate) or a certified copy of it;
(d) an application in Form RX1 for entry of the appropriate restriction(s) mentioned above (see *Restrictions*, page 500); and
(e) the fee payable (if applicable) (see *Fees*, page 221).

As to applications for the entry of a restriction, see *Restrictions*, page 500.

Transfer of land to a minor jointly with an adult

After 1996 a purported transfer to one or more minors and an adult or adults operates to vest the land in the adult or adults in trust for the minor or minors and the adult or adults (or if it purports to convey it to them in trust for any persons, for those persons) (TLATA, s 2(6) and Sch 1, para 1(2)). Such a transfer is capable of registration, but only the adult or adults will be registered as proprietors and an application should be made in Form RX1 for entry of a restriction in Form A, if this does not already appear in the register. Application may also be made in Form RX1 for entry of a restriction in Form B (LRR 2003, r 93(c). The wording of Form A and of Form B is shown above.

Since no evidence of the age of an applicant is required to be produced to the Registry, a conveyancer may discover that a person is under the age of 18 only after he has been registered as one of the proprietors. This will represent a mistake in the register and an application for alteration of the register should be made to remove the minor as proprietor and enter a Form A restriction, if this does not already appear in the register. Application may also be made in Form RX1 for entry of a restriction in Form B.

An applicant for alteration of the register should deliver to the Registry:

(a) an application in Form AP1;
(b) a statement by the conveyancer briefly summarising the facts and stating the alteration sought;
(c) evidence of minority (for example a birth certificate);
(d) an application in Form RX1 for entry of the appropriate restriction(s) mentioned above (see *Restrictions*, page 500); and
(e) the fee payable (if applicable) (see *Fees*, page 221).

As to applications for the entry of a restriction, see *Restrictions*, page 500.

Charge in favour of a minor or to a minor jointly with an adult

After 1996 any purported grant or transfer of a charge to one or more minors (or to one or more minors and one or more adults) operates in the same way as a purported transfer of land (TLATA, s 23(2) and Sch 1, para 1). Where the grant of a charge is to a minor, it cannot be registered, nor, since it is an interest under a trust of land, can a notice be entered in the register, but a Form A restriction should be entered. Where the grant of a charge or transfer of a charge is to a minor and an adult, the charge may be registered showing the adult as proprietor of the charge.

Where a minor has been registered as proprietor inadvertently, an application for alteration of the register should be made on the same lines as explained above in respect of a transfer of land.

MORTGAGE CAUTIONS

Under the LRA 1925, it was possible to protect a mortgage by a caution known as a mortgage caution. Its effect was to prevent the registration of any dealing with the registered title until notice had been served on the cautioner. The mortgage caution was used only rarely and no new mortgage caution (or sub-mortgage caution) has been capable of registration since 30 August 1977.

A proprietor of a sub-charge could (prior to 30 August 1977) protect that sub-charge by a sub-charge caution. Substantive registration of the sub-charge is not possible until the principal charge is itself substantively registered.

LRA (TP) Order 2003, art 16 preserves the position of mortgage cautions and sub-mortgage cautions under the LRA 2002, so that they continue to have the same effect under the LRA 2002 as they did under the 1925 Act.

It is possible to substantively register the charge protected by the mortgage caution (see *Legal charges*, page 333). The application must (where title to the protected mortgage is vested in someone other than the cautioner) include the documents proving devolution of title to the applicant. On registration, the following note will be added to the entry of the charge:

> This charge was formerly protected by a mortgage caution and has priority, under Article 16(5), Land Registration Act 2002 (Transitional Provisions) Order 2003, with effect from [*date*], the date on which the caution was entered.

If there are any existing charges in the register dated after the date of the caution, a corresponding note will be added to the existing charge entry.

It is not possible to apply to cancel a mortgage caution, but application may be made in Form WCT to remove it, accompanied by satisfactory evidence of the discharge of the mortgage. No fee is currently payable.

If an application for registration is lodged where a mortgage caution appears in the register and no withdrawal of the caution is lodged, the Registry will serve notice of the application on the mortgage cautioner. This notice will confirm that the mortgage caution cannot be removed, even where the cautioner fails to respond to the notice, as an application cannot have the effect of a warning-off of a mortgage caution.

NOTICES

A notice is an entry in the register in respect of the burden of an interest affecting a registered estate or a registered charge. The entry of a notice does not necessarily mean that the interest is valid, but does mean that the priority of the interest, if valid, is protected for the purposes of LRA 2002, ss 29 and 30 (LRA 2002, s 32). For details of this priority protection, see *Priorities*, page 452. Matters typically protected by a notice are contracts for sale and agreements for lease, adverse easements, leases, rentcharges, restrictive covenants, and home rights. Also orders of a court affecting the registered estate.

No notice may be entered in the register in respect of any of the following interests (LRA 2002, ss 33 and 90(4)):

(a)   an interest under a trust of land;
(b)   an interest under a settlement under the SLA 1925;
(c)   a leasehold estate in land which is granted for a term of 3 years or less from the date of the grant and which is not required to be registered;
(d)   a restrictive covenant made between a landlord and tenant, so far as relating to the demised premises;
(e)   an interest which is capable of being registered under the CRA 1965;
(f)   an interest in any coal or coal mine, the rights attached to any such interest and the rights of any person under Coal Industry Act 1994, ss 38, 49 or 51; and
(g)   leases created for PPPs relating to transport in London, within the meaning given by Greater London Authority Act 1999, s 218 (PPP leases).

In many cases a notice is entered by the Registry as a matter of course, without the need for a separate application, as part of the registration process. Such as notice is referred to as a 'registrar's notice' and takes effect as an agreed notice. For example, a notice may be entered by the Registry as a result of its examination of title on first registration (LRR 2003, r 35), or where it finds that the title is affected by an unregistered interest which overrides first registration and which is capable of being noted (LRA 2002, s 37). In the latter example, the Registry must give notice to the registered proprietor and to any person who appears to the Registry to be entitled to the interest protected by the notice or whom it otherwise considers appropriate (LRR 2003, r 89). The Registry need not give notice to a registered proprietor who applies for the entry of the notice or consents to the application for the notice. Nor need the Registry give notice to any other person if that person has applied for, or consented to, the notice, or whose name and address for service do not appear in the register of the title in question.

Where a registrable disposition requires completion of registration by the entry of a notice, the Registry must enter such a notice in the register (LRA 2002, s 38). This includes, for example, the entry of a notice of a lease in the landlord's title on the registration of a lease, or the entry of a notice in the grantor's title on the express grant of a legal easement.

Aside from the circumstances when a notice is entered by the Registry as described above, a notice may also be entered upon specific application. A person claiming to be entitled to the benefit of an interest affecting a registered estate or registered charge may apply for the entry of either an agreed notice or a unilateral notice. The right to apply for the entry of a notice must not be exercised without reasonable cause. This duty to act reasonably is owed to any person who suffers damage in consequence of its breach (LRA 2002, s 77). A person in breach of such duty is therefore liable in damages to a person who suffers loss in consequence.

Agreed notice

The Registry may approve the entry of an agreed notice only if:

(a)   the applicant is the registered proprietor of the estate or charge in question;
(b)   the applicant is a person entitled to be registered as proprietor of the estate or charge in question;
(c)   the registered proprietor of the estate or charge in question, or the person entitled to be registered as such, consents to the entry of the notice; or
(d)   the Registry is satisfied as to the validity of the applicant's claim (LRA 2002, s 34).

In respect of the following, an applicant cannot apply for entry of a unilateral notice and must apply for entry of an agreed notice (LRR 2003, r 80):

(a)   a home rights notice;
(b)   an IHT notice;
(c)   a notice in respect of an order under the ANLA 1992;
(d)   a notice of any variation of a lease effected by or under an order under Landlord and Tenant Act 1987, s 38, including any variation as modified by an order under s 39(4) of that Act;
(e)   a notice in respect of a public right; or
(f)   a notice in respect of a customary right.

An applicant for an agreed notice should deliver to the Registry:

(a) an application in Form AN1;

(b) a plan of the affected land (where the interest claimed affects only part of the land in the registered title);

(c) the deed, order or instrument giving rise to the interest claimed, or (if there is no such deed, order or instrument) other details of the interest claimed so as to satisfy the Registry as to the nature of the applicant's claim;

(d) (if the application is made with the consent of, rather than by, the registered proprietor or person entitled to be so registered) the relevant consent, which may be given in panel 11 of Form AN1, or (if the application is not made with such consent) evidence to satisfy the Registry as to the validity of the applicant's claim in accordance with LRA 2002, s 34(3)(c);

(e) (if the application is made by or with the consent of a person entitled to be registered as proprietor) evidence to satisfy the Registry of that person's entitlement to be registered as proprietor;

(f) where applicable, the appropriate SDLT certificate or other evidence (see *Stamp duty land tax*, page 541); and

(g) the fee payable (see *Fees*, page 221).

Before the Registry can enter an agreed notice in respect of an interest comprising a land transaction, it is obliged under Finance Act 2003, s 79(1) to ensure that the appropriate SDLT certificate accompanies the application where this is required.

Where the application is for entry of a home rights notice or its renewal, the appropriate application form is Form HR1 or Form HR2 (see *Home rights*, page 257).

An agreed notice must be entered in the charges register of the title affected. The agreed notice will give details of the interest protected and, in the case of a notice of a variation of an interest protected by a notice, details of the variation.

Cancellation of a notice other than a unilateral notice or a home rights notice

An applicant for the cancellation of a notice other than a unilateral notice or a home rights notice should deliver to the Registry:

(a) an application in Form CN1;

(b) (if the application relates to part only of the land to which the agreed notice relates) a plan or other sufficient details to allow the extent in question to be clearly identified on the Ordnance Survey map.

(c) evidence to satisfy the Registry that the interest has determined. Where appropriate, this should include evidence of devolution to prove determination of the interest and/or the right of the applicant to apply for the notice to be cancelled; and

(d)   the fee payable (see *Fees*, page 221).

Where the Registry is satisfied that the interest protected by the notice has come to an end, it must cancel the notice or make an entry in the register that the interest in question has come to an end. If the interest in question has come to an end in part only, an appropriate entry must be made in the register to reflect this (LRR 2003, r 87).

Unilateral notice

A unilateral notice may be entered without the consent of the registered proprietor and without the Registry having to be satisfied of the validity of the applicant's claim. Also, an application for entry of a unilateral notice may be preferred where the applicant does not wish the terms of the deed, order or document giving rise to the interest claimed to be open to public inspection and copying. Where the Registry enters a unilateral notice, it must give notice of the entry to the registered proprietor of the registered estate or registered charge affected.

An applicant for a unilateral notice should deliver to the Registry:

(a)   an application in Form UN1;

(b)   a plan of the affected land (where the interest claimed affects only part of the land in the registered title);

(c)   where applicable, the appropriate SDLT certificate or other evidence (see *Stamp duty land tax*, page 541); and

(d)   the fee payable (see *Fees*, page 221).

The statement in panel 11 or conveyancer's certificate in panel 12 of Form UN1 should be completed as appropriate, with the relevant details of the applicant's interest.

Before the Registry can enter a unilateral notice in respect of an interest comprising a land transaction, it is obliged under Finance Act 2003, s 79(1) to ensure that the appropriate SDLT certificate accompanies the application where this is required.

A unilateral notice must be entered in the charges register of the title affected. The first part of a unilateral notice in the register identifies that it is a unilateral notice and gives brief details of the interest protected. The second part identifies the beneficiary of the notice.

Registration of new or additional beneficiary of a unilateral notice

A person entitled to the benefit of an interest protected by a unilateral notice may apply to be entered in the register in place of, or in addition to, the existing registered beneficiary (LRR 2003, r 86). An applicant to be registered as beneficiary of an existing unilateral notice should deliver to the Registry:

(a)   an application in Form UN3;
(b)   evidence to satisfy the Registry as to the applicant's title to the interest protected by the unilateral notice (for example a transfer of the interest to the applicant);
(c)   where applicable, the consent of the existing registered beneficiary if he has not signed the Form UN3; and
(d)   the fee payable (see *Fees*, page 221).

Before entering the applicant in the register, the Registry will serve notice on the registered beneficiary of the unilateral notice, but need not do so if the registered beneficiary signs the Form UN3 or otherwise consents to the application, or if the applicant is the registered beneficiary's personal representative and evidence of his appointment accompanies the application. If the application is completed, details of the applicant will be entered in place of the existing registered beneficiary or jointly with that registered beneficiary as the case may be.

Removal of a unilateral notice

The registered beneficiary of a unilateral notice may apply in Form UN2 for the removal of the notice from the register (LRR 2003, r 85). No fee is currently payable. The application may also be made by the personal representative or trustee in bankruptcy of the registered beneficiary, in which case evidence of his appointment must accompany the application. If the Registry is satisfied that the application is in order, it must remove the unilateral notice.

Cancellation of a unilateral notice

The registered proprietor, or a person entitled to be registered as proprietor, of the registered estate or registered charge to which the unilateral notice relates, may apply at any time for the cancellation of that notice (LRA 2002, s 36).

The application must be made in Form UN4. No fee is currently payable. Where the application is by a person entitled to be registered as proprietor, it must be accompanied by evidence to satisfy the Registry of his entitlement, or his conveyancer must complete the certificate in panel 9 of Form UN4 to certify that he is satisfied that the applicant is entitled to be registered as proprietor. If the application relates to part only of the land to which the unilateral notice relates, a plan or other sufficient details to allow the extent in question to be clearly identified on the Ordnance Survey map must be lodged.

The Registry must give the registered beneficiary notice of the application and inform him that if he does not exercise his right to object within the relevant period, the Registry must cancel the unilateral notice. The relevant period is the period ending at 12 noon on the 15th working day after the date of issue of the notice or such longer period as the Registry may allow following a request by the beneficiary. The beneficiary must set out in such a request why a longer period should be allowed, and must make the request before the expiry of the period ending at 12 noon on the 15th working day after the date of issue of the notice. The Registry may, if it considers it appropriate, seek the views of the person who applied for cancellation. If, after considering such views and all other relevant matters, the Registry is satisfied that a longer period should be allowed, it may allow such period as it thinks appropriate, whether or not the period is the same as any period requested by the beneficiary. The longer period may never exceed a period ending at 12 noon on the 30th working day after the issue of the notice (LRR 2003, r 86). A working day is any day from Monday to Friday (inclusive) which is not Christmas Day, Good Friday or any other day either specified or declared by proclamation under Banking and Financial Dealings Act 1971, s 1 or appointed by the Lord Chancellor or certified by the Registry as being an 'interrupted day' due to delay or failure of a communication service or to some other event or circumstance causing substantial interruption in the normal operation of the Registry.

Only the person shown in the register as the beneficiary of the unilateral notice or a person entitled to be registered as the beneficiary of the unilateral notice may object to an application for cancellation of that notice (LRA 2002, s 73(3) and LRR 2003, r 86(7)). Where there are two or more persons who are shown in the register as beneficiary of the unilateral notice or who are entitled to be registered as beneficiary, each such person is a beneficiary of the unilateral notice and therefore has a right to object to its cancellation (LRR 2003, r 86(7)).

If the registered beneficiary or person entitled to be registered as beneficiary does not exercise his right to object to the cancellation of the unilateral notice within the relevant period, the Registry must cancel the unilateral notice (LRA 2002, s 36(3)).

Where the registered beneficiary or person entitled to be registered as beneficiary does wish to object to the cancellation of the unilateral notice, he must within the relevant period deliver to the Registry a written statement signed by him or his conveyancer (LRR 2003, r 19). The statement must give the full name of the beneficiary (or person entitled to be registered as beneficiary) and state that he objects to the cancellation of the unilateral notice and set out the grounds for the objection. If he wishes communications to be sent to an address other than his address for service, this should be stated.

Where an objection is made, if the Registry is satisfied that the objection is groundless, it need not give notice to the applicant and may cancel the unilateral notice. If the objection is not groundless, the Registry must give notice of it to the applicant for cancellation and may not cancel the unilateral notice until the objection has been disposed of (LRA 2002, s 73).

The beneficiary (or person entitled to be registered as beneficiary) and the applicant may still resolve their dispute by agreement. If, however, it is not possible to dispose of an objection by agreement, the Registry must refer the matter to the Tribunal. The Tribunal may, instead of deciding a matter itself, direct a party to the matter to commence proceedings, within a specified period, in the court for the purpose of obtaining the court's decision on the matter (LRA 2002, s 110(1)). A person aggrieved by a decision of the Tribunal may appeal to the Upper Tribunal (LRA 2002, s 111) (see *Disputes*, page 193).

NOTICES OF DEPOSIT

Instead of registering a mortgage with the Land Registry and holding a charge certificate, a lender used to be able to hold a borrower's land or charge certificate as security for the loan. Before 3 April 1995, the lender could apply for an entry to be made in the register giving notice that the certificate had been deposited with him. A notice of deposit, or notice of intended deposit, was entered in the register in respect of a lien created under LRA 1925, s 66. It has not been possible to make such an entry since the coming into force of the Land Registration Rules 1995 (SI 1995/140) on 3 April 1995. In the light of the decision in *United Bank of Kuwait v Sahib* [1997] Ch 107, it appears that it was not possible to create an equitable charge by deposit of a land certificate or charge certificate after the coming into force of the Law of Property (Miscellaneous Provisions) Act 1989, s 2 on 27 September 1989.

Where a notice of deposit, or a notice of intended deposit, of a land certificate or of a charge certificate has been entered in the register before 3 April 1995, it operates as a caution against dealings under the LRA 1925, s 54 (Land Registration Rules 1925, r 239(1) and LRA 2002, Sch 12, para 3). The transitional provisions contained in LRR 2003, rr 216 to 219 therefore apply. This is so even if the Registry has destroyed the land certificate or charge certificate in accordance with the power contained in LRA (TP) Order 2003, art 24(3) and (4).

Any entry of a notice of deposit or notice of intended deposit still subsisting in the register therefore continues to take effect as a caution against dealings (see *Cautions against dealings*, page 85). A notice of deposit, or notice of intended deposit, can be 'warned off' in the same way as a caution against dealings; a consent to cancellation may be given by the depositee or his personal representative or by his conveyancer.

When an entry of a notice of deposit or notice of intended deposit still subsists in the register and there is to be a transfer of part of the registered estate, or when a lease or rentcharge is to be granted out of the registered estate, a depositee usually provides a letter of consent which can then be sent to the Registry with the application to register the transfer or grant. When necessary, the consent must refer to a plan enabling the estate to which it relates to be identified on the title plan. A depositee's consent to a disposition may be by way of a letter or it may be endorsed by way of reply on a notice sent by the Registry to the depositee. Consent may be given by the depositee or his personal representative or by his conveyancer. A transfer of whole should be accompanied by a withdrawal of the notice of (intended) deposit.

The Registry will accept the following evidence as discharge for the purposes of cancelling an entry of a notice of deposit or notice of intended deposit:

(a)   an application in Form 86 to the Land Registration Rules 1925, provided it is dated before 13 October 2003;

(b)   the duplicate part of the original application Forms 85A, 85B or 85C for entry of the notice (under the Land Registration Rules 1925), provided it is dated before 13 October 2003;

(c)   a withdrawal in Form WCT by the chargee in whose favour the notice was made; or

(d)   an application in Form CCD by the proprietor of the registered estate or registered charge to which the notice relates, provided it is shown that the notice does not protect a valid interest, or that the interest has come to an end.

No fee is currently payable.

OFFICIAL COPIES AND INSPECTION

The LRA 2002 contains a general right to inspect and make copies which is much wider than was the case under the LRA 1925. This is in line with the Freedom of

Information Act 2000. LRA 2002, s 66(1) provides that any person may, subject to formalities and fee, inspect and make copies of:

(a)   the register of any individual registered title (including any title plan);
(b)   any document kept by the Registry which is referred to in the register;
(c)   any other document kept by the Registry which relates to an application to it; and
(d)   the caution register of an individual caution against first registration (including any caution plan).

However, the general right to inspect and make copies is subject to certain limitations imposed by LRR 2003, rr 133 and 135 which provide that the following 'excepted documents' are excepted from the general right:

(a)   exempt information documents;
(b)   an edited information document which has been replaced by another edited information document under LRR 2003, r 136(6) or r 138(4);
(c)   Form EX1A (reasons for exemption in support of an application to designate a document as an exempt information document);
(d)   Form CIT and any form which has been attached to Form CIT (application in connection with investigation or enforcement proceedings), together with any documents or copy documents prepared by the Registry in connection with the application;
(e)   any document relating to an application for a network access agreement under LRA 2002, Sch 5, para 1(4);
(f)   an 'identity document', i.e. any document within LRA 2002, s 66(1)(c) provided to, or prepared or obtained by, the Registry as evidence of identity of any person (such as an applicant);
(g)   an 'investigation of crime document', being any document within LRA 2002, s 66(1)(c) (other than an identity document) which relates to the prevention or detection of crime – *unless* it is a document:

(i)   lodged as part of or in support of either an application to the Registry or an objection to an application, or
(ii)   prepared by, or at the request of, the Registry as part of the process of considering an application or objection but which is not prepared principally in connection with the prevention or detection of crime.

In addition, correspondence and documents relating to claims for indemnity under LRA 2002, Sch 8 are also excepted from the general right. Also, the general right to inspect does not extend to the index of proprietors' names. However, these exceptions are in turn subject to special provision under LRR 2003, r 140, in relation to applications made in Form CIT in connection with court proceedings, insolvency and tax liability.

Personal inspection

A person may apply in Form PIC to make a personal inspection of the register and the documents referred to in LRA 2002, s 66(1) or (during the currency of a relevant notice given under LRR 2003, Sch 2) any part of them, subject to the exceptions referred to above. Land Registry offices are open to the public between the hours of 8.30am and 6pm Mondays to Fridays, excluding public holidays. Fees are payable for inspection, depending upon the subject matter. If the title number is not known, an additional fee may be payable. It is advisable to make an appointment to inspect, and to confirm the subject matter of what is to be inspected, in advance of a visit to a Land Registry office.

Official copies

An application may be made using Form OC1 for:

(a)   an official copy of an individual register or (during the currency of a relevant notice given under LRR 2003, Sch 2) any part of it;
(b)   an official copy of any title plan of an individual register;
(c)   an official copy of an individual caution register and caution plan; and
(d)   a certificate of inspection of any title plan.

A separate application must be made for each registered title or caution against first registration. A fee is payable (see *Fees*, page 221).

A certificate of inspection of a title plan will be issued by the Registry in Form CI and reveals whether the land in question is in the relevant title and whether it is affected by any colour or other reference shown on the title plan. The accuracy of the certificate will be guaranteed, but it will not confer on the applicant priority for the registration of any disposition.

An application may be made using Form OC2 for an official copy of any document referred to in the register of title and kept by the Registry, and any other document relating to an application that is kept by the Registry or (during the currency of a relevant notice given under LRR 2003, Sch 2) any part of such documents. Form EX2 is used for requests for official copies of exempt information documents (see 'Exempt information documents', below).

Official copies of registers and title plans are always timed and dated to show that they represent a true record at that specific time. Where there are pending substantive applications, the date and time will be backdated to immediately before receipt of the earliest pending application. An official search can also be made, to provide details of the pending application(s) if required. Official copies of documents are not dated because, once registered or otherwise referred to in the register, documents are not normally altered.

An official copy of the register, or of any document kept by the Registry which is referred to in the register or which relates to an application, is admissible in evidence to the same extent as the original (LRA 2002, s 67(1)). If there is a mistake in the official copy, a person who relies on that copy is not liable for loss suffered by another person by reason of the mistake (s 67(2)). A person is entitled to be indemnified by the Registry if he suffers loss by reason of a mistake in an official copy (LRA 2002, Sch 8, para 1(1)(d)) (see *Indemnity*, page 273).

Official copies are often of documents kept by the Registry which are not originals. As between the parties to a disposition relating to a registered title, the copy document kept by the registry is to be taken to be correct and to contain all the material parts of the original document (LRA 2002, s 120). No party to such disposition is to be affected by any provision of the original document not contained in the copy kept by the Registry, nor can any party require production of the original document.

Exempt information documents

A person may apply for the Registry to designate a document an 'exempt information document' if he claims that the document contains prejudicial information (LRR 2003, r 136). The document must be one referred to in the register of title, or one that relates to an application to the Registry, the original or a copy of which is kept by the Registry. Such application may accompany the application that will lead to the document being kept by the Registry. 'Prejudicial information' in this context means:

(a) information that relates to an individual who is the applicant and, if disclosed to other persons (whether to the public generally or specific persons) would, or would be likely to, cause substantial unwarranted damage or substantial unwarranted distress to the applicant or another; or

(b) information that if disclosed to other persons (whether to the public generally or specific persons) would, or would be likely to, prejudice the commercial interests of the applicant.

The application to designate a document an exempt information document must be made in Forms EX1 and EX1A. A fee is payable (see *Fees*, page 221). Form EX1A states the reasons for exemption. It should be borne in mind that Form EX1A is excepted from the general right of inspection and copying, but Form EX1 is not, nor are any accompanying letters. In addition to the document in question, the applicant must deliver to the Registry a copy which excludes the prejudicial information (with the words 'excluded information' inserted instead wherever information has been excluded within the document) and which is certified as being a true copy of the document from which the prejudicial information has been excluded except that it excludes the prejudicial information and includes the above wording instead.

Provided the Registry is satisfied that the applicant's claim is not groundless, it must designate the document an exempt information document and may make an appropriate entry in the register of any affected registered title. If, however, it considers that so designating it could prejudice the keeping of the register, it may cancel the application. Where a document is designated an exempt information document, the edited copy is known as the 'edited information document' and it is this which is supplied in response to a request for an official copy using Form OC2. The benefit of the designation of an exempt information document cannot be transferred to another person; for example on a transfer of the registered estate to which it relates.

Where a document has been designated an exempt information document, it is possible to make another application so that further information is excluded from the edited information document and a new edited information document is prepared (LRR 2003, r 136(6)).

It is possible for a person to apply for an official copy of an exempt information document using Form EX2 and stating why he considers that an official copy of the edited information document is not sufficient for his purposes. A fee is payable (see *Fees*, page 221). The applicant also has to state in Form EX2 why he considers that none of the information omitted from the edited information document is prejudicial information. Alternatively, if he accepts that some or all of the information is prejudicial information, he must give details and state why he considers that the public interest in providing an official copy of the exempt information document outweighs the public interest in not doing so.

The Registry must give notice of any such application to the person who applied for the document to be designated an exempt information document, unless it is satisfied that such notice is unnecessary or impracticable.

The Registry will supply an official copy of the exempt information document if it decides that none of the information excluded from the edited information document is prejudicial information. The Registry will also do so if it decides that, although some or all of the information excluded is prejudicial information, the public interest in providing an official copy of the exempt information document to the applicant outweighs the public interest in not doing so (LRR 2003, r 137). Application for an official copy of an exempt information document may also be made under LRR 2003, r 140 using Form CIT, in connection with court proceedings, insolvency or tax liability.

A person who applied for a document to be designated an exempt information document may apply in Form EX3 to have the designation removed. No fee is currently payable. The Registry must remove the designation and any entry in the register which relates to that designation, if it is satisfied that the application is in order. Where a document has been made an exempt document as a result of more than one application by different persons, the Registry must replace the existing edited information document with one that reflects only the current exemptions.

Freedom of Information Act 2000

The Freedom of Information Act 2000 came into force mainly on 1 January 2005 and generally allows inspection of all documents held by the Land Registry as a 'public authority'. Any person now has the right to ask a public authority for information and, if that authority holds it, to have that information disclosed to them unless there are justifiable reasons why this should not be done. Under the right of access provisions of the Freedom of Information Act:

(a)   a request must be in writing (which includes email or fax) and must include a name and address to which a response can be sent;
(b)   the request does not have to mention the Freedom of Information Act 2000;
(c)   the request can be made to any part of the public authority;
(d)   the authority must reply within 20 working days;
(e)   the authority has a duty to provide assistance to the applicant; and
(f)   the authority may charge a fee for providing the information.

A request to the Land Registry for information covered by the Freedom of Information Act 2000 may only be refused in the following circumstances:

(a)   where the Registry reasonably requires further information to identify and locate the information requested but the applicant has failed to supply it; or
(b)   where the request is 'vexatious' or repeated, for example where the Registry has previously complied with an identical or similar request from the same

applicant and a reasonable time has not elapsed between compliance with the previous request and the making of the current request; or

(c)   where the Registry estimates that the cost of complying with the request would exceed the 'appropriate limit' (currently £600); or

(d)   where an exemption applies and applying the 'public interest test' (if applicable) leads to the decision that it is not in the public interest to disclose the information (see below).

Exemptions from the obligation to disclose information can be absolute or non-absolute. If an absolute exemption applies, the information requested need not be disclosed and, in many cases, the Registry is not obliged to comply with the duty to confirm or deny whether it holds the requested information. Absolute exemption applies to requests for information reasonably accessible by other means. This means that the Freedom of Information Act 2000 does not apply, for example, to requests for official copies of registers, title plans, and documents relating to applications or to requests for historical copies of registers, as these are available under the general right under LRA 2002, s 66(1). Applications in that regard should therefore be made in the appropriate form, such as Form OC1 or as the case may be.

Information covered by the Registry's Publication Scheme is also absolutely exempt. The Freedom of Information Act 2000 requires the Registry to adopt and maintain a publication scheme setting out classes of information which it intends to make available to the public as a matter of course, the manner in which the information is to be made available and whether the information will be provided free or for a charge. The Registry's Publication Scheme is available on its website. Other examples of information covered by absolute exemption are information supplied by or relating to court records.

In the case of non-absolute exemptions, the Freedom of Information Act 2000 requires the Registry to consider whether or not the exemption applies and, if it does, then to consider the 'public interest test' before withholding or disclosing information. Examples of information covered by the non-absolute exemptions are personal information about third parties and information that constitutes a trade secret or the disclosure of which would, or would be likely to, prejudice the commercial interests of any person. Under the public interest test there is likely to be a public interest in disclosing information where it:

(a)   facilitates accountability and transparency in the spending of public money; or

(b)   allows individuals to understand decisions affecting their lives and, in some cases, assists individuals in challenging those decisions; or

(c)   brings to light information affecting public safety.

The LRA 2002 and the LRR 2003 were drafted to take account of the provisions of the Freedom of Information Act 2000, so it appears unlikely that inspection of exempt information would be allowed under that Act where it would not be allowed under the LRR 2003. However, it remains a possibility, which should be borne in mind when drafting documents relating to registered land.

In relation to a request under the Freedom of Information Act for personal inspection and copying, or for a copy of a document, or for historical information (as opposed to an application under the LRR 2003), the request should be made in accordance with the requirements set out above, for consideration by the Registry. There is no requirement to provide reasons for the request, but it may assist in cases where the public interest test needs to be applied.

In relation to a request for an official copy of an exempt information document under the Freedom of Information Act 2000 (as opposed to an application under the LRR 2003 in Form EX2), the request should be made in accordance with the requirements set out above, for consideration by the Registry. Again, there is no requirement to provide reasons for the request, but it may assist the Registry in deciding whether the full copy of the document can be provided.

Under the Freedom of Information Act 2000, the Registry may need to determine whether the excluded information is 'personal data' for the purposes of the Data Protection Act 1998 (see below), the disclosure of which would contravene any of the data protection principles in that Act. If it is, the information is exempt from the general right of access under the Freedom of Information Act 2000. If it is not, the Registry has to apply the public interest test in deciding whether a full copy of the document can be provided. The Registry will normally serve notice of the request upon any third party who may be affected by the decision and he will have the opportunity to make representations, which the Registry will take into account in making its decision.

A fee may be payable for a request under the Freedom of Information Act 2000. If the information cannot be provided within 20 working days, the Registry will inform the applicant in advance and provide an estimated time for dealing with the request. If the Registry decides to refuse a request for information, the applicant will be informed of this and the reasons for the decision.

Data Protection Act 1998

The Data Protection Act 1998 affects the Land Registry, but does not apply to the majority of the data that it holds because s 34 of that Act exempts information that is already publicly available; for example under the general right to inspect and make copies under LRA 2002, s 66(1). An application relating to such information should be made in the appropriate prescribed form, such as Form OC1 or as the case may be.

If a person as a 'data subject' makes a request under the Data Protection Act 1998 for personal data that is not already publicly available, it must be made in writing, accompanied by sufficient details to enable the Registry to locate the data, evidence of identity, and a fee of (currently) £10.

Under the Data Protection Act 1998, the Registry must deal with the request within 40 days. The response will provide details of the personal data held about the applicant, the purposes for which it is being used, and those to whom the data may be disclosed. If the data requested contains details about other living persons, the Registry may need to obtain their consent to divulge the data or it may edit the data to exclude those details. In this case, the 40-day period may be extended.

The General Data Protection Regulation ((EU) 2016/679) is directly applicable in all EU member states with effect from 25 May 2018. The new Regulation strengthens individuals' rights, and introduces new obligations on data controllers and data processors. The UK government has confirmed that it will adopt the new Regulation, and the Data Protection Bill 2017–19, once it receives Royal Assent, will supplement the Regulation and replace the 1998 Act.

OFFICIAL SEARCHES

In order to obtain up-to-date information as to all subsisting entries in the register of a title (including any which may have been made since an official copy of the register was obtained) and details of any pending applications in respect of a registered title, it is necessary to apply for an official search of the register. The LRA 2002 provides for a system of official searches of the register, which is operated in accordance with the LRR 2003. An application may be made for an official search with priority or an official search without priority. A fee is payable (see *Fees*, page 221).

Official search with priority

An official search with priority may be made only by a purchaser of the title in question. The search may be in respect of the individual register of a registered title or of a pending application for first registration (LRR 2003, r 147). A 'purchaser' for this purpose is a person who has entered into, or intends to enter into, a registrable disposition of a registered estate or registered charge for valuable consideration as disponee. 'Valuable consideration' does not include marriage consideration or a nominal consideration in money (LRA 2002, s 132(1)).

The purpose of such a search is to enable a purchaser to obtain an official certificate as to the entries in the register of the disponor's title immediately before completion and to ensure that (if he applies to register the disposition within the priority period conferred by the search) he will be unaffected by any entry made between the date of this certificate and the registration of their protectable disposition.

Lodging of official search

The application should be made in Form OS1 for a search of the whole of the estate in a registered title or application for first registration, and in Form OS2 for a search of part. No plan need accompany Form OS2 if the part affected is a numbered plot on an estate plan approved by the Registry relating to a developing estate, provided that the plot number(s) and the date of the Registry's approval are stated on the Form OS2. Where there is no approved estate plan, Form OS2 must be accompanied by a plan in duplicate; this plan should be a copy of the plan intended to be used in the protectable disposition.

The application can be made in paper form; or orally at any Land Registry Customer Service Centre (in the case of a search of whole); or, for Land Registry account holders only, by fax (in the case of an existing registered title only) or through the National Land Information Service (NLIS) or Business e-services or Business Gateway.

The 'search from' date

Application for an official search with priority must be from a date (the 'search from' date) which is the date shown on an official copy of the register of the individual registered title as the date on which the entries shown on that official copy were subsisting. A time is also printed on the official copy but this need not be quoted on an application for an official search. In the case of an electronic application, the search can be made from the date stated at the time of an access by remote terminal to the register of the individual registered title as the date on which the entries accessed were subsisting.

Official certificate of search

The result of a search is contained in an official search certificate issued by the Registry. It reveals details of any adverse entries made in the individual register on or after the day specified in the application as the 'search from' date. Details of any entries made in the register and subsequently cancelled during the period searched may not be given. It also reveals any pending application or pending official search with priority affecting the registered title entered on the day list. The date and time at which the priority period commences and expires are stated.

Additionally, in the case of a search in respect of an estate which is the subject of a pending application for first registration, the official search certificate will also enable the purchaser to satisfy himself that the estate searched is the subject of a pending first registration application, and will state by whom the application was made and on what date the application was received. It will not contain details of any entries that may be made in the register of title arising from the deeds or other evidence of title produced with the application for first registration. The same priority protection is conferred as that in relation to an official search of an existing registered title, but no guarantee is given that any registered title will be granted or, if granted, that it will be of the class of title sought.

Accuracy of an official search certificate is guaranteed and indemnity may be payable by the Registry as a result of any mistake in an official search (LRA 2002, Sch 8, para 1(1)(c)) (see *Indemnity*, page 273).

If the extent of the property to which the search relates is not wholly comprised within the registered title, the official search certificate will be limited to the extent which falls within the title. The details of the limitation and the reason for it will normally be included with the official search certificate, but the applicant should not seek to rely on this as a means of 'confirming' the registered proprietor's title and should instead rely on a proper investigation of that title.

Priority period of official search

The priority period provided by the official search is the period beginning at the time when the application for the official search is entered on the day list and ending at midnight marking the end of the 30th working day thereafter. A working day is any day from Monday to Friday (inclusive) which is not Christmas Day, Good Friday or any other day either specified or declared by proclamation under Banking and Financial Dealings Act 1971, s 1 or appointed by the Lord Chancellor or certified by the Registry as being an 'interrupted day' due to delay or failure of a communication service or to some other event or circumstance causing substantial interruption in the normal operation of the Registry.

See *Priorities*, page 452, for the position where two or more official search certificates with priority relating to the same registrable estate or charge or to the same registered land have been issued.

The priority period resulting from an official search in respect of a registrable disposition is also conferred on any prior registrable disposition affecting the same registered land on which that application is dependent (LRR 2003, r 151). For example, in the common situation where a person is purchasing registered land and is entering into a legal charge at the same time, a search by the intending chargee confers the same priority period on the intending transferee. The same applies where the search relates to a pending first registration. Where an application is lodged, or deemed to be lodged, at the same time as the priority period of a search expires, the application is taken as being made within that priority period (LRR 2003, r 154).

Effect of priority

An official search certificate with priority confers priority upon an application to register the protected disposition, over applications relating to other registrable dispositions and other matters which were not entered on the day list prior to that search and are not themselves protected by an earlier official search with priority.

An application protected by an official search with priority will have priority over an application protected by another official search with priority, in respect of the same registered estate or charge, where the first search is deemed to have been delivered before the second one.

If the completion of the protected disposition is delayed to an extent likely to preclude the delivery of the application for registration within the priority period, a second application for an official search may be made, whether the priority period under the first official search certificate is still subsisting or has expired. However, the second official search certificate will *not* operate to 'extend' the priority afforded by the first. It will only provide a separate priority period, which will not provide priority over any application lodged before its priority period commences.

Any entry made in the register during the priority period conferred by an official search will be postponed to a subsequent application to register the protectable disposition to which the priority period relates, unless the earlier entry was itself protected by an official search with a priority period ranking ahead of the one relating to the subsequent application (LRA 2002, s 72(2) and (3)). For this reason, where an official search with priority has not yet expired and has priority over an application on the day list, the Registry will not normally complete that application until the priority period of the search has expired (LRA 2002, s 72(5)).

Withdrawal of official search with priority

A person who has made an application for an official search with priority may withdraw that official search (LRR 2003, r 150). On withdrawal the priority period ceases to have effect. Where an entry has already been made in the register in respect of a disposition protected by the search, the search cannot be withdrawn.

Official search without priority

Any person may apply for an official search without priority using Form OS3 (LRR 2003, r 155). This form of official search is available to a person who is not a 'purchaser' (see above); for example, a mortgagee who intends to protect his mortgage in the register by entry of a notice. Such a search can only be made in respect of a registered title; it cannot be used to search against a pending first registration. The position with regard to plans for a search of part is the same as that for official searches in Form OS2 (see 'Official search with priority', above). The application can be made in paper form; or orally at any Land Registry Customer Service Centre (in the case of a search of whole); or, for Land Registry account holders only, by fax or through the NLIS (in the case of a search of whole or part) or through Business e-services (in the case of a search of whole).

Similar information is supplied with the result of an official search without priority as with the result of an official search with priority, but no priority period is given. The accuracy of the certificate is guaranteed but it will not confer on the applicant priority for the registration of any disposition.

Where an intending applicant is not a purchaser, so that only an official search without priority may be made, the possibility of reserving a period by means of an outline application should be considered.

Official search by a mortgagee in Form HR3

The proprietor of a registered charge or a mortgagee of registered land may search the register to enable him to comply with the provisions of FLA 1996, s 56(3) (see *Home rights*, page 257).

Outline applications

Previously, under LRR 2003, r 54 it was possible to use an outline application as a means of reserving a priority period for certain applications which could not be protected by an official search with priority, such as an application to register a registrable disposition not made for valuable consideration, or for entry of a restriction. The period reserved by the outline application commenced at the date and time it was entered on the day list and was a period expiring at 12 noon on the 4th working day following the day that the outline application was made. If, during that reserved period, the applicant delivered to the correct office of the Registry the relevant application form, together with the appropriate documentation and the prescribed fee, the application was dealt with in accordance with the date and time at which the outline application was received. The facility to make an outline application was withdrawn on 6 April 2018.

OFFICIAL SEARCHES OF THE INDEX

The Registry is obliged under LRA 2002, s 68 and LRR r 10 and 11 to keep certain indices. These are an index map, an index of verbal descriptions of relating franchises and manors and an index of proprietors' names. Both the index map and the index of verbal descriptions of relating franchises and manors are open to inspection and any person may apply for an official search of the indices. The index of proprietors' names is not open to general inspection, but the LRR 2003 provides for certain limited rights to make an official search of that index.

Search of the index map

The index map is a large scale map from which it is possible to ascertain, in relation to a parcel of land, whether there is:

(a) a pending application for first registration (other than in respect of title to a relating franchise);
(b) a pending application for a caution against first registration (other than where the subject of the caution is a relating franchise);
(c) a registered estate in land;
(d) a registered rentcharge;
(e) a registered profit à prendre in gross;
(f) a registered affecting franchise; or
(g) a caution against first registration (other than where the subject of the caution is a relating franchise).

If there is such a registered estate or caution, the index map provides the title number.

An affecting franchise is a franchise which relates to a defined area of land and is an adverse right affecting, or capable of affecting, the title to an estate or charge. A relating franchise is a franchise which is not an affecting franchise (see *Franchises*, page 240).

An application for an official search of the index map is made using Form SIM, or through the Land Registry Telephone Services, Business e-services or Business Gateway. The application must clearly describe the land to which it relates. The description should include the postal number or description, the road name, the locality, the town, the local authority serving the property, the post code and/or Ordnance Survey map reference (if known) and any known title number. If the search is in respect of a particular flat in a block of flats, this should be made clear in the description. A plan may not be necessary if the land can be identified by postal description. If, however, the Registry so requires, an applicant must provide a copy of an extract from the Ordnance Survey map on the largest scale published showing the land to which the application relates (LRR 2003, r 145). A fee is payable (see *Fees*, page 221).

The result of an official search of the index map will be in paper form and include the date and time of the official search certificate; a description of the land searched; details of any of the matters referred to in (a) to (g) above which affect the land; and, if there is a registered estate or caution, the title number.

It should be remembered that the index map is only an index and that any plan attached to the result of an official search is merely illustrative and does not define the extent of the land in a title. If more specific information is required about a title revealed by the result of a search of the index map, the applicant should obtain official copies of the register and title plan of that title (see *Official copies and inspection*, page 396).

Search of the index of relating franchises and manors

The index of relating franchises and manors is an index of verbal descriptions of:

(a) pending applications for first registrations of title to relating franchises;
(b) pending applications for cautions against first registration where the subject of the caution is a relating franchise;
(c) registered franchises which are relating franchises;
(d) registered manors; and

(e)   cautions against first registration where the subject of the caution is a relating franchise.

If there are any such registered estates and cautions, the index provides the title numbers arranged by administrative area.

An application for an official search of the index of relating franchises and manors is made using Form SIF. A fee is payable (see *Fees*, page 221).

In Form SIF the applicant must specify whether he is searching in respect of manors or relating franchises or both, and must also specify the administrative areas (that is, the relevant counties and/or unitary authorities) in respect of which he is searching.

The result of an official search of the index of relating franchises and manors will be in paper form and include the date and time of the official search certificate; a description of the administrative area(s) searched; details of any of the matters referred to in (a) to (e) above which affect the administrative area(s); and, if there is a registered estate or caution, the title number.

It should be remembered that the index of relating franchises and manors is only an index and that if more specific information is required about a title revealed by the result of a search of the index, the applicant should obtain official copies of the register and title plan of that title (see *Official copies and inspection*, page 396).

Search of the index of proprietors' names

The index of proprietors' names shows for each individual register the name of the proprietor of the registered estate and the proprietor of any registered charge together with the title number (LRR 2003, r 11). Until every register is kept electronically, the index need not contain the name of any corporate or joint proprietor of an estate or of a charge registered as proprietor prior to 1 May 1972. The index of proprietors' names is not open to general inspection. However, in addition to the special right to a search made in Form CIT (application in connection with court proceedings, insolvency and tax liability), any person may apply for a search to be made in the index in respect of either his own name, the name of a corporation aggregate, or the name of some other person in whose property he can satisfy the Registry that he is interested generally. For example, he may be interested as personal representative or trustee in bankruptcy.

An application for a search in the index of proprietors' names is made using Form PN1. Only one name can be searched on each form; where there is a former name or alternative name, a separate Form PN1 should be used for each. Every address which may have been used as an address for service in the register should be stated. A fee is payable (see *Fees*, page 221).

The reply to the application will state whether or not the person named in the search appears in the index and, if he does, the reply will also give the relevant title number(s). The reply does not constitute an official search for the purposes of the LRA 2002.

OPTIONS

An option to purchase, or to renew a lease of, registered land may be protected by the entry in the register of an agreed notice or a unilateral notice, and possibly (depending on the terms of the option agreement) a restriction. A notice does not necessarily mean that the option is valid but does mean that the priority of the option will be protected on any registered disposition (LRA 2002, ss 29, 30 and 32). A restriction does not confer any priority; it simply prevents an entry being made in the register in respect of any disposition, or a disposition of a specified kind, unless the terms of the restriction have (where applicable) been complied with. The protection given to the option may also extend to the subsequent estate contract when the option is exercised (*Armstrong & Holmes Ltd v Holmes* [1994] 1 All ER 826).

An option is not itself an interest within LRA 2002, Sch 1 or Sch 3 which overrides either first registration or registered dispositions. Its priority therefore needs to be protected by entry of a notice in the register.

However, even where an option relating to registered land is not protected by a notice, it may still override a later registered disposition for valuable consideration if, at the time of that later disposition, the person having the benefit of the option is in actual occupation of the land to which the contract relates. If he is in actual occupation of only part of the land to which the option relates, he has an overriding interest only in respect of the part he is occupying (LRA 2002, ss 29 and 30 and Sch 3, para 2).

The interest of the person in actual possession does not override a registered disposition if enquiry was made of him before the disposition and he failed to disclose the option when he could reasonably have been expected to do so. Nor does the option override a registered disposition if it belongs to a person whose occupation would not have been obvious on a reasonably careful inspection of the land at the time of the disposition, and if the person to whom the disposition is made does not have actual knowledge of the option at the time of the disposition (LRA 2002, Sch 3, para 2).

Where the option is contained in a lease that is an unregistered interest falling within LRA 2002, Sch 3, para 1 which overrides registered dispositions, the option may be protected by an entry in the register even where no entry may be made as to the lease itself (i.e. because the lease is for a term not exceeding 3 years and is not otherwise registrable). This applies even if the interest to be granted under the option is another lease which will be an interest which overrides registered dispositions.

The option should be granted and signed by the proprietor of the registered estate, or a satisfactory chain of title shown between the person granting the option and the registered proprietor. For example, if the registered proprietor has contracted to sell a registered title to A, and A then grants to B an option to purchase the land in the title, B's option can be protected by a notice, whether or not A's contract is also protected by a notice.

An option granted before the coming into force of the Perpetuities and Accumulations Act 2009 on 6 April 2010 may become void for remoteness if it breaches the rule against perpetuities (Perpetuities and Accumulations Act 1964, ss 9 and 10). An option granted after that date is no longer subject to the rule against perpetuities (Perpetuities and Accumulations Act 2009, s 1).

Before the Registry can enter an agreed notice or unilateral notice in respect of an interest comprising a land transaction, it is obliged under Finance Act 2003, s 79(1) to ensure that the appropriate SDLT certificate accompanies the application where this is required.

Agreed notice

In addition to the usual documents required (see *Notices*, page 389), an applicant should deliver to the Registry the original document granting the option or a certified copy of it.

Where the option is granted by a person with the benefit of a contract for sale, the contract or a certified copy of it should be included with the application. This is not necessary if there is already an agreed notice in respect of the contract in the register.

Where the consent of the registered proprietor is not available but, for example, the document granting the option is signed by him, this is likely to be sufficient to satisfy the Registry as to the validity of the applicant's claim for the purposes of LRA 2002, s 34(3)(c).

The agreed notice in the register will give details of the interest protected.

An application for entry of a unilateral notice may be preferred where the applicant does not wish the terms of the option to be open to public inspection and copying.

Unilateral notice

An applicant should deliver to the Registry the usual documents required (see *Notices*, page 389).

The statement in panel 11 or conveyancer's certificate in panel 12 of Form UN1 should be completed on the following lines to show the interest of the applicant:

> person having the benefit of an option [*to purchase*] *or* [*to renew a lease*] contained in a [*description of document*] dated [*date*] made between [*names*].

Where the option is granted by a person with the benefit of a contract for sale, the contract should also be referred to. The wording must establish the link between the registered proprietor and the person who is to be shown as the beneficiary of the notice.

The unilateral notice in the register will give brief details of the interest protected and identify the beneficiary of that notice.

Restriction

As a result of LRA 2002, s 42(2) no restriction may be entered for the purpose of protecting the priority of an interest which is, or could be, the subject of a notice. This does not, however, prevent the entry of a restriction in addition to the notice of the option, where appropriate. Although the notice will protect the priority of the option, a restriction may be used to ensure that any conditions in relation to another disposition by the registered proprietor are complied with. The consent of the registered proprietor to the entry of the restriction is required, unless the document granting the option contains a provision which limits the registered proprietor's powers to enter into any further disposition. The Registry must give notice of the application for a restriction to the proprietor of the registered estate or charge concerned, if it has not been made by or with the consent of such proprietor or a person entitled to be registered as such proprietor (LRA 2002, s 45).

An applicant should deliver to the Registry the usual documents required (see *Restrictions*, page 500).

If the application is made by a person who claims that he has a sufficient interest in the making of the entry, a statement in panel 12 of Form RX1 signed by the applicant or a certificate by his conveyancer in panel 13 of Form RX1 must be provided, setting out details of the option and of the provision in the document granting the option limiting the registered proprietor's powers to enter into a disposition.

Panel 9 of Form RX1 should be completed as to the required restriction(s). A restriction in a standard form contained in LRR 2003, Sch 4 does not require the approval of the Registry to the terms of the restriction under LRA 2002, s 43(3). A possible form of restriction based on Form L is:

> No disposition of the registered estate by the proprietor of the registered estate is to be registered without a written certificate signed by [*purchaser*] of [*address*] or their conveyancer that the provisions of [*clause, paragraph or other particulars*] of [*details of document granting the option*] have been complied with or that they do not apply to the disposition.

Form RX1 does not need to be used if the application is for a standard form restriction and is contained in either the 'additional provisions' panel of a prescribed form of transfer or assent, or in clause LR13 of a prescribed clauses lease (or any other lease containing clauses LR1 to LR14 of LRR 2003, Sch 1A) (LRR 2003, r 92(7)).

Options contained in registrable dispositions

Although an option may be granted by way of a separate transaction, it can also form part of the terms of a registrable disposition such as a transfer or a lease. In the case of a transfer of part of a registered title, the Registry must (where appropriate) make entries in the relevant registered title in respect of any rights, provisions or other matters created by the transfer which are capable of being so entered. However, the Registry need make no such entries where the relevant title numbers have not been given in panel 2 of Form AP1, unless separate application is made in respect of them (LRR 2003, r 72). Similar provisions apply in the case of a transfer of the whole of a registered title, or other registrable disposition (LRR 2003, r 72C).

In the case of a lease granted out of a registered estate in land which is required to be registered under LRA 2002, s 27(2)(b), LRR 2003, r 72A specifies certain entries which the Registry is obliged to make on registration of the lease. This applies to both prescribed clauses leases and other leases. On completion of such a lease by registration, the Registry must (where appropriate) make entries in the relevant registered title in respect of interests contained in the lease which are of the nature referred to in clause LR9 (rights of acquisition etc). However, where the lease is a prescribed clauses lease and the rights are not specified or referred to in clause LR9, the Registry need take no action in respect of them unless a separate application is made. Equally, the Registry need not make any entries where, in the case of a prescribed clauses lease, the title numbers of the relevant registered titles have not been given in clause LR2.2; or in any other case, the title numbers of the relevant registered titles required by clause LR2.2 have not been given in panel 2 of Form AP1 lodged for the purpose of completing the lease by registration, unless a separate application is made.

OVERREACHING

Overreaching occurs where there is a disposition of land, which is subject to a trust of land, and capital money arises; for example on a sale of the property. It is the mechanism under which the capital money is paid to not less than two trustees (or to a sole personal representative acting as such) or to a trust corporation, so that the equitable interests of the beneficiaries under the trust are transferred to the capital monies (such as the proceeds of sale), leaving the purchaser to take free of those interests (Law of Property Act 1925, ss 2 and 27).

In relation to registered estates which are subject to a trust of land, the entry of a restriction in Form A in the register reflects the existence of the trust and ensures that overreaching is effected on a disposition for value of the land (LRA 2002, s 42(1)(b) and LRR 2003, r 94).

Overreaching is discussed in more detail in the relevant sections of this book. See, in particular, *Joint proprietors*, page 286, *Personal representatives*, page 435, and *Trusts of land*, page 555.

OVERRIDING INTERESTS

Overriding interests (referred to in the LRA 2002 as 'interests which override') are unregistered interests which will override first registration or registered dispositions, as the case may be, notwithstanding that no entry in respect of them is made in the register. Unlike the LRA 1925, the LRA 2002 draws a distinction between unregistered interests which override first registration (as set out in LRA

2002, Sch 1 and s 90) and unregistered dispositions which override registered dispositions (as set out in LRA 2002, Sch 3 and s 90). Although many of the interests are the same in both schedules, there are certain important differences.

Unregistered interests which override first registration

On first registration, the registered estate is vested in the proprietor subject to any of the following interests which affect the estate at that time and which are not the subject of an entry in the register of that estate (LRA 2002, ss 11 and 12).

Leasehold estates in land

A lease of land granted for a term not exceeding 7 years from the date of the grant overrides first registration, unless such lease is one required to be registered under LRA 2002, s 4(1)(d), (e) or (f). A grant out of an unregistered freehold estate, or leasehold estate with more than 7 years to run, which is to take effect in possession after the end of the period of 3 months beginning with the date of the grant, is required to be registered under LRA 2002, s 4(1)(d). A grant of a lease out of an unregistered legal estate in land pursuant to HA 1985, Pt 5 (the right to buy) is required to be registered under LRA 2002, s 4(1)(e). A grant of a lease out of an unregistered legal estate in land in circumstances where HA 1985, s 171A applies (disposal by landlord which leads to a person's no longer being a secure tenant; the preserved right to buy) is required to be registered under LRA 2002, s 4(1)(f).

A lease granted for a term not exceeding 21 years was an overriding interest under LRA 1925, s 70(1)(k). Any such overriding interest subsisting in relation to a registered estate on 13 October 2003 continues to have overriding status (LRA 2002, Sch 12, para 12).

Interests of persons in actual occupation

An interest belonging to a person in actual occupation, so far as relating to land of which he is in actual occupation, except for an interest under a settlement under the SLA 1925, overrides first registration. Such an overriding interest extends only to land in the registered title which is actually occupied by the person having the interest. It is the interest, not the occupation, which takes effect as an overriding interest. The interest protected is not therefore confined to a right of occupation; for example, an option to purchase in favour of the person in actual occupation may be an overriding interest. However, the protection of the interest extends only to that land of which the person is in actual occupation; if a person only occupies part of the land to which an interest relates, the interest only has overriding status for that part. It should be noted that, unlike the position under the LRA 1925, the receipt of rents and profits is not sufficient for these purposes.

Easements and profits à prendre

A legal easement or profit à prendre overrides first registration. This will not be the case in relation to an equitable easement.

Customary rights

A customary right overrides first registration. Customary rights are rights enjoyed by members of a local community or a defined class of such community members. They are usually ancient in origin.

Public rights

A public right overrides first registration. Public rights are rights which are exercisable by any member of the public, such as a public right of way over a highway (*Overseas Investment Services Ltd v Simcobuild Construction Ltd* (1995) 70 P & CR 322). The vesting of the fee simple of a highway in the highway authority may be a public right for this purpose (*Secretary of State for the Environment, Transport and the Regions v Baylis (Gloucester) Ltd* [2000] EWCA Civ 361).

Local land charges

A local land charge overrides first registration (see *Local land charges*, page 367).

Mines and minerals

Certain interests relating to mines and minerals override first registration (see *Coal*, page 135, and *Mines and minerals*, page 380).

Franchise

A franchise was formerly an interest which overrode first registration. However, a franchise ceased to be an overriding interest at the end of 10 years from 13 October 2003 (LRA 2002, s 117(1)) (see *Franchises*, page 240).

Manorial rights

A manorial right was formerly an interest which overrode first registration. However, a manorial right ceased to be an overriding interest at the end of 10 years from 13 October 2003 (LRA 2002, s 117(1)) (see *Manors*, page 372).

Crown rents

A right to rent which was reserved to the Crown on the granting of any freehold estate (whether or not the right is still vested in the Crown) was formerly an interest which overrode first registration. A Crown rent includes, but may not be limited to, the rent payable to the Crown for freehold land in a manor of ancient demesne, or the rent reserved to the Crown under the grant of a freehold estate, whether or not that estate was situated in a manor of ancient demesne. In practice such Crown rents occur most commonly on conveyances of foreshore by the Board of Trade.

Such Crown rents ceased to be overriding interests at the end of 10 years from 13 October 2003 (LRA 2002, s 117(1)). The person having the benefit of the interest (if its priority has not already been previously defeated and it continues to subsist) should therefore protect it. In the case of unregistered burdened land, he should apply for a caution against first registration. If he does not do so, the priority of the interest is liable to be defeated on a subsequent first registration of unregistered burdened land (LRA 2002, ss 11 and 12). Until 12 October 2013, no fee was payable for such an application, but the normal fee will now apply.

A person applying for a caution against first registration should deliver to the Registry the usual documents required (see *Cautions against first registration*, page 88).

Either the cautioner (or at least one of them, if there is more than one cautioner), or someone authorised by the cautioner, or the cautioner's conveyancer must make the statement of truth in panel 10. No documents should be exhibited, as the statement should be self-contained. The statement of truth should be completed on the following lines to show the interest of the applicant:

> the person entitled to the benefit of a Crown rent of [*specify details*] charged on [*insert description*] arising by reason of [*summarise the basis on which the interest arises, including evidence of devolution to the applicant where necessary*] and which continues to be payable by [*specify relevant details*].

The interest stated in the Form CT1 will appear in the caution register, together with a description of the legal estate to which the caution relates. For the effect of the caution against first registration, see *Cautions against first registration*, page 88.

Non-statutory rights in respect of an embankment or sea or river wall

The benefit of a non-statutory right in respect of an embankment or sea or river wall overrides first registration (see *Embankments or sea or river walls*, page 202).

Rights to payment in lieu of tithe

A right to payment in lieu of tithe was formerly an interest which overrode first registration. In practice these rights are only likely to be corn rents where the liability to pay arises by an Act other than a Tithe Act and is in commutation of tithes.

Such rights ceased to be overriding interests at the end of 10 years from 13 October 2003 (LRA 2002, s 117(1)). The person having the benefit of the interest (if its priority has not already been previously defeated and it continues to subsist) should therefore protect it. In the case of unregistered burdened land, he should apply for a caution against first registration. If he does not do so, the priority of the interest is liable to be defeated on a subsequent first registration of unregistered burdened land (LRA 2002, ss 11 and 12). Until 12 October 2013, no fee was payable for such an application, but the normal fee will now apply.

A person applying for a caution against first registration should deliver to the Registry the usual documents required (see *Cautions against first registration*, page 88).

Either the cautioner (or at least one of them, if there is more than one cautioner), or someone authorised by the cautioner, or the cautioner's conveyancer must make the statement of truth in panel 10. No documents should be exhibited, as the statement should be self-contained. The statement of truth should be completed on the following lines to show the interest of the applicant:

> the person entitled to a right to payment in lieu of tithe [*specify details*] payable out of or charged on [*insert description*] arising under [*insert details of relevant statutory provision, and include details of devolution to the applicant where necessary*] and which continues to be payable by [*specify relevant details*].

The interest stated in the Form CT1 will appear in the caution register, together with a description of the legal estate to which the caution relates. For the effect of the caution against first registration, see *Cautions against first registration*, page 88.

Rights in respect of the repair of a church chancel

A right in respect of the repair of a church chancel was formerly an interest which overrode first registration. However, such rights ceased to be an overriding interest at the end of 10 years from 13 October 2003 (Land Registration Act 2002 (Transitional Provisions) (No 2) Order 2003 (SI 2003/2431)) (see *Chancel repair*, page 96).

Public-private partnership leases relating to transport in London

A PPP lease overrides first registration (see *Public-private partnership leases relating to transport in London*, page 473).

Rights acquired under the Limitation Act 1980

For the period of 3 years beginning on 13 October 2003, a right acquired under the Limitation Act 1980 before 13 October 2003 overrode first registration (LRA 2002, Sch 12, para 7). This applied even if the squatter was no longer in actual occupation. The 3-year period expired on 12 October 2006.

Unregistered interests which override registered dispositions

A registrable disposition for valuable consideration of a registered estate or registered charge is subject to any interest falling within LRA 2002, Sch 3 which affects the estate at the time of the disposition and which is not the subject of an entry in the register of that estate (LRA 2002, ss 29 and 30). Any interest which has been the subject of a notice in the register at any time on or after 13 October 2003 is not treated as falling within LRA 2002 Sch 3 for these purposes.

The unregistered interests which override registered dispositions are mainly the same as those described above as overriding first registration. The differences are as follows.

Leasehold estates in land

A lease the grant of which constitutes a registrable disposition does not override another registrable disposition. LRA 2002, Sch 12, para 12 provides that leases granted prior to 13 October 2003 for a term of less than 21 years retain the overriding status they enjoyed by virtue of the LRA 1925, s 70(1)(k).

Interests of persons in actual occupation

In addition to the exception of interests under settlements referred to above, the following interests of a person in actual occupation are not included in LRA 2002, Sch 3:

(a)   an interest of a person of whom enquiry was made before the disposition and who failed to disclose the right when he could reasonably have been expected to do so;

(b)   an interest which belongs to a person whose occupation would not have been obvious on a reasonably careful inspection of the land at the time of the disposition and of which the person to whom the disposition is made does not have actual knowledge at that time; and

(c)   a leasehold estate in land granted to take effect in possession after the end of the period of 3 months beginning with the date of the grant and which has not taken effect in possession at the time of the disposition.

Under the LRA 1925, s 70(1)(g) an interest could be an overriding interest by virtue of a person's receipt of rents and profits. Such an interest subsisting on 13 October 2003 will continue to override registered dispositions provided the receipt of rents and profits continues (LRA 2002, Sch 12, para 8). Such an interest does not override if enquiry was made of the person having the benefit of it before the disposition and that person failed to disclose the right when he could reasonably have been expected to do so.

Easements and profits à prendre

Although all legal easements and profits à prendre override first registration, the position is not the same for registered dispositions. Under LRA 2002, Sch 3, para 3, a legal easement or profit à prendre overrides a registered disposition only if:

(a)   at the time of the disposition it is within the actual knowledge of the person to whom the disposition is made; or

(b)   at the time of the disposition it would have been obvious on a reasonably careful inspection of the land over which the easement or profit is exercisable; or

(c)   the person entitled to the easement or profit proves that it has been exercised in the period of one year ending with the day of the disposition; or

(d)   in the case of a profit à prendre, it is registered under the CRA 1965.

Any easement or profit à prendre, however, which was an overriding interest immediately before 13 October 2003, but which would not fall within LRA 2002, Sch 3, para 3 if created on or after 13 October 2003, continues to be an overriding interest (LRA 2002, Sch 12, para 9). This includes equitable easements that were openly exercised and enjoyed as appurtenant to the dominant tenement which took effect as overriding interests on the registered servient title under the Land Registration Rules 1925, r 258.

For a period of 3 years beginning on 13 October 2003, the exceptions referred to in (a) to (d) above did not apply, so that any unregistered legal easement or profit à prendre overrode a registered disposition (LRA 2002, Sch 12, para 10). The 3-year period expired on 12 October 2006. Any unregistered easement or profit à prendre over registered land arising on or after 13 October 2003, will be a legal easement or profit only if it is an implied or prescriptive easement or profit.

Local land charges

Under LRA 2002, Sch 12, para 13, certain local land charges which had overriding status by virtue of LRA 1925, s 70(1)(i) will retain that status indefinitely (see *Local land charges*, page 367).

Crown rents

Crown rents ceased to be overriding interests at the end of 10 years from 13 October 2003 (LRA 2002, s 117(1)). The person having the benefit of the interest (if its priority has not already been previously defeated and it continues to subsist) should therefore protect it in the register. If he does not do so, the priority of the interest is liable to be defeated on a subsequent registration of a registrable disposition of registered burdened land for valuable consideration (LRA 2002, ss 29 and 30). In the case of registered burdened land he should apply for the entry in the register of an agreed notice or a unilateral notice. Until 12 October 2013, no fee was payable for such an application, but the normal fee will now apply.

In addition to the usual documents required (see *Notices*, page 389), a person applying for an agreed notice should deliver to the Registry the deed, order or instrument giving rise to the interest claimed or a certified copy of it, or (if there is no such deed, order or instrument) other details of the interest claimed so as to satisfy the Registry as to the nature of the applicant's claim.

Documentary evidence of the Crown rent will normally consist of a certified copy of the grant under which the Crown rent arises and, where the applicant is not the Crown, evidence of the devolution of the Crown rent to the applicant and confirmation that the Crown rent is still payable;

The agreed notice in the register will give details of the interest protected.

Where the registered proprietor does not consent to the entry in the register of an agreed notice and evidence to satisfy the Registry as to the validity of the applicant's claim cannot be lodged, an application for entry of a unilateral notice may still be made.

A person applying for a unilateral notice should deliver to the Registry the usual documents required (see *Notices*, page 389).

The statement in panel 11 or conveyancer's certificate in panel 12 of Form UN1 should be completed on the following lines to show the interest of the applicant:

> owner of the following Crown rent affecting the land: [*set out details of the Crown rent including details of the grant under which it arose and, where the applicant is not the Crown, details of the devolution of the Crown rent to the applicant and confirmation that the Crown rent is still payable*].

The unilateral notice in the register will give brief details of the interest protected and identify who are the beneficiaries of that notice.

Rights to payment in lieu of tithe

A right to payment in lieu of tithe ceased to be an overriding interest at the end of 10 years from 13 October 2003 (LRA 2002, s 117(1)). The person having the benefit of the right (if its priority has not already been previously defeated and it continues to subsist) should therefore protect it in the register. If he does not do so, the priority of the right is liable to be defeated on a subsequent registration of a registrable disposition of registered burdened land for valuable consideration (LRA 2002, ss 29 and 30). In the case of registered burdened land he should apply for the entry in the register of an agreed notice or a unilateral notice. Until 12 October 2013, no fee was payable for such an application, but the normal fee will now apply.

In addition to the usual documents required (see *Notices*, page 389), a person applying for an agreed notice should deliver to the Registry the deed, order or instrument giving rise to the interest claimed or a certified copy of it, or (if there is no such deed, order or instrument) other details of the interest claimed so as to satisfy the Registry as to the nature of the applicant's claim.

Documentary evidence of the right to payment in lieu of tithe will normally consist of confirmation as to the statutory provision on which the payment is based, evidence of the devolution to the applicant of the benefit of the right to the payment and confirmation that the payment is still payable;

The agreed notice in the register will give details of the interest protected.

Where the registered proprietor does not consent to the entry in the register of an agreed notice and evidence to satisfy the Registry as to the validity of the applicant's claim cannot be lodged, an application for entry of a unilateral notice may still be made.

A person applying for a unilateral notice should deliver to the Registry the usual documents required (see *Notices*, page 389).

The statement in panel 11 or conveyancer's certificate in panel 12 of Form UN1 should be completed on the following lines to show the interest of the applicant:

> owner of the following right to payment in lieu of tithe affecting the land: [*set out details of the corn rent or other payment, including details of the statutory provision on which the payment is based, details of devolution to the applicant where necessary and confirmation that the corn rent is still payable*].

The unilateral notice in the register will give brief details of the interest protected and identify who are the beneficiaries of that notice.

Rights acquired under the Limitation Act 1980

The provision in LRA 2002, Sch 12, para 7, which related to rights acquired under the Limitation Act 1980, did not apply on a registered disposition. Instead, for the period of 3 years beginning with 13 October 2003 there was included in LRA 2002, Sch 3 a right under Sch 12, para 18(1) (LRA 2002, Sch 12, para 11).

LRA 2002, Sch 12, para 18(1) provides that where a registered estate in land is held in trust for a person by virtue of the LRA 1925, s 75(1) immediately before 13 October 2003, he is entitled to be registered as the proprietor of the estate. The position under LRA 1925, s 75(1) was that where a registered proprietor's title had been extinguished by adverse possession, it was open to the squatter to apply for the closure of the registered proprietor's title which was deemed, in the meantime, to be held on trust for the squatter by the registered proprietor.

Interests which cannot take effect as overriding interests

Certain types of interest can never be overriding interests. These are:

(a) an interest under a settlement under the SLA 1925 (LRA 2002, Sch 1, para 2 and Sch 3, para 2(a)). However, an interest under a trust of land can have overriding status, if it otherwise qualifies;

(b) a pending land action, a writ or order affecting land issued or made by a court for the purpose of enforcing a judgment or recognisance, an order appointing a receiver or sequestrator, or a deed of arrangement (LRA 2002, s 87(3));

(c) a spouse's or civil partner's right of occupation under the FLA 1996 as amended by the Civil Partnership Act 2004 (FLA 1996, s 31(10), as amended by LRA 2002, Sch 11, para 34);

(d) in the case of registered dispositions only, a lease granted to take effect in possession more than 3 months ahead, and which has not taken effect in possession at the time of the disposition. This reflects the requirement to register such a lease (LRA 2002, Sch 3, para 2(d));

(e) rights of tenants arising from a desire notice under the Leasehold Reform Act 1967 (LRA 2002, Sch 11, para 8(2)(a));

(f) in the case of dispositions only, exercise of the Preserved Right to Buy (LRA 2002, Sch 11, para 18(10));

(g) rights under an access order made under the ANLA 1992 (LRA 2002, Sch 11, para 26(4));

(h) rights of tenants under the LRHUDA 1993 (LRA 2002, Sch 11, para 30(3)); and

(i) rights arising from a request to a landlord for the grant of an overriding lease under the Landlord and Tenant (Covenants) Act 1995 (LRA 2002, Sch 11, para 33(4)).

Duty to disclose overriding interests

A person applying for first registration must provide information to the Registry in Form DI about any of the overriding interests set out in LRA 2002, Sch 1 that affect the estate to which the application relates and are within the actual knowledge of the applicant, but are not apparent from the deeds and documents accompanying the application (LRR 2003, r 28). An applicant is not required to provide information about local land charges, or public rights, or a leasehold estate in land which falls within LRA 2002, Sch 1, para 1 but, at the time of the application, has one year or less to run. Form FR1 requires the applicant to confirm whether disclosable overriding interests affect the estate, and if so to enclose Form DI with the application.

A person applying to register a disposition of a registered estate must provide information to the Registry in Form DI about any of the overriding interests set out in LRA 2002, Sch 3 that affect the estate to which the application relates and are within the actual knowledge of the applicant (LRR 2003, r 57). An applicant is not required to provide information about local land charges, or public rights, or a leasehold estate in land which falls within LRA 2002, Sch 3, para 1 but, at the time of the application, has one year or less to run. The applicant must produce to the Registry any documentary evidence of the disclosed interest that is under his control. Form AP1 requires the applicant to confirm whether the application relates to a registrable disposition and disclosable overriding interests affect the estate, and if so to enclose Form DI with the application.

An applicant is not required, however, under either LRR 203, r 28 or r 57 to provide information about interests that, under LRA 2002, s 33 or s 90(4), cannot be protected by a notice. Such interests are:

(a) interests under a trust of land or under an SLA 1925 settlement;
(b) a leasehold estate in land granted for 3 years or less from the date of the grant and which is not required to be registered;
(c) a restrictive covenant between landlord and tenant, so far as relating to the demised premises;
(d) an interest which is capable of being registered under the CRA 1965;
(e) an interest in any coal or coal mine, or the rights attached to any such interest, or the rights of any person under Coal Industry Act 1994, ss 38, 49 or 51; and
(f) leases created for PPPs relating to transport in London, within the meaning given by Greater London Authority Act 1999, s 218.

The Registry may enter a notice in the register in respect of any overriding interest disclosed under LRR 2003, r 28 or r 57. Upon entry of such a notice, the interest ceases to be an overriding interest.

OVERSEAS INSOLVENCY PROCEEDINGS

Aside from the special provisions governing member states of the European Union (see below) and those governing the separate parts of the United Kingdom (see *Bankruptcy*, page 49), the general principle is that the courts of England and Wales will recognise that the courts of a foreign country have jurisdiction over a debtor if: (a) he was domiciled in that country at the time of presentation of the petition for insolvency; and (b) he submitted to the court by presenting the petition himself or by entering an appearance in the proceedings. A foreign bankruptcy order, even if recognised by the courts in England and Wales, will not have the effect of automatically vesting the debtor's assets in the foreign trustee in bankruptcy. Such a vesting may, however, be effected under an order of a court in England and Wales. In 2006, special provisions were introduced in relation to cross-border insolvency, as discussed below.

Insolvency proceedings commenced in another member state of the European Union

Where registered land in England and Wales is affected by proceedings under Regulation (EU) 2015/48 of the European Parliament and of the Council, a relevant person may apply for a note of a judgment opening insolvency proceedings within the meaning of EU Regulation, Art 3(1) to be entered in the register. For this purpose, 'relevant person' means any person or body authorised under the provisions of EU Regulation, Art 29 to request or require an entry to be made in the register in respect of the judgment opening insolvency proceedings the subject of the application (LRR 2003, r 171). In addition, any EU member state may require mandatory registration.

The application should be made in Form AP1 and be accompanied by such evidence of the judgment as the Registry may reasonably require; for example an official copy of the judgment with a certified translation of it. A fee is payable (see *Fees*, page 221). If the Registry is satisfied that the judgment opening insolvency proceedings has been made, it may enter a note of the judgment in the register.

If the debtor is the sole proprietor of a registered estate, the following entry will be made in the proprietorship register of the relevant title(s):

> By a judgment of the [*name of court or other body*] dated [*date*] insolvency proceedings within the meaning of Article 3(1) of Regulation (EU) No 2015/848 were opened which appear to relate to [*name of individual or body the subject of the proceedings*], the proprietor of the registered estate. Accordingly, the proprietor's right to exercise owner's powers may be limited. This entry is made following a request under Article 29 of that Regulation.
>
> NOTE: Copy judgment filed.

If the debtor is the sole proprietor of a registered charge, a similar entry (modified as appropriate so as to refer to the registered charge) will be made in the charges register of the relevant title(s).

The Registry will serve a notice of the application upon the debtor as the proprietor of the registered estate or charge.

If the debtor is one of joint proprietors of a registered estate or of a registered charge, no entry can be made.

It may be open to the insolvency office holder to apply in Form RX1 for entry of an appropriate restriction, either instead of or in addition to the entry of a note of the judgement (see *Restrictions*, page 500). However, a foreign insolvency office holder is not a trustee in bankruptcy for the purposes of the law of England and Wales, even if he has a similar title. Consequently, entry of a restriction in Form J or a bankruptcy restriction (see *Bankruptcy*, page 49) will not be appropriate.

Any application for a restriction (if not made by or with the consent of the registered proprietor) must therefore be accompanied by evidence to satisfy the Registry that the applicant has a sufficient interest in making the entry of the restriction applied for. This will normally require the applicant to supply evidence of the law of the country in which he was appointed, as it is that law which will govern the nature of his interest, if any, in the registered estate or charge. For example, a restriction in Form N may be appropriate in the case of a debtor who is a sole proprietor of a registered estate and the governing law would allow the insolvency office holder to prevent a disposition by the debtor. In the case of a debtor who is a joint proprietor, a restriction in Form II may be appropriate. The wording of Forms N and II is set out in Appendix IV, page 585.

Where an application is made in Form AP1 to register a trustee in bankruptcy (or its foreign equivalent comprised within EU Regulation, Art 2(5)) evidence of his entitlement to be registered should accompany the application. This will usually be on similar lines to the evidence required to register a trustee in bankruptcy appointed under the law of England and Wales (see *Bankruptcy*, page 49). A fee is payable (see *Fees*, page 221). The registrar will serve a notice of the application upon the debtor as the registered proprietor of the registered estate or charge.

Cross-Border Insolvency Regulations 2006

The Cross-Border Insolvency Regulations 2006 (SI 2006/1030) give effect to the United Nations Commission on International Trade Law Model Law on cross-border insolvency, which is intended to cover cases where, for example, a debtor has assets in more than one state. The Model Law provides for a court in England and Wales to determine whether a foreign proceeding is to be recognised and if so, whether as a 'main' or 'non-main' proceeding (depending on whether the foreign proceeding is taking place in the country where the debtor's main centre of operations is located). An order for recognition automatically triggers a suspension of the debtor's right to transfer, encumber or otherwise dispose of his assets, as if a bankruptcy order had been made against him. However, no bankruptcy order is made and no trustee in bankruptcy is appointed. This automatic suspension can be modified or terminated by an order of the court.

The Model Law also provides, in the alternative, for a court to grant either interim relief (during the period between the filing of the application for recognition and its determination) or discretionary relief upon recognition of the foreign proceeding to the foreign insolvency representative for the benefit of any recognised foreign proceeding. This includes relief to suspend the debtor's right to dispose of or encumber his assets.

Where an order is made by the court, the 2006 Regulations provide for the foreign representative to make the appropriate application to the registrar to give effect to the terms of the order. The form of application and the type of entry which can be made will depend upon whether the debtor is a sole registered proprietor or a joint registered proprietor.

Where the debtor is the registered proprietor of a registered estate which he holds for his own sole benefit, the application will be for entry of a restriction (see *Restrictions*, page 500). This will be in a non-standard form, to the effect that no disposition of the registered estate by the registered proprietor of that estate is to be completed by registration within the meaning of LRA 2002, s 27 except under a further order of the court. In any other case, the application will be for such entry as shall be necessary to reflect the effect of the court order.

The application should be made in Form RX1 accompanied a certified copy of the court order. A fee will be payable (see *Fees*, page 221).

It is possible that the court may direct the Registry to enter a restriction using its powers under LRA 2002, s 46. In such a case, the appropriate form of application will be in Form AP1 accompanied a certified copy of the court order. A fee will be payable (see *Fees*, page 221).

The same principles will apply where the debtor is the sole registered proprietor of a registered charge, except that the restriction will relate to dispositions of the registered charge rather than of the registered estate.

Where the debtor is a joint proprietor of a registered estate and holds a beneficial interest in the property under a trust of land, by analogy with the position in bankruptcy, only the beneficial interest of the debtor would be affected by a court order suspending his right to transfer, encumber or dispose of his assets.

In such circumstances, the foreign representative would normally have sufficient interest to apply for entry of a standard restriction in Form II, but not the non-standard restriction referred to above. A restriction in Form J (see *Bankruptcy*, page 49) would be inappropriate as there is no actual bankruptcy or appointment of a trustee in bankruptcy under the IA 1986. However, where the court has directed the Registry to enter a particular form of restriction under LRA 2002, s 46, the restriction will be entered notwithstanding that the debtor is not the sole proprietor.

PARTNERSHIPS

A partnership is the relationship which subsists between persons carrying on a business in common with a view to profit (Partnership Act 1890, s 1). A partnership is not a corporate body. For LLPs incorporated under the Limited Liability Partnerships Act 2000, see *Limited liability partnerships*, page 354, and for limited partnerships, see *Limited partnerships*, page 358.

Registration

A transfer or charge to a partnership must be to the names of the individual partners, not to the partnership name. If there are more than four partners, the transfer should be to four of them to hold the legal estate on trust for the partnership. No reference to the partnership is made in the register. In the case of a registered estate in land, as the beneficial interests are held under a tenancy in common, the Registry will enter a restriction in Form A in the proprietorship register in accordance with its obligation under LRA 2002, s 44(1). In the case of other registered estates, the proprietors should make an application for entry of such a restriction (LRR 2003, r 94(2A)).

The partners may also, if they wish, apply for entry of a restriction in Form Q.

If the partnership deed contains specific provisions requiring any consent to be obtained to a disposition, application should be made for entry of a restriction in Form B (TLATA, s 8(2) and LRR 2003, r 94(4)).

The wording of Forms A, B and Q is set out in Appendix IV, page 585.

An application for a restriction should be made in Form RX1. However, this form does not need to be used if the application is for a standard form restriction and is contained in either the 'additional provisions' panel of a prescribed form of transfer or assent, or in clause LR13 of a prescribed clauses lease (or any other lease containing clauses LR1 to LR14 of LRR 2003, Sch 1A) (LRR 2003, r 92(7)) (see *Restrictions*, page 500).

Although no reference to the partnership is made in the register, the proprietors may specifically apply to have any trading name entered in the proprietorship register. This will appear after the last address for service in the entry of the proprietors, in the form 'trading as [*trading name*]'.

PARTY WALL ETC ACT 1996

The purpose of the Party Wall etc Act 1996 is to regulate the manner in which works to party walls and other works adjacent to boundaries are carried out. In general, the Party Wall etc Act 1996 does not affect ownership of land and hence no notice or other entry may be made in the register in respect of any of the following arising under that Act:

(a) a party structure notice;
(b) a party wall award;
(c) a notice under s 1(2) of that Act in respect of a proposed new wall.

However, Party Wall etc Act 1996, s 14 provides that the expenses of building a party wall or party fence wall or carrying out works under that Act may be apportioned between the building owner and the adjoining owner (as defined in that Act). Until the adjoining owner has paid the appropriate share of the expenses to the building owner, the part of the party wall on the adjoining owner's land vests in the building owner.

If the adjoining owner's title is registered, the building owner can apply to protect his ownership rights by the entry of an agreed notice (using Form AN1) or a unilateral notice (using Form UN1) in the register (see *Notices*, page 389). The notice should be confined to the land affected and the position of the wall must be described sufficiently to enable a verbal description or a reference on the title plan to be given for so much of the wall as falls within the adjoining owner's title.

A party wall agreement may be made under the provisions of the Party Wall etc Act 1996 or under the general law; its effect for land registration purposes will depend upon its provisions.

A party wall agreement which provides that ownership of a wall or fence is split longitudinally between two neighbouring registered titles represents a 'provision as to boundary structures' and an application may be made in Form AP1 for the register to be altered to include an entry in respect of the agreement in the relevant title(s). A fee is payable (see *Fees*, page 221).

A party wall agreement may also contain the mutual grant of easements. If granted over a registered estate, these may constitute a registrable disposition required to be completed by registration (LRA 2002, s 27(2)(d)) and the appropriate application should be made in respect of them (see *Legal easements*, page 343).

PENDING LAND ACTIONS

A pending land action is defined as 'any action or proceeding pending in court relating to land or any interest in or charge on land' (Land Charges Act 1972, s 17(1)). For this purpose 'land' does not include a beneficial interest in land under a trust. A pending land action would include, for example, an application for a declaration as to the existence of an easement, or for forfeiture of a lease. However, an action for a pure money judgment, or for damages for breach of a restrictive covenant, would not constitute a pending land action. An action relating solely to a beneficial interest under a trust is not a pending land action, because an undivided share is excluded from the definition of 'land' for this purpose. However, it is arguable that an action which relates to the issue of whether the land is subject to a trust of land and/or to the appointment of a new or additional trustee may constitute a pending land action (see *Godfrey v Torpey & ors* [2006] EWHC 1423 (Ch)).

For the position where a pending land action relates to an application for a property adjustment order in matrimonial proceedings, see *Property adjustment orders*, page 468. For a pending land action relating to an application for an access to neighbouring land order, see *Access to neighbouring land orders*, page 1. For a pending land action relating to an application for a charging order, see *Charging orders*, page 100. For a pending land action relating to an application under the LRHUDA 1993, see *Collective enfranchisement*, page 136, and *Leases*, page 296.

A pending land action is treated as an interest affecting an estate or charge for the purposes of the LRA 2002 (LRA 2002, s 87(1)). It cannot, however, be an interest belonging to a person in actual occupation falling within LRA 2002, Sch 1, para 2 or Sch 3, para 2 which will override first registration or registered dispositions (LRA 2002, s 87(3)).

A pending land action may be protected by the entry in the register of an agreed notice or a unilateral notice, and possibly a restriction. The application may be made by the person taking the action or proceedings, or his assignee or chargee (LRR 2003, r 172). A notice will protect the priority of the pending land action as against a subsequent registered disposition for valuable consideration (LRA 2002, ss 29, 30 and 32). A restriction does not confer any priority; it simply prevents an entry being made in the register in respect of any disposition, or a disposition of a specified kind, unless the terms of the restriction have (where applicable) been complied with. The entry in the register in respect of a pending land action will only protect the action itself; if the court action is successful, a separate application should therefore be made to protect any order made by the court as appropriate. If the court action is unsuccessful, application should be made for removal from the register of an entry relating to the pending land action.

Agreed notice

In addition to the usual documents required (see *Notices*, page 389), an applicant should deliver to the Registry the sealed claim form and notice of issue.

As the consent of the registered proprietor is unlikely to be forthcoming in this situation, this is likely to be sufficient to satisfy the Registry of the validity of the applicant's claim in accordance with LRA 2002, s 34(3)(c).

The agreed notice in the register will give details of the interest protected.

Unilateral notice

Where the applicant wishes to apply for a unilateral notice he should deliver to the Registry the usual documents required (see *Notices*, page 389).

The statement in panel 11 or conveyancer's certificate in panel 12 of Form UN1 should be completed on the following lines to show the interest of the applicant:

> applicant in an action in the [*name* Division of the High Court] *or* [*name* County Court] [*set out full court reference and parties*] for [*state nature of the action*].

The unilateral notice in the register will give brief details of the interest protected and identify the beneficiary of that notice.

Restriction

As a result of LRA 2002, s 42(2) no restriction may be entered for the purpose of protecting the priority of an interest which is, or could be, the subject of a notice. This does not, however, prevent a restriction being entered in addition to a notice of the pending land action where appropriate. In most cases the existence of a pending land action will not make a disposition by the registered proprietor unlawful or invalid and the existence of the action itself will not be sufficient for the entry of a restriction; only in cases where the action gives rise to some limitation on the proprietor's powers of disposition would an application for a restriction be appropriate.

In addition to the usual documents required (see *Restrictions*, page 500), an applicant should deliver to the Registry the sealed claim form and notice of issue.

As the application for a restriction is unlikely to be made by or with the consent of the registered proprietor in this situation, the statement in panel 12 or conveyancer's certificate in panel 13 of Form RX1 must be completed, setting out details of the application to the court.

Panel 9 of Form RX1 should be completed as to the required restriction(s). The form of restriction sought depends on the nature of the pending land action. A restriction in a standard form contained in LRR 2003, Sch 4 does not require the approval of the Registry to the terms of the restriction under LRA 2002, s 43(3). A possible form of restriction based on Form N is:

> No [disposition *or specify type of disposition*] of the registered estate by the proprietor of the registered estate [*or by the proprietor of any registered charge not being a charge registered before the entry of this restriction*] is to be registered without a written consent signed by [*name*] of [*address*] [or [*their conveyancer or specify appropriate details*]].

The Registry must give notice of the application for a restriction to the proprietor of the registered estate concerned, if it has not been made by or with his consent or a person entitled to be registered as such proprietor (LRA 2002, s 45).

PERSONAL REPRESENTATIVES

Where a sole or sole surviving proprietor dies, the legal estate in registered land will vest in his executor or administrator by operation of law (Administration of Estates Act 1925, s 1(1)). This vesting is not a disposition which is required to be completed by registration in order to take effect at law (LRA 2002, s 27(5)). In the case of joint proprietors, the legal estate cannot be severed and can only be held on a legal joint tenancy (Law of Property Act 1925, ss 1(6), 34 and 36). The principle of 'survivorship' therefore applies, so that if one joint proprietor dies, the legal estate will automatically vest in the survivor(s) by operation of law regardless of devolution of the equitable interest. As to the death of a sole proprietor or joint proprietor, see *Death of a registered proprietor*, page 182, and *Joint proprietors*, page 286.

Registration of personal representative

On the death of a sole proprietor, or of the survivor of joint proprietors, of a registered estate or registered charge, the personal representative of such proprietor may apply to become registered as proprietor of that estate or charge. Although the personal representative is not obliged to become registered before exercising his powers of disposition, a disadvantage of not doing so is that the register remains out of date longer than it would if he was registered as soon as the grant of representation was made. Whilst the register is out of date, any notice sent by the Registry and addressed to the deceased proprietor may not be received by the personal representative.

The personal representative should deliver to the Registry:

(a)   an application in Form AP1;
(b)   evidence of the appointment of the personal representative in the form of either (LRR 2003, r 163(2):

  (i)   the original or a certified copy or office copy of the grant of probate or letters of administration to the estate of the deceased; or
  (ii)   a court order appointing the applicant as the deceased's personal representative, or a certified copy or office copy of it; or
  (iii) (where a conveyancer is acting for the applicant) a certificate given by the conveyancer that he holds the original or an office copy of such grant of probate, letters of administration or court order;

(c)   the appropriate confirmation or evidence as to identity (see *Identity evidence*, page 266); and
(d)   the fee payable (see *Fees*, page 221).

Where a personal representative is seeking to become registered jointly with another personal representative who is already registered as proprietor, the Registry will serve notice on that existing proprietor (LRR 2003, r 163(4)).

Where a personal representative is seeking to become registered in place of another personal representative who is already registered as proprietor, the application must also be accompanied by evidence to show that the appointment of the personal representative whom the applicant is replacing has been terminated (LRR 2003, r 163(2)).

Where the register states that the deceased was the administrator of the estate of a deceased proprietor, a grant of letters of administration *de bonis non* to the estate of that deceased proprietor must be obtained, and the administrator *de bonis non* can then apply to be registered as proprietor. Similarly, when the register states that the deceased was the executor of a deceased proprietor, but the executor has died intestate, his administrator is not entitled to be registered in the deceased executor's place; a grant of letters of administration *de bonis non* to the estate of the original testator is necessary, and the administrator *de bonis non* can then apply to be registered as proprietor. These exceptions apply because the 'chain of representation' does not apply in these circumstances.

A chain of representation arises where the executor of a deceased proprietor himself dies without having completed the administration of the estate. If the executor has left a will appointing an executor, then on proving that will, that latter executor also automatically becomes executor of the deceased proprietor's estate as well. The chain of representation only applies to executors not administrators and if the chain of successive executorships is broken then a grant *de bonis non* to the deceased proprietor's estate would then be required. If an applicant relies upon a chain of representation, evidence of any additional grant of probate showing the chain will also need to be lodged, as well as the grant to the deceased proprietor's estate.

Where the personal representative is registered as proprietor, the following is added after the personal representative's name:

> executor *or* executrix [*or administrator or administratrix*] of [*name*] deceased.

Where the land was settled before the death of the sole or last surviving joint proprietor and not by his will and the settlement continues after his death, an application to register the special personal representatives in whom the registered land vests under the Administration of Estates Act 1925 must be accompanied by the grant limited to the settled land (LRR 2003, Sch 7, para 11). In that case the following is added after the personal representative's name:

> special executor *or* executrix [*or administrator or administratrix*] of [*name*] deceased.

Entry of restrictions

A person dealing with a registered proprietor can assume that he has unlimited power to dispose of the registered estate or registered charge concerned, free from any limitation affecting the validity of the disposition, unless there is a restriction or other entry in the register limiting his powers, or a limitation imposed by or under the LRA 2002 (LRA 2002, s 26).

In the case of a personal representative, it is the duty of the executor or administrator to apply for any necessary restriction(s), although a person who has an interest in the due administration of the estate may also apply. A restriction does not confer any priority; it simply prevents an entry being made in the register in respect of any disposition, or a disposition of a specified kind, unless the terms of the restriction have (where applicable) been complied with.

Law of Property Act 1925, s 27(2) does not affect the right of a sole personal representative *acting as such* to give a valid receipt for capital money. Therefore the Registry will not automatically enter a restriction in Form A when registering a personal representative as proprietor of a registered estate. However, any existing such restriction will remain in the register because, in that case, the personal representative will be succeeding the deceased as trustee of the trust. For the same reason, the Registry will enter a restriction in Form A on first registration when registering the personal representative of a deceased proprietor who was a sole trustee or (except where he was the survivor of beneficial joint tenants) the last surviving trustee.

Where the personal representative holds the registered estate on a trust of land created by the deceased's will, or on a trust of land arising under the laws of intestacy which is subsequently varied, and his powers have been limited by TLATA 1996, s 8, he must apply for entry of a restriction in Form C (LRR 2003, r 94(3)). Where there are two or more personal representatives of a deceased proprietor, an application by one or more of them satisfies the obligation to apply for entry of the restriction. If an application is not made, any person who has an interest in the due administration of the estate may apply for entry of a restriction in Form C (LRR 2003, r 93(d)). The applicant should deliver to the Registry the usual documents required (see *Restrictions*, page 500).

Where the applicant is a person who has an interest in the due administration of the deceased's estate, the statement in panel 12 or conveyancer's certificate in panel 13 of Form RX1 should be completed on the following lines:

> The interest is that specified in rule 93(d) of the Land Registration Rules 2003, the applicant being a person interested in the due administration of the estate of [*name*] deceased.

Panel 9 of Form RX1 should be completed as to the restriction in Form C. The wording of Form C is set out in Appendix IV, page 585.

A restriction in Form C in LRR 2003, Sch 4 does not require the approval of the Registry to the wording of the restriction under LRA 2002, s 43(3).

The Registry must give notice of the application for a restriction to the proprietor of the registered estate concerned if it has not been made by or with his consent or a person entitled to be registered as such proprietor (LRA 2002, s 45).

Where a trust of land imposes limitations on the powers of the trustees under TLATA 1996, s 8, for example a requirement to obtain a consent before sale, and the legal estate is vested in the personal representatives of a sole or last surviving trustee, the personal representatives must apply for entry of a restriction in Form B (LRR 2003, r 94(4) and (7)). This does not apply if the land is held on charitable, ecclesiastical or public trusts. Where there are two or more persons registered as proprietor of the estate, an application by one or more of them satisfies the obligation to apply for entry of the restriction. If such an application is not made, any person who has an interest under the trust of land where the powers of the trustees are limited under TLATA 1996, s 8 may apply for the entry of a restriction in Form B (LRR 2003, r 93(c)). The applicant should deliver to the Registry the usual documents required (see *Restrictions*, page 500).

Where the applicant is a person who has an interest under a trust of land, the statement in panel 12 or conveyancer's certificate in panel 13 of Form RX1 should be completed on the following lines:

> The interest is that specified in rule 93(c) of the Land Registration Rules 2003, the applicant being a person who has an interest in the registered estate held under a trust of land where the powers of the trustees are limited by section 8 of the Trusts of Land and Appointment of Trustees Act 1996.

Panel 9 of Form RX1 should be completed as to the restriction in Form B. The wording of Form B is set out in Appendix IV, page 585.

A restriction in Form B in LRR 2003, Sch 4 does not require the approval of the Registry to the wording of the restriction under LRA 2002, s 43(3).

The Registry must give notice of the application for a restriction to the proprietor of the registered estate concerned if it has not been made by or with his consent or a person entitled to be registered as such proprietor (LRA 2002, s 45).

Dispositions by personal representatives

The personal representative may deal with the registered estate in accordance with his powers in that capacity, subject to any entry to the contrary in the register, whether or not he has been registered as proprietor in place of the deceased. For assents by personal representatives, see *Assents*, page 45. There are no prescribed forms of transfer by a personal representative and, whether the personal representative has been registered as proprietor or not, a transfer by him must therefore be in the appropriate prescribed form (see *Transfers*, page 551).

The Registry is not under a duty to investigate the reasons a transfer of registered land by a personal representative of a deceased sole proprietor or last surviving joint proprietor is made. Nor is it required to consider the contents of the will and, provided the terms of any restriction in the register are complied with, it must assume, whether or not it knows of the terms of the will, that the personal representative is acting correctly and within his powers (LRR 2003, r 162(2)).

In addition to the usual documents required (see *Transfers*, page 551), a person applying to register a transfer by a personal representative should deliver to the Registry evidence of the appointment of the personal representative (if not already registered as proprietor) in accordance with LRR 2003, r 162(1), being similar to that required by r 163(2) as specified in 'Registration of personal representative', above.

If a restriction in Form A appears in the register when the transfer is registered, it will be cancelled by the Registry if the transfer is by two or more personal representatives or a trust corporation, as the equitable interests under the trust of land will have been overreached (Law of Property Act 1925, ss 2 and 27). However, if the transfer is by a sole personal representative (not being a trust corporation) of a sole surviving proprietor, the application will be caught by the restriction as if it were an application to register a transfer on sale by the deceased. Therefore, unless the Registry is satisfied that the equitable interests have been overreached, it will be necessary either to appoint a new co-trustee to act jointly with the personal representative and give a joint receipt for the purchase money, or for evidence of the equitable title to be lodged so as to satisfy the Registry that the trust of land has come to an end. The reason for this is because although a sole personal representative *acting as such* can give a valid receipt for the purposes of overreaching, that will not apply where (as is the case in this situation) the personal representative is acting in a capacity of trustee under a trust of land.

Any other restrictions appearing in the register will also need to be complied with or cancelled or withdrawn, as appropriate. Thus, where a restriction in Form C appears in the register, the appropriate certificate, statutory declaration or statement of truth will need to be provided; on registration of the transfer the restriction will then be automatically cancelled.

First registration

Where a legal estate is currently unregistered, the vesting of that estate in the personal representative by operation of law will not 'trigger' compulsory first registration (LRA 2002, s 4(3)). However, an assent or conveyance of that estate may be a 'trigger' for compulsory first registration, in which case the appropriate application should be made (see *First registration*, page 222). Also, the personal representative may apply for voluntary first registration if desired, in which case the requisite evidence of his appointment (see 'Registration of personal representative', above) must accompany the application.

The Registry does not have the statutory protection conferred upon a 'purchaser' under Administration of Estates Act 1925, s 36(7). Nor does LRR 2003, r 162(2) apply in relation to an application for first registration. The Registry may therefore investigate the will or intestacy if it considers it necessary in order to satisfy itself that the applicant is entitled to apply. In practice, this will not normally be necessary except where a liability for IHT may arise.

Inheritance tax; capital transfer tax; death duties

In some circumstances a registered estate may be subject to a liability for IHT (formerly known as capital transfer tax) in respect of deaths occurring after 12 March 1975. This tax replaced death duties (in practice only estate duty) which applied in respect of deaths occurring on or before that date. The entry and/or removal of entries relating to IHT or death duties may therefore be relevant (see *Inheritance tax*, page 280).

PLANS

Land Registry title plans are produced using the Ordnance Survey's large scale digital map data. Although this data is supplied in a single consistent format, it is surveyed and digitised at different scales. It is not possible to achieve perfect accuracy in drawing features on a plan. The degree of variation between the actual position on the ground and that recorded on the map is known as the specified accuracy tolerance. This means that measurements scaled between features shown on Ordnance Survey mapping may not exactly match the actual distance measured between the same features on the ground. Different levels of accuracy apply dependent on the scale of the map and the original survey method used to create it. As a general guide, the width of a line on a 1:1250 Ordnance Survey map roughly represents 0.3 metres on the ground. The width of a line on a 1/2500 Ordnance Survey map roughly represents 0.6 metres on the ground. The Ordnance Survey publishes expected confidence levels in the accuracy of its maps in terms of relative and absolute accuracy.

Relative accuracy compares the scaled distance between features measured from the map data with distances measured between the same features on the ground. For example, if at a scale of 1:1250 the distances between well-defined points of detail 60 metres apart were measured on the ground, there would be an expectation that 95 per cent would be represented on the Ordnance Survey map by scaled distances of between 59.1 metres and 60.9 metres. Similarly, if at a scale of 1:2500 the measured distances between points of detail were 100 metres apart there would be an expectation that 95 per cent would be represented on the Ordnance Survey map by scaled distances of between 98.1 metres and 101.9 metres. Further information and examples appear on the Ordnance Survey's website at ww.ordnancesurvey.co.uk.

Absolute accuracy is the measure which indicates how closely the coordinates of a point in Ordnance Survey map data agree with the 'true' National Grid coordinates of the same point on the ground. As the true position can never be known exactly, the statistic is quoted relative to the best known position determined by precise survey methods.

Where an Ordnance Survey map has been enlarged from its original scale, the degree of accuracy remains the same as the original map specification. For example, a plan surveyed at 1:2500 and enlarged to 1:1250 will still be subject to the survey specifications of 1:2500 mapping. The copying, reducing or enlarging of a plan is likely to distort its accuracy.

The Ordnance Survey map shows permanent physical features, normally at ground surface level, together with a variety of descriptive information and symbols. Generally the Ordnance Survey map shows features more than 30cm high such as walls, fences, hedges or building outlines by firm black lines. Features less than 30cm high, such as kerbs or where two different surfaces meet, are shown by dotted black lines. Dotted black lines can also represent features that overhang, such as the outline of a building above ground surface level or where a roadway passes underneath.

The only features the Ordnance Survey map shows within private gardens are permanent buildings more than 12 square metres in area, and roads and tracks over 100 metres long.

The scale of the Ordnance Survey map also dictates how physical features are shown on a title plan. Where, for example, a hedge and a wall run close together on the ground, it may be that they are shown on the plan by a single firm black line because the gap between the two features cannot be shown at the scale in question. Even where only one physical feature is represented by a firm black line on the Ordnance Survey map, it may be a wide hedge or a narrow fence. Again a small projection in a boundary might be shown on a plan surveyed at 1:1250 scale where a plan surveyed at 1:2500 scale would show a straight line. Even if the latter plan is enlarged to 1:1250 scale, it will still not show the projection.

In *Alan Wibberley Building Ltd v Insley* [1999] UKHL 15, Lord Hope of Craighead said:

> The use of maps or plans such as those published by the Ordnance Survey is now widespread and has obvious advantages. Ordnance Survey maps are prepared to a high standard of accuracy and are frequently and appropriately used to fix boundaries by reference, for example, to Ordnance Survey field numbers. But like all maps they are subject to limitations. The most obvious are those imposed by scale. No map can reproduce to anything like the same scale of detail every feature which is found on the ground. Furthermore the Ordnance Survey does not fix private boundaries. The purpose of the survey is topographical, not taxative. Even the most detailed Ordnance Survey map may not show every feature on the ground which can be used to identify the extent of the owner's land. In the present case the Ordnance Survey map shows the hedge, but it does not show the ditch. So there is no reason in principle in this case for preferring the line on the map to other evidence which may be relevant to identify the boundary.

Plans for use in transfers of part or other deeds relating to an application to the Registry should be prepared bearing in mind the following guidelines. The plan should:

(a) be drawn to scale and show that scale;
(b) bear a north point;
(c) be at 1:1250 or 1:500 scale for urban properties or 1:2500 for rural properties;
(d) not be reduced in scale by copying;
(e) not be marked or referred to as for identification purposes only;
(f) not contain a disclaimer under the Property Misdescriptions Act 1991;
(g) show sufficient detail to be identified on the Ordnance Survey map;
(h) show buildings and other features in their correct or intended positions;
(i) show clearly the land in question, for example by edging, colouring or hatching;
(j) have edgings of a thickness that does not obscure any other detail;
(k) identify different floor levels (where appropriate);
(l) show intricate boundaries with a larger scale or inset plan;

(m) show measurements in metric units, to two decimal places;
(n) show undefined boundaries accurately and, where necessary, by reference to measurements; and
(o) show measurements that correspond as far as possible to scaled measurements.

As to title plans and boundaries, see *Boundaries*, page 77.

POSITIVE COVENANTS

Where the proprietor, or any previous proprietor, of a registered estate has given a positive covenant relating to that estate, the Registry may make an entry in respect of it in the proprietorship register (LRR 2003, r 64).

If the existence of the positive covenant is apparent from the register in some other way, the Registry need not make a separate entry. This might be the case where the positive covenant is included amongst restrictive covenants and is set out with them in the charges register. Where the Registry does make an entry, it must, where practicable, refer to the deed that contains the positive covenant.

There is no need to make a specific application for an entry in respect of a positive covenant when this is included in a deed lodged as part of an application in respect of a registrable disposition, such as a transfer. An entry will be made by the Registry as part of that application, if it considers it appropriate.

Where an entry has been made in respect of a positive covenant, the Registry must remove it from the register if it appears to the Registry that the covenant does not bind the current proprietor of the registered estate (LRR 2003, r 64(3)).

The burden of positive covenants does not run with freehold land (*Rhone v Stephens* [1994] 2 All ER 65 (HL)). Positive covenants may be made enforceable against successors in title of the covenantor by creating an estate rentcharge for a nominal amount. For the protection of estate rentcharges, see *Rentcharges*, page 486.

Positive covenants are sometimes protected by ensuring that a subsequent purchaser enters into a new deed of covenant with the person having the benefit of the original covenant. This arrangement may itself involve a positive covenant requiring that this be done and in the case of registered land may be supported by an application for a restriction.

Restriction

The consent of the registered proprietor to the entry of the restriction is required, unless the deed containing the positive covenant contains a provision which limits the registered proprietor's powers to enter into any further disposition.

In addition to the usual documents required (see *Restrictions*, page 500), an applicant for a restriction should deliver to the Registry (if the application is made by a person who claims that he has a sufficient interest in the making of the entry) a certified copy of the deed containing the positive covenant.

The statement in panel 12 of Form RX1 signed by the applicant or a certificate by his conveyancer in panel 13 of Form RX1 must be completed, setting out details of the deed and of the provision in the deed limiting the registered proprietor's powers to enter into a disposition.

Panel 9 of Form RX1 should be completed as to the appropriate restriction required. A restriction in a standard form contained in LRR 2003, Sch 4 does not require the approval of the Registry to the terms of the restriction under LRA 2002, s 43(3). A possible form of restriction based on Form L is:

> No disposition of the registered estate by the proprietor of the registered estate is to be registered without a written certificate signed by [*purchaser*] of [*address*] or their conveyancer that the provisions of [*clause, paragraph or other particulars*] of [*details of contract for sale*] have been complied with or that they do not apply to the disposition.

Alternatively, where the certificate of the registered proprietor of a specified title number is to be required, a similar restriction based upon Form M may be appropriate. If the consent of the person having the benefit of the positive covenant is to be required, then a restriction in Form N may be appropriate. A restriction in Form O may be appropriate where the consent of the registered proprietor of a specified title number, or the provision of a certificate as an alternative to such consent, is to be required (see Appendix IV, page 585 for the wording of these restrictions).

Form RX1 does not need to be used if the application is for a standard form restriction and is contained in either the 'additional provisions' panel of a prescribed form of transfer or assent, or in clause LR13 of a prescribed clauses lease (or any other lease containing clauses LR1 to LR14 of LRR 2003, Sch 1A) (LRR 2003, r 92(7)).

The Registry must give notice of the application for a restriction to the proprietor of the registered estate or charge concerned, if it has not been made by or with the consent of such proprietor or a person entitled to be registered as such proprietor (LRA 2002, s 45).

Positive covenants imposed by statute

Although normally the burden of a positive covenant does not run with the land, certain statutes make provision for a positive covenant entered into pursuant to that statute enforceable as though it was a restrictive covenant. Such statutes include Local Government (Miscellaneous Provisions) Act 1982, s 33; Mission and Pastoral Measure 2011, s 75; HA 1985, s 609; National Trust Act 1937, s 8; Wildlife and Countryside Act 1981, s 39; and Water Industry Act 1991, s 156.

The Registry will treat such covenants in the same way as restrictive covenants, but will omit the word 'restrictive' from the register entry.

POWERS OF ATTORNEY

A power of attorney is a deed by which one person (the donor) gives another person (the attorney) power to act on his behalf. It may be granted either for general purposes or for a specific purpose. If it is granted for a specific purpose, it should be ensured that it contains clear authority to enter into the disposition, as powers of attorney are interpreted strictly. It is not possible to note the appointment of an attorney by a registered proprietor in the register.

Any deed lodged for registration that has been executed under a power of attorney must be accompanied by one of the following (LRR 2003, r 61):

(a)   a certificate by a conveyancer in Form 1 in LRR 2003, Sch 3; or
(b)   the original power; or
(c)   a certified copy of the power in accordance with Powers of Attorney Act 1971 (PAA 1971), s 3.

The Registry will retain the evidence lodged in its files. If, therefore, the applicant wishes to keep the original, he should lodge a certified copy with the application (LRR 2003, r 203). The different types of power of attorney are as follows.

General powers under Powers of Attorney Act 1971, s 10

The PAA 1971 provides a short form of general power of attorney that can be used by a sole beneficial owner of land. Such a power must follow the form set out in Sch 1 to that Act or be in a form to the like effect and expressed to be made under that Act. The donor must execute the power as a deed. It confers upon the attorney authority to do anything that the donor can lawfully do by an attorney. However, powers in that form dated before 1 March 2000 are not appropriate for dealing with land of which the donor is a joint proprietor. Those dated after 29 February 2000 may only be used by a joint proprietor if certain conditions are satisfied under Trustee Delegation Act 1999, s 1 (see 'Powers of attorney by joint proprietors and other trustees', below). The donor may revoke such a power at any time and the death, bankruptcy or mental incapacity of the donor will automatically revoke it.

Other general and specific powers

As an alternative to the form set out in the PAA 1971, the donor of a power of attorney may use any form of wording, giving the attorney either general authority to act or limited powers. For example, in connection with a particular transaction or in relation only to a specified property. The donor must execute the power as a deed. Such a power may be used on behalf of a donor who is a joint proprietor only if certain conditions are satisfied under Trustee Delegation Act 1999, s 1 (see 'Powers of attorney by joint proprietors and other trustees', below). Unless it is a security power, the donor may revoke such a power and the death, bankruptcy or mental incapacity of the donor will automatically revoke it.

Security powers

A security power is a power of attorney that is expressed to be irrevocable and is given to secure a proprietary interest of the attorney; or the performance of an obligation owed to the attorney. While the attorney retains the interest or until the obligation is discharged, the donor can only revoke the power with the attorney's consent and the death, bankruptcy or mental incapacity of the donor does not revoke it.

Enduring powers of attorney

The Enduring Powers of Attorney Act 1985 was repealed by the Mental Capacity Act 2005 and in consequence no new enduring powers can be created after 30 September 2007. Enduring powers created before 1 October 2007 will continue to have effect, but are now subject to the provisions of Mental Capacity Act 2005, Sch 4 (see below). An enduring power must be in one of the prescribed forms according to the date of execution of the power.

Enduring powers dated after 29 February 2000 may be used by a donor who is a joint proprietor if certain conditions are satisfied under Trustee Delegation Act 1999, s 1 (see 'Powers of attorney by joint proprietors and other Trustees', below). There were transitional provisions for enduring powers dated before 1 March 2000 under which such powers could be used by a donor who was a joint proprietor until 1 March 2001. From 1 March 2001 an enduring power dated before that date can only be used by a donor who is a joint proprietor if:

(a)   the donor has a beneficial interest in the property and there is no indication in the power that the donor did not intend the attorney to exercise trustee functions; or
(b)   the power is registered with the Court of Protection following an application to the Court before 1 March 2001; or
(c)   an application made to the Court before 1 March 2001 for registration of the power has not been finally refused.

Enduring powers of attorney continue to be effective even after the donor has lost capacity, provided the power has been registered with the Court of Protection or the Public Guardian, as appropriate. Otherwise the attorney cannot use it to act on behalf of the donor if the donor lacks capacity.

If two or more attorneys are appointed jointly, they must all execute a deed on behalf of the donor. If they are appointed jointly and severally, only one need execute it.

If an enduring power of attorney has been registered at the Court of Protection or with the Office of the Public Guardian and any order or direction has been made by the court under Mental Capacity Act 2005, Sch 4, para 16 with respect to the power or to the donor or to the attorney, the order or direction, or an official copy or certified copy of it, must be lodged with the application for registration of a deed executed under the power (LRR 2003, r 61(2)).

Lasting powers of attorney

Lasting powers of attorney were introduced by the Mental Capacity Act 2005 and replaced enduring powers as the primary way for a donor to choose an attorney (or 'decision maker) to act in the event of loss of mental capacity. In addition to a 'property and financial affairs' lasting power, a donor is able to appoint an attorney to make decisions about his own welfare using a 'health and welfare' lasting power for a time when he lacks capacity to make such decisions himself.

Lasting Powers of Attorney, Enduring Powers of Attorney and Public Guardian Regulations 2007 (SI 2007/1253), Sch 1, part 1 prescribes the form which must be used for a 'property and financial affairs' lasting power of attorney and it must be executed in accordance with reg 9. A lasting power may only be used once it has been registered with the Office of the Public Guardian.

If two or more attorneys are appointed jointly, they must all execute a deed on behalf of the donor. If they are appointed jointly and severally, only one need execute it.

If a lasting power of attorney has been registered with the Office of the Public Guardian and any order or direction has been made by the court under Mental Capacity Act 2005, s 22 or s 23 with respect to the power or to the donor or attorney, the order or direction, or an official or certified copy of it, must be lodged with the application for registration of a deed executed under the power (LRR 2003, r 61(2)).

Powers of attorney by joint proprietors and other trustees

Trustees holding property upon trust (which includes joint owners who are holding on trust for themselves as beneficial joint tenants or tenants in common) can only delegate their duties and powers when they have authority to do so. However, several statutory provisions now allow for delegation.

It should be borne in mind that where overreaching is necessary, the attorney must act with at least one other person, unless the donor is a trust corporation, so as to ensure there is a valid receipt by at least two trustees in accordance with Law of Property Act 1925, ss 2 and 27. If a transfer is lodged which has been executed by only one person, both as proprietor and as attorney for the other proprietor or as attorney for all the proprietors, the Registry will return it for execution by the donor(s). If the transfer is not re-executed the Registry will enter a restriction in Form A in the register to reflect the fact that overreaching has not been effected and that there may therefore be beneficial interests that continue to subsist.

Trustee Act 1925, s 25

Under this section, a trustee can delegate the exercise of his powers for a maximum of 12 months from the start of the delegation or, if there is no provision for when the delegation starts, for 12 months from the execution of the power by the trustee. The power must be in the form set out in Trustee Act 1925, s 25(6) or in a form to the like effect and expressed to be made under s 25 of that Act.

Trustee Delegation Act 1999, s 1

This section allows a power of attorney to be used in relation to trust property after 1 March 2000 if there is no indication in the power that the donor does not intend the attorney to exercise trustee functions and, at the time the power of attorney is used, the donor has a beneficial interest in the property. This delegation is not limited in duration. This applies to general powers, certain enduring powers and lasting powers (see above).

A signed statement by the attorney made within 3 months of the date of the disposition will be conclusive evidence of the donor having had a beneficial interest at that time. The statement can be included within the transfer or other disposition or it may be made separately provided it is dated within 3 months of the date of the disposition.

If such a statement cannot be produced, the Registry will consider other evidence, such as a statutory declaration or statement of truth, confirming that the donor had a beneficial interest at the relevant time. In the absence of satisfactory evidence of the donor's beneficial interest, the disposition will need to be executed by the donor of the power.

Trusts of Land and Appointment of Trustees Act 1996, s 9

All the trustees of a trust of land may jointly delegate their functions to a beneficiary or beneficiaries of full age and beneficially entitled to an interest in possession. The delegation may be for any period or indefinite.

However, these 'beneficiary' attorneys are not treated as trustees for the purposes of receiving capital money, so that the trustees themselves will need to join in any disposition under which capital money arises in order to effect overreaching (TLATA 1996, s 9(7)). This type of power will therefore only be appropriate when no capital money is passing; for example on the grant of a lease without payment of a premium.

Statutory protection is given to a third party who in good faith deals with an attorney to whom trustee powers were delegated as a beneficiary, but who in fact was not a beneficiary to whom the trustee functions could be delegated. The attorney is presumed to have been a person to whom the trustee functions could be delegated unless the third party had knowledge that they were not such a person (TLATA 1996, s 9(2)). In consequence, where a beneficiary has executed a deed under a power of attorney, the Registry may require a statutory declaration or statement of truth from the disponee to confirm that he acted in good faith and had no knowledge at the time of completion of the disposition that the attorney was not a person to whom the functions of the trustees in relation to the land could be delegated. Alternatively, the disponee's conveyancer can provide a certificate to the effect that at the time of completion his client had no such knowledge (LRR 2003, r 63 and Forms 2 and 3 in Sch 3 (see Appendix V, page 593).

Gifts and dispositions at undervalue by an attorney

An attorney owes a fiduciary duty to the donor. In general therefore, an attorney cannot use the power to confer a benefit on himself or others to the detriment of the donor. Where an application for registration of such a disposition is lodged, the Registry's approach will depend upon the type of power used.

In the case of a general power, the Registry will regard the disposition as within the authority of the attorney even though, potentially, it could be set aside as being in breach of fiduciary duty. This is because the disposition is voidable rather than void, but the Registry will usually serve notice upon the donor as a precaution.

In the case of an enduring power or lasting power, there are considerable limitations upon gifts being made; the Registry will therefore reject applications to register such dispositions unless the disposition is re-executed in person by the donor or satisfactory evidence of authority to make the gift is lodged. For example, if an enduring power is registered and the disposition has been approved by the court under Mental Capacity Act 2005, Sch 4, para 16.

Where it is claimed, in relation to a disposition by an attorney under an enduring or lasting power granted by a joint proprietor, that there is no element of gift because the donor had no beneficial interest in the property, this may cause a consequential problem in relation to powers granted by a joint proprietor (see 'Powers of attorney by joint proprietors and other trustees', above).

Powers more than 12 months old – evidence of non-revocation

A purchaser from a person who has dealt with an attorney is entitled to assume that the power of attorney has not been revoked if the transaction in question took place within 12 months of the date when the power came into question. Although under LRR 2003, r 62, the Registry may require evidence of non-revocation if the power of attorney is more than 12 months old, such evidence will not normally be required. On the rare occasions when the Registry does require such evidence, this must be in Form 2 in LRR 2003, Sch 3, being either a statutory declaration or statement of truth made by the person dealing with the attorney or a certificate by that person's conveyancer (see Appendix V, page 593). As powers of attorney under Trustee Act 1925, s 25 can only operate for 12 months, evidence of non-revocation is unnecessary for such powers.

Execution of deeds by an attorney

There is no prescribed attestation clause, but the Registry has published forms of execution which are acceptable for land registration purposes.

Powers of attorney given to receivers in debentures

See *Debentures*, page 183.

PRIORITIES

The LRA 2002 contains specific provision for rules of priority in relation to registered land.

Basic rule of priority

The basic rule is that the priority of an interest affecting a registered estate or charge is not affected by a disposition of the estate or charge (LRA 2002, s 28). It makes no difference for this purpose whether the interest or disposition is registered. In effect, therefore, the basic rule is that the first in time by reference to date of creation prevails. This basic rule is, however, subject to considerable modification in the common event of a disposition for valuable consideration of a registered estate or a registered charge (as to which the special rule of priority discussed below applies), and also in the less common event of an Inland Revenue charge. For the relative priority of registered charges as between themselves, see *Legal charges*, page 333.

Special rule of priority

The LRA 2002 provides for the application of a special rule of priority in relation to a registrable disposition of a registered estate or of a registered charge which is completed by registration (LRA 2002, ss 29 and 30).

Registrable dispositions of registered estates for valuable consideration

A 'registrable disposition' means a disposition, such as a transfer or charge, which is required to be completed by registration under LRA 2002, s 27. 'Valuable consideration' does not include marriage consideration or a nominal consideration in money. Completion by registration of a registrable disposition for valuable consideration of a registered estate has the effect of postponing to the interest under the disposition any interest affecting the estate immediately before the disposition whose priority is not protected at the time of registration (LRA 2002, s 29). The priority of an interest is 'protected' for these purposes if it is a registered charge or the subject of a notice in the register; or it is an interest falling within LRA 2002, Sch 3 which overrides registered dispositions; or it appears from the register to be excepted from the effect of registration. Additionally, in the case of a disposition of a leasehold estate, the priority of an interest is also protected if the burden of the interest is incident to the estate; for example, covenants by a tenant contained in the registered lease.

For interests falling within LRA 2002, Sch 3 which override registered dispositions, see *Overriding interests*, page 416. Any interest which has been the subject of a notice in the register at any time on or after 13 October 2003 is not treated as an overriding interest for these purposes.

Where the grant of a leasehold estate in land out of a registered estate does not involve a registrable disposition, LRA 2002, s 29 has effect as if the grant involved such a disposition and the disposition were registered at the time of the grant (LRA 2002, s 29(4)). This would apply to the grant of a lease for a term of 7 years or less.

The following example illustrates the working of the rules of priority in LRA 2002, ss 28 and 29:

- A is registered proprietor of a freehold estate in land.
- On 5 January 2018, A enters into a restrictive covenant with B affecting the whole of the estate in A's title. B does not apply for a notice to be registered in A's title.
- On 5 February 2018, A grants C an estate contract affecting the whole of the estate and a notice of the estate contract is entered in the register on 9 February 2018.
- On 5 March 2018, A transfers part of the land in the title by way of gift to D and D is registered as proprietor of the new title so created on 9 March 2018.
- On 5 April 2018, A transfers the remainder of the land in the original title on sale to E and E is registered as proprietor on 9 April 2018.

Considering the relative priorities on 12 April 2018: B's interest has priority to C's interest under the basic rule in s 28, because they are both equitable interests and B's interest was created first in time. D's registered estate is subject to the interests of both B and C under the basic rule in s 28, because although the transfer to D was a registrable disposition, it was not made for valuable consideration and the special rule in s 29 does not therefore apply to it. E's registered estate is subject only to the interest of C, which was protected by notice at the relevant time, as the transfer to E was a registrable disposition for valuable consideration and it was completed by registration.

Registrable dispositions of registered charges for valuable consideration

A 'registrable disposition' means a disposition, such as a transfer or charge, which is required to be completed by registration under LRA 2002, s 27. 'Valuable consideration' does not include marriage consideration or a nominal consideration in money. Completion by registration of a registrable disposition for valuable consideration of a registered charge has the effect of postponing to the interest under the disposition any interest affecting the charge immediately before the disposition whose priority is not protected at the time of registration (LRA 2002, s 30). The priority of an interest is 'protected' for these purposes if it is a registered charge or the subject of a notice in the register; or it is an interest falling within LRA 2002, Sch 3 which overrides registered dispositions; or it appears from the register to be excepted from the effect of registration. Additionally, in the case of a disposition of a charge which relates to a leasehold estate, the priority of an interest is also protected if the burden of the interest is incident to the estate.

For interests falling within LRA 2002, Sch 3 which override registered dispositions, see *Overriding interests*, page 416. Any interest which has been the subject of a notice in the register at any time on or after 13 October 2003 is not treated as an overriding interest for these purposes.

Inland Revenue charges

The effect of a disposition of a registered estate or registered charge on a charge under Inheritance Tax Act 1984, s 237 is determined, not in accordance with LRA 2002, ss 29 and 30 as described above, but in accordance with Inheritance Act 1984, ss 237(6) and 238 (LRA 2002, s 31). This has the effect that a purchaser in good faith for money or money's worth takes free from the Inland Revenue charge in the absence of registration.

Priority of applications

The operation of the special rule of priority is subject to the operation of the rules applicable to the priority of applications, including the rules relating to the priority period conferred by an official search with priority. Where an application for an entry in the register is protected, any entry made in the register during the priority period relating to the application is postponed to any entry made in pursuance of it (LRA 2002, s 72(2)). An application for an entry is 'protected' for these purposes if it is one to which a priority period relates and it is made before the end of that period. LRA 2002, s 72(2) does not apply, however, if the earlier entry was itself made in pursuance of a protected application and its priority period ranks ahead of the later application. If it appears to the Registry that LRA 2002, s 72(2) might apply to an entry, it may defer dealing with the application for such entry.

Where a court makes an order under LRA 2002, s 46(3) that an entry is to have overriding priority, this prevails over an application for another entry.

A purchaser may obtain a priority period for his application by applying for an official search with priority using Form OS1 or Form OS2, as appropriate (see *Official searches*, page 404). The priority period is the period beginning at the time when the application for the official search is entered on the day list and ending at midnight marking the end of the 30th working day thereafter. A working day is any day from Monday to Friday (inclusive) which is not Christmas Day, Good Friday or any other day either specified or declared by proclamation under Banking and Financial Dealings Act 1971, s 1 or appointed by the Lord Chancellor, or certified by the Registry as being an 'interrupted day' due to delay or failure of a communication service or to some other event or circumstance causing substantial interruption in the normal operation of the Registry.

Where two or more official search certificates with priority relating to the same registrable estate or charge or to the same registered land have been issued and are in operation, the certificates take effect, in respect to the priority conferred, in the order the applications for search were entered on the day list, unless the applicants agree otherwise. Where one transaction is dependent upon another, the Registry must assume, unless the contrary appears, that the applicants have agreed that their applications for search have priority so as to give effect to the sequence of the documents effecting the transactions (LRR 2003, r 153).

Where two or more applications relating to the same registered title are made at the same time by the same applicant, they rank in such order as he may specify. Where the applications are not made by the same applicant, they rank in such order as the applicants specify that they have agreed. If the applicants have not specified the agreed order of priority, the Registry notifies them and requests them to agree within a specified time. Should the applicants not agree within this period, the Registry proposes the order of priority and serves notice of its proposal on the applicants. If any applicant objects to this proposal, there is in consequence a dispute between the applicants (see *Disputes*, page 193 as to how such a dispute may be resolved). Where one transaction is dependent upon another, the Registry must assume, unless the contrary appears, that the applicants have specified that the applications are to have priority so as to give effect to the sequence of the documents effecting the transactions (LRR 2003, r 55).

PROFITS À PRENDRE

A profit à prendre is a right to take something from another person's land, such as the right to take fish, game or peat. A legal profit must subsist for an interest equivalent to an estate in fee simple absolute in possession or a term of years absolute (Law of Property Act 1925, s 1(2)(a)). Under the LRA 1925, the benefit of a profit à prendre appurtenant (that is, one attached to land) could be registered as appurtenant to a registered estate in land, but the benefit of a profit in gross (that is, one not attached to any land) could not be registered. However, the LRA 2002 provides for profits à prendre in gross to be capable of substantive registration in their own right (LRA 2002, s 2). It is not, however, compulsory to apply for first registration of the title to a profit à prendre in gross. It is not possible to register a profit which is appurtenant to land separately from that land (LRA 2002, s 59(1)).

A 'right of common' is a form of profit à prendre and some rights of common will be profits à prendre in gross. However, not all profits à prendre in gross will be rights of common. This distinction is important, because rights of common over land capable of being registered under the CRA 1965 cannot be registered under the LRA 2002. Nor can the burden of such rights be the subject of a notice in the register of land subject to them (LRA 2002, s 33(d)).

Legal profits à prendre on first registration

Beneficial profits à prendre

On first registration of title, the estate is vested in the registered proprietor together with all interests subsisting for the benefit of the estate (LRA 2002, ss 11(3) and 12(3)). This includes the benefit of any subsisting appurtenant legal profits, whether or not these are the subject of an entry in the register. If, at the time of first registration, the Registry is satisfied that a right subsists as a legal estate and benefits the registered estate, it may enter the benefit of that appurtenant right in the register (LRR 2003, r 33(1)). This will be as the result of the Registry's examination of the title or its consideration of a written application providing details of the right and evidence of its existence. Where the profit has arisen by implication or prescription, the evidence will usually be in the form of a statutory declaration or statement of truth (see 'Prescriptive profits à prendre', below). If the Registry is not satisfied that the right subsists as a legal interest benefiting the registered estate, it may enter details of the right claimed in the property register with such qualification as it considers appropriate (LRR 2003, r 33(2)).

The applicant must therefore lodge evidence that the grantor had power to grant the profit, otherwise the Registry may either omit the right or enter a qualification note to an entry in the register relating to the appurtenant profit.

Where the burdened estate is registered, the consent of any chargee of that estate, whose charge has priority over the grant of the profit and who has not joined in the grant, should be lodged. If the chargee has not consented to the grant, the profit is liable to be overridden if the chargee exercises his power of sale. If the consent cannot be lodged, the application may be completed but with a note along the following lines being added to the register entry for the benefiting title:

> NOTE: The consent of the proprietor of the charge dated [*date*] in favour of [*name*] affecting title(s) [*title number(s)*] was not produced on registration and the rights [*referred to above or as the case may be*] may be overridden in the event of the exercise of the power of sale.

The note can be cancelled without fee if an application is subsequently made in Form AP1 enclosing the consent. Any restriction (including a restriction in favour of a chargee) in the register of the burdened title must be complied with so far as necessary. If there is a caution against dealings or a notice of (intended) deposit in the register of the burdened title and the consent to the registration of the profit does not accompany the application, the Registry may serve notice upon the cautioner or depositee.

Where the burdened estate is unregistered, evidence of the grantor's title to it, commencing with a good root more than 15 years old at the date of the application, must accompany the application. The consent of any legal mortgagee of the burdened estate to the grant of the profit should also be lodged, unless he has joined in the grant. If this consent is not lodged, the application may be completed but with a note being added to the register entry for the benefiting title in the form referred to above. In addition, if the grantor's title is leasehold, full evidence of title to any superior leasehold titles (whether of the land or profit) relating to the burdened land should be lodged.

If the profit was granted over an unregistered estate that has since been registered, it may be necessary for a notice as to the burden of the profit to be entered in the register of the burdened title at the same time as the benefit is entered in the register of the benefiting title. This will be done by the Registry as part of the first registration, normally after service of notice on the proprietor of the burdened title.

Subjective profits à prendre

On first registration, the estate is vested in the registered proprietor subject to any profit which is an interest which overrides first registration under LRA 2002, Sch 1, or is the subject of an entry in the register in relation to the estate, and/or, in the case of a leasehold title, which is incident to the leasehold estate (LRA 2002, ss 11(4)(a) and 12(4)(a) and (b)). The Registry must enter a notice in the register of the burden of any profit which appears from its examination of the title to affect the registered estate, except any which appears to it to be of a trivial or obvious character, or the entry of a notice in respect of which would be likely to cause confusion or inconvenience (LRR 2003, r 35). No notice may be entered in the register in respect of a profit which is a right of common capable of being registered under the CRA 1965 (LRA 2002, s 33(d)). Even where no entry is made as to a subjective legal profit on first registration, it is an interest falling within LRA 2002, Sch 1, para 3 which therefore overrides first registration.

A person applying for first registration must provide information to the Registry in Form DI about any legal profits which are within his actual knowledge and affect the estate to which the application relates, other than any which are capable of being registered under the CRA 1965 (see 'Duty to disclose overriding interests', page 426). The Registry may enter a notice in the register in respect of any such legal profit (LRR 2003, r 28).

Legal profits à prendre arising after first registration

The express grant or reservation of a legal profit (other than one capable of being registered under the CRA 1965 and other than a grant as a result of the operation of Law of Property Act 1925, s 62) over registered land must be completed by registration if it is to operate at law. The profit may be created in either a deed of grant, a transfer or a lease. Registration in the case of an appurtenant legal profit is completed by the entry of a notice of the profit in the register of the burdened estate and, if the benefiting estate is registered, an entry in the property register of that estate (LRA 2002, s 27(2)(d) and (7) and Sch 2, para 7). Until completed by registration, such a profit is only equitable. In the case of a legal profit in gross, the grantee must be registered as proprietor of the profit and a notice in respect of the profit must be entered in the register (LRA 2002, Sch 2, para 6) (see 'Registration of profit à prendre in gross created over registered land', below).

If the grant of a profit over a registered burdened estate is a registrable disposition, an application to complete the grant by registration *must* be made in Form AP1 or AN1 in order to meet the registration requirements. This is the case even if only the burdened estate is registered (LRR 2003, rr 13 and 90). Therefore an application for entry of an agreed or unilateral notice in Form UN1 will *not* meet the registration requirements. In that event, a subsequent application may be made in Form AP1 to complete the profit by registration so that it does take effect at law. Until then, it takes effect in equity only and, if it is an appurtenant profit, the benefit cannot be registered in the register of the benefiting estate (if registered).

Where the profit is contained in a transfer or charge of part of a registered estate, only an application to register the transfer or charge is necessary; no separate application in respect of the profit is required. The Registry will make the necessary entries as a matter of course when registering the transfer, provided the relevant title numbers are provided in panel 2 of Form AP1 or separate application is made (LRR 2003, r 72(4) and (5)). On registration of the transfer or charge, entries are made in the new title created and the retained or uncharged title, in respect of any appurtenant legal profits granted or reserved in the transfer or charge. An entry in respect of a profit in gross is made in the burdened title and a new title created in respect of the profit. In the case of a charge of part such entries are made only if the Registry decides that the charged part is to be comprised in a separate registered title from the uncharged part.

An applicant for registration of the benefit of an appurtenant legal profit contained in a deed of grant should deliver to the Registry:

(a)   an application in Form AP1;
(b)   the deed of grant or a certified copy of it;
(c)   any consents or certificates required in respect of mortgages, charges or restrictions relating to the burdened title;
(d)   (if the right is granted over unregistered land) an abstract or epitome showing the grantor's title to the unregistered estate;
(e)   the appropriate confirmation or evidence as to identity (see *Identity evidence*, page 266);
(f)   the appropriate SDLT certificate or other evidence (see *Stamp duty land tax*, page 541); and
(g)   the fee payable (see *Fees*, page 221).

The title numbers of all the registered titles involved must be specified in panel 2 of Form AP1, otherwise the Registry is not obliged to make any entry unless separate application is made (LRR 2003, r 72C(3)). The profit will be completed by registration, with entries being made in the register of the burdened estate and (if registered) the benefiting estate (r 72C(2)).

Where the grant or reservation of a profit is not a registrable disposition, it will be effective at law when made. However, an application may be made for the benefit of the profit to be registered as appurtenant to a registered benefiting estate (LRR 2003, r 73A(1)(a)). The application must be made in Form AP1, accompanied by an abstract or epitome showing the grantor's title to the unregistered burdened land and any consents or certificates required in respect of mortgages, charges or restrictions relating to the burdened land. Where the Registry is not satisfied that the right claimed subsists as a legal estate appurtenant to the applicant's registered estate, it may enter details of the right claimed in the property register with such qualification as it considers appropriate.

Where the benefiting estate having the benefit of a profit appurtenant is unregistered, or an unregistered profit in gross exists, application may be made for the entry of a notice in respect of such a profit where it affects a registered estate. Where it appears to the Registry that a registered estate is subject to a legal profit à prendre, it may enter a notice in the register in respect of that profit (LRA 2002, s 37). In that case the Registry must give notice to the registered proprietor and to any person who appears to it to be entitled to the interest protected by the notice or whom the Registry otherwise considers appropriate (LRR 2003, r 89). However, if the registered proprietor applies for the entry of the notice, or consents to an application for such an entry, the Registry is not obliged to give notice to him. The Registry is also not obliged to give notice under r 89 to any person who has applied for, or consented to, the entry of the notice, nor is it so obliged if that person's name and address for service are not set out in the registered title in question.

Prescriptive profits à prendre

Prescription is the acquisition of a right through long use or enjoyment (user) so that the law presumes that the right was lawfully granted. There are three methods of acquiring a profit by prescription: at common law; by lost modern grant; and under the Prescription Act 1832 (except that this Act does not apply to a profit in gross). Whichever method is relied on, the user must have been exercised:

(a) for at least 20 years (or at least 30 years if the claim to a profit appurtenant is made under the Prescription Act 1832);

(b) as of right, that is, without force, without secrecy and without permission;

(c) by or on behalf of a freehold owner against another freehold owner, so that where the burdened land is occupied by a tenant, the user must normally have started before the tenancy began; and

(d) continuously, with no long, unexplained periods of non-user. Where the claim is made under the Prescription Act 1832, a break is not treated as an 'interruption' in user for the purposes of that Act until acquiesced in for one year.

In addition, the right claimed must be one that could have been lawfully granted. This point was considered by the House of Lords in *Bakewell Management Ltd v Brandwood* [2004] UKHL 14. In consequence, if the right could not have been lawfully granted by deed, then it cannot be acquired by prescription.

A prescriptive profit over a registered estate that has arisen by prescription does not have to be completed by registration to take effect at law and it will subsist either in gross or (as the case may be) for the benefit of any registered or unregistered estate to which it is appurtenant, notwithstanding that it is not the subject of an entry in the register. However, its validity will only be guaranteed for registration purposes if it is registered as a profit in gross or (as the case may be) as appurtenant to a registered estate.

An application for registration of the benefit of a prescriptive profit appurtenant may be made in either Form FR1 at the time of an application for first registration of the benefiting estate (LRR 2003, r 33); or Form AP1 at any time subsequently (LRR 2003, r 73A). If the burdened estate is registered, the title number must be given in the application form. Where the application is only to note the burden of a profit, the application should be made in Form AN1 for entry of an agreed notice or Form UN1 for entry of a unilateral notice (see *Notices*, page 389), as appropriate.

The application must be accompanied by satisfactory supporting evidence, normally in the form of a statement of truth (which may be in Form ST4 in LRR 2003, Sch 1) or statutory declaration by the applicant and any predecessors in title setting out the relevant details of the user of the profit claimed, for the requisite period of 20 years or more. If the title to the applicant's estate is unregistered, he should lodge evidence of his title. Similarly, the applicant should lodge evidence of title in respect of the burdened estate if that is unregistered. If an inspection of the land is necessary, an additional fee to cover the cost of this will also be payable.

If the application is completed, the register entries made by the Registry will depend upon whether both the benefiting estate and burdened estate are registered or only one of them is registered. Also, where the burdened estate is unregistered, whether satisfactory evidence of title to it has been lodged.

Where both the benefiting estate and burdened estate are registered, the Registry will give notice of the application to the registered proprietor and any registered chargee of the burdened title. If no objection is received, the benefit of the profit will be registered as appurtenant to the benefiting estate and a notice as to the burden will be entered in the burdened estate.

Where the benefiting estate is registered but the burdened estate is unregistered, if the applicant lodges evidence of title to the burdened estate and the address of the freehold owner, the Registry will give notice of the application to the freehold owner and any other person who may have an interest in the burdened land. If no objection is received, the benefit of the profit will be registered as appurtenant to the benefiting estate. However, if (as may often be the case) the applicant is not able to lodge evidence of title to the burdened estate and the address of the freehold owner, the Registry is likely to make only a note in the register to the effect that the applicant claims the benefit of the profit (LRR 2003, r 73A(5)). This entry will be in the following form:

> The registered proprietor claims that the land has the benefit of a right [*terms of profit as claimed by claimant*]. The right claimed is not included in this registration. The claim is supported by [*dates and details of statement(s) of truth or statutory declaration(s) and who has made them*].

Where the burdened estate is registered but the benefiting estate is unregistered, the Registry will give notice of the application to the registered proprietor and any registered chargee of the burdened estate. If no objection is received, a notice as to the burden will be entered in the burdened estate in the appropriate form, depending upon whether the application is for an agreed notice or a unilateral notice.

Where the benefit of a prescriptive profit appurtenant is entered in the register of a registered benefiting estate, the entry will indicate that the right was acquired through long user and will refer to the statement(s) of truth or statutory declaration(s) lodged in support of the application, which will be open to inspection and copying.

If a valid objection is received in response to a notice of an application which cannot be disposed of by agreement, the matter will have to be dealt with in accordance with LRA 2002, s 73 (see *Disputes*, page 193). Similar procedures, adapted as necessary, apply where a profit has arisen by implied grant rather than by prescription.

Unregistered legal profits à prendre which override registered dispositions

Although all legal profits à prendre override first registration, the position is not the same for registered dispositions. In the light of LRA 2002, Sch 3, para 3, a legal profit overrides a registered disposition only if:

(a)   at the time of the disposition it is within the actual knowledge of the person to whom the disposition is made; or

(b)   at the time of the disposition it would have been obvious on a reasonably careful inspection of the land over which the profit is exercisable; or

(c)   the person entitled to the profit proves that it has been exercised in the period of one year ending with the day of the disposition; or

(d)   it is registered under the CRA 1965.

Any profit, however, which was an overriding interest immediately before 13 October 2003, but which would not fall within LRA 2002, Sch 3, para 3 if created on or after 13 October 2003, continues to be an overriding interest (LRA 2002, Sch 12, para 9). For a period of 3 years beginning on 13 October 2003 any unregistered legal profit overrode a registered disposition (LRA 2002, Sch 12, para 10). An unregistered profit over registered land arising on or after 13 October 2003 is a legal profit only if it is an implied or prescriptive profit; the grant of a profit which constitutes a registrable disposition will be equitable unless completed by registration.

A person applying to register a registrable disposition of a registered estate must provide information to the Registry in Form DI about any legal profits (other than those capable of being registered under the CRA 1965) falling within LRA 2002, Sch 3, para 3 which are within his actual knowledge and affect the estate to which the application relates (see 'Duty to disclose overriding interests', page 426). The applicant must produce to the Registry any documentary evidence of the existence of any such legal profits as is under his control. The Registry may enter a notice in the register in respect of any such legal profit (LRR 2003, r 57).

First registration of profit à prendre in gross

In addition to the usual documents required (see *First registration*, page 222), an applicant should deliver to the Registry:

(a)   sufficient details, by plan or otherwise, so that the area of land which is affected by the profit can be clearly identified on the Ordnance Survey map;

(b)   in the case of a leasehold profit in gross, the lease, if in the control of the applicant (and a certified copy, if the applicant wishes for the original to be returned).

If the grantor's title is leasehold, full evidence of title to any superior leasehold titles (whether of the land or profit) relating to the burdened land should be lodged.

If there are any rights, interests or claims affecting the profit which are known to the applicant, other than those disclosed in the title deeds or Form DI, these should be disclosed in Form FR1. This would include, for example, a disputed third party claim relating to the profit. As to first registration generally, see *First registration*, page 222.

Leases of profits à prendre in gross may only be the subject of first registration if at the date of the application more than 7 years of the term are unexpired (LRA 2002, s 3(3)). The provision in LRA 2002, s 3(4), which enables discontinuous leases of any length to be the subject of first registration, relates only to an estate in land. The Registry may decide to grant only a qualified class of title, if the term of a discontinuous lease is not sufficiently clear for the purposes of s 3(3). Notice of a lease of an unregistered profit à prendre in gross may be entered in the register of an affected servient registered title even if less than 7 years of the term are unexpired.

The property register of a registered profit à prendre in gross must contain a description of the profit and, where practicable, sufficient particulars of any instrument which created it to enable it to be identified (LRR 2003, rr 5 and 7). An easement over other land can exist as appurtenant to a profit à prendre in gross. On first registration, the title to the profit à prendre in gross will be examined and appurtenant easements to which good title can be shown will be registered. Rights which are effectively part of the profit à prendre in gross, such as a right of access over land adjoining a river bank in order to exercise a right to fish, will form part of the description of the profit à prendre in gross in the register.

Where the applicant for first registration is unable to produce a full documentary title, the application must be supported by evidence to account for this, usually in the form of a statutory declaration or statement of truth, exhibiting any appropriate supporting documents. A statement of truth may be in Form ST3 in LRR 2003, Sch 1 (see *Lost or destroyed title deeds*, page 369).

Where two or more persons apply to be registered as proprietors of a profit à prendre and a sole proprietor or the survivor of joint proprietors will not be able to give a valid receipt for capital money, application must be made for entry of a restriction in Form A (LRR 2003, r 94(2A)) (see *Joint proprietors*, page 286).

Registration of profit à prendre in gross created over registered land

The express grant of a profit à prendre in gross out of a registered estate (other than one capable of being registered under the CRA 1965) is a registrable disposition (LRA 2002, s 27(2)(d)). In the case of a deed of grant, an applicant should deliver to the Registry:

(a)   an application in Form AP1;
(b)   the deed creating the profit or a certified copy of it;
(c)   any consents or certificates required in respect of mortgages, charges or restrictions in the grantor's title;
(d)   Form DI giving the information as to overriding interests required by LRR 2003, r 57, including any documentary evidence of the interests (see 'Duty to disclose overriding interests', page 426);
(e)   the appropriate confirmation or evidence as to identity (see *Identity evidence*, page 266);
(f)   the appropriate SDLT certificate or other evidence (see *Stamp duty land tax*, page 541); and
(g)   the fee payable (see *Fees*, page 221).

On registration of the profit, it is allotted its own title number. Notice of the registered profit is entered on the grantor's registered title without any need for a separate application or further fee. Where two or more persons apply to be registered as proprietors of a profit à prendre and a sole proprietor or the survivor of joint proprietors will not be able to give a valid receipt for capital money, application must be made for entry of a restriction in Form A (LRR 2003, r 94(2A)) (see *Joint proprietors*, page 286). Where the disposition consists of the grant of a lease of a profit à prendre in gross out of a registered estate, this will be a registrable disposition, regardless of the length of the term (LRA 2002, s 27(2)(d)). As to the registration of such a lease, see *Leases*, page 296. In the case of a discontinuous lease, the Registry may decide to enter a qualifying note in the leasehold title, if the lease is being substantively registered with its own title and the term of the lease is not sufficiently clear for the purposes of the registration requirements in LRA 2002, Sch 2, para 6.

Dispositions of a registered profit à prendre in gross

The proprietor of a registered profit à prendre in gross may transfer or lease it subject to any rule of law, express provision in the grant of the profit, or entry in the register to the contrary (LRA 2002, s 23). A lease of a registered profit à prendre in gross is a registrable disposition, regardless of the length of the term (LRA 2002, s 27(2)(d)). As to the registration of such a lease, see *Leases*, page 296. The transfer or lease may be in respect of the whole of the registered profit, or part of it. In the latter case, the part may relate to either a geographical division of the area over which the profit subsists (for example by splitting off a right to fish in a specific part of the river over which the right subsists), or a division of the subject matter of right (for example by splitting off a right to fish for salmon from a general right to fish in a river).

Extinguishment of profits à prendre

When a profit is referred to in the register of title and has been extinguished, an appropriate application may be made for the relevant entry or entries to be removed. Extinguishment may occur by virtue of statute; release (express or implied); or merger by unity of ownership and possession. In that event, application may be made for removal of the relevant entry or entries and/or (in the case of a registered estate consisting of a profit à prendre in gross) closure of the registered title. The application must be accompanied by evidence to satisfy the Registry that the profit has been extinguished. If a valid objection is received in response to a notice of the application served by the Registry which cannot be disposed of by agreement, the matter will have to be dealt with in accordance with LRA 2002, s 73 (see *Disputes*, page 193). In the case of a registered profit à prendre in gross, or a profit appurtenant which has been registered in a registered benefiting title, the application should be made in Form AP1. Otherwise (where only the burden has been noted in the register of a registered burdened estate), the application should be in Form CN1 (for cancellation of an agreed notice), Form UN2 (for removal of a unilateral notice) or Form UN4 (for cancellation of a unilateral notice), as appropriate (see *Notices*, page 389).

Related matters

An equitable profit à prendre may exist. In such a case, reference may usefully be made to the principles applicable to equitable easements (see *Equitable easements*, page 212). As to legal easements, see *Legal easements*, page 343.

PROPER OFFICE

Unless lodged electronically or in accordance with a written arrangement as to delivery made between the Registry and the applicant or his conveyancer, all applications and correspondence should be delivered to the 'proper office', as designated by an order of the Lord Chancellor as the proper office for the receipt of applications (LRA 2002, s 100(3)) or if no such order subsists, to the Registry under the provisions of any relevant direction by the registrar under LRA 2002, s 100(4) as to the address to be used for the delivery of applications (LRR 2003, r 15(3)(a)).

The Land Registration (Proper Office) Order 2013 (SI 2013/1627) came into force on 1 October 2013 and designated all 14 Land Registry offices (as listed in the Schedule to that Order) as proper offices for the receipt of applications under the LRA 2002. It replaced the previous Land Registration (Proper Office) Order, which designated a particular office as the proper office, depending on the administrative area in which the land concerned was situated. The aim of the 2013 Order was to evenly distribute paper applications for registration, when paper records were held at different Registry offices.

However, as the register is held in electronic form shared across all Registry offices and most applications are delivered electronically, the 2013 Order was revoked on 6 April 2018. Those applications still sent in paper go to a single address for scanning and electronic distribution. The Registry has published recommendations as to where an applicant should send his application, based on whether he is a business user or member of the public, as the case may be.

The address for members of the public is: HM Land Registry Citizen Centre, PO Box 74, Gloucester GL14 9BB.

Conveyancers and other business users of land registration services who have a written arrangement as to delivery should send applications to their designated 'Customer Team' within a Registry office. Other such business users should send their applications to the relevant office in accordance with the Registry's recommendation (currently being the applicant's closest office).

The Royal Mail address for business customers is: HM Land Registry, [*insert customer team's office name, or if none, the name of the closest office*], PO Box 75, Gloucester GL14 9BD.

The DX address for business customers is: HM Land Registry, [*insert customer team's office name, or if none, the name of the closest office*], DX 321601 Gloucester 33.

For electronic applications, see *Electronic services*, page 200.

PROPERTY ADJUSTMENT ORDERS

An application for a property adjustment order under Matrimonial Causes Act 1983, s 24, or under the equivalent provisions in Civil Partnership Act 2004, s 72 and Schs 5 and 7, which affects the legal estate in registered land is a pending land action (see *Pending land actions*, page 433). As such, it is treated as an interest affecting an estate or charge for the purposes of the LRA 2002 (LRA 2002, s 87(1)). It cannot, however, be an interest belonging to a person in actual occupation falling within LRA 2002, Sch 1, para 2 or Sch 3, para 2 which overrides first registration or registered dispositions (LRA 2002, s 87(3)). Such an application may be protected by entry in the register of an agreed notice or a unilateral notice.

An application for a property adjustment order which does not affect the legal estate in registered land is not a pending land action and cannot be protected by entry of a notice. For example, an application for an order only in respect of a beneficial interest held by the other spouse or civil partner under a trust of land, where the dispute is not as to the existence of the trust, but as to who is entitled to a beneficial interest under it. This is because the interest in dispute does not constitute 'land' for this purpose. By contrast, an application where the existence of the trust is in dispute (for example, an application for a declaration that a sole proprietor holds on an implied trust), or an application for the appointment of a new or additional trustee, may affect the legal estate and is therefore arguably a pending land action which may be protected by entry of a notice (see *Godfrey v Torpey & others* [2006] EWHC 1423 (Ch)).

Where the spouses or civil partners already hold the property as beneficial joint tenants, consideration should be given to severing the equitable joint tenancy (see *Severance of a beneficial joint tenancy*, page 533).

Once the court has made a final order, there will no longer be a 'pending' action and the appropriate action will need to be taken in respect of the order itself. A property adjustment order affecting the legal estate may be protected by entry of an agreed notice or a unilateral notice, although in most cases it will be more appropriate to complete and register a disposition (such as a transfer or charge) giving effect to its terms.

The order of the court may provide for the immediate sale of the property and the distribution of the proceeds of sale. Such an order does not require to be the subject of an entry in the register.

Where the order provides that one party should enter into a charge in favour of the other, the protection of such charge depends on whether it is a registrable charge or an equitable charge (see *Legal charges*, page 333, and *Equitable charges*, page 207 as appropriate).

A property adjustment order that has the effect only of either creating a trust of land, or of declaring the beneficial interests under a trust of land, cannot be protected by entry of a notice (LRA 2002, s 33(a)). Such an order may be protected by entry of a restriction, where appropriate, in which case the form of the restriction will depend upon the nature of the order. Where the order has the effect of creating a trust, or of severing an existing beneficial joint tenancy, application should be made for a restriction in Form A, if such a restriction has not already been entered in the register. A restriction does not confer any priority; it simply prevents an entry being made in the register in respect of any disposition, or a disposition of a specified kind, unless the terms of the restriction have (where applicable) been complied with.

Agreed notice

In addition to the usual documents required (see *Notices*, page 389), an applicant should deliver to the Registry a certified copy of the petition or answer claiming relief, or a certified copy of the property adjustment order made by the court, as the case may be.

As the consent of the registered proprietor is unlikely to be forthcoming in this situation, this is likely to be sufficient to satisfy the Registry of the validity of the applicant's claim in accordance with LRA 2002, s 34(3)(c).

The agreed notice in the register will give details of the interest protected.

Unilateral notice

An applicant should deliver to the Registry the usual documents required (see *Notices*, page 389).

Where the application relates to an application for a property adjustment order, the statement in panel 11 or conveyancer's certificate in panel 12 of Form UN1 should be completed on the following lines to show the interest of the applicant:

> applicant for a property adjustment order under the [*Matrimonial Causes Act 1973*] or [*Civil Partnership Act 2004*] in the [*name of court*] [*set out full court reference and parties*].

Where the application relates to a property adjustment order which has been made by the court, the statement in panel 11 or conveyancer's certificate in panel 12 of Form UN1 should be completed on the following lines to show the interest of the applicant:

> person who has obtained a property adjustment order under the [*Matrimonial Causes Act 1973*] *or* [*Civil Partnership Act 2004*] dated [*date*] made in the [*name of court*] [*set out full court reference and parties*] which provides that [*set out the effect of the order*].

The unilateral notice in the register will give brief details of the interest protected and identify the beneficiary of that notice.

Restriction

In addition to the usual documents required (see *Restrictions*, page 500), an applicant should deliver to the Registry a certified copy of the property adjustment order made by the court.

As the application for a restriction is unlikely to be made by or with the consent of the registered proprietor in this situation, the statement in panel 12 or conveyancer's certificate in panel 13 of Form RX1 must be completed, setting out details of the applicant's interest under the property adjustment order.

Panel 9 of Form RX1 should be completed as to the appropriate restriction(s).

If there is no restriction in Form A already in the register, a person having a beneficial interest under a trust of land has a sufficient interest for the purposes of LRA 2002, s 43(1)(c) to apply for entry of a restriction in Form A, to ensure that a survivor of the joint proprietors (unless a trust corporation) will not be able to give a valid receipt for capital money (LRR 2003, r 93(a)). The wording of Form A is set out in Appendix IV, page 585.

The person having a beneficial interest under a trust of land also has a sufficient interest for the purposes of LRA 2002, s 43(1)(c) to apply for entry of a restriction in Form II to ensure that he receives notice of a disposition. The wording of Form II is set out in Appendix IV, page 585.

This restriction does not of itself prevent a disposition, provided its terms are complied with. This is because the interest of the beneficiary will be overreached where the requirements of Form A have been met (Law of Property Act 1925, ss 2 and 27).

A restriction in standard Form A or Form II in LRA 2002, Sch 4 does not require the approval of the Registry to the wording of the restriction under LRA 2002, s 43(3).

The Registry must give notice of an application for a restriction to the proprietor of the registered estate or charge concerned if it has not been made by or with his consent or a person entitled to be registered as such proprietor (LRA 2002, s 45).

PROPRIETARY ESTOPPEL

Where the owner of land creates an expectation in another person that that person will receive some right or interest over the land and that person acts to his detriment as a result of that expectation, an equity may arise in favour of that person by estoppel. If the owner refuses to grant the right or interest in question, an application for relief may be made to the court. The court has discretion as to the form of relief it grants (see for example *Crabb v Arun District Council* [1976] Ch 179; *Taylor Fashions v Liverpool Victoria Friendly Society* [1981] 1 All ER 897; and *Gillett v Holt* [2001] Ch 210). In recent years, the courts have sometimes sought to limit the circumstances in which an estoppel may arise (see for example *Yeoman's Row Management Ltd v Cobbe* [2008] UKHL 55).

There has been doubt as to the nature of the interest after the proprietary estoppel has arisen but before the court has made its decision. LRA 2002, s 116 declares for the avoidance of doubt that, in relation to registered land, an equity by estoppel has effect from the time the equity arises as an interest capable of binding successors in title, subject to the rules about the effect of dispositions on priority. For the rules about the effect of dispositions on priority, see *Priorities*, page 452. LRA 2002, s 116 applies to estoppels created both before and after that section came into force on 13 October 2003.

Between the time the equity by estoppel arises and the time the court gives effect to it, the interest may be protected by entry of a notice. If the person claiming the equity is in actual possession of the land over which the equity is claimed, it may take effect as an interest falling within LRA 2002, Sch 1, para 2 or Sch 3, para 2 which overrides first registration and registered dispositions. If an application for entry of a notice is made, this will normally be for a unilateral notice, unless the facts claimed to give rise to the interest are unequivocal, in which case application may be made for an agreed notice.

Agreed notice

In addition to the usual documents required (see *Notices*, page 389), an applicant should deliver to the Registry details of the facts claimed to have given rise to the proprietary estoppel, including the name of the proprietor of the registered estate against whom the equity is claimed to have arisen, together with any documentary evidence available.

As the consent of the registered proprietor is unlikely to be forthcoming in this situation, the evidence lodged must be sufficient to satisfy the Registry as to the validity of the applicant's claim in accordance with LRA 2002, s 34(3)(c).

The agreed notice in the register will give details of the interest protected.

Unilateral notice

An applicant should deliver to the Registry the usual documents required (see *Notices*, page 389).

The statement in panel 12 or conveyancer's certificate in panel 13 of Form UN1 should be completed on the following lines to show the interest of the applicant:

> person having an equity arising by proprietary estoppel as a result of [*set out facts which give rise to the proprietary estoppel, including the name of the proprietor of the registered estate against whom the equity is claimed to have arisen*].

The unilateral notice in the register will give brief details of the interest protected and identify the beneficiary of that notice.

PUBLIC AUTHORITY CERTIFICATES OF TITLE

The Registry has made arrangements with a number of local and other public authorities whereby when the authority sells unregistered land, it gives the purchaser a certificate as to the title in an agreed form, instead of deducing title in the ordinary way. The certificate contains a statement of the incumbrances that affect the land. The Registry will accept this statement, and accordingly, when the purchaser applies for first registration of his title, he need not produce the normal conveyancing evidence of the authority's title. It also makes it unnecessary for a Land Charges search to be made by the purchaser against the name of the authority.

This procedure will be used, for example, on purchases of property under the right to buy scheme. Under HA 1985, s 154(2), a landlord is obliged to give to a tenant who exercises his right to buy under that Act a certificate of title in a form approved by the Registry. Three such forms of certificate of title have been so approved: PSD1 (where the landlord conveys a freehold dwelling house); PSD2 (where the landlord owns the freehold and grants a lease of a house or grants a shared ownership lease of a house or flat); and PSD3 (where the landlord does not own the freehold and grants an underlease of a house or flat).

Similarly, Forms PSD13, PSD14 and PSD15 have been approved for use in preserved right to buy cases and Form PSD16 has been approved for use in extended right to buy cases. Form PSD17 has been approved for use on the conveyance, lease or assignment of housing land or buildings, where the disposal is subject to a preserved right to buy or is a voluntary disposal with the consent of the Secretary of State, or is a disposal by a Housing Action Trust. Forms PSD11 (freehold dwelling) and PSD12 (leasehold dwelling) have been approved for use in relation to the compulsory registration of title to defective dwellings repurchased under HA 1985, Sch 20, para 17.

These forms of certificate of title are only for use in the specified cases and should not be used in any other circumstances. The certificate must be signed as provided and, in the case of a local authority, by the chief executive officer or by some other officer approved by the Registry. In reliance upon the certificate, the property will be registered subject to any incumbrances specified in the certificate, any contained in the deed inducing registration, and any created by the applicant. The authority is responsible for the accuracy of the certificate and must refund to the Registry any indemnity paid because the certificate was incorrect.

PUBLIC-PRIVATE PARTNERSHIP LEASES RELATING TO TRANSPORT IN LONDON

PPP leases for the purposes of the LRA 2002 are leases created for PPPs relating to transport in London within the meaning given by Greater London Authority Act 1999, s 218. No application for voluntary registration of such a lease may be made, nor does the requirement of registration apply on the grant or transfer of a leasehold estate in land under a PPP lease (LRA 2002, s 90(1) and (2)).

The grant of a term of years absolute under a PPP lease is not required to be completed by registration. The express grant of an interest falling within Law of Property Act 1925, s 1(2) (for example a legal easement), is not required to be completed by registration where the interest is created for the benefit of a leasehold estate in land under a PPP lease (LRA 2002, s 90(3)).

No notice may be entered in the register in respect of an interest under a PPP lease (LRA 2002, s 90(4)).

A PPP lease is an unregistered interest which overrides first registration and registered dispositions, as though it were included within LRA 2002, Schs 1 and 3 (LRA 2002, s 90(5)). An applicant is not, however, required to provide any information about a PPP lease under the duty to disclose interests which override those imposed by LRR 2003, rr 28 and 57 (see 'Duty to disclose overriding interests', page 426).

RECEIVERS APPOINTED UNDER THE LAW OF PROPERTY ACT 1925

Receivers appointed either under the statutory powers of appointment conferred by Law of Property Act 1925, s 109, or under an express power contained in a mortgage or debenture, who do not meet the requirements for an administrative receiver, are commonly referred to as 'Law of Property Act' or 'LPA' receivers. For administrative receivers, see *Administrative receivers*, page 5; for receivers appointed under the Mental Health Act 1983, see *Mental incapacity*, page 375; and for receivers appointed by court order, see *Receivers appointed by order of the court*, page 479.

A receiver is more commonly appointed where the mortgagor is a company, but appointment is also possible where the mortgagor is an individual. Where more than one receiver is appointed, the instrument of appointment must make it clear whether they can act jointly and severally, or jointly only.

In the case of a mortgage or debenture created by deed, a statutory power arises when the mortgage money has become payable and the power of sale is exercisable (Law of Property Act 1925, ss 101(1), 103 and 109). This statutory power may be varied, extended or excluded by the mortgage or debenture, which may contain an express power to appoint (Law of Property Act 1925, ss 109(3) and 101(4)).

In the case of a company mortgagor, where an administrator has been appointed prior to the appointment of the receiver, the consent of the administrator (or the permission of the court) to the appointment of the receiver must be lodged with any application to register a disposition by the receiver, otherwise the Registry will serve notice on the administrator, giving him the opportunity to object, before the application can proceed further. The appointment of a receiver does not prevent an administrator being subsequently appointed, although the receiver is not automatically dismissed if this occurs. However, the receiver must vacate office if required to do so by the administrator.

An entry in respect of the mortgage or debenture under which the receiver is appointed should already appear in the register by virtue of it having been registered as a registered charge or protected by entry of a notice. As the property remains vested in the mortgagor, the receiver cannot be registered as proprietor nor can a note of the receiver's appointment be entered in the register. The receiver may, however, make an application for any necessary changes to the mortgagor's address for service in the register.

Address for service

The receiver should ensure that the mortgagor's address for service shown in the register is such as will allow notices to be received. If an additional address for service (up to three are permitted) or an amended address for service is required the receiver should deliver to the Registry:

(a) an application in Form AP1;
(b) a certified copy of the appointment of the receiver;
(c) evidence that the receiver has power to apply on behalf of the mortgagor; and
(d) a certified copy of the debenture or charge under which the receiver is appointed (if not already noted or registered and a copy filed with the Registry).

No fee is currently payable.

Sale by a receiver

A receiver has only limited statutory powers under Law of Property Act 1925, s 109 and these powers are normally extended by the mortgage or debenture. The statutory powers must be extended if the receiver is to have power to dispose of the mortgagor's property.

An LPA receiver has no statutory power to execute on behalf of the company. The mortgage or debenture will normally include a power of attorney in favour of the receiver. Such a power is not a security power and will not survive liquidation if the mortgagor is a company. If the receiver executes as attorney under such a specific power, even if the power is under 12 months old, the application for registration of the disposition will need to be accompanied by a statutory declaration or statement of truth confirming that the applicant did not, at the time of the completion of the transaction, know of any revocation of the power or know of the occurrence of any event (such as the winding-up of a company mortgagor or bankruptcy, death or mental incapacity of an individual mortgagor) which had the effect of revoking the power. A conveyancer's certificate to the like effect may be provided instead.

Usually the mortgage or debenture will also give the receiver the right to sell or otherwise dispose of the mortgagor's property and this includes the power to execute in the name and on behalf of the mortgagor. If the receiver executes under such a power, evidence of non-revocation will not be required.

In the case of a company mortgagor, a deed can also, at the direction of the receiver, be sealed by the company using its common seal in the presence of the duly authorised officers of the company, or signed as a deed by a director and secretary or by two directors of the company (or by a single director if that signature is witnessed and attested).

A receiver is the agent of the mortgagor. On liquidation of a company mortgagor this agency comes to an end, but the receiver continues to have power to act for the purposes of holding and disposing of the company's property and may use the company's name for that purpose (*Sowman v David Samuel Trust Ltd* [1978] 1 All ER 616).

In a winding-up of a corporate mortgagor by the court, any disposition of the company's property after commencement of the winding-up is void unless sanctioned by an order of the court (IA 1986, s 127). However, where a debenture has been created prior to the winding-up, any subsequent disposition by the debenture holder or receiver under powers contained in the debenture does not require an order of the court.

The IA 1986 makes provision for transactions at an undervalue, preferences, extortionate credit transactions and the avoidance of certain floating charges (IA 1986, ss 238 to 241, 244 and 245) which may have the effect of invalidating the debenture wholly or in part. When making an application for registration of a disposition by a receiver, the applicant must therefore disclose any such challenge of which he is aware and if there is any suggestion that the liquidator may be seeking to have the debenture avoided under these provisions, the Registry may serve notice upon the liquidator, giving him the opportunity to object. If a valid objection is received which cannot be disposed of by agreement, the matter will have to be dealt with in accordance with LRA 2002, s 73 (see *Disputes*, page 193). Similar considerations are likely to apply where it appears that a trustee in bankruptcy may seek to avoid the mortgage under IA 1986, ss 339, 340, 343 or 423 (while having regard to the provisions of s 342(2) and (2A)).

If the debenture confers a power of attorney upon the receiver, this power is not a security power and it will be revoked by the winding-up of the company. However, the right to sell, or otherwise dispose of, the company's property will include the right to execute in the name and on behalf of the company and such a right will continue after winding-up commences (*Barrows v Chief Land Registrar, The Times*, 20 October 1977).

A receiver is the agent of the mortgagor not of the mortgagee or debenture holder and therefore has no power to discharge the mortgagor's property from any mortgage or charge (including the mortgage or debenture under which he was appointed), regardless of the date of creation of the mortgage or charge. Consequently, on a sale of a property by a receiver, the purchaser must, where appropriate, ensure that a release or discharge is obtained for all mortgages and charges, including the mortgage or debenture under which the receiver was appointed.

In addition to the usual documents required (see *Transfers*, page 551), a transferee of a registered title from a receiver should deliver to the Registry:

(a)   a certified copy of the receiver's appointment;
(b)   a certified copy of the mortgage or debenture under which the receiver was appointed (unless this is already noted in the register and a copy is filed at the Registry);
(c)   evidence that the power of appointment of a receiver under the mortgage has arisen (which may be in the form of a certificate by the mortgagee, or by a conveyancer on his behalf, that the power of appointment under the mortgage has arisen, unless this is evident from a full copy of the mortgage or debenture filed at the Registry);
(d)   if the receiver executes as attorney, evidence of non-revocation where appropriate:
(e)   a discharge or release in respect of any charges appearing in the title;
(f)   details of any challenge to the validity of the debenture that is within the actual knowledge of the receiver or the applicant. Where the mortgagor is a company and the challenge is by a liquidator or administrator of the company, or the mortgagor is an individual and the challenge is by a trustee in bankruptcy, details of the name and address of the liquidator, administrator or trustee in bankruptcy should be provided;
(g)   the consent of any previously appointed administrator, or the permission of the court, to the appointment of the receiver where required.

Any existing restrictions in the register will need to be complied with. If a restriction in Form A appears in the register, consideration must be given both as to whether the terms of the restriction have been complied with so as to enable the transfer to be registered and, if so, as to whether overreaching has been effected so as to enable the existing restriction to be cancelled from the register.

If there are joint mortgagors, a transfer executed by a single receiver on their behalf will comply with the restriction and can be registered, as it is not a disposition by a sole proprietor. This reflects the fact that the joint mortgagors (as trustees) have power to mortgage the land and can delegate to the receiver the power to sell and convey the mortgaged land. Delegation by more than one mortgagor to a single receiver will be effective for registration purposes, as it represents 'collective delegation' for the purposes of Trustee Act 2000, s 11, so that the joint mortgagors are acting through a single agent. However, execution by a single receiver would not appear to fulfill the requirements for overreaching to be effected under Law of Property Act 1925, ss 2(1)(ii) and 27 (Trustee Delegation Act 1999, s 7). As the transfer is not by the mortgagee, the overreaching provisions relating to a conveyance by a mortgagee contained in Law of Property Act 1925, s 2(1)(iii) will not apply. In consequence, upon registration of the transfer, the restriction will not be automatically cancelled by the Registry pursuant to LRR 2003, r 99, as it will not be in a position to be satisfied that the beneficial interests under the existing trust of land have necessarily been overreached. Although application may be made under LRR 2003, r 97 for the restriction to be cancelled, such an application would have to be supported by evidence to satisfy the Registry that the restriction is no longer required because the mortgagors were the only persons with a beneficial interest in the land and the land was not, or is no longer, subject to any beneficial interest in favour of a third party.

If there are joint mortgagors and the transfer is executed by two or more joint receivers on their behalf, this will both comply with the restriction in Form A and effect overreaching, so that the restriction will be cancelled on registration of the transfer.

If there is a sole mortgagor, a transfer executed by either a single receiver or joint receivers on his behalf cannot be registered as it is a disposition by a sole proprietor and so caught by the restriction in Form A; nor will it effect overreaching.

The position will be similar if the disposition is a lease granted out of the mortgaged registered title, except that if the lease is registered in circumstances where a restriction in Form A appears in the register of the mortgaged title and overreaching has not been effected, the restriction will not be carried forward to the register of the new leasehold title. The powers of the receiver would have to have been extended beyond the limited statutory powers in the Law of Property Act 1925, to enable such a lease to be granted.

RECEIVERS APPOINTED BY ORDER OF THE COURT

An order appointing a receiver is treated as an interest affecting an estate or charge for the purposes of the LRA 2002 (LRA 2002, s 87(1)(c)). It cannot, however, constitute an interest belonging to a person in actual occupation falling within LRA 2002, Sch 1, para 2 or Sch 3, para 2 which overrides first registration and registered dispositions (LRA 2002, s 87(3)). No notice of an order appointing a receiver may be entered in the register (LRA 2002, s 87(2)). Such an order may, however, be protected by the entry of a restriction.

The receiver is to be regarded as a person having a sufficient interest in the entry of a restriction for the purposes of LRA 2002, s 43(1)(c) if he is applying for a restriction in Form L or Form N (LRR 2003, r 93(s)). A restriction does not confer any priority; it simply prevents an entry being made in the register in respect of any disposition, or a disposition of a specified kind, unless the terms of the restriction have (where applicable) been complied with.

For administrative receivers, see *Administrative receivers*, page 5. For LPA receivers, see *Receivers appointed under the Law of Property Act 1925*, page 474. For receivers appointed under the Mental Health Act 1983, see *Mental incapacity*, page 375.

Restriction

In addition to the usual documents required (see *Restrictions*, page 500), the receiver should deliver to the Registry a certified copy of the order of the court appointing the receiver.

As the application for a restriction is unlikely to be made by or with the consent of the registered proprietor in this situation, the statement in panel 12 or conveyancer's certificate in panel 13 of Form RX1 should be completed on the following lines:

> The interest is that specified in rule 93(s) of the Land Registration Rules 2003, the applicant being the receiver appointed by [*name*] Court on [*date*].

Panel 9 of Form RX1 should be completed as to the appropriate restriction. A restriction in a standard form contained in LRR 2003, Sch 4 does not require the approval of the Registry to the terms of the restriction under LRA 2002, s 43(3).

A possible form of restriction based on the wording of Form L is:

> No [disposition *or specify type of disposition*] of the registered estate by the proprietor of the registered estate [*or by the proprietor of any registered charge not being a charge registered before the entry of this restriction*] is to be registered without a certificate signed by [*name*] of [*address*] [or [*their conveyancer or specify appropriate details*]] that the provisions of [*specify clause, paragraph or other particulars*] of [*specify details*] have been complied with [or that they do not apply to the disposition].

A possible form of restriction based on the wording of Form N is:

> No [disposition *or specify type of disposition*] of the registered estate by the proprietor of the registered estate [*or by the proprietor of any registered charge not being a charge registered before the entry of this restriction*] is to be registered without a written consent signed by [*name*] of [*address*] [or [*their conveyancer or specify appropriate details*]].

A restriction in standard Form L or Form N does not require the approval of the Registry to the wording of the restriction under LRA 2002, s 43(3).

The Registry must give notice of the application for a restriction to the proprietor of the registered estate concerned, if it has not been made by or with his consent or a person entitled to be registered as such proprietor (LRA 2002, s 45).

RECTIFICATION

For the purposes of the LRA 2002, 'rectification' is an alteration of the register which involves the correction of a mistake and which prejudicially affects the title of a registered proprietor (LRA 2002, Sch 4, para 1). Rectification is therefore a form of alteration, but not all alterations amount to rectification. For alterations which do not amount to rectification, see *Alteration of the register*, page 39. Where there is an issue of rectification, indemnity may be payable by the Registry to a person who suffers loss as a result, see *Indemnity*, page 273. A person may apply to the court for an order for rectification of the register under LRA 2002, Sch 4, para 2. A person may also apply to the Registry for rectification of the register under LRA 2002, Sch 4, para 5. The power to rectify the register extends to changing for the future the priority of any interest affecting the registered estate or charge concerned (LRA 2002, Sch 4, para 8). The effect of rectification is therefore prospective and takes effect for the future only; it does not operate retrospectively from the time of the original mistake.

Rectification pursuant to an order of the court

Where rectification of a title to a registered estate in land by court order is sought and the proprietor of that estate is in possession of the land, the court can make such an order only if:

(a) the proprietor consents to it; or
(b) he has caused or substantially contributed to the mistake by fraud or lack of proper care; or
(c) it would be for any other reason unjust for the alteration not to be made.

A proprietor is in possession of the land if it is physically in his possession or in that of a person who is entitled to be registered as the proprietor. Land in the possession of a tenant is treated as in the possession of the landlord, and similarly in the cases of mortgagee and mortgagor, licensee and licensor, and beneficiary and trustee (LRA 2002, s 131). A proprietor's title, for this purpose, includes his title to any registered estate which subsists for the benefit of his registered estate in the land; for example, a beneficial easement.

Where rectification of a registered estate in land by court order is sought and the proprietor of that estate is not in possession of the land, the court must make such an order if it has power to do so, unless there are exceptional circumstances which justify its not doing so (LRA 2002, Sch 4, para 3(3)).

A court order for alteration of the register must state the title number of the title affected and the alteration that is to be made. It must also direct the Registry to make the alteration (LRR 2003, r 127(1)). Service on the Registry of such an order must be made by making an application for the Registry to give effect to the order, accompanied by the order (r 127(2)).

An applicant for an alteration of the register pursuant to an order of the court should deliver to the Registry:

(a) an application in Form AP1;
(b) the court order for alteration of the register or a sealed copy of that court order; and
(c) the fee (if applicable) (see *Fees*, page 221).

Rectification other than pursuant to an order of the court

Where application is made direct to the Registry for an alteration which amounts to rectification, the same principles as to the protection of a proprietor in possession of a registered estate in land apply. Equally, where the proprietor is not in possession and the Registry has power to make the alteration, the application must be approved, unless there are exceptional circumstances which justify not making the alteration.

An application for alteration, other than under a court order, must be supported by evidence to justify the alteration (LRR 2003, r 129). The Registry may make such enquiries as it thinks fit and must give notice of the proposed alteration to any person who would be affected by it, unless it is satisfied that such notice is unnecessary (LRR 2003, r 128). Rule 128 does not, however, apply to alteration of the register in the specific circumstances covered by any other rule.

An applicant for an alteration of the register otherwise than pursuant to a court order should deliver to the Registry:

(a)   an application in Form AP1;
(b)   a statement of the alteration being applied for;
(c)   all relevant evidence held by the applicant which is relevant to the application to alter the register; and
(d)   the fee (if applicable) (see *Fees*, page 221).

Where the application leads to a valid objection which cannot be disposed of by agreement, any dispute will have to be dealt with in accordance with LRA 2002, s 73 (see *Disputes*, page 193).

REGISTERED SOCIAL LANDLORDS AND PRIVATE REGISTERED PROVIDERS

In England, but not Wales, the regulation of social housing was amended by the Housing and Regeneration Act 2008, and again by the Localism Act 2011. Registered providers of social housing are therefore affected by different regulatory regimes depending upon whether they are English or Welsh.

In England, Homes England (previously the Homes and Communities Agency) maintains a register of providers of social housing, which may be public (for example local authorities) or private (for profit or not for profit). Such private providers were formerly known as registered social landlords but are now referred to as private registered providers.

In Wales, private providers continue to be referred to as registered social landlords where they are registered within the register maintained by the Welsh Ministers under HA 1996, s 1.

In either case, such a body may be a registered charity which is a housing association. Alternatively, it may be a registered society or a registered company which satisfies the conditions for registration. For housing associations which are unregistered social landlords, see *Housing associations*, page 263. For registered societies, see *Registered societies*, page 485.

Registration of registered social landlords or private registered providers as proprietor

If an applicant for registration as proprietor of a registered estate or registered charge is, or holds on trust for, a private registered provider of social housing, or a registered social landlord within the meaning of the HA 1996, the application must include a certificate to that effect (LRR 2003, r 183A(1)). This is in addition to any requirements arising from the fact that the applicant is a charity, a registered society or a company, for which see *Charities*, page 104; *Registered societies*, page 485; or *Companies*, page 154, respectively.

If a registered estate in land is held on trust for a private registered provider or a registered social landlord and two or more trustees are being entered as proprietors, a restriction in Form A will be entered by the Registry in the register. If an unregistered housing association is a charity, a charity restriction will be entered where appropriate.

In England, disposal of a dwelling by a private registered provider requires the consent of Homes England, if the dwelling is social housing (Housing and Regeneration Act 2008, s 172). Where a private registered provider is registered as proprietor of land a restriction on the following lines is entered:

> No disposition of the registered estate by the proprietor of the registered estate is to be completed by registration without a certificate by the registered proprietor signed by their secretary or by two trustees if a charitable trust or by their conveyancer that the provisions of section 172 of the Housing and Regeneration Act 2008 have been complied with or that they do not apply to the disposition.

Previously, the required consent was that of the Homes and Communities Agency or the Housing Corporation or the Office for Tenants and Social Landlords (Tenant Services Authority), depending upon the date of the disposition.

In Wales, a registered social landlord has power under HA 1996, s 8, but not otherwise, to dispose of land. That power is subject to the consent of the Welsh Ministers (HA 1996, s 9). Where a registered social landlord is registered as proprietor of land, a restriction on the following lines is entered:

> No disposition by the proprietor of the land is to be registered without the consent of the Welsh Ministers when such consent is required under the provisions of section 9 of the Housing Act 1996.

Previously, the required consent was that of the Housing Corporation. In certain circumstances as set out in HA 1996, s 10, consent is not required. These include disposals to tenants under the right to buy or right to acquire.

Dispositions by registered social landlords or private registered providers

Applications to register dispositions by private registered providers or registered social landlords should meet the requirements of any restriction in the register. If a private registered provider or registered social landlord is a charity, the appropriate charity statement should be included within the disposition where necessary (see *Charities*, page 104).

Where a house is sold by a private registered provider or registered social landlord at a discount, the transfer will contain a covenant to repay a proportion of the discount if the purchaser disposes of the house within 3 years. This takes effect as a charge and an entry in respect of it is entered in the charges register of the purchaser's title.

Where the disposal is of a house in a National Park, an area of outstanding natural beauty or an area designated as a rural area, the transfer or conveyance may contain a covenant limiting the freedom of the purchaser to dispose of the property. In such case a restriction in Form Y is entered automatically in the proprietorship register (LRA 2002, s 44(2) and LRR 2003, r 95(2)(h)). The wording of Form Y is set out in Appendix IV, page 585.

Where the disposal consists of a lease, application may be made for entry of a restriction in Form KK in the register of the title to the lease. The wording of Form KK is set out in Appendix IV, page 585.

REGISTERED SOCIETIES

Registered societies are registered under the Co-operative and Community Benefit Societies Act 2014 (CCBSA 2014). They replaced industrial and provident societies and all existing societies that were registered under the Industrial and Provident Societies Act 1965 became registered societies on 1 August 2014.

The purpose of the CCBSA 2014 was to consolidate the existing legislation relating to industrial and provident societies, co-operatives, community benefit societies, and other societies registered under the Industrial and Provident Societies Act 1965.

Registered societies registered after 1 August 2014 can be either co-operative societies or community benefit societies.

They are corporate bodies which, unless their rules state to the contrary, possess the power to purchase or take a lease of land in their own name. Once registered as proprietors of land they may sell, lease, exchange or mortgage it.

Many (but not all) housing associations are registered societies.

The Financial Conduct Authority (FCA) maintains the register of registered societies. Although registered societies are treated as companies for tax purposes and the Companies Act 2006 requires the name of a registered society to be registered in the Companies House index of company names, they are regulated by the FCA and have to register any charges over their assets with the FCA, not at the Companies Registry. Charges by registered societies are therefore not subject to the filing requirements for companies under Companies Act 2006, Pt 25, or to the requirement in LRR 2003, r 111.

A purchaser, assignee, mortgagee or tenant is not bound to enquire as to the authority for any such dealing with the land by the society. As a result, a restriction does not need to be entered in the proprietorship register merely because the proprietor is a registered society.

On an application to register a registered society as proprietor, a copy of its registered rules, or a certificate by its conveyancer in Form 8 in LRR 2003, Sch 3, should be lodged (LRR 2003, r 183). In practice, arrangements are often made by registered societies with the head office of the Land Registry so that the rules do not need to be lodged with every application. For the position where the society is also a charity, housing association or private registered provider or registered social landlord, see respectively *Charities*, page 104,

Housing associations, page 263, and *Registered social landlords and private registered providers*, page 482. See also *Credit unions*, page 178.

The registration number of a registered society will be entered in the proprietorship register immediately after the name of the society.

A registered society may execute deeds either under its common seal authenticated in accordance with the society's rules and expressed to be a deed; or by being signed by a member of the committee and its secretary or by two members of the committee and expressed (in whatever form of words) to be executed by the society (CCBSA 2014, s 53).

RENTCHARGES

A rentcharge is any sum of money charged on land payable annually or periodically, other than rent reserved by a lease or interest charged under a mortgage (Rentcharges Act 1977, s 1). 'Land' for this purpose has the same meaning as in Law of Property Act 1925, s 205(1). Rentcharges are sometimes described in deeds as rent charges, chief rents, quit rents, fee farm rents or some similar term. A rentcharge is usually perpetual, but can be granted for a term of years so that it is terminable. The land affected by a rentcharge can be either freehold or leasehold; in the latter case, the rentcharge will always be terminable because the lease itself will eventually come to an end.

A rentcharge is usually created by way of a conveyance or transfer, where the vendor of the land reserves an annual rent, payable to him and his successors in title and charged upon the land sold. In modern times, most new rentcharges created are 'estate rentcharges', which are discussed below. A rentcharge is capable of being bought and sold or charged. A rentcharge may be capable of being substantively registered with its own title and the burden of it may be the subject of a notice in the register of registered land affected by it.

The Rentcharges Act 1977 made a number of important changes to the law relating to rentcharges. It provides for the extinguishment, apportionment and redemption of certain rentcharges and limits the scope for the creation of new rentcharges. Its main provisions came into operation on 22 August 1977. After 21 August 1977 the only new rentcharges which may be created (either at law or in equity) are those falling within Rentcharges Act 1977, s 2, including rentcharges arising out of an order of the court, and estate rentcharges. In practice the only new rentcharges likely to be created are estate rentcharges. An estate rentcharge is defined by Rentcharges Act 1977, s 2(4) and (5) as being a rentcharge of either:

(a) a nominal amount for the purpose of making covenants to be performed by the owner of the land affected by the rentcharge enforceable by the rent owner against the owner for the time being of the land; or

(b) a reasonable amount to meet, or contribute towards, the cost of the performance by the rent owner of covenants for the provision of services, the carrying out of maintenance or repairs, the effecting of insurance or the making of any payment by him for the benefit of the land affected by the rentcharge or for the benefit of that and other land.

Rentcharges Act 1977, s 3 provides (subject to certain exceptions) for the extinguishment of rentcharges after a period of 60 years. Sections 4 to 10 of that Act deal with apportionment and redemption.

Rentcharges created out of unregistered land

In relation to an estate which is subject to a rentcharge, on first registration of title to that estate, the estate is vested in the registered proprietor subject to any rentcharges which are the subject of an entry in the register in relation to the estate (LRA 2002, ss 11(4) and 12(4)). The Registry must enter a notice in the register of the burden of any rentcharge which appears from its examination to affect the registered estate (LRR 2003, r 35).

In relation to the title to an unregistered rentcharge, it is not compulsory to register the title to a legal rentcharge created out of unregistered land, either on its creation or on a subsequent sale or transfer. However, it is possible to make a voluntary application to register a legal rentcharge which is either perpetual, or is held for a term of years of which more than 7 years are unexpired at the date of the application for first registration of the rentcharge (LRA 2002, s 3). The rentcharge must be based either on a deed dated before 22 August 1977; or on a deed dated on or after 22 August 1977 where its creation is not prohibited by Rentcharges Act 1977, s 2. The fact that a rentcharge is subject to extinguishment in accordance with the provisions of the Rentcharges Act 1977 does not of itself prevent it from being 'perpetual' or for a term of years 'absolute' for the purposes of registration. It was also possible to register a legal rentcharge under the LRA 1925. Rentcharges that subsist as equitable interests only, for example because of the mode of their creation or because they are informally apportioned parts of a legal or equitable rentcharge, cannot be registered but they may be protected in the register by means of a notice (see below).

In addition to the usual documents required (see *First registration*, page 222), an applicant for first registration of a legal rentcharge should deliver to the Registry:

(a)   sufficient details, by plan or otherwise, so that the area of land which is affected by the rentcharge can be clearly identified on the Ordnance Survey map;

(b)   the deed creating the rentcharge and those deeds proving devolution of title to the applicant.

If there are any rights, interests or claims affecting the rentcharge which are known to the applicant, other than those disclosed in the title deeds or Form DI, these should be disclosed in the Form FR1. This would include, for example, any rights in the course of being acquired over the rentcharge by adverse possession, or a disputed third party claim relating to the rentcharge. For first registration generally, see *First registration*, page 222.

Where the applicant for first registration is unable to produce a full documentary title, the application must be supported by evidence to account for this, usually in the form of a statutory declaration or statement of truth, exhibiting any appropriate supporting documents. A statement of truth may be in Form ST3 in LRR 2003, Sch 1 (see *Lost or destroyed title deeds*, page 369).

Where two or more persons apply to be registered as proprietors of a rentcharge and a sole proprietor or the survivor of joint proprietors will not be able to give a valid receipt for capital money, application must be made for entry of a restriction in Form A (LRR 2003, r 94(2A)) (see *Joint proprietors*, page 286).

Registration of rentcharge created over registered land

The express grant or reservation of a legal rentcharge over registered land is a registrable disposition which must be completed by registration (LRA 2002, s 27(2)(e)). Until completed by registration, the rentcharge takes effect in equity only. The registration requirements are:

(a)   In the case of a rentcharge granted in fee simple or for a term of more than 7 years, the grantee must be registered as proprietor of the rentcharge and a notice of the rentcharge must be entered in the register of the title out of which it was created.

(b)   In the case of a rentcharge granted for a term of less than 7 years, a notice of the rentcharge must be entered in the register of the title out of which it was created. (LRA 2002, s 27 and paras 6 and 7 of Sch 2, part 1).

A legal rentcharge may be created as a disposition of registered land in one of two ways. It may be the subject of a deed of grant by the proprietor of the land; or it may be granted in a transfer or lease of registered land by the transferee or tenant to the transferor or landlord, charged upon the land transferred or demised.

Typically, the latter will be the case where there is a transfer or lease of a plot on a developing estate, where an estate rentcharge is imposed on each plot. In both cases an application for the registration of the rentcharge should be made in Form AP1.

In the case of a rentcharge granted for a term of less than 7 years, application for entry of a notice of the rentcharge in the grantor's title may be made in Form AP1 or AN1 (LRR 2003, r 90).

In the case of a rentcharge granted in a transfer or lease, a single Form AP1 can cover both registration of the land and registration of the rentcharge if desired. The Registry is not obliged to substantively register the rentcharge unless specific application is made in the Form AP1 (LRR 2003, rr 72(6) and 72C(4)). The rentcharge cannot be registered until the transfer or lease itself has been completed by registration and therefore taken effect at law.

If a legal rentcharge is granted out of leasehold land registered with good leasehold title, and more than a qualified title to the rentcharge is desired, satisfactory evidence must be produced to show that the lease (and any superior lease) was validly granted.

Every deed creating a rentcharge out of registered land must contain a reference to the title number of that land (LRR 2003, r 212(3)) and particulars, by plan if necessary, to enable the land charged to be identified on the title plan of the grantor's title (r 213).

If completed by registration, the rentcharge will be substantively registered under its own individual title (where it is capable of substantive registration) and/or a notice of the burden will be entered in the register of title of the land charged.

If not completed by registration, the rentcharge will take effect in equity only, although the burden will still be capable of being protected by a notice in the register of the title to the land charged (see below).

A right of re-entry relating to a rentcharge created out of registered land on or after 13 October 2003 must itself be completed by registration if it is to take effect at law (LRA 2002, s 27(2)(e)). In the case of such a right created in a lease for a term of years absolute which is itself a registrable disposition, LRR 2003, r 77 provides that completion by registration of the lease will be sufficient to meet the registration requirements for the right of re-entry and no additional entry will need to be made in respect of it.

An applicant for registration of a rentcharge granted by a deed of grant should deliver to the Registry:

(a) an application in Form AP1;

(b) the deed creating the rentcharge (and a certified copy, if the applicant wishes for the original to be returned);

(c) any consents or certificates required in respect of mortgages, charges or restrictions in the grantor's title;

(d) Form DI giving the information as to overriding interests required by LRR 2003, r 57, including any documentary evidence of the interests (see 'Duty to disclose overriding interests', page 426);

(e) the appropriate confirmation or evidence as to identity (see *Identity evidence*, page 266);

(f) the appropriate SDLT certificate or other evidence (see *Stamp duty land tax*, page 541); and

(g) the fee payable (see *Fees*, page 221).

Where two or more persons apply to be registered as proprietors of a rentcharge and a sole proprietor or the survivor of joint proprietors will not be able to give a valid receipt for capital money, the Registry will not automatically enter a restriction in Form A and instead application must be made for entry of the restriction (LRR 2003, r 94(2A)) (see *Joint proprietors*, page 286).

Rentcharges granted by a UK company or UK limited liability partnership

Previously, such rentcharges were specifically exempted from the requirement for registration at the Companies Registry. However, as a result of the Companies Act 2006 (Amendment of Part 25) Regulations 2013 (SI 2013/600), which came into force on 6 April 2013, it appears that this specific exemption may no longer apply. Where necessary therefore, when an application for substantive registration of such a rentcharge granted on or after 6 April 2013 is made to the Land Registry, evidence of registration at the Companies Registry (see 'Registration of a charge created by a company', page 156 and 'Registration of charge created by a UK limited liability partnership', page 355 should be lodged. If this is not done, the Land Registry may enter a note in the register of the rentcharge title, indicating that it is subject to the provisions of Companies Act 2006, s 859H if and so far as that section applies to the rentcharge.

Rentcharges which cannot be registered

Rentcharges which subsist only as equitable interests cannot be registered, but the burden of such rentcharges should be protected in the register of the title to the land out of which they were created, where that land is registered.

When an equitable rentcharge is created out of a registered estate, a notice of the burden of the rentcharge should be entered in the register of the title to the estate charged. If an equitable rentcharge is created by the transferee in a transfer of a registered estate, a notice of the burden will be entered in the register of the transferee's title as a matter of course when the transfer is registered (LRR 2003, rr 72(4) and 72C(2)).

If an equitable rentcharge is created by the tenant in a prescribed clauses lease and the requisite details are inserted in clause LR12, a notice of the burden will be entered in the register of the tenant's title as a matter of course when the lease is registered (LRR 2002, r 72A(2) and (3)). If created in a non-prescribed clauses lease, a notice of the burden will be entered in the register of the tenant's title as a matter of course when the lease is registered (r 72C(2)) (see *Leases*, page 296).

In any other case of an equitable rentcharge created out of a registered estate, a separate application should be made to enter a notice of the rentcharge in the register of the title of the estate charged.

Entry of notice of rentcharge

When an estate is first registered, a notice of the burden of any subsisting rentcharge, whether legal or equitable, charged on the estate and appearing in the title, will be entered in the charges register of the title to the estate charged, together with details of any apportionments and exonerations.

On the completion by registration of a legal rentcharge created out of a registered estate, a notice of the burden of the rentcharge will be entered in the register of the title to the estate charged, in accordance with the registration requirements (see above).

If a rentcharge is a registrable disposition under LRA 2002, s 27 but is not completed by registration, it takes effect in equity only, but the burden of it will still be capable of being protected by entry of a notice in the register of the title to the estate charged. In the case of a rentcharge granted in a transfer or lease, the Registry will enter such a notice as a matter of course when registering the transfer or lease itself (LRR 2003, rr 72(4), 72A(2) and 72C(2)).

On the creation, out of a registered estate, of a rentcharge which cannot be registered, a specific application for the entry of an agreed notice or a unilateral notice in respect of the rentcharge in the register of the title to the estate out of which the rentcharge issues will be necessary. The application should be made in Form AN1 for entry of an agreed notice or Form UN1 for entry of a unilateral notice, as appropriate (see *Notices*, page 389).

Dispositions of registered rentcharges

A registered rentcharge can be transferred, leased or charged in the same way and subject to the same rules as a registered estate in land, so far as the nature of a rentcharge permits. The guidance appearing elsewhere in this book, whilst primarily relating to registered estates in land, also applies generally to registered rentcharges (see, in particular, *Transfers*, page 551, and *Leases*, page 296). However, a rentcharge owner cannot create easements or restrictive covenants.

Any transfer of a rentcharge should provide for the express assignment of the benefit of the grantor's covenant to pay the rent, as such a covenant does not run at law with the rentcharge so as to enable the rentcharge owner to sue under it.

Dispositions of rentcharges have the same SDLT requirements as other dispositions of registered land, as a rentcharge is for this purpose 'land' (see *Stamp duty land tax*, page 541).

Transfer of registered estate subject to a rentcharge

LRR 2003, r 69 makes provision in relation to implied covenants in respect of such a transfer (see *Implied covenants*, page 268).

Apportionment and redemption of rentcharges

Apportionment is the division of a rentcharge. A formally apportioned rentcharge can be dealt with separately in its own right.

Exoneration is the release of part of the land charged from any liability for payment.

An apportionment or an exoneration may each be formal or informal. There are two types of formal apportionment. The most common is by a ministerial order (or certificate of apportionment) given by the Secretary of State. The other is a deed made between all the relevant parties. To be formal (and to have full effect at law), all the owners of the land affected by the rentcharge and the rentcharge owner must join in the deed.

An informal apportionment or exoneration arises where not all the relevant parties join in the deed; this often occurs where there is a transfer or lease of part of the land in a registered title and the rentcharge owner is not a party to the apportionment or exoneration.

A registered title which relates to an estate in land or to a rentcharge may be affected by a ministerial order apportioning a rentcharge or by a ministerial certificate that a rentcharge has been redeemed. If it is not known whether the title to the land or rentcharge is registered, a search of the index map may be made in Form SIM (see *Official searches of the index*, page 409).

An application should be made for effect to be given to the order or the certificate in the registered title(s) affected. Where an apportionment is made conditional on the redemption of the rentcharge, the application should not be made until after the redemption has taken place. The application should be made in Form AP1, referring to 'Apportionment of rentcharge' or 'Redemption of rentcharge' as the case may be. It should be supported by an official copy of the order and/or an official copy of the certificate of redemption as appropriate. A fee is payable (see *Fees*, page 221). However, no fee is payable if the application is accompanied by an application upon which a scale fee is payable; for example where the order or certificate has been obtained in anticipation of a sale of the registered land or rentcharge and the application for the registration of the order or certificate is lodged with the application for the registration of the transfer on sale of the land or rentcharge.

Where a rentcharge has been formally exonerated, this acts as an extinguishment of the rentcharge.

Extinguishment of rentcharges

Rentcharges Act 1977, s 3(1) provides that, subject to certain exceptions, every rentcharge shall (if it has not then ceased to have effect) be extinguished at the expiry of the period of 60 years beginning with the passing of that Act (22 July 1977), or the date on which the rentcharge first became payable, whichever is later. This section will not extinguish any rentcharge payable wholly or partly in lieu of tithes or of a kind referred to in Rentcharges Act 1977, s 2(3) (disregarding s 2(5), which relates to estate rentcharges). Variable rentcharges are also excluded from extinguishment under Rentcharges Act 1977, s 3(1), but where a variable rentcharge ceases to be variable s 3(1) will apply as if the date on which the rentcharge first became payable was the date on which it ceased to be variable.

Apart from extinguishment under the 1977 Act, a rentcharge may also be determined or extinguished by a number of other means, including;

(a)   merger;
(b)   a deed of release whereby the rentcharge owner releases the rentcharge to the owner of the land charged;
(c)   re-entry after an order of the court, where the rentcharge owner has obtained possession of the land charged by order of the court;
(d)   a certificate of redemption given by the Secretary of State (see above);
(e)   effluxion of time, in the case of a terminable rentcharge;
(f)   adverse possession where, by virtue of non-payment of the rent, the rentcharge has become statute barred (see below);
(g)   cessation of the estate in the land charged; for example on forfeiture of a leasehold estate subject to a terminable rentcharge; and
(h)   informal letter or receipt from the rentcharge owner.

An application following the extinguishment of a rentcharge, other than by ministerial certificate, should be made supported by appropriate evidence of extinguishment. The application should be made in Form AP1 (where both the land and the rentcharge are registered, or only the rentcharge is registered). Otherwise, it should be made in Form CN1 for cancellation of an agreed notice, or Form UN4 for cancellation of a unilateral notice (where only the land charged is registered) (see *Notices*, page 389). A fee is payable (unless the application is accompanied by an application upon which a scale fee is payable, when no fee is payable) (see *Fees*, page 221).

Adverse possession of registered rentcharges

A person may be in adverse possession of a rentcharge if he fails to pay the rent due under the rentcharge, or if he pays the rent to a person who is not entitled to receive it. In the first case, the proprietor of the estate subject to the charge is in adverse possession of the rentcharge. In the second, the person who receives the rent from him is in adverse possession of the rentcharge. The period of adverse possession runs from the date at which the proprietor of the charge received the last rent (Limitation Act 1980, ss 15(1) and 38(8)).

The LRA 2002 and the LRR 2003 make provision for adverse possession of a registered rentcharge. LRR 2003, r 191 (made pursuant to the power contained in LRA 2002, Sch 6, para 14) applies the provisions of LRA 2002, Sch 6 to rentcharges in the modified form set out in LRR 2003, Sch 8. This provides for a procedure similar to that in respect of adverse possession of registered land (see *Adverse possession*, page 11). Accordingly, a person may apply under LRA 2002, Sch 6, para 1 (as modified) to be registered as proprietor of the registered rentcharge if he has been in adverse possession of the registered rentcharge for a period of 10 years ending on the date of the application. The registered rentcharge need not have been registered throughout this period. A person may not make such an application if:

(a) he is a defendant in proceedings by the registered proprietor of the registered rentcharge for recovery of the rent or to enter into possession of the land out of which the registered rentcharge issues;
(b) judgment in favour of the registered proprietor of the registered rentcharge in respect of proceedings of the nature mentioned in sub-paragraph (a) has been given against him in the last 2 years; or
(c) the registered proprietor of the registered rentcharge of which that person was in adverse possession has entered into possession of the land out of which the registered rentcharge issues.

If a person given notice of an application requires that it is dealt with under LRA 2002, Sch 6, para 5 (as modified), the applicant is entitled to be registered as the new proprietor only if either of the following conditions in para 5 (as modified) is met.

The first condition is that:

(a) it would be unconscionable because of an equity by estoppel for the registered proprietor to seek to assert his title to the registered rentcharge against the applicant; and
(b) the circumstances are such that the applicant ought to be registered as the proprietor.

The second condition is that the applicant is for some other reason entitled to be registered as the proprietor of the registered rentcharge. The third condition in Sch 6, para 5 which applies in relation to adverse possession of a registered estate in land, does not apply to adverse possession of a rentcharge and this condition is therefore omitted from Sch 6 (as modified).

Where the applicant cannot bring himself within either condition his application is rejected. He may then make a further application to be registered as proprietor of the registered rentcharge under LRA 2002, Sch 6, para 6 (as modified) if he is in adverse possession of that rentcharge from the date of the application until the last day of the period of 2 years beginning with the date of its rejection.

There are restrictions on making applications, similar to those relating to applications based on adverse possession of land (see *Adverse possession*, page 11, and LRR 2003, Sch 8).

Where a person is entitled to be registered as proprietor of a registered rentcharge under LRA 2002, Sch 6 (as modified) as a result of non-payment of the rentcharge, the registered rentcharge title is closed or (if the title also comprises other rentcharges) the registered rentcharge is cancelled; this reflects the fact that the rentcharge has effectively been merged with the applicant's existing estate. This does not apply if, were that person to be registered as proprietor of that rentcharge, he would be subject to a registered charge or registered lease or other interest protected in the register (LRR 2003, r 192). Where a person is entitled to be registered as proprietor of a registered rentcharge as a result of having received the payment of rent due under the rentcharge, the Registry will not remove the entry of the rentcharge from the register but will instead register the applicant as the new proprietor.

Where as a result of an application under LRA 2002, Sch 6 (as modified), a person is registered as proprietor of a registered rentcharge or that registered title is closed or the registered rentcharge is cancelled (the title comprising also other rentcharges), no previous registered proprietor of the rentcharge may recover any rent due under the rentcharge from a person who has been in adverse possession of the rentcharge (LRR 2003, r 193). This applies whether the adverse possession arose as a result of non-payment of the rent or by receipt of the rent from the person liable to pay it.

Application under Land Registration Act 2002, Sch 6, para 1 (as modified) for registration by a person in adverse possession of registered rentcharge

An applicant making an application under LRA 2002, Sch 6, para 1 (as modified) should deliver to the Registry:

(a)   an application in Form ADV1;
(b)   a statutory declaration or statement of truth made by the applicant not more than one month before the application, together with any necessary supporting statutory declarations or statements of truth, to provide evidence of adverse possession of the rentcharge against which the application is made for a period of not less than 10 years ending on the date of application. A statement of truth may be made in Form ST2 in LRR 2003, Sch 4, although its use is not compulsory;
(c)   any additional evidence which the applicant considers necessary to support the claim;
(d)   a list in duplicate in Form DL of all the documents delivered;
(e)   the appropriate confirmation or evidence as to identity (see *Identity evidence*, page 266); and
(f)   the fee payable (see *Fees*, page 221).

The statutory declaration or statement of truth by the applicant must also contain:

(a) confirmation that LRA 2002, Sch 6, para 1(2) (as modified) does not apply. Paragraph 1(2) provides that a person may not make an application if he is a defendant in proceedings by the registered proprietor of the rentcharge for recovery of the rent or to enter into possession of the land out of which the rentcharge issues, or if judgment in such proceedings has been given against him in the last 2 years. It also provides that he may not make such an application if the registered proprietor of the rentcharge of which he was in adverse possession has entered into possession of the land out of which the rentcharge issues;

(b) confirmation that to the best of his knowledge the restriction on applications in LRA 2002, Sch 6, para 8 (as modified) does not apply (see *Adverse possession*, page 11, and LRR 2003, Sch 8);

(c) confirmation that to the best of his knowledge the rentcharge is not, and has not been during any of the period of alleged adverse possession, subject to a trust (other than one where the interest of each of the beneficiaries is an interest in possession);

(d) confirmation that the proprietor of the registered rentcharge has not re-entered the land out of which the rentcharge issues; and

(e) if, should a person given notice of the application require that it be dealt with under LRA 2002, Sch 6, para 5 (as modified), it is intended to rely on one or both of the conditions set out in that paragraph, the facts supporting such reliance.

The applicant must also supply such additional evidence as the Registry may require after the application has been considered (LRR 2003, r 17).

Application under Land Registration Act 2002, Sch 6, para 6 (as modified) for registration by person in adverse possession of registered rentcharge

Where an applicant has had an application under LRA 2002, Sch 6, para 1 (as modified) rejected, he may be able to make a further application under LRA 2002, Sch 6, para 6 (as modified) if he has been in adverse possession of the registered rentcharge for a further 2 years from the date of rejection. However, a person may not make an application under this paragraph if:

(a) he is a defendant in proceedings by the registered proprietor of the registered rentcharge for recovery of the rent or to enter into possession of the land out of which the registered rentcharge issues;

(b) judgment in favour of the registered proprietor of the registered rentcharge in respect of proceedings of the nature mentioned in sub-paragraph (a) has been given against him in the last 2 years; or

(c) the registered proprietor of the registered rentcharge of which that person was in adverse possession has entered into possession of the land out of which the registered rentcharge issues.

The special form of notice required by Sch 6, para 2 (as modified) and the right to require the application to be dealt with under Sch 6, para 5 (as modified) do not apply to such applications. Instead, under LRR 2003, r 17, 15 working days' notice of the application will be served by the Registry on the proprietor of the registered rentcharge and certain other persons (see *Adverse possession*, page 11).

An applicant should deliver to the Registry:

(a) an application in Form ADV1;
(b) a statutory declaration or statement of truth made by the applicant not more than one month before the application, together with any necessary supporting statutory declarations or statements of truth, to provide evidence of adverse possession of the rentcharge against which the application is made for a period of not less than 2 years beginning with the date of rejection of the original application and ending on the date of application. A statement of truth may be made in Form ST2 in LRR 2003, Sch 4, although its use is not compulsory;
(c) any additional evidence which the applicant considers necessary to support the claim;
(d) a list in duplicate in Form DL of all the documents delivered;
(e) the appropriate confirmation or evidence as to identity (see *Identity evidence*, page 266); and
(f) the fee payable (see *Fees*, page 221).

The statutory declaration or statement of truth by the applicant must also contain:

(a) full details of the previous rejected application;
(b) confirmation that to the best of his knowledge the restriction on applications in LRA 2002, Sch 6, para 8 (as modified) does not apply (see *Adverse possession*, page 11, and LRR 2003, Sch 8);
(c) confirmation that to the best of his knowledge the rentcharge is not, and has not been during any of the period of alleged adverse possession, subject to a trust (other than one where the interest of each of the beneficiaries is an interest in possession);
(d) confirmation that the proprietor of the registered rentcharge has not re-entered the land out of which the rentcharge issues; and
(e) confirmation that LRA 2002, Sch 6, para 6(2) (as modified) does not apply. Paragraph 6(2) (as modified) provides that a person may not make an

application if he is a defendant in proceedings by the registered proprietor of the rentcharge for recovery of the rent or to enter into possession of the land out of which the rentcharge issues, or if judgment in such proceedings has been given against him in the last 2 years. It also provides that he may not make such an application if the registered proprietor of the rentcharge of which he was in adverse possession has entered into possession of the land out of which the rentcharge issues.

The applicant must also supply such additional evidence as the Registry may require after the application has been considered (LRR 2003, r 17).

The effect of registration under LRA 2002, Sch 6, paras 1 or 6 (as modified), including that in relation to registered charges (and the provision for apportionment of charges, where appropriate) is similar to that in relation to a registered estate in land (see *Adverse possession*, page 11, and LRR 2003, Sch 8).

Transitional provisions

Under LRA 2002, Sch 12, para 18(5) and LRR 2003, r 224, if title to a rentcharge was acquired by adverse possession prior to 13 October 2003, and it was held in trust under LRA 1925, s 75(1) immediately before that date, the beneficiary of that trust may apply either to be registered as proprietor of the rentcharge, or for the registration of the rentcharge to be cancelled (see *Adverse possession*, page 11, and LRR 2003, Sch 8).

Adverse possession of unregistered rentcharges

Adverse possession may arise in relation to a rentcharge the title to which is unregistered; in such a case reference may usefully be made to the principles applicable to adverse possession of an unregistered estate in land (see *Adverse possession*, page 11).

The position regarding adverse possession of rentcharges, both registered and unregistered, has (at least potentially) been affected by the amendments made to the Limitation Act 1980 by Tribunals, Courts and Enforcement Act 2007, Pt 3, s 86; Pt 4, s 146; Sch 14, paras 35 to 37; Sch 23, Pt 4, which came into force on 6 April 2014.

REQUISITION, REJECTION AND CANCELLATION POLICY

Under LRR 2003, r 16, if an application appears to the Registry to be substantially defective, it may reject it on delivery or it may cancel it at any time thereafter. If an application is not in order, the Registry may raise such requisitions as it considers necessary and specify a period (being not less than 20 working days) within which the applicant must comply with the requisitions. If the applicant fails to do so, the Registry may cancel the application or may extend the period when this appears to be reasonable in the circumstances.

Under LRR 2003, r 17, if it considers it necessary or desirable, the Registry may refuse to complete or proceed with an application until further documents or evidence are supplied or notice is given.

If it will not be possible to reply to requisitions in the time specified an extension must be requested. The request should:

(a) state the reason for the delay;
(b) explain what is being done to resolve the problem; and
(c) indicate when it is expected that a full reply to the requisition can be supplied.

If such a request is made and supported by a proper reason an extension may be allowed, but if no request is made the application will be cancelled. Land Registry Practice Guides 49, *Return and rejection of applications for registration*, and 50, *Requisition and cancellation procedures*, contain full details of its policy and practice on the rejection of defective applications and on requisitions and cancellation. These are available to view and download on the Registry's website at www.gov.uk/government/publications.

RESTRICTIONS

A restriction is an entry in the register regulating the circumstances in which a disposition of a registered estate or charge may be the subject of an entry in the register. It therefore represents a limitation on the exercise of the 'owner's powers' contained in LRA 2002, s 23, for the purposes of ss 26 and 52 of that Act. It may prohibit the making of an entry in respect of any disposition, or of certain kinds of disposition; indefinitely or for a specified period or until the occurrence of a specified event. For example, a restriction may prohibit the registration of a disposition of a registered estate without the written consent of a named person.

Where a restriction is entered in the register, no entry may be made in respect of a disposition to which the restriction applies unless it is in accordance with the terms of the restriction or the Registry makes an order. The Registry may by order disapply or modify a restriction in respect of a particular disposition or class of dispositions (LRA 2002, s 41).

A restriction affecting a registered estate may also affect a charge that is subsequently registered, if its wording is sufficiently wide to catch dispositions by both a registered proprietor and a registered chargee; it will not, however, affect a charge which was registered prior to the entry of the restriction. A restriction affecting a registered charge will not catch dispositions by the proprietor of the registered estate and a separate restriction in that regard would be necessary. Nor will it affect a charge which was registered prior to the entry of the restriction.

LRA 2002, s 42(1) provides that the Registry may enter a restriction if it appears to it that it is necessary or desirable to do so for the purpose of:

(a) preventing invalidity or unlawfulness in relation to dispositions of a registered estate or charge;
(b) securing that interests which are capable of being overreached on a disposition of a registered estate or charge are overreached; or
(c) protecting a right or claim in relation to a registered estate or charge.

Although most restrictions are entered as a result of an application, the Registry may enter such restriction without an application having been made. If it does so, it must give notice of the entry to the registered proprietor (LRA 2002, s 42(3)). The Registry is obliged to enter a restriction in certain circumstances (see 'Obligatory restrictions', below). The court may make an order requiring the Registry to enter a restriction if it appears necessary or desirable to do so for the purposes of protecting a right or claim in relation to a registered estate or registered charge (see 'Court order for entry of restriction', below).

No restriction may be entered, however, for the purpose of protecting the priority of an interest which is, or could be, the subject of a notice (LRA 2002, s 42(2)). This does not necessarily prevent the entry of a restriction in addition to a notice. Although the notice will protect the priority of the interest, a restriction may be used to ensure that any conditions in relation to another disposition by the registered proprietor are complied with. For example, a notice may be entered to protect the priority of a right of pre-emption and at the same time a restriction entered to ensure that there is no disposition of the land to a third party without the written consent of the person having the benefit of the right of pre-emption.

A right or claim may only be protected under LRA 2002, s 42(1)(c) if it relates to a registered estate or registered charge; that is, to the legal estate. This does not therefore include rights or claims that relate only to an equitable interest in an estate or charge under a trust of land, which can generally be the subject of a restriction for the purposes of s 42(1)(a) or (b). In most cases, entry of a restriction in Form A will be appropriate, to ensure that overreaching takes place on a disposition that gives rise to capital monies. A specific exception to this is a charging order affecting a beneficial interest under a trust, which may nevertheless be protected by a restriction in Form K entered under s 42(1)(c) (see *Charging orders*, page 100).

The right to apply for the entry of a restriction must not be exercised without reasonable cause (LRA 2002, s 77(1)). This duty to act reasonably is owed to any person who suffers damage in consequence of its breach (s 77(2)).

Application for entry of restriction

A person may apply for the entry of a restriction if he is the registered proprietor or entitled to be so registered; or if he has the consent of the registered proprietor or the person entitled to be so registered; or if he otherwise has a sufficient interest in the making of the entry (LRA 2002, s 43(1)). LRR 2003, r 93 lists various different classes of person who are automatically regarded as having sufficient interest in the making of an entry. These are dealt with in the appropriate sections of this book. This list is not exhaustive, but a person not falling within any of the categories listed will have to lodge evidence that he has a sufficient interest in the entry of the restriction.

An applicant for entry of a restriction should deliver to the Registry:

(a)   an application in Form RX1 (but see also below);

(b)   (if the application is made with the consent of, rather than by, the registered proprietor or person entitled to be so registered) the relevant consent unless this is given in panel 11 of Form RX1 or the applicant's conveyancer certifies in panel 8 of Form RX1 that he holds such consent;

(c)   (if the application is made by or with the consent of a person entitled to be registered as proprietor) evidence to satisfy the Registry of that person's entitlement to be registered as proprietor. This may take the form of a certificate by the applicant's conveyancer in panel 8 of Form RX1 that he is satisfied that the applicant, or the person consenting to the application, is entitled to be registered as proprietor and that he holds the originals of the documents that contain evidence of that person's entitlement, or an application for registration of that person as proprietor is pending at the Registry;

(d)   (if the application is made by a person who claims that he has a sufficient interest in the making of the entry) a statement in panel 12 of Form RX1 signed by the applicant or a certificate by his conveyancer in panel 13 of Form RX1, giving details of the nature of the applicant's interest in the entry of the required restriction (or, if the interest is one of those specified in LRR 2003, r 93, stating which of them) and details of how the applicant's interest arose. Any supporting documents should be listed in panel 5 of Form RX1 or in a separate Form DL; and

(e)   the fee payable (see *Fees*, page 221).

Panel 9 of Form RX1 should be completed as to the required restriction(s). If a restriction requires notice to be given to a person, or requires a person's consent or certificate, or is a standard form restriction that refers to a named person and requires his address, that person's address for service must be stated. A restriction in one of the standard forms set out in LRR 2003, Sch 4 does not require the approval of the Registry to the wording of the restriction under LRA 2002, s 43(3). For non-standard restrictions, such approval will be required, see 'Forms of restriction', below.

If the restriction affects the registered estate, it will be entered in the proprietorship register. If it affects a registered charge, it will be entered in the charges register.

An application for a restriction need not be made in Form RX1 provided it is for a *standard* form of restriction and the application is instead made in one of the following:

(a)   the additional provisions panel of a prescribed form of transfer or assent in Forms TP1, TP2, TR1, TR2, TR4, TR5, AS1, AS2 or AS3;

(b)   clause LR13 of a prescribed clauses lease (or any other lease containing clauses LR1 to LR14 of LRR 2003, Sch 1A and which is required to be completed by registration under LRA 2002, s 27(2)(b) or is the subject of an application for first registration of title to it);

(c)   panel 8 of Form CH1, or in a charge which has first been approved by the Registry, or in an electronic document to which LRA 2002, s 91 applies where the form of the document (including the application for the restriction) has first been approved by the Registry;

(d)   (in the case of application for a Form A restriction following the severance of a beneficial joint tenancy by agreement or notice) Form SEV.

Notice of the application for entry of a restriction and of the right to object to it is given to the registered proprietor, unless the application was made by him or with his consent, or by or with the consent of a person entitled to be registered as proprietor, or the application was required to be made by LRR 2003, r 94 (which lists various cases where an application must be made). Notice is also not given where the restriction reflects a limitation under an order of the court or the Registry, or under an undertaking given in place of such an order (LRA 2002, s 45). The Registry may not determine the application before the end of the specified period unless each person notified has indicated that he is not objecting or his objection has been disposed of. The specified period is the period ending at 12 noon on the 15th working day after the date of issue of the notice or, if more than one such notice is issued, after the date of issue of the latest notice. A working day is any day from Monday to Friday (inclusive) which is not Christmas Day, Good Friday or any other day either specified or declared by proclamation under Banking and Financial Dealings Act 1971, s 1 or appointed by the Lord Chancellor, or certified by the Registry as being an 'interrupted day' due to delay or failure of a communication service or to some other event or circumstance causing substantial interruption in the normal operation of the Registry. For the position where the registered proprietor objects to the entry of the restriction, see *Disputes*, page 193.

Forms of restriction

Standard forms of restriction are set out in LRR 2003, Sch 4. Some of the standard forms contain variables and LRR 2003, r 91A allows certain amendments to be made to the standard forms. Other than that, the amendment of a standard form will result in a restriction being non-standard. Use of the standard forms of restriction is recommended if at all possible. If no standard form is suitable, application may be made to enter a non-standard form of restriction. Where an application is made for a non-standard restriction, the Registry may approve the application only if it appears to it that the terms of the restriction are reasonable and that applying the restriction would be straightforward and would not place an unreasonable burden on the Registry (LRA 2002, s 43(3)). Before the terms of a non-standard restriction are formally agreed between parties, it is therefore prudent to check with the Registry that an application for such restriction will be approved. For example, it is unlikely that the Registry will accept an application for a restriction that expressly prevents the entry of a notice.

The standard forms of restriction are set out in full in Appendix IV, page 585.

Court order for entry of restriction

If it appears to the court that it is necessary or desirable to do so for the purpose of protecting a right or claim in relation to a registered estate or charge, it may make an order requiring the Registry to enter a restriction in the register (LRA 2002, s 46(1)). This may be a standard or non-standard restriction, but such an order may not be made for the purpose of protecting the priority of an interest which is, or could be, the subject of a notice. Although the order may be addressed directly to the Registry, a formal application for the restriction to be entered should be made, as the Registry may not otherwise be aware of the order. It is not necessary to use Form RX1 to apply for the entry of the restriction; instead the court order and Form AP1 should be delivered to the Registry, together with the fee payable (see *Fees*, page 221).

The court may include in such an order a direction that the entry of the restriction made in pursuance of the order is to have overriding priority. Where this is done, an entry is made in the register to ensure that the priority of the restriction ordered by the court is apparent. Since such a direction of the court overrides an existing priority protection given by an official search with priority, the Registry must give notice of the entry to the person who applied for the official search (or the conveyancer or agent who applied on his behalf), unless the Registry is satisfied that such notice is unnecessary (LRR 2003, r 100).

Obligatory restrictions

In addition to the making of a court order made under LRA 2002, s 46(1), there are certain other circumstances where a restriction must be entered by the Registry without an application being made.

Where two or more persons are registered as proprietors of a registered estate in land, the Registry must enter a restriction in Form A unless the survivor will be able to give a valid receipt for capital money (LRA 2002, s 44(1) and LRR 2003, r 95(2)(a)). This is for the purpose of securing that interests which are capable of being overreached on a disposition of a registered estate or charge are overreached.

Certain statutes require a restriction to be entered, for example HA 1996, s 13 (see *Registered social landlords and private registered providers*, page 482). Details of some of these statutory provisions and the appropriate restrictions to be entered are set out in LRR 2003, r 95(2). These restrictions are dealt with in the appropriate sections of this book.

A bankruptcy restriction is required to be entered under LRA 2002, s 86(4) (see *Bankruptcy*, page 49).

Compliance with a restriction

An application must, where necessary, comply with the terms of a restriction before it can be completed. LRR 2003, r 91B contains provisions relating to a certificate or consent by a corporation required under the terms of a restriction.

Application for an order that a restriction be disapplied or modified

An applicant who appears to the Registry to have a sufficient interest in a restriction may apply for the Registry to make an order disapplying or modifying the restriction (LRA 2002, s 41(3)). For example a restriction might require the consent of a person who has transferred his responsibility to a third party and an application then be made to modify the restriction by substituting the name of the third party in the entry.

An applicant should deliver to the Registry an application Form RX2 setting out (LRR 2003, r 96):

(a)   whether the application is to disapply or modify the restriction and, if the latter, the details of the modification sought;

(b)   why the applicant has a sufficient interest in the restriction to make the application;

(c)   details of the disposition or the kind of disposition that will be affected by the order; and

(d)   why the applicant considers that the Registry should make the order.

A fee is payable (see *Fees*, page 221).

The Registry may make such enquiries and serve such notices as it thinks fit and it may require the applicant to supply further evidence. If an order is made it must, if appropriate, be noted in the register.

Cancellation of a restriction

Any person may apply to cancel a restriction that is no longer required. The application must be made in Form RX3 and no fee is currently payable. The application must be accompanied by evidence to satisfy the Registry that the restriction is no longer required (LRR 2003, r 96). If the Registry is satisfied with the evidence it must cancel the restriction. Where the restriction gives an address for service for any person who is not the applicant for cancellation, notice of the application is sent to that person. For the position where the person objects to the cancellation of the restriction, see *Disputes*, page 193.

When registering a disposition of a registered estate, the Registry must cancel a restriction entered for the purpose of protecting an interest, right or claim arising under a trust of land if it is satisfied that such estate is no longer subject to that trust of land (LRR 2003, r 99). Thus the Registry will, for example, automatically cancel a restriction in Form A where the beneficial interests under the trust of land have clearly been overreached on a transfer on sale.

The Registry may cancel a restriction without an application being made where it is satisfied that the entry is superfluous (LRA 2002, Sch 4, para 5(d)). For example, a restriction requiring the consent of the proprietor of a registered charge is cancelled when the charge is discharged, or a restriction may reflect a limitation on the powers of a previous proprietor, which does not apply to the current proprietor.

Withdrawal of a restriction

A person with the benefit of a restriction may apply for it to be removed from the register without regard to the question of whether it still serves any purpose (LRA 2002, s 47). The application must be made in Form RX4 and no fee is currently payable. The application must be accompanied by the required consent (LRR 2003, r 98), which is either:

(a) where the restriction requires the consent of a specified person, the consent of that person;
(b) where the restriction requires a certificate to be given by a specified person, the consent of that person;
(c) where the restriction requires notice to be given to a specified person, the consent of that person;
(d) where the restriction requires the consent of a specified person, or alternatively a certificate to be given by a specified person, the consent of all such persons;
(e) in any other case, the consent of all persons who appear to the Registry to have an interest in the restriction.

A certificate may be given by the applicant's conveyancer that he holds any consents required. This certificate may be given in panel 10 of Form RX4.

In general, a 'voluntary' restriction (that is, one applied for voluntarily rather than entered in pursuance of an obligation under the LRA 2002) cannot be removed from the register as a matter of course when a disposition is registered, even where the terms of the restriction have been complied with and the disposition is a transfer on sale, for example. Therefore, if it is intended that the restriction should not remain in the register following the registration of the disposition, an express withdrawal should normally be obtained.

No application may be made to withdraw a restriction that:

(a)   is entered to prevent invalidity or unlawfulness in relation to dispositions and reflects some limitation on the registered proprietor's powers of disposition imposed by statute or the general law;

(b)   is entered by someone who was under an obligation to apply under LRR 2003, r 94;

(c)   the Registry is obliged to enter;

(d)   reflects a limitation under an order of the court or of the Registry, or an undertaking given in respect of such an order; or

(e)   the court has ordered the Registry to enter under LRA 2002, s 46.

Restrictions entered under the Land Registration Act 1925

The LRA 2002 applies to restrictions entered in the register prior to 13 October 2003 in the same way that it applies to restrictions entered on or after that date under the LRA 2002. The effect of a restriction under the LRA 1925 is preserved. For example, a restriction preventing the noting of a disposition is not treated as preventing the entry of a unilateral notice, since the restriction would not have prevented the entry of a caution against dealings.

Inhibitions entered under the Land Registration Act 1925

Although it has not been possible to enter a new inhibition in the register since 13 October 2003, an inhibition entered before that date will continue to have effect and will be treated as a restriction for the purposes of the LRA 2002. Inhibitions prohibit, wholly or partially, the exercise of a proprietor's powers of disposition. Inhibitions, other than bankruptcy inhibitions (see *Bankruptcy*, page 49), are very uncommon. An application to cancel an inhibition must be made to the court if the inhibition was originally entered pursuant to an order of the court; otherwise it must be made to the Registry. No fee is currently payable for cancellation.

RESTRICTIVE COVENANTS

The LRA 2002 is a register of legal estates and interests and does not therefore provide for the entry of the benefit of equitable rights in the register. Consequently, no entry can be made in the register of the benefit of a restrictive covenant, as such a benefit is an equitable not a legal right. Entitlement to the benefit of a restrictive covenant must therefore subsist 'off the register'. The burden of a restrictive covenant usually needs to be protected by way of a notice in the register. For restrictive covenants between a landlord and tenant, however, see 'Restrictive covenants in leases', page 320. The fact that an interest is the subject of a notice does not necessarily mean that the interest is valid, but does mean that the priority of the interest, if valid, is protected (LRA 2002, s 32(3)).

Restrictive covenants on first registration

When the deeds and documents lodged on first registration show that the estate is subject to restrictive covenants, notice of the covenants will be entered in the register (LRR 2003, r 35(1)). This does not apply to covenants between a landlord and tenant affecting the demised premises in the lease (LRA 2002, s 33(c)). The entry in the charges register will refer to the deed containing the covenants and provide details of the covenants (including any covenanting clause) either by setting out the covenants verbatim in the register or by referring to a filed document containing them. Sometimes neither the original deed nor a certified copy nor examined abstract will accompany the application. The action taken by the Registry will then depend on the circumstances:

(a) If an unverified copy or abstract of the covenants accompanies the application and the Registry considers the risk of it being inaccurate to be so small that it can properly be treated as though it were verified (for example, if the evidence consists of an apparently accurate typewritten copy or a photocopy), it will be so treated and an entry made in the register as above.

(b) If an unverified copy or abstract of the covenants accompanies the application but cannot properly be treated as though it were verified and if a solicitor so requests, an entry will (in accordance with an agreement made between The Law Society and the Registry) be made in the charges register along the following lines:

> A [*Conveyance*] of the land in this title [*and other land*] dated [*date*] made between [*parties*] contains restrictive covenants but no verified particulars of them were produced on first registration. The details set out [*in the schedule of restrictive covenants hereto*] of what purport to be the said covenants were provided by (*solicitor*) acting for a vendor in [*specify details*].

As this entry is qualified, no indemnity will be payable by the Registry if the details referred to are not complete or correct.

(c)   If an unverified copy or abstract of the covenants accompanies the application, but cannot be treated as verified and is not the subject of a request by a solicitor as in (b) above, an entry will be made in the register referring to the deed containing the covenants and stating that it contains restrictive covenants but that:

> ... neither the original deed nor a certified copy nor an examined abstract thereof was produced on first registration.

Such an entry will also be made when no particulars, verified or unverified, of the covenants or stipulations accompany the application.

Particulars of the words of covenant should be provided whenever possible, but when only particulars of restrictive stipulations without the words of covenant accompany an application, a modified form of entry indicating that the words of covenant were not available, will be used. The fact that a notice in the register does not necessarily mean that a restrictive covenant is valid means that the entry on first registration of a restrictive covenant which was void for non-registration as a Land Charge does not confer any fresh validity on such a covenant.

Restrictive covenants and registered land

If a transfer of the whole or part, or other registrable disposition, of a registered estate under LRA 2002, s 27(2) imposes restrictive covenants, a notice of these covenants will be entered automatically in the register of the burdened title upon registration of the transfer or other disposition. However, if the transfer or other disposition imposes restrictive covenants on any other title, the relevant title number(s) must be given in panel 2 of the Form AP1, otherwise the Registry is not obliged to make any entry in that title and a specific application for entry of a notice of the covenants on that title will be necessary (LRR 2003, rr 72(5) and 72C(3)).

If restrictive covenants are imposed upon a registered estate otherwise than in a transfer or other registrable disposition, for example by a deed of covenant, an application must be made for entry of a notice in the register of title to the burdened estate. It is important to identify the burdened estate clearly (by plan if necessary) and also to identify the estate intended to be benefited by the covenants. The application may be for entry of an agreed notice or a unilateral notice.

Agreed notice

In addition to the usual documents required (see *Notices*, page 389), an applicant should deliver to the Registry the deed of covenant or a certified copy of it.

Where the consent of the registered proprietor is not available but, for example, the deed of covenant is signed by him, this is likely to be sufficient to satisfy the Registry as to the validity of the applicant's claim for the purposes of LRA 2002, s 34(3)(c).

The agreed notice in the register will give details of the interest protected.

Unilateral notice

An applicant should deliver to the Registry the usual documents required (see *Notices*, page 389).

The statement in panel 11 or conveyancer's certificate in panel 12 of Form UN1 should be completed on the following lines to show the interest of the applicant:

> person having the benefit of restrictive covenants contained in a Deed dated [*date*] made between [*parties*] [as varied by *a Deed dated [date] made between [parties]*].

The unilateral notice in the register will give brief details of the interest protected and identify the beneficiary of that notice.

Release, waiver or modification of restrictive covenants

An application for entry of a notice in respect of a deed of release or variation should be made in Form AN1 for an agreed notice or Form UN1 for a unilateral notice, if made by the person claiming the benefit of the covenants (see *Notices*, page 389); or in Form AP1 if made by the registered proprietor of the burdened title. In the case of an agreed notice of a variation of an interest protected by a notice, the entry in the register must give details of the variation (LRR 2003, r 84(4)).

An application for cancellation of an existing notice (other than a unilateral notice) in respect of restrictive covenants based upon a deed of release should be made in Form CN1 (see *Notices*, page 389). In practice it is usually difficult, if not impossible, to prove that a deed purporting to release, waive, discharge or modify restrictive covenants is fully effective, because of the difficulty in identifying the extent of the estate having the benefit of the covenants and ensuring that all parties having an interest in the covenants have joined into the deed. It is therefore the practice of the Registry in most cases (unless the position is beyond doubt) to retain the original notice of the covenants in the register and enter a notice of such a deed in the register stating that it is 'expressed' to release or vary the covenants (LRR 2003, r 87(4)).

Where it is claimed that restrictive covenants protected in the register by a notice (other than a unilateral notice) are void for non-registration as a Land Charge following first registration, application may be made in Form CN1 to cancel the notice, accompanied by evidence to satisfy the Registry that the covenants are void (LRR 2003, r 87(1)). It should be noted that:

(a)   registration as a Land Charge is not necessary for matters contained in a deed dated after 27 July 1971 which attracts compulsory registration (Land Charges Act 1972, s 4(3));

(b)   under the Land Registry 'D31 procedure' (abolished in March 1976), Land Charge registrations were cancelled on completion of first registration of title. The fact the Land Charge no longer appears may not therefore be conclusive that it was not registered at the relevant time;

(c)   land charges in favour of local authorities are not void for want of registration as a Land Charge, if registered as local land charges before 1 August 1977; and

(d)   in relation to a disposition which is *not* to a purchaser, such as a deed of gift to a donee or an assent to a beneficiary, the disponee (not being a purchaser) will be bound by the covenant even if it has not been not registered as a Land Charge.

If the existing notice in respect of restrictive covenants is a unilateral notice, application may be made in Form UN2 for removal or in Form UN4 for cancellation of the notice (see *Notices*, page 389).

When the Upper Tribunal (Lands Chamber) – formerly the Lands Tribunal – has made an order under Law of Property Act 1925, s 84 as to modification or discharge of restrictive covenants, application may be made for this to be reflected in the register. The action taken by the Registry will depend upon the terms of the order.

Positive covenants imposed by statute

Although normally the burden of a positive covenant does not run with the land, certain statutes make provision for a positive covenant entered into pursuant to that statute enforceable as though it was a restrictive covenant. Such statutes include Local Government (Miscellaneous Provisions) Act 1982, s 33; Mission and Pastoral Measure 2011, s 75; HA 1985, s 609; National Trust Act 1937, s 8: Wildlife and Countryside Act 1981, s 39; and Water Industry Act 1991, s 156.

The Registry will treat such covenants in the same way as restrictive covenants. but will omit the word 'restrictive' from the register entry.

RETENTION, DESTRUCTION AND RETURN OF DOCUMENTS

The Registry may destroy any document which it retains if it is satisfied that it has made and retained a sufficient copy of the document or further retention of the document is unnecessary (LRR 2003, r 203). The Registry may release any document retained by it upon such terms, if any, for its return as it considers appropriate (LRR 2003, r 205).

See also *Applications to HM Land Registry*, page 44 and *First registration*, page 222.

RIGHT TO BUY AND RIGHT TO ACQUIRE UNDER THE HOUSING ACTS

Many tenants of local authorities and certain other public sector landlords have the right to buy their houses or flats under the HA 1985. This right to buy was originally introduced by the Housing Act 1980 and is now dealt with in HA 1985, Pt V. Many other tenants of registered social landlords have the right to acquire their houses or flats under the HA 1996. The right to acquire operates in the same way as the right to buy, but only applies to qualifying tenants of registered social landlords who live in houses or flats provided with public money and which have remained in the social rented sector.

In the case of a freehold house, the freehold is transferred to the tenant when he exercises his right to buy and, in the case of a flat or leasehold house, a lease is granted to him, usually for 125 years (depending upon the nature of the landlord's reversionary title). The tenant is given a discount on the purchase price.

Charges on landlord's title

Where the right to buy is exercised, no discharge or release is required in respect of any registered or noted charge, nor is the consent of any chargee under a restriction required (HA 1985, Sch 6, paras 20 and 21).

In the case of the exercise of the right to acquire from a registered social landlord, the procedure in Housing (Right to Acquire) Regulations 1997 (SI 1997/619), Sch 1, para 41(g) applies. The tenant receives either evidence of the release from the charge provided by the chargee or a certificate from the landlord given under HA 1985, Sch 6, para 23(1) or (3) (inserted by Housing (Right to Acquire) Regulations 1997, Sch 1, para 41(g)). Such a certificate is effective to release the house or flat from the charge.

Rentcharges

A transfer under the right to buy or right to acquire is made subject to any existing rentcharge. Where the property being transferred is, with other land, subject to the rentcharge, the transfer must contain a covenant by the landlord to indemnify the tenant and his successors in title in respect of any liability arising under the rentcharge (HA 1985, Sch 6, para 21(3)). A lease granted under the right to buy or right to acquire is not affected by any rentcharge on the landlord's interest (HA 1985, Sch 6, para 20).

Statutory easements

Unless excluded or modified, a transfer or lease under the right to buy or right to acquire is deemed to include a grant and reservation of the easements contained in HA 1985, Sch 6, para 2. These include rights of support, rights of light and air, and rights of drainage and other domestic services. An entry in respect of these statutory easements is automatically made in the register when the transfer is registered. A transfer or lease may also include non-statutory easements, as well as restrictive and other covenants.

Discount charges

Where a tenant exercises the right to buy or right to acquire, he is entitled to a discount on the purchase price. The tenant covenants in the transfer to repay the discount if there is a disposal within a certain period. This period was formerly 3 years, but was extended to 5 years as from 18 January 2005 by the Housing Act

2004. Certain disposals do not result in the repayment of discount (HA 1985, s 160). The covenant takes effect as a charge (HA 1985, s 156) and an entry is made automatically on registration of the transfer.

Right of first refusal

Under the HA 1985, s 156A (as inserted by the Housing Act 2004, s 188) and the Housing (Right of First Refusal) (England) Regulations 2005 (SI 2005/1917), right to buy disposals by local authorities and right to acquire disposals by registered social landlords of land in England dated on or after 10 August 2005 may contain a covenant not to dispose of the land unless certain prescribed conditions, relating to a right of first refusal in favour of the landlord, are satisfied. The Housing (Right of First Refusal) (Wales) Regulations 2005 (SI 2005/2680) allow such disposals of land in Wales dated on or after 28 September 2005 to contain a similar covenant. The covenant applies to disposals made within a period of 10 years beginning with the date of the conveyance or grant by the landlord. Certain disposals are exempted or do not constitute relevant disposals for this purpose.

The Registry must enter in the register a restriction reflecting the limitation imposed by any such covenant (HA 1985, s 156A(12)). The restriction entered will be to the effect that no disposition within the relevant period is to be registered unless accompanied by a certificate from the relevant authority that the transfer or lease complies with the requirements of HA 1985, s 156A or is an exempt disposal or is otherwise not a relevant disposal.

Acquisition on rent to mortgage terms

Formerly, the HA 1985 conferred a right for a tenant to acquire his property on rent to mortgage terms. As from 18 July 2005, such a right (subject to certain transitional provisions) is no longer exercisable (HA 1985, s 142A as inserted by the Housing Act 2004, s 190(1)).

Where the tenant exercised the right to buy on rent to mortgage terms under HA 1985, s 143, the provisions of Sch 6A to that Act (as inserted by the LRHUDA 1993, s 117) applied. It was not possible to exercise the right to acquire from a registered social landlord on rent to mortgage terms.

The landlord's share was secured by a legal charge in favour of the landlord which should have been lodged for registration at the same time as the transfer to the tenant was registered. That charge had priority over the discount charge. The transfer to the tenant contained provisions relating to the paying off of the landlord's share.

Property to which Housing Act 1985, s 37 or s 157 applies

Where the sale to the tenant is of a house in a National Park, an area of outstanding natural beauty or an area designated as a rural area, the transfer or conveyance may contain a covenant limiting the freedom of the purchaser to dispose of the property. In such case where the sale is under the right to buy, a restriction in Form V is entered automatically in the proprietorship register (LRA 2002, s 44(2) and LRR 2003, r 95(2)(c)). The wording of Form V is set out in Appendix IV, page 585.

Where the sale is a voluntary sale to which HA 1985, s 37 applies, a restriction in Form U is entered automatically in the proprietorship register (LRA 2002, s 44(2) and LRR 2003, r 95(2)(b)). The wording of Form U is set out in Appendix IV, page 585.

Preserved right to buy

Where public sector landlords dispose of their housing stock to social or private sector landlords, the tenant's right to buy may be preserved, even though the new landlord is not one which would otherwise be subject to the right to buy. Where this occurs, the transfer to the new landlord must contain a statement that the transfer is, so far as it relates to dwelling houses occupied by secure tenants, a transfer to which HA 1985, s 171A applies. It must also contain a list of the dwelling houses transferred which are occupied by secure tenants (HA 1985, Sch 9A, para 1). Such a statement may be along the following lines:

> Section 171A of the Housing Act 1985 applies to this deed so far as it relates to dwelling houses occupied by secure tenants. The [*purchaser*] *or* [*lessee*] applies for entry of the notice and restriction required by paragraph 4 of Schedule 9A to that Act.

A transfer of unregistered land, or a lease out of unregistered land, to which HA 1985, s 171A applies is subject to compulsory registration (LRA 2002, s 4(1)(b) and (f)) (see *First registration*, page 222).

On registration of a transfer containing a statement that HA 1985, s 171A applies, a notice of the rights of the qualifying tenants and a restriction in Form W are entered automatically in the register (HA 1985, Sch 9A, para 4, LRA 2002, s 44(2) and LRR 2003, r 95(2)(f)). The wording of Form W is set out in Appendix IV, page 585.

The rights of the tenant having the preserved right to buy are not interests within LRA 2002, Sch 3 which override registered dispositions and so the priority of such rights is liable to be postponed under LRA 2002, s 29 in favour of a registered disposition for valuable consideration unless protected by a notice in the register. Where the tenants are moved to another registered property, the landlord should apply for the notice and restriction to be entered in respect of that registered title, if there is no entry in that title.

Where the registered proprietor supplies a certificate that the registered title, or a specified part of it, is not subject to any rights of a qualifying person under the preserved right to buy, application may be made for the notice and restriction to be cancelled or modified (see *Notices*, page 389), as appropriate.

In certain circumstances, a transfer by a local authority or a housing action trust requires the consent of the Secretary of State or the Welsh Ministers. A transferee of housing stock following such consent may itself be subject to a requirement for similar consent on a subsequent transfer. A statement to this effect should be made in the transfer and a restriction in Form X is entered automatically in the proprietorship register. The wording of Form X is set out in Appendix IV, page 585.

Exempt disposals as defined by the HA 1988, s 81(8) are:

(a) the disposal of a dwelling house to a person having the right to buy it under HA 1985, Pt V (whether the disposal is in fact made under that Part or otherwise);

(b) the disposal of a dwelling house to a person having the right to buy it under HA 1996, Pt I (whether or not the disposal is in fact made under provisions having effect by virtue of s 17 of that Act);

(c) a compulsory disposal within the meaning of HA 1985, Pt V;

(d) the disposal of an easement or rentcharge;

(e) the disposal of an interest by way of security for a loan;

(f) the grant of a secure tenancy or what would be a secure tenancy but for any of HA 1985, Sch 1, paras 2 to 12;

(g) the grant of an assured tenancy or an assured agricultural occupancy, within the meaning of HA 1988, Pt I, or what would be such a tenancy or occupancy but for any of Sch 1, paras 4 to 8 to that Act; and

(h)   the transfer of an interest held on trust for any person where the disposal is made in connection with the appointment of a new trustee or in connection with the discharge of any trustee.

RIGHT TO MANAGE COMPANIES

Commonhold and Leasehold Reform Act 2002, Pt 2 came into force on 30 September 2003 and makes provision for the management functions of the landlord (and certain third parties) to be exercisable by a right to manage (RTM) company in place of the landlord. An RTM company is a special company limited by guarantee, the membership of which is restricted to qualifying tenants (generally a tenant under a long lease).

The practice of the Registry is that applications to protect an RTM company by way of entry of an agreed notice or unilateral notice (in the case of a registered estate), or registration of a caution against first registration (in the case of an unregistered estate) under the LRA 2002 are not appropriate, because the RTM is not an adverse right affecting the landlord's title.

LRR 2003, r 79A does, however, allow for application to be made in Form AP1 for an entry to be made in the proprietorship register to record the acquisition of the RTM by an RTM company. Such an application must be accompanied by evidence to satisfy the Registry that:

(a)   the applicant is an RTM company;
(b)   the right to manage is in relation to the premises comprised in the registered estate;
(c)   the registered proprietor of the registered estate is the landlord under a lease of the whole or part of the registered estate; and
(d)   the right to manage the premises has been acquired, and remains exercisable, by the RTM company.

Such evidence may be provided by way of a conveyancer's certificate. If the Registry is so satisfied, it must make the appropriate entry in the proprietorship register. The entry does not guarantee that the RTM has been acquired or that, if acquired, it remains exercisable, but it does highlight to those proposing to deal with the landlord's title that there is an RTM company which claims to have acquired the RTM in respect of the premises concerned. A fee is payable (see *Fees*, page 221).

RIGHTS OF LIGHT AND AIR

Rights of light and air may subsist as easements (see *Equitable easements*, page 212, and *Legal easements*, page 343). A transfer or conveyance or other document may contain an agreement or declaration as to rights of light and air; this may be the case where, for example, an owner sells off part of the land comprised in his registered title.

The existence of an agreement which prevents the statutory period of prescription beginning to run does not create an incumbrance on the property (*Smith v Colbourne* [1914] 2 Ch 533 (CA)). The benefit of an agreement preventing the acquisition of rights of light or air will not therefore be entered as appurtenant to a registered estate.

However, if it appears to the Registry, either on first registration or on the registration of a registrable disposition, that an agreement prevents the acquisition of rights of light or air for the benefit of the registered estate, it may make an entry in the property register of that estate (LRR 2003, rr 36 and 76).

RIGHTS OF PRE-EMPTION

The grant of a right of pre-emption imposes an obligation upon the grantor as owner of the land not to sell it without first giving the grantee the right to purchase it. Following the decision of the Court of Appeal in *Pritchard v Briggs* [1980] Ch 338, the status of a right of pre-emption as an interest in land has remained doubtful. However, in the case of rights of pre-emption created on or after 13 October 2003, LRA 2002, s 115 provides that a right of pre-emption in relation to registered land has effect from the time of creation as an interest capable of binding successors in title, subject to the rules about the effect of dispositions on priority. For the rules about the effect of dispositions on priority, see *Priorities*, page 452.

A right of pre-emption in respect of registered land may be protected by the entry in the register of an agreed notice or a unilateral notice, and possibly (depending on the terms of the agreement and whether it expressly or impliedly limits the registered proprietor's powers of disposition) by a restriction. A notice does not necessarily mean that the right of pre-emption is valid but does mean that the priority of that right will be protected on any registered disposition (LRA 2002, ss 29, 30 and 32). A restriction does not confer any priority; it simply prevents an entry being made in the register in respect of any disposition, or a disposition of a specified kind, unless the terms of the restriction have (where applicable) been complied with.

A right of pre-emption is not itself an interest within LRA 2002, Sch 1 or Sch 3 which overrides either first registration or registered dispositions. Its priority therefore needs to be protected by entry of a notice in the register.

However, even where a right of pre-emption relating to registered land is not protected by a notice, it may still override a later registered disposition for valuable consideration if, at the time of that later disposition, the person having the benefit of the right of pre-emption is in actual occupation of the land to which the contract relates. If he is in actual occupation of only part of the land to which the right of pre-emption relates, he has an overriding interest only in respect of the part he is occupying (LRA 2002, ss 29 and 30 and Sch 3, para 2).

The interest of the person in actual possession does not override a registered disposition if enquiry was made of him before the disposition and he failed to disclose the right of pre-emption when he could reasonably have been expected to do so. Nor does the right of pre-emption override a registered disposition if it belongs to a person whose occupation would not have been obvious on a reasonably careful inspection of the land at the time of the disposition, and if the person to whom the disposition is made does not have actual knowledge of the right of pre-emption at the time of the disposition (LRA 2002, Sch 3, para 2).

Where the right of pre-emption is contained in a lease that is an unregistered interest falling within LRA 2002, Sch 3, para 1 which overrides registered dispositions, the right of pre-emption may be protected by an entry in the register even where no entry may be made as to the lease itself (i.e. because the lease is for a term not exceeding 3 years and is not otherwise registrable).

The right of pre-emption should be granted and signed by the proprietor of the registered estate, or a satisfactory chain of title between the person granting the right of pre-emption and the registered proprietor shown. For example, if the registered proprietor has contracted to sell a registered title to A, and A then grants to B a right of pre-emption in respect of the land in the title, B's right of pre-emption can be protected by a notice, whether or not A's contract is also protected by a notice.

A right of pre-emption granted before the coming into force of the Perpetuities and Accumulations Act 2009 on 6 April 2010 may become void for remoteness if it breaches the rule against perpetuities (Perpetuities and Accumulations Act 1964, ss 9 and 10). A right of pre-emption granted after that date is no longer subject to the rule against perpetuities (Perpetuities and Accumulations Act 2009, s 1).

Agreed notice

In addition to the usual documents required (see *Notices*, page 389), an applicant should deliver to the Registry the original document granting the right of pre-emption or a certified copy of it.

Where the right of pre-emption is granted by a person with the benefit of a contract for sale, the contract or a certified copy of it should be included with the application. This is not necessary if there is already a notice of the contract in the register.

Where the consent of the registered proprietor is not available but, for example, the document granting the right of pre-emption is signed by him, this is likely to be sufficient to satisfy the Registry as to the validity of the applicant's claim for the purposes of LRA 2002, s 34(3)(c).

The agreed notice in the register will give details of the interest protected.

An application for entry of a unilateral notice may be preferred where the applicant does not wish the terms of the pre-emption to be open to public inspection and copying.

Unilateral notice

An applicant should deliver to the Registry the usual documents required (see *Notices*, page 389).

The statement in panel 11 or conveyancer's certificate in panel 12 of Form UN1 should be completed on the following lines to show the interest of the applicant:

> person having the benefit of a right of pre-emption contained in a [*description of document*] dated [*date*] made between [*names*].

Where the right of pre-emption is granted by a person with the benefit of a contract for sale, the contract should also be referred to. The wording must establish the link between the registered proprietor and the person who is to be shown as the beneficiary of the notice.

The unilateral notice in the register will give brief details of the interest protected and identify the beneficiary of that notice.

Restriction

As a result of LRA 2002, s 42(2), no restriction may be entered for the purpose of protecting the priority of an interest which is, or could be, the subject of a notice. This does not, however, prevent a restriction from being entered in addition to the notice of the right of pre-emption. Although the notice will protect the priority of the right of pre-emption, a restriction may be used to ensure that any conditions in relation to another disposition by the registered proprietor are complied with. The consent of the registered proprietor to the entry of the restriction is required, unless the document granting the right of pre-emption contains a provision which limits the registered proprietor's powers to enter into any further disposition.

In addition to the usual documents required (see *Restrictions*, page 500), an applicant should deliver to the Registry (if the application is made by a person who claims that he has a sufficient interest in the making of the entry) a certified copy of the document granting the right of pre-emption. The statement in panel 12 or conveyancer's certificate in panel 13 of Form RX1 must be completed, setting out details of the right of pre-emption and of any provision in the document granting the right of pre-emption which limits the registered proprietor's powers to enter into a disposition.

Panel 9 of Form RX1 should be completed as to the required restriction(s). A restriction in a standard form contained in LRR 2003, Sch 4 does not require the approval of the Registry to the terms of the restriction under LRA 2002, s 43(3). A possible form of restriction based on Form L is:

> No disposition of the registered estate by the proprietor of the registered estate is to be registered without a written certificate signed by [*purchaser*] of [*address*] or their conveyancer that the provisions of [*clause, paragraph or other particulars*] of [*details of document granting the right of pre-emption*] have been complied with or that they do not apply to the disposition.

Form RX1 does not need to be used if the application is for a standard form restriction and is contained in either the 'additional provisions' panel of a prescribed form of transfer or assent, or in clause LR13 of a prescribed clauses lease (or any other lease containing clauses LR1 to LR14 of LRR 2003, Sch 1A) (LRR 2003, r 92(7)).

The Registry must give notice of the application for a restriction to the proprietor of the registered estate or charge concerned, if it has not been made by or with the consent of such proprietor or a person entitled to be registered as such proprietor (LRA 2002, s 45).

Rights of pre-emption contained in registrable dispositions

Although a right of pre-emption may be granted by way of a separate transaction, it can also form part of the terms of a registrable disposition such as a transfer or a lease. In the case of a transfer of part of a registered title, the Registry must (where appropriate) make entries in the relevant registered title in respect of any rights, provisions or other matters created by the transfer which are capable of being so entered. However, the Registry need make no such entries where the relevant title numbers have not been given in panel 2 of the Form AP1, unless separate application is made in respect of them (LRR 2003, r 72). Similar provisions apply in the case of a transfer of the whole of a registered title, or other registrable disposition (LRR 2003, r 72C).

In the case of a lease granted out of a registered estate in land which is required to be registered under LRA 2002, s 27(2)(b), LRR 2003, r 72A specifies certain entries which the Registry is obliged to make on registration of the lease. This applies to both prescribed clauses leases and other leases. On completion of such a lease by registration, the Registry must (where appropriate) make entries in the relevant registered title in respect of interests contained in the lease which are of the nature referred to in clause LR9 (rights of acquisition, etc). However, where the lease is a prescribed clauses lease and the rights are not specified or referred to in clause LR9, the Registry need take no action in respect of them unless a separate application is made. Equally, the Registry need not make any entries where, in the case of a prescribed clauses lease, the title numbers of the relevant registered titles have not been given in clause LR2.2; or in any other case, the title numbers of the relevant registered titles required by clause LR2.2 have not been given in panel 2 of the Form AP1 lodged for the purpose of completing the lease by registration, unless a separate application is made.

RIGHTS OF REVERTER

In the 19th century, various statutes made provision to facilitate the donation of land for certain purposes, for example as a site for the erection of a school or a place of worship. To overcome difficulties which could arise from alienation of such land by way of gift, in particular in relation to land which was settled land, these statutes included provision for a right of reverter in favour of the grantor.

The effect of such a right was that, if the land ceased to be used for the purpose for which it had been granted, title to it would revert to the grantor or his successors. A grant subject to such a right of reverter took effect as a determinable fee simple, but this did not prevent it from being a legal estate. The statutes in question (the relevant enactments) were the School Sites Acts of 1841, 1844, 1849, 1851 and 1852; the Literary and Scientific Institutions Act 1854; and the Places of Worship Sites Act 1873.

The Reverter of Sites Act 1987 came into force on 17 August 1987. It was intended to overcome some of the problems which could arise where an event triggering determination of the determinable fee simple and reverter of title (a reversion event) occurred. Section 1 of that Act provides that where any relevant enactment provides for reverter, that enactment shall have effect (and be deemed always to have had effect) so that instead of reverting automatically to the grantor, the land is to be held on trust after the reversion event. The trustees are the persons who held it immediately before the reversion event and they hold it on a trust of land for the revertee. The trustees will be under a duty to convey the land to a revertee who is of full age and capacity, but they do have a power of sale whilst the land is vested in them. Accordingly, a sale by two or more trustees or a trust corporation will overreach the beneficial interest of the revertee.

There are two exceptions to the imposition of such a trust:

(a)   Where the trustees have extinguished the right of a revertee before 17 August 1987 (Reverter of Sites Act 1987, s 1(4)). This would be the case where, for example, the trustees had, prior to that date, been in possession of the land for more than 12 years after the reversion event. In such a case, the trustees will hold the land on trust, but there will be no beneficiary of the trust and the trustees' powers are limited to those that they could have exercised if the 1987 Act had not been passed, or to applying to either the Charity Commission or the Secretary of State for Education for a Charity Commission's Scheme or Education Act Scheme (as the case may be) in accordance with the provisions of the 1987 Act.

(b)   Where the trustees have traced the beneficiaries, but either the beneficiaries do not want to claim the property or for some other reason it is felt desirable that actual or potential beneficiaries should have their rights extinguished and a charitable purposes scheme created. In such a case, the trustees may apply under Reverter of Sites Act 1987, s 2 or s 5 to either the Charity Commission or the Secretary of State for Education for a Charity Commission's Scheme or Education Act Scheme (as the case may be) in accordance with the provisions of the 1987 Act.

Restriction

Where a registered estate becomes subject to a trust of land, other than on a registrable disposition, or where the estate is held on a trust of land and there is a change in the trusts, and a sole or last surviving trustee will not be able to give a valid receipt for capital money, the registered proprietor must apply for entry of a restriction in Form A (LRR 2003, r 94(1) and (2)). If such an application is not made, a revertee entitled to the beneficial interest in the land has a sufficient interest for the purposes of LRA 2002, s 43(1)(c) to apply for entry of such a restriction, to ensure that a survivor of the joint proprietors (unless a trust corporation) will not be able to give a valid receipt for capital money (LRR 2003, r 93(a)). The wording of Form A is set out in Appendix IV, page 585.

A restriction does not confer any priority; it simply prevents an entry being made in the register in respect of any disposition, or a disposition of a specified kind, unless the terms of the restriction have (where applicable) been complied with.

An applicant should deliver to the Registry the usual documents required (see *Restrictions*, page 500).

No fee is currently payable where the application is in respect of a restriction in Form A only.

Where the applicant is a person who has an interest under a trust of land, the statement in panel 12 or conveyancer's certificate in panel 13 of Form RX1 should be completed on the following lines:

> The interest is that specified in rule 93(a) of the Land Registration Rules 2003, the applicant being a person who has an interest in the registered estate held under a trust of land as a result of [*set out details of provision for reverter and of the reversion event*].

Panel 9 of Form RX1 should be completed as to Form A set out above. A restriction in Form A in LRR 2003, Sch 4 does not require the approval of the Registry to the wording of the restriction under LRA 2002, s 43(3).

The Registry must give notice of the application for a restriction to the proprietor of the registered estate concerned if it has not been made by or with his consent or a person entitled to be registered as such proprietor (LRA 2002, s 45).

Transfer to revertee

If a revertee becomes beneficially entitled, he should take a transfer of the land from the trustees and apply for registration in the usual way (see *Transfers*, page 551). The application should be accompanied by a letter confirming, if such be the case, that the land is not affected by anything done by the revertee prior to 17 August 1987, the validity of which is preserved by Reverter of Sites Act 1987, s 1(4).

SEQUESTRATORS

Sequestrators appointed by the court under a writ of sequestration have a duty to enter on the property of the contemnor and take possession of all his estate. An order appointing a sequestrator is treated as an interest affecting an estate or charge for the purposes of the LRA 2002 (LRA 2002, s 87(1)). It cannot, however, be an interest belonging to a person in actual occupation falling within LRA 2002, Sch 1, para 2 or Sch 3, para 2 which overrides first registration or registered dispositions (LRA 2002, s 87(3)). Nor can a notice of an order appointing a sequestrator be entered in the register (LRA 2002, s 87(2)). Such an order may therefore only be protected by entry of a restriction in the register.

The sequestrator may be treated as a person having a sufficient interest for the purposes of LRA 2002, s 43(1)(c) if he is applying for entry of a restriction in Form L or Form N (LRR 2003, r 93(s)). A restriction does not confer any priority; it simply prevents an entry being made in the register in respect of any disposition, or a disposition of a specified kind, unless the terms of the restriction have (where applicable) been complied with.

Restriction

In addition to the usual documents required (see *Restrictions*, page 500), the sequestrator should deliver to the Registry a certified copy of the court order appointing the sequestrator.

As the application for a restriction is unlikely to be made by or with the consent of the registered proprietor in this situation, the statement in panel 12 or conveyancer's certificate in panel 13 of Form RX1 should be completed on the following lines:

> The interest is that specified in rule 93(s) of the Land Registration Rules 2003, the applicant being the sequestrator appointed by [*name*] Court on [*date*].

Panel 9 of Form RX1 should be completed as to the wording of the appropriate restriction. A restriction in a standard form contained in LRR 2003, Sch 4 does not require the approval of the Registry to the terms of the restriction under LRA 2002, s 43(3). A possible form of restriction based on the wording of Form L is:

> No [disposition *or specify type of disposition*] of the registered estate by the proprietor of the registered estate [*or by the proprietor of any registered charge not being a charge registered before the entry of this restriction*] is to be registered without a certificate signed by [*name*] of [*address*] [or [*their conveyancer or specify appropriate details*]] that the provisions of [*specify clause, paragraph or other particulars*] of [*specify details*] have been complied with [or that they do not apply to the disposition].

A possible form of restriction based on the wording of Form N is:

> No [disposition *or specify type of disposition*] of the registered estate by the proprietor of the registered estate [*or by the proprietor of any registered charge not being a charge registered before the entry of this restriction*] is to be registered without a written consent signed by [*name*] of [*address*] [or [*their conveyancer or specify appropriate details*]].

The Registry must give notice of such an application to the proprietor of the registered estate or charge concerned if it has not been made by or with his consent or a person entitled to be registered as such proprietor (LRA 2002, s 45).

SETTLEMENTS

Registered land which is settled land must be registered in the name of the tenant for life or the statutory owner or the special personal representatives in whom the legal estate would be vested if the land were unregistered. The rights of beneficiaries, which are overreached by dispositions under the SLA 1925, do not appear in the register but are protected by the entry of appropriate restrictions in the register. An interest under a settlement under the SLA 1925 is not an unregistered interest which overrides first registration or registered dispositions even where the interest belongs to a person in actual occupation of the land (LRA 2002, Sch 1, para 2 and Sch 3, para 2). No notice can be entered in the register in respect of an interest under a SLA 1925 settlement (LRA 2002, s 33(a)).

No new settlement under the SLA 1925 can be created after 31 December 1996 (TLATA, s 2). As regards existing settlements, LRA 2002, s 89 provides that rules may make provision in relation to the application of the SLA 1925 to registered land and this is dealt with in LRR 2003, r 186 and Sch 7.

Settled land forms of restriction

Applications for first registration of settled land must be accompanied by an application for entry of a restriction in Form G, H or I as appropriate. There is a similar requirement where registered land is transferred into settlement or bought with capital money of the settlement. In addition to those forms of restriction, the registered proprietor of settled land is under a duty to apply for such other restrictions as may be appropriate. In that case the application should be completed to show that the restrictions applied for are required for the protection of the beneficial interests and powers under the settlement in accordance with the LRR 2003, Sch 7, para 7(2). Forms G *(Tenant for life as registered proprietor of settled land, where there are trustees of the settlement)*, H *(Statutory owners as trustees of the settlement and registered proprietors of settled land)* and I *(Tenant for life as registered proprietor of settled land – no trustees of the settlement)* are contained in LRR 2003, Sch 4, and the wording of those restrictions is set out in Appendix IV, page 585.

A house is not a mansion house if it is usually occupied as a farmhouse or where the site of the house and grounds does not exceed 25 acres (SLA 1925, s 65).

The restrictions may be modified on application or as the Registry sees fit, according to the circumstances. Where one of the prescribed restrictions should have been entered in the register and has not been, any person who has an interest in the settled land can apply for such restriction (modified if appropriate) to be entered. The persons interested under the settlement may apply for any additional restriction(s) necessitated by the provisions of the settlement.

Except in the instances referred to in LRR 2003, Sch 7, para 8 (proprietor ceasing in his lifetime to be the tenant for life) and para 14 (discharge of registered land from beneficial interests and powers under a settlement), the restrictions bind the proprietor in his lifetime but do not affect dispositions by his personal representatives.

Transfer of land into settlement

A transfer of registered land into settlement must include the following provisions, with any necessary alterations and additions (LRR 2003, Sch 7, para 4):

The Transferor and the Transferee declare that—

(a)   the property is vested in the Transferee upon the trusts declared in a trust deed dated *(date)* and made between *(parties)*,

(b)   the trustees of the settlement are (*names*),

(c)   the power of appointment of new trustees is vested in (*name*),

(d)   the following powers relating to land are expressly conferred by the trust deed in addition to those conferred by the Settled Land Act 1925: (*insert additional powers*).

or, if the tenant for life is a minor and the transferees are the statutory owner—

(a)   the property is vested in the Transferee as statutory owner under a trust deed dated (*date*) and made between (*parties*),

(b)   the tenant for life is (*name*), a minor, who was born on (*date*),

(c)   the trustees of the settlement are (*names*),

(d)   during the minority of the tenant for life the power of appointment of new trustees is vested in the Transferee,

(e)   the following powers relating to land are expressly conferred by the trust deed in addition to those conferred by the Settled Land Act 1925: (*insert additional powers*).

An application must also be made for a restriction in Forms G, H or I as appropriate.

Registered land bought with capital money

Where registered land is acquired with capital money, the transfer must include the following provisions, with any necessary alterations and additions (LRR 2003, Sch 7, para 6):

The Transferee declares that—

(a)   the consideration has been paid out of capital money,

(b)   the property is vested in the Transferee upon the trusts declared in a trust deed dated (*date*) and made between (*parties*),

(c)   the trustees of the settlement are (*names*),

(d)   the power of appointment of new trustees is vested in (*name*),

(e)   the following powers relating to land are expressly conferred by the trust deed in addition to those conferred by the Settled Land Act 1925: (*set out additional powers*).

An application must also be made for a restriction in Forms G, H or I as appropriate.

Registered land brought into settlement

Where registered land has been settled and the existing registered proprietor is the tenant for life under the settlement, the registered proprietor must make a declaration in Form 6 in LRR 2003, Sch 3 and apply for a restriction in Form G modified as appropriate. This arises only where the settlement is a variation of a settlement created before 1 January 1997, or derives from such a settlement, and falls within the TLATA, s 2(2).

For the wording of Form 6, see Appendix V, page 593.

Proprietor ceasing in his lifetime to be tenant for life

Where a registered proprietor ceases in his lifetime to be a tenant for life and has not become absolutely entitled, he must transfer the land to his successor in title, or, if the successor is a minor, to the statutory owner. On the registration of the successor in title or statutory owner, the trustees of the settlement, if the settlement is continuing, must apply for any necessary alteration in the restrictions in the register.

Registration of special personal representatives

Where land was settled before the death of the sole or last surviving joint registered proprietor and not by his will, and the settlement continues after his death, the personal representatives in whom the registered land vests under the Administration of Estates Act 1925 may apply to be registered as proprietor in place of the deceased proprietor. The application must be accompanied by the grant of probate or letters of administration of the deceased proprietor limited to the settled land. The personal representatives must be registered in place of the deceased proprietor and the following added (LRR 2003, Sch 7, para 11):

> special executor or executrix (or administrator or administratrix) of [*name*], deceased.

Transfer on death of tenant for life

Where the settlement continues after the death of the registered proprietor who was tenant for life, the personal representatives will assent the land using Form AS1 or AS2 to the person entitled. In addition to the usual documents required (see *Assents*, page 45), an applicant should deliver to the Registry:

(a) (if the personal representatives are not already registered as proprietors) the grant of probate or letters of administration limited to, or including, settled land;

(b) an application for entry of a restriction in Form G or Form H, as appropriate. This may be made in the additional provisions panel of Form AS1 or Form AS2 or in Form RX1.

The assent in Form AS1 or Form AS2 must contain the following provisions with any necessary alterations or additions (LRR 2003, Sch 7, para 12):

The Personal Representatives and the Transferee declare that—

(a) the property is vested in the Transferee upon the trusts declared in [a trust deed dated (*date*) and made between (*parties*)] *or* [the will of *(name of deceased)* proved on *(date)*],
(b) the trustees of the settlement are (*names*),
(c) the power of appointment of new trustees is vested in (*name*),
(d) the following powers relating to land are expressly conferred by the [trust deed] *or* [will] in addition to those conferred by the Settled Land Act 1925: (*set out additional powers*).

Where the settlement ends on the death of the proprietor, an application by the personal representatives to register a transfer to the person entitled should be accompanied by the grant of probate or letters of administration (if the personal representatives are not already registered as proprietors) and Form RX3 for cancellation of the restriction relating to the settlement.

Registration of statutory owner during a minority otherwise than on death

If a minor becomes entitled in possession to registered land otherwise than on a death (or will be so entitled on attaining full age) the statutory owner during the minority is entitled to have the land transferred to him and to be registered as proprietor. The transfer must be in Form TR1 and must not refer to the settlement. An application to register the transfer must be accompanied by an application for a restriction in Form H.

Minority where settlement arises under a will or intestacy

During a minority, the personal representatives under a will or intestacy of a person who died before 1 January 1997 under which a settlement of registered land is created or arises, must be registered as proprietors and will have all the powers conferred by the SLA 1925 on a tenant for life and on the trustees of the settlement.

When the minor becomes beneficially entitled to an estate in fee simple or a term of years absolute in registered land or would, if he were of full age, be or have the powers of a tenant for life, the personal representatives must (unless they are themselves the statutory owner) during the minority give effect in the register to the directions of the statutory owner. The statutory owner must direct the personal representatives to apply for a restriction in Form H.

The Registry is under no duty to call for any information regarding why an application is made, or the terms of the will or devolution under the intestacy, or the directions of the statutory owner. Instead the Registry can assume that the personal representatives are acting according to the directions given and that the directions were given and were correct.

A disponee dealing with the personal representatives who complies with the Form H restriction is not concerned to see or enquire whether any directions have been given by the statutory owner with regard to the disposition to him.

Changes to settlement

As changes take place under a settlement of registered land, the registered proprietor or his personal representatives must execute the instruments necessary to give effect to the changes in the register and must apply for any necessary changes in the restrictions appearing in the register. An appropriate prescribed form in LRR 2003, Sch 1 should be used, modified where necessary according to the facts.

New trustees are appointed in the usual way (see *Trusts of land*, page 555). Where, however, a restriction in Form G appears in the register, an application to modify the restriction by substituting the new names is necessary. This should be made in Form RX2 signed by any continuing trustees and the new trustees or their respective conveyancers (see *Restrictions*, page 500). Deaths of trustees must be proved by death certificates.

End of settlement other than on death

Where the settlement comes to an end otherwise than on the death of the registered proprietor, the trustees of the settlement may enter into a deed of discharge in accordance with SLA 1925, s 17. An application to cancel the restriction relating to the settlement should be made in Form RX3 accompanied by the deed of discharge (see *Restrictions*, page 500).

SEVERANCE OF A BENEFICIAL JOINT TENANCY

A registered proprietor may sever a beneficial joint tenancy. The severance may be effected by a deed of declaration entered into by the joint proprietors, but is more commonly effected by one of the joint proprietors serving notice on the other joint proprietor(s) under Law of Property Act 1925, s 36(2). Severance may also occur where, for example, one of the joint proprietors has been declared bankrupt or has charged his beneficial share to a third party. Where there has been severance, the proprietors of a registered estate must apply for entry of a restriction in Form A, since the estate is held on a trust of land and, as a result of a change in the trusts, the survivor of joint proprietors will not be able to give a valid receipt for capital money (LRR 2003, r 94(1)(b)).

Restriction in Form A

An applicant for entry of a restriction in Form A should deliver to the Registry an application in Form RX1 or (where the severance has been effected by agreement or by the service of notice) in Form SEV. No fee is payable where the application is in respect of a restriction in Form A only.

If applying in Form RX1, panel 9 should be completed as to the wording of Form A, which is set out in Appendix IV, page 585.

If the application has not been made by or with the consent of all the registered proprietors, the statement in panel 12 or conveyancer's certificate in panel 13 of Form RX1 must be completed, setting out details of the severance. In the case of Form SEV, the details in panel 8 should be completed as appropriate. In addition, whether Form RX1 or Form SEV is used, the application must be accompanied (where the severance was effected by notice) by either:

(a) the original or a certified copy of the notice of severance given by one proprietor to the other(s) together with a certificate by the applicant or his conveyancer confirming that notice has been served on the other proprietor(s); or

(b) the original or a certified copy of the notice of severance signed by the proprietor(s) on whom it has been served, or a certificate by the applicant's conveyancer confirming that he holds the original of such a notice.

Where severance has been effected by a document, such as a deed of declaration signed by all of the registered proprietors, the original or a certified copy of the document should be lodged, or a certificate by the applicant's conveyancer confirming that he holds the original or a certified copy of such a document. If the application has been made by or with the consent of all the registered proprietors, evidence of the severance need not be lodged.

Where the application has not been made by all the registered proprietors or with their consent, the Registry is not obliged to give notice of the application for a restriction to the other proprietor(s) of the registered estate or charge concerned under LRA 2002, s 45. This is because the application is one which the applicant is obliged to make under LRR 2003, r 94; the Registry will, however, notify the other proprietor(s) of completion of the application.

A restriction does not confer any priority; it simply prevents an entry being made in the register in respect of any disposition, or a disposition of a specified kind, unless the terms of the restriction have (where applicable) been complied with. A restriction in Form A reflects, rather than effects, the severance. It ensures that a survivor of the joint proprietors (unless a trust corporation) will not be able to give a valid receipt for capital money and that the beneficial interests will be overreached on a sale under Law of Property Act 1925, ss 2 and 27.

For the position where the beneficial joint tenancy has been severed as a result of the bankruptcy of one of the joint proprietors, see 'Bankruptcy of a joint proprietor', page 56. For the position where the beneficial joint tenancy has been severed as a result of a charging order being created over the beneficial share of one of the joint proprietors, see *Charging orders*, page 100. For joint proprietors generally, see *Joint proprietors*, page 286.

SHARED OWNERSHIP LEASES

A shared ownership lease differs from a conventional lease in allowing a tenant to purchase a share in the equity of the property. This assists tenants who might otherwise be unable to afford to buy a property outright. The purchaser, as tenant, is granted a lease of the property at a premium which represents the value of the share purchased. The rent is calculated to take account of the value of the share in the property that has not been purchased. Provisions in the lease allow the tenant to purchase further shares in the property, a procedure called 'staircasing'. The rent is reduced when further shares are purchased. There may also be further provisions allowing the tenant the option to call for a transfer of the landlord's interest in the property or, in the case of a flat, to call for a conventional lease of the flat.

Tenants who had the right to buy under the HA 1985 but who did not qualify for the maximum mortgage had the right to be granted a shared ownership lease. That right was abolished by LRHUDA 1993, s 107.

A shared ownership lease sometimes contains a discount charge, for example under HA 1996, s 11 where the landlord is a registered social landlord. A notice of the discount charge is entered in the charges register.

HA 1988, s 5(5A) permits a landlord to include within a shared ownership lease a right of pre-emption in his favour, and to enforce that right.

A shared ownership lease granted out of a registered estate in land must normally be in the form of a prescribed clauses lease (see *Leases*, page 296).

Registration of the lease

An application for registration of a shared ownership lease is made in the same way as for a conventional lease. Where the lease is granted out of a registered estate, see *Leases*, page 296.

On registration of the lease, it is allotted its own title number. Notice of the registered lease is entered in the landlord's registered title without any need for a separate application or further fee. Where the lease contains an option for the tenant to call for a transfer of the landlord's interest or to call for the grant of a lease in conventional form, notice of the option is entered in the landlord's title. No entry as to such option is made in the tenant's title.

Where the lease contains a provision requiring the tenant to offer a surrender to the landlord if the tenant wishes to assign before he has purchased all the equity in the property, a note of this obligation is made in the property register of the tenant's title. A note will also be entered if the lease contains a right of pre-emption in favour of the landlord.

Where the lease is granted out of unregistered land, see *First registration*, page 222.

Where the lease contains an option for the tenant to call for a transfer of the landlord's interest or to call for the grant of a lease in conventional form, no entry as to such option is made in the tenant's title. A C(iv) Land Charge should be registered in respect of the landlord's unregistered title.

Where the lease is granted by a registered social landlord, application may be made in Form RX1 or clause LR13 of a prescribed clauses lease (or a lease containing the prescribed clauses) for entry of a restriction in Form KK. The wording of Form KK is set out in Appendix IV, page 585.

The tenant may assign the benefit of any options in the lease granted in his favour. This may be done when the tenant mortgages the leasehold estate. No entry is made in the register of any such assignment.

Staircasing

The acquisition by the tenant of further shares in the property does not require any entry to be made in the register unless, at the same time, a deed is entered into varying the terms of the lease, usually by reducing the rent, or a discount charge arises on such acquisition.

Where there is a deed of variation of the lease, the tenant should deliver to the Registry:

(a)   an application in Form AP1;
(b)   the deed of variation or a certified copy; and
(c)   the fee payable (see *Fees*, page 221).

If satisfied that the variation has effect at law, the Registry will make an entry relating to the deed in the property register of the tenant's title, together with a notice in the landlord's title (if registered).

Where the further shares are acquired at a discount and the liability to repay the discount takes effect as a charge, specific application should be made to register the charge or enter a notice in respect of it, as appropriate.

SOUVENIR LAND

During the 1970s and 1980s, schemes were set up for the sale of very small plots of land which had sentimental or commemorative value only and which were often promoted for conservation purposes. All such land was known as 'souvenir land'. At that time, the small size of the plots and the number of titles in a very small area posed considerable potential problems for the Registry. In consequence, the Land Registration (Souvenir Land) Rules 1972 (SI 1972/985) provided that the Registry could declare an area of land to be subject to a souvenir land scheme if that area consisted wholly or mainly of land which had been, or was proposed to be, disposed of in souvenir plots. A plot of souvenir land was defined by Land Registration and Land Charges Act 1971, s 4(5) as:

> any piece of land which being of inconsiderable size and little or no practical utility, is unlikely to be wanted in isolation except for the sake of pure ownership or for sentimental reasons or commemorative purposes.

The effect of that declaration was that disposals of individual plots within the designated area took effect as if the title were not registered. An entry on the following lines appeared in the property register of the affected title:

> The land [*edged and numbered (number) in blue on the filed plan*] is subject to a Souvenir Land scheme.
>
> NOTE: Declaration dated ... filed.

Only a few registered titles were affected by such a declaration. A souvenir land declaration could also be made in respect of unregistered land. It is no longer possible to make a souvenir land declaration in relation to either registered or unregistered land and dispositions must now be registered, or (as the case may be) the subject of an application for first registration, in the normal way.

Where a souvenir land declaration has been entered in the register and any unregistered transaction with that land has been made, the proprietor must not dispose of that land otherwise than in a manner which gives effect to the interests of any third parties who have become entitled to apply to be registered as proprietor of any part of that land (LRA (TP) Order 2003, art 11).

The particulars of the declaration entered in the register take effect as a restriction and the Registry may amend the register to substitute for the declaration in the property register a restriction in the proprietorship register (LRA (TP) Order 2003, art 11(4) and (5)). The wording of the restriction is:

> No disposition is to be registered without the consent of the person or persons (if any) entitled to apply to be registered as proprietor of the land disposed of, or any part of it, as the result of any unregistered transaction effected since [*the date of the declaration as noted in the register*].

Cancellation of entries relating to souvenir land

Where the registered proprietor can establish to the satisfaction of the Registry that there has been no unregistered transaction with the souvenir land after the declaration was made, so that no third party has become entitled to be registered as proprietor of it, he may apply using Form AP1 for cancellation of the entry in the register relating to the souvenir land. The application may be made in respect of a particular part of the souvenir land only.

Application for registration by a third party

A third party may apply to be registered as proprietor of part of the souvenir land using application Form AP1 if he is able to establish to the satisfaction of the Registry that one or more unregistered transactions were effected since the declaration was made and that, as a result of them and any other events that have taken place:

(a)   the legal estate in the land is vested in him; or
(b)   a legal estate granted out of the land is vested in him; or
(c)   a legal estate such as is referred to in (a) or (b) has been transferred to him, directly or indirectly, by the person in whom it has become vested.

The Registry will give notice of such application to the registered proprietor. The restriction referred to above must be complied with, where appropriate.

SPECIAL POWERS OF APPOINTMENT

A special power of appointment is a power under which the donee of the power, who may not be the registered proprietor, is able to appoint the property among a limited class of persons. Such a power of appointment takes effect in equity (Law of Property Act 1925, s 1(7)) and allows the donee of the power to transfer an equitable interest only.

A power of appointment cannot be protected by entry of a notice in the register (LRA 2002, s 33). However, the donee of a special power of appointment has a sufficient interest for the purposes of LRA 2002, s 43(1)(c) to apply for the entry of a restriction in relation to the registered land affected by the power (LRR 2003, r 93(e)). A restriction does not confer any priority; it simply prevents an entry being made in the register in respect of any disposition, or a disposition of a specified kind, unless the terms of the restriction have (where applicable) been complied with.

Restriction

An applicant should deliver to the Registry the usual documents required (see *Restrictions*, page 500).

Where the applicant is a person who is the donee of a special power of appointment, the statement in panel 12 or conveyancer's certificate in panel 13 of Form RX1 should be completed on the following lines:

> the applicant's interest is that specified in rule 93(e) of the Land Registration Rules 2003, the applicant being the donee of a special power of appointment which affects the registered estate.

Panel 9 of Form RX1 should be completed as to the wording of the appropriate restriction. A restriction in a standard form contained in LRR 2003, Sch 4 does not require the approval of the Registry to the terms of the restriction under LRA 2002, s 43(3). A possible form of restriction based on Form N is:

> No [disposition *or specify type of disposition*] of the registered estate by the proprietor of the registered estate [*or by the proprietor of any registered charge not being a charge registered before the entry of this restriction*] is to be registered without a written consent signed by [*name*] of [*address*] [or [*their conveyancer or specify appropriate details*]].

The Registry must give notice of the application for a restriction to the proprietor of the registered estate concerned if it has not been made by or with his consent or a person entitled to be registered as such proprietor (LRA 2002, s 45).

SPORTING RIGHTS

Sporting rights are those relating to shooting, fishing and hunting and may potentially be of considerable commercial value. Most sporting rights will take effect as profits à prendre, although fishing rights may relate to a corporeal fishery.

Profits à prendre, franchises and manorial rights

Sporting rights which are profits à prendre mainly exist in gross rather than as appurtenant to land. Profits à prendre in gross may be the subject of a voluntary application for first registration; an application for first registration is never compulsory. For the registration and protection of profits à prendre in gross and appurtenant profits, see *Profits à prendre*, page 456.

As a result of Law of Property Act 1922, Twelfth Schedule, there are preserved to the lord of the manor in relation to copyhold land enfranchised under that Act, the rights, franchises, royalties or privileges of the lord in respect of any rights of chase or warren, piscaries or other rights of hunting, shooting, fishing, fowling, or otherwise taking game, fish or fowl. Copyhold Act 1852, s 48 and Copyhold Act 1894, s 23 excepted similar rights in respect of enfranchisement under those Acts. Any franchises of forest, free chase, park or free warren were abolished by Wild Creatures and Forest Laws Act 1971, s 1(1). For the registration and protection of franchises and manorial rights, see *Franchises*, page 240, and *Manors*, page 372.

Corporeal fisheries

There is a presumption that the owner of a several fishery in a non-tidal river is the owner of the bed of the river (*Hanbury v Jenkins* [1901] 2 Ch 401). This presumption prevails over the better known presumption that the owner of the land abutting a non-tidal river owns the bed to the middle of the stream. Both presumptions are rebuttable on the particular facts of a case. A similar presumption arises, in the case of a several fishery in a tidal river, that ownership of the fishery includes the soil under the fishery. Such a fishery must have been created by a grant of the Crown before Magna Carta 1297 (see for instance *Duke of Beaufort v John Aird and Co* (1904) 20 TLR 602 where the evidence commenced with an extract from the Domesday Book). After Magna Carta 1297 such a fishery would have to have been created by statute.

A corporeal fishery, being land, is subject to compulsory first registration in the usual way (see *First registration*, page 222). Although no longer possible under the LRA 2002, for the period of 2 years from 13 October 2003 the owner of an unregistered corporeal fishery could under transitional provisions register a caution against first registration in respect of that land. Such a caution will, however, have ceased to have effect at the end of that period of 2 years, except in relation to applications for first registration made before the end of that period. Any caution against first registration registered by such an owner under LRA 1925, s 53 continues to have effect and the relevant provisions of the LRA 2002 now apply to it (see *Cautions against first registration*, page 88).

STAMP DUTY LAND TAX

SDLT is a tax payable on certain land transactions completed on or after 1 December 2003. It was introduced by the Finance Act 2003 and replaced stamp duty for most land transactions. 'Land transaction' means the acquisition of a chargeable interest in land located in the United Kingdom. 'Chargeable interest' is defined in Finance Act 2003, s 48(1) and includes freehold and leasehold estates in land, and rights over another's land. The definition includes both legal and beneficial interests. A wide range of transactions are therefore within the scope of SDLT. It is payable in respect of transactions rather than deeds. A liability to SDLT can therefore arise even in cases where no deed has been executed; for example, the surrender of a lease by operation of law.

The rate of tax is a percentage of the 'chargeable consideration' for the transaction, which for SDLT purposes comprises anything given for the transaction in money or money's worth. It therefore includes not only monetary consideration but also other forms of consideration such as the release or assumption of a debt; the provision of works and services; or the transfer of other property. Certain reliefs may be available in appropriate cases; such reliefs must be applied for.

Currently, different rates apply to residential property and to non-residential and mixed use property. A 'higher rate' of SDLT is currently chargeable on the purchase of an 'additional residential property' such as a buy-to-let property or a holiday home.

Most land transactions are 'notifiable', which means HMRC must be informed about the transaction, even in cases where it is of a type which will not attract SDLT. Notification is given by means of the submission of a return in form SDLT1. The Land Registry cannot register the transaction (or enter a notice in the register in respect of it) unless the application is accompanied by evidence that HMRC has been notified. Such evidence will be either a Land Transaction Return certificate (Form SDLT5), or a printed submission certificate as generated when a person applies electronically for an SDLT5 certificate.

Other transactions and interests which are exempt from SDLT or outside the scope of SDLT do not require notification to HMRC. A 'self certificate' in Form SDLT60 was previously required for these, but this was abolished with effect from 12 March 2008. Exempt interests are described in Finance Act 2003, s 48(2) and include, for example, a legal or equitable charge, a discharge of a charge or a contract for sale. Certain transactions are exempt transactions (as opposed to exempt interests) and thus do not need to be notified to HMRC. These are defined in Finance Act 2003, Sch 3 and include transactions in connection with divorce and assents. Certain other transactions, although not exempt transactions (as defined in Sch 3), are also not notifiable. These include a transaction dated on or after 22 July 2004 but before 12 March 2008 that consists entirely of residential property where the total consideration for the transaction (together with any linked transaction) is less than £1,000. The Registry can register such transactions without SDLT evidence being lodged, but in cases where the position is not clear, a covering letter confirming the position should be lodged with the application.

There are still a few transactions on which stamp duty (rather than SDLT) is payable. These will mainly be based on pre-11 July 2003 contracts. Where a document is lodged which is endorsed with stamp duty and, if appropriate, with a 'produced' stamp, no query will be raised and no covering letter is necessary. A transfer for value (not relating to a share) dated after 30 November 2003 on which stamp duty would still be payable but which is below the stamp duty threshold, should be lodged with a Form L(A)451 and a covering letter of explanation. Where appropriate, a transfer may contain a certificate under the Stamp Duty (Exempt Instruments) Regulations 1987 (SI 1987/516) and should be lodged with a covering letter explaining why the certificate is appropriate.

On 1 April 2015 the Land and Buildings Transaction Tax (LBTT) replaced SDLT in Scotland. From April 2018, Land Transaction Tax (LTT) replaced SDLT in Wales.

Further details concerning SDLT are available on the HMRC website at www.hmrc.gov.uk/sdlt.

STATEMENTS OF TRUTH

The LRR 2003 make provision for use of a statement of truth as a means of providing evidence in support of an application to the Registry; for example, an application based upon adverse possession or a prescriptive easement. It provides an alternative to the use of a statutory declaration in most circumstances. Its use has been available since 10 November 2008, when the Registry adopted statements of truth as an alternative form of evidence, following the precedent set by the civil courts. Except where a prescribed application form incorporates a statement of truth (such as Forms ADV2 and CT1), an applicant may use a statutory declaration for supporting evidence if preferred.

Certain standard forms of statement of truth, to cover common forms of application, are contained in LRR 2003, Sch 1, although their use is not compulsory:

(a)   Form ST1 – Statement of truth in support of an application for registration of land based upon adverse possession.
(b)   Form ST2 – Statement of truth in support of an application for registration of a rentcharge based upon adverse possession.
(c)   Form ST3 – Statement of truth in support of an application for registration of land based on lost or destroyed title deeds.
(d)   Form ST4 – Statement of truth in support of an application for registration and/or noting of a prescriptive easement.

Also available is Form ST5 – Statement of truth in support of an application to cancel a Form A restriction.

For land registration purposes, a statement of truth is defined in LRR 2003, r 215A and must comply with the following requirements:

(a)   it must be made by an individual in writing;
(b)   it must contain a declaration of truth in the following form: 'I believe that the facts and matters contained in this statement are true';
(c)   it must (except where he is unable to read or sign it) be signed by the person who makes it;
(d)   it need not be sworn or witnessed;
(e)   if a conveyancer makes the statement of truth or signs it on someone's behalf, the conveyancer must sign in his own name and state his capacity.

If a statement of truth is made by a person who is unable to read, it must be signed in the presence of a conveyancer and contain a certificate made and signed by the conveyancer in the form set out in r 215A(4)(b). If a statement of truth is made by a person who is unable to sign it, it must state the person's name, be signed by a conveyancer at his direction, and contain a certificate made and signed by the conveyancer in the form set out in r 215A(5)(c).

STATUTORY CHARGES

Statutory charges are charges created by or under a statute. Some statutory charges will be local land charges, such as a charge imposed under Public Health Act 1936, s 291, in favour of a local authority (see *Local land charges*, page 367). Other statutory charges, such as those in favour of the Lord Chancellor, in relation to legal aid, on property recovered or preserved (Legal Aid Act 1988, s 16(6); Access to Justice Act 1999, s 10(7); or Legal Aid, Sentencing and Punishment of Offenders Act 2012, s 25(1) (see *Legal aid*, page 332) are not local land charges.

A statutory charge which is not a local land charge and which charges the legal estate must be completed by registration and does not operate at law until the registration requirements are met (LRA 2002, s 27). Such a statutory charge may be protected by entry of an agreed notice or unilateral notice in the register, but will take effect in equity only, until it is completed by registration.

Registration

An applicant to register a statutory charge should deliver to the Registry:

(a)   an application in Form AP1;
(b)   a statement of charge (for example, in the case of a charge under Legal Aid, Sentencing and Punishment of Offenders Act 2012, s 25(1)), a statement given by a person stated to hold the rank of, or equivalent to, Civil Service Grade 7 or above) or a certified copy of it;
(c)   (where the charge has priority over existing charges (see below) an application in Form SC; and
(d)   the fee payable (see *Fees*, page 221).

Some charges created by or under a statute have effect to postpone a charge which at the time of registration of the statutory charge is entered in the register or is the basis for an entry in the register. Where application Form SC is lodged and the Registry is satisfied that the statutory charge has the priority specified in that form, an entry must be made in the charges register showing that priority. If the applicant does not satisfy the Registry that the statutory charge has that priority, but the Registry considers that the applicant has an arguable case, an entry may be made in the charges register that the applicant claims that priority. In either case, the Registry must give notice of the statutory charge to the proprietor of any registered charge appearing in the affected title at the time of registration of the statutory charge. It must also give notice to any person who appears to be entitled to a charge protected by a notice in the register where that person's name and address appear in the register of the title in question. A person who suffers loss by reason of a failure by the Registry to give such notice may be entitled to indemnity (see *Indemnity*, page 273).

Where an entry as to claimed priority has been made, LRR 2003, r 105(5) to (8) makes provision for an application to be made for the entry to be removed, or to be replaced with an entry that the statutory charge in question does have the priority specified in the Form SC. The applicant must provide evidence to satisfy the Registry that it should take the action sought by the applicant. The Registry must serve notice of the application upon the proprietors of registered charges affected by the application.

Restriction

Where a statutory charge takes effect as a charge over a beneficial interest in registered land, rather than as a charge on the legal estate, it cannot be registered or protected by entry of a notice. It may, however, be capable of protection by entry of a restriction. If the statutory charge has the effect of severing a beneficial joint tenancy, application may be made for entry of a restriction in Form A, if such a restriction does not already appear in the register. The purpose of this restriction is to ensure that a survivor of the joint proprietors (unless a trust corporation) will not be able to give a valid receipt for capital money and that the requirements for overreaching in Law of Property Act 1925, ss 2 and 27 are complied with.

Where a statutory charge has arisen in favour of the Lord Chancellor under Legal Aid Act 1988, s 16(6), Access to Justice Act 1999, s 10(7) or Legal Aid, Sentencing and Punishment of Offenders Act 2012, s 25(1) over a beneficial interest in registered land held under a trust of land, he has a sufficient interest for the purposes of LRA 2002, s 43(1)(c) to apply for entry of a restriction in Form JJ (LRR 2003, r 94(w)). The wording of Form JJ is set out in Appendix IV, page 585.

Where a statutory charge has arisen in favour of a local authority under Health and Social Services and Social Security Adjudications Act 1983, s 22 on the beneficial interest of an equitable joint tenant in a registered estate, it has a sufficient interest for the purposes of LRA 2002, s 43(1)(c) to apply for entry of a restriction in Form MM (LRR 2003, r 94(x)). The wording of Form MM is set out in Appendix IV, page 585.

Such a statutory charge does not have the effect of severing such a beneficial joint tenancy (Health and Social Services and Social Security Adjudications Act 1983, s 22(5)). Where the charge charges the beneficial interest of an equitable tenant in common in a registered estate, it is not possible to apply for a restriction in Form MM.

An applicant for entry of a restriction should deliver to the Registry the usual documents required (see *Restrictions*, page 500).

Panel 9 of Form RX1 should be completed as to the required restriction(s). A restriction in a standard form contained in LRR 2003, Sch 4 does not require the approval of the Registry to the terms of the restriction under LRA 2002, s 43(3).

The Registry must give notice of the application for a restriction to the proprietor of the registered estate or charge concerned, if it has not been made by or with the consent of such proprietor or a person entitled to be registered as such proprietor (LRA 2002, s 45).

STATUTORY VESTING

There are a number of statutory provisions under which land may be transferred automatically and vest in a particular person or body by operation of law. In the case of unregistered land, a vesting by operation of law will not 'trigger' compulsory first registration (LRA 2002, s 4(3)), but a voluntary application may be made. A transfer of unregistered land pursuant to a court order will, however, be a 'trigger' for compulsory first registration (LRA 2002, s 4(1)(c)) (see *First registration*, page 222).

In relation to a registered estate, the compulsory purchase or statutory vesting will need to be completed by registration in order to take effect at law, including situations where there is a vesting by operation of law (LRA 2002, s 27(5)). In the case of a transfer by virtue of a court order, an application for registration should be made accompanied by the court order (LRR 2003, r 127(2) or r 161(2)) (see *Transfers*, page 551).

SUBROGATION

Subrogation is a remedy not a cause of action. It is available in a wide variety of situations to reverse the defendant's unjust enrichment (*Boscawen v Bajwa* [1995] 4 All ER 769 (CA)).

Where a lender makes a loan and that money is used to pay off an existing registered charge on the property, that lender may be subrogated to the rights of the original chargee, even though the entry in respect of the registered charge has been removed from the register. This may even be the case where the lender contemplated making only an unsecured loan, if otherwise a third party would be unjustly enriched at the lender's expense (*Banque Financière de la Cité v Parc (Battersea) Ltd* [1998] UKHL 7). A lender who obtains some security, but less than what he bargained for, is not necessarily precluded from claiming further security by subrogation (*Cheltenham & Gloucester plc v Appleyard* [2004] EWCA Civ 291). Where a lender's legal charge over a property is defective, it may be entitled by subrogation to an unpaid vendor's lien over the property, on the basis that the owner has been unjustly enriched at the lender's expense (*Bank of Cyprus UK Ltd v Menelaou* [2015] UKSC 66).

An example of where subrogation could arise might be when a lender makes a loan to be secured by a first charge and part of the money advanced is used to discharge an existing charge. The application to register the lender's charge is not made during the priority period of the official search relating to it and, before the application for registration is lodged, an application to register another charge is lodged by a third party. The third party's charge will therefore have priority over the lender's unprotected charge (LRA 2002, s 29). The lender may, however, be entitled to be subrogated to the original charge to the extent that its loan was used to redeem the original charge.

Where it is considered that a person has an interest in land as a result of subrogation, an application to protect that interest by entry of a notice may be made. In practice, the fact that documentation is usually not immediately available to satisfy the Registry as to the validity of the applicant's claim means that application for a unilateral notice rather than for an agreed notice is more likely to be appropriate.

Unilateral notice

An applicant should deliver to the Registry the usual documents required (see *Notices*, page 389).

The statement in panel 11 or conveyancer's certificate in panel 12 of Form UN1 should set out the nature of the interest claimed and how it has arisen by subrogation.

The unilateral notice in the register will give brief details of the interest protected and identify the beneficiary of that notice.

TIME SHARE

In a time share lease, the right to possession under the lease is discontinuous. A single property may be the subject of several discontinuous leases, under each of which the tenant is entitled to occupy the property for a specified period; typically, a specific week or specific weeks every year for a certain number of years.

Such a lease may be the subject of an application for first registration no matter how short a period of the term is unexpired (LRA 2002, s 3(4)). First registration, on the grant of such a lease out of unregistered land or the transfer or first mortgage of such an unregistered lease, is compulsory only where the term at the time of the grant, transfer or mortgage has more than 7 years to run. A grant is also subject to compulsory registration where it is out of an unregistered freehold, or leasehold with more than 7 years to run, and it is to take effect in possession after the end of the period of 3 months beginning with the date of the grant (LRA 2002, s 4).

A time share lease takes effect as a lease for a single term equivalent to the aggregate of the individual periods during which the tenant is entitled to occupy the demised premises (*Cottage Holiday Associates Limited v Customs and Excise Commissioners* [1983] QB 735). For example, the term of a lease for 2 specified weeks every year for 25 years is 50 weeks.

A grant of a term of years absolute out of a registered estate in land under which the right to possession is discontinuous is required to be completed by registration (LRA 2002, s 27(2)). Where necessary, this should be in the form of a prescribed clauses lease (see 'Prescribed clauses leases', page 300).

Prior to the coming into force of the LRA 2002, most leases granted for a term not exceeding 21 years were overriding interests under LRA 1925, s 70(1). A lease which was an overriding interest under the LRA 1925 immediately before 13 October 2003 continues to be an unregistered interest which overrides both first registration and registered dispositions (LRA 2002, Sch 12, para 12).

For applications for first registration of leases, see *First registration*, page 222, and for applications for registration of leases which are registrable dispositions, see 'Leases which are registrable dispositions', page 297. A copy of any calendar used to define the weeks during which the tenant is entitled to occupy the land (where such a calendar does not form part of the lease) should accompany any application for registration.

No notice may be entered in the register in respect of a lease which is granted for a total term of 3 years or less from the date of the grant and is not required to be registered (LRA 2002, s 33(b)).

TITLE INFORMATION DOCUMENT

Although it is not required by the LRR 2003, as a matter of practice the Registry issues a Title Information Document whenever an application is 'marked off' (i.e. completed). The document consists of a frontsheet with an official copy of the register attached. It is envisaged that a conveyancer will pass this document on to his client.

TOWN OR VILLAGE GREENS

As a result of the CRA 1965, all town or village greens in England and Wales were required to be registered with the appropriate council specified in that Act during a period ending on 31 July 1970. After that date no land capable of being registered under the CRA 1965 is deemed to be a town or village green unless so registered. 'Town or village green' is defined in the CRA 1965 as land which has been allotted by or under any Act for the exercise or recreation of the inhabitants of any locality; or on which the inhabitants of any locality have a customary right to indulge in lawful sports and pastimes; or on which the inhabitants of any locality have indulged in such sports and pastimes as of right for not less than 20 years.

The purpose of the CRA 1965 was to establish a record of land in England and Wales which was either common land, a town green or a village green; the rights of common existing over such land; and the ownership of the land. The Commons Act 2006 is not fully in force yet, but when it is, it will repeal the CRA 1965 and the regulations passed under its authority. As to common land, see *Commons*, page 150. Common land does not include a town or village green. No person was to be registered as owner of any land the freehold estate to which was already registered at the Land Registry. Once ownership had been registered under the CRA 1965 (unless provisional only), the land was subject to compulsory registration at the Land Registry on sale, even in areas which at that time were not compulsory areas. The application had to be made within 2 months of the sale. Where this requirement has been overlooked, an application may be made to the Registry for an order under LRA 2002, s 6(5) extending the period for registration. The application may be made by letter and should explain the reasons the period for registration should be extended.

Once a town or village green is registered at the Land Registry, the Registry notifies the appropriate council accordingly. The council then deletes the registration of ownership and indicates that the land is registered at the Land Registry.

CRA 1965, s 11 exempts from the effect of that Act the New Forest, Epping Forest and the Forest of Dean and any land exempted by an order of the Minister (see *Commons*, page 150 for a list of areas in respect of which such an order was made).

Where a town or village green was registered under the CRA 1965 and the Commons Commissioner, following enquiry, was not satisfied that any person was the owner of the land, he could direct the registration authority to register as owner the parish council or other appropriate local authority as set out in CRA

1965, s 8. On registration under s 8, the land vested in that local authority. Any such direction should be revealed on a subsequent application for first registration of the land.

Where, after 2 January 1970, any land becomes a town or village green, an application for that land, and for the rights of common over it and claims of ownership to it, to be entered in the appropriate registers maintained under the CRA 1965, should be made in accordance with the Commons Registration (New Land) Regulations 1969. For the position where there are any rights of common over such a town or village green, see *Commons*, page 150.

The Common Land (Rectification of Registers) Act 1989 made provision for removal from the register of town or village greens, on application by the owner, of dwelling houses and land ancillary to dwelling houses. Any such application had to be made by 22 July 1992. A copy of any order made under that Act should be lodged with any application for first registration of the land in question.

The Commons Act 2006 provides for application to be made by any person for registration of a town or village green where a significant number of the inhabitants of any locality, or of any neighbourhood within a locality, have indulged as of right in lawful sports and pastimes on the land for a period of at least 20 years; and they continue to do so at the time of the application. The 2006 Act also makes provision for such an application to be made in certain circumstances where such use of the land by the inhabitants has previously ceased. Growth and Infrastructure Act 2013, ss 14, 15 and 16 amends the Commons Act 2006 so as to impose certain limitations upon the scope to apply for such registration; currently only s 16 is in force.

Town and village greens do not consist only of open areas of grassland; they may also consist of a lake, woodland or even a beach. See, for example, *Newhaven Port and Properties Ltd, R (on the application of) v East Sussex County Council & Anor* [2013] EWCA Civ 276. In recent years, some applications for registration as a town or village green have been made as a means of opposing development of the land. See, for example, *Oxfordshire CC v Oxford CC* [2006] UKHL 25 and *R (Lewis) v Redcar & Cleveland BC* [2010] UKSC 11.

First registration of a town or village green

In addition to the usual documents required (see *First registration*, page 222), an applicant should deliver to the Registry a copy of the entries in the register of common land, town greens and village greens.

Where there is a discrepancy between the town or village green's ownership register and the deeds, this must be accounted for. Registration as owner under the CRA 1965 is not conclusive proof of ownership; evidence of the applicant's title must be produced to the Registry in the normal way. An exception to this is where the land has been vested in a local authority under s 8 as mentioned above.

As to first registration generally, see *First registration*, page 222.

The applicant may be registered with absolute title if the Registry is of the opinion that the applicant's title is such as a willing buyer could properly be advised by a competent professional adviser to accept. In considering the applicant's title, the Registry may disregard the fact that the title appears to it to be open to objection if it is of the opinion that the defect will not cause the holding under the title to be disturbed (see *Classes of title*, page 130).

Dispositions of a registered town or village green

A transfer, lease or other disposition must, where appropriate, be completed by registration in the normal way.

TRANSFERS

A transfer of a registered estate must be in Forms TP1, TP2, TR1, TR2, TR5, AS1 or AS3, as appropriate, unless it is effected by an electronic document to which LRA 2002, s 91 applies (LRR 2003, r 58). Forms AS1 and AS3 are transfers by way of assent (see *Assents*, page 45).

Form TP1 is a transfer of part of the registered estate comprised within one or more registered titles and Form TP2 is a similar transfer by the proprietor of a registered charge under power of sale. Form TR1 is a transfer of whole of one or more registered titles and TR2 is a similar transfer by the proprietor of a registered charge under the power of sale. Form TR5 is a transfer of a portfolio of titles, comprising the whole or part of the registered estate comprised within each of the titles in the portfolio.

A transfer of a registered charge must be in Form TR4 or Form AS2, as appropriate (LRR 2003, r 116). Form TR4 is a transfer of a charge or portfolio of charges (see *Legal charges*, page 333). Form AS2 is a transfer by way of assent (see *Assents*, page 45).

A transfer affecting two or more registered titles may, on the written request of the applicant, be registered as to some or only one of the registered titles (LRR 2003, r 56). The applicant may later apply to have the transfer registered as to any other of the registered titles affected by it.

A transfer of part of the land in a registered title must have attached to it a plan signed by the transferor and clearly identifying the land transferred (LRR 2003, r 213). If the land transferred is clearly identified on the title plan, it may instead be described by reference to the title plan.

Where any registered estate is transferred wholly or partly in consideration of a transfer of another estate, it must still be effected by a transfer in one of the prescribed forms, such as Form TR1 or Form TP1, as appropriate. A receipt for any equality money must be given in the receipt panel and the following provision must be included in the additional provisions panel (LRR 2003, r 59):

> This transfer is in consideration of a transfer [*or conveyance, or as appropriate)*] of [*brief description of property exchanged*] dated today [*if applicable* and of the sum stated above paid for equality of exchange].

If a transfer is made by way of exchange, a separate transfer should be used for each part of the exchange, with the 'receipt' and 'additional provisions' panels in each transfer being completed as appropriate.

In the case of a sale and sub-sale, a single form of transfer may be used, with the registered proprietor being the transferor and the sub-purchaser being the transferee. Details of the sub-vendor should be included in the 'additional provisions' panel in the transfer, along with any other relevant details or provisions as appropriate. However, if there is to be a specific transfer by the sub-vendor to the sub-purchaser, two separate transfers should be used.

If a transfer subject to a charge is being effected, the 'consideration' and 'additional provisions' panels in the transfer should be completed with the relevant details or provisions as appropriate, including any release by the chargee (who should be made a party to the transfer) and any covenant(s) in respect of the charge.

Where a transfer is made in connection with the transfer of an equitable share in the registered estate, the assignment of the share and the transfer of the legal estate may be effected by separate instruments. However, a single form of transfer to effect the whole transaction may be used, with the 'consideration' and 'additional provisions' panels in the transfer being completed with the relevant details or provisions as appropriate. Any existing Form A restriction in the register will not be cancelled, unless application is made in Form RX3 for its cancellation, accompanied by evidence lodged to satisfy the Registry that it is no longer required (see *Joint proprietors*, page 286).

A transfer of a registered estate is required to be registered and does not operate at law until the transferor or his successor in title is entered in the register as the proprietor (LRA 2002, s 27 and Sch 2). In the case of a transfer of part of a registered estate, the following entries are also made in the registered title of the retained land (LRR 2003, r 72):

(a) an entry in the property register referring to the removal of the estate comprised in the transfer; and
(b) (where appropriate) entries relating to any rights, restrictive covenants, provisions, and other matters created by the transfer which are capable of being so entered. However, the Registry need make no such entries where the relevant title numbers have not been given in panel 2 of the Form AP1, unless separate application is made in respect of them.

Instead of making the entry referred to at (a) above, the Registry may make a new edition of the registered title out of which the transfer is made and, if it considers it desirable, it may allot a new title number to that title.

Entries are also made in the new registered title and any other affected titles relating to any rights, restrictive covenants, provisions, and other matters created by the transfer which are capable of being so entered. However, the Registry need make no such entries in any other affected titles where the relevant title numbers have not been given in panel 2 of the Form AP1, unless separate application is made in respect of them.

In the case of a transfer of the whole of a registered estate, entries are made in the registered title and any other affected titles relating to any rights, restrictive covenants, provisions and other matters created by the transfer which are capable of being so entered. However, the Registry need make no such entries in any other affected titles where the relevant title numbers have not been given in panel 2 of the Form AP1, unless separate application is made in respect of them (LRR 2003, r 72C).

A transfer of a registered leasehold estate in land which contains a legal apportionment of or exoneration from the rent reserved by the lease must include the following statement, with any necessary alterations and additions (LRR 2003, r 60(1)):

> Liability for the payment of [*if applicable* the previously apportioned rent of *(amount)* being part of] the rent reserved by the registered lease is apportioned between the Transferor and the Transferee as follows –

    (*amount*) shall be payable out of the Property and the balance shall be payable out of the land remaining in title number (*title number of retained land*) *or*

    the whole of that rent shall be payable out of the Property and none of it shall be payable out of the land remaining in title number (*title number of retained land*) *or*

    the whole of that rent shall be payable out of the land remaining in title number (*title number of retained land*) and none of it shall be payable out of the Property.

A person applying to register a transfer of a registered estate must provide information to the Registry in Form DI about any of the overriding interests (subject to certain exceptions such as local land charges or public rights) set out in LRA 2002, Sch 3 that affect the estate to which the application relates and are within the actual knowledge of the applicant (LRR 2003, r 57). For details, see 'Duty to disclose overriding interests', page 426. The applicant must produce to the Registry any documentary evidence of the interest which is under his control. The Registry may enter a notice in the register in respect of any such interest.

Registration of transfer

An applicant to register a transfer should deliver to the Registry:

(a)   an application in Form AP1;

(b)   a transfer in the appropriate prescribed form or a certified copy;

(c)   Form DI giving the information as to overriding interests required by LRR 2003, r 57, including any documentary evidence of the interest (see 'Duty to disclose overriding interests', page 426);

(d)   the appropriate confirmation or evidence as to identity (see *Identity evidence*, page 266);

(e)   the appropriate SDLT certificate or other evidence (see *Stamp duty land tax*, page 541); and

(f)   the fee payable (see *Fees*, page 221).

Related topics

For transfers under power of sale, see *Legal charges*, page 333. For transfers relating to mines and minerals, see *Mines and minerals*, page 380. For transfers to two or more proprietors, see *Joint proprietors*, page 286. For implied covenants in transfers, see *Implied covenants*, page 268. For Land Registry forms in general, see *Forms*, page 238.

TRIBUNAL

LRA 2002, s 108 makes provision for the Tribunal to determine:

(a) objections referred to it under LRA 2002, s 73(7) (see *Disputes*, page 193); and

(b) appeals under LRA 2002, Sch 5, para 4 relating to e-conveyancing network access agreements (see *Electronic services*, page 200).

Also, the Tribunal may make any order which the High Court could make for the rectification or setting aside of a document which effects a qualifying disposition of a registered estate or charge or is a contract to make such a disposition or effects a transfer of an interest which is the subject of a notice in the register (LRA 2002, s 108(2)). For this purpose a 'qualifying disposition' is a registrable disposition required to be completed by registration under LRA 2002, s 27, or a disposition which created an interest which may be the subject of a notice in the register (s 108(3)). An application for such rectification or setting aside should be made direct to the Tribunal and not to the Registry. An appropriate application may be made to the Registry if such an order is made (see *Alteration of the register*, page 39).

The Tribunal is staffed by specialist judges versed in the field of land registration and property law. It deals with matters in accordance with the Tribunal Rules.

The functions of the Adjudicator to HM Land Registry, who previously dealt with the above matters, were transferred to the Tribunal on 1 July 2013. The office of the Adjudicator was abolished and consequential amendments were made to the LRA 2002 (Transfer of Tribunal Functions Order 2013 (SI 2013/1036)),

TRUSTS OF LAND

The TLATA 1996 reformed the law relating to trusts of land and the appointment of trustees. It defines a 'trust of land' as any trust of property which consists of or includes land, except for settled land (as defined in the SLA 1925) and land to which the Universities and Colleges Estates Act 1925 applies (TLATA 1996, s 1). This definition includes a trust created before the commencement of TLATA 1996 and also includes any description of trust, whether express, implied, resulting or constructive. It therefore includes a bare trust or a trust for sale, but not a settlement under the SLA 1925. 'Land' for this purpose includes an undivided share in land.

Where a sole owner of land holds both the legal estate (in the case of registered land, the registered title) and the underlying equitable or beneficial interest, the legal estate and equitable interest are merged and there is no trust of land. The essential characteristic of a trust of land is that the legal estate to the land is separated from the equitable interest, with the legal estate being vested in the trustee(s) and the equitable interest being vested in the beneficiary or beneficiaries. A trust of land may:

(a)   be expressly created in writing (Law of Property Act 1925, s 53(1)(b));

(b)   be a 'bare trust' arising where the trustee is merely the nominee for a beneficiary of full age (see *Bare trusts*, page 73);

(c)   arise by operation of law as an implied, resulting or constructive trust (for example, where the proprietor has purchased the land using funds provided by a third party) (see *Constructive, resulting and other implied trusts*, page 165); or

(d)   arise by operation of law as a statutory trust; for example, the statutory trust automatically imposed by Law of Property Act 1925, ss 34 and 36 where two or more persons own land jointly, so that they hold the legal estate on a trust of land even if they are holding the equitable interest on trust for themselves (see *Joint proprietors*, page 286).

A trust of land may therefore exist where the trustees are holding on trust for themselves only; for themselves and a third party; or for a third party only. The legal estate can never be severed and can only be held by two or more persons as beneficial joint tenants (Law of Property Act 1925, ss 1(6) and 34). Upon the death of one of the trustees, the legal estate will pass by 'survivorship' and vest automatically in the surviving trustee(s) (or in the personal representative of a deceased sole or sole surviving trustee), regardless of the devolution of the equitable interest (see *Joint proprietors*, page 286).

Land which is held on a trust of land should be vested in the trustees. In relation to registered land, the register records the ownership of the legal estate, not the beneficial interests. The Registry is not affected with notice of a trust (LRA 2002, s 78).

It is not possible to enter a notice in the register to protect an interest under a trust of land (LRA 2002, s 33(a)). The trustees should apply for the entry of appropriate restrictions to reflect any limitations on their powers of disposition contained in the trust deed.

Registration of trustees

There are no prescribed forms specifically for dispositions to trustees; the standard forms prescribed in LRR 2003, Sch 1 must be used where the title is already registered (see *Assents*, page 45, and *Transfers*, page 551). In the case of the grant of a lease out of a registered estate, this should where necessary be in the form of a prescribed clauses lease (see 'Prescribed clauses leases', page 300).

As with unregistered land, the number of trustees of a private trust of registered land cannot exceed four; if more than four are named, only the first four named who are able and willing to act will be registered as proprietors. This limitation does not apply to charitable trusts (see *Charities*, page 104).

The basis upon which the applicants are holding the land on trust, whether for themselves as equitable joint tenants or tenants in common or otherwise upon trust, should be made clear in the appropriate panel of the transfer, assent or prescribed clauses lease or (where the application is for first registration) of Form FR1. Alternatively, Form JO may be used. In a new lease of land granted out of a registered title, an appropriate declaration should be included within the prescribed clauses (if used) or within a clause in the lease. If this is not done, the Registry may have to enter a restriction in Form A by default in pursuance of its obligation under LRA 2002 s 44(1) (see 'Entry of restrictions', below).

Entry of restrictions

A person dealing with a registered proprietor can assume that he has unlimited power to dispose of the registered estate or registered charge concerned, free from any limitation affecting the validity of the disposition, unless there is a restriction or other entry in the register limiting his powers, or a limitation imposed by or under the LRA 2002 (LRA 2002, s 26). In the context of a trust of land, this means that, if two or more persons are registered as joint proprietors, a purchaser can safely acquire the legal estate from them, or from the survivor of them, unless there is a restriction or other entry to the contrary in the register.

A restriction does not confer any priority; it simply prevents an entry being made in the register in respect of any disposition, or a disposition of a specified kind, unless the terms of the restriction have (where applicable) been complied with.

In the case of a private trust (that is, one not for charitable, ecclesiastical or public purposes), it is the duty of the trustees to apply for any necessary restriction(s), although a beneficiary may also apply. The Registry is obliged to enter a restriction without application in only one circumstance, though it may do so in certain other cases if it appears to be necessary or desirable.

If the Registry enters two or more registered proprietors of a registered estate in land, it must enter a Form A restriction where the survivor of them will not be able to give a valid receipt for capital money (LRA 2002, s 44(1)). In the case of other registered estates, the proprietor(s) should make an application for entry of such a restriction (LRR 2003, r 94(2A)). The wording of Form A is set out in Appendix IV, page 585.

The Registry will not enter a restriction in Form A in respect of a registered charge, because although a charge can be held on trust, the survivor of the registered chargees is always able to give a valid receipt for the money secured by it (LRA 2002, s 56).

When a trust corporation applies to be registered as sole proprietor of an estate, which it holds on trust, it must apply for a Form A restriction. Although it will be able to give a valid receipt for capital money arising on a disposition, the restriction is needed in case the proprietor ceases to be a trust corporation at any time, or is replaced by another trustee.

Law of Property Act 1925, s 27(2) does not affect the right of a sole personal representative *acting as such* to give a valid receipt for capital money. Therefore, the Registry will not automatically enter a restriction in Form A when registering a personal representative as proprietor of a registered estate. However, any existing such restriction will remain in the register because, in that case, the personal representative will be succeeding the deceased as trustee of the trust. For the same reason, the Registry will enter a restriction in Form A on first registration when registering the personal representative of a deceased proprietor who was a sole trustee or (unless he was the survivor of beneficial joint tenants) the last surviving trustee.

Where a registered estate becomes subject to a trust of land, other than on a registrable disposition, or where the estate is held on a trust of land and there is a change in the trusts, and a sole or last surviving trustee will not be able to give a valid receipt for capital money, the registered proprietor must apply for entry of a restriction in Form A (LRR 2003, r 94(1) and (2)). Where there are two or more persons registered as proprietor of the estate, an application by one or more of them satisfies the obligation to apply for entry of the restriction. If such an application is not made, any person who has an interest under the trust of land has a sufficient interest for the purposes of LRA 2002, s 43(1)(c) to apply for the restriction in Form A (LRR 2003, r 93(a)). An applicant should deliver to the Registry the usual documents required (see *Restrictions*, page 500).

No fee is currently payable where the application is for a Form A restriction only.

Where the applicant is a person who has an interest under a trust of land, the statement in panel 12 or conveyancer's certificate in panel 13 of Form RX1 should be completed on the following lines:

> The interest is that specified in rule 93(a) of the Land Registration Rules 2003, the applicant being a person who has an interest in the registered estate held under a trust of land as a result of [*set out relevant details*].

Panel 9 should be completed as to the restriction in Form A. A restriction in Form A in LRR 2003, Sch 4 does not require the approval of the Registry to the wording of the restriction under LRA 2002, s 43(3).

The Registry must give notice of the application for a restriction to the proprietor of the registered estate concerned if it has not been made by or with his consent or a person entitled to be registered as such proprietor (LRA 2002, s 45).

Where the trust imposes limitations on the powers of the trustees under TLATA 1996, s 8 (for example, the requirement to obtain a consent before effecting any sale), the registered proprietors must apply for entry of a restriction in Form B (LRR 2003, r 94(4)). This does not apply if the land is held on charitable, ecclesiastical or public trusts, but does apply where the legal estate is vested in the personal representatives of a sole or last surviving trustee. Where there are two or more persons registered as proprietor of the estate, an application by one or more of them satisfies the obligation to apply for entry of the restriction. If such an application is not made, any person who has an interest under the trust of land where the powers of the trustees are limited under TLATA 1996, s 8 has a sufficient interest for the purposes of LRA 2002, s 43(1)(c) to apply for entry of the restriction in Form B. An applicant should deliver to the Registry the usual documents required (see *Restrictions*, page 500).

Where the applicant is a person who has an interest under a trust of land, the statement in panel 12 or conveyancer's certificate in panel 13 of Form RX1 should be completed on the following lines:

> The interest is that specified in rule 93(c) of the Land Registration Rules 2003, the applicant being a person who has an interest in the registered estate held under a trust of land where the powers of the trustees are limited by section 8 of the Trusts of Land and Appointment of Trustees Act 1996.

Panel 9 should be completed as to the restriction in Form B. The wording of Form B is set out in Appendix IV, page 585.

A restriction in Form B in LRR 2003, Sch 4 does not require the approval of the Registry to the wording of the restriction under LRA 2002, s 43(3).

The Registry must give notice of the application for a restriction to the proprietor of the registered estate concerned if it has not been made by or with his consent or a person entitled to be registered as such proprietor (LRA 2002, s 45).

Where personal representatives hold a registered estate on a trust of land created by the deceased's will, or on a trust of land arising under the laws of intestacy which is subsequently varied, and their powers have been limited by TLATA 1996, s 8, they must apply for entry of a restriction in Form C (LRR 2003, r 94(3)). Where there are two or more personal representatives of a deceased proprietor, an application by one or more of them satisfies the obligation to apply for entry of the restriction. If such an application is not made, any person who has an interest in the due administration of the estate has a sufficient interest for the purposes of LRA 2002, s 43(1)(c) to apply for entry of a restriction in Form C (LRR 2003, r 93(d)). An applicant should deliver to the Registry the usual documents required (see *Restrictions*, page 500).

Where the applicant is a person who has an interest in the due administration of the deceased's estate, the statement in panel 12 or conveyancer's certificate in panel 13 of Form RX1 should be completed on the following lines:

> The interest is that specified in rule 93(d) of the Land Registration Rules 2003, the applicant being a person interested in the due administration of the estate of [*name*] deceased.

Panel 9 of Form RX1 should be completed as to the restriction in Form C. The wording of Form C is set out in Appendix IV, page 585.

A restriction in Form C does not require the approval of the Registry to the wording of the restriction under LRA 2002, s 43(3).

The Registry must give notice of the application for a restriction to the proprietor of the registered estate concerned if it has not been made by or with his consent or a person entitled to be registered as such proprietor (LRA 2002, s 45).

TLATA 1996, s 6(6) provides that the powers of an absolute owner of land conferred by that section shall not be exercised in contravention of, or of any order made in pursuance of, any other enactment or any rule of law or equity. TLATA 1996, s 6(8) provides that where any enactment other than that section confers on trustees authority to act subject to any restriction, limitation or condition, trustees of land may not exercise the powers conferred by that section to do any act which they are prevented from doing under the other enactment by reason of the restriction, limitation or condition. Any person who has a sufficient interest in preventing a contravention of TLATA 1996, s 6(6) or (8) has a sufficient interest for the purposes of LRA 2002, s 43(1)(c) to apply for a restriction in order to prevent such a contravention (LRR 2003, r 93(b)).

Dispositions by trustees

There are no prescribed forms specifically for dispositions to trustees; the standard forms prescribed in LRR 2003, Sch 1 must be used where the title is already registered (see *Assents*, page 45, and *Transfers*, page 551). In the case of the grant of a lease out of a registered estate, this should where necessary be in the form of a prescribed clauses lease (see 'Prescribed clauses leases', page 300).

Any restriction(s) in the register will, where necessary, need to be complied with before a disposition by the trustees can be registered. In the case of a restriction in Form A, where capital money arises as a result of the disposition and a sole or sole surviving trustee (not being a trust corporation) cannot give a valid receipt, at least one new co-trustee will need to be appointed to join in the disposition. The appointment may be effected within the form of disposition, such as a transfer, or by separate deed. In the case of a restriction in Form B, the appropriate certificate, statutory declaration, or statement of truth will need to be provided.

In certain circumstances, an existing restriction may be cancelled automatically following completion of a disposition by registration. Thus a restriction in Form A will be cancelled on registration of a transfer on sale by two or more trustees or a trust corporation (except where the transfer is to one or more of the existing proprietors) under LRR 2003, r 99. A restriction in Form B will be cancelled on registration of a transfer on sale by the trustees when the appropriate certificate, statutory declaration, or statement of truth has been provided. In other cases, application may be made to cancel a restriction where appropriate. The application should be made in Form RX3, accompanied by evidence to satisfy the Registry that the restriction is no longer required. If the Registry is so satisfied, it must cancel the restriction (LRR 2003, r 97) (see *Restrictions*, page 500).

Powers of attorney granted by trustees

There are several statutory provisions enabling trustees to delegate their functions, individually or collectively (see *Powers of attorney*, page 446). Under TLATA 1996, s 9, the trustees, acting jointly, can delegate their functions to a beneficiary or beneficiaries by means of a power of attorney. But the attorneys cannot give a valid receipt for capital money, even if they are two or more

(TLATA 1996, s 9(7)). If capital money arises on a disposition, the trustees (or their individual attorneys appointed under Trustee Act 1925, s 25) will therefore have to execute the deed in order to give the receipt. An attorney under TLATA 1996, s 9 can, however, execute a disposition under which no capital money arises.

Vesting of registered land in new trustees

It is important that the names and addresses for service of trustees in the register are kept up to date and that any change of trustees is reflected in the register. An appointment of a new trustee will not be effective to vest the registered title in the new and any continuing trustees until it has been completed by registration. There are a number of methods of effecting the appointment and discharge of trustees of land.

Where new trustees have been appointed in place of existing trustees, the simplest course is to proceed by way of a transfer in Form TR1 from the registered proprietors to the new trustees. The additional provisions panel of the transfer should include a statement that the transfer is made for the purpose of giving effect to the appointment of new trustees. The legal estate passes to the new trustees only when they are registered as proprietors (LRA 2002, s 27) (see *Transfers*, page 551).

Where a deed of appointment or retirement of trustees has an express or implied vesting declaration to which Trustee Act 1925, s 40 applies, an application may be made to register this disposition by operation of law without executing a transfer (LRA 2002, s 27(5)). This might be appropriate, for example, where a person other than the existing registered proprietors has the power of appointing new trustees. The limitations on using this procedure in respect of charges and leases requiring a consent to alienation should be noted (Trustee Act, s 40(4)). An applicant to register such a disposition should deliver to the Registry:

(a)   an application in Form AP1;
(b)   the deed of appointment or retirement or a certified copy of it;
(c)   a certificate from the conveyancer acting for the persons making the appointment or effecting the retirement that they are entitled to do so, or other evidence to satisfy the Registry that the persons making the appointment or effecting the retirement are entitled to do so (LRR 2003, r 161(3));
(d)   Form DI giving the information as to overriding interests required by LRR 2003, r 57, including any documentary evidence of the interest (see 'Duty to disclose overriding interests', page 426);

(e)   the appropriate confirmation or evidence as to identity (see *Identity evidence*, page 266);

(f)   the appropriate SDLT certificate or other evidence (see *Stamp duty land tax*, page 541); and

(g)   the fee payable (see *Fees*, page 221).

Under Trustee Act 1925, s 41, the court may by vesting order appoint a new trustee. Where it relates to a registered estate, such an order must be completed by registration (LRA 2002, s 27(5)). Where the court has made a vesting order an applicant should deliver to the Registry:

(a)   an application in Form AP1;

(b)   the vesting order (LRR 2003, r 161(2)) or a certified copy of it;

(c)   Form DI giving the information as to overriding interests required by LRR 2003, r 57, including any documentary evidence of the interest (see 'Duty to disclose overriding interests', page 426);

(d)   the appropriate confirmation or evidence as to identity (see *Identity evidence*, page 266);

(e)   the appropriate SDLT certificate or other evidence (see *Stamp duty land tax*, page 541); and

(f)   the fee payable (see *Fees*, page 221).

In certain cases where trustees may be appointed or discharged by resolution of a meeting of the trustees or other persons, for example under Trade Union and Labour Relations (Consolidation) Act 1992, ss 13 and 129, a vesting declaration is implied by statute in the memorandum or written record of the resolution. If the trust property is a registered estate or a registered charge, this declaration has to be completed by registration (LRA 2002, s 27(5)). The existing registered proprietors may execute a transfer to the new and any continuing trustees. Alternatively, application may be made to register the implied vesting declaration itself, which should accompany the application.

Where an implied vesting declaration has arisen, an applicant should deliver to the Registry:

(a)   an application in Form AP1;

(b)   a certified copy of the memorandum or resolution and evidence of the provision under which it operates to vest the estate in the trustees (LRR 2003, r 161(1));

(c)   Form DI giving the information as to overriding interests required by LRR 2003, r 57, including any documentary evidence of the interest (see 'Duty to disclose overriding interests', page 426);

(d)   the appropriate confirmation or evidence as to identity (see *Identity evidence*, page 266);

(e)   the appropriate SDLT certificate or other evidence (see *Stamp duty land tax*, page 541); and

(f)   the fee payable (see *Fees*, page 221).

In the case of unregistered land, the appointment of a new trustee may be a 'trigger' for compulsory first registration (see *First registration*, page 222).

When a trustee has died, an application to remove his name from the register, or an application to register a disposition by the remaining trustees, should be accompanied by evidence of the death (LRR 2003, r 164).

UNINCORPORATED ASSOCIATIONS

An unincorporated association consists of a group of individuals who have come together to achieve some common purpose, such as clubs, societies (including unincorporated friendly societies) and trade unions. In general, there are three types of unincorporated association: partnerships formed for profit; not for profit associations which are not (or not exclusively) charitable; and associations formed for charitable purposes. Unlike corporate bodies, unincorporated associations do not have their own legal personality and cannot therefore be registered in their own right as the proprietor of registered land. Instead, where an unincorporated association holds land, the legal estate must be vested in trustees, or a trust corporation, in trust for the members of the association. For the position where an unincorporated association is a charity, see *Charities*, page 104.

Registration of trustees

A transfer or charge to an unincorporated association must be to the names of the individual members, not to the association itself. If there are more than four members and the unincorporated association is not a charity, the transfer should be to four of them to hold the legal estate on trust for all the members of the association. The names of the trustees in the proprietorship register may be followed by an appropriate description such as: 'the trustees of the [*name of unincorporated association*]'.

As a sole trustee or the survivor of two or more trustees (unless a trust corporation) will be unable to give a valid receipt for capital money, entry of a restriction in Form A will be required, and if necessary should be applied for. In the case of a registered estate in land, the Registry will, when entering joint proprietors, enter a restriction in Form A in the proprietorship register in accordance with its obligation under LRA 2002, s 44(1). In the case of other registered estates, the proprietor(s) should make an application for entry of such a restriction (LRR 2003, r 94(2A)).

If no other restriction is entered, the proprietors' powers of disposition are taken, in favour of any disponee, as being free from any limitation affecting the validity of a disposition (LRA 2002, s 26). The trustees should therefore consider applying for any further restriction, such as one to ensure compliance with club rules. For example a restriction in Form R may be applied for.

If the rules of the association contain any limitation on the trustees' powers of disposition, application should be made for entry of a restriction in Form B (TLATA, s 8(2) and LRR 2003, r 94(4)).

The wording of Forms A, B and R is set out in Appendix IV, page 585.

Dispositions by trustees

The trustees shown in the register as proprietors must execute any disposition by the trustees of an unincorporated association. If any of them have died, evidence of death must be lodged and the survivor(s) must execute the deed and comply with the terms of any restriction in the register.

Change of trustees

The normal rules on the appointment, retirement or removal of trustees apply to the trustees of an unincorporated association. For the position where the registered estate is to be vested in new trustees of an unincorporated association, see 'Vesting of registered land in new trustees', page 562.

UPGRADE OF CLASS OF TITLE

Where a registered estate has been awarded a class of title which is less than absolute, an application to upgrade it may be made under LRA 2002, s 62. For the classes of title which may be granted in relation to registered titles, see *Classes of title*, page 130. The Registry has power to upgrade the class of title where it is satisfied as to the title, applying the same standards as on an application for first registration. This usually means that the defect that resulted in the grant of the particular class of title on first registration has been remedied. Before approving an application for upgrading, the Registry may require the production of further documents or evidence, or serve such notices, as it considers necessary or desirable.

An application for upgrading of title must be made in Form UT1 (LRR 2003, r 124(1)). The applicant must state the class of title to which he is applying for the title to be upgraded and also state in what capacity he is entitled to apply for upgrading of title. Confirmation must be given that no claim adverse to the title of the proprietor has been made by virtue of an estate, right or interest whose enforceability is preserved by virtue of the existing entry about the class of title. However, this confirmation is not necessary where the application is to upgrade a good leasehold title which was granted prior to 19 June 2006 because the consent of a superior landlord and/or the landlord's mortgagee was not lodged at the time of registration of the lease.

The Registry may upgrade a possessory freehold title to absolute freehold if satisfied as to the title to the estate. It may upgrade a possessory leasehold title to good leasehold if satisfied as to the title to the estate or to absolute leasehold if satisfied both as to the title to the estate and as to the superior title. Evidence of title so as to overcome the defect which caused the possessory class of title to be granted in the first place will need to be lodged. For example, where lost pre-registration title deeds subsequently come to light after first registration has taken place.

The Registry may also upgrade a possessory freehold title to absolute where (in the case of a freehold estate in land) the estate has been registered with possessory title for a period of at least 12 years. It may upgrade a possessory leasehold title to good leasehold where (in the case of a leasehold estate in land) the estate has been registered with possessory title for a period of at least 12 years. A proprietor is in possession if the land is physically in his possession, or in that of a person who is entitled to be registered as the proprietor of the registered estate. Land in the possession of a tenant is treated as being in the possession of the landlord. Land in the possession of a mortgagee is treated as being in the possession of the mortgagor. Land in the possession of a licensee is treated as being in the possession of the licensor. Land in the possession of a beneficiary is treated as being in the possession of the trustee (LRA 2002, s 131).

The Registry may upgrade a good leasehold title to absolute if it is satisfied as to the superior title. Evidence will therefore need to be lodged to establish that the landlord had power to grant the lease.

The Registry may upgrade a qualified freehold title to absolute freehold if satisfied as to the title to the estate. The Registry may upgrade a qualified leasehold title to good leasehold if satisfied as to the title to the estate or to absolute leasehold if satisfied both as to the title to the estate and as to the superior title. Documentary evidence must therefore be lodged to satisfy the Registry as to the title.

An application to upgrade the class of title of a registered estate may be made by the proprietor of that estate or a person entitled to be registered as proprietor. Such an application may also be made by the proprietor of a registered charge affecting that estate or a person interested in a registered estate which derives from that estate.

None of the powers to upgrade the title in LRA 2002, s 62 is exercisable if there is outstanding any claim adverse to the title of the registered proprietor which is made by virtue of an estate, right or interest the enforceability of which is preserved by virtue of the existing entry about the class of title (LRA 2002, s 62(6)). For the effect of a caution against conversion registered under the Land Registration Rules 1925, see *Cautions against conversion*, page 84.

Where a registered freehold or leasehold estate is upgraded to absolute, the proprietor ceases to hold the estate subject to any estate, right or interest the enforceability of which was preserved by virtue of the previous entry about the class of title. This also applies where the title is upgraded to good leasehold, except that then the upgrading does not affect or prejudice the enforcement of any estate, right or interest affecting, or in derogation of, the title of the landlord to grant the lease (LRA 2002, s 63).

Upgrading possessory or qualified freehold to absolute

An applicant should deliver to the Registry:

(a) an application in Form UT1;
(b) documentary evidence to satisfy the Registry as to the title (this is not required where the title to a registered estate in freehold land has been registered as possessory for at least 12 years and panel 10 of Form UT1 has been completed to show the proprietor is in possession);
(c) where the application is by a person entitled to be registered as the proprietor of the estate sought to be upgraded, evidence of that entitlement;
(d) where the application is by a person interested in a registered estate which derives from the estate sought to be upgraded, evidence of the applicant's interest where this is not apparent from the register (panel 9 of Form UT1 must also be completed with details of the interest claimed); and

(e)   the fee payable (see *Fees*, page 221).

Upgrading possessory or qualified leasehold to good leasehold

An applicant should deliver to the Registry:

(a)   an application in Form UT1;
(b)   documentary evidence to satisfy the Registry as to the title (this is not required where the title to a registered estate in leasehold land has been registered as possessory for at least 12 years and panel 10 of Form UT1 has been completed to show the proprietor is in possession);
(c)   where the application is by a person entitled to be registered as the proprietor of the estate sought to be upgraded, evidence of that entitlement;
(d)   where the application is by a person interested in a registered estate which derives from the estate sought to be upgraded, evidence of the applicant's interest where this is not apparent from the register (panel 9 of Form UT1 must also be completed with details of the interest claimed); and
(e)   the fee payable (see *Fees*, page 221).

Upgrading good leasehold to absolute

An applicant should deliver to the Registry:

(a)   an application in Form UT1;
(b)   documentary evidence to satisfy the Registry as to any superior title which is not registered;
(c)   where any superior title is registered with possessory, qualified or good leasehold title, documentary evidence to satisfy the Registry that that title qualifies for upgrading to absolute title;
(d)   evidence of any consent to the grant of the lease required from any chargee of any superior title and any superior landlord;
(e)   where the application is by a person entitled to be registered as the proprietor of the estate sought to be upgraded, evidence of that entitlement;
(f)   where the application is by a person interested in a registered estate which derives from the estate sought to be upgraded, evidence of the applicant's interest where this is not apparent from the register (panel 9 of Form UT1 must also be completed with details of the interest claimed); and
(g)   the fee payable (see *Fees*, page 221).

No fee is currently payable where the application is accompanied by an application upon which a scale fee is payable or by a letter confirming that it is made on the sole basis that good leasehold title was granted because the consent of a superior landlord and/or the landlord's mortgagee was not lodged at the time of registration of the lease (see below). Since the effect of registration with an absolute title is to confer an absolute title to any easements granted in the lease, the title of the landlord to grant the easements should also be shown. Where the Registry is not satisfied on this point, an entry may be made in the register excluding the easement concerned from the registration.

Where good leasehold title was granted prior to 19 June 2006 because the consent of a superior landlord and/or the landlord's mortgagee was not lodged at the time of registration of the lease, application may be made to upgrade to absolute title if the consent can be produced. Alternatively, such an application can be made if accompanied by a covering letter requesting the upgrade to be made on the basis of the current Registry practice introduced on that date, which is to grant absolute title where the consent is not lodged, but to make protective entries in the register (see *First registration*, page 222). An application on that basis will, however, result in those protective entries having to be made in the register of the upgraded title.

Upgrading possessory or qualified leasehold to absolute

An applicant should deliver to the Registry:

(a) an application in Form UT1;
(b) documentary evidence to satisfy the Registry as to the title to the estate sought to be upgraded (this is not required where the title to a registered estate in land has been registered as possessory for at least 12 years and panel 10 of Form UT1 has been completed to show the proprietor is in possession);
(c) documentary evidence to satisfy the Registry as to any superior title which is not registered;
(d) where any superior title is registered with possessory, qualified or good leasehold title, documentary evidence to satisfy the Registry that that title qualifies for upgrading to absolute title;
(e) evidence of any consent to the grant of the lease required from any chargee of any superior title and any superior landlord;
(f) where the application is by a person entitled to be registered as the proprietor of the estate sought to be upgraded, evidence of that entitlement;
(g) where the application is by a person interested in a registered estate which derives from the estate sought to be upgraded, evidence of the applicant's interest where this is not apparent from the register (panel 9 of Form UT1 must also be completed with details of the interest claimed); and
(h) the fee payable (see *Fees*, page 221).

Since the effect of registration with an absolute title is to confer an absolute title to any easements granted in the lease, the title of the landlord to grant the easements should also be shown. Where the Registry is not satisfied on this point, an entry may be made in the register excluding the easement concerned from the registration.

VENDOR'S LIENS

A vendor's lien arises when a binding contract for sale of the land is made, and subsists until the purchase money is paid. It can continue even though the vendor has executed a transfer of the land and given possession to the purchaser. If the vendor has agreed that he will take some other form of security for the purchase money, then the lien does not arise.

A vendor's lien is a type of equitable charge which arises automatically by operation of law. It gives the vendor the right to apply to court for an order for sale under which he will be paid the money due (see *Barclays Bank plc v Estates & Commercial Ltd (In Liquidation)* [1997] 1 WLR 415).

If a registrable disposition of a registered estate is made for valuable consideration, completion of the disposition by registration has the effect of postponing to the interest under the disposition any interest affecting the estate immediately before the disposition the priority of which is not protected at the time of registration (LRA 2002, s 29). Since a vendor's lien is an interest affecting the estate *before* the transfer (as it arises on creation of the contract), on registration of the transfer the purchaser of the registered estate takes free of the vendor's lien unless the vendor has already protected the lien before registration of the transfer. In that event, although the purchaser will still be obliged to honour his contractual obligations under the contract and the vendor may be able to sue the purchaser for the unpaid amount, if the purchaser does not pay him, the vendor cannot request the court to order that the property be sold to repay him. The vendor should therefore protect his lien by entering an agreed notice or a unilateral notice against his own title before completing the transfer.

If the vendor's lien has arisen on a sale of unregistered land, the Registry will, if it is apparent from its examination of the title that the lien has arisen, enter a notice of it in the register (LRR 2003, r 35).

If the vendor remains in actual occupation of the land, the vendor's lien may take effect as an interest falling within LRA 2002, Sch 1, para 2 or Sch 3, para 3 which overrides first registration or registered dispositions. An overriding interest of that nature is subject to the duty of disclosure under LRR 2003, rr 28 and 57 (see 'Duty to disclose overriding interests', page 426). For liens arising under LRHUDA 1993 s 32(2), see *Collective enfranchisement*, page 136.

Agreed notice

In addition to the usual documents required (see *Notices*, page 389), the vendor should deliver to the Registry the contract or a certified copy of it.

The agreed notice in the register will give details of the interest protected.

Application for entry of a unilateral notice may be preferred where the applicant does not wish the terms of the contract giving rise to the lien to be open to public inspection and copying.

Unilateral notice

The vendor should deliver to the Registry the usual documents required (see *Notices*, page 389).

The statement in panel 11 or conveyancer's certificate in panel 12 of Form UN1 should be completed on the following lines to show the interest of the applicant:

> person having the benefit of a vendor's lien arising under an agreement for sale dated [*date*] made between [*registered proprietor*] and [*purchaser*].

The unilateral notice in the register will give brief details of the interest protected and identify the beneficiary of that notice.

WRITS OR ORDERS AFFECTING LAND

A writ or order of the kind mentioned in Land Charges Act 1972, s 6(1)(a) is treated as an interest affecting an estate or charge for the purposes of the LRA 2002 (LRA 2002, s 87(1)). It cannot, however, be an interest belonging to a person in actual occupation within LRA 2002, Sch 1, para 2 or Sch 3, para 2 which overrides first registration or registered dispositions (LRA 2002, s 87(3)). Such a writ or order is one affecting land issued or made by any court for the purposes of enforcing a judgment or recognisance. A writ or order which relates to an undivided share under a trust of land, or which has the effect of creating an interest under a trust of land, is not an interest affecting land for this purpose, as it does not affect the legal estate.

A writ or order affecting land may be protected by application for the entry in the register of an agreed notice or a unilateral notice, and possibly a restriction. The application may be made by the person who has obtained such a writ or order, or his assignee or chargee (LRR 2003, r 172). In practice, an application for an agreed notice will be the usual course of action. The entitlement to apply for entry of a restriction and the form of restriction will depend on the nature of the writ or order; LRR 2003, r 93 specifies the form of restriction for which persons having the benefit of certain types of writ or order will be entitled to apply. A restriction does not confer any priority; it simply prevents an entry being made in the register in respect of any disposition, or a disposition of a specified kind, unless the terms of the restriction have (where applicable) been complied with.

Agreed notice

In addition to the usual documents required (see *Notices*, page 389), an applicant should deliver to the Registry the writ or order or a certified copy of it.

In the case of an application for entry of an agreed notice, where the consent of the registered proprietor is not available the Registry may only approve the application where it is satisfied of the validity of the applicant's claim (LRA 2002, s 34(3)(c)).

The agreed notice in the register will give details of the interest protected.

Unilateral notice

An applicant should deliver to the Registry the usual documents required (see *Notices*, page 389).

The statement in panel 11 or conveyancer's certificate in panel 12 of Form UN1 should be completed on the following lines to show details of the interest of the applicant:

> person having the benefit of a [*insert details of writ or order in question*] of the [*name* Division of the High Court] *or* [*name* County Court] dated [*date*] [*set out full court reference and parties*].

The unilateral notice in the register will give brief details of the interest protected and identify the beneficiary of that notice.

Restriction

An applicant should deliver to the Registry the usual documents required (see *Restrictions*, page 500).

Panel 9 of Form RX1 should be completed as to the required restriction(s). A restriction in a standard form contained in LRR 2003, Sch 4 does not require the approval of the Registry to the terms of the restriction under LRA 2002, s 43(3). The form of restriction sought will depend on the nature of the writ or order.

Where the writ or order relates to the legal estate in the registered title and imposes a limitation upon dispositions, an application may be made for entry of an appropriate form of restriction to reflect this limitation (see, for example, *Freezing orders, restraint orders and interim receiving orders*, page 248).

Where the writ or order relates to an undivided share under a trust of land, or has the effect of creating an interest under a trust of land, the interest cannot be protected by the entry of a notice. Instead, application may be made for entry of a restriction in Form A, if such a restriction does not already appear in the register. In such a case, a person having a beneficial interest under a trust of land has a sufficient interest for the purposes of LRA 2002, s 43(1)(c) to apply for entry of a restriction in Form A, to ensure that a survivor of the joint proprietors (unless a trust corporation) will not be able to give a valid receipt for capital money (LRR 2003, r 93(a)). The wording of Form A is set out in Appendix IV, page 585.

A beneficiary under a trust of land created by such a writ or order may where appropriate also have a sufficient interest to apply for entry of a restriction in Form II. For example, if the effect of the writ or order is that the registered proprietor holds the registered title on a trust of land for himself and the beneficiary. The purpose of the restriction is to ensure that the beneficiary receives notice of a disposition. The wording of Form II is set out in Appendix IV, page 585.

This restriction does not of itself prevent a disposition, provided its terms are complied with. This is because the interest of the beneficiary will be overreached where the requirements of Form A have been met (Law of Property Act 1925, ss 2 and 27).

The Registry must give notice of the application for a restriction to the proprietor of the registered estate or charge concerned, if it has not been made by or with his consent or a person entitled to be registered as such proprietor (LRA 2002, s 45).

APPENDIX I
HM LAND REGISTRY OFFICES[1]

Head Office/Croydon Office Trafalgar House Bedford Park Croydon CR0 2AQ DX 313101 Croydon 47	Birkenhead Office Rosebrae Court Woodside Ferry Approach Birkenhead CH41 6DU DX 312901 Birkenhead 18	Coventry Office Earlsdon Park Coventry 55 Butts Road, Coventry CV1 3BH DX 729440 Coventry 3
Durham Office Southfield House Southfield Way Durham DH1 5TR DX 313201 Durham 24	Fylde Office Wrea Brook Court Lytham Road Warton Preston PR4 1TE DX 313501 Lytham 7	Gloucester Office Twyver House Bruton Way Gloucester GL1 1DQ DX 313301 Gloucester 31
Hull Office Earle House Colonial Street Hull HU2 8JN DX 313401 Hull 24	Leicester Office Westbridge Place Leicester LE3 5DR DX 313601 Leicester 43	Nottingham Office Castle Wharf House 2 Canal Street Nottingham NG1 7AU DX 313701 Nottingham 55
Peterborough Office Stuart House West Wing City Road Peterborough PE1 1QF DX 313801 Peterborough 29	Plymouth Office Seaton Court 2 William Prance Road Plymouth PL6 5WS DX 313001 Plymouth 26	Telford Office Parkside Court Hall Park Way Telford TF3 4LR DX 313901 Telford 15

---

[1] Reproduced with kind permission of HM Land Registry.

Wales Office Ty Cwm Tawe Phoenix Way Llansamlet Swansea SA7 9FQ DX 314001 Swansea 25	Weymouth Office Melcombe Court 1 Cumberland Drive Weymouth Dorset DT4 9TT DX 314101 Weymouth 5	Land Charges Department PO Box 292 Plymouth PL5 9BY DX 8249 Plymouth 3
Agricultural Credits Department PO Box 292 Plymouth PL5 9BY DX8249 Plymouth 3	Royal Mail address for business customers: Land Registry [*insert customer team's office name or, if none, name of customer's closest office*] PO Box 75 Gloucester GL14 9BD	DX address for business customers: Land Registry [*insert customer team's office name or, if none, name of customer's closest office*] DX 321601 Gloucester 33
Address for members of the public: Land Registry Citizen Centre PO Box 74 Gloucester GL14 9BB	Bankruptcy applications Land Registry Bankruptcy Unit (LRBU) PO Box 292 Plymouth PL5 9BY DX8249 Plymouth 3	Insolvency applications Land Registry Insolvency Unit PO Box 292 Plymouth PL5 9BY DX8249 Plymouth 3

APPENDIX II
LIST OF FORMS[2]

Schedule 1 forms

ADV1	Application for registration of a person in adverse possession under LRA 2002, Sch 6
ADV2	Application to be registered as a person to be notified of an application for adverse possession
AN1	Application to enter an agreed notice
AP1	Application to change the register
AS1	Assent of whole of registered title(s)
AS2	Assent of charge
AS3	Assent of part of registered title(s)
CC	Entry of a note of consolidation of charges
CCD	Application to cancel a caution against dealings
CCT	Application to cancel a caution against first registration
CH1	Legal charge of a registered estate
CH2	Application to enter an obligation to make further advances
CH3	Application to note agreed maximum amount of security
CI	Certificate of inspection of title plan
CN1	Application to cancel a notice (other than a unilateral notice)
CS	Continuation sheet for use with application and disposition forms
CT1	Caution against first registration
DB	Application to determine the exact line of a boundary
DI	Disclosable overriding interests
DL	List of documents
DS1	Cancellation of entries relating to a registered charge
DS2	Application to cancel entries relating to a registered charge
DS3	Release of part of the land from a registered charge
EX1	Application for the registrar to designate a document as an exempt information document

---

EX1A	Reasons for exemption in support of an application to designate a document as an exempt information document
EX2	Application for official copy of an exempt information document
EX3	Application to remove the designation of a document as an exempt information document
FR1	First registration application
HC1	Application for copies of historical edition(s) of the register/title plan held in electronic form
HR1	Application for registration of a notice of home rights
HR2	Application for renewal of registration in respect of home rights
HR3	Application by mortgagee for official search in respect of home rights
HR4	Application for cancellation of a notice of home rights
NAP	Notice to the registrar in respect of an adverse possession application
OC1	Application for official copies of register/plan or certificate in Form CI
OC2	Application for official copies of documents only
OS1	Application by purchaser for official search with priority of the whole of the land in a registered title or a pending first registration application
OS2	Application by purchaser for official search with priority of part of the land in a registered title or a pending first registration application
OS3	Application for official search without priority of the land in a registered title
PIC	Application for a personal inspection under LRA 2002, s 66
PN1	Application for a search in the index of proprietors' names
PRD1	Request for the production of documents
PRD2	Notice to produce a document, LRA 2002, s 75 and LRR 2003, r 201
RX1	Application to enter a restriction
RX2	Application for an order that a restriction be disapplied or modified
RX3	Application to cancel a restriction
RX4	Application to withdraw a restriction
SC	Application for noting the overriding priority of a statutory charge
SEV	Application to enter a restriction in Form A on severance of joint tenancy by agreement or notice
SIF	Application for an official search of the index of relating franchises and manors
SIM	Application for an official search of the index map

ST1	Statement of truth in support of application for registration based upon adverse possession
ST2	Statement of truth in support of application for registration based upon adverse possession of a rentcharge
ST3	Statement of truth in support of application for registration of land based upon lost or destroyed title deeds
ST4	Statement of truth in support of application for registration and/or noting of a prescriptive easement
TP1	Transfer of part of registered title(s)
TP2	Transfer of part of registered title(s) under power of sale
TR1	Transfer of whole of registered title(s)
TR2	Transfer of whole of registered title(s) under power of sale
TR4	Transfer of a charge or portfolio of charges
TR5	Transfer of portfolio of titles (whole or part)
UN1	Application to enter a unilateral notice
UN2	Application to remove a unilateral notice
UN3	Application to be registered as beneficiary of an existing unilateral notice
UN4	Application for the cancellation of a unilateral notice
UT1	Application for upgrading of title
WCT	Application to withdraw a caution

Schedule 3 forms

Form 1	Certificate as to execution of power of attorney (LRR 2003, r 61)
Form 2	Statutory declaration/certificate/statement of truth as to non-revocation for powers more than 12 months old at the date of the disposition for which they are used (LRR 2003, r 62)
Form 3	Statutory declaration/certificate/statement of truth in support of power delegating trustees' functions to a beneficiary (LRR 2003, r 63)
Form 4	Certificate as to vesting in an incumbent or other ecclesiastical corporation (LRR 2003, r 174)
Form 5	The like certificate under LRR 2003, r 175
Form 6	Transfer where the tenant for life is already registered as proprietor (LRR 2003, r 186 and Sch 7, para 5)
Form 7	Certificate of powers of overseas corporations (LRR 2003, r 183)
Form 8	Certificate of powers of corporations other than overseas corporations (LRR 2003, r 183)

Commonhold forms

CM1	Application to register a freehold estate in commonhold land
CM2	Application for the freehold estate to cease to be registered as a freehold estate in commonhold land during the transitional period
CM3	Application for the registration of an amended commonhold community statement and/or altered memorandum and articles of association
CM4	Application to add land to a commonhold registration
CM5	Application for the termination of a commonhold registration
CM6	Application for the registration of a successor commonhold association
COE	Notification of change of extent of a commonhold unit over which there is a registered charge
CON1	Consent to the registration of land as commonhold land
CON2	Consent to an application for the freehold estate to cease to be registered as a freehold estate in commonhold land during the transitional period
COV	Application for registration with unit holders
SR1	Notice of surrender of development right(s)

Other forms

ACD	Application for approval of a standard form of charge deed and allocation of official Land Registry reference
CNG	Change of gender
COG1	Update registered owner's contact address
DJP	Application to remove from the register the name of a deceased registered proprietor
DS2E	Application to cancel entries relating to a registered charge
ID1	Evidence of identity for a private individual
ID2	Evidence of identity for a corporate body
ID3	Evidence of identity for use with FR1 only
JO	Trust information
PN1ID	IOPN search: evidence of identity
RD1	Request for the return of an original document(s)
RQ	Request for a restriction by owner(s) not living at the property
RQ(Co)	Request for a restriction by a company

APPENDIX III
LAND REGISTRATION RULES 2003,
SCHEDULE 1A:
PRESCRIBED CLAUSES LR1 TO LR14

- *All words in italicised text and inapplicable alternative wording in a clause may be omitted or deleted.*
- *Clause LR13 may be omitted or deleted.*
- *Clause LR14 may be omitted or deleted where the Tenant is one person.*
- *Otherwise, do not omit or delete any words in bold text unless italicised.*
- *Side-headings may appear as headings if this is preferred.*
- *Vertical or horizontal lines, or both, may be omitted.*

LR1. Date of lease	
LR2. Title number(s)	**LR2.1 Landlord's title number(s)** *Title number(s) out of which this lease is granted. Leave blank if not registered.*
	LR2.2 Other title numbers *Existing title number(s) against which entries of matters referred to in LR9, LR10, LR11 and LR13 are to be made.*
LR3. Parties to this lease *[Give full names and addresses of each of the parties. For UK incorporated companies and limited liability partnerships, also give the registered number including any prefix. For overseas companies, also give the territory of incorporation and, if appropriate, the registered number in the United Kingdom including any prefix.]*	**Landlord** **Tenant** *Other parties* *Specify capacity of each party, for example "management company", "guarantor", etc.*

LR4. Property *Insert a full description of the land being leased* *or* *Refer to the clause, schedule or paragraph of a* *schedule in this lease in which the land being* *leased is more fully described.* *Where there is a letting of part of a registered* *title, a plan must be attached to this lease and* *any floor levels must be specified.*	**In the case of a conflict between this clause and the remainder of this lease then, for the purposes of registration, this clause shall prevail.**
LR5. Prescribed statements etc. *If this lease includes a statement falling within* *LR5.1, insert under that sub-clause the relevant* *statement or refer to the clause, schedule or* *paragraph of a schedule in this lease which* *contains the statement.* *In LR5.2, omit or delete those Acts which do not* *apply to this lease.*	*LR5.1 Statements prescribed under rules 179 (dispositions in favour of a charity), 180 (dispositions by a charity) or 196 (leases under the Leasehold Reform, Housing and Urban Development Act 1993) of the Land Registration Rules 2003.* *LR5.2 This lease is made under, or by reference to, provisions of:* **Leasehold Reform Act 1967** **Housing Act 1985** **Housing Act 1988** **Housing Act 1996**

LR6. Term for which the Property is leased
Include only the appropriate statement (duly completed) from the three options.
NOTE: The information you provide, or refer to, here will be used as part of the particulars to identify the lease under rule 6 of the Land Registration Rules 2003.
	From and including
	
	To and including
	
	   OR
	
	The term as specified in this lease at clause/schedule/paragraph
	
	   OR
	
	The term is as follows:

LR7. Premium *Specify the total premium, inclusive of any VAT where payable.*	
LR8. Prohibitions or restrictions on disposing of this lease *Include whichever of the two statements is appropriate.* *Do not set out here the wording of the provision.*	This lease does not contain a provision that prohibits or restricts dispositions. *OR* This lease contains a provision that prohibits or restricts dispositions.
LR9. Rights of acquisition etc. *Insert the relevant provisions in the sub-clauses or refer to the clause, schedule or paragraph of a schedule in this lease which contains the provisions.*	**LR9.1 Tenant's contractual rights to renew this lease, to acquire the reversion or another lease of the Property, or to acquire an interest in other land** **LR9.2 Tenant's covenant to (or offer to) surrender this lease** **LR9.3 Landlord's contractual rights to acquire this lease**
LR10. Restrictive covenants given in this lease by the Landlord in respect of land other than the Property *Insert the relevant provisions or refer to the clause, schedule or paragraph of a schedule in this lease which contains the provisions.*	
LR11. Easements *Refer here only to the clause, schedule or paragraph of a schedule in this lease which sets out the easements.*	**LR11.1 Easements granted by this lease for the benefit of the Property** **LR11.2 Easements granted or reserved by this lease over the Property for the benefit of other property**
LR12. Estate rentcharge burdening the Property *Refer here only to the clause, schedule or paragraph of a schedule in this lease which sets out the rentcharge.*	

LR13. Application for standard form of restriction *Set out the full text of the standard form of restriction and the title against which it is to be entered. If you wish to apply for more than one standard form of restriction use this clause to apply for each of them, tell us who is applying against which title and set out the full text of the restriction you are applying for.* *Standard forms of restriction are set out in Schedule 4 to the Land Registration Rules 2003.*	The Parties to this lease apply to enter the following standard form of restriction [against the title of the Property] *or* [against title number]
LR14. Declaration of trust where there is more than one person comprising the Tenant *If the Tenant is one person, omit or delete all the alternative statements.* *If the Tenant is more than one person, complete this clause by omitting or deleting all inapplicable alternative statements.*	The Tenant is more than one person. They are to hold the Property on trust for themselves as joint tenants *OR* The Tenant is more than one person. They are to hold the Property on trust for themselves as tenants in common in equal shares *OR* The Tenant is more than one person. They are to hold the Property on trust *Complete as necessary*

APPENDIX IV
LAND REGISTRATION RULES 2003,
SCHEDULE 4:
STANDARD FORMS OF RESTRICTION

Form A (Restriction on dispositions by sole proprietor)

No disposition by a sole proprietor of the registered estate (except a trust corporation) under which capital money arises is to be registered unless authorised by an order of the court.

Form B (Dispositions by trustees — certificate required)

No [disposition *or specify type of disposition*] by the proprietors of the registered estate is to be registered unless one or more of them makes a statutory declaration or statement of truth, or their conveyancer gives a certificate, that the [disposition *or specify type of disposition*] is in accordance with [*specify the disposition creating the trust*] or some variation thereof referred to in the declaration, statement or certificate.

Form C (Dispositions by personal representatives — certificate required)

No disposition by the personal representative of [*name*] deceased, other than a transfer by way of assent, is to be registered unless such personal representative makes a statutory declaration or statement of truth, or their conveyancer gives a certificate, that the disposition is in accordance with the terms of

[*choose whichever bulleted clause is appropriate*]

- the will of the deceased [as varied by [*specify date of, and parties to, deed of variation or other appropriate details*]]
- the law relating to intestacy as varied by [*specify date of, and parties to, deed of variation or other appropriate details*]

or some [further] variation thereof referred to in the declaration, statement or certificate, or is necessary for the purposes of administration.

Form D (Parsonage, diocesan glebe, church or churchyard land)

No disposition of the registered estate is to be registered unless made in accordance with

[*choose whichever bulleted clause is appropriate*]

* [*in the case of parsonage land*] the Parsonages Measure 1938
* [*in the case of church or churchyard land*] the New Parishes Measure 1943
* [*in the case of diocesan glebe land*] the Endowments and Glebe Measure 1976

or some other Measure or authority.

Form E (Non-exempt charity — certificate required)

No disposition by the proprietor of the registered estate to which section 36 or section 38 of the Charities Act 1993 applies is to be registered unless the instrument contains a certificate complying with section 37(2) or section 39(2) of that Act as appropriate.

Form F (Land vested in official custodian on trust for non-exempt charity – authority required)

No disposition executed by the trustees of [*name of charity*] in the name and on behalf of the proprietor is to be registered unless the transaction is authorised by an order of the court or of the Charity Commission, as required by section 22(3) of the Charities Act 1993.

Form G (Tenant for life as registered proprietor of settled land, where there are trustees of the settlement)

No disposition is to be registered unless authorised by the Settled Land Act 1925, or by any extension of those statutory powers in the settlement, and no disposition under which capital money arises is to be registered unless the money is paid to [*name*] of [*address*] and [*name*] of [*address*], (the trustees of the settlement, who may be a sole trust corporation or, if individuals, must number at least two but not more than four) or into court.

[Note — If applicable under the terms of the settlement, a further provision may be added that no transfer of the mansion house [shown on an attached plan or otherwise adequately described to enable it to be fully identified on the Ordnance Survey map or title plan] is to be registered without the consent of the named trustees or an order of the court.]

Form H (Statutory owners as trustees of the settlement and registered proprietors of settled land)

No disposition is to be registered unless authorised by the Settled Land Act 1925, or by any extension of those statutory powers in the settlement, and, except where the sole proprietor is a trust corporation, no disposition under which capital money arises is to be registered unless the money is paid to at least two proprietors.

[Note — This restriction does not apply where the statutory owners are not the trustees of the settlement.]

Form I (Tenant for life as registered proprietor of settled land — no trustees of the settlement)

No disposition under which capital money arises, or which is not authorised by the Settled Land Act 1925 or by any extension of those statutory powers in the settlement, is to be registered.

Form J (Trustee in bankruptcy and beneficial interest — certificate required)

No disposition of the

[*choose whichever bulleted clause is appropriate*]

- registered estate, other than a disposition by the proprietor of any registered charge registered before the entry of this restriction,
- registered charge dated [*date*] referred to above, other than a disposition by the proprietor of any registered sub-charge of that charge registered before the entry of this restriction,

is to be registered without a certificate signed by the applicant for registration or their conveyancer that written notice of the disposition was given to [*name of trustee in bankruptcy*] (the trustee in bankruptcy of [*name of bankrupt person*]) at [*address for service*].

Form K (Charging order affecting beneficial interest — certificate required)

No disposition of the

[*choose whichever bulleted clause is appropriate*]

- registered estate, other than a disposition by the proprietor of any registered charge registered before the entry of this restriction.

- registered charge dated [*date*] referred to above, other than a disposition by the proprietor of any registered sub-charge of that charge registered before the entry of this restriction,

is to be registered without a certificate signed by the applicant for registration or their conveyancer that written notice of the disposition was given lo [*name of person with the benefit of the charging order*] at [*address for service*], being the person with the benefit of [an interim *or* a final] charging order on the beneficial interest of [*name of judgment debtor*] made by the [*name of court*] on [*date*] (Court reference [*insert reference*]).

Form L (Disposition by registered proprietor of a registered estate or proprietor of charge — certificate required)

No [disposition *or specify type of disposition*] of the registered estate [(other than a charge)] by the proprietor of the registered estate [, or by the proprietor of any registered charge, not being a charge registered before the entry of this restriction,] is to be registered without a certificate signed by

[*choose* **one** *of the bulleted clauses*]

- a conveyancer
- the applicant for registration [or their conveyancer]
- [*name*] of [*address*] [or their personal representatives] [or [their conveyancer or *specify appropriate details*]]
- [*name*] of [*address*] [or their personal representatives] and [*name*] of [*address*] [or their personal representatives] [or [their conveyancer *or specify appropriate details*]]
- [*name*] of [*address*] and [*name*] of [*address*] or the survivor of them [or by the personal representatives of the survivor] [or [their conveyancer *or specify appropriate details*]]
- [*name*] of [*address*] or [after that person's death] by [*name*] of [*address*] [or [their conveyancer *or specify appropriate details*]]

that the provisions of [*specify clause, paragraph or other particulars*] of [*specify details*] have been complied with [or that they do not apply to the disposition].

Form M (Disposition by registered proprietor of registered estate or proprietor of charge certificate of registered proprietor of specified title number required)

No [disposition *or specify type of disposition*] of the registered estate [(other than a charge)] by the proprietor of the registered estate [, or by the proprietor of any registered charge, not being a charge registered before the entry of this restriction,] is to be registered without a certificate signed by the proprietor for the time being of the estate registered under title number [*specify title number*] [or [their conveyancer *or specify appropriate details*]] that the provisions of [*specify clause, paragraph or other particulars*] of [*specify details*] have been complied with [or that they do not apply to the disposition].

Form N (Disposition by registered proprietor of registered estate or proprietor of charge — consent required)

No [disposition *or specify type of disposition*] of the registered estate [(other than a charge)] by the proprietor of the registered estate [, or by the proprietor of any registered charge, not being a charge registered before the entry of this restriction,] is to be registered without a written consent signed by

[*choose **one** of the bulleted clauses*]

- [*name*] of [*address*] [or their personal representatives] [or [their conveyancer *or specify appropriate details*]].
- [*name*] of [*address*] [or their personal representatives] and [*name*] of [*address*] [or their personal representatives] [or [their conveyancer *or specify appropriate details*]].
- [*name*] of [*address*] and [*name*] of [*address*] or the survivor of them [or by the personal representatives of the survivor] [or [their conveyancer or *specify appropriate details*]].
- [*name*] of [*address*] or [after that person's death] by [*name*] of [*address*] [or [their conveyancer or *specify appropriate details*]].

Form O (Disposition by registered proprietor of registered estate or proprietor of charge — consent of registered proprietor of specified title number or certificate required)

No [disposition or *specify type of disposition*] of the registered estate [(other than a charge)] by the proprietor of the registered estate [, or by the proprietor of any registered charge, not being a charge registered before the entry of this restriction,] is to be registered without a written consent signed by the proprietor for the time being of the estate registered under title number [*specify title number*] [or [their conveyancer *or specify appropriate details*]].

[*The text of the restriction may be continued as follows, to allow for the provision of a certificate as an alternative to the consent.*]

or without a certificate signed by

[*choose **one** of the bulleted clauses*]

- a conveyancer
- the applicant for registration [or their conveyancer]
- [*name*] of [*address*] [or [their conveyancer *or specify appropriate details*]]

that the provisions of [*specify clause, paragraph or other particulars*] of [*specify details*] have been complied with [or that they do not apply to the disposition].

Form P (Disposition by registered proprietor of registered estate or proprietor of charge — consent of proprietor of specified charge or certificate required)

No [disposition *or specify type of disposition*] of the registered estate [(other than a charge)] by the proprietor of the registered estate [, or by the proprietor of any registered charge, not being a charge registered before the entry of this restriction,] is to be registered without a written consent signed by the proprietor for the time being of the charge dated [*date*] in favour of [*chargee*] referred to in the charges register [or [their conveyancer *or specify appropriate details*]].

[*The text of the restriction may be continued as follows, to allow for the provision of a certificate as an alternative to the consent* .]

or without a certificate signed by

[*choose **one** of the bulleted clauses*]

- a conveyancer
- the applicant for registration [or their conveyancer]
- [*name*] of [*address*] [or [their conveyancer *or specify appropriate details*]]

that the provisions of [*specify clause, paragraph or other particulars*] of [*specify details*] have been complied with [or that they do not apply to the disposition].

Form Q (Disposition by registered proprietor of registered estate or proprietor of charge — consent of personal representatives required)

No [disposition *or specify type of disposition*] of the

[*choose whichever bulleted clause is appropriate*]

- registered estate by the proprietor of the registered estate
- registered charge dated [*date*] referred to above by the proprietor of that registered charge

is to be registered after the death of [*name of the current proprietor(s) whose personal representatives' consent will be required*] without the written consent of the personal representatives of the deceased.

Form R (Disposition by registered proprietor of registered estate or proprietor of charge — evidence of compliance with club rules required)

No [disposition *or specify type of disposition*] of the registered estate [(other than a charge)] by the proprietor of the registered estate [, or by the proprietor of any registered charge, not being a charge registered before the entry of this restriction,] is to be registered unless authorised by the rules of the [*name of club*] of [*address*] as evidenced by

[*choose whichever bulleted clause is appropriate*]

- a resolution of its members.
- a certificate signed by its secretary or conveyancer.
- [*specify appropriate details*].

Form S (Disposition by proprietor of charge — certificate of compliance required)

No [disposition or *specify type of disposition*] by the proprietor of the registered charge dated [*date*] referred to above is to be registered without a certificate signed by

[*choose **one** of the bulleted clauses*]

- a conveyancer
- the applicant for registration [or their conveyancer]
- [*name*] of [*address*] [or their personal representatives] [or [their conveyancer or *specify appropriate details*]]
- [*name*] of [*address*] [or their personal representatives] and [*name*] of [*address*] [or their personal representatives] [or [their conveyancer or *specify appropriate details*]]
- [*name*] of [*address*] and [*name*] of [*address*] or the survivor of them [or by the personal representatives of the survivor] [or [their conveyancer or *specify appropriate details*]]
- [*name*] of [*address*] or [after that person's death] by [*name*] of [*address*] [or [their conveyancer or *specify appropriate details*]]
- the proprietor for the time being of the sub-charge dated [*date*] in favour of [*sub-chargee*] [or [their conveyancer or *specify appropriate details*]]

that the provisions of [*specify clause, paragraph or other particulars*] of [*specify details*] have been complied with [or that they do not apply to the disposition].

Form T (Disposition by proprietor of charge consent required)

No [disposition or *specify type of disposition*] by the proprietor of the registered charge dated [*date*] referred to above is to be registered without a written consent signed by

[*choose **one** of the bulleted clauses*]

- [*name*] of [*address*] [or their personal representatives] [or [their conveyancer *or specify appropriate details*]].
- [*name*] of [*address*] [or their personal representatives] and [*name*] of [*address*] [or their personal representatives] [or [their conveyancer *or specify appropriate details*]].
- [*name*] of [*address*] and [*name*] of [*address*] or the survivor of them [or by the personal representatives of the survivor] [or [their conveyancer *or specify appropriate details*]].
- [*name*] of [*address*] or [after that person's death] by [*name*] of [*address*] [or [their conveyancer *or specify appropriate details*]].
- the proprietor for the time being of the sub-charge dated [*date*] in favour of [*sub-chargee*] [or [their conveyancer *or specify appropriate details*]].
-

Form U (Section 37 of the Housing Act 1985)

No transfer or lease by the proprietor of the registered estate or by the proprietor of any registered charge is to be registered unless a certificate by [*specify relevant local authority*] is given that the transfer or lease is made in accordance with section 37 of the Housing Act 1985.

Form V (Section 157 of the Housing Act 1985)

No transfer or lease by the proprietor of the registered estate or by the proprietor of any registered charge is to be registered unless a certificate by [*specify relevant local authority or housing association etc*] is given that the transfer or lease is made in accordance with section 157 of the Housing Act 1985.

Form W (Paragraph 4 of Schedule 9A to the Housing Act 1985)

No disposition (except a transfer) of a qualifying dwelling-house (except to a qualifying person or persons) is to be registered without the consent of—

(a) in relation to a disposal of land in England, the Secretary of State, or

(b) in relation to a disposal of land in Wales, the Welsh Ministers,

where consent to that disposition is required by section 171D(2) of the Housing Act 1985 as it applies by virtue of the Housing (Preservation of Right to Buy) Regulations 1993.

Form X (Section 81 or 133 of the Housing Act 1988 or section 173 of the Local Government and Housing Act 1989)

No disposition by the proprietor of the registered estate or in exercise of the power of sale or leasing in any registered charge (except an exempt disposal as defined by section 81(8) of the Housing Act 1988) is to be registered without the consent of—

(a) in relation to a disposal of land in England, the Secretary of State, and

(b) in relation to a disposal of land in Wales, the Welsh Ministers,

where consent to that disposition is required by [*as appropriate* [section 81 of that Act] *or* [section 133 of that Act] *or* [section 173 of the Local Government and Housing Act 1989]].

Form Y (Section 13 of the Housing Act 1996)

No transfer or lease by the proprietor of the registered estate or by the proprietor of a registered charge is to be registered unless a certificate by [*[specify relevant registered social landlord]*] is given that the transfer or lease is made in accordance with section 13 of the Housing Act 1996.

Form AA (Freezing order on the registered estate)

Under an order of the [*name of court*] made on [*date*] (Court reference [*insert reference*]) no disposition by the proprietor of the registered estate is to be registered except with the consent of [*name*] of [*address*] or under a further order of the Court.

Form BB (Freezing order on charge)

Under an order of the [*name of court*] made on [*date*] (Court reference [*insert reference*]) no disposition by the proprietor of the registered charge dated [*date*] referred to above is to be registered except with the consent of [*name*] of [*address*] or under a further order of the Court.

Form CC (Application for freezing order on the registered estate)

Pursuant to an application made on [*date*] to the [*name of court*] for a freezing order to be made under [*statutory provision*] no disposition by the proprietor of the registered estate is to be registered except with the consent of [*name of the person applying*] of [*address*] or under a further order of the Court.

Form DD (Application for freezing order on charge)

Pursuant to an application made on [*date*] to the [*name of court*] for a freezing order to be made under [*statutory provision*] no disposition by the proprietor of the registered charge dated [*date*] referred to above is to be registered except with the consent of [*name of the person applying*] of [*address*] or under a further order of the Court.

Form EE (Restraint order or interim receiving order on the registered estate)

Under [a restraint order or an interim receiving order] made under [*statutory provision*] on [*date*] (Court reference [*insert reference*]) no disposition by the proprietor of the registered estate is to be registered except with the consent of [*name of prosecutor or other appropriate person*] of [*address*] or under a further order of the Court.

Form FF (Restraint order or interim receiving order on charge)

Under [a restraint order or an interim receiving order] made under [*statutory provision*] on [*date*] (Court reference [*insert reference*]) no disposition by the proprietor of the registered charge dated [*date*] referred to above is to be registered except with the consent of [*name of prosecutor or other appropriate person*] of [*address*] or under a further order of the Court.

Form GG (Application for restraint order or interim receiving order on the registered estate)

Pursuant to an application for [a restraint order *or* an interim receiving order] to be made under [*statutory provision*] and under any order made as a result of that application, no disposition by the proprietor of the registered estate is to be registered except with the consent of [*name of prosecutor or other appropriate person*] of [*address*] or under a further order of the Court.

Form HH (Application for restraint order or interim receiving order on charge)

Pursuant to an application for [a restraint order or an interim receiving order] to be made under [*statutory provision*] and under any order made as a result of that application no disposition by the proprietor of the registered charge dated [*date*] referred to above is to be registered except with the consent of [*name of prosecutor or other appropriate person*] of [*address*] or under a further order of the Court.

Form II (Beneficial interest that is a right or claim in relation to a registered estate)

No disposition of the registered estate, other than a disposition by the proprietor of any registered charge registered before the entry of this restriction, is to be registered without a certificate signed by the applicant for registration or their conveyancer that written notice of the disposition was given to [*name*] at [*address*].

Form JJ (Statutory charge of beneficial interest in favour of [the Lord Chancellor])

No disposition of the

[*choose whichever bulleted clause is appropriate*]

- registered estate, other than a disposition by the proprietor of any registered charge registered before the entry of this restriction,
- registered charge dated [*date*] referred to above, other than a disposition by the proprietor of any registered sub-charge of that charge registered before the entry of this restriction,

is to be registered without a certificate signed by the applicant for registration or their conveyancer that [written notice of the disposition was given to the Lord Chancellor at [address and Lord Chancellor's reference number]].

Form KK (Lease by registered social landlord or non-profit registered provider of social housing)

No deed varying the terms of the registered lease [of property in Wales] is to be registered without the consent of

[...]
[...]

– the Welsh Ministers of [*address*].

Form LL (Restriction as to evidence of execution)

No disposition of the

[*choose whichever bulleted clause is appropriate*]

- registered estate by the proprietor of the registered estate
- registered charge dated [*date*] referred to above by the proprietor of that registered charge is to be registered without a certificate signed by a conveyancer that that conveyancer is satisfied that the person who executed the document submitted for registration as disponor is the same person as the proprietor.

Form MM (Interest in beneficial joint tenancy subject to charge under section 22(1) of the Health and Social Services and Social Security Adjudications Act 1983 or under the terms of a deferred payment agreement within the meaning of section 68(2) of the Social Services and Well-being (Wales) Act 2014)

No disposition of the registered estate made after the death of [*specify the name of the person whose beneficial interest under a beneficial joint tenancy is subject to a charge under* section 22(1) of the Health and Social Services and Social Security Adjudications Act 1983 or under the terms of a deferred payment agreement within the meaning of section 68(2) of the Social Services and Well-being (Wales) Act 2014], or after that person has become the sole proprietor of the registered estate, is to be registered unless—

(1)   the disposition is by two or more persons who were registered as proprietors of the legal estate at the time of that person's death,

(2)   notice of a charge under section 22(1) or (6) of the Health and Social Services and Social Security Adjudications Act 1983 or under the terms of a deferred payment agreement within the meaning of section 68(2) of the Social Services and Well-being (Wales) Act 2014 for the benefit of [*name and address of the local authority*] has been entered in the register or, where appropriate, such charge has been registered, or

(3)   it is shown to the registrar's satisfaction that no such charge is subsisting.

Form NN (Disposition by registered proprietor of registered estate or proprietor of charge — consent or certificate required)

No [*disposition or specify type of disposition*] of the registered estate [(other than a charge)] by the proprietor of the registered estate [, or by the proprietor of any registered charge, not being a charge registered before the entry of this restriction,] is to be registered without a written consent signed by

[*choose one of the bulleted clauses*]

- [*name*] of [*address*] [or their personal representatives] [or [their conveyancer *or specify appropriate details*]],
- [*name*] of [*address*] [or their personal representatives] and [*name*] of [*address*] [or their personal representatives] [or [their conveyancer or *specify appropriate details*]],
- [*name*] of [*address*] and [*name*] of [*address*] or the survivor of them [or by the personal representatives of the survivor] [or [their conveyancer or specify appropriate details]],
- [*name*] of [*address*] or [after that person's death] by [*name*] of [*address*] [or [their conveyancer or *specify appropriate details*]],

or a certificate signed by

[*choose one of the bulleted clauses*]

- a conveyancer
- the applicant for registration [or their conveyancer]
- [*name*] of [*address*] [or [their conveyancer or *specify appropriate details*]]

that the provisions of [*specify clause, paragraph or other particulars*] of [*specify details*] have been complied with [or that they do not apply to the disposition].

Form OO (Disposition by proprietor of charge consent or certificate required)

No [disposition *or specify type of disposition*] by the proprietor of the registered charge dated [*date*] referred to above is to be registered without a written consent signed by

[*choose one of the bulleted clauses*]

- [*name*] of [*address*] [or their personal representatives] [or [their conveyancer or *specify appropriate details*]].
- [*name*] of [*address*] [or their personal representatives] and [*name*] of [*address*] [or their personal representatives] [or [their conveyancer or *specify appropriate details*]].
- [*name*] of [*address*] and [*name*] of [*address*] or the survivor of them [or by the personal representatives of the survivor] [or [their conveyancer or specify appropriate details]].
- [*name*] of [*address*] or [after that person's death] by [*name*] of [*address*] [or [their conveyancer *or specify appropriate details*]].

- the proprietor for the time being of the sub-charge dated [*date*] in favour of [*sub-chargee*] [or [their conveyancer *or specify appropriate details*]].

[or a certificate signed by

[*choose one of the bulleted clauses*]

- a conveyancer
- the applicant for registration [or their conveyancer]
- [*name*] of [*address*] [or [their conveyancer or *specify appropriate details*]]

that the provisions of [*specify clause, paragraph or other particulars*] of [*specify details*] have been complied with [or that they do not apply to the disposition].

Form PP (Disposition by registered proprietor of registered estate or proprietor of charge — certificate of landlord etc, or of a conveyancer, required)

No [disposition *or specify type of disposition*] of the registered estate [(other than a charge)] by the proprietor of the registered estate [, or by the proprietor of any registered charge, not being a charge registered before the entry of this restriction,] is to be registered without a certificate signed by

[*choose one of the bulleted clauses*]

- the proprietor for the time being of the registered estate comprising the reversion immediately expectant on the determination of the registered lease,
- the proprietor for the time being of the estate registered under title number [*specify title number*],
- [*name*] of [*address*] [or by [*name*] of [*address*]],

or by a conveyancer, that the provisions of [*specify clause, paragraph or other particulars*] of [*specify details*] have been complied with [or that they do not apply to the disposition].

Form QQ (Land included in a list of assets of community value maintained under section 87(1) of the Localism Act 2011)

No transfer or lease is to be registered without a certificate signed by a conveyancer that the transfer or lease did not contravene section 95(1) of the Localism Act 2011.

Form RR (Deputy appointed under section 16 of the Mental Capacity Act 2005 – solely owned property)

No disposition during the lifetime of [*name of person who lacks capacity*] of the [registered estate] [registered charge dated [*date*]] is to be completed by registration unless made pursuant to an order of the court under the Mental Capacity Act 2005.

Form SS (Trustee appointed in place of a person who lacks capacity – jointly owned property)

No disposition of the [registered estate] [registered charge dated [*date*]] made during the lifetime of [*name of person who lacks capacity*] is to be completed by registration without the written consent of the Court of Protection.

...

APPENDIX V
LAND REGISTRATION RULES 2003,
SCHEDULE 3:
FORMS REFERRED TO IN RULE 206

Form 1 – Certificate as to execution of power of attorney (rule 61)

Date of power of attorney: ....

Donor of power of attorney: ....

Donee of power of attorney: ....

I/We ....

of ....

....

certify that

- the power of attorney ("the power") is in existence [and is made and, where required, has been registered under (*state statutory provisions under which the power is made and, where required, has been registered, if applicable)*],
- the power is dated (*insert date*),
- I am/we are satisfied that the power is validly executed as a deed and authorises the attorney to execute the document on behalf of the donor of that power, and
- I/we hold [the instrument creating the power] *or* [a copy of the power by means of which its contents may be proved under section 3 of the Powers of Attorney Act 1971] *or* [a document which under section 4 of the Evidence and Powers of Attorney Act 1940, paragraph 16 of Part 2 of Schedule 1, or paragraph 15(3) of Part 5 of Schedule 4 to the Mental Capacity Act 2005] is sufficient evidence of the contents of the power.

Signature of conveyancer .... Date ....

Form 2 – Statutory declaration/certificate/statement of truth as to non-revocation for powers more than 12 months old at the date of the disposition for which they are used (rule 62)

Date of power of attorney: ....

Donor of power of attorney: ....

I/We ....

of ....

do [solemnly and sincerely declare] *or* [certify] *or* [state] that at the time of completion of the .... to me/my client I/my client had no knowledge—

- • of a revocation of the power, or
- • of the death or bankruptcy of the donor or, if the donor is a corporate body, its winding up or dissolution, or
- • of any incapacity of the donor where the power is not a valid lasting or enduring power of attorney, or

Where the power is in the form prescribed for a lasting power of attorney—

- • that a lasting power of attorney was not created, or
- • of circumstances which, if the lasting power of attorney had been created, would have terminated the attorney's authority to act as an attorney, or

Where the power is in the form prescribed for an enduring power of attorney—

- • that the power was not in fact a valid enduring power, or
- • of an order or direction of the Court of Protection which revoked the power, or
- • of the bankruptcy of the attorney, or

Where the power was given under section 9 of the Trusts of Land and Appointment of Trustees Act 1996—

- • of an appointment of another trustee of the land in question, or
- • of any other event which would have the effect of revoking the power, or
- • of any lack of good faith on the part of the person(s) who dealt with the attorney, or

- that the attorney was not a person to whom the functions of the trustees could be delegated under section 9 of the Trusts of Land and Appointment of Trustees Act 1996, or

Where the power is expressed to be given by way of security—

- that the power was not in fact given by way of security, or
- of any revocation of the power with the consent of the attorney, or
- of any other event which would have had the effect of revoking the power.

Where a certificate is given—

Signature of conveyancer .... Date ....

Print name ....

Firm name or employer (if any) ....

Capacity (e.g. acting for ...) ....;

or

Where a Statutory Declaration is made—

And I make this solemn declaration conscientiously believing the same to be true and by virtue of the provisions of the Statutory Declarations Act 1835.

Signature of Declarant .... Date ....

DECLARED at .... before me, a person entitled to administer oaths.

Name ....

Address ....

Qualification ....

Signature ....;

or

Where a statement of truth is made—

I believe that the facts and matters contained in this statement are true.

Signature .... Date ....

Print name ....

Firm name or employer (if any) of any conveyancer signing ....

Capacity of any conveyancer signing (e.g. acting for ...) ....

WARNING
1. If you dishonestly make a statement which you know is, or might be, untrue or misleading, and intend by doing so to make a gain for yourself or another person, or to cause loss or the risk of loss to another person, you may commit the offence of fraud under section 1 of the Fraud Act 2006, the maximum penalty for which is 10 years' imprisonment or an unlimited fine, or both.
2. Failure to complete the form with proper care may result in a loss of protection under the Land Registration Act 2002 if, as a result, a mistake is made in the register.
3. Under section 66 of the Land Registration Act 2002 most documents (including this form) kept by the registrar relating to an application to the registrar or referred to in the register are open to public inspection and copying. If you believe a document contains prejudicial information, you may apply for that part of the document to be made exempt using form EX1, under rule 136 of the Land Registration Rules 2003.

Form 3 – Statutory declaration/certificate/statement of truth in support of power delegating trustees' functions to a beneficiary (rule 63)

Date of power of attorney: ....

Donor of power of attorney: ....

I ....

of ....

do [solemnly and sincerely declare] or [certify] or [state] that at the time of completion of the .... to me/my client I/my client had no knowledge—

- of any lack of good faith on the part of the person(s) who dealt with the attorney, or
- that the attorney was not a person to whom the functions of the trustees could be delegated under section 9 of the Trusts of Land and Appointment of Trustees Act 1996.

Where a certificate is given—

Signature of conveyancer .... Date ....

Print name ....

Firm name or employer (if any) ....

Capacity (e.g. acting for ...) ....;

or

Where a Statutory Declaration is made—

And I make this solemn declaration conscientiously believing the same to be true and by virtue of the provisions of the Statutory Declarations Act 1835.

Signature of Declarant .... Date ....

DECLARED at .... before me, a person entitled to administer oaths.

Name ....

Address ....

Qualification ....

Signature ....;

or

Where a statement of truth is made—

I believe that the facts and matters contained in this statement are true

Signature .... Date ....

Print name ....

Firm name or employer (if any) of any conveyancer signing ....

Capacity of any conveyancer signing (e.g. acting for ...) ....

WARNING
1. If you dishonestly make a statement which you know is, or might be, untrue or misleading, and intend by doing so to make a gain for yourself or another person, or to cause loss or the risk of loss to another person, you may commit the offence of fraud under section 1 of the Fraud Act 2006, the maximum penalty for which is 10 years' imprisonment or an unlimited fine, or both.
2. Failure to complete the form with proper care may result in a loss of protection under the Land Registration Act 2002 if, as a result, a mistake is made in the register.
3. Under section 66 of the Land Registration Act 2002 most documents (including this form) kept by the registrar relating to an application to the registrar or referred to in the register are open to public inspection and copying. If you believe a document contains prejudicial information, you may apply for that part of the document to be made exempt using form EX1, under rule 136 of the Land Registration Rules 2003.

Form 4 – Certificate as to vesting in an incumbent or other ecclesiastical corporation (rule 174)

(*Date*). This is to certify that the registered estate (*or* registered charge *or* that part of the registered estate) comprised in a [*describe the transfer*] under the provisions of [*state the Act or Measure*] (*if such transfer were a conveyance under such Act or Measure*), vests in the incumbent of .... (*or* the bishop of .... *as the case may be*) and his successors immediately (*or as the case may be*) upon the happening of the event following, namely, the [*state event*].

(To be sealed by the Church Commissioners)

Form 5 – The like certificate under rule 175

(*Date*). This is to certify that the [*describe scheme, instrument or transfer, &c.*] operates to vest immediately (*or,* on publication in the "London Gazette", *or at some subsequent period, as the case may be*), the registered estate (*or* registered charge *or* that part of the registered estate [*include description by reference to a plan or to the register if possible*]) in the [*describe the corporation or person*].

(To be sealed by the Church Commissioners)

Form 6 – Transfer where the tenant for life is already registered as proprietor (rule 186 and paragraph 5 of Schedule 7)

(*Date*). Pursuant to a trust deed of even date herewith, [made between A.B. (*name of tenant for life*) and C.D. and E.F. (*names of trustees of the settlement*)], I, the said A.B., hereby declare as follows —

(a) The land is vested in me upon the trusts from time to time affecting it by virtue of the said trust deed.

[(b) The said C.D. and E.F. are the trustees of the Settlement.

(c) The following powers relating to land are expressly conferred by the said trust deed in extension of those conferred by the Settled Land Act 1925 (*fill in the powers, if any*).]

(d) I have the power to appoint new trustees of the settlement.

(To be executed as a deed)

Form 7 – Certificate of powers of overseas corporations (rule 183)

I ....

of ....

(*insert workplace address, including country*) certify that—

- I give this certificate in respect of .... (the corporation),
- I practise law in .... (*insert territory*) (the territory) and am entitled to do so as a qualified lawyer under the law of the territory,
- I have the requisite knowledge of the law of the territory and of the corporation to give this certificate,
- the corporation is incorporated in the territory with its own legal personality, and
- the corporation has no limitations on its powers to hold, mortgage, lease and otherwise deal with, or to lend money on a mortgage or charge of, land in England and Wales.

Signature .... Date ....

Form 8 – Certificate of powers of corporations other than overseas corporations
(rule 183)

I ....

of ....

(*insert workplace address*) certify that—

- ....(the corporation) has its own legal personality, and
- the corporation has no limitations on its powers to hold, mortgage, lease and otherwise deal with, or to lend money on a mortgage or charge of, land.

Signature of conveyancer .... Date ....

APPENDIX VI
LAND REGISTRATION RULES 2003,
SCHEDULE 9:
FORMS OF EXECUTION

Note: All dispositions other than assents must be executed as a deed. In the case of an assent the words "as a deed" may be omitted.

A. Where the instrument is to be executed personally by an individual —

Signed as a deed by (*full name of individual*) in the presence of:	*Signature*

Signature of witness ....

Name (in BLOCK CAPITALS) ....

Address ....

....

....

....

B. Where the instrument is to be executed by an individual directing another to sign on his behalf —

Signed as a deed by (*full name of person signing*) at the direction and on behalf of (*full name of individual*) in [his][her] presence and in the presence of:

Sign here the name of the individual and your own name, eg: John Smith by Jane Brown

Signature of first witness ....

Name (in BLOCK CAPITALS) ....

Address ....

....

....

....

Signature of second witness ....

Name (in BLOCK CAPITALS) ....

Address ....

....

....

....

C. Where the instrument is to be executed by a company registered under the Companies Acts, or an unregistered company, using its common seal

Executed as a deed by affixing the common seal of (*name of company*) in the presence of:

Common seal of company

Signature of director ....

Signature of [director] [secretary] ....

D(i). Where the instrument is to be executed by a company registered under the Companies Acts, or an unregistered company, without using a common seal, acting by a director and its secretary or by two directors —

Executed as a deed by (*name of company*) acting by [a director and its secretary] [two directors]	*Signature*
	
	                                      Director
	
	Signature
	
	                    [Secretary][Director]

D(ii). Where the instrument is to be executed by a company registered under the Companies Acts, without using a common seal, acting by a director—

Executed as a deed by (*name of company*) acting by a director in the presence of:	*Signature* Director

Signature of witness ....

Name (in BLOCK CAPITALS) ....

Address ....

....

....

....

E. Where the instrument is to be executed on behalf of an overseas company without using a common seal —

Executed as a deed by (*name of company*), a company incorporated in (territory) acting by (full name(s) of person(s) signing), who, in accordance with the laws of that territory, [is][are] acting under the authority of the company.	*Signature in the name of the company* Signature of Authorised [signatory] [signatories]

Note: In the case of an overseas company having a common seal, the form of execution appropriate to a company registered under the Companies Acts may be used, with such adaptations as may be necessary, in place of execution by a person or persons acting under the authority of the company.

F(i). Where the instrument is to be executed by a limited liability partnership incorporated under the Limited Liability Partnerships Act 2000, without using a common seal, acting by two members—

[Executed] as a deed by (*name of limited liability partnership*) acting by two members	*Signature* Member *Signature* Member

F(ii). Where the instrument is to be executed by a limited liability partnership incorporated under the Limited liability Partnerships Act 2000, without using a common seal, acting by a single member—

Executed as a deed by (*name of limited liability partnership*) acting by a member in the presence of:	*Signature* Member

Signature of witness ....

Name (in BLOCK CAPITALS) ....

Address ....

....

....

....

Index

References are to page numbers

Absolute title: introduction   130–131,
133, 371–372, 565–570
Access to neighbouring land orders   1–3,
390, 426
see also Party walls
Accretion and diluvion   3–4, 237
see also Rivers; Sea
Actual occupation, interests of persons in:
introduction   417–418, 422, 527
Addresses for service: introduction   4–5
Administrative receivers   5–8, 217, 266,
474
see also LPA receivers; Receivers
appointed by the court
Administrators
of companies: introduction   8–11
of estates *see* Personal representatives:
introduction
Adverse possession: introduction   11–30
general introduction   11–16, 23–24,
30, 198–199, 214–215, 237, 379
first registration and   12, 25–27, 28,
29, 130–131, 132, 215, 228
leasehold land and   12, 18, 27–30
LRA 2002 Sch 6 and   12, 13–14, 15,
16–24, 27–28, 28, 198–199
transitional provisions   12, 24–25,
27, 29, 30
overriding interests and   421, 425
of rentcharges   488, 494–499
Advowsons   30–31
Agreements to pay further consideration
37–38
Agricultural property   148, 263, 517,
528

Air, rights of   230, 295, 514, 519
Airspace   38–39, 220
Alteration
of application or accompanying
document   174–175, 185–186
of the register: introduction   39–41,
179
cautions register   94–96
see also Deeds: introduction, effecting
dispositions, amendment;
Rectification: introduction
Amalgamation of registered titles   42–
43, 193
Annuities   43–44
see also Rentcharges: introduction
Applications to the Registry: introduction
44–45, 179–181, 201, 500, 506
bulk applications   83–84, 193, 222
death of applicant   181–182
disputes   193–199
errors   174–175, 185–186
evidence in support: introduction
542–543
fees: introduction   221–222
forms: introduction   238–240
requistions, rejection, cancellation:
introduction   500
small scale applications   84
Arrangement, deeds of   277, 426
see also Family arrangement, deeds of;
Individual voluntary arrangements
(IVAs): introduction
Assents: introduction   45–48, 182, 266,
267, 283, 441, 512, 542
Assets of community value   48–49

Bankruptcy   49–72
  introduction   49–55, 59–60, 266
    entries under LRA 1925   52–53, 59
  after-acquired property   63–64
  annulment   62–63
  bankrupt's home   61–62, 66–69, 100
  copies and inspection of documents
    relating to   397, 398, 401, 411
  discharge   60–62
  disclaimer by trustee   69–72, 328
  insolvent estates   58–59
  joint proprietors   56–57, 62, 429, 430
  powers of attorney and   447, 476
  proceedings started outside England
    and Wales   72, 427–431
  protection of purchasers   55–56, 65
  searches   201
  voidable dispositions   64–66, 476–477
Bare trusts   26, 46, 73, 225
Bona vacantia   19, 74–75, 76, 357, 366
Boundaries   20, 77–83, 190, 191, 234–
  235
  between land and water *see* Rivers; Sea
  encroachment   12, 28–30
  see also Party walls; Plans: introduction
Bulk applications   83–84, 193, 222

Capital transfer tax   280, 281, 282
  see also Inheritance tax
Cautions
  against conversion   84–85
  against dealings: introduction   85–88
  against first registration: introduction
    88–96, 194, 241–242, 273, 397, 398,
    409
  mortgage cautions   388
Certificates of title (of public authorities)
  162, 165, 276, 472–473
Certified copies: introduction   45, 227–
  228
Chancel repair   96–99, 421
Change of name   99–100, 119, 266, 267
Channel Islands   235
Channel Tunnel   285
Charges *see* Charging orders:
  introduction; Equitable charges:
  introduction; Land charges; Legal
  charges: introduction; Limited owner's
  charge; Local land charges:
  introduction; Statutory charges:
  introduction
Charging orders: introduction   100–104
Charities   104–119
  introduction   104–106, 154, 286, 557
  changes affecting   117–119, 223
  dispositions by   105, 109–116, 117
    Church of England and   106, 120–
      123, 126, 128
  dispositions in favour of   105, 106–
    109
  exempt, meaning   105, 121, 252
  see also Reverter, rights of; Trusts of
    land: introduction, charitable trusts,
    land held on
Children *see* Minors
Church of England   120–130
  introduction   25, 120, 154, 286
  advowsons   30–31
  chancel repair   96–99, 421
  charity law and   106, 120–123, 126, 128
  ecclesiastical trusts, land held on   154,
    286, 439, 559
  redundant churches   96, 125, 129–130
  tithes   96, 420–421, 424–425, 493
  see also Reverter, rights of
Church in Wales   31, 96
Civil partnerships
  change of name and   99–100
  home rights and   66–67, 257–261,
    339, 390, 408, 426
  leases determinable on   303–304
  property adjustment orders   468–471
Classes of title: introduction   42, 84–85,
  130–135, 371–372
  absolute title: introduction   130–131,
    133, 371–372, 565–570
  good leasehold title: introduction   84,
    133–134, 371–372, 566–567, 568–
    569
  possessory title: introduction   84, 130–
    131, 132, 134–135, 372, 566, 567–
    568, 569–570
  qualified title: introduction   84, 132,
    134, 567–568, 569–570

upgrade: introduction 84–85, 274, 372, 565–570
see also Estate, right or interest in land: introduction
Co-operative societies *see* Registered societies: introduction
Coal 135–136, 152, 230, 381, 384–385, 389, 427
Collective enfranchisement: introduction 136–148
  introduction 136
  acquisition order 136, 143–147
  lease back 143
  notice under LRHUDA 1993 s 13 137
  post-enfranchisement registration 142–143, 147
  right of first refusal to purchase reversion 147–148
  vendor's lien 143
  vesting order: Landlord and Tenant Act 1987 147
  vesting order: LRHUDA 1993 s 24(4) or s 25(6) 141, 142
  vesting order: LRHUDA 1993 s 26(1) 138–141, 142
Commonhold 148–150
Commons 26, 150–153, 230, 389, 423, 427
  status in context of profits à prendre 150, 152, 153, 456, 458, 463
  see also Town or village greens
Community benefit societies *see* Registered societies: introduction
Companies: introduction 26, 100, 154–160, 267, 411
  application for counter-fraud restriction 248
  conversion to LLP status 356
  debentures: introduction 156–157, 183–185, 231–234
  dissolution: introduction 6, 7, 157, 184, 266, 328
    bona vacantia 19, 74–75, 76, 357, 366
    sales by LPA receivers and 475, 476, 477

overseas companies 100, 155, 157, 159–160, 366
  see also Administrative receivers; Administrators, of companies: introduction; LPA receivers; Receivers appointed by the court
Compensation by the Registry *see* Indemnity: introduction
Compulsory acquisition of land 160–165, 193, 224, 261, 263
Constructive trusts 165–168
Contracts for sale: introduction 35, 37–38, 168–171, 214, 541, 555
  interaction with options and rights of pre-emption 413, 414, 520, 521
  vendor's liens 37, 143, 570–571
Conversion of title, cautions against 84–85
  see also Upgrade of title: overview
Conveyancers, meaning 171
Copies *see* Documents: introduction, official copies and inspection
Copyhold 171–174, 375, 382, 384, 540
  see also Manors: introduction
Cornwall, Duchy of *see* Crown, the
Costs
  arising from breach of requirement for first registration 225
  in court proceedings 275
    legal aid 332–333, 543, 544, 545
  in Registry proceedings
    payable by the Registry 40, 41, 175–177
    payable by a third party 177–178
  in Tribunal cases 177, 196, 197
Court proceedings: miscellaneous matters
  copies and inspection of documents in connection with 397, 398, 401, 411
  costs in *see* Costs, in court proceedings
  freedom of information requests to the Registry and 402
  protection of orders by notice 389
  transfers pursuant to court order, registration 546
  writs and orders affecting land: introduction 571–573
  see also entries for other topics

Covenants: introduction
    forfeiture of lease for breach   329, 330
    implied: introduction   256, 268–273,
        276, 321–322
    indemnity: introduction   276–277
    positive: introduction   276, 444–446,
        512–513
    relevance of history of title   256
    restrictive   214, 230, 256, 276, 370,
        372, 509–513
Credit unions   178–179
Crown, the
    adverse possession and   18, 19, 25, 27
    corporeal fisheries and   540
    Crown rents   419–420, 423–424
    demesne land   75, 81, 89, 187–189,
        223, 224
        foreshore *see* Foreshore
        mines and minerals and   188, 381,
            382
    see also Compulsory acquisition of
        land; Franchises: introduction;
        Manors: introduction
Customary rights   390, 418
    see also Town or village greens

Day list: introduction   179–181
Death
    of applicant for registration   181–182
    leases determinable on   303–304
    of registered proprietor *see* Assents:
        introduction; Inheritance tax; Joint
        proprietors: introduction; Personal
        representatives: introduction
Death duties   280–281, 441
    see also Inheritance tax
Debentures: introduction   156–157, 183–
    185, 231–234
    created by LLPs   355–356
    see also Administrative receivers;
        Administrators, of companies:
        introduction; LPA receivers;
        Receivers appointed by the court
Deeds: introduction
    accompanying application for first
        registration   227–228

effecting dispositions, amendment
    175, 185–187
lost or destroyed   226–227, 228, 266,
    273, 369–372
see also Documents: introduction
Demesne land   75, 81, 89, 187–189, 223,
    224
    foreshore *see* Foreshore
    mines and minerals and   188, 381, 382
    see also Crown, the, Crown rents
Destruction of documents
    destroyed or lost title deeds:
        introduction   226–227, 228, 266,
        273, 369–372
    Registry practice   45, 513
Developing estates   190–192, 200, 267,
    489
Developing schemes   193
Diluvion and accretion   3–4, 237
    see also Rivers; Sea
Disclaimer of property   69–72, 74–75,
    325, 328, 362–366
Division of registered titles   199–200
Documents: introduction
    accompanying application for first
        registration   227–228
    deeds *see* Deeds: introduction
    official copies and inspection   149,
        179, 180, 396–404
    retention, destruction and return by the
        Registry   45, 513
Dwellings *see* Residential premises:
    miscellaneous matters

Easements: introduction
    equitable: introduction   212–213, 320,
        418, 423
    grants of exclusive use, whether
        easements   217–219
    legal: introduction   343–352, 372,
        418, 422–423
    lost or destroyed title deeds and   372
    quasi-easements   334–335, 343
    relevance of history of title   256
    statutory   142, 514
    see also Profits à prendre: introduction

Electronic services of the Registry:
introduction 200–202, 228, 239, 555
Embankments 202–204, 420
see also Rivers; Sea
Encroachment 12, 28–30
Enlargement of long leases 204–207,
292
Equitable charges: introduction 207–
212
see also Debentures: introduction;
Notices of deposit
Equitable easements: introduction 212–
213, 320, 418, 423
Equitable interests: introduction 214,
556
see also Mere equities: introduction
Errors *see* Alteration; Deeds:
introduction, effecting dispositions,
amendment; Rectification: introduction;
Slip rule
Escheat 69, 75–77, 188, 363, 365–366
Estate duty *see* Death duties
Estate management schemes 295–296
Estate rentcharges 302, 444, 486–487,
489, 493
Estate, right or interest in land:
introduction 214–215
Estoppel 19, 198–199, 323, 353, 471–
472, 495
European Convention on Human Rights
15, 97
European Union
data protection law 404
EEIGs 215–217
EGTCs 217–219
insolvency proceedings in a non-UK
member state 427
Exclusive use, grants of 219–221
Exempt information documents 149,
179, 180, 397, 398, 399–401

Facility letters 267
Family arrangement, deeds of 282–283
Fees: introduction 221–222
First registration: introduction 222–231
breach of requirements 225, 255

cautions against: introduction 88–96,
194, 241–242, 273, 397, 398, 409
death of applicant 181
lost or destroyed title deeds and:
introduction 226–227, 228, 266,
369–372
pending applications, official searches
and 404, 405, 406, 407, 408, 409,
410
unregistered interests overriding:
introduction 226, 230, 416–421,
426, 427
First-tier Tribunal *see* Tribunal
Fishing rights 152, 237, 375, 456, 464,
466, 539–540
Flats 78, 191, 410
application for variation of long lease
306
collective enfranchisement *see*
Collective enfranchisement:
introduction
exclusion from certain provisions of
Leasehold Reform Act 1967 292,
307
extended (substitute) lease under
LRHUDA 1993 310–317
management
appointment of manager under
Landlord and Tenant Act 1987
148
RTM companies 518
options in shared ownership leases
535
tenure granted under 'right to buy'
legislation 513
see also Commonhold; Residential
premises: miscellaneous matters
Floating charges: introduction 231–234
see also Administrative receivers;
Administrators, of companies:
introduction; Debentures:
introduction; LPA receivers;
Receivers appointed by the court
Flying freeholds 148, 234–235
Foreclosure 339, 340
Foreign law: introduction 235–236

Foreshore   18, 25, 188, 236–238
    see also Crown, the, Crown rents; Sea
Forfeiture of leases   325, 328–330, 380
Forgery *see* Fraud and forgery
Forms: introduction   238–240
Franchises: introduction   240–245, 297–
    298, 375, 409–410, 410–411, 418, 540
Fraud and forgery   25, 93, 245–248,
    249–250, 274, 283, 380, 481
    see also Identity evidence: introduction
Freehold title: introduction
    change from leasehold to *see*
        Copyhold; Leases: introduction,
        change from leasehold to freehold
    commonhold   148–150
    determination *see* Escheat
    flying freeholds   148, 234–235
    merger of leasehold and freehold   75,
        224, 293–294, 325–326
    see also Classes of title: introduction
Freezing orders   248–249, 249–251
    see also Inhibitions
Friendly societies   251–254, 564

Gender, change of   99
Gifts: introduction   254–256, 451, 512
Glossary and note   xxvii–xxix
Good leasehold title: introduction   84,
    133–134, 371–372, 566–567, 568–569

Highways   1, 15, 374, 418
Historical information kept by the
    Registry   256–257, 291, 403
Home rights   66–67, 257–261, 339, 390,
    408, 426
Housing action trusts   261–262, 276, 473
Housing associations   154, 155, 263–265

Identity evidence: introduction   266–
    268, 397
Implied covenants: introduction   256,
    268–273, 276, 321–322
Implied trusts: introduction   165–168
Indemnity: introduction   273–276, 397
Indemnity covenants   276–277
Index *see* Official searches: introduction,
    of the index: introduction

Individual voluntary arrangements
    (IVAs): introduction   277–280
    supervisors and identity evidence   266
Industrial and provident societies *see*
    Credit unions; Registered societies:
    introduction
Inheritance tax   46, 280–283, 357, 390,
    441, 454
    copies and inspection of documents in
        connection with tax   397, 398, 401,
        411
    Inland Revenue charge   280–282, 452,
        454
Inhibitions   250, 283–285, 508
    bankruptcy inhibitions   52–53, 59, 62
    where registered proprietor was
        incumbent of benefice   125
Insolvency
    copies and inspection of documents in
        connection with   397–398
    corporate *see* Companies: introduction,
        dissolution: introduction
    insolvent estates   58–59
    office holders, and identity evidence
        266–267
    personal *see* Bankruptcy; Individual
        voluntary arrangements (IVAs):
        introduction
Inspection of documents *see* Documents:
    introduction, official copies and
    inspection
Interim receiving orders   249–251
Internal waters   285
    see also Rivers; Sea
Isle of Man   235
Isles of Scilly   236, 285

Joint proprietors: introduction   286–290
    business partners as *see* Limited
        partnerships; Partnerships
    consisting of minor(s) and adult(s)
        386–387
    death of sole survivor *see* Personal
        representatives: introduction
    index of proprietors' names and   411
    insolvency and   56–57, 62, 278, 429,
        430

powers of attorney by 447, 448, 449–451

severance of beneficial tenancy in common: introduction 282–283, 286, 379, 468, 469, 503, 533–534, 545

see also Trusts of land: introduction

Lancaster, Duchy of *see* Crown, the

Land charges

equitable charges over unregistered land as 207

equitable easements over unregistered land as 212

home rights over unregistered land 66–67, 257–261, 339, 390, 408, 426

Inland Revenue charge 280–282, 452, 454

local *see* Local land charges: introduction

pending land actions: introduction 426, 433–435

restrictive covenants: introduction 214, 230, 256, 276, 370, 372, 509–513

searches 26, 60, 201, 226, 472

writs and orders affecting land: introduction 571–573

Land Registry: introduction 194, 290–291

applications to *see* Applications to the Registry: introduction

compensation by *see* Indemnity: introduction

day list: introduction 179–181

documents and *see* Documents: introduction

electronic services: introduction 200–202, 228, 239, 555

fees: introduction 221–222

forms: introduction 238–240

geographical extent of LRA 2002 285

historical information kept by 256–257, 291, 403

proper office: introduction 179–180, 467–468

Land transaction tax (LTT) (in Wales) 542

see also Stamp duty land tax (SDLT): introduction

Large scale applications (bulk applications) 83–84, 193, 222

Leasehold valuation tribunal 136, 143, 148, 306, 312, 330

Leases: introduction 296–333

general introduction 296–300

agreements for 31–34, 35, 36

apportionment of rent 321–322

change from leasehold to freehold

collective enfranchisement *see* Collective enfranchisement: introduction

conversion to commonhold 149, 150

enlargement 204–207, 292

leasehold enfranchisement 205, 291–296

see also Copyhold

classes of leasehold title: introduction 133–135

see also Classes of title: introduction

determination 324–332

overview 324–325, 331–332

disclaimer 69–72, 74–75, 325, 328, 362–365

effluxion of time 325, 328

enlargement 204–207, 292

forfeiture 325, 328–330, 380

frustration 325, 331

leases for life or determinable on death, marriage or civil partnership 303–304

merger 75, 224, 293–294, 325–326

notice 325, 330–331

surrender 28, 300–301, 306–307, 312, 323, 325, 326–327, 541

easements and: introduction 212, 302, 303, 317–320, 325

equitable mortgages 211

extension

by substitute lease under LRHUDA 1993 310–317

under Leasehold Reform Act 1967 292, 307–310

other 322–324

Leases: introduction *(continued)*
  first registration   89, 222, 223–224,
    230–231, 254, 296–297, 382
    breach of requirements   225, 255
  of flats *see* Flats
  leases for life or determinable on death,
    marriage or civil partnership   303–
    304
  notices of deposit and   396
  noting: introduction   300, 331
    interests that cannot be protected by
      notice   230, 300, 389, 474
  options and: introduction   412, 413,
    415–416
  overriding interests and: introduction
    417, 421–422, 426–427
  prescribed clauses leases: introduction
    300–301
  rectification   305–306
  registrable dispositions: procedure
    301–303
  restrictive covenants in: introduction
    230, 302, 320–321, 325, 389, 427, 509
  sub-leases   71, 75, 224, 307, 327, 329,
    362, 363, 364
  variation   186–187, 300–301, 304–
    307, 390, 536
Legal aid   332–333, 543, 545
Legal charges: introduction   333–343
  general introduction   333–336, 343,
    352, 353
  amendment and variation   187, 338
  collateral charges   337
  consolidation   338
  debentures *see* Debentures:
    introduction
  discharge   340–342
  further advances   336–337
  home rights search by mortgagee   261,
    408
  mortgage cautions   388
  mortgage receivers *see* LPA receivers
  priorities and: introduction   337–338
  remedies of registered chargee:
    introduction   339–340
    appointment of receiver *see* LPA
      receivers

  sub-charges   342–343
  subrogation   546–547
  substituted security   293, 323
  transfer: introduction   343
Legal easements: introduction   343–352,
  372, 418, 422–423
Legal estates: introduction   352
Legal interests: introduction   352–353, 556
Licences: introduction   353–354
Light, rights of   230, 295, 514, 519
Limited liability partnerships (LLPs)
  100, 154, 334, 354–357, 490
Limited owner's charge   357–358
Limited partnerships   358–360
Liquidators *see* Companies: introduction,
  dissolution: introduction
Local land charges: introduction   230,
  367–369, 418, 423, 426–427, 512
  statutory charges   295–296, 367–368,
    543, 545
Lost title deeds: introduction   226–227,
  228, 266, 273, 369–372
LPA receivers   217, 266, 339, 474–479

Manors: introduction   150, 222, 297–
  298, 372–375, 409, 419, 540
  see also Copyhold
Marriage
  change of name and   99–100
  home rights and   66–67, 257–261,
    339, 390, 408, 426
  leases determinable on   303–304
  property adjustment orders   468–471
Mental incapacity: introduction   266–
  267, 375–379
  see also Powers of attorney:
    introduction; Receivers appointed by
    court order
Mere equities: introduction   379–380
  see also Equitable interests:
    introduction
Merger: introduction
  leasehold and freehold estates   75,
    224, 293–294, 325–326
  legal and equitable interests   556
  see also Profits à prendre: introduction;
    Rentcharges: introduction; Tithes

Mines and minerals: introduction 43, 200, 274, 380–385, 418
  coal 135–136, 152, 230, 381, 384–385, 389, 427
Minors 26, 66, 171–174, 385–386, 529, 531–532
Mortgages *see* Equitable charges: introduction; Legal charges: introduction

Name
  change 99–100, 119, 266, 267
  index of proprietors' names 397–398, 409, 411–412
Northern Ireland 72, 154, 157, 183, 235, 354, 355
Notices: introduction 194, 389–395, 427
Notices of deposit 395–396

Official copies and inspection 149, 179, 180, 396–404
Official searches: introduction
  of the index: introduction 409–412
    index map: introduction409-410
    index of proprietors' names 397–398, 409, 411–412
    index of verbal descriptions of relating franchises and manors 244, 373, 409, 410–411
  of the register: introduction 179, 399, 404–409, 455–456
  home rights searches 261, 339
Options: introduction 270, 277, 299, 328, 412–416
  see also Pre-emption, rights of: introduction
Outline applications: introduction 408–409
Overages 37–38
Overreaching: introduction 286–288, 449, 450, 501, 502, 505, 507
Overriding interests: introduction 416–427
Overriding priority 249, 455, 505, 508
Overseas addresses 5
Overseas companies 100, 155, 157, 159–160, 366

Overseas insolvency proceedings 366, 427–431
Overseas limited partnerships 359
Overseas LLPs 357

Partners
  business *see* Partnerships
  civil *see* Civil partnerships
Partnerships 289, 431–432
  conversion to LLP status 356
  limited partnerships 358–360
  LLPs 100, 154, 334, 354–357, 490
  PPPs 6, 222, 230, 297, 300, 389, 421, 427, 473–474
Party walls 1, 79, 432–433
  see also Access to neighbouring land orders
Pending land actions: introduction 426, 433–435
Personal representatives: introduction 181–182, 224, 266, 267, 411, 435–441
  insolvent estates 58–59
  of a joint proprietor *see* Joint proprietors: introduction
  special personal representatives 437, 527, 530
  trusts of land and 438, 439, 440, 558, 559, 560
  see also Assents: introduction; Inheritance tax
Plans: introduction 77–83, 201, 256–257, 397, 398, 441–444
Positive covenants: introduction 276, 444–446, 512–513
Possessory title: introduction 84, 130–131, 132, 134–135, 372, 566, 567–568, 569–570
Postponement, deeds of 337–338
Powers of appointment, special 538–539
Powers of attorney: introduction 266, 267, 446–452
  see also Mental incapacity: introduction
Pre-emption, rights of: introduction 519–523
  see also Options: introduction
Prescribed clauses leases: introduction 300–301

Priorities: introduction   452–456
    official searches with priority   404–
        408, 455–456
    overriding priority   249, 455, 505, 508
Private fund limited partnerships   359
Private registered providers of social
    housing *see* Registered social landlords
    and private registered providers:
    introduction
Profits à prendre: introduction   42, 384,
    409, 418, 456–466, 539–540
    rights of common, status of   150, 152,
        153, 456, 458, 463
    whether overriding interests   353, 418,
        422–423, 458, 463
    see also Commons; Easements:
        introduction
Proper office of the Registry: introduction
    179–180, 467–468
Property adjustment orders   468–471,
    542
Public authority certificates of title   162,
    165, 276, 472–473
Public rights   230, 237–238, 390, 418,
    426–427
Public trusts, land held on   154, 286,
    439, 559
Public-private partnerships (PPPs)   6,
    222, 230, 297, 300, 389, 421, 427, 473–
    474

Qualified title: introduction   84, 132,
    134, 567–568, 569–570
Quasi-easements   334–335, 343

Receivers *see* Administrative receivers;
    Interim receiving orders; LPA
    receivers; Mental incapacity:
    introduction; Receivers appointed by
    court order
Receivers appointed by court order
    479–480
Rectification: introduction   39, 176–177,
    245–246, 273–274, 275, 276, 379–380,
    480–482
    rectification by Tribunal   199, 555
Redundant churches   96, 125, 129–130

Registered social landlords and private
    registered providers: introduction
    262, 264, 482–484, 535, 536
    see also Right to buy and right to
        acquire: introduction
Registered societies: introduction   485–
    486
Rentcharges: introduction   88, 272–273,
    339, 352, 353, 409, 486–499
    estate rentcharges   302, 444, 486–487,
        489
    see also Annuities; Tithes
Requisitions: introduction   500
Residential premises: miscellaneous matters
    adverse possession   15
    bankrupt's home   61–62, 66–69, 100
    on common land   153
    compulsory purchase   163–164
    flats *see* Flats
    forfeiture of leases of   329–330
    home rights   66–67, 257–261, 339,
        390, 408, 426
    housing action trusts and   262–263
    mansion houses   528
    parsonages and houses of residence
        120, 122, 123, 128, 130
    repurchase of defective dwellings   473
    SDLT and   541, 542
    social housing *see* Social housing:
        introduction
    on town or village greens   550
    see also Exclusive use, grants of
Restraint orders: introduction   249–251
    see also Inhibitions
Restrictions: introductions   500–508
Restrictive covenants: introduction   214,
    230, 256, 276, 370, 372, 509–513
Resulting trusts   165–168
Retention, destruction and return of
    documents by the Registry   45, 513
Reverter, rights of   120, 148–149, 523–
    526
Right to buy and right to acquire:
    introduction   262–263, 270, 417, 473,
    484, 513–516, 535
    preserved right to buy   223, 224, 298,
        417, 426, 473, 516–518

service charge loans 267

Right to manage 518

see also Flats, management, appointment of manager under Landlord and Tenant Act 1987

Rights of way 349, 418

Rivers

accretion and diluvion of land 3–4, 237

bed, ownership 540

tidal waters in *see* Foreshore; Internal waters

walls and embankments 202–204, 375, 420

see also Fishing rights

RTE companies *see* Collective enfranchisement: introduction

RTM companies *see* Right to manage

School sites, reverter of *see* Reverter, rights of

Scotland 72, 154, 183, 215, 235, 354, 355, 359, 542

Sea

foreshore 18, 25, 188, 236–238

see also Crown, the, Crown rents

internal waters 285

mean sea level 39

walls and embankments 202–204, 237, 375, 420

Searches

bankruptcy searches 201

commons registration searches 26

company searches 26

home rights searches 261, 339

Land Charges searches 26, 60, 201, 226, 472

official searches of the register and index *see* Official searches: introduction

Secure tenancies 143, 223, 224, 262–263, 297, 298, 517

Sequestration 426, 526–527

Settlements: introduction 230, 357–358, 389, 427, 437, 527–532

see also Annuities

Severance of beneficial tenancy in common: introduction 282–283, 286, 379, 468, 469, 503, 533–534, 545

Shared ownership leases 534–536

Slip rule 198

Social housing: introduction 482–483

repurchase of defective dwellings 473

see also Housing associations; Registered social landlords and private registered providers: introduction; Registered societies: introduction; Right to buy and right to acquire: introduction

Souvenir land 536–538

Special personal representatives 437, 527, 530

Special powers of appointment 538–539

Sporting rights 172, 375, 456, 539–540

fishing *see* Fishing rights

sports and pastimes *see* Town or village greens

Spouses *see* Marriage

Stamp duty 541, 542

Stamp duty land tax (SDLT): introduction 391, 392, 541–542

copies and inspection of documents in connection with tax 397, 398, 401, 411

Statements of truth: introduction 542–543

Statutory charges: introduction 273, 352, 353, 543–546

estate management schemes 295–296

Inland Revenue charge 280–282, 452, 454

legal aid charge 332, 333, 543, 544, 545

local authority charges 367–368, 543, 545

Statutory vesting: introduction 546

Sub-charges 266, 333, 338, 342–343, 388

Sub-leases 71, 75, 224, 307, 327, 329, 362, 363, 364

Sub-sale 169, 170, 221, 552

Subrogation 546–547

Tax
  capital transfer tax   280, 281, 282
  copies and inspection of documents in
    connection with   397, 398, 401, 411
  death duties   280–281, 441
  inheritance tax *see* Inheritance tax
  LTT (in Wales)   542
  SDLT: introduction   391, 392, 541–542
  stamp duty   541, 542
Time shares   547–548
Tithes   96, 420–421, 423–424, 493
Title: introduction
  amalgamation   42–43, 193
  classes: introduction *see* Classes of
    title: introduction
  deeds: introduction *see* Deeds:
    introduction
  division   199–200
  estate, right or interest in land:
    introduction   214–215
  freehold: introduction *see* Freehold
    title: introduction
  leasehold: introduction *see* Leases:
    introduction
  merger: introduction *see* Merger:
    introduction
  public authority certificates   162, 165,
    276, 472–473
  title information documents   548
Town or village greens   150, 151, 549–
  551
  see also Commons
Transfers: introduction   186, 238, 551–
  554
Tribunal   xxix, 130, 177, 195–199, 555
  see also Leasehold valuation tribunal;
    Upper Tribunal (Lands Chamber)
Trusts of land: introduction   214, 389,
  555–564
  bare trusts   26, 46, 73, 225
  charitable trusts, land held on   106,
    119, 154, 286, 439, 559
  ecclesiastical trusts, land held on   154,
    286, 439, 559
  first registration and   222, 223, 224,
    230, 254

  home rights and   258
  implied: introduction   165–168
  mental incapacity of trustee   377–378
  nil-rate band discretionary trusts   282–
    283
  overreaching and: introduction   416
  overriding interests under: introduction
    426
  personal representatives and   438,
    439, 440, 558, 559, 560
  powers of attorney by trustees   447,
    449–451
  public trusts, land held on   154, 286,
    439, 559
  scope of pending land actions and
    433, 468
  see also Annuities; Joint proprietors:
    introduction; Minors; Reverter, rights
    of; Settlements: introduction

Unincorporated associations   252, 564–
  565
  see also Partnerships
Upgrade of title: overview   84–85, 274,
  372, 565–570
Upper Tribunal (Lands Chamber)   129–
  130, 164, 198, 512

Vendor's liens   37, 143, 570–571
Village greens *see* Town or village
  greens

Wales: introduction
  assets of community value   48
  Church in Wales   31, 96
  commons, former law about vehicles
    349
  compulsory purchase   162, 163
  social housing   263, 264, 265, 482,
    483, 484, 515
  tax   542
  UK internal waters   285
  Welsh language   178, 238, 253, 268,
    354
Writs and orders affecting land:
  introduction   571–57